Hindu Mission, Christian Mission

SUNY series in Religious Studies

Harold Coward, editor

Hindu Mission, Christian Mission

Soundings in Comparative Theology

REID B. LOCKLIN

SUNY
PRESS

Published by State University of New York Press, Albany

Printed in the United States of America

For information, contact State University of New York Press, Albany, NY
www.sunypress.edu

Library of Congress Cataloging-in-Publication Data

Name: Locklin, Reid B., author.
Title: Hindu mission, Christian mission : soundings in comparative theology / Reid B. Locklin.
Description: Albany : State University of New York Press, [2024]. | Series: SUNY series in religious studies | Includes bibliographical references and index.
Identifiers: LCCN 2023039269 | ISBN 9781438497402 (hardcover : alk. paper) | ISBN 9781438497426 (ebook) | ISBN 9781438497419 (pbk. : alk. paper)
Subjects: LCSH: Hinduism—Missions. | Conversion—Hinduism. | Missions. | Chinmaya Mission. | Ramakrishna Mission. | Advaita. | Vedanta.
Classification: LCC BL1243.32 .L63 2024 | DDC 294.5/72—dc23/eng/20231026
LC record available at https://lccn.loc.gov/2023039269

For Jolie

Contents

List of Illustrations ix

Acknowledgments xi

Introduction: Beyond the Conversion Controversy 1

Part I. Constructing Missionary Advaita

Chapter 1 Toward a Comparative Theology of Mission 9

Chapter 2 A History of Missionary Advaita in Late Modernity 43

Chapter 3 Paradigms and Styles of Advaita Mission 81

Part II. Fruits of Encounter

Chapter 4 A Gospel of Inner Experience? Transcending Limits of Language and Culture 121

Chapter 5 Conquest of the Quarters? Crossing Borders and Charting New Geographies 151

Chapter 6 All Selves, and Whole Selves? Striving for Social and Political Liberation 183

List of Illustrations

Figure 5.1	The B-M-I Chart offers a symbolic, interiorized map for the Chinmaya Mission.	159
Figure 5.2	The floor labyrinth of Grace Cathedral, San Francisco, closely resembles that of Chartres Cathedral.	175
Table 5.1	Three retellings of Ādi Śaṅkarācārya's conquest.	161

Acknowledgments

From one point of view, I can trace the origin of this book to November 1999. I was in Chennai, studying the great eighth-century Advaitin Ādi Śaṅkarācārya's independent treatise *Upadeśasāhasrī* with a teacher in the tradition, when Pope John Paul II—now honored as Saint John Paul II—made a pastoral visit to India. The visit was controversial, for reasons discussed in chapter 1, so I had several conversations with my teacher about it. I perceived at least some affinities between the missionary vision of the pope and the Advaita text we were studying together. Was I crazy? My teacher suggested that I might gain insight about this by visiting the nearest Chinmaya Mission center to purchase a small book entitled *Śaṅkara the Missionary*.

I presented a paper offering an interpretation of *Śaṅkara the Missionary* for the first time in 2005, after I had completed my doctoral studies and taken up my current post in Toronto, and I co-authored a related journal article in 2009. Slowly, the project ballooned well beyond this one short treatise. The monograph has remained in the background of my other teaching and research since that time, occasionally thriving, often languishing, not infrequently arising unexpectedly in my mind as I worked on more urgent projects. All books, at some level, are the works of communities rather than individuals, but this is even more the case for an undertaking like this one, which has had such a long gestation.

I am grateful for the support of several institutions and research communities, which provided space, time, and resources for me to reflect comparatively on questions of mission. These include, first, my professional home at the University of Toronto. I have benefitted enormously from the encouragement of colleagues in both the St. Michael's College Christianity and Culture Program and the Department for the Study of Religion, and I owe a debt of gratitude to the faculty and staff of the John M. Kelly Library at the University of St. Michael's College. At least half of the writing was completed during two successive research leaves: first, as a Senior Research Fellow with the impressive student fellows and colleagues of the Martin Marty Center at the University of Chicago Divinity School, in 2010–2011; and, subsequently, as a Resident Scholar at the Collegeville Institute of Saint John's Abbey and University in Minnesota, and a Visiting Scholar at the Faculty of Divinity of the University of Cambridge, in the winter and spring, respectively, of 2018. At Cambridge, I am especially grateful for the collegiality of Professors Ankur Barua and Sarah Coakley, as well as financial support from the Teape Trust.

This study would have been impossible without the incredible hospitality of organizations and individuals associated with the Advaita movements profiled herein. Since my graduate studies, I have been blessed with opportunities to attend lectures, retreats, and *satsangs* with Arsha Vidya Gurukulam, Arsha Vidya Ontario, and the Chinmaya Mission. The community at Chinmaya Shivalaya and then the Chinmaya Vedic Heritage Center have welcomed me warmly since I took up my position in Toronto, particularly in the persons of Peter Rebele, Swamini Shivapriyananda, Dev Acharya, and Gina Acharya. I received a similarly warm reception at the Chinmaya International Foundation in Kerala for a short retreat in January 2008, and I appreciated the opportunity to attend regular classes at Vivekananda Vedanta Society of Chicago and Chinmaya Mission Chicago in the winter and spring of 2011. The dynamic young leaders of the Chinmaya Yuva Kendra were particularly generous with their time and made a very strong impression. Dennis Hartel graciously arranged a short visit to Arunachala Ashrama in Nova Scotia in August 2017. Peter Fell did the same for the Vedanta Society and Arunachala Ashrama of New York in January 2018, and, in the course of our commute to and from the NYC suburb of Jamaica, he helpfully disrupted many of my assumptions about Jagadguru Śrī Candraśekhara Bhāratī and the Śaṅkarācāryas of Śṛṅgeri. At the Jamaica ashram, Bandhu was kind enough to gift me a copy of Ramana Maharshi's *Upadeśa*

Saram, which deepened and transformed my engagement with the Maharshi. I am, finally, grateful to Mary Frohlich, RSCJ, for talking with me about her early experiences with Transcendental Meditation and to Cynthia Ann Humes for sharing chapters of her own unpublished manuscript on TM. Though I suspect that these friends and benefactors may not agree with every one of my interpretations and conclusions—and should in no case be held responsible for any of them—I hope that my affection and admiration is evident in the pages that follow.

A number of students provided research and writing support for this volume through directed research courses, the University of Toronto work study program, and the President's Research Fund of the University of St. Michael's College. These include Noreen Ahmed, Lori Frias, Tristan Gosselin, Ren Ito, Connor Kokot, Julia Lauwers, Aldea Mulhearn, Iakoiehwáhtha Patton, Adriano Parravani, Matthew Remedios, and Stephen Skierski. The following colleagues provided feedback on the manuscript, in part or in whole: Chad Bauman, Bennett Comerford, Nika Kuchuk, Jeffery D. Long, Nadya Pohran, Anantanand Rambachan, Daniel Soars, two anonymous referees, and the winter 2018 community of Collegeville Institute Resident Scholars, including Tom Fate, Jim Hofmann, Jaisy Joseph, Bob Kitchen, Ernest Simmons, David Smoker, and Toppo Takamura. Special thanks are due to my amazing writing group colleagues at the University of Toronto, who have, over the decade and a half that this study has been percolating, included Caitriona Brennan, Matthew Dougherty, Iris Gildea, Jennifer Harris, Ella Johnson, Alison More, Michael O'Connor, Colleen Shantz, Natalie Wigg-Stevenson, and Terezia Zoric. I am also deeply grateful for the skillful guidance of James Peltz and the production team at SUNY Press, especially John Britch, Diane Ganeles, Aimee Harrison, and John Wentworth. Tristan Gosselin and Bernadette Guthrie provided invaluable assistance with the index. The book is much stronger due to the contributions, corrections, and suggestions of these students and colleagues. Of course, all errors remain my own.

Several chapters of this book incorporate previously published material. Chapter 2 is a revised and expanded version of Reid B. Locklin, "A Century of Advaita Mission: Tracing a Lineage and Opening a Conversation," *Journal of Ecumenical Studies* 52.4 (2017): 488–526. Copyright © 2017 *Journal of Ecumenical Studies*. Reused with permission of the University of Pennsylvania Press. Chapter 3 is a lightly revised version of Reid B. Locklin, "Paradigms and Styles of Advaita Mission: An Experiment in Interpretation," *International Journal of Hindu Studies* 20.1 (2016): 1–49, Springer Nature. Chapter 5 draws its central exposition from two previously published works: Reid B. Locklin and Julia Lauwers, "Rewriting the Sacred Geography of Advaita: Swami Chinmayānanda and the *Śaṅkara-dig-vijaya*," *The Journal of Hindu Studies* 2.2 (2009): 179–208; and Reid B. Locklin, "Migration and Spiritual Conquest: Emplacing Contemporary Comparative Theology in a Hindu Theology of the 'Quarters' (*dik*)," in *Strangers in this World: Multi-Religious Reflections on Immigration*, ed. Hussam S. Timani, Allen G. Jorgenson, and Alexander Y. Hwang (Minneapolis, MN: Fortress Press, 2015), 11–29. Chapter 7, similarly, incorporates material previously published in two venues: Reid B. Locklin, "Non-Dual Belonging: Sanskritization and the Dissolution of the Multiple in Advaita Missionary Movements," *Journal of Hindu-Christian Studies* 28 (2015): 88–99; and Reid B. Locklin, "Non-Dual Conversion and Non-Dual Belonging: Trajectories of Religious Transformation in Missionary Advaita Vedānta," in *Hindu-Christian Dual Belonging: Both, Between, and Beyond*, ed. Nadya Pohran and Daniel Soars (New York: Routledge, 2022), 122–39. Copyright © 2022 Routledge. Reused with permission of Taylor & Francis Group. Profound thanks to these publishers for their permission to re-present the content of these articles and chapters in the present volume.

I mentioned at the top of these acknowledgments that I presented my first paper related to the present study in 2005. A year later, I was joined by my spouse Jolie in marriage, and the project has thus lurked around the edges of our entire partnership. In part for this reason, I dedicate *Hindu Mission, Christian Mission* to Jolie. I could never have asked for, nor imagined, a more inspiring friend and life companion.

Introduction

Beyond the Conversion Controversy

On December 11, 2014, then Parliamentary Affairs Minister M. Venkaiah Naidu of the reigning Hindu nationalist Bharatiya Janata Party (BJP) raised a storm of criticism when he proposed a ban on all religious conversions throughout India. At issue was the alleged forced conversion of some two hundred Muslim families to Hinduism by activists associated with the Rashtriya Swayamsevak Sangh (RSS) in Agra earlier in the same month.[1] It was, if nothing else, savvy politics: once Naidu had changed the conversation from the converting practices of this activist group to conversion as such, the secular Congress party quickly went on the defensive. "Can Mr. Naidu stop anyone from converting willingly to any other religion?" asked Congress leader Digvijay Singh, "It will be an infringement of fundamental rights conferred by the Constitution. It is the fundamental right of an individual to choose his/her religion."[2] Two weeks later, *The Hindu* newspaper ran a "Sunday Anchor" feature with articles considering the social and political issues raised by the issue. Its title was "Conversion Confusion."[3]

This was not the first such episode in the so-called "conversion controversy" in India and the wider South Asian diaspora, nor would it be the last. Indeed, to at least some extent, this controversy has shaped Hindu-Christian relations since the arrival of Vasco da Gama on the shores of India in 1498. The controversy has, however, acquired a distinctive shape in the nineteenth, twentieth, and early twenty-first centuries, corresponding closely to the full consolidation and eventual dissolution of the British colonial project.[4] Beginning perhaps with the polemics of Swami

Dayananda Saraswati (1824–1883) and his founding of the Ārya Samāj in nineteenth-century Gujarat and continuing through Mohandas K. Gandhi's (1869–1948) exchanges with Bishop V. S. Azariah in the mid-1930s, the real and imagined threat of Western missionary powers cast a long shadow across the movement for Indian independence from colonial rule.

Eventually, the debates of Dayananda and Gandhi on conversion became woven into the very fabric of the sovereigntist project. During and well beyond the independence struggle, various affiliates of the Hindu nationalist Sangh Parivar movement added a militant dimension to their critique, echoed and fostered in part by such Hindu apologists as Ram Swarup (1920–1998), Sita Ram Goel (1921–2003), and Arun Shourie (1941–).[5] Several rites of reconversion, "purification" (*śuddhi*), or "welcoming" (*parāvartan*) had been developed by Dayananda and others in the nineteenth century, and these were deployed aggressively by the Vishwa Hindu Parishad (VHP) and other activist movements in the 1980s and 1990s to stem a perceived tide of conversions to Christianity and Islam, by directly converting non-Hindus or, more commonly, as a means of integrating or "Sanskritizing" those marginalized caste groups and *Ādivāsī* or tribal communities believed to be particularly vulnerable to Christian mission work.[6] Several Indian states enacted anti-conversion legislation, from 1967 to the present day.[7] In 1998, the BJP Prime Minister Atal Bihari Vajpayee called for a "national debate on conversions" in light of Christian missionary work in *Ādivāsī* communities, and this call was punctuated—not coincidentally, in the view of some—by the brutal murder of the Australian missionary Graham Staines and his two young sons in January 1999 in a tribal region of Orissa. The flames of the controversy have been fanned more recently by, among other factors, the 2008 anti-Christian riots in Kandhmal and the return of the BJP to power with the 2014 election and 2019 re-election of the Hindu nationalist government of Prime Minister Narendra Modi.[8]

This controversy can be understood in multiple ways, from the philosophical to the political to the sociological or ethnographic. A good case can be made—and has been made—that the public conversion controversy has far more to do with the complex interplay of the social divisions of class and caste than anything specific to Christianity, Islam, or Hinduism.[9] Nevertheless, the question has often been posed, and debated, on theological terms, and thus invites theological engagement.[10]

In this book, I attempt such an engagement through a comparative Hindu–Christian study of mission and missiology. Though I have titled the study *Hindu Mission, Christian Mission,* I undertake my comparative inquiry in reference not to "Hinduism" as such but to only one of its many strands: the non-dualist tradition of Advaita Vedānta, as embodied in the teaching of the eighth-century teacher Śaṅkara and his many, diverse successors in the medieval, modern, and contemporary periods. Advaita was among the first and most successful traditions to articulate a theology of worldwide mission in the late nineteenth century, a theology expressed most clearly in Swami Vivekananda's (1863–1902) repeated calls to "conquer the world through our spirituality."[11] I contend that the distinctive theologies of mission articulated by Vivekananda and his successors have deep roots and a complex development from the medieval period to the present day, and that they offer both a significant challenge and intriguing points of resonance with missiological proposals emerging from contemporary Catholicism and the mainline ecumenical movement.[12]

Both sides of the comparative inquiry attempted in *Hindu Mission, Christian Mission* are by design limited and particular. For reasons to be explained more fully in chapter 1, I judge that it makes good practical and methodological sense to seek clarity on a broad point of interpretation by attending to a single, delimited case study. As Canadian philosopher Bernard Lonergan once put the matter, "[I]t seems a mistaken method to seek generalization before one has tried to understand the particular."[13] In this case, I hope to demonstrate, a single, sustained, comparative inquiry can point us beyond some of the false oppositions of the conversion controversy toward a more holistic, fruitful encounter of distinctive missionary theologies and their visions of integral transformation. If successful, this study will open space for other such studies, engaging a fuller range of similarly distinct missionary traditions of Hinduism, Christianity, and other religious paths.

The argument of the book proceeds in two major movements. Part I, in three chapters, provides an initial description and defense of "missionary Advaita" as an historical phenomenon and interpretive category. As a first step in the analysis, chapter 1 lays the methodological ground for a comparative theology of mission, suggesting several scholarly developments that point a way beyond ossified positions on both sides of the conversion debate in India and abroad. Chapter 2 goes on to trace the historical emergence of Advaita Vedānta as an explicitly missionizing movement in the late nineteenth and early twentieth centuries. It does this by establishing "historical markers" that profile the distinctive character of several Advaita organizations, as well as defining successive stages in the development of a broader, relatively coherent mission movement. Chapter 3 shifts the attention from these contemporary movements to their roots in the ancient and medieval rivalries among *saṃpradāyas* or teaching traditions in the broader Hindu stream. Drawing on the Christian missiological scholarship of David Bosch, M. Thomas Thangaraj, Stephen B. Bevans, and Roger P. Schroeder, this chapter attempts to articulate the most distinctive "paradigms" and "styles" of Advaita mission from the tradition's remembered past. Such paradigms reach from the "compassionate teacher" of eighth-century teacher Ādi Śaṅkarācārya through the "servant-conqueror" of the late medieval Śaṅkara hagiographies to the image of the Buddha in the teachings of Swami Vivekananda, and they are further enriched by the various styles of missionary witness symbolized by Śaṅkara's four legendary disciples.

In part II of the book, four chapters move from this descriptive analysis toward a more explicitly comparative and constructive engagement. In each chapter I trace distinctive points of engagement that characterize these Advaita traditions and, in and through their careful exploration, bring them into dialogue with selected currents of Christian missiology. Chapter 4 explores the frequent appeal to "pure experience" as a transcultural ideal and key to the translation of Advaita Vedānta into new contexts and new idioms. No figure is more closely associated with an experiential approach than the sage Ramana Maharshi (1879–1950); hence, the Maharshi serves as a focal point for the inquiry in this chapter, both through his distinctive reinterpretation of such ancient authorities as Śaṅkara and the classic Advaita treatise, the *Vivekacūḍāmaṇi*, and through his subsequent contestation and retranslation by other missionary Advaitins. After this, in chapter 5, I engage the transformation of "locality" in missionary Advaita, focusing particularly on the creative rereading of the Śaṅkara hagiographies by Swami Chinmayananda (1916–1993) and the international Chinmaya Mission. Rather than simply shedding a traditional emphasis on the sacred geography of India in favor of a universalized, transcultural ideal, I suggest that these Advaita teachers and disciples engage in a more complex hermeneutical process, imaginatively relocating the sacred geography itself so that it comprehends the universal reach of their movements.

Having addressed questions of translation and quantitative, geographical extension in chapters 4 and 5, in chapter 6, I trace a more qualitative extension of Advaita mission from a strictly interior, spiritual liberation to include embodied concepts of empirical, social, and political liberation. Of special interest in this chapter is the gradual emergence of Advaita as a form of political theology, including the vigorous engagement of Transcendental Meditation and the Natural Law Party in traditional electoral politics and the more radical Advaita theology of liberation propounded by the ostensibly traditionalist Advaita theologian Anantanand Rambachan. Chapter 7, finally, returns to the question of conversion. After exploring several narratives of conversion in Advaita traditions, I suggest that metaphors of Sanskritization and nondualist belonging can reframe the imaginative construction of such conversions from the language of shifting allegiance to that of transformation, purification, and integrative ascent

One purpose of part II, and of the volume as a whole, is serious, sustained engagement with Advaita theologies of mission in their distinctiveness—beyond the polemics of the conversion controversy or these theologies' too-easy dismissal as mere imitative reversals of evangelical Christianity. I thus hope that the exposition and analysis in these chapters may advance the study of late modern and contemporary Advaita traditions, on their own terms. At the same time, my own purpose in studying missionary Advaita is ultimately constructive. Hence, in the concluding section of each chapter of this second part of *Hindu Mission, Christian Mission,* I take the additional step of offering comparative reflections. Chapters 4 and 5 consider themes of translation, recollection, and pilgrimage as aspects of Christian mission, and chapter 6 engages the political theologies of the Chinmaya Mission, Transcendental Meditation, and Anantanand Rambachan with comparable Christian theologies of social responsibility and "integral mission." Finally, in chapter 7,

I attempt to learn from Advaita models of conversion by looking at recent scholarship on the Christian convert *par excellence*: Paul the Apostle. Such scholarship, when read in the light of Advaita mission, opens the door to reconsidering Christian mission in terms of "Christification" rather than conversion.

It would be naïve to presume that the politics of the conversion controversy can be resolved by a single comparative inquiry, conducted mostly in the settler state of Canada by a Catholic theologian of North European ancestry who also happens to be a student of Advaita Vedānta. Indeed, as the comparativist Francis Clooney has noted in another context, it may be too much to ask of comparative theology that it engage every issue or social conflict. Not every important question is properly theological.[14] "We need to be careful," Clooney writes, "since it does no service to theology to use the word too broadly, or in contexts where, despite what we wish, it no longer obtains."[15] Perhaps the conversion controversy is a matter best left to journalists, social scientists, and political leaders in India and abroad.

I readily concede that theology may not be everything. Neither, however, is it nothing. If, as I contend in this volume, both Advaita Vedānta and Christianity offer robust theologies of mission that challenge and clarify each other in significant ways, then the encounter of these theologies may help us think more productively about Hindu–Christian relations, about the disputed question of conversion and, ultimately, about mission itself. That, at least, is the wager I am making in this study. Readers can decide for themselves whether it is a wise bet.

Feast of Saint Thomas the Apostle
July 2023
Williams Treaty Territory

Part I

Constructing Missionary Advaita

1

Toward a Comparative Theology of Mission

One of the more provocative books written on the conversion controversy in the last several years is is Goldie Osuri's *Religious Freedom in India: Sovereignty and (Anti) Conversion*.[1] For Osuri, the issue of conversion and the controversies that engulf it in India are fundamentally non-theological. They concern the ongoing construction of "a normative understanding of India's religious identity,"[2] and, more specifically, "relio-cultural, political, and juridical struggles for sovereignty."[3] Many scholars have noted that anxiety over the formation and maintenance of an Indian state looms large in the histories of conversion inquiries and anti-conversion legislation.[4] Osuri, informed by Carl Schmitt, Michel Foucault, and Georgio Agamben, goes further. She places the conversion controversy at the very center of the sovereigntist project. From the first anti-conversion legislation in the colonial-era princely states well into the contemporary period, the positioning of conversion as a threat to "public order," from which minoritized *Ādivāsīs*, Dalits, women and children require state protection, facilitates the consolidation of a majoritarian identity on the part of Hindu nationalists and secularists alike.[5] Even the language of religious freedom borrowed from the United Nations, Osuri contends, can be enlisted by organizations such as the Hindu American Foundation to advance the "religio-cultural" and "biopolitical" construction of sovereign power.[6]

Osuri's work is thoughtful, well documented, and persuasive. At the same time, her treatment of religion as an element of culture, and her nearly exclusive focus on the sociopolitical construction of

Hindu identity, differentiates her from those theorists who engage the intellectual content of the arguments more directly. In his aptly titled *Debating "Conversion" in Hinduism and Christianity*, for example, Ankur Barua suggests that the controversy over conversion is fundamentally philosophical, insofar as diverse Christian and Hindu traditions do in fact advance conflicting claims about the highest, unsurpassable truth and the achievement of final liberation. "[T]he Hindu-Christian debates over 'conversion,'" he writes, "are ultimately over the question of what is, in fact, the true Religion."[7] Barua readily concedes that conversion is politically freighted, noting the impact of contemporary historiographies of Christian missions, Hindu nationalism, and the rise of postcolonial theory in the Indian academy.[8] But he also argues that any strictly political or sociological reading of the controversy risks obscuring the internal diversities of both traditions, as well as truly relevant differences in their respective frameworks. Such differences include the integration of material well-being in most Christian visions of our highest end, or the way *karma* theory in Hinduism functions to render any "conversion" to highest truth merely less urgent rather than less desirable.[9]

"In short," Barua concludes, "the conflicts at the conceptual heart of Hindu-Christian encounters over 'conversion' should be understood in terms not so much of a tolerant Hinduism being subjected to the missionary depredations of an intolerant Christianity but of the opposition between two somewhat divergent schemes, each of which claims to be the fullness of 'the *Religion*' which can encompass the partial truths of 'the religions.'"[10] Though one should not neglect very real questions of history and identity, then, Barua insists that the controversy depends for its resolution on either the clear, rational establishment of one or the other tradition's truth-claims, or, perhaps more realistically, a deeper account of tolerance and the fruitful role of substantive disagreement in public life.[11]

Barua's arguments are also persuasive, and I will return to his monograph at several points in this work. But it is worth noting that both Barua and Osuri, for all their differences, treat conflicts over conversion more or less as they present themselves: as conflicts, whether they are understood as rhetorical constructions for the purposes of majoritarian Hindu politics or as the authentic result of philosophical disagreement. In this chapter, by contrast, I propose to ask what we might learn if we transpose the conversion controversy from the language of conflict into the language of engagement, conversation, and mutual transformation. Like Barua, I take up the controversy from an explicitly philosophical and theological perspective. I take such an approach not merely because these are the areas of my scholarly expertise, or because I judge that theological accounts have consequences and are worth engaging on their own terms, but also because a sustained engagement on these questions may serve as an occasion to re-think and to re-imagine the theology of mission in Christian and—at least potentially—Hindu traditions. That is, the conversion controversy can, if engaged in a comparative, conversational mode, emerge as a resource for renewed theological reflection.

Such a transposition into a more conversational mode is, I believe, facilitated by three strategic decisions. First, we benefit if we widen our view beyond "conversion" as an event or moment of decision to include those wider visions of "mission" and "missionary activity" that might motivate such conversions and render them meaningful. Second, we stand to gain if we refrain from generalizing too broadly but instead focus on the engagement of specific Hindu and Christian traditions in their particularity. In the case of this book, I argue for a specific engagement of Catholic and mainline ecumenical theologies of mission with the mission theologies that emerge from a diverse but relatively coherent group of Hindu movements associated with the non-dualist tradition of Advaita Vedānta. Finally, I suggest that such a particularist engagement of Hindu and Christian mission theologies may be most fruitfully pursued in the mode of contemporary comparative theology, as this subdiscipline has emerged in North America in the late twentieth and early twenty-first centuries.

I will develop and defend each of these propositions in turn. But first, it will be useful to linger a bit longer on the conversion controversy itself and its most typical discursive form—namely, a narrative of imperialist conquest and one-sided oppression. From such an examination, I suggest, we will be better positioned to explore the possibility of, and the pressing need for, an alternative mode of engagement.

"Conversion Is Violence": Parallel Narratives of Conquest and Oppression

In his own study of conversion controversies, *In Search of Identity*, Sebastian Kim has pointed out that Hindu and Christian controversialists have, from the colonial period to the present day, tended to talk past one another, due to the different frameworks they bring to the question. Christians have, for example, tended to argue for religious freedom from a liberal Enlightenment perspective on human rights. Hindus have, instead, appealed to the close relation of Indian culture and Hindu identity and to Hindu traditions of religious tolerance against the disruptive forces of proselytization.[12] "The Hindu-Christian debate of 1998–99," he writes, "helps us to see that interpretation of religious conversion requires more than an examination of personal changes of religious commitment or the sociopolitical changes taking place in a community. Study of the debate . . . suggests that it is also due to a clash of two radically different religious frameworks."[13] Kim's contention here coheres strongly with Barua's argument in *Debating "Conversion."* Barua too argues that Hindu and Christian views of religious diversity, and thus of conversion, flow from their more fundamental differences on "the nature of the divine reality, human personhood, and the human capacity to know the ultimate."[14]

Though my argument in this book will ultimately support Kim's and Barua's shared judgment on this point, I have also been struck by the fact that the impasse between Hindu and Christian controversialists can be traced not only to what differentiates them but also to what they share at a rhetorical level: namely, a common narrative structure of one-sided aggression and victimization.[15] To illustrate this common thread, I turn to public arguments of the Hindu teachers Swami Dayananda Saraswati and Sita Ram Goel, on the one hand, and the Christian theologians C. V. Mathew and Jose Kuruvachira, on the other.

A first instance of this narrative pattern can be found in an open letter published by the popular Advaita teacher Swami Dayananda Saraswati (1930–2015)—not to be confused with the nineteenth-century figure of the same name—in November 1999. In this letter, written on the occasion of a visit to India by Pope John Paul II, Dayananda calls on the pope to announce a "freeze" on all conversions in India and, ideally, throughout the world. He writes:

> Among the world's religious traditions, there are those that convert and those that do not. The non-converting religious traditions, like the Hindu, Jewish and Zoroastrian, give others the freedom to practise their religion whether they agree with the others' tenets or not. They do not wish to convert. I would characterise them as non-aggressive. Religions that are committed by their theologies to convert, on the other hand, are necessarily aggressive, since conversion implies a conscious intrusion into the religious life of a person, in fact, into the religious person.[16]

Hinduism is in a special situation, Dayananda contends, because Hinduism is deeply, inextricably bound up with Indian culture. Unlike Christianity, which can move between cultures, Hindu and Indian identity are inextricably entwined.

More importantly, due precisely to its Indianness, Hinduism is a non-converting religion. It stands defenseless and unarmed before the Christians' "one-sided aggression":

> In any tradition, it is wrong to strike someone who is unarmed. In the Hindu tradition, this is considered a heinous act, for which the punishment is severe. A Buddhist, a Hindu, a Jew, are all unarmed, in that they do not convert . . . We don't believe in conversion, even though certain Hindu organisations have taken back some converted people. Thus, conversion is not merely violence against people; it is violence against people who are committed to non-violence.[17]

There is no evidence that John Paul II read the letter, or that he would have been receptive to its sentiments if he had. A little over a week after the publication of Swami Dayananda's letter, during his visit in Delhi, the Pope occasioned still more intense controversy when he spoke of a "great harvest of faith" in his apostolic exhortation *Ecclesia in Asia*.[18]

Dayananda's letter had important political consequences in its own right,[19] but my purpose in introducing it here is to illustrate its relatively simple, rhetorical construction of the dispute, with "converting" Christian aggressors on one side and defenseless, "non-converting" Hindus on the other. This construction recurs frequently, even in treatments that extend well beyond a brief, open letter.[20] In his prodigious *History of Hindu-Christian Encounters*, for example, Sita Ram Goel offers a valuable documentary archive, with many diverse views and long, largely unedited quotations. This complex history of many voices is, however, framed by a similarly simple narrative structure. Christianity, Goel claims, exists for no other purpose than to advance its "dogma" as "a subterfuge for forging and wielding an organizational weapon for aggression against other people."[21] This represents a state of "permanent war," waged "on non-Christian societies and cultures with a view to conquer and convert them completely."[22] The preferred weapons of this war are force, symbolized by the sixteenth-century Jesuit missionary Francis Xavier, and fraud, symbolized by Roberto De Nobili and his successors in today's Christian ashram movement.[23] The deepest fraud is the Christian preaching of Christ itself, which has no credible basis in theology, spirituality or history.[24]

In a companion volume, *Jesus Christ: Artifice for Aggression*, Goel writes that "Nobody can beat the Christian theologians, not even Hegel, when it comes to camouflaging with pompous rhetoric and linguist tricks the complete collapse of their logic."[25] The shame is that the Hindus, overwhelmed by the financial resources of Western colonial and neocolonial powers, lacking the requisite intellectual resources and intrinsically and self-defeatingly disposed to generosity for others in their midst, repeatedly fall victim to this massive deception.[26] Deliberately evoking Adolf Hitler, Goel dismisses the Christian proclamation as a "big lie" and its gospels as the "First Nazi Manifesto."[27] Sita Ram Goel's language is far more inflated and deliberately provocative, but his narrative corresponds more or less seamlessly with that offered by Swami Dayananda. Christian missionaries are aggressive would-be conquerors; the Hindus are innocent victims; and the primary weapon of their victimization is conversion.

Indian Christians, more than anyone, perceive the clear and present danger to their communities in the rhetoric of Dayananda, Goel, and their fellow travelers, and they have not hesitated to respond in kind. In 1999, the same year that Swami Dayananda published his open letter, for example, theologian C. V. Mathew published a broad, synthetic study of what he viewed as a single, relatively coherent

"Saffron Mission" of Brahmanical Hinduism in India and the West, and this was followed by several more pointed and polemic studies by a Salesian priest, Jose Kuruvachira, between 2006 and 2008.[28]

For Mathew, the emergence of distinctively modern movements like the Ramakrishna Mission in the late nineteenth century and the reconversion work of the Rashtriya Swayamsevak Sangh (RSS) and other Hindu nationalist organizations can ultimately be traced back to much older patterns of Sanskritization and Brahminization embodied in the Vedic dictum *kṛṇvanto viśvamāryam*, "Let the whole world become Aryan."[29] While Kuruvachira more strongly emphasizes the novelty of this development in the modern period, he also interprets processes of Sanskritization, so-called "reconversion" rites like *śuddhi* and *parāvartan*, and especially the nineteenth-century teacher Swami Vivekananda's oft-quoted exhortations, "Up, India, conquer the world with your spirituality" and "the world must be conquered by India" as an unambiguous mandate to convert.[30] "In the course of time," Kuruvachira writes, "increased travel facilities, modern communications networks, globalisation, rise of Hindu cultural nationalism, better organisation and animation of the Hindu diaspora and so on have contributed greatly in making Hinduism emerge as an 'aggressive' missionary religion, seeking followers not only in India but also overseas, especially in the West."[31]

Kuruvachira's language here echoes that of Swami Dayananda—deliberately, it would seem—and he is candid about his intention to respond to Goel and other Hindu apologists.[32] Perhaps, then, it is no great surprise that Kuruvachira's account reveals significant structural affinities with that of Goel, just with different actors in the assigned roles. In this case, the primary aggressors are Hindu missionaries, particularly the RSS, Vishva Hindu Parishad (VHP), and other affiliates of the nationalist Sangh Parivar coalition in the latter half of the twentieth century. These reactionaries, according to Kuruvachira, propagate a vision of "one religion, one race and one culture," fundamentally opposed to religious freedom and motivated by "hatred of persons belonging to other faiths and communities."[33] They advance this agenda, again, through deception, including social service, school programs and curricular reforms, through large amounts of funding from international sources, and even through the use of "enticement and allurement"—here echoing common accusations against Christian missionaries.[34]

The biggest deception, in this case, is the claim not to proselytize or convert in the name of Hinduism: indeed, such a claim, belied by reconversionary activity in India and the work of the Ramakrishna Mission, Transcendental Meditation, and the International Society of Krishna Consciousness (ISKCON) abroad, represents nothing but a "big lie."[35] The worst part of this deception, Kuruvachira goes on to claim, is the extreme vulnerability of its victims, who include oppressed religious minorities, Dalits and *Ādivāsīs* in India; credulous, hospitable, and overly accommodating Indian Christians; and even unsuspecting Westerners, whose increasing secularism make them particularly susceptible to Hindu missions.[36] Finally, in a recurring leit-motif, Kuruvachira draws frequent parallels between the Hindu nationalists in particular and Adolf Hitler.[37] It is Sita Ram Goel and his Hindu peers who, on this reading, represent the actual Nazis and true perpetrators of violence against those committed to nonviolence.[38]

Obviously, my brief overview here does not do full justice to the arguments of either Goel or Kuruvachira. None of the claims, on either side, are entirely without merit.[39] My point in presenting these two narratives in parallel here, then, is not to discredit them but simply to illustrate their striking resemblance. Sita Ram Goel and Jose Kuruvachira disagree fundamentally about who should be identified as the real oppressor, the real victims, and the real Nazis of this controversy. Yet, they do so within a highly coherent, shared interpretive framework with many of the same categories and reference points.

It is worth noting, finally, that this interpretive framework also functions beyond the purview of explicit controversialists. I offer just two examples here. First, we can turn to the Hindu comparativist Arvind Sharma's contribution to the recent *Oxford Handbook of Religious Conversion*, entitled "Hinduism and Conversion."[40] This is the first chapter in a section dedicated to the meaning and means of conversion in diverse religious traditions. Yet, the main argument of the chapter instead adopts a modified version of Swami Dayananda's categorical distinction between "converting" and "non-converting" traditions, transposed here into the language of "proselytizing" and "non-proselytizing" religions—with "proselytization" described as any explicit effort to seek adherents.[41] The chapter details Hinduism's fundamental status as a "non-proselytizing" tradition, elaborates Hindu objections to proselytization by Muslims and Christians, and ultimately traces a fairly straight line from Christian proselytization to the 2008 violence in Kandhmal.[42] Christians were among the worst victims of this violence, Sharma recognizes, but he also seems to imply that the conflict was provoked by the foreign, inherently oppressive practice of proselytization brought to India with the advent of Christianity and Islam.

On the other side of the ledger, we find Robert Eric Frykenberg's account of missionary movements in his 2009 survey *Christianity in India*, especially its chapter entitled "Indian Christians and 'Hindu Raj.' "[43] In this account, Frykenberg makes the counterintuitive case that the British Raj, built on networks of patronage and power knitted piecemeal by the East India Company, actually represented Brahmanical Hindu interests and thwarted grassroots Christian movements at nearly every turn. "Nothing suited or supported the imperial Raj," he writes in another place, "better than the construction of such an imperialistic Hinduism."[44] The true successors of this hegemonic regime, on Frykenberg's reading, are not the Christians of contemporary India but the forces of Hindu nationalism that oppose and oppress them through the coercive use of state power.[45] The conflictual, conversionary work that most fully embodies the history of British colonialism is that of the RSS and the VHP.

Unlike Goel and Kuruvachira, Sharma and Frykenberg are souls of scholarly care in these and other works. Sharma's chapter in the *Handbook of Religious Conversions* contains many caveats, and here and elsewhere he distinguishes carefully between the missionary theologies of evangelical and liberal Christianities.[46] Frykenberg too is acutely aware of the diversities of both Hinduism and Christianity, and he concedes that Hindu fundamentalism and indeed all fundamentalisms of South Asia bear the mark of "profoundly intrusive forms of radical conversion movements exported to South Asia from Europe," "fiercely antitheistic forces of the Enlightenment," and "Indological Orientalism."[47] Nevertheless, even in the work of such erudite scholars we encounter similar framings of at least some forms of conversion as acts of violence propagated by powerful elites, and the positioning of Hindus or Christians, respectively, in the role of oppressed victims.

Is this, however, the only way to conceive of mission and conversion, in either or both of the Hindu and Christian traditions? In the remainder of this chapter, we will explore how Hindus and Christians might imagine dialogical possibilities beyond this shared narrative, and what the consequences might be in terms of their mutual relation and respective self-understandings.

Pathways to Conversation

One place where Goel and Kuruvachira agree is on the fundamental nature of conversion—or, at least, the nature of conversion in the *other* tradition. Goel draws his working definition from a 1947 Christian pamphlet entitled *The Right to Convert*. According to this pamphlet, conversion consists of "changes of faith, together with the outward expressions that such changes normally involve, and efforts to promote such changes."[48] Though Goel notes that Christians may describe their missionary work in many ways, this is mere subterfuge designed to lure victims into the "missionary trap" of conversion and destruction of other religions.[49] Kuruvachira, as we have seen, accuses Hindu militants of a deeper deceit: to deny their own doctrine of conversion, particularly by disguising it as a mere return of converts to their natural, pre-Christian or pre-Muslim state. "But upon closer examination," he writes, "one can understand that the so-called *shuddhi* or 'reconversion' is a semantic misnomer": "In essence it is another term for religious conversion which involves missionary work, preaching, teaching and the use of specified rituals and ceremonies on the part of Hindus, and acceptance of new doctrines, creeds, practices and ways of life, and a change in mental attitudes on the part of the converted."[50] Goel and Kuruvachira thus agree on what theorist Gauri Viswanathan calls the "most transparent" meaning of conversion: namely, a "change of religion."[51] It might seem to follow from this definition that the most transparent meaning of a missionary or "proselytizing" religious tradition would be a tradition that sets out to effect such changes of religion in the persons and communities it encounters.

In some Orientalist literature of the late nineteenth and early twentieth centuries, such transparent meanings of "conversion," "mission," and "missionary traditions" were used to distinguish the "higher" world religions such as Christianity or Buddhism from such merely "ethnic" or national religions such as Hinduism.[52] These categorical distinctions have, however, fallen out of scholarly use in recent years. On the one hand, any transparent understanding of "mission" as comprehending only—or even primarily—geographical or demographic expansion has come under serious scrutiny in many of the Christian traditions in which the term carries its main currency, including the missiologies of Catholicism and mainline ecumenical churches. On the other, the very concepts of "religion" and "world religion" developed in the Orientalist canon have come under scathing critique, increasingly replaced by a more textured, particularist focus on diverse Christianities and Hinduisms, attentive both to their indigenization in specific cultural contexts and their participation in wider transnational social formations. In this section, I will examine each of these developments in turn, followed by an account of the conceptual space they open for the comparative and constructive missiological study proposed in this book.

Beyond Conversion: Recent Developments in Christian Missiology

In his *Debating "Conversion,"* Ankur Barua devotes several chapters to untangling various strands of Christian mission theology, in the colonial era and in the present age. One dynamic that he highlights is the tension between European missionaries and indigenous converts in India, and their conflicting visions of Christian leadership and mission in South Asia.[53] This relates to questions of indigenization, which I will take up in the next section. A second dynamic highlighted by Barua relates to these same European missionaries' continual re-evaluation of the imperial project, of social reform, of the place (or not) of caste in their churches, and of the church's relation to South Asian religions.[54] These latter discussions pertain more directly to the meaning and significance of the term "mission" as a Christian practice and as a category of interpretation.

Barua is not alone in highlighting mission as problematic in modern and contemporary Christianity. In a short book intended for pastoral use, Roger P. Schroeder describes the twentieth-century transformation in Catholic missiology in particularly stark terms in a chapter title: "From Ransoming Pagan Babies to Mission on Every Continent."[55] The first phrase in this formulation refers to Schroeder's immature understanding of mission as a child, in the 1960s:

> "Pagan" babies (or adults) needed to be saved from the fires of hell by the act of baptism that would bring them safely on board the church—that is, the *Roman Catholic Church,* the ark of salvation. The stereotypical missionary picture was that of a white priest baptizing a non-white person in such mission lands as Africa, Asia, and the Pacific . . . The twofold motivation for mission was the salvation of souls and the establishment of the visible church around the world.[56]

Schroeder contrasts this vision from his childhood against a more contemporary, more mature, and far more all-embracing vision of mission as "*proclaiming, serving, and witnessing to God's reign of love, salvation and justice.*"[57] It is the latter understanding, he argues, that better represents the dominant missiology of the Catholic Church and other mainline churches.

This changed formulation encapsulates at least two major shifts in the missionary self-understanding of Catholicism and ecumenical Christianity. The first of these is usually referred to as a renewed understanding of Christian mission in terms of *missio Dei,* or the "mission of God." This theme is well captured in a 1966 *World Mission Report* of the United Church of Canada: "The mission with which the church is entrusted . . . is a mission from God to men [*sic*], not a mission from Christian men to non-Christian men."[58] This theology of *missio Dei* shifts the emphasis from missionary effort as a task initiated and undertaken by the Christian churches themselves toward mission as shared participation in a work already underway in the wider world—a work initiated, sustained, and brought to perfection not by any human institution but by the Triune God.[59] Second, precisely as a graced participation in the work of God, mission has come to be seen as encompassing not merely the addition of new members to the community but a wider range of activities. From a survey of both official teaching documents and scholarly conversations, Stephen B. Bevans suggests that an emerging ecumenical consensus on mission comprehends "six operative elements: (1) witness and proclamation; (2) liturgy, prayer, and contemplation; (3) justice, peace, and the integrity of creation; (4) dialogue with women and men of other faiths and ideologies; (5) inculturation; and (6) reconciliation."[60] Here, though mission may include conversion, such conversion has been re-positioned as one possible result of missionary activity rather than as its main objective.

What accounts for such a dramatic shift? As Catholic missiologists, Bevans and Schroeder attribute great significance to the teachings of the Second Vatican Council (1962–1965) of the Catholic Church and the post-conciliar magisterium, drawing special attention to Vatican II's decree on missionary activity, *Ad Gentes* (1965), Pope Paul VI's apostolic exhortation on evangelization in the modern world, *Evangelii Nuntiandi* (1975), and Pope John Paul II's encyclical *Redemptoris Missio* (1990).[61] Behind this development in the Catholic world lay the emergence of the global ecumenical movement with the World Missionary Conference in Edinburgh in 1910, the formal establishment of the World Council of Churches in 1948, and the ongoing work of its Commission on World Mission and Evangelism. It is worth noting that the theology of *missio Dei* that animates the decree *Ad Gentes* received its first public articulation not at the Vatican Council or in any specifically Catholic context but at a 1952 meeting of the International Missionary Conference in Willingen, Germany.[62] Finally, alongside Vatican II and the world ecumenical movement, Christian historians in the late twentieth century began to draw attention to the relatively recent, contingent character of the nineteenth- and early twentieth-century missionary theology that Schroeder encountered in his youth, unfolding instead a tremendous variety of such theologies, from the New Testament period to the present day.[63]

In contemporary Catholic and ecumenical Christian missiologies, then, "mission" cannot be reduced to conversion or to evangelical preaching; it encompasses a wider range of functions within a far more expansive theological horizon. To illustrate the valence that the category carries in the contemporary period, and its potential as a site for interreligious exchange, we can turn to two documents from significant authorities in the global Christian movement. The first of these is the 2011 ecumenical statement "Christian Witness in a Multi-Religious World," which stands out among such statements due to its release by the more conservative World Evangelical Alliance, alongside the World Council of Churches and the Catholic Church.[64] Unlike *Ad Gentes* or the 1966 *World Mission Report*, "Christian Witness" does not offer a full theology of mission. It focuses instead on several "practical issues" of witness and proclamation in the contemporary, pluralistic world ("Preamble"). Nevertheless, it provides a useful framework. As a foundation, the document cites 1 Peter 3:15, pairing the obligation of believers to give an accounting for their hope with the no-less-pressing obligation to do this with "gentleness and respect" ("Basis," no. 1). On one side of this formula, the authors note that the Christian hope of salvation rests not in the witness of Christians themselves but in the "supreme witness" of Jesus Christ and "the work of the Holy Spirit" who "blows where the Spirit wills in ways over which no human being has control" ("Basis," nos. 2, 7). On the other side, the twin obligations of "gentleness and respect" commend an attitude of "dialogue" with those to whom one offers Christian witness and rules out coercion and other unworthy means of evangelization ("Basis," nos. 4, 7).

These themes of dialogue and respect recur in the document's "Principles" (nos. 6–10, 12), alongside calls for authentic healing, "acts of service and justice," and the personal "integrity, charity, compassion and humility" that are part and parcel of authentic discipleship (nos. 3–5). "Christian witness," the document's authors contend, consists most fully in a profound imitation of the teachings and example of Christ, and in Christians' testimony to the "God [who] is the source of all love" through their own "lives of love" ("Principles," nos. 1–2). True witness cannot be reduced to demographics or strategies of church growth; it demands a holistic practice of life- and grace-filled sharing in the ministry of Christ.

Our second example brings out the idea of mission as a praxis of love more forcefully and at far greater length: Pope Francis's apostolic exhortation *Evangelii Gaudium*, "On the Proclamation of the Gospel in Today's World" (hereafter *EG*).[65] Written as a synthesis of a synodal meeting on the topic of the "New Evangelization," *EG* identifies three primary spheres of missionary proclamation: ordinary pastoral ministry, conversion of those already baptized to a deeper experience of faith, and "preaching the Gospel to *those who do not know Jesus Christ or who have always rejected him*" (no. 15). But these activities, according to the Pope, comprehend only a small portion of the wider mission to which the church has been called by God. Citing John Paul II's 1990 encyclical *Redemptoris Missio,* Francis insists that "missionary outreach is *paradigmatic for all the Church's activity*" (no. 15). For this reason, the five chapters of the exhortation comprehend a staggering array of topics, from reform of the Vatican curia to effective homiletics, and from a scathing critique of unbridled market capitalism (nos. 53–60, 202–208) to ardent praise for the "rich complementarity" Christians share with Jews (no. 249).

For our purposes, the core of Francis's missionary theology in this document can be located in chapters 3 and 4. The third chapter, on the question of explicit gospel preaching, draws attention both to the prior initiative of God in mission and to the universality of God's offer of salvation (nos. 112–13), in accord with an underlying theology of *missio Dei*. Francis also emphasizes the vital importance of cultural diversity and popular piety as, in themselves, important witnesses to the Gospel (nos. 115, 122–26). When Francis turns to verbal proclamation, then, it comes as no surprise that he again underscores this principle of diversity, drawing together such diverse activities as intimate, "personal dialogue" between neighbors and friends (no. 128), the "creative apologetics" of scientists and academics (nos. 133–34), and the Sunday homily (nos. 135–59) as key elements of mission. Evangelization in this chapter is primarily something that happens within the church, and Francis cautions that it should not be seen "exclusively or primarily in terms of doctrinal formation" (no. 161). Instead, it consists in a full life of love, formed by continual re-immersion in the Gospel *kerygma* (nos. 164–65) and manifested in a practice of gentle accompaniment that "teaches us to remove our sandals before the sacred ground of the other" (no. 169). When Francis turns his attention more fully to the church's evangelical outreach beyond its own boundaries, as he does in chapter 4, the focus shifts nearly entirely from its preaching to its prophetic action in defense of the poor and marginalized (nos. 177–237) and to its mutual, "social dialogue" with the natural sciences, with other Christians, and with followers of other religious paths (nos. 238–58).

These two examples—one the product of consensus in the world ecumenical movement, the other from the highest authority of the Catholic Church—clearly highlight the breadth and complexity of Christian mission in the contemporary world. It is telling that "Christian Witness" refers only once to "conversion" and does so only to remind Christians that it is the exclusive work of the Holy Spirit ("Basis," no. 7). Of the eleven appearances of the term in EG, it refers nearly exclusively to something that must be undertaken by baptized Christians (no. 15), pastoral ministers (nos. 25–26), and the structures of the Catholic Church in their continual processes of repentance and reform (nos. 27, 30, 32), as well as in the church's summons to engage in prophetic social action in pursuit of the common good (nos. 182, 201). About the evangelization of non-Christians, Francis offers the following recommendation: "All of them [non-Christians] have a right to receive the Gospel. Christians have the duty to proclaim the Gospel without excluding anyone. Instead of seeming to impose new obligations, they should appear as people who wish to share their joy, who point to a horizon of beauty, and who invite others to a delicious banquet. It is not by proselytizing that the Church grows, but 'by attraction' " (no. 15).[66] Conversion is clearly not excluded here but neither is it held up as the highest or sole objective of Christian witness. Elsewhere, in discussing interreligious dialogue, Francis argues that Christians should strive neither for Christian hegemony nor a privatizing secularity in the public sphere but that they should instead advocate for a "healthy pluralism, one which genuinely respects differences and values them as such" (no. 255).[67]

Hindu critics of Christianity are often suspicious of such irenic calls for pluralism and dialogue, and history provides ample ground for suspicion. However, my purpose in introducing "Christian Witness" and *Evangelii Gaudium* here is more analytic than apologetic. In both of these documents, we witness contemporary Christian visions of mission that are capacious, complex, and explicitly open to dialogue and relational exchange—that is, visions of a mission beyond mere conversion, conventionally understood.

Such a capacious understanding of mission has three important consequences for the present project. First of all, by including interreligious exchange as an important element of mission, distinct from proclamation, they provide an important *prima facie* warrant for theological inquiries beyond the boundaries of Christian tradition.[68] Second, perhaps more importantly, both visions insist that mission belongs to God, and that its scope extends more widely than the Christian communion. They thus open the possibility of reflection on how other traditions also participate in this mission. Wilfred Cantwell Smith stated this idea clearly in 1967: "The mission of the Church is world-wide; but it is not God's only mission. It is not even his only world-wide mission. Anyone who accepts the doctrine of the Holy Spirit, without setting ecclesiastic frontiers to his activity, already admits to this in theory, though many have yet to see and feel it in their hearts."[69] Presently, Smith contends, Christians know little of the comparable "missions" of Islam, Hinduism, Buddhism, and rabbinical Judaism. "But we can learn."[70]

Finally, the more capacious and holistic account of mission offered in documents like "Christian Witness" and *Evangelii Gaudium* offers a useful conceptual bridge for such interreligious learning to take place, precisely by distinguishing Christian mission as a participation in God's saving work from any single, specific form such participation may take. Stated more simply: if mission is not reducible to conversion, then an interreligious inquiry into mission need not start with conversion, or even with the presumption that all traditions "convert." Such questions can be deferred, in preference to deeper questions about God and humanity, about final liberation and its consequences in human history, and about the manifold ways that persons and institutions come to share in this liberation and these histories. Conveniently, the Advaita movements that will occupy our attention in these pages have reflected deeply on these questions, and their reflections can be fruitfully brought into conversation with Christian missiology. Questions of conversion will come, but later, as part of a wider, more holistic, and hopefully more interesting conversation on mission.

Before moving to this wider conversation, however, it will be useful to look more closely at what could or should count as a "religion" or a "tradition" in this, or any, interreligious inquiry—and, in particular, to justify a focus on the particulars of a tradition like modern and contemporary Advaita Vedānta rather than "Hinduism." It is to these questions that we now turn.

Beyond Hindu India and Christian Europe: Indigenization and Transnationalism

In her study *The Invention of World Religions*, Tomoko Masuzawa offers a genealogical history of the categories of "religion" and "world religions" as discourses that emerged hand in hand with the European colonial project. While in principle a rhetoric that concedes the existence of religious plurality might seem to represent a kind of progress, Masuzawa suggests that it preserves the logic of European hegemony in a new form. She writes:

> What is at stake here is far more fundamental than the problem of border violations between historical science and theology; rather it is a question of whether the world religions discourse can be in any way enlisted, and trusted, on the side of historical scholarship. Or, put another way, whether the idea of the diversity of religion is not, instead, the very thing that facilitates the transference and transmutation of a particular absolutism from one context to another—from the overtly exclusivist hegemonic version (Christian supremacist dogmatism) to the openly pluralistic universalist one (world religions pluralism)—and at the same time makes this process of transmutation very hard to identify and nearly impossible to understand.[71]

In making a case for the cultural particularity of "religion," Masuzawa is far from alone. Inspired in part by the seminal work of Edward Said, a significant number of scholars have problematized "religion" and, in some cases, called for its radical revision or thorough abandonment as a discipline of scholarly study.[72]

The critique of "religion" has a particular resonance in the context of India, and particularly troublesome consequences in contemporary debates about religious conversion. Though it would be rare these days to encounter the argument that Hinduism is an invention of the modern period, few contemporary scholars dispute the formative role of British Orientalists in positioning the diverse Vedic and Sanskritic traditions of India as a singular, reified "world religion" on the model of Protestant Christianity.[73] This ideological construction was never innocent. "The missionary construction of 'Hinduism' and the understanding of the significance of missionary activity," writes Barua, "formed two sides of the same coin: if 'Hinduism' consisted of systemised structures of superstition, then the mission to the Hindus could be conceived of as the attempt to demolish these structures."[74] But it also had unforeseen consequences, as modern Hindus from Swami Vivekananda to Sita Ram Goel adopted this constructed vision as their own, invoking it to consolidate an ethno-religious identity for India as a nation-state and eventually deploying it to castigate Christian intolerance and aggression.[75]

The missionaries' ideological construction of Hinduism had yet another troubling legacy: its parallel construction of "Christianity" itself as a similarly singular, doctrinally uniform, reified, and quintessentially European "world religion." Fueled in part by postmodern currents in anthropology and sociology, however, a new generation of historians, archivists, and ethnographers—not to mention Indian Christian theologians themselves—have attempted to reverse this bias. In North America, the transition to a new style of scholarship can perhaps be marked by the publication of two important works: Susan Bayly's *Saints, Goddesses and Kings* in 1989, and Selva J. Raj and Corinne M. Dempsey's edited collection *Popular Christianity in India* in 2002.[76] In the former, Bayly broke new ground by taking up six case studies of Muslims and Christians in South India between 1700 and 1900 and illustrating their thorough acculturation to indigenous traditions of status and sacred power. In the latter, originating in a 1997 panel at the American Academy of Religion, Raj and Dempsey consolidated the work of ethnographers and other scholars studying festival rites, processions, liturgies, scriptural study, healing, and exorcism in the popular, hybrid practice of local Christian communities—Protestant, Catholic, Orthodox, and Assyrian, from throughout the subcontinent.

These more textured, particularist studies of Christianity in South Asia collectively assert its indigenous character.[77] As Bayly puts the matter: "Once dismissed as alien or marginal implants of European colonial rule, the manifestations of Islam and Christianity which took root in south India should now be seen as fully 'Indian' religious systems. Their underlying principles of worship and social organisation derived from a complex and dynamic process of assimilation and cross-fertilization."[78] In his study of the practice of vow rituals (*nerccai*) at three Catholic shrines in rural Tamil Nadu, Selva Raj similarly notes that, with the exception of a few "identity markers" such as crosses and scapulars, "there is very little difference between Catholic and Hindu *nerccai* ritual performance. This suggests that, with some minor variations, Catholics and Hindus share a common ritual system."[79] Based in part on his ethnographic work, Raj would eventually become one of the leading advocates for including Christianity, as well as Judaism and Islam, in survey texts and courses on the indigenous religions of South Asia.[80]

Recognizing the highly indigenized, hybrid forms Christianity took in South Asia is of vast importance for addressing the specter of "de-nationalism," as it functions to marginalize Christians in the conversion debate in India. But it has also become important for understanding the local, indigenized character of the Christianities propagated by the Western missionaries themselves. In his *Christianity in India,* for example, Robert Frykenberg draws attention not merely to the agency of Dalit and tribal communities who adopted Christianity in their own idiom and on their own terms but also to the distinctive stamp left on Goan religious life by an intra-Catholic struggle between the Portuguese *Padroado Real* and the Roman *Propaganda Fide*.[81] David Mosse has persuasively argued that the robust adoption of indigenous patterns of divine patronage in many rural shrines in nineteenth-century Tamil Nadu had as much or more to do with their French Jesuit pastors' dreams of restoring something like the recently lost European *ancien regime* in India than any particularly enlightened views of inculturation.[82] Finally, we can adduce the curious case of *malars* or *alrupangal,* small images of body parts offered to the deity or saint as either petition or thanksgiving for healing in South India.[83] Commonly regarded by Hindus and Christians alike as an originally Hindu practice, and sometimes therefore condemned as superstition, it now seems certain that the use of such images originated in rural shrines in southern Europe.[84] Here, it appears, an indigenous Christian practice in Europe became part of Hindu practice in South India, before then becoming a mark of the authentic indigenization of Christianity in South Asia.

This final example, of course, points to the fact that the Hindu traditions that dominate the religious fabric of most parts of India are also themselves deeply implicated in dynamics of adaptation and indigenization. As scholars increasingly discovered the irreducible locality of Christian traditions, they also turned their attention to the capacity of Hindu traditions to transcend the local—or, better, to become local elsewhere than South Asia. Often coded as the study of Hinduism "in the diaspora," these studies note the ways that Hindu communities adopt congregational or denominational structures of authority, reimagine the sacred geography of North America and Europe, and engage with U.S. or Canadian traditions of pluralism and secularity.[85] Where Christians in India may adapt Hindu traditions of vow-taking and sacred power, to cite just one example, Hindus in the United States can also adapt their traditions in creative ways, reimagining codes against ritual pollution to permit the hosting of blood drives on temple grounds and promoting organ donation across boundaries of birth and class.[86] Finally, of course, we should note that the Hindu diaspora of these studies is often treated as one part of a wider diaspora of South Asian religious traditions, including Syro-Malabar, Syrian Orthodox, and other distinctively South Asian Christianities.[87]

One of the most fruitful insights from this body of scholarship has been the increasingly common shift from "diaspora" to "transnationalism" as the category of choice in the study of South Asian traditions, illustrating the complex currents of influence to and from the Indian subcontinent and destabilizing assumptions about premodern ritual or social forms as pristine archetypes.[88] Sometimes this takes the form of narrow case studies, such as Maya Warrier's inquiry into the diverse apprehensions of "modernity" in the experiences of both Western and South Asian devotees of Mata Amritanandamayi.[89] It can also comprehend a wider sweep of transnational social formations, such as Srinivas Aravamudan's intriguing account of "Guru English,"[90] or the critical genealogies of contemporary yoga by Elizabeth De Michelis, Sarah Strauss, and Andrea Jain.[91] In all these cases, Hindu traditions are no longer South Asian in a restrictive sense; nor are they "world religions" in the sense of the nineteenth-century Orientalists. They are translocal, vernacular, and continually reinvented in the cross-currents and contestations of cultures.

The particular traditions examined by Warrier and De Michelis are transnational in another important sense: that is, their disciples are no longer exclusively, or even primarily, South Asian in origin.

They are ethnically and geographically diverse. Stated another way, the study of Hinduism as a transnational phenomenon has also highlighted the fact that a number of Hindu traditions have emerged as implicitly or explicitly missionary in character, even in the restricted, conventional sense critiqued above.[92] Between 2009 and 2013, several edited collections provided glimpses into the distinctive profiles of both South Asian and Western gurus, who advance the teachings of particular Hindu *saṃpradāyas*, attract new followers and, in many cases, institutionalize their movements as formal missions.[93] Sunrit Mallick's *The First Hindu Mission to America* profiles Protap Chadra Majumdar (1840–1905) and his work as a missionary of the Brahmo Samāj, beginning in 1883.[94] In her *Transcendent in America,* Lola Williamson takes up a second generation of twentieth-century "Hindu-Inspired Meditation Movements" that can be regarded as indigenous to North America despite their South Asian origins.[95] E. Burke Rochford has, in two volumes, traced the origins, decline, and transformation of the evangelical Vaiṣṇava International Society of Krishna Consciousness (ISKCON) or Hare Krishna movement, founded in New York City in 1966.[96] Finally, the last four decades have produced a number of scholarly treatments of the international Ramakrishna Mission, founded by Swami Vivekananda in the wake of his famous presentations at the 1893 World's Parliament of Religions in Chicago.[97]

One of these works, Carl T. Jackson's *Vedanta for the West* (1994), stands out for special attention because of its final chapter, in which Jackson compares the mission theology of the Ramakrishna movement with those of the Self-Realization Fellowship, Transcendental Meditation, and ISKCON.[98] The comparison is short, Jackson's purview limited primarily to questions of strategy, and his view more or less entrenched in what Masuzawa excoriates as a discourse of "world religions pluralism."[99] Nevertheless, he notes how these diverse traditions manifest different mission theologies, with consequences for the aggressiveness of their outreach and their respective levels of openness to adapting South Asian practices to the North American context and appointing local leadership.

Jackson's interests are primarily ethnographic, but his brief treatment well reveals how the study of a particular Hindu missionary tradition can raise questions of constructive theology, including the theology of mission. It seems evident that, if such an inquiry can take place between different forms of missionary Hinduism, it can also occur between these particular traditions and the no less particular missionary theologies of the Catholic Church and ecumenical Christianity, surveyed in the previous section. In his Apostolic Exhortation *Evangelii Gaudium*, for example, Pope Francis commends interreligious dialogue as part and parcel of the church's evangelical vocation, and he describes such dialogue as a "process" of "mutual listening," enrichment, and purification (no. 250). It seems reasonable to suppose that engagement in this process need not merely express the mission of the church but might also extend to a rethinking of the church's own theology of mission, in and out of its interreligious exchange.

Beyond the Monological: A Comparative Theology of Mission

The idea of exploring the theology of mission in a conversational, comparative mode is not original to this book, or even to this century. We have already briefly noted Wilfred Cantwell Smith's evocation of "world-wide missions" beyond the Christian fold, which he advanced in 1967. In a short article for the 1987 *Dictionary of Mission*, Peter Antes and Hans Waldenfels too suggested that the time had come for a more inclusive approach to their discipline. They write: "For a long time 'mission' was considered an exclusively Christian term, its use being restricted to activities propagating the Christian faith. Even in the phenomenology of religions (at least in Europe), "mission" was often reserved for Christianity alone. Consequently, there are few systematic, cross-cultural, and comparative studies of missions that have yet been produced. But the encounter of religions in our time calls for a correction in this respect."[100] Such calls for further comparative study of missions and missiology have been echoed by François Böspflug in 2006 and by Stanley H. Skreslet in 2012, among others.[101]

Responses to these calls are still, on the whole, fairly thin on the ground. Most have focused on the so-called "great missionary traditions" of Christianity, Buddhism, and Islam, sometimes broadened to include Manichaeism or Marxism.[102] But comparative inquiry on the question of mission has also extended to Hinduism. Several volumes have drawn particular Hindu traditions into comparative studies of conversion, most notably Rowena Robinson and Sathianathan Clarke's *Religious Conversion in India* in 2003, Rudolf C. Heredia's *Changing Gods* in 2007, Lewis Rambo and Charles Farhadian's *Oxford Handbook of Religious Conversion* in 2014, and Peter Berger and Sarbeswar Sahoo's *Godroads* in 2020.[103] Klaus K. Klostermeier's contribution to the edited volume *Mixed Messages* takes a wider view. Klostermeier carefully distinguishes among the various theological traditions of Hinduism, as well as between "domestic" and "foreign" missionary strategies.[104] He concludes that, due to this diversity, "the Hindu missionary influence is multidimensional and will not likely result in large-scale conversions to a 'Hindu Church.'"[105]

Klostermeier's purpose, like that of the other comparative studies surveyed above, is descriptive and sociological. Two other comparative studies are more ambitious. Aaron J. Ghiloni's 2015 edited collection *World Religions and Their Missions*, for example, takes a broad approach to the question of mission.[106] Part of the problem with studying this theme comparatively rests in the ambiguity of the term. It is by no means clear, for instance, that Buddhism is "missionary" in the same sense as many forms of Christianity.[107] And the case becomes still more complex when we turn to missionary traditions of Hinduism, some of which emerge in explicit contrast to missionary Christianity.[108] Embracing such ambiguity, Ghiloni contends in *World Religions and Their Missions* that "a variety of missions" among diverse traditions "implies a variety of *meanings* of mission, even within a single religion."[109] Thus, in addition to individual chapters on missionary traditions of Atheism, Bahá'í, Buddhism, Christianity, Hinduism, Islam, and the Church of Jesus Christ of Latter-day Saints, two subsequent chapters attempt to discern common themes and paths forward in dialogue.

In his self-conscious retrieval of the Orientalist term "missionary religions," Ghiloni discerns several performative, heuristic guides for comparative study. Missionary traditions are, he suggests, characterized by a sense of duty, vocation, or special calling; an orientation to geographic or world historical movement; a desire to communicate a truth; and a "relational embrace" of community life.[110] In a chapter on missionary Hinduism, Ferdinando Sardella draws on his own expertise in modern Vaiṣṇava traditions along with research on other mission movements to develop more specific themes, including "compassion," "enlightenment," "liberation" from the false self, and "access to the world of divine love," as shared reference points.[111] Whereas Klostermeier and other contributors to *Mixed Messages* focus on the particularities of missionary traditions, *World Religions and Their Missions* attempts to formulate responsible generalizations, cognizant of these particularities but not confined by them.

Arvind Sharma's *Hinduism as a Missionary Religion* strikes a similar note with a narrower case study.[112] His work is explicitly constructive. While acknowledging a prevailing consensus that Hindus remained "non-missionary" at least well into the modern era, Sharma makes a forceful case against this consensus. "Hinduism," he writes, "has always possessed a missionary character."[113] He locates some of the most compelling evidence in the Vedic and Classical periods, adducing the Ṛg-Veda, *Manusmṛti,* and epic literature to suggest that foreigners could be, and often were, reconstrued as "lapsed Hindus," rendering them eligible for incorporation into the twice-born castes.[114] At this point, however, Sharma also finds the received terminology an obstacle, especially the language of conversion. Parsing terms carefully, he insists that, even as a "missionary religion," Hinduism does not "seek converts," and he redefines conversion in non-exclusive terms as "acceptance of a universal point of view."[115] Stated another way, there are now and have been missionary forms of Hinduism and even "conversion" to these traditions, but their distinctive theologies transform the meanings of both terms.[116]

In *Hinduism as a Missionary Religion,* Sharma treats Hinduism basically as a single, cohesive whole, without lingering on its internal complexity or its embeddedness in transnational processes of exchange. At the same time, he also brings the Hindu traditions he studies into direct conversation with Christian theologies of mission, proselytization, and conversion for the purpose of mutual illumination.[117] In this latter respect, as well as his self-interested location within the tradition he is studying, Sharma shows strong affinities with a scholarly approach highlighted but not developed by Ghiloni: contemporary comparative theology.[118]

Comparative theology—or, better, the "new" or "contemporary" comparative theology[119]—has emerged as a promising subdiscipline of Christian theology in the last three decades. In Anglophone North America, it is closely identified with the work of the Jesuit theologian Francis X. Clooney, one of its most committed advocates. On Clooney's reading, the "new" comparative theology stands in a complex genealogical relation both to the sixteenth- and seventeenth-century missionary theologies of his fellow Jesuits Francis Xavier (1506–1552) and Roberto de Nobili (1579–1656), on the one hand, and the post-Enlightenment "classic comparative theology" of F. Max Müller (1823–1900) and other European Orientalists, on the other.[120] Rooted in the explicit faith commitment of the former and the painstaking scholarly commitment of the latter, comparative theology in its contemporary variant aims to embody "an interreligious learning that is neither merely academic nor merely spiritual, a weaving together of intellectual inquiry with spiritual vulnerability." One's faith commitment and one's academic inquiry are self-consciously "allowed to challenge and purify one another."[121] Beyond this integration of faith and vulnerability in the scholarly project, contemporary comparative theology also stands apart from many older forms of comparative religion by its choice of specific examples, its narrow, aspectual focus, and its reluctance to generalize.[122] It aims at transformation of theological traditions, not by the articulation of some grand theory but by specific encounters of persons and traditions.[123]

And how does such transformation take place? For Clooney, this relates closely to an aspect of his research program that has occasioned some controversy: his nearly exclusive focus on texts.[124] Noting the ways that many religious traditions place emphasis on disciplined reading and commentary as practices of transformation, Clooney's work engages in the creative juxtaposition of texts, with the intention of extended signification: "To contextualize, to read one's Text along with other texts, is to create new meanings. Established meanings, simple or complex, are extended through previously unintended juxtapositions. Something of the independent, first meaning of one's Text may be changed, even distorted or lost, while new meanings, not intended by the author, occur to the reader." [125] Clooney's use of "Text" here refers to more than just a piece of writing. The particular works at the center of any inquiry evoke that full heritage of authoritative writings, traditions, and practices that endow a particular religious path with meaning and value. It is this broader Text that is destabilized and resignified in the process of comparative re-reading. The generation of new meanings can be subtle, and sometimes such new meanings are adverbial rather than nominal: they may refer to the "how" of our faiths, the manner of their practice and expression, rather than the "what" of our distinctive truth claims.[126]

Catherine Cornille has helpfully classified the various ways that comparative theologians learn from other traditions into distinctive heuristic patterns: "*intensification*" or "*reaffirmation*" of the home tradition or particular aspects of it, "*recovery*" of forgotten or suppressed elements of this tradition, "*rectification*" of erroneous understandings of religious others, "*reinterpretation* of one tradition in light of another," and "actual *appropriation* of new insights, experiences, and practices" from another religious path.[127] Clooney's own work tends to focus on intensification and reaffirmation, and particularly on recovery. Thus, in his first significant work in the field, *Theology after Vedānta,* Clooney re-reads and comparatively retrieves portions of Thomas Aquinas's *Summa Theologiae* and its subcommentaries in and out of a thorough immersion in the commentarial tradition of Advaita Vedānta.[128] In 2014's *His Hiding Place Is Darkness,* on the other hand, he seeks a renewed, powerless, risky surrender to Christ as the beloved, through deep immersion in and juxtaposition of a Vaiṣṇava devotional hymn with the Song of Songs.[129] In these and other works, Clooney more often affirms distinctive elements of the Christian proclamation rather than challenging them, even as the affective character of such affirmations is persistently unsettled and set on a new, interreligious footing.

Thus conceived, contemporary comparative theology reveals strong affinities with the more local, contextualized studies of Hindu and Christian traditions surveyed in the previous section. Its modesty, its specificity, its willingness to reconsider Christian traditions in light of comparative inquiry, and its acknowledgment of the provisional, unfinished character of all theological inquiry recommend it as one useful resource for engaging the "postcolonial situation."[130] Most importantly for the present study, comparative theology suggests a new and designedly indirect response to the "conversion controversy." Rather than refuting one or the other narrative of oppression—or even both of them together—a comparative theological approach to the question will attempt to construct a provisional alternative, one in which distinctively Hindu and distinctively Christian theologies of mission may become resources for a mutual practice of re-reading, resignification, and at least potentially, renewal. Such a contemporary comparative theology of mission will not proceed by generating a new cross-cultural theory of mission, or by attempting to articulate the missionary theology of "Hinduism" or even "Christianity" as cohesive wholes. It will instead proceed by small steps, and it will focus resolutely on the particular.

"Mission" as Comparative Category and Site of Transformation

In the first section of this chapter, I examined the public contestations of Swami Dayananda Saraswati, Sita Ram Goel, C. V. Mathew, and Jose Kuruvachira, adducing their parallel narratives of conquest and oppression. These narratives, I suggested, pose an obstacle to mutual understanding between Hindus and Christians in India and abroad. In the intervening section, I have now surveyed three recent developments that may be read to disrupt the terms of this debate and to open space for conversation: the late twentieth- and early twenty-first-century reformulation of Christian missiology in terms of *missio Dei* and holistic transformation; increasing recognition of the indigeneity of South Asian Christianities and the transnationalism of global Hinduisms in contemporary scholarship; and the emergence of comparative missiology and comparative theology as fields of scholarly inquiry over the last several decades. Each development, on its own, provides impetus and resources for reconsidering the conversion controversy. Taken together, I suggest, they recommend something like a comparative theology of mission, as attempted in the chapters that follow.

Any particular comparative theology of mission will, according to my understanding, be limited and provisional by design. There may be many such theologies, as new texts and traditions come into view. In the case of this comparative theology of mission, the data from which I draw are the history and contemporary teachings of Catholic and ecumenical Christian traditions, on one side, and the history and contemporary teachings of several movements associated with the non-dualist Hindu tradition of Advaita Vedānta, on the other.

The choice of Advaita as the Hindu dialogue partner in this study will be problematic for some readers, insofar as it may seem to presume an Orientalist preoccupation with Vedānta as the "essence" of Hinduism.[131] This is not my understanding of the Advaita tradition, however, nor my intention for the present volume. In part, my selection of Advaita follows simply from the fact that this is the tradition on which I have focused significant scholarly energy for the past two decades. The choice is, in this respect, arbitrary.[132] There are nevertheless intrinsic reasons for focusing on Advaita Vedānta in a Hindu-Christian theology of mission. Not least, as noted earlier, these include the prominence of the Advaita teacher Swami Vivekananda (1863–1902) and the Ramakrishna Mission in any discussion of Hindu missionary movements in the modern period. Vivekananda is frequently portrayed as "the first major missionary of Hinduism in the West."[133] The contestation of this status by some rivals,[134] while raising legitimate questions of history, nevertheless tends to reaffirm the prominence of the claim itself in both scholarly literatures and public understandings of modern Hinduism.

In addition, certain distinctive characteristics of Advaita teaching—including especially its appeal to a self-knowledge beyond culture, beyond ethnicity, and beyond the phenomenal realm of name and form—challenge key teachings of Catholic and other Christian churches and also, paradoxically, function to render the tradition similarly transcultural in appeal. As Thomas A. Forsthoefel puts the matter, Advaita "has proven itself to be a most efficient philosophical instrument to serve the transmission of Hinduism to the West."[135] Of course, the very teachings that have made Advaita so effective in this regard distinguish it not only from Christian traditions but also from other obvious conversation partners in the broader Hindu stream, such as the explicitly evangelical and theistic ISKCON tradition of Gauḍīya Vaiṣṇavism.[136] Far from enshrining Advaita Vedānta as the essence of Hinduism, then, I hope that the particularist approach taken here elicits the historical contingency of the tradition and its complex, contested relations with other traditions in South Asia and in its transnational context.

The operative category of my comparative inquiry, like those of Ghiloni, Klostermeier, and Sharma, is "mission"—and this too may be problematic for some readers. First of all, few would dispute that, at least in its contemporary usage, this is a Christian category with little parallel in premodern South Asia. The English term is derived from the Latin *missio,* itself a translation of the Greek verb *apostellō,* referring to the act of sending or being sent. A dictionary of ecclesiastical Latin offers the following definition:

> **missio:** mission; the task entrusted to the Church by Jesus to proclaim the gospel to the world and make disciples of all people; the word mission is often used to indicate a parish that has no resident priest but is regularly served by a priest from a neighboring parish; in the plural the word missions often refers to the activity involved in spreading the faith in foreign and/or non-Christian areas.[137]

It appears evident that most interpreters presume a definition quite like this one when they argue for or against an understanding of Hinduism as a "missionary religion." Thus, Sharma states that a religion can be called "missionary" in a broad sense if it "accepts converts"; it becomes a "proselytizing religion" insofar as it "not merely accepts but also seeks converts."[138] In his monograph, he adds to the general notion of "bringing others into one's fold" an element of intention: "To be a missionary religion, one must have a *conscious* sense of that mission."[139] Though Sharma abstracts from common Christian ecclesiastical definitions to make his case for missionary Hinduism, the basic structure remains more or less intact.

In my account of contemporary Catholic and mainline ecumenical Christian missiologies, above, I have argued that the valence of mission can be further generalized even in intra-Christian conversations, and Ghiloni's volume offers further examples of this in a comparative context. Despite its Christian provenance, the category can be read to possess a degree of historical malleability and semantic breadth that render it capable of comparative inquiry. In the language of the philosopher and comparativist Wesley Wildman, we might say that the category of mission can be and has been rendered sufficiently "vague" to permit fruitful comparison. The category can be meaningfully applied to different, even contradictory, phenomena.[140]

In fact, Wildman's account of comparative method clarifies a number of points. First, and perhaps most important, he cautions against seeking purity or imagining we could ever achieve perfect neutrality in our analytic categories. Instead, he recommends seeking pragmatic methods to manage the inevitable risk of distortion. For Wildman, this entails a "self-conscious dialectic approach" in which categories are continuously reformulated in response to new data, ideally in a collaborative context that includes experts and adherents in a process of mutual correction.[141] As a philosopher of religion, Wildman's comparative method embodies what Cornille calls a "meta-confessional" approach, distinct from the explicitly "confessional" orientation of Clooney and other comparative theologians.[142] Nevertheless, Wildman helpfully notes that all comparisons, of whatever type, are "interested"—that is, they are "conditioned by the interests of interpreting beings."[143]

This, in turn, points us to another, more concrete respect in which mission is problematic as a comparative category. For the particular Christian missionary theologies that emerged out of the colonial project—the mission theologies embodied in the ecclesiastical definition of *missio*, presented above—are widely regarded as ethically questionable to many Hindus and also to a significant number of Christian persons and traditions seeking new ways to engage religious plurality in the contemporary world.[144] The conversion controversy illustrates this dimension of mission as a historical and theological problematic, as does the ever-more-pressing need of Christian churches to produce documents like "Christian Witness in a Multi-Religious World" and *Evangelii Gaudium*. I would contend, however, that mission is valuable as a locus of Hindu-Christian comparative inquiry precisely because it has become a controverted source of argument for Christianity as well as for Hinduism. The category is fruitfully problematic insofar as it facilitates comparative inquiry into a set of contested theological questions that could be, and are being, pursued by other theologians of mission in other ways.[145] It positions "mission" not merely as a tool for analysis but also—at least ideally—as a site of theological transformation.

Even the most fervent desire for transformation and renewal, of course, does not remove the need for careful management. In this book, I develop my comparison in two movements, which attempt, first, to specify mission as a comparative category and then, in a second interpretive act, to use it constructively. In the first part of the study, I offer a sustained interpretation of Advaita Vedānta as a missionary tradition, moving from the *a priori* discussion in this chapter to a chronological account of five major modern and contemporary Advaita mission movements in chapter 2 and a more historical and synthetic analysis, from the eighth century to today, in chapter 3. The goal of these chapters is rich description, albeit a rich description specifically motivated by the exigence of mission as an interpretive category. In the book's second section, I move into a more explicitly constructive mode, taking up several distinctive themes of Advaita mission, elaborating each theme with reference to several of the movements profiled in the second chapter, and exploring points that resonate, challenge, and invite renewed reflection on particular aspects of Catholic and ecumenical Christian missiologies. The themes are: the Advaita promise of liberative experience in chapter 4, the resignification of place in chapter 5, the transformation of social realities in chapter 6, and the question of conversion in chapter 7. In a short conclusion, I attempt to consolidate the insights generated by the comparison, as well as to trouble them a bit as we reflect on their practical significance and concrete application.

In the first half of the book, then, I respecify *mission* as a category of Advaita life and thought; in the second half, I deploy the category—as respecified—to reflect on comparable themes of Christian mission.[146] In the terms set out by Cornille, the study aims to be self-consciously and rigorously "confessional" in method and approach. This means that its descriptive and constructive portions are, inevitably, mutually imbricated. As Cornille writes: "The confessional approach to comparative theology . . . renders explicit the fact that one's understanding of the other religion is always colored by certain religious prejudices and that the process of learning from the other also involves some degree of transformation or reinterpretation of the self-understanding of the other."[147] Stated differently, although the organization of the work privileges careful description of missionary Advaita prior to its theological reinterpretation in dialogue with missionary Christianity, such description already constitutes a constructive intervention in both traditions. The themes that I have deployed to bring out shared themes and missionary dimensions of the Advaita movements selected for study, for example, are the fruit of my own creative engagement and theoretic interests as a Christian student of Advaita Vedānta. They do not, in most cases, follow unambiguously from direct statements of Ādi Śaṅkarācārya, Swami Vivekananda, or other teachers I profile in the pages that follow. I am nevertheless hopeful that members of these movements will recognize themselves and their teachings in my interpretation, and perhaps even be assisted in their ongoing re-articulations of Advaita theology.

The success or failure of this project, thus described, will depend in no small part upon close attention to the teachings, texts, and histories of particular Advaita movements, and a careful accounting of their missionary theologies. Conveniently, beginning in the late nineteenth century, not a few Advaita movements did some of the analytic work for us, referring to themselves as "missions" and setting themselves in explicit relation to various missionary Christianities, in India and abroad. Hence, our survey can begin with one of these movements—the Ramakrishna Mission of Swami Vivekananda—and the legacy it offered for other teachers and organizations and for the construction of missionary Advaita as a transnational phenomenon.

2

A History of Missionary Advaita in Late Modernity

> The whole of the Western world is on a volcano which may burst tomorrow, go to pieces tomorrow. They have searched every corner of the world and have found no respite. They have drunk deep of the cup of pleasure and found it vanity. Now is the time to work so that India's spiritual ideas may penetrate deep into the West. Therefore young men of Madras, I specially ask you to remember this. We must go out, we must conquer the world through our spirituality and philosophy.
>
> —Swami Vivekananda, "The Work Before Us"[1]

Swami Vivekananda (1863–1902) repeatedly called his hearers to "conquer the world through our spirituality."[2] These calls are often taken as the first articulations of a worldwide Hindu missionary mandate in the modern period.[3] In his *Indische Mission und neue Frömmigkeit in Westen*, for example, Reinhart Hummel places Vivekananda at a crucial juncture in the modern transformation of Hinduism from a merely ethnic or regional tradition into a full-fledged, missionary "world religion" (*Weltreligion*). This transformation began with the reception of Hindu themes by European philosophers and American Transcendentalists in the early nineteenth century; reached a decisive turning point with Vivekananda's speeches at the 1893 World's Parliament of Religions and the development of organized mission societies in its wake; and came to fruition through a renewed profusion of gurus and broadly Hindu religious groups after World War II.[4] On this telling, the precise content of Vivekananda's missionary message is less important than its role as a catalyst for the emergence of a relatively coherent, if also necessarily complex and pluriform, Hindu mission to the West.

But this is not the only way to interpret the influence of this influential teacher and movement initiator. Although Swami Vivekananda did indeed purport to speak for Hinduism at the 1893 Parliament, he also stood in a very particular theological tradition: namely, the non-dualist Hindu teaching tradition of Advaita Vedānta, distinct from classical Vaiṣṇavism, Śaivism, or even the nineteenth-century Brahmo Samāj. When Vivekananda argued at the Parliament that the "common religion" of all Indian "sects" is the struggle of the individual self to "become one with Brahman" and to "realise the Lord as the perfection, the reality, of its own nature and existence,"[5] he was issuing a challenge not only to Westerners but also to fellow Hindus, both in India and abroad. When, seven years later in San Francisco, he urged his hearers to "cast off these kindergartens of religion" in favor of Advaita Vedānta as the future religion of humankind, he includes in his sweeping denunciation not merely the various traditions of Christianity but also the religions of "Buddhas and Shivas and Vishnus," and even "orthodox" Hinduism.[6] If, from a sociological point of view, Swami Vivekananda can be classified as one among many witnesses to a confident reassertion and reversal of what European Orientalists had positioned as a merely passive "mystic East,"[7] he engaged this hermeneutical project from a specific theological vantage, with its own distinctive history and lineage in South Asia.[8]

With these considerations in mind, I propose in this chapter to trace a slightly different historical and theological trajectory from Swami Vivekananda's famous speeches in 1893 than that developed by Hummel and other interpreters. That is, I do not narrate the emergence of Hinduism as a "world religion"; instead, I attend to the more particular emergence of Advaita Vedānta as a distinctive missionary movement in the nineteenth and twentieth centuries, manifested in several social and institutional forms. It is the missiological transformation of Advaita theologies that occupy our primary attention here, rather than the historical construction of contemporary Hinduism, as such.[9]

This interpretive choice should not be regarded as self-evident or innocent. Others have made defensible cases for "Yoga," "Vedantic-Yoga," or "Hindu-Inspired Meditation Movements" as more suitable classifications for several of the movements treated here.[10] Nevertheless, as argued in the previous chapter, there are several good reasons to focus on Advaita Vedānta. These include the organic relationship that can be adduced between the emergence of these Advaita mission movements in the twentieth century and the "internal" proselytism between different Hindu teaching traditions that continued well into the modern period.[11] Though Advaita Vedānta—or "the Vedānta"—has often been deployed as the quintessence of Hinduism and the true foundation of all religions, these claims should not distract us from the fact that it has also functioned as one or many *saṃpradāya*s in fierce competition with rivals for membership, social status, and political patronage.[12] Both Advaita's ambitious, theological claim as the essence of Hinduism and its actual, concrete rootedness in the historical development of a particular *saṃpradāya* recommend it as a useful site of constructive inquiry.

The chapter proceeds in several steps. In the first section, I set some limits on the category of "Advaita Vedānta" as applied to these modern and contemporary religious movements. Then, in the bulk of the chapter, I offer successive portraits of five movements that illumine stages in the development of missionary Advaita, as well as its particular dimensions. The selected movements include the Ramakrishna Mission founded by Swami Vivekenanda at the end of the nineteenth century, as well as several twentieth-century successors: Ramanasramam, the Chinmaya Mission, Transcendental Meditation, and the Sringeri Vidya Bharati Foundation. Finally, I note a few common themes and set the stage for the wider-scale and more synthetic inquiry that will occupy us in chapter 3.

This survey is not nearly exhaustive. Nevertheless, as I hope to demonstrate, these five movements represent a sufficiently wide cross-sample to generalize, as well as to invite substantive theological inquiry. In the second part of this volume, we will engage this inquiry in comparative mode. For the moment, however, the focus remains on the first, necessary step of tracing the emergence and establishing the rough contours of missionary Advaita as a social and theological reality in the contemporary world.

Setting Some Limits

In an important article from 1992, Raymond Brady Williams suggested five "trajectories" of adaptation followed by South Asian communities in the diaspora, including "individual," "national," "ecumenical," "ethnic," and "hierarchical" patterns of social life and religious practice.[13] More recently, in the preface to their 2005 collection *Gurus in America*, Thomas A. Forsthoefel and Cynthia Ann Humes instead classify the traditions in volume chapters according to "one of four substreams of Hindu thought and practice: Yoga, Advaita Vedanta, Bhakti, and Tantra."[14] Taken together, these two systems of classification nicely delimit the scope of missionary Advaita, at least for our purposes here. First, all of the movements profiled below fall broadly into Williams's "hierarchical" trajectory insofar as they are focused on loyalty to a guru or guru lineage, they differentiate religious identity from regional language or ethnic identity, and they thereby "attempt to make converts from several national or ethnic groups" within and also, to different degrees, beyond the transnational South Asian community.[15] Second, they are all recognizably Advaitin in their religious orientation. In neither case do the types fit perfectly: the Ramakrishna Mission definitely reveals characteristics of what Williams terms an "ecumenical" strategy of adaptation, for example, and most if not all of these movements incorporate elements from other streams of Hindu thought and practice—notably Tantra in the case of Transcendental Meditation. Nevertheless, all can be broadly classified as hierarchical or guru-based religious movements emerging from the tradition of Advaita Vedānta.

This tradition can be further delimited both theologically and sociologically. The Chinmaya Mission, for example, encapsulates the Advaita teaching with a popular half-verse:

> Brahma satyam jagan-mithyā // Jīvo brahmaiva nāparaḥ
>
> (Brahman, the Absolute, alone is real; this world is unreal (māyā); and the jīva or the individual soul is not different from Brahman.)[16]

Ultimate liberation, according to this teaching, does not consist in the achievement of a higher birth or surrender to divine grace, though both have important roles to play. It consists simply in knowing—or better, in these traditions, *realizing*—one's identity with *Brahman*. At least on the face of it, culture, ethnicity, and even religious identity itself are all radically relativized to the status of mere "names and forms" (*nāma-rūpa*) obscuring the true, divine, ever-liberated reality of each and every conscious being. This is the good news, the gospel of Advaita for the world.

But, of course, things are never quite so simple in the phenomenal world of human experience. Speaking historically, no matter how universal its message, the Advaita tradition took shape in fairly narrow Brahmanical religious circles, and it has traditionally been preserved by a monastic federation called the Daśanāmī Order, presided over by several Śaṅkarācāryas or "world-teachers" (*jagad-gurus*) in important religious centers or *maṭhas* throughout India.[17] It is therefore also significant that all of the movements profiled here have claimed some form of filiation—albeit sometimes a contested one—with the Daśanāmī Order.[18] In the case of the Sringeri Vidya Bharati Foundation, the link is direct. But the Ramakrishna Mission and the Chinmaya Mission also authorize their teaching with reference to the Śṛṅgeri *maṭha* in the southern state of Karnataka. Transcendental Meditation claims a connection to Jyotir in Uttarakhand, and Ramanasramam traditionally enjoyed a close relationship with Kāñcī in Tamil Nadu.[19] Other movements claim similar filiations, and several also make Advaita central to their teaching. A few of these, such as the Divine Life Society and Arsha Vidya Gurukulam, will emerge at the edges of our treatment here and in subsequent chapters. By selecting only five movements for special attention in this chapter, however, we can gain an initial sense of this wider tapestry and trace major features of its historical development from the late nineteenth century to the present day.

In the first place in this development, due to his chronological priority as well as his enduring significance, stands Swami Vivekananda and the Ramakrishna movement.

1893: Swami Vivekananda at the World's Parliament of Religions

The beautiful new facility of the Vivekananda Vedanta Society of Chicago features a small permanent exhibit entitled "Chicago, A

Sacred Pilgrimage, in the Footsteps of Swami Vivekananda." A series of still photographs offer a view into this great personality, the 1893 Columbian Exhibition that brought him to the city, various homes where he resided during his visit, and other landmarks, including above all the present-day Art Institute, the site of the first World's Parliament of Religions that same year. Below a large portrait, the exhibit features Vivekananda's legendary proclamation: "Haribhai, I am going to America. Whatever you hear of as happening there . . . is all for this (striking his own chest). For this (me) alone everything is being arranged." The exhibit well illustrates the sense of destiny with which the Society regards Vivekananda's role in the Parliament—or, better, the Parliament's role in advancing Vivekananda's historic mission. As both the exhibit and the Society's website make clear, Chicago has become a *tīrtha* or sacred pilgrimage site.[20] In this sacred place, at the cusp of the twentieth century, Swami Vivekananda emerged as "the harbinger of a modern and dynamic form of missionary Hinduism to the West."[21]

Storming the White City

It seems safe to venture that this was not what the organizers of the World's Parliament of Religions originally had in mind. Richard Seager has drawn attention to the highly ambivalent character of this event, illustrated by two defining features of its physical environment in the Columbian Exposition: the so-called "White City" or Court of Honor on the shore of Lake Michigan, and the Midway Plaisance, extending west from the Exhibition grounds.[22] The White City, on Seager's reading, symbolized the distinctly modern "Anglo-Protestant" myth of progress that framed the Parliament in the minds of many of its organizers.[23] Strolling through the White City, Parliament Chairman John Henry Barrows imagined that the gates might aptly have been inscribed with the prophecy, "The kingdoms of this world shall become the kingdoms of our Lord and of his Christ."[24] Though the Christians who attended the Parliament undoubtedly held diverse views of the event, a good case can be made that the dominant sense was a form of Christian fulfillment, looking toward the unity of world religions on liberal Protestant terms.[25]

The role that other religions were supposed to play in this vision of Christian progress can, again following Seager, be symbolized by the Midway Plaisance, a mile-long strip of ethnographic displays and concessions that placed African and Asian civilizations in a quasi-evolutionary order from the "savages" at furthest remove to the ethnic German and Italian hamlets at the gates of the White City.[26] Of the nearly two hundred delegates at the Parliament, forty-one representatives were from outside the Christian fold, including thirty representing religions of Asia: twelve Buddhists, eight Hindus, and considerably smaller delegations from Confucian, Taoist, Shinto, Zaroastrian, and Jain traditions.[27] Like the exotic displays of the Midway Plaisance, this modest smattering of religious others in an overwhelmingly Christian gathering was expected, by a widely shared if unspoken consensus, to confirm the myth of "nineteenth-century America as embodying a new Greece or Rome, a repristinated Christianity, and the most highly evolved and enlightened civilization in history."[28]

Though his importance is sometimes exaggerated, a general consensus holds that Swami Vivekananda was among the most effective Asian delegates in challenging this neat schema of Christian progress.[29] In his opening message, he thanked the assembled gathering in the name of "the most ancient order of monks in the world" and "the mother of all religions."[30] In his paper on Hinduism, he further identified Advaita Vedānta as the essence of the Hindu tradition,[31] and then issued a sweeping declaration about the unity of all religions:

> . . . if there is ever to be a universal religion, it must be one which will have no location in place or time; which will be infinite like the God it will preach, and whose sun will shine upon the followers of Krishna and of Christ, on saints and sinners alike; which will not be Brahminic or Buddhistic, Christian or Mohammedan, but the sum total of all these, and still have infinite space for development . . . It will be a religion which will have no place for persecution or intolerance in its polity, which will recognise divinity in every man and woman, and whose whole scope, whose whole force, will be centred in aiding humanity to realise its own true, divine nature.[32]

The challenge presented by Swami Vivekananda and the other Asian delegates was not merely rhetorical. In Hummel's estimation, as noted above, the Parliament marked the definitive moment when the dissemination of Asian religious traditions, which had previously been the preserve of Western intellectuals, passed into the hands of Asian religious leaders.[33]

After the Parliament, Protap Chandra Majumdar delivered some two hundred lectures and reaffirmed ties between the Unitarian Church and his own Brahmo Samāj; Anagirika Dharmapāla pursued missionary work in Britain and America in connection with the Mahā Bodhi Society, a pan-Buddhist organization he had founded in 1891; and Shaku Sōen would eventually dispatch his student D. T. Suzuki to the United States to spread the teaching of Zen.[34] Most famously, Swami Vivekananda carried his message of universal religion into the United States, France, and Britain, initiated select Western followers into renunciant life, and established the nascent Vedanta Society in 1895.[35] Thereafter, in one of the series of addresses he offered upon his return to India in 1897, he announced:

> The work that has been done by me in the Western world has been very little; there is no one present here who could not have done a hundred times more work in the West than has been done by me. And I am anxiously waiting for the day when mighty minds will arise, gigantic spiritual minds, who will be ready to go forth from India to the ends of the world to teach spirituality and renunciation—those ideas which have come from the forests of India and belong to Indian soil alone.[36]

Vivekananda would not wait long for that day to arrive. Before the end of the year, he had established the Ramakrishna Mission Association and consolidated the foundation for what is now the worldwide Ramakrishna movement.[37] As proclaimed by Swami Budhananda in a small introduction to the movement, Swami Vivekananda launched a "redemptive gospel for the regeneration of mankind [*sic*]," a true "world mission" oriented toward "total regeneration."[38]

Many aspects of this historical development have been the subject of scholarly dispute. First of all, a number of studies have challenged received narratives of the movement's namesake Sri Ramakrishna and the continuity between Ramakrishna's devotional mysticism and Vivekananda's Advaita.[39] Beyond this, historians have also raised questions about Vivekananda's own personal development and the precise origins of his missionary impulse.[40] In a massive collection of papers produced by the Ramakrishna Mission to celebrate the centenary of the Parliament, several essays cite a series of addresses prior to his departure, in which he described his "mission to the West."[41] In Madras, for example, he reportedly spelled out his agenda in very explicit terms: "The time has come for the propagation of our Faith. The time has come for the Hinduism of the ṛṣis to become dynamic . . . Shall we remain passive, or shall we become aggressive, as in days of old, preaching unto the nations the glory of the Dharma?"[42]

This speech, along with a "call from above" that Vivekananda reportedly received from Ramakrishna in his sleep, can be enlisted to support the claim that he had a very clear missionary intention prior to 1893.[43] Yet, neither the Madras address nor any report of this vision can be found in Vivekananda's collected writings. Both are reported by disciples after his death. Closer study of the primary sources suggests instead that the idea of establishing a Hindu mission emerged only gradually during Vivekananda's travels. The Parliament, on this second reading, represented less a platform than a catalyst for the founding of the Ramakrishna movement.[44] Either way, the significance of the event probably cannot be overstated: without the 1893 Parliament's World of Religions, it is difficult to imagine the emergence of Vivekananda as an assertive, evangelical Vedāntin and the foundation of the first worldwide Advaita mission.

The Good News of Practical Vedānta

Less subject to dispute are the particular teachings that made Vivekananda's initiative such a success, particularly his notion of "practical Vedānta."[45] In a short collection disseminated by the movement, his core teachings are summarized as follows:

> Each soul is potentially divine.
> The goal is to manifest this divinity within by controlling nature, external and internal.
> Do this either by work or worship or psychic control or philosophy—by one or more or all of these—and be free.
> This is the whole of religion. Doctrines or dogmas or rituals or books or temples or forms are but secondary details.[46]

In Vivekananda's writings, this outline is filled in so as to render it both recognizably Advaitin and eminently practical—and, remarkably, both at the same time.[47]

Advaita Vedānta is "practical," first, because it can be accommodated to any person's natural temperament through flexible combinations of the *yogas* of knowledge (*jñāna-yoga*), mental control (*raja-yoga*), devotion (*bhakti-yoga*), and selfless service (*karma-yoga*).[48] Social service is strongly valorized and made central on the path to liberation by the conviction that, since the divine *Brahman* is the innermost self of all conscious beings, worldly striving on such beings' behalf becomes a form of worship.[49] Yet, Vedanta's practicality is still further revealed by its esoteric teaching on the ultimate *māyā* or provisional character of this same world. For this enables spiritual seekers to claim their true, ever-liberated divine identity, here and now. Vivekananda writes:

> This very world becomes heaven, which formerly was hell. To the eyes of the bound it is a tremendous place of torment, but to the eyes of the free it is quite otherwise . . . This is the view of Vedanta, and this is its practicality. When we have become free, we need not go mad and throw up society and rush off to die in the forest or in a cave. We shall remain where we were, only we shall understand the whole thing.[50]

In this sense, Vivekananda's teaching transvalues the meaning of "practicality" itself. Though it might seem more practical to set aside otherworldly religious concerns and focus exclusively on the material world, only the spiritual teaching of Advaita holds the key to true freedom.[51]

Such a transvaluation relates to another key aspect of Swami Vivekananda's teaching: the contrast and mutual exchange between the spiritual East and the materialist West.[52] "Just as the western ideal is to keep up luxury in practical life," he writes, "so ours is to keep up the highest form of spirituality, to demonstrate that religion is not merely frothy words but can be carried out, every bit of it, in this life."[53] Or again, contrasting the "Oriental" and "Occidental" ideals: "The present adjustment will be the harmonising, the mingling of these two ideals. To the Oriental, the world of the spirit is as real as to the Occidental is the world of the senses . . . Each calls the other a dreamer. But the oriental ideal is as necessary for the progress of the human race as is the occidental, and I think it is more necessary."[54]

Today, it is widely acknowledged that, in drawing such a contrast between East and West, "Orient" and "Occident," spiritual and material, Vivekananda both mirrored and reversed the colonialist construction of the "mystic Orient."[55] Yet, it is no less widely acknowledged that this contrast and Vivekananda's call for mutual exchange provided a highly coherent organizational structure for his movement. In India, the Ramakrishna Mission committed itself primarily to direct service, famine relief, education, and building up the material conditions of the Indian people—that is, it brought the material values of the West to the spiritually rich Orient. In the United States and Europe, by contrast, the Vedanta Societies focused primarily on spreading the spiritual teachings of Advaita. This duality has also profoundly affected the received image of Swami Vivekananda himself as simultaneously a progressive spiritual innovator and a conservative symbol of Indian nationalism.[56]

Most contemporary members of the Ramakrishna movement will, of course, remind his interpreters that there was just one Swami Vivekananda, and, despite different emphases in different social contexts, just one missionary movement. Vedanta Societies in North America host soup kitchens or sponsor free medical clinics, and the Ramakrishna Math and Mission has never failed to offer spiritual instruction.[57] Though the growth of the movement has been modest in terms of pure numbers, particularly outside of India,[58] there is no question that it has dramatically impacted the development of comparative religion, the presentation and self-representation of Hinduism worldwide, and the work of many scholars and political leaders.[59] Swami Budhananda even perceives the clear influence of Vivekananda and the Ramakrishna movement in the teaching of the Second Vatican Council of the Catholic Church in 1962–1965.[60] Most importantly for our purposes, the Ramakrishna movement offered a rationale and template for other Advaita movements. Some would reject this template, and no one would accept it without adaptation. But, to the degree that later Advaitins do articulate alternatives, they do so largely on terms set for them by Swami Vivekananda, in and out of his experience at the 1893 World's Parliament of Religions.

1934: *A Search in Secret India* and the Legacy of Ramana Maharshi

In 1930, British journalist Paul Brunton (1898–1981, also named Raphael Hurst) set out in search of what he would later describe as "an India which has been hidden from prying eyes for thousands of years," namely, the mystic India of ancient yogis and rishis.[61] In the 1934 book describing this quest, *A Search in Secret India*, Brunton relates a journey full of purported holy men—some fraudulent, others genuine. A high point came when, on the advice of the Śaṅkarācārya of Kañcī, he stayed at a small ashram on the southern face of the hill Arunachala, in Tamil Nadu. He relates his first experience of the sage at the center of ashram life:

> There is something in this man which holds my attention as steel filings are held by a magnet . . . One by one, the questions which I prepared in the train with such meticulous accuracy drop away. For it does not seem to matter whether they are asked or not, and it does not matter whether I solve the problems which have hitherto troubled me. I know only that a steady river of quietness seems to be flowing near me; that a great peace is penetrating the inner reaches of my being, and that my thought-tortured brain is beginning to arrive at some rest.[62]

After a short visit, Brunton continued his travels, only to return, prompted by a series of coincidences and an irresistible inner voice.[63] This time he received more instruction, engaged in rigorous self-inquiry, and arrived at "spiritual certitude" about humankind's ultimate identity with God and the "eternal refuge" deep within.[64] He offers a summary: "I can only say that in India I found my faith restored . . . This faith was restored in the only way a sceptic would have it restored, not by argument but by the witness of an overwhelming experience. And it was a jungle Sage, an unassuming hermit who had formerly lived for twenty years in a mountain cave, who promoted this vital change in my thinking."[65] This "jungle Sage" was the widely venerated Ramana Maharshi (1879–1950).

The Prophet of Self-Inquiry

Brunton was not the first European to meet the Maharshi, nor the first to communicate his teachings to a Western audience.[66] Nevertheless, the account in *A Search for Secret India* led to a dramatic increase in visitors to the ashram, as well as providing an accessible précis of Ramana's teaching for Westerners and Indians alike.[67] In this case—more so than in the case of Swami Vivekananda—the content of the message is inextricable from the person of the sage.[68] Born Venkataraman Ayyar in a small village near Madurai, the Maharshi had what even the most devotional accounts reckon a relatively unremarkable childhood. Nevertheless, at the age of seventeen, he had something that could be called, following Arvind Sharma, a "conversion experience," the "pivot on which the rest of his life was destined to turn."[69] Seized by a sudden fear of death, the young Ramana spontaneously lay down and began imitating a corpse, stiffening his limbs, holding his breath, and imagining himself in the funeral pyre. Then, he began a rigorous process of internal self-examination:

> . . . with the death of this body, am "I" dead? Is the body "I"? This body is silent and inert. But I felt the full force of my personality and even the sound "I" within myself,—apart from the body. So "I" am a spirit, a thing transcending the body . . . "I" was something very real, the only real thing in that state and all the conscious

> activity that was connected with my body was centred on that. The "I" or my "self" was holding the focus of attention by a powerful fascination from that time forwards. Fear of death had vanished at once and forever.[70]

This was in 1896, at precisely the moment—carefully noted by one of Ramana's later Western disciples[71]—when Swami Vivekananda was concluding his transatlantic journey and laying the foundation for what would become the Ramakrishna movement. Ramana's path, however, followed a very different course. Within the year, he abandoned family and home, journeyed to Arunachala, and took up a life of silent contemplation, first in and around the temple compound in the town of Tiruvannamalai and then in a cave on the hill. He slowly attracted disciples, eventually including his own mother, and upon her death in 1922, he took up residence in an ashram constructed by devotees, Ramanasramam.

As Brunton's narrative well demonstrates, Ramana Maharshi's preferred mode of teaching was silence.[72] He did offer brief written expositions in response to requests and gradually, as he underwent a slow "process of return to outer activity" after his initial absorption, began to grant personal interviews.[73] In a work considered among his most comprehensive and authoritative, *Reality in Forty Verses*, one verse aptly captures the gist of his teaching: "When the mind turns inward seeking 'Who am I?' and merges in the Heart, then the 'I' hangs down his head in shame and the One 'I' appears as Itself. Though it appears as 'I-I,' it is not the ego. It is Reality, Perfection, the Substance of the Self."[74] Ramana called this method simply *vichara*, or "self-inquiry," and it emerged as the central discipline of self-knowledge, for which meditative practice and other disciplines functioned as remote preparation.[75] "Śrī Ramaṇa's emphasis on this method is so great," writes Advaita philosopher T. M. P. Mahadevan, "that we may rightly describe him as the Prophet of Self-inquiry."[76] Condensed very briefly, the method entails a relentless asking of the question, "who am I?" or, stated differently, a continual pursuit of "that which sees"—from "that which sees" the body, to "that which sees" the mind, and so on.[77] Such a process of negation—which, in essence, recapitulates Ramana's own spontaneous conversion, described above—leads ineluctably to the extinction of the individual mind, ego-sense, and world of thought, and, with this extinction, the spontaneous self-revelation of the effulgent *ātman*, the "I-I" or perhaps the "I of the I" as the sole true existent.[78] This divine "I-I" is symbolized by the incorporeal, spiritual heart, on the right side of the chest, where people instinctively point when they say, "it is I."[79]

The Silent Mission of the Silent Sage

The precise relation of this teaching to classical Advaita Vedānta has been a subject of considerable discussion among both devotees and scholars. On the one hand, both Ramana and his disciples insist that the sage's self-realization was not preceded by any study of Vedānta. When asked about the source of his teaching, Ramana reported, "Bhagavan's teaching is an expression of his own experience and realization. Others find that it tallies with Sri Shankara's," that is, with classical Advaita Vedānta.[80] He refused to receive formal initiation as a renunciant, counting himself an *atyāśramin*, outside the traditional stages of life, and he commended interior, spiritual renunciation among his disciples.[81] Moreover, in his *Forty Verses*, he appears sharply to qualify the value of study, discussion, or even meditation on scripture to facilitate liberation: "The natural and true Reality forever resides in the Heart of all. Not to realize It there and stay in It, but to quarrel: 'It is,' 'It is not'; 'It has form,' 'It has not form'; 'It is one,' 'It is two,' 'It is neither,' this is the mischief of *maya*."[82]

On the other hand, Ramana never resisted those who identified his teaching with that of Śaṅkara, and he eventually produced original Tamil translations of Advaita classics he considered particularly conducive to self-inquiry, such as the *Vivekacūḍāmaṇi* or *Crest-Jewel of Discrimination*.[83] He accepted traditional Advaitin emphases on the need for a guru to attain self-knowledge, while also modifying this requirement to include the possibility of spiritual gurus or other interior "catalysts" of liberation.[84] Finally, his disciples have emphasized the fundamental coherence of *vichara* with the four *yogas* of knowledge, discipline, devotion, and service, as earlier articulated by Swami Vivekananda.[85]

However deep or shallow its roots in the classical tradition, Ramana Maharshi's teaching made a significant mark on the subsequent development of Advaita. Ramana did not himself found an explicitly missionary movement; on this score, as Phillip Charles Lucas has observed, he stands in explicit contrast not only to Swami Vivekananda but also to Swami Chinmayananda and Maharishi Mahesh Yogi, treated below.[86] Nevertheless, the "Ramana Effect" took on a life of its own, by virtue of its portability, its universality, and its deep affinity with aspects of a growing, contemporary movement toward "liberal spirituality."[87] Ramana's legacy has been preserved and disseminated through the original Ramanasramam and its Board of Trustees, through almost fifty affiliate centers or individual *satsang* groups throughout India, Europe, North America, Australia, and Mauritius, and through an active publishing division.[88] A lay devotee named Bhagawat Prasad Singh, led by a series of spiritual visions of the Maharshi in both the United States and India, founded the Arunachala Ashrama in New York in 1966 and an affiliate retreat center in rural Nova Scotia in 1972.[89] The New York ashram now disseminates its own newsletter, publications, and other media, including a documentary film, *The Sage of Arunachala*, produced in 1992.[90] More significant, perhaps, has been the reception of Ramana's teaching into the work of other Advaita movements, such as the Divine Life Society and the Chinmaya Mission, as well as the teachings of such influential European and North American teachers as Eckhart Tolle, Gangaji, and Arunachala Ramana.[91]

This indirect, assimilative process of reception should not be taken as accidental, nor as a sign of the teaching's limited scope. Rather, it reveals the distinctive character of this particular missionary movement. When asked why he did not travel and preach like other teachers, Ramana reportedly replied, "How do you know that I am not doing it? . . . Preaching is simple communication of knowledge. It may be done in Silence too."[92] The editors of the short volume *Hunting the "I"* similarly insist that "Sri Ramana Maharshi and his message need neither backing nor propaganda; they have found their silent way all over the world to those hearts that were ripe and ready for them."[93] Ramana's Western disciple Arthur Osborne goes further, suggesting that, with the passing of the Maharshi, he became the inner guru of every conscious being and initiated a new spiritual path uniquely suited to the present age.[94] He writes:

> The story is no more ended than the story of Christ was ended upon the cross. It is, indeed, not a new religion that Sri Bhagavan brought upon the earth, but a new hope, a new path, for those who understand and aspire from every land and religion in this age of spiritual darkness. It was not for his body's lifetime only. To those who feared that the guidance might end with death he replied curtly, 'You attach too much importance to the body.' Now, as then, he guides whoever approaches him and whoever submits to him he supports. To all who seek he is here.[95]

The mission of Ramana Maharshi may challenge many prevailing assumptions about missionary activity—not least, a presumption that mission always follows from self-conscious intention and agency. Instead, this mission works anonymously, in a way uniquely suited to a silent sage.

1951: Swami Chinmayananda and the Jñāna Yajña Ideal

On December 23, 1951, in the early years of Indian Independence, Swami Chinmayananda Saraswati (1916–1993) arrived in the city of Poona by train, fresh from his studies of Vedānta in Rishikesh and Uttarkashi, in the sacred Himalayas. That same evening, he delivered a lecture, provocatively entitled "Let Us Be Hindus." After drawing attention to the apparent irony of this title, attached to an address for an audience of Hindus in front of a Hindu temple, Chinmayananda offers a brief rationale:

> It has become a new fashion with the educated Hindu to turn up his nose and sneer in contempt at the very mention of his religion in any discussion. Personally I too belong in my sympathies to these critics of our religion. But when this thoughtless team begins to declare that we would benefit ourselves socially and nationally by running away from our sacred religion, I pause to reconsider my own stand . . . My proposal is that the

> wise thing would be for us to try and bring about a renaissance of Hinduism so that under its greatness—proved through many centuries—we may come to grow into the very heights of culture and civilization that was ours in the historical past.[96]

In the speech, Chinmayananda goes on to describe the "decadent" state of modern Hinduism, laying blame primarily on the deteriorating quality of the Brahmin and Kshatriya classes, the machinations of the "selfish, arrogant, power-mad priest caste," and the "overgrowth" of mythologies, commentaries, and other *śāstras* that have obscured the true nature of Hinduism.[97] His solution? A "Upanishad Jnana Yagna" or "sacrifice of knowledge" dedicated to the *Kena Upaniṣad*. He concludes: "During these hundred days of the Upanishad Jnana Yagna, we shall be trying to discover the eternal happiness and bliss that is the succulent essence of all true religions . . . In a spirit of communal living for these one hundred days we shall come to discover the Science of Perfection, the true essence of Hinduism."[98]

The Yagna commenced in January 1952 and, at least according to sources within the Chinmaya movement, attendance grew quickly from an initial group of eighteen to overflow the temple hall. The event eventually comprehended a full program of daily discourses on the *Kena Upaniṣad*, bhajans, morning meditation, *satsang* discussions over tea, a continuous forty-day chant of the *Mahā Mantra*, publication and distribution of the discourses in small booklets, and, midway through the program, a literal *yajña* in the form of a Vedic Havan ritual, presided over by Brahmin priests but conducted together with gathered "women, businessmen and lower caste students."[99] Thus Chinmayananda initiated his "Yagna Plan" to communicate the teachings of Vedānta to the educated middle classes throughout India and beyond. As he would sometimes summarize the matter, he had initiated his lifelong mission "to convert Hindus to Hinduism."[100]

Re-Awakening Mother Śruti

In his public teaching, Swami Chinmayananda frequently invoked the legacy of Swami Vivekananda; indeed, on the dust jacket of a commentary on the *Bhagavad-Gītā,* Chinmayananda himself is "hailed as the second Swami Vivekananda."[101] Ramana Maharshi is perhaps a more important influence on the actual content of his teaching, however, both through Swami Sivananda and the Divine Life Society, where Chinmayananda received his initial training and formal initiation into renunciant life, and through his own brief personal encounters with the sage as a young man and shortly before the first Jnana Yagna.[102] Swami Chinmayananda, like Ramana, sometimes characterizes the Advaita teaching as a process of destroying the ego or attaining a state of "thought-extinction."[103]

More typically, however, he offers various schematics of the human constitution, as befits a "science of perfection."[104] Thus, he categorizes phenomenal existence according to the five "sheaths" of food, vital air, mind, intellect, and bliss, or the threefold experience of the "world-of-objects" through the body (*śarīra*), the "world-of-feelings" through the mind (*manas*), and the "world-of-ideas" through the intellect (*buddhi*).[105] Beginning in 1955, he began using the so-called Body-Mind-Intellect (BMI) Chart to illustrate the latter analysis and the ultimate foundation of embodied life in the "Divine Principle"—the "Self" and true "Subject" of all possible experiences, symbolized in the chart by the sacred syllable *oṃ* (see figure 5.1).[106] Obscuring the Divine Principle, at the source of our individuality and all sensory experiences, stand the *vāsanās*, subjective impressions, and tendencies inherited from past experience in this and previous lives. Hence, the state of self-knowledge and liberation, sometimes characterized as thought-extinction, is more correctly identified as the exhaustion or destruction of these *vāsanās*.[107]

Like many other modern Vedāntins, Swami Chinmayananda accepted a number of *yogas* or alternate means through which the process of *vāsanā*-exhaustion can proceed, depending upon personal temperament and level of maturity.[108] But he also refocused attention on the scriptural sources of the teaching, described as "Mother Śruti," the "direct experiences and revelation" of the ancient rishis, the cold waters of the Ganges that startle us free from our dreamlike experiences of the world.[109] Such awakening is accomplished primarily by means of the traditional threefold Advaita method of hearing the scriptures, reflection, and contemplation, tellingly re-specified as hearing (*śravaṇa*), personal study of the *Upaniṣads*, the *Bhagavad-Gītā*, and other spiritual literature (*svādhyāya*), and repeated contemplation of a mantra (*japa*)—the latter of which culminates in "a thriller mood of choiceless contemplation" or simply "meditation" (*dhyāna*).[110] Thus, in addition to periodic fortnight or longer Jnana Yagnas offered by Swami Chinmayananda and other renunciant teachers on core Vedānta scriptures, the movement also developed a distinctive structure of small weekly discussion groups, led by laypeople and structured according to a progressive "Scheme of Study," along with ample opportunities for devotional *pūja* and instruction in *japa* and meditation. Whereas *pūja* and selfless action in the world purify the mind and prepare it to receive the teaching, it is only through hearing, study, and contemplation that it can become quiet, "hitched to one line-of-thought," and eventually, at least for brief moments, perfectly silent and actionless in a state of "Absolute Bliss."[111]

Spirituality and Cultural Nationalism

Viewed against the examples set by Vivekananda and Ramana Maharshi, Swami Chinmayananda's teaching can be interpreted as a return to more classical methods and sources of Advaita Vedānta. It is fitting, then, that he also rationalized his innovations by appeal to a deeply traditional authority: the eighth-century Advaitin *par excellence*, Ādi Śaṅkarācārya. Whereas Swami Vivekananda appealed to Buddhism as the world's first missionary religion, born from the heart of the Hindu fold,[112] Chinmayananda instead constructed his movement on the model of this famous Vedāntin, "one of the most vigorous missionaries in our country," who rediscovered in the *Upaniṣads* "the true cultural basis of our nation" and led a dramatic "revivalist movement" better characterized as a "revolution."[113] Though Śaṅkara's faith and erudition represented his primary "weapons" in this revolution, a

> pen alone would not have won the war of culture for our country. He showed himself to be a great organizer, a far sighted diplomat, and courageous hero and a tireless servant of the country. Selfless and unassuming, this mighty angel strode up and down the length and breadth of the country serving his motherland and teaching his country-men to live up to the dignity and

> glory of *Bhārat*. Such a vast programme can neither be accomplished by an individual nor sustained without institutions of great discipline and perfect organisation. Establishing the *maṭha-s*, opening temples, organizing halls of education, and even prescribing certain ecclesiastical codes, this mighty Master left nothing undone in maintaining what he achieved.[114]

With this as a model, it makes good sense that Chinmayananda's own mission was also characterized by teaching throughout India and, beginning with his first "*Dik-Vijay Yatra*" or global conquest in 1965, the world.[115] It was also characterized by systematic institutionalization. The Chinmaya Mission, incorporated in 1953, quickly gave birth to a number of institutions dedicated to fostering cultural and religious "revival" in India and in the diaspora.[116] In addition to numerous Mission centers worldwide, these include the Bal Vihar and Chinmaya Yuva Kendra (CYK) programs for children and young adults beginning in 1959; Sandeepany Sadanalaya, a kind of seminary system centralized in Mumbai in 1963; a network of private and state schools, beginning in 1965; Chinmaya Mission West in 1975; a research center, located at the traditional maternal home of Śaṅkara, in 1990, and Chinmaya Vishvavidyapeeth, a university with campuses in Kochi and Pune, in 2016.[117] Swami Chinmayananda placed special emphasis on the full inclusion of women in the Chinmaya Mission, and, from the early 1980s onward, the empowerment of marginalized Indian women became one of the primary emphases of the Chinmaya Organisation for Rural Development (CORD).[118]

The institution associated with the Mission that has attracted the most scholarly attention, however, is not among those that bear the name "Chinmaya." This institution is the Hindu nationalist Vishwa Hindu Parishad (VHP), which Swami Chinmayananda co-founded in 1964.[119] It seems evident that Chinmayananda himself can be safely classified as a type of Hindu nationalist: before taking up renunciant life and the study of Vedānta, he had worked as a political activist and journalist for the Independence movement, and his interpretation of Śaṅkara as a missionary engaged in a "war of culture" for sacred India strikes an unmistakably nationalist chord.[120] In a 1993 interview, he expressed forceful support of the VHP, its sister organization the Rashtriya Swayamsevak Sangh (RSS), and the destruction of the Muslim Babri Masjid in Ayodhya by militant nationalists the previous year.[121] At the same time, some interpreters have noted that, over time, Chinmayananda distanced himself from VHP ideology, and one of the authorized histories of the Chinmaya Mission describes a self-conscious break between the two organizations.[122] The most recent such history mentions the VHP only briefly in passing, in recounting Chinmayananda's relationship with the Dalai Lama.[123] This recent history also draws attention to Chinmayananda's assertion, in a letter to a devotee, that "Ours is not a political organization, and we have no political program."[124]

When asked about the matter shortly before his death, Chinmayananda offered a reply that bears directly on the nature of his missionary vision:

> When *your* pope came to India [Paul VI in December 1964], he said he was going to convert 125 people to Christianity. Public opinion made him withdraw his plan but I was in Bombay and announced that I would convert 200 people to Hinduism and I did. Then I had the idea to start a group to work for conversions. I didn't have enough people of my own so I asked the RSS for their help. Guruji [RSS head, Golwalkar] liked the idea and had thousands of workers everywhere. The VHP has grown into a mighty force. It is all over the world. After I started the VHP, I returned to my own mission as spiritual teacher of vedanta. Anyone can do the work of the VHP . . .[125]

On the one hand, then, Swami Chinmayananda seems to approve of conversion to Hinduism, presumably referring here to the rites of "purification" (*śuddhi*) or "homecoming" (*parāvartan*) originally developed by the Ārya Samāj in the late nineteenth century and adapted by the VHP to "re-convert" Indian Muslims and Christians and to integrate low-caste and tribal communities into the Hindu fold.[126] On the other hand, this was not Swami Chinmayananda's own mission, nor the most valuable task at hand—"Anyone" can do *that* kind of work. The Chinmaya Mission ostensibly exists for a different kind of conversion: a moral and spiritual conversion to the higher truth of Vedānta, the essence of Hinduism and of every true religion the world has ever seen.

1992: Transcendental Meditation, the Natural Law Party, and the Raam Rajya

In the summer of 1992, a year before Swami Chinmayananda's interview on the matter of the VHP, I was visiting a good friend and his family in my hometown. My friend announced unexpected news: he had been selected as one of the delegates to the U.S. Electoral College for the upcoming presidential election, albeit for a third-party candidate: the quantum physicist Dr. John Hagelin. I had not heard of Hagelin or his Natural Law Party up to that point, but in the letters he had written to delegates like my friend, as well as in subsequent interviews and debates, he emerged as an intelligent, articulate politician with a wry sense of humor and progressive ideas about campaign finance reform, sustainable energy, and holistic health policy. Hagelin did not win that election, of course, but he ran again in 1996 and briefly led a coalition platform with the Reform Party in 2000. Regional branches of the Natural Law Party also forged state coalitions and supported other third-party candidates, such as Ralph Nader and the Green Party in 2004.[127] That same year, Hagelin and his party made a policy decision that would have surprised my friend and me back in 1992: he founded a parallel structure called the U.S. Peace Government, charged with governing the country and fostering peace "from the crucial level of collective consciousness."[128] For, unbeknownst at least to me, in 1992 my friend and I had encountered a very distinctive form of missionary Advaita: Transcendental Meditation (TM).

The "Mechanical Path" of Self-Realization

Of all the movements surveyed in this article, TM arguably has the strongest public profile in North America and Europe, not least due to the association of its founder Maharishi Mahesh Yogi (1914–2008) with the Beatles and other celebrities in the 1960s and 1970s. TM has been studied as a cult, as an expression of hybrid

New Age religiosity, and as a test case, along with TM-inspired health and wellness personalities such as Deepak Chopra and Sri Sri Ravi Shankara, for interrogating contemporary patterns of spiritual consumerism.[129] But TM is also rooted in Advaita Vedānta. In Maharishi Mahesh Yogi's programmatic 1963 work *Science of Being and Art of Living*, for example, the Maharishi gives a précis of the "science" of his title in the explicit language of non-dualism: "*I am That eternal Being, thou art That and all this is That eternal Being in its essential nature.*"[130] In our conscious experience, according to his teaching, human beings are suspended between two fundamental, contradictory realities: the interior, absolute reality of Being and the exterior, relative reality of breath, mind, and worldly phenomena, generated by a beginningless cycle of *karma*. The relative exists only in and through the Absolute, like waves on the surface of a deep ocean, branches and roots enlivened by the sap of the tree, or the changing states of ice, water, and steam on the underlying reality of H_2O.[131] All of this resonates with classical Advaita, as well as with modern Vedāntins like Vivekananda, Ramana Maharshi, and Chinmayananda. However, here Maharishi Mahesh Yogi takes his argument a step further, claiming that the great mistake of prior teachers in the tradition has been to seek the solution to this dilemma by withdrawing from the material world or seeking escape from it. The goal is rather to harmonize the relative with the Absolute, to continue to interact with and indeed positively to transform the world of *karma* in a way that does not perpetuate bondage to it.[132]

More to the point, the Maharishi suggests that the traditional mode of teaching liberation has been precisely backward, insofar as Advaita teachers have postulated the highest contemplative experience of *samādhi* at the end of long practice in devotion, inquiry, or even meditative discipline, rather than as their source and starting point.[133] Hence, in place of self-inquiry or the threefold method of hearing, reflection, and contemplation, the Maharishi reduces the entire teaching to one "simple formula" or "practical technique": Transcendental Meditation, or simply TM.[134] Disciples enter the practice of TM through two introductory lectures, a ceremonial *pūja* ceremony, initiation into a *mantra*, training by a licensed teacher, and then a simple routine of two twenty-minute sessions each day.[135] According to the Maharishi, the vibrations of the *mantra*'s sound, irrespective of whether the disciple understands its meaning, generate a kind of positive interference with the person's own subtle vibrations. The mind is set free and led inward, following its own natural attraction, from the sensory experience of speech to subtler strata of thoughts and, from there, to the Absolute.[136] "When it transcends the subtlest state of thought, the conscious mind transcends the subtlest state of relative experience and arrives at the state of the transcendental Being, the state of pure consciousness or self-awareness."[137] But this is, as already noted, only the beginning:

> From this state of pure Being the mind comes back again to experience the thought in the relative world. Through constantly going into the realm of the transcendent and back out into the field of relativity, the familiarity with the essential nature of the Being deepens and the mind becomes gradually more aware of its own essential nature. With more and more practice, the ability of the mind to maintain its essential nature while experiencing objects through the senses increases. When this happens the mind and its essential nature, the state of transcendental Being, become one, and the mind is then capable of retaining its essential nature—Being—while engaged in thought, speech or action.[138]

The reduction of a Hindu teaching to the repeated practice of a meditative technique was not entirely new, at least in the North American context: the way had already been paved by the Kriya Yoga movement of Swami Yogananda (1893–1952) and the Self-Realization Fellowship in the early twentieth century.[139] The Maharishi's originality can perhaps be located instead in his resolute consistency in upholding what he called the "mechanical path" of self-realization—his gloss for *karma-yoga,* reinterpreted in terms of repeated practice of TM—to the exclusion of all others. Even more striking is his supreme confidence that this "simple formula" represented a panacea not only for individual liberation from bondage to *karma* but also for improved health, reduced crime, and the complete transformation of modern society.[140]

A New Global Order

If the Maharishi's interpretation of Advaita Vedānta may seem radical compared with a more traditional teacher like Swami Chinmayanananda, it is worth keeping in mind that he consistently claimed to have received this teaching from one of the most traditional Vedānta authorities one can imagine: "Gurudev," Brahmananda Swaraswati, the Śaṅkarācārya of Jyotir Maṭh from 1941 to 1953.[141] As Cynthia Ann Humes has argued, taking this claim seriously lends a degree of intelligibility to the movement's otherwise opaque history. There is wide agreement on the facts of the case. TM grew rapidly after the Maharishi initially brought it to the United States in 1959 and hit its peak in membership and public exposure in 1975 when Merv Griffin and other famous celebrities extolled its virtues. But its membership sharply declined in 1976–1977, following a New Jersey court decision excluding it from public schools and prisons as a "religious" practice and the Maharishi's own introduction of the controversial "TM-Sidhi" technique and "Yogic flying" for advanced practitioners. After this, TM developed a more rigid institutional structure, a more assertive commitment to maintaining the purity of the teaching, and a more explicitly Indian and Hindu public profile, introducing a complete line of Ayurvedic healing products and food supplements, Vedic rituals for priests and lay practitioners, Vedic music, Vedic architectural designs, and Hindu astrology.[142]

Scholars have proposed a variety of explanations for the transformations of 1976–1977, including the possible influence of Swami Muktananda (1908–1982) and his Siddha Yoga movement, or an increased need for supernaturalist "compensators" in the face of the precipitous membership decline.[143] Humes proposes that the transformations were, more simply, a reassertion of the movement's explicitly Advaita religious and cultural roots after the initial strategy of suppressing this language in favor of a Western scientific idiom had proved less fruitful than desired in spreading the practice of TM. She writes:

> TM was supported by personal experience and, since the early seventies, empiricism and numerous scientific studies. As Maharishi gradually incorporated many fac-

> ets commonly understood as "Hinduism," distinguished from the old, unimproved Vedic wisdom by his unique spellings and his name-brand recognition, all individual experience and even one's body came to be interpreted through the advaitic belief system Maharishi provides. Thus, despite declaring his insights to be "perennial," "primordial," timeless truth accessible to each person, for Maharishi, the perennial truth is fundamentally Vedic.[144]

In his early writings, despite the more neutral language of "Being" and the "Absolute," the Maharishi made it clear that his teaching was rooted in Advaita scriptures like the *Upaniṣads* and the *Bhagavad-Gītā*, whose true meaning had been lost until being rediscovered by Brahmananda Saraswati.[145] As TM membership grew, then declined, and eventually stabilized around a core of devotees and a wider circle of more casual consumers of Ayurvedic products and of TM itself, this identity re-emerged more explicitly and aggregated a wider range of ostensibly Vedic accoutrements. The development of the movement is not entirely linear: beginning in 2005, for example, the positioning of TM as a purely secular, therapeutic practice has been recovered and actively promoted by the David Lynch Foundation for Consciousness-Based Education and World Peace as a formally distinct, complementary structure to the main TM organization.[146]

Perhaps the most fascinating aspect of TM, well demonstrated by John Hagelin and the Natural Law Party, is the Maharishi's conviction that those who self-consciously take up TM represent but a small slice of those who could be transformed through its intrinsic power to heal divisions and foster world peace.[147] In 1972, the Maharishi launched the World Plan to provide at least one TM teacher for every thousand people worldwide, and he later proclaimed the so-called "Maharishi Effect," which promised a steep drop in crime, conflict, and other social problems in any community with one TM practitioner for every hundred citizens, or the square root of that number of advanced TM-Sidhi "Yogic flyers."[148] One social institution sprang up after another in rapid succession, each dedicated to collaborate on public issues through conventional means like research and community organizing and to intervene directly through TM spiritual practice. These associations include not only the

U.S. Natural Law Party but also the Indian *Ajeya Bharat* Party and other similar political movements worldwide, collectively embodying what the Maharishi referred to as the sovereignty of the god Rama, Raam Rajya. This process culminated in the inauguration of the Global Country of World Peace in 2000.[149] The Global Country has its own king, the Lebanese physiologist Dr. Tony Nader—Maharaja Adhiraj Rajaraam—and in 2002 it also launched its own currency, the Raam, and established a world capital in Maharishi Vedic City, Iowa. This is just north of Fairfield, itself a community thoroughly transformed by the foundation of the accredited Maharishi University of Management in 1974 and the many other institutions that followed, including a grand meditation Dome, an Ecovillage, a separated community of "pandits" offering Vedic sacrifices for the world, and Hagelin's own U.S. Peace Government.[150]

In 1959, according to TM advocate Jack Forem, Maharishi Mahesh Yogi embarked to the United States in the hopes of spreading the teaching of "Gurudev" back to India and indeed to the whole world.[151] Today, the United States has become one center of a still more ambitious mission: the creation, through spiritual practice, of a new age of peace and an ideal global order.

2010: The Śṛṅgeri Maṭh Comes to Etobicoke

In July 2005, acclaimed film director David Lynch established his eponymous Foundation for Consciousness-Based Education and World Peace "to ensure that every child anywhere in the world who wanted to learn to meditate could do so." This secularizing initiative attempted to divest TM of its Hindu trappings and to spread it among at-risk youth, prisoners, and military veterans suffering from PTSD.[152] Just one month later, in the west Toronto neighborhood of Etobicoke, a representative of the Jagadguru or "world-teacher," Śri Bharathī Thīrtha Mahāswamigal, presided over the inauguration of a center dedicated, by all appearances, to something close to the opposite purpose: the Sringeri Vidya Bharati Foundation (SVBF).

SVBF Canada was incorporated in 2005 as "a non-profit, charitable organization to propagate Sanathana Dharma in communities across Canada" and as an "overseas affiliate" of the Śrī

Śāradā Pīṭhaṃ in Śṛṅgeri, Karnataka.[153] An impressive temple of Śrī Śāradāmbā, the presiding wisdom goddess of the Śṛṅgeri Pīṭham, was consecrated with great fanfare in a ten-day Mahābhiṣekam ritual in June 2010, attended by local and national political figures, devotees, and representatives of other temples and teaching traditions.[154] Southern Ontario became home to one of the most recognizably Hindu institutions imaginable—the Śṛṅgeri *maṭha*, an ancient, authoritative center of Advaita teaching and a beating heart of the Daśanāmi monastic federation.

A Beacon of Dharma

At the beginning of this chapter, I argued for filiation with the Daśanāmi federation as one significant marker to locate the Ramakrishna Mission, Ramanasramam, Chinmaya Mission, and TM securely within the wide stream of "orthodox" Advaita tradition. Interestingly, in its self-presentation as a "beacon light of Sanatana Dharma,"[155] the SVBF places less emphasis on the message of Advaita than do any of these other movements. It would seem more closely to embody what Raymond Brady Williams has classified as an "ecumenical" trajectory of adaptation common to many temples in North America, emphasizing broadly shared Hindu traditions rather than the teachings of a particular *saṃpradāya*.[156]

In an introductory video posted on the center's website, for example, prominent leaders describe the purposes of SVBF as threefold:

1. To "reinforce the principles of Sanatana Dharma in people who left India in pursuit of wealth and settled in the West" and to provide affordable priestly services;
2. To help a younger generation, raised in North America, in "understanding fundamental principles inherent in our Dharma," by providing classes and inspiring models of *dharmic* living;
3. To help devotees gain "awareness of your own self and awareness about others also," through contact with those who are marginalized in the wider society.[157]

Sanātana dharma—loosely translated, a "timeless" or "transcendent" pattern of life—is common parlance for the patrimony shared by all Sanskritic traditions of Hinduism, irrespective of particular gurus or teaching traditions. Given SVBF's self-declared role as a beacon of such *dharma*, it makes good sense that its temple includes *mūrtis* of ten deities, including Śiva, Viśnu, the fierce goddess Durgā, the monkey god Hanuman, and the elephant-headed Ganeśa, in addition to the central figure of Śāradāmbā. The webpage presents testimonies from devotees of several traditions, and the video feed even includes a lecture by a popular Vaiṣṇava interpreter of and television actor for Vedānta Deśika (1268–1370)—one of the sharpest polemicists against Advaita in the classical period![158] Were it not for the omnipresence of Ādi Śaṅkarācārya and his successors in the imagery of the center, one could be forgiven for thinking that the SVBF had little connection at all to Advaita, much less to its missionary forms.

In the next chapter, I will try to make a historical case for the centrality of Śṛṅgeri in the development of missionary Advaita in premodern times. For our present purposes, however, it is sufficient to note that its seemingly conflicted identity has deep roots in the *maṭh*'s tradition and legacy. The SVBF website and *maṭh*-friendly publications assert that the Śrī Śāradā Pīṭhaṃ was founded by Ādi Śaṅkarācārya himself and that its teaching lineage and authority have continued unbroken from Śaṅkara's direct disciple Sureśvara to the present Śaṅkarācārya, Bhāratī Tīrtha, and his designated successor.[159] Neither assertion stands uncontested. Kañci and other rival *maṭhas* in South India have advanced similar, conflicting status claims,[160] and recent historical scholarship suggests that the *maṭh* may have originally been Śaiva in orientation, well into the twelfth century.[161] Most interpreters agree that by 1346 the Śṛṅgeri *maṭha* is recognizably Advaitin and thoroughly enmeshed in the politics of the Vijayanagara Empire (1336–1570). In that year, Harihara I (1336–1356) bestowed a land grant of nine villages on the temple complex and its leadership, presumably in gratitude for its advice and possibly its financial assistance in founding the empire.[162]

For some six centuries, under the patronage of successive sovereigns—Hindu, Muslim, and colonial British—the *maṭha* thrived as both an enclave of Advaita teaching and a temporal authority.[163]

One result of this history is a dual mission and identity that Glenn Yocum captures with reference to the physical geography of the Śṛṅgeri village. Yocum focuses especially on the bridge that joins the town, temples, and administrative centers on the north bank of the Tuṅga River to the monastic residence of the Śaṅkarācārya and several disciples on the south bank: "The binary opposition between dharma and moksha, this world and its transcendence, is symbolically, spatially, and conceptually present at Sringeri, but the matha and its head exist on both sides of the spiritual divide, so beautifully and appropriately demarcated by the river Tunga. The matha marks a *tirtha,* a literal crossing of a river and a spiritual transformation."[164] We can see both sides of this *tīrtha*—between *dharma* and *mokṣa,* between temporal and spiritual concerns—in the progressive development of Śṛṅgeri in the modern era.

On the one hand, the teachers and administrators of the *maṭha* have functioned as legal authorities in temporal matters, both in relation to their own holdings until the mid–twentieth century and also, well up to the present day, through their interpretation of the *dharma-śāstra* and *dharma-sūtra* codes of conduct to a wide, predominantly Brahmin religious public.[165] On the other, in addition to literally moving his residence across the Tuṅga to the south bank, the formidable Jagadguru Saccidānanda Śivābhinava Nṛsiṃha Bhāratī (1866–1912) undertook several initiatives to foster a Vedic and Sanskrit culture conducive to the spiritual teaching of Advaita. These included a renewed tradition of all-India tours; a celebration of Śaṅkara's own such victory tour on the anniversary of his birthday each spring (*Śaṅkara-jayanti*); several schools of Vedic studies (*veda-pāṭha-śālā*) for qualified boys and young men; and a regular gathering of Sanskrit scholars of Advaita for vigorous scholastic debate (*vidvat-sabhā*).[166]

Importantly for my present purpose, Saccidānanda Śivābhinava Nṛsiṃha Bhāratī also founded remote affiliates of the *maṭha* in Bangalore in 1907 and in Kalaḍi, the traditional birthplace of Śaṅkara, in 1910.[167] This program of geographical extension, which had begun in a preliminary way in the sixteenth century, continued to intensify throughout the twentieth century. It would culminate, eventually, in the establishment of the Sringeri Vidya Bharati Foundation as an overseas affiliate, first in Stroudsburg, Pennsylvania, and then in west Toronto.[168]

A Wide Reach and a Narrow Path

With this background in mind, we can perhaps make sense of the development of the Śṛṅgeri *maṭha* as yet another form of Advaita mission—one that precedes the emergence of movements like the Vedanta Society and the Chinmaya Mission while also drawing creatively on the models they provide. The website of the main *maṭha* clearly identifies its primary identity as "an institution to spread the truths of Advaita Vedanta."[169] In his public teaching, however, Jagadguru Bhāratī Tīrtha concedes that few persons actually possess the social and intellectual competence to undertake Vedānta study. For the overwhelming majority of seekers, Bhāratī Tīrtha instead prescribes the fulfillment of *dharma*—the obligatory duties associated with one's caste or social context—along with fervent devotion to God and the guru, as remote preparation and mental purification.[170] In principle, as world teacher (*jagadguru*), the Śaṅkarācārya reaches out to all persons to facilitate their eventual passage to liberating self-knowledge; in practice, this only rarely takes the form of explicit Advaita teaching.[171]

A similar twofold vision is developed in a series of articles highlighted as "Teachings" on the SVBF USA website.[172] One piece on "Vaidika Samskaras," for example, begins with the universalist assertion that "The Hindu Faith aims at enabling every human being to the realization of this Absolute Truth or the Self, and proclaims that, this realization is the only goal for every one to reach." But the author, Dr. S. Yegnasubramanian, immediately cautions that "this realization may not be possible for most because of the thickness of the impurity accumulated over several cycles of birth," necessitating an arduous process of ritual and ethical self-purification in this and future lives.[173] In commentaries on the classical Advaita texts, *Upadeśa Pañcakam* and *Tattva Bodha*, Yegnasubramanian somewhat extends the reach of the teaching, relativizing traditional caste restrictions and introducing the category of "internal *saṃnyāsin*" to describe a person who renounces means and ends mentally, without recourse to formal renunciation.[174] Yet, in these articles, he again contends that the central task before most seekers is to make steady progress through the stages of life and to strive for the requisite personal and mental refinement that will eventually qualify them for Vedānta study.[175]

A more secure indication about how the *maṭha* works to advance the teaching of Advaita can perhaps be found by shifting one's attention from Yegnasubramanian's prose to his bibliographies. For his exposition relies heavily on selected publications of the Chinmaya Mission and, in every case, public lectures by the Advaita teacher Swami Paramarthananda of Chennai, India.[176] Paramarthananda is among the most prominent disciples of Swami Dayananda Saraswati (1930–2015), whom we encountered briefly in chapter 1. Formed in the Chinmaya Mission, Dayananda eventually established his own network of self-identified "traditional" teachers dedicated to *ārṣa vidyā*, the knowledge of the ancient rishis. This network includes ashrams in Rishikesh and Coimbatore, India, and Saylorsburg, Pennsylvania—right around the corner from the Stroudsburg branch of the Sringeri Vidya Bharati Foundation.[177]

The close relationship between Śṛṅgeri and the Arsha Vidya *paraṃparā* is well illustrated by the unprecedented decision of Jagadguru Bhāratī Tīrtha to honor Swami Dayananda with the inaugural Ādi Śaṅkarācārya Award on April 26, 2012.[178] Bhāratī Tīrtha's remarks at the award ceremony are worth quoting at length:

> As all of you know, Dayananda Saraswati Swamiji has been taking lot of efforts towards spreading the Advaita Siddhanta and Sanatana Dharma . . . He has exactly the same attitude of shraddha-bhakti [faith and devotion] towards Adi Shankara Bhagavatpāda, as do I. He is ever intent on communicating to everyone the messages of His [Shankaracharya's] Bhāshyas, and always interested in strengthening the shraddha of the people towards Bhagavatpāda. He wishes to convey the message of Advaita to everyone. While I am trying to do all these within Bhārata [India], keeping with certain niyamas (rules for Peethadhipatis), Swamiji is doing the same even outside Bhārata.[179]

Swami Dayananda receives the first-ever Ādi Śaṅkarācārya Award for doing what the Jagadguru, due to his distinctive position and role, cannot undertake on his own. He is commended for spreading Advaita beyond the geographical boundaries of India to "everyone."

We need not press the particular relationship between Śṛṅgeri and the Arsha Vidya *paraṃparā*. We can, instead, read this as exemplifying the broader, complex, and differentiated connections fostered by the Śṛṅgeri *maṭha* with a variety of such movements. The Chinmaya and Ramakrishna Missions, we recall, also claim filiation with Śṛṅgeri, and these filiations are embodied in concrete patterns of exchange and mutual recognition. As just one example, the senior *ācārya* of the Toronto Vedanta Society inaugurated a religious education center at the Sringeri Vidya Bharati Foundation in Etobicoke, and Vedanta Society teachers continued to animate some of the classes that it offers.[180]

A center such as SVBF Canada—like the Śṛṅgeri *maṭha* itself—exists to foster the liberating self-knowledge of Advaita, first and always. It pursues this mission primarily through its teaching of *dharma*, Sanskrit, devotional practice, and other remote means that purify the mind for the discipline of knowledge. For those few who have become suitably qualified, it offers direct instruction. Yet, its own reach, by tradition and by self-conscious intention, is limited to India and the Hindu diaspora. Hence, Śṛṅgeri also spreads the Advaita message by one further means: vital relations with Arsha Vidya, the Chinmaya Mission, the Vedanta Society, and other movements that push beyond these limits, "even outside Bhārata." It advances its own mission by advancing theirs.

Conclusion

In this chapter, I have traced a historical trajectory of missionary Advaita in late modernity, from the World's Parliament of Religions at the end of the nineteenth century to the crowning of the Raja Raam of the Global Country of Peace and the establishment of a Toronto affiliate of the Śṛṅgeri *maṭha* in the early years of the twenty-first century. Across this period of just over one hundred years, I suggest we can speak intelligibly of an emerging, transnational movement of missionary Advaita. As the discussion also reveals, however, this is a movement of considerable diversity and internal complexity.

The fundamental teaching of Advaita Vedānta stands at the center of each of these movements, and it represents one of the primary keys of their transcultural appeal. In both its classical and modern formulations, Advaita draws sharp distinctions between phenomenal experience and the true, innermost self of all beings, between the Body-Mind-Intellect and the Divine Principle, between the relative and the absolute. Such distinctions, in turn, suggest a further distinction between the teaching in its purity and any context in which it happens to find itself. The Advaita teaching must of necessity be communicated through various names and forms, and these vary extraordinarily, from the strident nationalism of Swami Chinmayananda to the silent introspection of Ramana Maharshi, from the grand syntheses of Swami Vivekananda to the insistent reduction of the whole teaching to "one simple formula" in Transcendental Meditation. All of these movements undeniably root their teaching in one or another ideal of Advaita Vedānta; yet, the coherence of that ideal across its various instantiations may seem as asymptotic and elusive as Ramana Maharshi's "I-I."

As a first approximation, however, we can note at least one common theme: a vision of mission as a collective, spiritual work of return and reform. In her work *Religious Freedom in India,* Goldie Osuri interprets conversion as "an event and site of exception" that functions to consolidate the identity of the Hindu state.[181] Rites of purification and return, such as *śuddhi* and *parāvartan,* represent a kind of double exception in her analysis, insofar as "reconversion to a Hindutva version of Hinduism is not regarded as conversion" by the sovereign regime.[182] Conversion is not conversion when it is coded as return.

In several of the movements surveyed here, we do encounter readings of Advaita Vedānta that seem to justify a kind of ethno-religious nationalism and politicized rhetoric of return. The concern of the teachers of SVBF Canada to offer a "beacon," bringing materialist South Asian immigrants and their unmoored children back to a *sanātana dharma* that is their ancestral patrimony, strikes a nationalist chord, as does Swami Chinmayananda's reinterpretation of Ādi Śaṅkara's legendary conquest as warrant to foster a new "renaissance" of Hindu life and thought. So, too, Vivekananda wraps the Ramakrishna Mission in the language of religious and cultural reform, and he appeals freely to a romanticized narrative of India's glorious past. In Maharishi Vedic City, finally, ancient *śāstras* are brought to bear on suburban architecture, the conduct of government, and a rotating community of Brahmin *pandits* meditating for world peace.[183] In each of these cases, the Advaita message calls its hearers back to an ethno-cultural, Sanskritized identity as their native condition and ancestral birthright.

Yet, Maharishi Vedic City sits in the suburbs of Fairfield, Iowa, not India, and vanishingly few of its residents are South Asian in origin. According to Maharishi Mahesh Yogi, the true native condition of all conscious beings is neither cultural nor, strictly speaking, religious: it is each such conscious being's "own essential nature, the state of transcendental Being."[184] For all of these movements, entirely aside from their particular religious and political ideologies, the most authentic "return" is that which calls hearers back to their own already-achieved, innate state of liberation, here and now. "When we have become free," proclaims Vivekananda, "we need not go mad and throw up society and rush off to die in the forest or in a cave. We shall remain where we were, only we shall understand the whole thing."[185]

The modern Advaitins profiled in this chapter speak variously of the exhaustion of the *vāsanās* and identification with the *oṃ* at the source of body, mind, and intellect, the dissolution of the ego, or the gradual purification of the mind for Vedāntic study. These differences are real, and they chart subtly different paths to liberation. But, in every case, the goal is an ontological, inward turn to the self. "When the mind turns inward seeking 'Who am I?' and merges in the Heart, then the 'I' hangs down his head in shame and the One 'I' appears as Itself."[186] Any outward reform of society or external reclamation of one's identity as an ethnic "Hindu," as a follower of *sanātana dharma,* or as a traditional or progressive Advaitin is predicated on hearers' far more profound return to their own *ātman.* Such an emphasis would seem clearly to distinguish missionary Advaita from missionary Christianity, and from many, if not most, other forms of missionary Hinduism as well.

We will have ample opportunities to explore—and to trouble—this point of comparison and contrast in several of the chapters that follow. First, however, we turn to a more immediate and pressing question of historical interpretation. Specifically, what is the relationship between the Advaita mission movements that begin to emerge in the late nineteenth century and classical Vedānta? Is this a strictly modern development, or does it have antecedents in prior tradition? In chapter 3, I propose to address these questions and, in so doing, to explore further the distinctive form and character of an Advaita theology of mission.

3

Paradigms and Styles of Advaita Mission[1]

In an important 2004 article entitled "Images of Śaṃkara," Jacqueline G. Suthren Hirst offered the eighth-century Advaita teacher's "method of negation" as a useful way to approach contemporary reconstructions and re-imaginings of his life and legacy.[2] "For example," she writes with reference to Śaṅkara's exegetical practice, his oft-cited analogies of

> the clay-pot, rope-snake and magician-magic are all used to illuminate the relation of Brahman to the world. Individually, each is misleading; together they purify one another. The first might suggest that Brahman is a nonconscious material cause that really changes into the world, its effect. The rope-snake excludes real change or materiality from the process. However, as an example of error through superimposition, it might locate *avidyā*, which gives rise to the superimposed world, solely in the individual. Though this was a view taken by later Advaita, Śaṃkara refuses such an easy solution. The magician-magic example forces the pupil's attention back to Brahman, as sole cause. And so on.[3]

Similarly, surveying a number of modern and contemporary approaches to the study of Śaṅkara—the "philosophical," the "traditional-textual," "sociopolitical," and "experiential"—Suthren Hirst suggests that each, taken on its own, inevitably distorts our view, whereas, when taken together, they may be mutually purifying. The eighth-century teacher eludes being captured in his totality by any of these approaches or even by all of them taken together. Nevertheless, the most fruitful approximations will be those that carefully attend to the ways that Śaṅkara's work is "not unphilosophical," "not untextual," "not socially and politically ungrounded," and "not ungrounded in religious experience."[4]

Most importantly for my present purpose, Suthren Hirst initiates each of these four idealized "types" of scholarly study with reference to four very particular, personal, and concrete embodiments of Śaṅkara's legacy from the early to mid–twentieth century: Sarvepalli Radhakrishnan (1888–1975), Swami Saccidānandendra Sarasvatī (1880–1975), His Holiness Śrī Śaṃkarācārya Candraśekharendra Sarasvatī (1894–1994), and Ramana Maharshi (1879–1950).[5] This interpretive choice reflects a deep instinct, pervasive in the literature of Advaita and other traditions in its Sanskrit milieu, to symbolize institutions and broader social and intellectual currents personally by evoking the images of great figures and their disciples in the teaching tradition.[6] Thus, when Suthren Hirst evokes the image of Saccidānandendra, she deploys his individual, personal model of engagement to characterize a wider interpretive *paraṃparā* that includes Paul Hacker, Francis X. Clooney, and, not least, Suthren Hirst herself.[7]

In this chapter, I attempt to follow the same deep instinct and to deploy a similar interpretative strategy to address a different issue entirely. Having traced the nineteenth- and twentieth-century emergence of Advaita Vedānta as a transnational missionary movement in the previous chapter, here I attempt to trace the historical roots of this movement and to establish, with somewhat greater precision, its theological specificity. As we know from previous chapters, the status of Advaita and other Hindu traditions as "missionary" has been a subject of considerable dispute. Some apologists have argued that the Hinduism is fundamentally non-missionary in character. Others concede a missionary dimension to the tradition. At some risk of oversimplifying, these latter interpreters may be divided into two broad schools. One group views the emergence of missionary forms of Hinduism as an entirely modern development, taking shape either as a direct imitation of Western missionaries in India[8] or as a response to broader patterns of globalization and the transformed conditions of modernity.[9] For interpreters like

C. V. Mathew and Arvind Sharma, on the other hand, the emergence of movements like the Ramakrishna Mission and the International Society of Krishna Consciousness can be traced to older patterns of Sanskritization and interreligious competition.[10] Sharma is particularly insistent on this score, declaring that "Hinduism has always possessed a missionary character."[11]

Presented with these two lines of interpretation, with Suthren Hirst in mind, we might hypothesize that the truth lies somewhere in the middle and that the mutual differences of these lines of interpretation might function to purify each approach of possible distortions. Perhaps, in other words, it may be possible to conclude that contemporary, ostensibly missionary forms of non-dualist Hinduism are "not ungrounded in ancient traditions," but that they are also "not without exigencies distinctive to the modern period." I hope to illustrate precisely such a conclusion in this chapter. This will require that we reach behind the movements surveyed in the previous chapter to premodern Advaita traditions that flourished between the eighth and sixteenth centuries, while also tracing a coherent, if also internally complex, theological trajectory from these medieval traditions to the missionary Advaitas of the present day.

My argument proceeds in three layers, which move from the more particular to the more general and from the concrete to the speculative. In a first, preliminary discussion, I return to the field of contemporary Christian missiology, from chapter 1, focusing on the claim of many missiologists that the history of Christianity reveals no singular understanding of "mission," but diverse—even incommensurable—missionary paradigms, models, or types. In the second section, I attempt to apply this insight to the historical development of Advaita Vedānta by highlighting what I judge to be three major "paradigms" of Advaita mission: (1) the compassionate teacher depicted in Ādi Śaṅkarācārya's eighth-century, independent treatise *Upadeśasāhasrī*; (2) the image of Śaṅkara himself as a conquering *avatāra* of Śiva in the late medieval hagiographical tradition (*dig-vijaya*); and (3) the image of the Buddha as the first "Hindu missionary" in the speeches of Swami Vivekananda. Without claiming to be comprehensive, I argue that these three idealized paradigms reveal both significant historical continuity and substantive diversity—even incommensurability—in advancing Advaita as a missionary movement. Finally, in a more speculative vein, I suggest that the distinctive profiles of the four disciples depicted in the most prominent hagiography, Mādhava's *Śaṅkaradigvijaya,* might serve to rationalize different forms or styles that Advaita mission has taken, and can take, in the modern and contemporary periods. My interest in this chapter is both historical and constructive. That is, I hope to add further clarity to our understanding of Advaita as a distinct missionary movement in South Asia and to bring to light fruitful interpretive tools for interpreting the diverse missionary activities and movements that define this tradition in the contemporary world.

Paradigms, Types, and Styles of Christian Mission

As discussed in chapter 1, the English term "mission" is derived from the Latin *missio* and the Greek *apostellō,* "to send or to be sent." In most contemporary parlance, it is understood in primarily Christian terms as "the task entrusted to the Church by Jesus to proclaim the gospel to the world and make disciples of all people" as well as "the activity involved in spreading the faith in foreign and/or non-Christian area."[12] It would seem that it was only by analogy to this definition, or something similar, that such teachers as Vivekananda and Chinmayananda were empowered to christen the institutions they founded as "missions," and it is this definition, rendered suitably vague to permit comparative inquiry, that provides the primary heuristic for the present, interreligious study.

But is such a definition truly as stable as it appears, even in Christian tradition? A kind of revolution on this question was provoked by the 1991 publication of *Transforming Mission: Paradigm Shifts in Theology of Mission* by the South African Reformed theologian David J. Bosch (1929–1992). The first page of Bosch's study features a definition of mission similar to that quoted above and an analysis of this definition into its constituent elements, namely, "(a) propagation of the faith, (b) expansion of the reign of God, (c) conversion of the heathen, and (d) the founding of new churches." Having introduced this normative definition, however, Bosch immediately calls it into question:

> Still, all these connotations attached to the word "mission," familiar as they may be, are of recent origin. Until the sixteenth century the term was used exclusively with reference to the doctrine of the Trinity, that is, of the sending of the Son by the Father and of the Holy Spirit by the Father and the Son. The Jesuits were the first to use it in terms of the spread of the Christian faith among people (including Protestants) who were not members of the Catholic Church.[13]

The key phrase here is "of recent origin." According to Bosch, the normative definition of mission with which he begins his study is also a thoroughly modern one, and—as he contends quite strongly—as much a product of as a pretext for European colonial regimes.[14]

As an historian of the Christian movement, Bosch is fully aware that the development of Christian missiology cannot be reduced to this particular use of a Latin term. The Christian movement spread fairly rapidly throughout the Mediterranean world and beyond from an early date, beginning almost from its inception in Western Asia. Hence, the bulk of Bosch's volume traces the various distinctive patterns and frameworks by which Christians have construed their "sending" and "being sent" from the time of the New Testament to the twentieth century. Following the historian of science Thomas Kuhn (via the Catholic theologian Hans Küng), he classifies these patterns as mutually incommensurable, comprehensive "paradigms" of mission particular to different eras of Christian history.[15] The first section of the book traces three distinct perspectives within the "apocalyptic-eschatological pattern of early Christianity" as articulated in the New Testament gospels of Matthew and Luke and the letters of Paul the Apostle; the second takes up four "historical paradigms" of Eastern Christianity, medieval Roman Catholicism, the Protestant Reformation, and the post-Enlightenment; and the third draws out no fewer than thirteen elements of an "Emerging Ecumenical Missionary Paradigm" for the late twentieth century. The details of these different paradigms need not delay us here, and Bosch's reconstructions can be and have been criticized on historical grounds.[16] What is most significant is that Bosch insisted on talking about mission in a plural rather than a singular idiom, attentive to both continuity and discontinuity in the messy processes of historical transformation.

To cite just one example relevant to the present topic, Bosch notes that the modern prominence of one classic Christian mission text—the "Great Commission" of Matthew 28:18–20—can be traced to a single, influential tract by the Baptist missionary William Carey (1761–1834) in the context of British colonial expansion. The text in question is Carey's famous (or notorious) *An Enquiry into the Obligations of Christians to use Means for the Conversion of the Heathens,* published just a year before his departure for Calcutta in 1793.[17] With this text in mind, it becomes possible to imagine that the emergence of what would become a consensus understanding of "mission" in Christian modernity and the advent of an Advaita missionary like Swami Vivekananda may be mutually imbricated, separated as they were by a little more than a century and a little less than twenty kilometers.[18]

Be this as it may, Bosch's influence on the discipline of Christian missiology, at least in the English-speaking world, would be difficult to overstate. Stephen Bevans and Roger Schroeder note a widespread opinion that "after the twentieth century, any missiology can be done only as a footnote to the work of David Bosch."[19] At the same time, recent scholarship has complicated the picture he constructed by unhinging dominant paradigms or models from a too-firm connection with one or another era of Christian history. Thus, M. Thomas Thangaraj identifies eight "models" of mission that trace a rough historical development without being strictly chronological: Mission as "Kerygmatic Presence," as "Martyrdom," as "Expansion," as "Monastic Service," as "Conversion of Heathens," as "Mission Societies," as "Education," and as "Joint Action for Justice and Peace."[20] Bevans and Schroeder themselves classify three "types" of missionary theology that continually interact in distinctive ways to shape diverse movements at every moment of Christian history: "Mission as Saving Souls and Extending the Church"; "Mission as Discovery of Truth"; and "Mission as Commitment to Liberation and Transformation."[21] From their own surveys, Thangaraj, Bevans, and Schroeder also offer constructive proposals for new, synthetic missionary models suited to the present context—"*Missio Humanitatis*" in the case of Thangaraj, "prophetic dialogue" in the case of the Bevans and Schroeder—but there seems little reason to believe that these models will not also be subject to further revision.[22] Adaptation to new historical contexts, then, does not merely apply to the practice of individual missionaries or missionary organizations; it cuts to the fundamental understanding of "mission" itself, as a category of thought, practice, and comparative inquiry.

It is worth noting that, even in this scholarship, the meaning of mission is never totally relativized. If Bosch's key insight was to draw attention to discontinuity in this history, it remains the case that the same history also reveals points of continuity. Christians of every era judged that they were "sent" to communicate the gospel and to work for the building of God's reign in some respect; but the imagined recipients of this communication, the intended results, and the means to be employed varied widely from one social and historical context to the next.

So also, as we turn to Advaita history to discern its missionary character beyond the particular narratives of individual teachers and movements, we might reasonably expect to encounter multiple paradigms or models, bound together by a broad family resemblance but distinct in their particulars. As in Arvind Sharma's *Hinduism as a Missionary Religion,* and indeed in any investigation of "mission" in Hindu traditions for the foreseeable future, we will necessarily build analogies to the Christian traditions from which the distinctively modern usage of this term emerged. At the same time, disciplined by this recent work in Christian missiology, we can do so in a self-consciously plural idiom. We will attempt to build an analogy, in other words, not to any particular usage or historical practice of mission in Christian tradition (though that might well be possible) but to the whole complex process of historical development and transformation. The key element of this interpretive transposition will be the notion—articulated by Bosch and developed further by Thangaraj, Bevans, and Schroeder—of missionary "paradigms" or "models," those distinctive patterns of thought and practice that may be read to punctuate this historical process and to render it susceptible to systematic inquiry.

Three Historical Paradigms of Advaita Mission

Given the limits of space and of my own expertise, I will not attempt in this chapter to offer a comprehensive history of Advaita mission comparable to Bosch's *Transforming Mission* or Bevans and Schroeder's *Constants in Context*. Instead, in this section, I will briefly sketch just three paradigms from what I take to be decisive moments in the ongoing construction of Advaita: the eighth-century teaching of Ādi Śaṅkara; the late medieval hagiographical tradition exemplified in the *Śaṅkaradigvijaya* attributed to Mādhava; and the speeches of Swami Vivekananda at the turn of the twentieth century. No doubt, other eras and alternative paradigms are worthy of note. Should the proposal in this chapter prove convincing, the ground will be laid for a richer historical narrative in future scholarship.[23]

Even confining the inquiry to these periods and figures, however, we must face the question: what would define a model or paradigm of mission in Advaita tradition? As a Christian theologian, Bosch chooses emblematic verses from the New Testament to capture the fundamental impulse of each era. Thus, according to his analysis, "for God so loved the world" (John 3:16) well captures the self-giving, communal, and cosmic paradigm of the Eastern churches, whereas the more menacing "compel them to come in" (Luke 14:23) defines the approach of medieval Catholicism.[24] In the case of Advaita, following the example provided by Suthren Hirst, we might prefer a more embodied, personal representation. That is, given the centrality of the authorized teacher in the tradition, I propose to seek out its paradigmatic expressions in the idealized images of such teachers constructed by leading exponents of the tradition.[25] Note that these are treated as *idealized images*, not as historical portraits. Though some historical context will be necessary, our interest will be focused on the fictive image of a model *ācārya* constructed by Śaṅkara in the eighth century, rather than on Śaṅkara himself, and so on. Such idealized constructions do not quite attain the level of systematic rationality characteristic of Hindu "theology," as Francis X. Clooney or Jonathan Edelmann might require.[26] They can nevertheless be treated as "pre-theological" works, each of which provides an intelligible, coherent vision of the tradition, amenable to further inquiry and analysis.

The Compassionate *Ācārya* of the *Upadeśasāhasrī*

Years ago, Reinhart Hummel made the prescient observation that most missionary movements in modern Hinduism have an organic relationship with the "internal" competition that existed (and exists) among rival *saṃpradāyas* from ancient times well into the modern period.[27] Such competition among Śaivas, Vaiṣṇavas, and other diverse teaching traditions could be fierce. Not infrequently, it included an explicit rhetoric of conversion, and it was supported, from time to time, by programs of religiously authorized coercion.[28] Late medieval thinkers would produce doxographies that sharply distinguish *nāstika* from *āstika* by their relation to Vedic authority and position the *āstika* traditions as ever-greater approximations of the home tradition. Yet, earlier Vedānta, Buddhist, and Jain traditions reveal little such irenicism or strategies of inclusion.[29] "In pre-twelfth-century India," writes Andrew Nicholson, "many thinkers today labeled 'Hindu' went to great efforts to disprove one another's teachings, including use of *ad hominem* attacks, straw man arguments, and other questionable means. There was no understanding then that all of these thinkers were part of a shared orthodoxy."[30]

Among those Nicholson paints with a sectarian brush is the eighth-century Advaita teacher, Ādi Śaṅkarācārya. Writing in the twentieth century, as we have seen, Swami Chinmayananda and his followers would offer a portrait of Śaṅkara as a great reconciler, and his non-dualist teaching as a force of "universal brotherhood and mutual understanding . . . no matter what paths were followed."[31] In making such a claim, Chinmayananda reflects what has become a defining trope of modern Vedānta. Nicholson, by contrast, notes that in his certainly authentic writings Śaṅkara "issued scathing attacks on *āstika* and *nāstika* alike, hardly distinguishing between the two."[32] As is well known, a major section of Śaṅkara's commentary on the *Brahmasūtra*s is dedicated to dismantling other systems of thought,[33] and in his commentaries on the *Upaniṣads* he will periodically pause to attempt a sweep of major opponents. Recent scholarship has drawn attention to apologetic and even polemic features of the great teacher's writings, as he defines clear boundaries against Sāṃkhyas, Buddhists, and rival, theistic traditions of Vedānta.[34] *Bhedābheda* Vedāntins such as Śaṅkara's rough contemporary Bhāskara readily returned the favor.[35] In many places, it seems safe to presume that Śaṅkara's adversaries are fictive or remote, and that the debates are scripted for strictly pedagogical purposes. However, Suthren Hirst sees in the harsh rhetoric of his commentary on *Bṛhadāraṇyaka Upaniṣad* 2.1.20 the implied presence of actual, contemporary rivals, "plausibly a Vaiṣṇava Vedāntin group, whom Śaṅkara seeks to manoeuvre out of competition."[36]

Positioning Śaṅkara as a sectarian teacher in a competitive religious milieu runs counter to the received image of him in modern Advaita, but it also opens the possibility of reading his certainly authentic works with an eye toward an implied missiology—albeit one distinctive to Śaṅkara's eighth-century context. As a possible starting point for such a reading, we can turn to his independent treatise, the *Upadeśasāhasrī*.[37] In the sixteenth verse chapter of this work, for example, Śaṅkara engages in a broad refutation, first of the Buddhist traditions he will later categorize as "the way of self-negation" (*nir-ātma-vāda*, USP 16.68) in verses 23–44, and then of those Sāṃkhyas and Vaiśeṣikas he lumps together as "dualist" (*dvaya-vāda*, 16.68) in verses 45–63. He does not rank these traditions according to their approximation of the truth,[38] as we will encounter in late medieval doxographies, but simply calls for their thorough renunciation: "Therefore, assumptions concerning bondage, final release, etc., [which are] other than this are indeed confused ideas. The assumptions of the Sāṃkhyas, of the followers of Kaṇāda, and of the Buddhists are lacking in profound consideration. As [their assumptions] contradict the scriptures and reasoning, they should never be respected. Their faults can be pointed out hundreds and thousands of times. . . . Therefore, having abandoned the teaching of other scriptures, a wise person should make firm his understanding of the true meaning of the *Vedānta* and also of Vyāsa's thought, with faith and devotion and without any crookedness" (USP 16.64–67).[39]

The result of the refutation and renunciation of alternative traditions is, in this text, virtually identified with establishment in the higher view. "Seekers after final release," Śaṅkara concludes, "being free from doubts which arise from the views of others, become firm on the path of knowledge" (USP 16.68). This is, from a strictly rhetorical point of view, strong language of competition, exclusion, and identity formation.

The primary agent for freeing prospective disciples from the doubts that arise from other teachings and establishing them on this path is the authorized *ācārya*. In the concluding section of the seventeenth verse chapter, the role of this teacher is summarized as follows:

> Concentrating upon *ātman* the love which is [now set] on external things—for they end in suffering, are inconstant and exist for *ātman*—a seeker after truth should resort to a teacher who is tranquil, wise, released, actionless, and established in *Brahman*, since the *śruti* says, "One who has a teacher knows . . ." and the *smṛti* also says, "Learn to know this." If a student is disciplined and properly qualified, the teacher should immediately transport him over his great interior ocean of darkness in the boat of the knowledge of *Brahman*. (17.50–52)

If USP 16 emphasizes the incoherence and threat posed by rival teaching traditions in Śaṅkara's pluralistic milieu, this passage privileges the home tradition as the sole true alternative to these other views, aptly symbolized by the boat of knowledge. The teacher, characterized here as peaceful, wise, and established in *Brahman* (*brahmaṇi sthita*), functions as the pilot of this boat and is thus a suitable object of refuge.[40]

Śaṅkara describes this authorized teacher twice in the prose portion of *Upadeśasāhasrī*, at the beginning of each of the first and the second chapters (USG 1.6; 2.45). The two descriptions differ somewhat in their particulars, but the image that emerges is nevertheless coherent.[41] The longer description occurs in USG 1.6:

> And the teacher is able to consider the pros and cons [of an argument], is endowed with understanding, memory, tranquility, self-control, compassion, favor and the like; he is versed in the traditional doctrine; not attached to any enjoyments, visible or invisible; he has abandoned all the rituals and their requisites; a knower of *Brahman*, he is established in *Brahman*; he leads a blameless life, free from faults such as deceit, pride, trickery, wickedness, fraud, jealousy, falsehood, egotism, self-interest, and so forth; with the only purpose of helping others he wishes to make use of knowledge.

In this passage, Śaṅkara places exterior, observable virtues of intellectual acuity, facility with the scriptural traditions, personal detachment, and compassion alongside fundamental affirmations of the teacher's interior, unobservable self-knowledge. In the *Upadeśasāhasrī*'s second prose chapter, he focuses more narrowly on these interior qualities: the teacher is described as "a knower of *Brahman*" (*brāhmaṇa*), "established in *Brahman*" (*brahmaniṣṭha*), and "sitting at ease" (*sukhamāsīna*; USG 2.45).

Reading these two passages together with the brief description provided in USP 17, above, we can say that one qualification emerges most consistently: the teacher is a knower of *Brahman*, firmly established in *Brahman*, one who is—to adopt a later formulation—liberated in life (*jīvan-mukta*). This is no great surprise. On the one hand, affirmation of the teacher's *mukti* functions to authorize both this individual teacher and the entire teaching lineage.[42] On the other hand, such an affirmation also introduces a paradox, insofar as this *mukta*, described as actionless and sitting at leisure, with nothing left to accomplish, nevertheless takes up the intentional, goal-oriented activity of examining prospective disciples, determining who is worthy, and offering instruction (e.g., USG 1.2–5).[43] Part of the paradox is resolved by appeal to *prārabdha karma*: until the fall of the body, the inertia of past actions that have begun to bear fruit, including virtues like compassion, continue to operate.[44] But a deeper answer is given by Śaṅkara in USG 1.6, when he writes that the *ācārya* acts solely for the purpose of doing good for others (*kevalaparānugrahaprayojanaḥ*). That is, this teacher's activity and perhaps even his continued embodiment stems from the world's great need rather than his own desires.[45]

Insofar as the *ācārya* in the *Upadeśasāhasrī* may be read as exemplifying a particular model or paradigm of Advaita mission, this model emerges only in part from these few passages of explicit description. A more elaborate portrait arises from the *ācārya*'s actual teaching activity, as depicted in the first two prose chapters and implied throughout the verse chapters. From such a fuller reading, at least three points merit special attention. First, although in some places in the prose chapters one can discern the implied presence of Buddhist or theist Vaiṣṇava competitors,[46] the focus remains on the scriptural and reasoned dialogue between a single teacher and a single disciple. Second, Śaṅkara's vision is explicitly elitist: the qualified recipient is normed in the *Upadeśasāhasrī* as a high-caste, Brahmin male, a renunciant or celibate student possessed of superlative intellectual and moral virtues who has approached the teacher in search of final release (USG 1.2–3; 2.45).[47] Finally, despite this very narrow field of prospective disciples, Śaṅkara is by no means indifferent to the need to identify them and bring them to liberating knowledge. At USG 1.3, he identifies the final goal of the *ācārya*'s teaching activity by setting two terms in parallel: *śreyas*, presumably the preferable or superior state of liberation, and *vidyā-santati*, the diffusion, continuity, or sustained practice of knowledge. Thus, continuance of the teaching tradition stands alongside liberation itself as one of its core objectives. The teaching of Advaita may proceed one disciple at a time, but its vision of liberation demands continual dissemination.[48]

It is tempting to read the prose descriptions of the *Upadeśasāhasrī* as a kind of autobiography, describing Śaṅkara's actual self-understanding and teaching practice. But this would exceed the evidence. Do we know that Śaṅkara never sought out disciples but received them only when approached? We cannot know this with certainty. Indeed, we can only guess at the intended audience of the *Upadeśasāhasrī*. In the person of the *ācārya*, however, we can speak more securely about Śaṅkara's idealized, theological vision of the tradition. He envisions an exclusivist path of self-knowledge, which entails complete rejection of alternative Vedic and Buddhist ways of life for authentic seekers on this path. In principle, his vision is universalist, insofar as he teaches liberation by knowledge of the innermost self of each and every conscious being; in practice, at least in the *Upadeśasāhasrī*, he restricts access to a small set of high-caste renunciants, and idealized teachers communicate the message of liberation by means of intimate, one-on-one dialogue. It is, in this regard, a mission focused more on securing the firm identity of insiders than on any kind of world conquest. Though it seems likely that Śaṅkara propagated his teaching in fierce competition with actual rivals in his South Indian religious milieu, the primary goal of such competition appears to be the maintenance of the *paraṃparā* and continuance of the teaching practice. The size of the community, in Śaṅkara's idealized vision, may matter less than its perdurance as a living, liberating option for those few Brahmin elites from one generation to the next who possess the *adhikāra* to receive its teaching aright.

The Servant-Conqueror of the Śaṅkara Hagiographies

The eighth-century missionary paradigm of Ādi Śaṅkarācārya, if we may call it that, stands out for its social elitism, uncompromising exclusion of all rival teaching traditions, and insider discourse. We encounter a strikingly different vision in the *vijayas*, that body of hagiographical literature dating from about the fourteenth century onward. The primary motif of this literature, including not only the Śaṅkara hagiographies but also those dedicated to other leading renunciant-teachers, is the *digvijaya* or "conquest of the quarters," a triumphant tour of the Indian subcontinent modeled on the conquests and ritual enthronements of legendary kings.[49] "The *digvijaya*," writes Jonathan Bader in his survey of the leading Śaṅkara hagiographies, "is, strictly speaking, appropriate only for a king. But the hagiographers transpose this ritual method of legitimizing authority from the sphere of politics to the realm of metaphysics."[50] Śaṅkara emerges in these narratives as a true conqueror of the subcontinent, albeit one who conquers with no goal except release for those caught in *saṃsāra* and no weapon except the liberating words of his Advaita teaching.[51]

The hagiographies have attracted attention with respect to their reliability, or unreliability, as sources for learning about the life of Śaṅkara.[52] Yet, at least arguably, they are far more significant as sources for understanding theological developments in the Advaita tradition during the late medieval and early modern periods.[53] The most prominent of these works, the *Śaṅkaradigvijaya* attributed to Mādhava (ŚDV), represents a compilation and synthesis of prior narratives. It appears to have been brought into its final form sometime between 1650 and 1740.[54] Whereas Śaṅkara described his idealized teacher rather simply as a self-knower, established in *Brahman* and equipped with the intellectual and moral virtues of a sage, the idealized Śaṅkara of the ŚDV draws authority from his more exalted status as an *avatāra* of Śiva, who has come to Earth to restore the Vedic tradition and destroy ignorance.[55] After a prologue that establishes this cosmological context (ŚDV 1.27–59) and the precedent set by Skanda in the form of Kumārila Bhaṭṭa (1.60–98), the ŚDV follows Śaṅkara from his miraculous birth through his initiation into renunciant life and the tradition of Advaita Vedānta in its first half (ŚDV 2.1–7.58), and then, in the second half, traces a pilgrimage and victory tour across every corner of India, in which the great teacher engages in a series of verbal contests with rival Mīmāṃsākas, Vaiṣṇavas, Śaivas, Buddhists, and Jains (7.59–15.174). The ŚDV concludes in the mountains of Kashmir, where Śaṅkara defeats an army of such opponents and ascends a "throne of omniscience" (*sarvajñapīṭha*) as his reward (16.54–93). William S. Sax identifies the "*digvijaya* ideal" reflected in this and other hagiographical texts as explicitly missiological, insofar as their vision self-consciously mirrors the "proselytizing tours" of significant Vaiṣṇavas in the medieval period and establishes the "lordship" of the teaching tradition by "encompassing ('converting') their opponents rather than destroying them."[56] In the *Upadeśasāhasrī*, rival teachings are renounced; in the *Śaṅkaradigvijaya*, they are rendered subject to the authority of Advaita.

If we were to treat terms like "mission" and "proselytism" as univocal terms and wanted to find an origin for such motifs in Advaita tradition, it would be tempting to follow Sax in tracing such a missionary impulse to the *vijaya* literature, rather than to an earlier source like the *Upadeśasāhasrī*. Whereas the latter engages in respectful, reasoned dialogue (*vāda*) between teacher and student, only the former depicts the Advaita teacher engaging in a kind of argumentation that aims for defeat and conversion of the opponent.[57] But, as suggested in my brief review of Bosch above, univocal definitions may not be adequate to the complexity of this (or any) historical development. On the one hand, the scripted dialogues of the *Upadeśasāhasrī* seem clearly to presume a competitive, polemic religious milieu. In places—such as USP 16, quoted above—this comes explicitly to the surface. On the other, the South Indian social and political context of the *vijayas* included elements of both mutual accommodation and fierce competition, as rival Smārta, Vaiṣṇava, and other traditions vied for royal patronage in a shared, pluralistic network of rulers, temples, *maṭhas*, and leading *ācāryas*.[58] The present inquiry, then, does not aim to discover which of these traditions is more robustly or authentically missionary, according to some stable norm. It aims instead to discern how the distinctive missionary paradigm of the *vijayas* transforms the similarly distinctive paradigm of a text like the *Upadeśasāhasrī* in ways particular to these late medieval and early modern contexts. Insofar as possible, mirroring the work of Bosch and his successors, we can allow the scope and character of Advaita mission to emerge from these texts and traditions, rather than asking whether they fit into some pre-existing frame.

We can begin a comparison of these two paradigms with their respective attitudes toward rival teaching traditions. In both cases, debates establish the superiority of the Advaita position. In the *Upadeśasāhasrī*, the positions of such adversaries are embedded in the real and implied dialogues among those either already established as Advaita teachers or who have come as seekers, with the intended result that such seekers can securely abandon rival views and become inoculated against their errors. In the ŚDV and other hagiographies, by contrast, the debates take place in public, identify Śaṅkara's opponents by name, frequently receive arbitration by some supernatural authority, and typically conclude with the conversion or destruction of the adversary.[59] If the vision of the *Upadeśasāhasrī* may be read as a form of sectarianism, then the ŚDV envisions the creation of what Elaine M. Fisher has called a "sectarian public," an account of Advaita that engages a far wider world of lay devotees, imperial politics, and active contestation in a pluralist milieu.[60]

Consider, for example, the most extended contest in the ŚDV: the debate with Śaṅkara's elder contemporary, the Mīmāṃsāka, householder and rival Advaitin, Maṇḍana Miśra. After an initial dispute in the presence of Vyāsa and Jaimini (8.14–31), Śaṅkara stipulates unambiguous terms for the true contest, namely that the loser agrees to become a disciple of the victor (*anyonyaśiṣyatvapaṇā*), effectively converting to the victor's teaching tradition (8.36). The Goddess Sarasvatī, in the form of Maṇḍana's wife, Ubhayabhāratī, moderates the discussion and bestows garlands on both disputants; upon his defeat by Śaṅkara, Maṇḍana's garland withers and fades (8.132), and he abandons his teaching to become Śaṅkara's disciple, Sureśvara. Though there is no arbitrator for Śaṅkara's debate with Bhāskara, the defeat of this important rival has a similarly dramatic effect, resulting in the destruction of Bhāskara's *bhedābheda* teaching and the spread of Advaita (15.140). So too, Śaṅkara's ascent to the throne of omniscience is tested—and witnessed—in public, by a host of Vaiśeṣika, Nyāya, Sāṃkhya, Buddhist, Jain, and Pūrva Mīmāṃsā scholars, and this result is again validated by the intervention of Sarasvatī (16.62–92).

Somewhat in tension with this public, confrontational image of the idealized teacher, the Śaṅkara of the ŚDV also adopts a more irenic and inclusivist view than we witness in the *Upadeśasāhasrī*. In the narrative, Śaṅkara frequents and even establishes temples dedicated to Viṣṇu, Śiva and the Goddess, and it is only in the *vijaya* literature that he seems to have gained credit for establishing the six devotional traditions of Smārta orthodoxy.[61] In the practice of the Daśanāmī monastic federation, this served to sanction the extension of the Advaita tradition from the near-exclusive preserve of *saṃnyāsins* to include an active, supporting role for lay devotees.[62] Such an inclusive vision also extends, in a limited way, to social diversity. In one of the most famous episodes of the ŚDV, Śaṅkara and his disciples attempt to avoid contact with a hunter from an outcaste tribe (*śvapaca*). The hunter immediately reminds them that the authentic teaching of Advaita admits no supposition of difference between *brāhmaṇa* and *śvapaca* (6.29). Śaṅkara promptly recognizes the hunter as a knower of the self (*ātmavid*; 6.34), worthy of reverence as a *guru* (6.38). This does not lead to social revolution: the *śvapaca* is later revealed as Śiva in disguise (6.40–43), and the ŚDV proclaims Śaṅkara's central mission as the "uplifting of the twice-born" (1.48).[63] The episode nevertheless signals a deepened reflection on the universal presence of the *ātman* in all conscious beings, regardless of class or caste.[64]

Andrew Nicholson has highlighted the fundamentally inclusive vision of late medieval doxographies. Among these, he draws special attention to the influential *Sarvadarśanasaṃgraha* produced by Mādhava, the fourteenth-century Advaitin teacher and advisor to Vijayanagara kings also traditionally identified as the author of the ŚDV.[65] In his doxography, Mādhava clearly differentiates *āstika* from *nāstika* traditions on the basis of their attitudes to Vedic authority and positions them in hierarchical sequence, with each teaching tradition correcting an error in the preceding one until they culminate in the highest truth of Advaita Vedānta.[66] While the attribution of ŚDV to Mādhava may be difficult to sustain, it seems clear that the ŚDV and the other *vijayas* draw on a similar, integrative interpretive paradigm, one with little basis in the certainly authentic works of Śaṅkara but strong affinities with the doxographies of both Advaitins and their rivals in the late medieval and early modern periods. The *Upadeśasāhasrī* offers a vision of a marginal, contrast community, which engages other traditions only for the purpose of defining boundaries and establishing identities for disciples on the path. Such engagement—alternately antagonistic and accommodating—moves to the center of the *vijayas*' missionary paradigm, even as the Advaita tradition itself moves to the center of their authors' vision of religious, political, and social life.

Why the shift? If one accepts an early date for the *vijaya* traditions and an origin in the Vijayanagara Empire, then, as noted earlier, competition for royal patronage may be the decisive factor. Both Nicholson and Sax also adduce the influence of a monolithic military and religious "other" in the form of Islam.[67] Though some Islamic influence is certainly possible, the notion of Islam as a monolithic other seems to reflect the concerns and stereotypes of a later period. For Mādhava and other Advaitins who produced *vijayas* with Śaṅkara as the conquering hero, a more proximate and likely far more threatening model was provided by the rapid spread of various Vaiṣṇava *bhakti* traditions throughout late medieval India.[68] This threat was far from remote: though the Advaitin teacher Vidyāraṇya and the Śṛṅgerī *maṭha* enjoyed a special relationship with early Vijayanagara kings, later dynasties favored Mādhva and Śrī Vaiṣṇava temples and traditions.[69] Daniel Sheridan has gone so far as to argue that the narrative of the ŚDV may actually be based directly on the traditional biography of Madhva, the Dvaita Vedāntin, Vaiṣṇava and great critic of Śaṅkara. On this reading, the Śaṅkara *vijaya* represents a kind of rear-guard, defensive maneuver in the face of a superior enemy.[70]

Whatever the motive and original sources of the *vijaya* literature, the image of Śaṅkara one finds therein clearly presents a missionary paradigm distinct from that embodied by the authorized *ācārya* of the *Upadeśasāhasrī*. It is more public and confrontational; it positions Advaita at the foundation of what is emerging as a unified *āstika* or Vedic social and religious orthodoxy; and it deploys the teaching of non-dualism not merely to distinguish Advaita from rivals but also to subject them and incorporate them under the aegis of its higher view. In so doing, it provides an important link between the eighth-century writings of Ādi Śaṅkarācārya and the distinctively modern missionary paradigm of Svāmi Vivekananda and other Vedāntins in the nineteenth, twentieth, and twenty-first centuries.

The Missionary Buddha in the Speeches of Swami Vivekananda

We have already had occasion to note the frequent designation of Swami Vivekananda as the "first Hindu missionary" from India to North America and Europe.[71] "Vivekananda," writes Torkel Brekke, "was a missionary of Hinduism. His motivation for going to America was straightforward. On the one hand he wished to bring money and technology to India . . . On the other he wished to flood the West with Hinduism."[72] The great teacher was also, adds David Miller, "heralded by many of his followers as a Second Śaṅkara, who through the synthesis of the old and the new created a New Hinduism."[73]

Having examined the paradigms of the idealized *ācārya* of the eighth-century treatise *Upadeśasāhasrī* and the idealized image of Śaṅkara in the *vijaya* literature, the label "Second Śaṅkara" naturally suggests an appropriation of one or the other missionary ideal. And this, as we know from the previous chapter, is what we do find in the rhetoric of Swami Chinmayananda and his Chinmaya Mission in the late twentieth century. In the case of Vivekananda at the turn of the previous century, however, the picture is considerably more complex.[74] We do find traces of the *vijaya* narrative, such as when Vivekananda observes that "Shankara was regarded by many as an incarnation of Shiva" (CWSV 7: 40) and compares plans to visit his ailing mother to a similar episode in the *Śaṅkaradigvijaya* (CWSV 8: 490; see ŚDV 14.29–50). Vivekananda also freely described his own work, particularly in India, as a reforming mission analogous to Śaṅkara's *vijaya* (CWSV 2: 139; 3: 216–17, 535–36; 4: 326, 462–63; 5: 217). In a speech from 1897, he declared that from the time of Śaṅkara to his own campaign, "the whole work in India is a reconquest of this Buddhistic degradation by the Vedanta" (3: 265).

Aside from such passing allusions, however, Vivekananda portrays Śaṅkara less as the conquering hero of the hagiographies and more as a "great Advaitic philosopher" and "the greatest teacher of the Vedanta philosophy" (CWSV 3: 229; 8: 6). He recognizes him as the foremost exponent of Advaita teaching and his work as a sublime, rational synthesis of the Vedānta (1: 363; 2: 139; 3: 325–26, 341; 7: 59; 8: 6). But he also accuses the great sage of imposing his own, narrow interpretation on the scriptural texts (3: 348, 439; 7: 40–41, 155–56).[75] Taking the integrative strategy of the late medieval doxographies to yet another level, Vivekananda positions Śaṅkara as one in a series of spiritual masters that includes not only Vivekananda's own teacher, Ramakrishna, but also the Buddha and many of Advaita's fiercest critics, such as Rāmānuja, Madhva, and Caitanya (3: 219; 4: 332, 369, 462; 5: 217; 7: 261, 330).[76] In the same breath, he praises Śaṅkara's razor-sharp intellect and faults him for his cold heart and deficit of "liberality" (7: 117). Elsewhere he states, "Ramanuja's heart was greater" (3: 265), and, with reference to Ramakrishna, "the time was ripe for one to be born who in one body would have the brilliant intellect of Shankara and the wonderfully expansive, infinite heart of Chaintanya" (3: 267). Finally, in an oft-quoted passage that goes to the heart of Vivekananda's missionary paradigm, he pronounces that "Shankara left this Advaita philosophy in the hills and forests, while I have come to bring it out of those places and scatter it broadcast before the workaday world and society" (7: 162). Here the exclusivist vision of a work like the *Upadeśasāhasrī* is clearly recognized, named, and rejected.

Where, then, does Swami Vivekananda derive a paradigm to warrant the movement of Advaita out of the forest, and not only into the workplaces and cities of India but also beyond the shores of the subcontinent? Not from the image of Śaṅkara the philosophical genius or from the image of Śaṅkara as world conqueror. For this rhetorical purpose, he turns instead to a very particular constructed image of Gautama Buddha. The image itself owes many of its most distinctive features to the recent "discovery" of Buddhism in Western, Orientalist scholarship;[77] but, as with Orientalist constructions of Vedānta and "Hinduism" itself, Swami Vivekananda successfully redeploys these features to his own distinctive, missionary project.[78]

Gwilym Beckerlegge has previously drawn attention to the sharp distinction Vivekananda draws between the person of the Buddha and the tradition that followed in his name.[79] Buddhism, from at least Śaṅkara's era to Vivekananda's own day, is described as a corrupting force, in need of correction and conquest (e.g., CWSV 1: 21; 2: 507; 3: 527; 5: 217 8: 103–4). The Buddha himself, on the other hand, receives praise as "God incarnate" (1: 21), "my Ishta – my God" (6: 227), "the sanest philosopher the world ever saw" (3: 528–29), and "the greatest soul that ever wore a human form" (4: 326). Most importantly, the teaching of the Buddha—unlike the materialism and atheism of his later followers—was none other than the teaching of Advaita Vedānta (7: 59). In a lecture on Advaita philosophy delivered in London in 1896, Vivekananda identified the Buddha and Śaṅkara as the two great figures who deployed this teaching to rescue India from crass materialism. "Buddha," he pronounces, "brought the Vedanta to light, gave it to the people, and saved India" (2: 139). In a dialogue with a disciple two years later at Belur Math, he credits the Buddha with transforming Advaita from an obscure teaching recorded on "a few palm leaves" to a philosophy applicable to "the everyday life of the people. In a sense, *he* was the living embodiment of the Vedanta" (7: 118–19).

At one level, in incorporating the Buddha into his own religious vision, Swami Vivekananda was simply following a long tradition of Vaiṣṇava theologies of *avatāra* and other strategies of appropriation.[80] The last quotation cited above, however, highlights an element of this construction of the Buddha that served to shift the tradition in the direction of Vivekananda's distinctively modern project: namely, his construction as a popular preacher and even evangelist of Advaita. In one of his addresses at the World's Parliament of Religion, Vivekananda famously declared that it was the Buddha's "glory" that "he had the large-heartedness to bring out the truths from the hidden Vedas and throw them broadcast all over the world. He was the first being in the world who brought missionarising into practice—nay, he was the first to conceive the idea of proselytizing" (CWSV 1: 22). In his London lecture, discussed above, he credits the Buddha for carrying the message of Vedānta out of "the forests" and preaching it to "the masses" (1: 138)—thus attributing to the Buddha success in the precise mission he so dramatically set for himself. In a number of places, he makes the parallel explicit, declaring, "I have a message to the West as Buddha had a message to the East" (5: 314), and "Other sects and parties have carried spirituality all over India, but since the days of Buddha we have been the first to break bounds and try to flood the world with missionary zeal" (5: 225). Or, as he states in a famous passage from his programmatic 1897 lecture, "The Work Before Us":

> There have been great conquering races in the world. We also have been great conquerors. The story of our conquest has been described by that noble Emperor of India, Asoka, as the conquest of religion and of spirituality. Once more the world must be conquered by India. This is the dream of my life, and I wish that each one of you who hear me today will have the same dream in your minds, and stop not until you have realised the dream. (3: 276)

Here the reference is to Aśoka rather than to the Buddha (see also 1: 390–91; 3: 530–31; 4: 194–95, 308, 312, 376–77, 486–87; 6: 289; 7: 288–89, 347; 9: 368). It appears clear, however, that Aśoka is depicted as faithfully carrying forward an initiative pioneered by the Buddha, and he thus similarly authorizes the work of Vivekananda and his fellow disciples.

We could, in principle, conclude our discussion of Vivekananda's idealized portrait of the Buddha here, with the command to "conquer the world with spirituality." It may be worth noting, however, that Vivekananda also uses this portrait to draw out yet another, distinctive element of his missionary paradigm: namely, an Advaita imperative for compassion, service, and equality in the broader, social sphere. In the same speech at the World's Parliament cited above, for example, Vivekananda notes that "the great glory of the Master [Buddha] lay in his wonderful sympathy for everybody, especially the ignorant and poor" (CWSV 1: 22). The Buddha is praised repeatedly for his compassion, patience, "large-heartedness," and extraordinary selflessness (1: 438; 2: 140, 352, 496; 5: 240; 6: 227; 7: 59, 118). Vivekananda proceeds to trace the early success of Buddhism in India to "the marvelous love which, for the first time in the history of humanity, overflowed a large heart and devoted itself to the service not only of all men but of all living beings—a love which did not care for anything except to find a way of release from suffering for all beings" (8: 99–100). Such love translated, in the case of the Buddha, into a critique of the caste system (2: 485; 3: 527; 8: 97) and a preaching that emphasized "this one idea of equality" (1:424–25; cf. 7: 430). "[W]hat Buddha did was to break wide open the gates of that very religion which was confined in the Upanishads to a particular caste" (6: 225). Although the Buddha long preceded the era of Śaṅkara, the image of the former is deployed strategically to complement or correct distortions introduced by the latter. In one speech, Vivekananda explains, "we want today that bright sun of [Shankara's] intellectuality joined with the heart of Buddha, the wonderful infinite heart of love and mercy" (2: 140). In practical terms, this provides a warrant for his movement's commitment both to the teaching of Advaita Vedānta and to a program of social uplift to all humankind and all living beings, regardless of class or caste.

It may be worth reminding ourselves, at this point, that in looking at Vivekananda's construction of the Buddha as a missionary paradigm, we are largely prescinding from questions about its historical accuracy or the correspondence between these high ideals and the actual structure or practices of Vivekananda's Ramakrishna Mission. In addition, we can note that, precisely as an idealized construction, this missionary paradigm does not simply replace earlier paradigms. The image Vivekananda constructs of the Buddha, and especially of Aśoka's missionary conquests, for example, draws forward a number of themes already developed in the *vijaya* literature.[81] And his fierce polemics and debate obviously resonate with the spirited dialogues depicted in the *Upadeśasāhasrī*.

One might wonder, then, why Vivekananda so firmly transposes the subject of these themes from Śaṅkara to the Buddha. No doubt, this follows in part simply from Vivekananda's admiration for the teaching and example of the Buddha.[82] Another motivating factor may be a sense of rivalry with prominent Buddhist reformers such as Vivekananda's fellow representative at the World's Parliament, the Sri Lankan, Anāgārika Dharmapāla.[83] But it also seems clear that the choice served a strategic function. By appealing to an earlier, popular teaching of "Advaita" that reaches behind those articulated in Śaṅkara's writings or the *vijaya* literature, for example, Vivekananda claims license to innovate in the tradition. Given that he spoke of the Buddha most frequently with Western audiences, he likely was also deliberately appropriating an Orientalist construction of Buddhism as a "universal religion" comparable to Christianity.[84] This gains further support from the several places where Vivekananda pairs the Buddha with Christ, and sometimes Krishna, as exemplary figures (CWSV 6: 134; 7: 27, 76; 8: 28, 180–81, 229).

Whatever Vivekananda's primary motive, the results of his interpretative strategy are clear. In the figure of the Buddha, he constructs an image of Advaita that promotes its application to everyday life, its active dissemination beyond the shores of India, and its engagement in questions of service and social justice.[85] Such a paradigm would be distinctively well-suited to the new, transnational religious context in which Swami Vivekananda found himself and to which he made a significant contribution.[86] The universality of the Advaita message of liberation finds, in his teaching, a new idiom and a new social expression.

Four Styles of Contemporary Advaita Mission

The temptation at this point, touched on already, may be to declare that only in the teaching of Vivekananda did Advaita Vedānta transcend its distinctively Indian, ethnic origins and emerge for the first time as an authentically missionary movement and genuine "world religion."[87] The work of David Bosch and his successors in Christian missiology, however, suggests a far more modest conclusion—if also one richer in interpretive possibility. First, we should note that the Ramakrishna Mission never transcended ethnicity in any absolute sense; instead, its distinctive teachings and structure brought it into complex negotiations with the various cultures it encountered, in India and in the West.[88] In this respect, it looks much like many forms of Christianity, from the first century to the present day. Second, to the extent that the movement initiated by Vivekananda cast a wider geographical net than that envisioned by Śaṅkara or the *vijaya* literatures—which would, I think, be difficult to contest—this conceptual shift possesses a complex, genetic relationship with prior theological formulations of the tradition, only two of which have been brought out here. If the advent of modernity and postmodernity may have accelerated these shifts and their accompanying social formations, then this too corresponds with the historical experience of most Christian traditions, among many others. All Vedāntas are Neo-Vedāntas, we might say, or none is.[89]

We could perhaps stop at this point, having offered one possible narrative of the historical development of missionary Advaita across these three paradigms. However, given the proliferation of Advaita movements in the wake of Vivekananda's historic speeches at the World's Parliament of Religion, as documented in the previous chapter, I propose to take the analysis one step further. That is, I wish to briefly explore the possibility of further differentiating distinctive elements of Advaita mission by appealing to the image of the four disciples of the *Śaṅkaradigvijaya*.

In the previous section, my intent was primarily descriptive and genealogical; here, it is more speculative and systematic. To the best of my knowledge, my interpretation here is original and does not correspond directly to the teachings of any Advaita tradition, ancient or modern.

This does not mean my correlation has no roots in such teachings, however. In particular, I take my start from a work we have encountered earlier: *Śaṅkara the Missionary*. In this book, we recall, Swami Chinmayananda and his followers offer a creative retelling of the *Śaṅkaradigvijaya* as a missional narrative for the international Chinmaya Mission. Most important for my present purpose, the authors of *Śaṅkara the Missionary* re-organize this narrative in distinct ways, lifting the portraits of Śaṅkara's four primary disciples out of the retelling of Śaṅkara's *vijaya* for separate treatment. In one chapter, entitled "The Four *Maṭha*-s and the Four Disciples," the authors connect the narratives of Padmapāda, Sureśvara, Hastāmalaka, and Toṭaka to the founding of the Daśanāmī Order in the traditional Advaita centers of Purī, Śṛṅgeri, Dvārakā, and Jyotir.[90] In a second chapter—an appendix in the 1978 original edition—they draw on the noted Śṛṅgerī teacher Swami Jñānānanda Bhāratī to draw correlations between the disciples and the mental faculties of *ahaṃkāra, buddhi, citta,* and *manas,* as well as various verses from the *Bhagavad-Gītā*.[91] Such symbolic associations, they note, emerge to an extent in the *Śaṅkaradigvijaya* itself.[92] "Thus," they conclude, "we have in these four great disciples of *Śaṅkara* an exemplification of the various levels and various paths, a rare phenomenon in the spiritual history of the country, nay, of the whole world."[93] On the one hand, then, the image of the four disciples simply represents the diversity of differently qualified students of the teaching; on the other, it also possesses a deeper symbolic valence in the narrative—one that makes it suitable for representing the diversity of the tradition itself.

It seems a short step from the interpretation of the disciples offered in *Śaṅkara the Missionary* to ask whether they might also serve as an additional typology for contemporary missionary Advaita. As with the paradigms discussed above, the models provided by the disciples are personal and embodied rather than textual or abstract. The social expression of the tradition takes the form of an idealized portrait of a leading *ācārya*. These models, however, do not seem to function as paradigms insofar as they do not define particular movements or historical periods in their totality. Instead, I have designated them as missionary *styles*, that is, distinctive modes of communicating and deploying the Advaita teaching which may—and generally do—appear in combination rather than in isolation from one another.[94]

The Padmapāda Style: Revalorization of Tradition

The authors of *Śaṅkara the Missionary* associate Śaṅkara's lead disciple, Padmapāda, with the *ahaṃkāra*, the basis of self-identity, as well as with a path of fervent devotion and surrender to the master (*praṇipāta*).[95] Of all the disciples in the ŚDV, Padmapāda is the first to appear, and he approaches the teacher in the most traditional manner, as outlined in a work like the *Upadeśasāhasrī*: he presents himself for examination, establishes his social and intellectual *adhikāra* to receive the teaching, and professes his detachment from all earthly and heavenly benefits (ŚDV 6.1–15; cf. USG 1.2–5). One full chapter of the *Śaṅkaradigvijaya* is dedicated to Padmapāda's pilgrimage across the subcontinent, which precedes and, in some ways, anticipates Śaṅkara's own conquest (ŚDV 14). Padmapāda's defense of the tradition also includes the limited, sanctioned use of violence, as he tears apart a hostile Kāpālika Śaiva by taking the form of Nṛsiṃha (11.37–44) and employs the power of *oṃ* to reverse a curse cast by the great sage Abhinavagupta, with deadly results (16.30–32). Finally, apart from the narrative of the ŚDV, the centrality of Padmapāda is attested by the fact that he alone among the earliest layer of Śaṅkara's disciples is widely—if not unambiguously—credited with composing a subcommentary on the *Brahmasūtrabhāṣya*, the first four verses of which are preserved as the *Pañcapādikā*.[96]

Gathering these strands together, it may be fair to claim that the distinctive missionary style represented in Padmapāda relates to the preservation and defense of Advaita tradition *qua* tradition, and as a firm assertion of that traditioned identity, rendered in both spiritual and social terms. Swami Vivekananda's impassioned defenses of Hinduism at the 1893 World's Parliament of Religions could easily be interpreted in this light, as he positioned himself as a spokesperson not only for Advaita but for Hinduism, and indeed the whole subcontinent. Just as the Padmapāda style includes assertion through conquest and even limited use of force, so also Vivekananda's missionary vision came to include the rhetoric of nationalist revival and even, potentially, a form of political Hinduism—though the precise scope and character of Vivekananda's religious nationalism remains a source of significant debate.[97]

A clearer example of this missionary style can, perhaps, be found in the life and work of Swami Chinmayananda himself. In his preface to *Śaṅkara the Missionary*, we recall, Chinmayananda praises the hero of the *vijaya* literature as a kind of "spiritual general" whose conquest effected a rediscovery and renewal of "the true cultural basis of our nation."[98] Earlier than this, in the address that inaugurated his first *Upaniṣad-Jñāna-Yajña*, he lamented what he characterized as the Hindu tradition's two-hundred-year decline, a decline accelerated by its loss of "any patronage from the state."[99] No doubt, Chinmayananda specifies the true essence of Hinduism as a transcendent, spiritual "science of perfection" founded on the Advaita teaching.[100] But his project is clearly as much cultural and political as gnoseological. Hence, it finds appropriate expression not only in a life of scriptural teaching but also in renewed connections with the traditional structures of the Daśanāmī monastic federation and the eventual co-founding of the nationalist Vishva Hindu Parishad.[101]

Some interpreters might be tempted to dismiss such political initiatives as foreign to the essence of Advaita teaching, or perhaps to reduce the tradition as a whole to a conservative social or political agenda. However, neither perspective adequately accounts for the complexity of both ancient and modern Advaita movements. Adopting Suthren Hirst's method of negation, these traditions should not be reduced to a political agenda, but neither can they be regarded as "socially and politically ungrounded."[102] In the image of Padmapāda, we may find an ideal-typical representation that begins to capture both sides of this dynamic. Swami Chinmayananda, like Padmapāda, assumes the role of *ahaṃkāra* for the tradition—that is, a role of self-assertion and personal agency. It seems only suitable that such a missionary style would draw on all available resources to advance the Advaita teaching and to reverse those forces that oppose it, repositioning this teaching as a powerful agent of cultural identity and transformation.

The Hastāmalaka Style: The Power of Presence

To associate a particular discursive style with one of the four disciples implies, by virtue of the association, that this style does not exhaust the tradition. Hence, we turn to a second model of missionary discipleship, and one that may be positioned as something close to the opposite of that represented by Padmapāda: that is, the model of Hastāmalaka. In the ŚDV, as discussed above, Padmapāda approaches Śaṅkara in the traditional manner to receive instruction. By contrast, Hastāmalaka does not approach the teacher at all and, it seems, receives no explicit instruction. Instead, Śaṅkara comes across him accidentally, as the mute and unlearned son of a village *pandit*. Hastāmalaka falls prostrate before Śaṅkara and, when addressed, pronounces a short verse summary of the whole Advaita teaching (ŚDV 12.38–62). By virtue of his achievement in past lives, Śaṅkara explains, Hastāmalaka was a self-knower at birth—or at least from a very early age (see 13.34–38)—and does not require the external mediation of dialogue and debate. The emblematic silence of this disciple is indirectly attested by his modest literary production: the *Hastāmalakaślokāḥ* remains the sole work attributed to him.[103] This, the Śaṅkara of the ŚDV explains, followed from the disciple's complete, uninterrupted immersion in the contemplation of *Brahman*, which rendered him unsuitable for scholarly endeavors (ŚDV 13.22–32). Hence, the authors of *Śaṅkara the Missionary* conclude, Hastāmalaka is aptly symbolized by Krishna's phrase, "with mind ever concentrated upon Me."[104]

Arguably, no modern or contemporary Advaita teacher more closely corresponds to the model provided by Hastāmalaka than Ramana Maharshi. As we discussed in the previous chapter, Ramana's missionary movement is one that defies conventional ideas of action and agency. The Maharshi began teaching Advaita explicitly only after twenty years of silent contemplation, and even then he preferred silence. "Preaching," he insisted, "is simple communication of knowledge. It may be done in Silence too."[105] Arvind Sharma captures this emphasis with a verse traditionally attached to the *Dakṣināmūrtistotram*: "A young master is sitting with aged disciples under a banyan tree // The master teaches in silence and the doubts of the students are dispelled."[106] Here, it is not the words of the teaching but rather the liberated and liberating presence of the self-realized teacher that receives pride of place in communicating the Advaita message.

One might hesitate to recognize the teaching and example of Ramana Maharshi as a form of missionary Advaita. Instead of dismissing it as non-missionary, however, it may make better sense to position it as a highly distinctive style of Advaita mission, roughly consistent with the received image of the disciple Hastāmalaka. As such, it significantly qualifies the idealized image of Śaṅkara or Padmapāda as vigorous debaters and victorious conquerors. According to this missionary style, the liberating message of Advaita finds its most efficacious expression not in public events such as Swami Chinmayananda's celebrated *jñāna-yajña*s but in the subtle, inherently attractive witness of a silent sage.

The Toṭaka Style: Devoted Service

Perhaps no feature of contemporary Advaita movements has been more widely recognized as distinctive to the modern period than the integration of social service into their wider missionary agendas.[107] This is a major emphasis of the Ramakrishna movement,[108] and one that receives support in Vivekananda's idealized image of the Buddha, as discussed above. But we also encounter the theme elsewhere and defended in other terms. As one particularly vivid example, consider the biographical narrative of Swami Chinmayananda's teacher, Swami Sivananda (1887–1963), as preserved in the tradition of his Divine Life Society.[109] Central to this narrative is the image of Sivananda as a medical professional, who traveled to Rishikesh and received *saṃnyāsa* after a prosperous career in Malaysia and Singapore. Before the founding of the Divine Life Society, he reports that he alternated between spiritual practice and providing medical care to the poor and sick on the banks of the Ganges.[110] Eventually, he would attract many disciples, publish his writings in pamphlets and books, found hospitals and schools, and contribute significantly to the contemporary yoga movement.[111] But across these initiatives the image of the compassionate servant and physician remained primary.

In his work *Practice of Karma Yoga*, for instance, Sivananda called for a "thorough overhauling of the organization of this fourth order of life—Sannyasa," issuing a summons for a "drastic form of service" and citing the image of Śaṅkara as a model "Karma Yogi."[112] In an appendix to the work, he offers the following advice:

> Serve poor, sick people. There is no Yajna that is greater than this. Serve everyone with Bhav, Prem and full Shraddha. Serve the Lord in all. Serve your country and society. Serve your parents, brothers and sisters, the Sadhus, Sannyasins, Bhaktas, Mahatmas and your spiritual teachers with devotion and a full heart. Shampoo the legs of poor people. Feel that you are touching the body of the Lord (Virat). Feel that the energy of Hiranyagarbha (cosmic energy) is flowing through your hands. Tap the very source, the store-house of cosmic energy.[113]

The scope of this injunction is breathtaking. Although it incorporates a wide range of activities, including traditional service to the guru, Sivananda most strongly emphasizes care for the sick and poor. Indeed, the most vulnerable members of society are recast as a kind of embodiment of the guru. It is not primarily by gathering firewood for the teacher, it would seem, but by shampooing the legs of the destitute that one connects with the power of a divine master.

It would be quite easy to identify in the rhetoric of Swami Sivananda traces of comparable Christian discourses of service and of the poor as a privileged place of encounter with the Lord. Nothing in our discussion of missionary paradigms and styles precludes the creative deployment of themes drawn from other traditions—just as Vivekananda adopted Orientalist conceptions of the Buddha and the authors of the *vijaya* literature drew creatively on tropes elicited from their Vaiṣṇava rivals. But it is worth noting that one can also identify a model closer to hand: that is, the image of the disciple Toṭaka in the *Śaṅkaradigvijaya*. Toṭaka received his name from one short work attributed to him, the *Śrutisārasamuddharaṇam*, which sets an imagined dialogue between teacher and student to verse in the *toṭaka* meter.[114] Compared to the decisive contribution of Padmapāda or the copious output of Sureśvara, this represents a rather limited intellectual project. The *vijaya* literature rationalizes this modest legacy in a way parallel to the silence of Hastāmalaka. In the ŚDV narrative, a disciple named Giri is identified not as a self-knower from birth but as a slow learner who excels at service. When, on one occasion, he is late to join the group of disciples for instruction, Śaṅkara infuses him directly with knowledge of the *Śrutisārasamuddharaṇam*, which Toṭaka then recites flawlessly, to everyone's amazement (ŚDV 12.70–86). The work, in other words, emerged in the disciple's mind not as the result of his own immanent understanding but as a reward for his loving service. Hence, the authors of *Śaṅkara the Missionary* associate Toṭaka with the one "who does actions for me" (*mat-karma-kṛt*) of the *Bhagavad-Gita* 11.55 and with the *manas*, "the restless mind, ever engaged in all kinds of service to the Master."[115]

No doubt, in the work of a teacher like Sivananda, the scope of what might count as service to the master has been considerably widened. Or, perhaps better, any person in need is symbolically rendered *as* the Lord, as the master, as the authorized teacher. With such a transposition—modest from a theological point of view but dramatic in its practical consequences—the received image of Toṭaka can provide a framework for situating social service in relation to other aspects of Advaita mission. As such, it emerges as a distinct missionary style, of central importance to the therapeutic vision of the Divine Life Society but also operative in a much wider range of modern and contemporary Advaita movements.

The Sureśvara Style: Polemics and Innovation

Sureśvara has been reserved in the final place in this survey of the four disciples, in part because his distinctive model or style of mission is most difficult to categorize. On the one hand, he was by far the most prolific of Śaṅkara's immediate disciples, authoring a massive subcommentary (*vārttika*) on the *Bṛhadāraṇyakopaniṣadbhāṣya*, another *vārttika* on the *Taittirīyopaniṣadbhāṣya*, and the independent treatise, *Naiṣkarmyasiddhi*. A commentary on the *Dakṣinamūrtistotram* and a number of other works are also attributed to him. On the other hand, all of these works are in some sense marginal to the *Brahmasūtrabhāṣya* as the core Advaita text and central focus of the commentarial tradition.[116] The narrative of the *Śaṅkaradigvijaya* blames this state of affairs on the interference of Padmapāda, who did not trust Sureśvara to write such subcommentary on the *Brahmasūtrabhāṣya* due to his prior career as Maṇḍana Miśra (ŚDV 13.1–21). Sureśvara is thus positioned in the ŚDV as both an insider and an outsider, resolute in his commitment to the tradition while at the same time embodying a persistent risk of disruption. This ambivalent status renders Sureśvara's style distinct from the more straightforward valorization of tradition typical of Padmapāda.

This distinctive style can also claim some modest basis in Sureśvara's writings themselves. In a work like *Naiṣkarmyasiddhi*, for example, Sureśvara strongly advances core teachings of Śaṅkara against such adversaries as Maṇḍana Miśra and supports his own arguments with extensive quotations from his teacher's *Upadeśasāhasrī*, thus inscribing himself firmly in the tradition;[117] yet, in his *vārttika* on the *Bṛhadāraṇyakopaniṣadbhāṣya* he freely, self-consciously sets his interpretations against those of his teacher on such significant topics as eligibility for *saṃnyāsa*.[118] Finally, the symbolic associations with Sureśvara in *Śaṅkara the Missionary* reveal a similar, dynamic ambivalence. He is commended for his fervent devotion to the teaching as one who "worships me" (*madyājin*; *Bhagavad-Gita* 9.34, 18.65) and "looks upon me as the Supreme" (*matparama*; *Bhagavad-Gita* 11.55); but he is also characterized as "questioning" (*paripraśna*) and as a symbol of the *buddhi* or discriminating intellect because "he would not yield until he was convinced."[119] He is styled, it appears, both as a fervent advocate of the Advaita teaching and as its loyal opposition.

If we earlier associated Padmapāda with the preservation, defense, and revalorization of tradition, it may be possible to perceive in the image of Sureśvara a parallel, more polemic, and more inward strategy of re-traditioning and innovation. Swami Chinmayananda's teaching, for example, can be characterized as a form of cultural nationalism, as discussed above, but Chinmayananda himself also polemicized harshly against Brahmin priests even as he moved out of the ambit of his guru Sivananada and developed new institutional forms to bring the teaching of the Upanishads to the Indian middle-class.[120] Chinmayananda's student Swami Dayananda would eventually go on to break with the Chinmaya Mission, found his own Arsha Vidya Gurukulam, and polemicize against the teachings of "modern teachers of Vedanta," including such modern lights as Vivekananda, Ramana Maharshi, Sivananda, and Chinmayananda himself.[121] One of Dayananda's lay disciples, Anantanand Rambachan, has in turn brought his teacher's critique forward in two major works that seek to reclaim Śaṅkara's teachings from these modern teachers.[122] From this ostensibly traditionalist foundation, however, Rambachan also launched strong criticisms of caste discrimination, homophobia, gender bias, and other oppressive structures in Hindu traditions and in the teaching of Śaṅkara himself.[123] In a subsequent work, he has gone so far as to articulate a distinctively Advaita theology of political liberation.[124] At each step in this *paraṃparā*, from Sivananda to Rambachan, we witness successive moments of affirmation and critique, traditionalization and transformation.

In his studies of the Divine Life Society and the Ramakrishna Mission several years ago, David Miller noted that contemporary interpreters of Hindu traditions err if we attempt to draw too sharp a contrast between the "traditional" and the "modern." In these movements, the affirmation of tradition can become a source of innovation, and modern values take root in the teaching lineage by means of a complex, contested process of re-traditioning.[125] Arguably, this observation rings true to some extent for all of the figures I have surveyed in this and the previous chapter, from a renunciant teacher like Śaṅkara in the eighth century to an academic theologian like Rambachan today. But when this dialectic of affirmation and critique, polemic and innovation moves to the forefront and takes conscious expression, I suggest, it becomes something like a distinct missionary style.

Compared with the other three styles surveyed thus far, this one is perhaps least likely to be mistaken for a comprehensive, coherent paradigm. One could, in theory if not in practice, imagine a missionary movement based wholly on silent witness, service, or cultural nationalism, but the dynamic practice of re-traditionalization works at the boundaries of existing traditions, defending these traditions, subjecting them to searching critique, and developing new formulations for them. It is an Advaita missionary style that exists in necessary relation with others. It stands as both a permanent challenge to these other styles and, perhaps, as a key to their ongoing vitality and renewal. As such, it might gain clarity and imaginative depth by appeal to Sureśvara, a prominent Advaitin disciple who claimed the center of the tradition from a position closer to its margins.

Conclusion

In his "Hindu Theology as Churning the Latent," Jonathan Edelmann draws on the eighteenth-century Gauḍīya Vaiṣṇava scholar Viśvanātha Cakravartin to define constructive theology as a "churning of the ocean," distilling the "latent meanings" of a scriptural text by means of such hermeneutical tools as "ordering," "internal overcoding," "exegesis," and "signification."[126] The articulation of Hindu theology employs hermeneutical tools, but it is not reducible to them; it also depends upon the theologian's personal formation in a particular Hindu tradition, including both intellectual discipline and ethical conduct.[127]

In this chapter, I have attempted to bring out some of the latent, theological significance of the *Upadeśasāhasrī*, the *Śaṅkaradigvijyaya*, and the speeches of Swami Vivekananda, as these latent meanings might inform the analysis of missionary Advaita in the modern and contemporary periods. As noted, this proposal falls short of Edelmann's notion of "Hindu theology" in several ways. I have, first, drawn latent meanings not from the Upanishads or another Advaita scriptural text, but from the rhetorical constructions of selected Advaita teachers. Perhaps more important, as a Christian comparativist, my social location would certainly fall short of the spiritual and ethical disposition that might qualify me as an Advaita theologian. It is possible that my position more closely resembles that of the antigods than that of the gods in the famous *Bhāgavata Purāṇa* episode that gives Edelmann's essay its title.[128] If I am hopeful that I can help churn this particular ocean of milk, one might say, I do so with little or no expectation of the same immortal reward.

Then why all the churning? First of all, in identifying key paradigms of Advaita mission across history, we have the opportunity to move beyond false dichotomies and facile application of the label "mission" to one or another Hindu movement, as well as the tendency to position Hindu missionary movements exclusively in relation to colonialist Christianity. It matters little to my analysis whether these missionary paradigms are entirely unique to Advaita: we have in several places noted points of continuity with the missionary visions of implied or named adversaries, and it seems a sound historical principle that most phenomena will reveal more similarities than differences with other, comparable phenomena from the same social and cultural milieu. So too, the analysis conducted here may be read to imply that almost any tradition that aspires to survive for longer than a single generation can be characterized as missionary in some respect. The interesting question, then, is not *what* classifies a particular tradition as "missionary" or "non-missionary" as binary categories, but *how* any tradition may articulate and understand its missionary dimensions in diverse, particular times and places. The *santati* of Śaṅkara's *Upadeśasāhasrī*, the *vijaya* of the Śaṅkara hagiographies, the "large-heartedness" of Vivekananda's Buddha—each of these is susceptible to a missiological reading, but they are not susceptible to being read univocally, separately or together, as expressions of one and the same Advaita missionary paradigm. As interpretive paradigms, they remain incommensurable at a fundamental level. And the picture becomes still more complex when we add the similarly diverse symbolic images of Padmapāda, Hastāmalaka, Toṭaka, and Sureśvara.

Simply noting this complexity may be sufficient for the purposes of description. Yet, once such a description has been offered—once the ocean has undergone its first round of churning—we can begin to explore its constructive possibilities. We recall that David Bosch, Stephen Bevans and Roger Schroeder, and M. Thomas Thangaraj each suggest, in their respective Christian contexts, that the historical analysis of missiological paradigms, types, or styles opens space for the formulation of new, integrative visions for the twenty-first century. Such a higher, integrative theology of Advaita mission, in itself, is not the object of our present inquiry; that important work awaits a suitably qualified and motivated Advaita theologian. We can nevertheless make an initial attempt to discern the deeper coherence and intelligibility of the theological tapestry we have uncovered, with an eye to the further comparative inquiry and constructive reappropriation attempted in the chapters that follow.

Jacqueline Suthren Hirst's article "Images of Śaṅkara," with which we began the inquiry of this chapter, may chart an initial way forward. We recall that, in her reconstruction of Śaṅkara's Advaita theology, well-worn tropes such as the rope mistaken for a snake or the magician's illusion function not by aggregation but by mutual restriction, as each removes an error implicit in the others.[129] The truth is not found in any of the images, or even in all of them together, but in the space opened among them by their fruitful juxtaposition. So also the vitality of the Advaita movements surveyed in the previous chapter may perhaps be sought not in some fixed ideal they all share, but in the shared space they open to negotiate competing Advaita ideals. It is telling that, although I have drawn examples from particular movements to illustrate particular missionary styles, none of these movements can be reduced entirely to a single paradigm or style. The chauvinism of the Padmapāda style finds itself tempered by Toṭaka's spirit of service, and the silent witness of Hastāmalaka is inevitably challenged to assert itself socially, culturally, and even politically, as Padmapāda might require. And all of these approaches may be affirmed, challenged, and transformed by the unrelenting *buddhi* of Sureśvara.

The *amṛta* or nectar of immortality that gives these Advaita theologies of mission life and intelligibility, we might say, emerges *in* the tension among diverse paradigms and styles rather than in their systematic resolution. This tension manifests itself first diachronically, in the process of historical transformation traced in the first half of the chapter. But the tension also functions synchronically, both within and between particular Advaita mission movements and their particular theological constructions. And it does so, in part, because the tension between various teaching tropes, between the transcendence of final liberation and its contingent expression in human language, and indeed between the duality of empirical experience and the true, non-dualist reality of *Brahman* define Advaita Vedānta, both as a teaching tradition and as a soteriological project.

The path of knowledge consists less in fully resolving these points of tension than in identifying them correctly and allowing them to effect a radical reorientation of meaning and value—what Suthren Hirst has called an "epistemic shift."[130] Points of tension can, when skillfully deployed, become catalysts of liberating self-knowledge. It is to such points of tension—and their liberative potential in the comparative theological project—that we now turn.

Part II

Fruits of Encounter

4

A Gospel of Inner Experience?

Transcending Limits of Language and Culture

Few Western scholars have made as strong a case for the cross-cultural appeal of missionary Advaita as Thomas A. Forsthoefel. In his essay "Weaving the Inward Thread to Awakening," Forsthoefel offers what might be described as a phenomenological apologetic for the tradition of Ramana Maharshi.[1] While conceding the Maharshi's integrity and other personal qualities as compelling reasons for his widespread influence, Forsthoefel places strongest emphasis on the intrinsic attraction of his experiential claim. "[T]he source of Ramana's perennial appeal," he writes, "lies in his paradigmatic experience of realization and his repeated insistence that such experience is accessible and available to all, regardless of cultural or social conditions."[2] Forsthoefel contrasts the "externalist" teaching of Śaṅkara, which roots the Advaita teaching in a particular cultural and institutional context, against the more "internalist" focus of Ramana Maharshi, which sets it free from these limitations to appeal not only to interested Westerners but indeed to any person, from any cultural or religious background.[3] He writes: "What we see is a genuine universalism that follows from a harmony of Advaita theory and practice: the theory is the metaphysic of non-dualism and the practice is a decisive internalist epistemology of religious experience. The result is a form of Advaita that transcends the social and cultural settings of South Asia."[4] The offer of non-dualist experience and appeals to Advaita's ostensibly "internalist" epistemology, on this reading, are key to understanding the cross-cultural appeal of Ramana Maharshi.

This is true not only for the great sage of Arunachala, of course, but also for most other expressions of late modern Advaita Vedānta.[5] Anantanand Rambachan and Elizabeth De Michelis have well demonstrated the centrality of the meditative state of *samādhi* and spiritual experience in the teaching of Swami Vivekananda.[6] In his account of Ramana's universal appeal, moreover, Forsthoefel tellingly invokes Robert K. C. Forman and the famous Katz-Forman debate on the question of religious experience. In doing so, Forsthoefel might have noted that Forman received his core convictions through his early connections not with Ramana Maharshi but with Transcendental Meditation.[7] In his *Science of Being and Art of Living,* to cite just one example, Maharishi Mahesh Yogi describes TM as a "practical message of the direct experience of Being as the ultimate reality," and he elaborates a gradual process of mental refinement through which the gross, bodily senses become suffused by a blissful, liberating awareness of divine Being.[8] Even as traditional an authority as the 35th Sṛṅgeri Jagadguru Śrī Abhinava Vidyātīrtha Mahāswāmigal (1917–1989)[9] will argue that "a true Advaitin is one who has realized as a matter of experience that one is the Supreme Brahman."[10]

Despite these witnesses to the centrality of direct, non-dualist experience as both presupposition and goal of the Advaita teaching, however, it is not at all clear how well their accounts comport to one another, or to classical Advaita. One strong dissenting voice is that of Swami Dayananda Saraswati (1930–2015), discussed briefly in chapter 2. In his short pamphlet *The Teaching Tradition of Advaita Vedanta,* Dayananda takes direct aim at the language of experiential "realization" and subjects it to a searching critique. "According to modern Vedānta," he writes, "self-knowledge is intellectual while self-realization is experiential, and because of this difference the study of the śāstra is meant for self-knowledge while something else will become the means for self-realization."[11] But such a view is confused, and a distortion of the authentic teaching. According to Dayananda, liberating knowledge comes through study of the Vedic scriptures, not in any other way. Yet, even here, the efficacy of the scripture and its ability to confer direct knowledge seem to follow from the enduring, self-evident presence of the divine *ātman* in the hearer's immanent consciousness.[12] Is this not a different, albeit more subtle, appeal to experience?

In this chapter, I explore various appeals to inner, non-dualist experience as a cross-cultural ideal in missionary Advaita. As even this brief initial discussion reveals, such an appeal is both pervasive and contested. That is, the claim to direct experience of *ātman* cannot be called a source of shared agreement among missionary Advaitins. Nevertheless, I suggest, it can be interpreted as a site of what Kathryn Tanner calls "common investment and engagement" across the history of the tradition and, thus, a significant locus of shared identity.[13] To develop this idea, I trace several layers of engagement on this theme in Advaita tradition, beginning with Śaṅkara and classical Advaita, continuing through three late modern commentaries on the popular *Vivekacūḍāmaṇi,* and then turning to the ongoing reception of Ramana Maharshi's "direct path" (*mārgaḥ ārjavāt*) of self-inquiry and extinction of the mind. At each level, I contend, appeals to liberative experience—along with their contestations—function productively for the tradition, providing both a pretext for missionary activity and an interpretive space to adapt the Advaita message to new contexts and social conditions.

Finally, in the first of four comparative theological "soundings" that distinguish the second part of this study from its first three chapters, I draw on the influential historian and missiologist Lamin Sanneh to redescribe Advaita and Christian missionary traditions in terms of translation, recollection, and liberative experience. On this reading, mission proceeds by a dynamic, contested process of translation, seeking ever-new cultural expressions to draw hearers' attention back to their own selves—back, that is, to a liberating but elusive experience of transformed selfhood that defines human existence even as it remains persistently unrecognized by most persons most of the time. The preaching of these respective messages of freedom does not consist in a simple exportation of doctrine; instead, it implicates teachers and students in a complex, discursive, and collective practice of recollection, an ever-provisional engagement of God and one another at the depths of their personal and historical experience.

Experiencing Liberation in Śaṅkara and Classical Vedānta

By raising the question of experience in modern and contemporary Advaita Vedānta, we enter well-traveled and well-contested terrain. Scholars have debated the status of the so-called "experience of liberation" (*anubhava*) or the deep meditative state of *nirvikalpa samādhi* in the teaching of Ādi Śaṅkarācārya and, in many cases, drawn a sharp contrast between his early medieval teaching and that of late modern teachers like Swami Vivekananda and Sarvepalli Radhakrishnan (1888–1975).[14] Even recent apologies for an experiential approach by Forsthoefel and Arvind Sharma have tended to distinguish the teachings of Ramana Maharshi and other late modern Vedāntins from Śaṅkara and classical Vedānta.[15] Forstoefel, as we have seen, differentiates the "internalist" epistemology of Ramana from the "externalist," scripturalist emphasis of the classical tradition.[16] Sharma draws this distinction with characteristic economy, writing, "Ramana may be said to be the chief spokesman of *experiential* Advaita just as the philosopher Śaṅkara . . . is looked upon as the leading expositor of *doctrinal* Advaita."[17] The category of pure or non-dualist experience is deployed here to distinguish one strand of the tradition from others rather than to reveal any deep affinity or mutual identity.

The reality, however, may be less simple. In his characteristically penetrating analysis, for example, Wilhelm Halbfass has suggested that the difference between classical Vedānta and late modern Vedāntins on the question of experience may follow from the fact that the concept of "experience" in question is distinctively modern—and, indeed, that it is specific to the colonial context.[18] Thus, after reviewing the use and function of *anubhava* in the works of Śaṅkara, Padmapāda, and other teachers in their classical milieu, Halbfass concludes that the use of this term by Radhakrishnan and other "neo-Vedāntin" interpreters has little basis in "traditional Hinduism." "The changes," he writes, "are not only a matter of emphasis; they reflect a radically new situation—the encounter of the Indian tradition with Western science and philosophy."[19] Beginning with Rammohan Roy (1772–1833) and reaching well into the twentieth century, Halbfass demonstrates how leading Indian thinkers often adapted Western idioms of experiential verification to advance their particular understandings of Hinduism. But he also shows how these Western conceptualizations were often attributed, by the philosophers, historians, and psychologists who articulated them, to Hindu sources.[20] The Western theories of experience borrowed by Hindu apologists originated, in part, in distinctively Western readings of classical Hindu sources. Late modern Hindu appeals to liberative, non-dualist experience may, in other words, owe their origin neither to the East nor the West but to their colonial encounter.

The main sources Halbass uses to establish classical or "traditional" Hindu approaches to experience are Ādi Śaṅkarācārya's eighth-century commentaries on the *Brahma-sūtras* and Upaniṣads, as well as his independent treatise, the *Upadeśasāhasrī*.[21] The last of these is a particularly useful reference point. For, in the longest verse chapter of this work, Śaṅkara addresses the question of experience directly, through his extended refutation of an opposing view called "*prasaṃkhyāna-vāda*."[22] According to the *prasaṃkhyāna-vāda*, which may originate with Śaṅkara's elder contemporary and rival Advaitin Maṇḍana Miśra,[23] the merely "relational" or "indirect" knowledge provided by the Vedic scriptures reaches its liberating fulfillment in an unmediated, experiential knowledge acquired through a meditative practice called *prasaṃcakṣā* (USP 18.9) or *prasaṃkhyāna* (USP 18.12, 18.17).[24] Śaṅkara fervently refutes this argument across the 233 verses of *Upadeśasāhasrī Padyabandha* 18. Stated briefly, he argues that no finite effort or empirical experience can ever be identified with a liberation that is none other than the innermost, changeless self of every hearer, here and now (e.g., USP 18.19–25, 196–97, 208–11). This self can be realized directly by a discriminating mind immediately upon hearing a Vedic sentence such as the great saying, "That thou art" (*tat-tvam-asi*), with no need for subsequent practice (e.g., USP 18.96, 169–71, 178–79, 188–90).[25] "The knowledge that one is ever-free arises from the sentence," he concludes, "and not from anything else" (USP 18.188a).

And what about experience more generally? As a rule, Śaṅkara paints all empirical experiences, including experiences of meditation, with the same brush. The yogic term *samādhi*, often interpreted by contemporary scholars in terms of contemplative experience, appears in only three verses of the *Upadeśasāhasrī*, and it can be read in every case as an evanescent property of the mind, distinct from the changeless *ātman* (USP 13.14; 13.17; 14.35).[26] This also seems to be the thrust of Śaṅkara's comment on *Brahma-sūtra* 2.1.9, where the state of *samādhi* is equated to deep sleep.[27] There are certainly places where Śaṅkara prescribes meditation (e.g., USP 10; USG 3), and he commends yoga as a secondary means for purifying the mind.[28] Nevertheless, the evidence of the *Upadeśasāhasrī* affirms Halbfass's conclusion that "Śaṅkara does not invoke any extraordinary 'psychological events,' and he does not try to validate the truth of non-dualism by referring to 'visionary' or 'mystical' experiences of extraordinary persons."[29]

This picture of classical Vedānta, however, becomes more complicated if one widens one's view from Śaṅkara and a text like the *Upadeśasāhasrī* to include its wider Advaita milieu. Whether or not the *prasaṃkhyāna-vāda* of USP 18 can be traced directly to the teaching of Maṇḍana Miśra, it appears clear that Śaṅkara is contending against a rival form of Advaita that privileges some form of contemplative experience on the path to liberation.[30] It is this rival tradition and its distinctive use of such terms as *anubhava* and *samādhi* that establish a framework for argument, enabling the debate that unfolds across the verses of USP 18. More complicating still is another, no less classical Vedānta work often attributed to Śaṅkara but emblematic of what Halbfass describes cryptically as "a different approach": the *Vivekacūḍāmaṇi* or *Crest-Jewel of Discrimination*.[31] Like the *Upadeśasāhasrī*, the *Vivekacūḍāmaṇi* is an independent treatise, apparently written to introduce Advaita to new students. Whereas the former is a composite of loosely related prose and verse chapters, the latter presents a single, linear dialogue between a teacher and disciple, running some 580 verses in one widely available recension.[32]

Both of these treatises enforce what Thomas Forsthoefel has called a normative "culture of liberation." Thus, the *Vivekacūḍāmaṇi* identifies the qualified disciple as a Brahmin male endowed with a prescribed set of personal and intellectual virtues (VC 2–4, 19) and upholds a traditional process of hearing (*śruti*), reflection (*manana*), and meditation (*dhyāna*) on the path to liberation (70).[33] The *Vivekacūḍāmaṇi*, however, unfolds this traditional process in a way that the author of the *Upadeśasāhasrī* would—at least arguably—scarcely recognize. Beginning with VC 70, the state of liberation is described as a consciousness of "extinction" (*nirvāṇa*, 70), as a "supreme, undifferentiated state" (*a-vikalpaṃ paraṃ*, 70), as a destroying of the mind (*mano'naśyati*, 277), and as an unmediated achievement of one's "own experience" (*sva-anubhūti*, 477).[34] The *Vivekacūḍāmaṇi*, moreover, devotes over a hundred verses (352–463) to detail a series of contemplative practices that Francis X. Clooney and Hugh Nicholson call "Vedāntic yoga," that is, a "project of concentration and ultimate integral unity (*samādhi*)." Having arrived at a perfect state of *samādhi* as the culmination of his instruction and meditative practice (480), the model disciple goes on to describe his liberated consciousness at length, in vivid, experiential terms (479–519).[35] "Although there are slightly different epistemological emphases in the process of liberation," writes Forsthoefel of this treatise, "*anubhava* appears to be the decisive, internally accessed, and self-established saving moment for the *mumukṣu*."[36]

Placing the arguments of the *Upadeśasāhasrī* and the *Viveka-cūḍāmaṇi* side by side, it is hard to avoid concluding that classical Advaita Vedānta—and possibly the great teacher Śaṅkara himself, if one accepts traditional attributions—speaks in more than one register about the status and content of experience. Such ambiguity, moreover, does not end with these two texts. It continues to define the tradition's development in the late medieval and early modern periods. First of all, the emergence of rival Vivaraṇa and Bhāmatī schools of Advaita scholasticism from the first generation of Śaṅkara's disciples to the fourteenth century may be read, at least from one point of view, to turn on this very issue.[37] And, as Advaita continues its development into the early modern period, we witness the emergence of what Andrew O. Fort has termed "Yogic Advaita."[38] In works like the *Yogavāsiṣṭha* and the fourteenth-century teacher Vidyāraṇya's *Jīvanmuktiviveka*, strong emphasis is placed on the control of the mind through meditative discipline, the elimination of mental impressions or *vāsanās*, and the elevated "state of consciousness" of the liberated self-knower.[39] Though Vidyāraṇya does not hesitate to invoke the *Upadeśasāhasrī* in his *Jīvanmukti-viveka*,[40] it is arguably the vision of a text like *Vivekacūḍāmaṇi* that more significantly shapes his account of final liberation.

Vidyāraṇya, as we recall from the previous chapter, is a deeply traditional figure closely associated with the Śṛṅgeri *maṭha*, the composition of the *Śaṅkaradigvijaya*, and even the Vivaraṇa scholastic tradition.[41] Yet, his *Jīvanmuktiviveka* includes a full chapter on yogic discipline and the "destruction of the mind" (*mano-nāśa*) as the pre-eminent means of liberation.[42] This experientialist current appears to have claimed something like a place of pride, at what would eventually emerge as one of the hearts of Advaita orthodoxy, as well as one of the major catalysts of the tradition as a missionary movement.

Experience as a Site of Engagement in Three Commentaries

At considerable risk of oversimplification, we might borrow the language of Thomas Forsthoefel to interpret the history of Advaita Vedānta on the question of liberative experience in terms of a gradual shift from a more "externalist" pole of interpretation on the relation of Vedic teaching, contemplative practice, and self-knowledge, loosely represented in a text like Śaṅkara's *Upadeśasāhasrī*, toward another "internalist" pole, more appreciative of *samādhi* and the epistemic significance of meditative practice, broadly anticipated by the *Vivekacūḍāmaṇi*.[43] Nevertheless, as revealed especially in a synthetic, hybrid figure like Vidyāraṇya, neither side of the debate ever claims final victory. The conversation continues from one generation to the next, unfolding new interpretive possibilities in its wake and drawing in new interlocutors.

To appreciate the significance of this complex pattern of engagement and contestation, we may be helped by the theoretical approaches of the South Asianist Lawrence A. Babb and Christian theologian Kathryn Tanner. In his study *Redemptive Encounters*, for example, Babb sets out to discern unifying features of three ethnographic case studies self-consciously drawn from the margins of Hindu tradition.[44] "There is no such thing as a Hindu worldview," he suggests, "or at least not in the narrow meaning of this expression."[45] Nevertheless, Babb identifies a fundamental coherence among these diverse Hindu traditions, not in doctrine or content of teaching but in "constant themes" or "loosely floating images."[46] In elucidating these themes, Babb distinguishes clearly between coherence and consensus. "Here unity is not necessarily expressed as concord and harmony; it consists, rather, of agreement on certain cultural ground rules that can be invoked (if only implicitly) even in debate and conflict."[47] Arguing along similar lines, Tanner has sharply criticized past attempts to ground Christian identity in terms of purportedly shared values and beliefs, a process of doctrinal development or invariant discursive rules.[48] Instead, she suggests that Christian identity emerges in the shared task of discipleship and an "extended argument" about the significance of Jesus and the life of faith.[49] Coherence in this case again does not flow from consensus. Quite the opposite. What unites Christian practices "is nothing internal to the practices themselves. What unites them is concern for true discipleship, proper reflection in human words and deeds of an object of worship that always exceeds by its greatness human efforts to do so."[50]

Returning to the history of missionary Advaita, we might venture that the categories of *anubhava*, *samādhi*, and other experiential tropes do not unify the tradition by forging a shared consensus on the content of the teaching. Instead, they function more like the "loosely floating images" of Babb's study or the "concern for true discipleship" valorized by Tanner: they give shape to Advaita as a missionary tradition through a coherent, generative process of "extended argument" and discursive discord.[51]

Insofar as inner experience functions as such a site of engagement for missionary Advaita, this engagement takes place across a wide range of diverse ashrams, schools, and devotee homes, in public lectures, private conversations, and scriptural commentaries. It is possible, however, to gain a glimpse into this wider conversation by looking at diverse interpretations of a shared text, a classical text that places the question of experience at the center of its own inquiry: namely, the independent treatise *Vivekacūḍāmaṇi*, discussed briefly in the previous section. As noted in chapter 2 of this study, Ramana Maharshi judged that the *Vivekacūḍāmaṇi* cohered with his own experience and method of self-inquiry, and he eventually produced his own Tamil translation (hereafter RamanaVC).[52] The text also attracted the special interest of the thirty-fourth Śaṅkarācārya of Śṛṅgeri, Jagadguru Śrī Candraśekhara Bhāratī (1892–1954).[53] The jagadguru produced an incomplete commentary, which was discovered by a devotee in 1958 and eventually released to him by Candraśekhara Bhāratī's successor, Abhinava Vidyātīrtha, and published in English translation in 1973 (hereafter CBVC).[54] Finally, the *Vivekacūḍāmaṇi* became one of the central texts for Swami Chinmayananda and the Chinmaya Mission. Early in his *jñāna yajna* plan, in the mid-1950s, Chinmayananda began supplementing his discourses on the major Upaniṣads and the *Bhagavad-Gītā* with selections from the *Vivekacūḍāmaṇi* and other classical texts. Teachings on the first hundred verses of the *Vivekacūḍāmaṇi* were published serially in the journal *Tyagi* and brought out as a small volume shortly thereafter. Then, in 1970, Swami Chinmayananda published a commentary on the full text (hereafter ChinmayaVC).[55]

As translators and commentators on the *Vivekacūḍāmaṇi*, Ramana Maharshi, Candraśekhara Bhāratī, and Swami Chinmayananda all offer broadly experientialist readings of the liberated state. All three, echoing the *prasaṃkhyāna-vāda* of USP 18, develop a strong contrast between an initial, theoretical, or indirect knowledge gained from the scriptures and the subsequent verification of such knowledge in yogic *samādhi* or some form of immediate, contemplative apprehension of the highest truth (e.g., RamanaVC, 249–50 [362]; CBVC 377 [376]; ChinmayaVC 136, 223, 474–75 [473–74]). At the same time, their different accounts of the text stake out distinctive positions on this liberative experience, as well as the means of its communication and attainment by prospective hearers of the Advaita message.

The three commentators differ, first, on the ideal relation of disciple, text, and teacher. Candraśekhara Bhāratī, as one might expect, accepts and even strengthens the *Vivekacūḍāmaṇi*'s social restrictions. Only *saṃnyāsins*, who alone truly renounce the world of means and ends, can become eligible for instruction in Vedānta, and only male Brahmins are eligible for *saṃnyāsa* (CBVC 2, 8, 19–20, 45 [43]). Others should endeavor in the practice of *karma* until they achieve birth as a Brahmin and the perfect detachment of the renunciant state, in this life or a future birth (2, 72 [70]). Similarly, though the practice of *samādhi* and direct realization of *Brahman* may be the culmination of the teaching practice, it can bear fruit only if preceded by study of the *śruti* as the *pramāṇa* or unique means of liberating knowledge (e.g., 67 [65], 277 [276]). The jagadguru writes: "The jīva is Brahman only; the entire world too is Brahman only. Mokṣa is abiding in infinitude; that is, being as Brahman. Brahman is without a second. For all of this the śrutis are the ground. It is said 'pramāṇam' in the singular because though the śrutis are many, the knowledge generated by them all is identical" (479 [478]). Candraśekhara Bhāratī does recognize exceptions, such as the ancient sage Vāmadeva who achieved self-knowledge in his mother's womb, but such exceptions are reinscribed into the normative pattern by appeal to *sādhanas* and scriptural study completed by the seeker in previous lives (61 [59]; cf. 268 [267]).

Ramana Maharshi and Swami Chinmayananda, by contrast, strive assiduously in their commentaries to soften these restrictions and thus to broaden the reach of the teaching to a wider group of prospective disciples. Ramana, in his free translation, strengthens several passages that relativize the *śāstras*, including such great sayings as "I am *Brahman*" (*aham-brahma-asmi*), in favor of his appeal to "direct experience" as the true means of liberation (e.g., RamanaVC 218–19 [60–65]).[56] Chinmayananda places greater emphasis on the *śruti*. But he also notes that scriptures are effective only when used as intended, and not for empty speculation (e.g., ChinmayaVC 7, 70, 267–70). The key is a nuanced, practical "intellectual understanding" (59–61).

These interpretive patterns repeat themselves in discussions of eligibility (*adhikāra*) in the text. Ramana Maharshi explicitly dismisses the social restrictions placed by the *Vivekacūḍāmaṇi* on prospective disciples. "[E]ven though all of the above qualifications may not be obtained," he writes, "liberation is assured through the grace of the Lord if only three conditions are obtained: that is human birth, intense desire for liberation, and association with sages" (RamanaVC 212 [2–3]). Though he does not follow Ramana in directly refuting such traditional restrictions on the teaching, Swami Chinmayananda does suggest they have been culpably misinterpreted, with exclusionary intent, by "the orthodoxy," "hasty paṇḍitas," and "a perverted set of priests" (ChinmayaVC 2, 14, 25). On his reading, the *Vivekacūḍāmaṇi*'s descriptions of qualified disciples should be interpreted figuratively, such that "man" (*jana*) comes to refer to the virtues of courage and balance, "Brahmin" (*vipra*) to personal maturity, and "renunciant" (*yati*) to anyone seeking liberation, irrespective of state of life (2, 436 [435]). The criteria of *adhikāra*, he further insists, are to be applied only for the "self-scoring of seekers themselves" and never to enforce social boundaries (14, 22). Anyone whose interior disposition leads her to seek the teaching also reveals that she possesses the *adhikāra* to receive it.

Swami Chinmayananda can generalize social restrictions and transpose them into the language of interiority in part because that is how he interprets the scriptures as a whole—that is, as the ancient rishis' indirect, categorical accounts of "the Truth of their own experiences" (e.g., ChinmayaVC 7). The intended goal of scriptural instruction is perforce also described in experiential terms, as an "intuition," "revelation," or "trans experience" (117). The teaching culminates in an extinction of thought and transcendence of the mind (151, 178, 186–87, 244, 259, 567 [566]) or, stated differently, in an experiential identification with the infinite (340 [339], 354 [353]). Seekers are enjoined to cultivate "desireless desires" (542 [541]), "thoughtful" feeling (264), or "feelingful understanding" (301) in order to apprehend the teaching of the scriptures and to make the experience of the ancient rishis their own.

As suggested by a term like "desireless desire," Swami Chinmayananda freely employs the language of paradox to preserve an interpretive space for non-dualist experience without describing it directly. He notes, for example, that the subjective experience of contemplative *nididhyāsana* cannot be captured in language (ChinmayaVC 394 [393]) and that it is referred to as "bliss" only by analogy (131, 261). He suggests that seekers can gain an approximate sense of such bliss through a process of abstraction, by mentally removing the sense of finitude from ordinary enjoyments in life (131) or by adding conscious awareness to the perfect rest of dreamless sleep (70, 107, 207, 383 [382], 402 [401], 527 [526]). In accord with his broader teaching, Chinmayananda also characterizes the message of the *Vivekacūḍāmaṇi* as a "Science of Life."[57] He introduces the categories of the B-M-I chart early in the commentary (124) and describes the path to liberation as the systematic elimination of *vāsanās* (e.g., 277, 317–18, 388 [387]). In accord with its status as a science, this path appears to be mechanical and automatic. Yet, Swami Chinmayananda also insists that our efforts merely prepare the way for liberating knowledge to dawn of its own accord (148, 197). The discipline of meditation represents a "hopeful and expectant waiting for Awareness to reveal Itself," "like a lover waiting for the promised visit of his beloved" (318). Chinmayananda's commentary thus executes a delicate dance, insisting on the verifiable fact of liberative experience and the scientific means of its attainment, while also conceding its inaccessibility to categorical language or finite striving. Liberation depends entirely, in the end, on the gracious self-revelation of *ātman*.

Candraśekhara Bhāratī and Ramana Maharshi are more reticent than Swami Chinmayananda to give an account of liberative experience, but it is no less central to their respective readings of the *Vivekacūḍāmaṇi*. Candraśekhara Bhāratī states that *nididhyāsana*, the final phase of the threefold Advaita method, aims specifically at *su-anubhava*, "direct realisation," a final perfecting of the incomplete, fleeting *anubhava* attained through hearing and reasoning (CBVC 2, 420 [419]). Even among those Brahmin renunciants who achieve such realization, however, there are further gradations and levels of attainment, according to the subtlety and focus of their mental concentration (454 [453]). For Ramana, by contrast, the point of any form of contemplative practice is to press behind the language of graded progress to arrive at what he calls *sahaja samādhi,* referring here less to an achievement of focused concentration than to "a particular kind of innate state (*sahaja sthiti*) that transcends all concepts and dualities."[58] Hearing, reflection, meditation—all of these stand in roughly parallel positions as diverse aids to self-inquiry, to the discovery of the "I-I" behind all possible experience (RamanaVC, 226–27 [125, 135]).[59] "This supreme Self," Ramana offers as his reading of VC 535, "is self-effulgent with manifold powers (*shakti*), incapable of being known by anyone, and yet is experienced as the 'I-I' in the Heart" (RamanaVC, 265). If for Candraśekhara Bhāratī the pure experience of *Brahman* is veiled behind layers of social restriction and years or decades of spiritual practice, for Ramana it is hidden in full view. Either way, it remains just off stage and out of plain sight.

Following Halbfass, it seems reasonable to concede that all three of these commentators employ the category of experience in a way distinct from the teaching of Ādi Śaṅkarācārya and classical Vedānta. This certainly reflects the exigence of late modernity and the colonial encounter. At the same time, their accounts do not arise out of thin air. They are rooted in their common engagement with a classical text, and their respective interpretations reflect concerns that would be widely shared, even by rival forms of Advaita. As a site of shared engagement, moreover, the category of experience is highly productive. Liberative experience sets the Brahmin *saṃnyāsīs* of Śṛṅgeri apart from the general population and authorizes the *maṭha*'s authoritative interpretation of the Vedas, according to Candraśekhara Bhāratī. For Ramana Maharshi, by contrast, it radically relativizes all such institutional restrictions, in favor of the much more malleable and informal conditions of "human birth, intense desire for liberation, and association with sages." For Swami Chinmayananda, the promise of attaining transcendent "Awareness" both motivates a lifelong discipline of ethical purification and "self-scoring" and calls all such striving into question, in a kind of engaged, practical mysticism of ordinary life. In each case, in and through their diverse and even contradictory interpretations, the language of inner experience provides a necessary pretext for these traditions' missionary projects, as well as a creative space for working out pragmatic questions about the transmission and fruitful reception of the teaching.

Contesting Ramana Maharshi and the "Direct Path" of Liberation

In his *Presuppositions of India's Philosophies*, Karl H. Potter draws a useful distinction between "path" and "leap" philosophies of liberation. For "path" philosophers such as Śaṅkara and many of his Hindu and Buddhist rivals, Potter argues, liberation is positioned at the end of a process of gradual self-refinement and continually deepening insight into higher reality.[60] For "leap philosophers" such as the medieval Advaitins Sureśvara and Prakāśānanda, on the other hand, liberation arises as a sudden unraveling of phenomenal experience.[61] "When we become free," Potter writes, "nothing comes to be; therefore, none of the problems about becoming that puzzle progress philosophers arises for the leap philosopher."[62]

Potter offers these categories as ideal types rather than absolutes: Śaṅkara's direct disciple Sureśvara actually appears in both columns, relative to different questions of interpretation.[63] Nevertheless, the typology can help us discern different emphases and approaches among missionary Advaitins on the question of liberative experience. As commentators on the *Vivekacūḍāmaṇi*, for example, it seems evident that Candraśekhara Bhāratī most fully exemplifies a path approach and Ramana Maharshi a leap approach, with Swami Chinmayananda somewhere in the middle. For Ramana, emphasis falls firmly on the immediacy of *ātman* and the universal availability of its experiential recollection. Ankur Barua notes a revealing exchange between the Maharshi (M) and a disciple (D):

> [M]: Who is it who has or has not realized?
>
> [D]: There is only one self.

> [M]: The question can arise only if there be two. Abandon the wrong identification of the Self with the non-self.
>
> [D]: I mean the higher stage of consciousness.
>
> [M]: There are no stages.[64]

For Candraśekhara Bhāratī, and to a lesser extent Swami Chinmayananda, emphasis falls instead on the necessity of the teaching tradition to create the proper conditions for self-recollection and to translate it into the lived experience of qualified seekers.

At one level, these are just differences of interpretation; at another, they illustrate the difficulty of accounting for non-dualist experience, as well as its vitality as a site of engagement. But this raises a further question. What happens if the experiential appeal is ruled out altogether, as seems to be the case with a figure like Swami Dayananda Saraswati, discussed briefly at the beginning of this chapter? Are there forms of missionary Advaita that prescribe a different "path," or a different "leap," altogether?

One place to explore this question is in the thirty verses of Ramana Maharshi's *Upadeśa Sāram*, or "Essence of the Teaching" (hereafter RamanaUS),[65] and its reception by Swami Dayananda and the Arsha Vidya teaching tradition. Written in 1927 at the request of the acclaimed poet Muruganar, the *Upadeśa Sāram* represents itself as a teaching of Śiva to a group of ascetics. Ramana composed it in Tamil *undiyār* verse to fit into a larger composition of Muruganar; within a year, he had translated it into Sanskrit, Telugu, and Malayalam.[66] The work emphasizes self-inquiry (*ātma-vicāra*) while drawing attention to the organic relation of this practice to other spiritual disciplines (*RamanaUS* 10). Detached action, ritual worship, and devotional *japa* are positioned as "preparatory *sādhanās*" in verses 1–6. Subsequent verses unfold a series of progressively more subtle and interiorized disciplines, including devotional meditation (7–9), breath control, and contemplative annihilation of the mind (11–14), the practice of *ātma-vicāra* (16–20), and the Advaita discipline of self-knowledge (21–29).[67] The work concludes with an admonition: "The shining of the self, free from the ego—this is real penance [*tapas*]. This is Ramana's teaching" (30).

Read as a linear narrative, the *Upadeśa Sāram* would appear to propose a well-defined "path" to liberation, beginning with detached action and devotional practice and leading eventually—by stages—to one's experiential transformation, and a number of commentators interpret the work in precisely this way. However, it is also possible to read the first half of the text as a simple enumeration of diverse, more or less effective supports to facilitate an experiential leap, a moment when the disciple comes "to see through the substantival unreality of the mind."[68] In several places in the second half of the text, for example, Ramana refers to liberation as a direct apprehension, vision, or "seeing" (*darśana*) of the true, innermost self (RamanaUS 16, 25–26, 28). Perhaps more important, he consistently assesses the various *sādhanās* in terms of their capacity—or incapacity—to extinguish thoughts or to annihilate the individual ego. Thus, the highest form of devotional meditation is one that establishes the devotee in a state "devoid of any thought" (*bhāva-śunya*; RamanaUS 9). While breath control can suspend one's thoughts temporarily, Ramana teaches, only extraordinary mental focus can facilitate the mind's "annihilation" (*vināśana*; 13), its "going to destruction" (*nāśam-eti*; 14), or the attainment of a completely "destroyed mind" (*naṣṭa-mānasa*; 15). Similarly, the divine "I-I" (*aham-ahaṃtā*) is described as shining forth in its own self-illuminating nature upon the collapse (*pat-*) or annihilation (*nāśa-bhāj*) of the individual sense of "I" (*aham*; 19–20). "When an inquiry is made into what exactly is this mind," Ramana notes at a key point of transition, "it will be found that there is no mind at all. This is the direct path for realization of the self" (17). The use of "direct path" (*marga ārjavāt*) here is telling. Other paths may provide support, but only self-inquiry leads directly to the annihilation, dissolution, or experiential falsification of individual selfhood.[69]

As a work that offers the teaching of Ramana Maharshi in a concise, accessible form, the *Upadeśa Sāram* has generated a modest commentarial tradition. The multiple translations of the text by Ramana himself function as a kind of initial gloss, as the Telugu and Malayalam accounts in particular clarify certain points in the canonical Sanskrit version.[70] However, beginning with the scholar and devotee Ganapati Muni in 1928, teachers associated with Ramanasramam have also produced several authorized commentaries.[71] These commentators offer a consistently experiential reading of the text, and one that places strong emphasis on the cessation of thoughts and dissolution of the mind as the direct path to liberation. In his comment on verse 9, for example, D. M. Sastri distills the "central message" of the whole text as "stilling the mind and remaining free from thoughts," and he dismisses thought itself as an "obstacle" to self-realization.[72] "We have always known ourself as we really are," writes Michael James, commenting on the Tamil original. "We will not experience self-knowledge as something newly attained."[73] On the contrary: because our true nature is merely obscured by the workings of our individual minds—like the sun obscured by passing clouds—the experience of liberation emerges spontaneously when we arrive at a perfectly tranquil "thought-free state."[74]

The main goal of these commentaries is to clarify elements of Ramana's teaching, but they also function to establish the authoritative status of the *Upadeśa Sāram* in the Vedānta tradition. Several commentators emphasize that the thirty verses of the text are not based on "second-hand knowledge" but on Ramana's "*direct experience*"[75] and that this experience itself should be regarded as "prior to and superior to any scriptures."[76] It is true that Ramana's text never cites the Vedas or any other scriptural authority to support its claims; instead, the teachers of Ramanasramam regard the *Upadeśa Sāram* itself as a form of scripture, especially in its Sanskrit edition. "Since Sanskrit happens to be the language of the Vedas," writes Rao, "the Sanskrit version [of the text] is accorded a special status, and is recited alongside the Vedas daily at the time of the Veda-parayana in the *Ashram*."[77]

The claim that the *Upadeśa Sāram* may have special status as a kind of scripture of late modern, missionary Advaita is attested, at least in part, by the role that it has come to play in other movements beyond the direct legacy of Ramana Maharshi. Swami Chinmayananda, for instance, included the *Upadeśa Sāram* alongside the Upaniṣads, the *Vivekacūḍāmaṇi*, and other classical Advaita texts in his public teaching and in the scheme of study for small groups.[78] At least as recently as 2005, no less significant an authority than Chinmayananda's direct successor, Swami Tejomayananda, offered public lectures on the *Upadeśa Sāram*—just as he would on the Vedic scriptures or the teachings of Ādi Śaṅkarācārya.[79] So also, somewhat remarkably, has the *Upadeśa Sāram* continued to be reckoned as authoritative in the Arsha Vidya *paraṃparā* founded by Swami Dayananda, after his departure from the Chinmaya Mission. From the 1980s to the present day, long after the works of Swami Chinmayananda had been conclusively dropped from the curriculum, Arsha Vidya teachers continue to offer public discourses on Ramana Maharshi's most important teaching text.[80]

Swami Dayananda's *Talks on Upadesa Sāram* was first published in 1987, shortly after his break with Chinmayananda and the Chinmaya Mission, and this work invites special attention for its spirited engagement on the question of inner, non-dualist experience. Arguably, Dayananda uses his commentary to reinscribe Ramana's experiential teaching within a framework consistent with his own, ostensibly more traditionalist vision of Advaita. He begins his commentary by offering an account of Ramana's biography, and he concedes that the great sage "*said* that his teaching was based on his own experience and what he understood," rather than any study of the scriptures.[81] Nevertheless, Dayananda equates Ramana's fundamental method of self-inquiry to the *Upaniṣadic* dictum *tattvamasi*, "you are that," and suggests that the *Upadeśa Sāram* should be understood as the essence not of Ramana's own teaching but of "the message of the Upaniṣads, the Gita and other books."[82]

Throughout the first half of his commentary, Dayananda locates multiple opportunities to insist that Ramana's teaching receives its final confirmation not in the student's own experience but in the revelation of the Vedic *śruti* and the judgment of other more authoritative teachers in the tradition.[83] In his comment on the initial verses, for instance, Dayananda offers extensive discussions of the action and knowledge portions of the Veda, as well as detailing the traditional sixfold qualification (*adhikāra*) for Vedāntic study—none of which is attested or even alluded to in the original text.[84] When Ramana offers a meditation on *soham*, "I am that," as the prescribed "view" (*matā*) in verse 8, Dayananda glosses the term *matā* as "accepted as true by all scriptures and validated by the wise";[85] and when Ramana describes his teaching as "confirmed" (*niścitam*) in verse 10, Dayananda interprets this as "ascertained by Śruti."[86] In the hands of Swami Dayananda, then, a text that appears to speak from the authority of immanent experience is revealed as resting instead on the authority of the Vedic scriptures and classical Vedānta.

Given Dayananda's apparently "externalist" orientation, it comes as no surprise that the most difficult portions of the *Upadeśa Sāram* for him are those that speak of the cessation of thoughts and dissolution of the mind as the direct means of liberation. Throughout his commentary on verses 9–10 and 13–20 in particular, Dayananda operates from the realist principle that "Knowledge, any form of knowledge, must take place in the mind"—including liberating self-knowledge.[87] Hence, wherever the *Upadeśa Sāram* refers to the destruction of the mind or annihilation of the ego, this must be referred not to some extraordinary, supra-cognitive state but merely to the resolution of superficial doubts, anxieties, and dualistic conceptions.[88] "Elimination of thoughts is not knowledge," he writes, with just a touch of polemic; "it is not self-discovery."[89] In his comment on verse 10, Dayananda develops this point by introducing, and quickly disposing of, a *pūrva-pakṣa* or opposing point of view: "How to remove self-ignorance? They say, 'You transcend the mind and the Self will reveal itself.' Self is unopposed to ignorance; it is already revealed but is not recognised. That you are ignorant, is known to you. By transcending the mind, you get stoned or fall asleep . . . Thoughts are never totally transcended. Even if they are transcended what happens after transcending the mind? Nothing."[90] Elsewhere in the commentary, Dayananda will refer to this misconception as "'submarine' philosophy," a school of thought that imagines the divine *ātman* as "a submarine to surface out from the debris of thoughts."[91] He traces the origins of this view to the classical yoga of Patañjali, and he dismisses the "modern" and "distorted" forms of Advaita that have integrated yoga into their teaching.[92] "Neither absence of thoughts is enlightenment nor their presence bondage . . . Negating all thoughts is a good experience but does not enlighten."[93]

Dayananda summarizes his alternative interpretation of the tradition as follows: "Vedanta is a *pramāṇa,* the means to Self-knowledge. The inquiry 'Who am I?' must be done with the help of the teaching of a guru. Then it works."[94] This, he contends, is the true "essence" (*sāram*) of the *Upadeśa Sāram* and, by extension, the central message of Ramana Maharshi. Those who interpret the great sage in terms of non-dualist experience and the transcendence of the mind, he implies, have simply misunderstood. Perhaps with these other interpreters in mind, Dayanananda observes that Ramana teaches "in a cryptic method" and thus may be prone to confusion.[95]

Interestingly, even as Swami Dayananda criticizes "submarine" philosophies and modern, experientialist forms of Vedānta, he nevertheless recognizes the existence of some kind of "liberative experience." That is, he concedes that a particular conscious state of non-dualist awareness does arise in *nirvikalpa samādhi*, as well as in more ordinary occasions of joy, deep sleep, and even the momentary pauses between successive intonations of a sacred *mantra*.[96] The difficulty with such non-dualist experiences, according to Dayananda, is that they do not last, and they do not explain themselves.[97] Thus, toward the end of the work, he writes: "Experientially you are with yourself in sleep and in every moment of joy. Only you do not recognise that. Since you have this experience of limitlessness, Śruti can communicate with you . . . You do pick up happiness even with ignorance, but knowledge makes you recognise the happiness as yourself. It was always there, but not recognised. Vedanta makes you recognise this fact."[98] A few pages later, he describes such experience as "the basis for learning," a foundation from which the scriptures and the teacher can facilitate disciples' liberating recognition.[99]

In his commentary, Dayananda clearly sets himself against Ramana Maharshi and his own teacher Swami Chinmayananda on such questions as the extinction of the mind, the transcendence of thought, and the value of contemplative experience. But he also echoes many of their core convictions about the reality and significance of experience, as such. According to D. M. Sastri, Ramana taught that the liberated sage becomes conscious of "the Heart" or "the centre of spiritual experience . . . by a sort of feeling recollection made while he is with bodily awareness."[100] Asked by a disciple, "How can we conceive such a heart?," Ramana reportedly replied, "Why should you conceive of anything? You have only to see from where the 'I' springs."[101] The liberation that disciples seek is already given, in reality and in their own, immanent experience. This is one important key to Advaita Vedānta's cross-cultural appeal. But it is a problematic, disruptive key: it evokes controversy and requires a continual process of argument, adaption, and (re)translation into new idioms and frameworks of interpretation. Recollection, translation, argument—all of these go hand in hand in the ongoing dissemination and reception of the teaching.

Reaping the Fruits: Mission as Translation and Liberating Recollection

The present chapter began with what Thomas Forsthoefel celebrates as the "genuine universalism" of Ramana Maharshi, rooted in the sage's "internalist epistemology" and appeal to a pure, liberative experience free of the limitations of culture, social class, or geographical origin.[102] In the intervening pages, the notion of liberative experience has been explored and tested at several levels, beginning with the tension between the eighth-century teaching of Śaṅkara and rival Advaita traditions of the *prasaṃkhyāna-vāda,* the *Vivekacūḍāmaṇi,* and late medieval advocates of "Yogic Advaita." The interpretations of the *Vivekacūḍāmaṇi* by Ramana Maharshi, Śrī Candraśekhara Bhāratī, and Swami Chinmayananda have brought subtle distinctions to the experientialist side of this engagement. Swami Dayananda's revisionist reading of the *Upadeśa Sāram* represents a rejoinder from the opposite pole, more indebted to the scripturalist approach of Śaṅkara but no less universalist in scope and intent.

Among the movements selected for the wider study of this volume, the traditions of Ramana, Śṛṅgeri and Chinmayananda have occupied most of our attention in this chapter, and the Ramakrishna Mission and Transcendental Meditation have receded to the background. Nevertheless, as noted at the outset of the inquiry, these latter traditions also appeal in different ways to a contemplative, non-dualist experience of *ātman* in their respective teachings. What we might call a good news or "gospel" of inner experience emerges as a significant site of shared identity for all of these movements, and it is one key to their universalizing claims.[103] In the terms provided by Kathryn Tanner, the theme functions as a defining "focus of common investment and engagement" for late modern missionary Advaita, in the midst of its diversity.[104] It possesses such status in these modern and contemporary traditions, at least in part, because the question of experience has been a site of engagement for the tradition more widely, tracing back at least to the eighth century—and arguably further in the history and prehistory of Vedānta.[105]

Though the focus of this chapter has been on shared engagement rather than common agreement, significant motifs recur across these accounts. Notably, notwithstanding their important disagreements, Ramana Maharshi, Candraśekhara Bhāratī, Swami Chinmayananda, and Swami Dayananda all speak of the non-dualist awareness of *ātman* less as a particular kind of experience than as a perduring dimension of all experience. Again following Forsthoefel, we might see in their teachings not the communication of some new, elevated experience *of Brahman* but rather a liberating recollection of an "experience which *is* Brahman," already and eternally present in every hearer's immanent self-awareness.[106] Such recollection does not arise spontaneously, at least not ordinarily.[107] It requires translation into ordinary human language. This includes the language of the Vedic scriptures to be sure, especially for a self-identified "traditional teacher" like Swami Dayananda, but it also comprehends texts like the *Upadeśasāhasrī*, *Vivekacūdamāṇi*, and *Upadeśa Sāram*, translations and commentaries of prominent missionary teachers, and the personal, face-to-face encounters of these teachers, these teachers' disciples, and *their* disciples with new communities and generations of hearers.

It is in this process of translation that the disagreements among the various *ācārya*s spills into view. Does liberative experience follow immediately from a correct hearing of the scriptures, or does it require verification through some form of meditative discipline? Is it the preserve of social and religious elites, or is it available to anyone? Does it arise in one great leap, or at the end of a long process? Does it happen by means of ordinary mental cognition, or does it require the dissolution of the intellect? If the liberating recollection of *ātman* is by definition singular, its translation into the particular languages, practices, and institutional cultures of diverse Advaita movements is demonstrably plural. There is no way around translation, as such, in the missionary enterprise.

One scholar who has reflected deeply on the role and significance of translation in the theology of mission, as well as on the fruitfulness of comparing diverse missionary traditions, is the late Gambian missiologist Lamin Sanneh (1942–2019). A convert to Catholicism, Sanneh completed his doctoral studies in Islamic history at the University of London, and his influential 1989 book *Translating the Message* attempts a preliminary, typological comparison of mission in Christianity and Islam.[108] He distinguishes two understandings of religious universalism, which he labels "mission by *diffusion*" and "mission *by translation*."[109] According to the former type, "religion expands by means of its founding cultural warrants and is implanted in other societies primarily as a matter of cultural adoption."[110] A diffusionist universalism defined the worldview of the earliest Jewish Christians, as well as that of medieval Christendom and colonial Europe. This worldview ultimately generated imperialist and colonialist forms of the faith, as well as sinister moments of violence and even genocide. However, Sanneh identifies diffusionist universalism most strongly with Islam, with its emphasis on rooting out non-Islamic patterns of life in the process of conversion and its typical retention of Arabic as the sole language of scriptural study and worship wherever it spreads.[111]

Authentic Christianity, on Sanneh's reading, represents a mirror image reversal of Islam, as well as its own imperialist and colonial distortions, insofar as it has more consistently identified its universality not with its capacity to absorb others into a single religious culture but rather with its capacity to become culturally and sociologically plural through continual, intrinsically liberating processes of translation.[112] Sanneh places great weight on the fact that the language of the Christian New Testament writings is neither Aramaic nor Hebrew—the mother tongues of Jesus—but Greek.[113] From this original, revelatory moment of translation followed a series of further transformations, from Paul the Apostle's arguments against circumcision and food laws for Gentile converts to the creation of the Vulgate Bible in the fourth century and the Slavonic liturgies of Cyril and Methodius in the ninth, and then, subsequently, from the revolutionary composition of the first English Bible in the sixteenth century to the proliferation of vernacular Bibles and catechetical materials in Asia and Africa up to the present day.[114] For Sanneh, the spread of Christianity by translation represents more than a fact of history. It reveals something essential about Christianity itself, as a distinct type of missionary tradition. "Christianity is a translated religion without a revealed language," he writes. "Translation is the church's birthmark as well as its missionary benchmark: the church would be unrecognizable or unsustainable without it."[115]

In the discussion of Advaita mission movements in this chapter, the motif of translation arose in close connection with a liberating recollection or recognition of the divine *ātman* in the experience of the hearer. Intriguingly, Sanneh also suggests that gospel translation facilitated a kind of liberating recollection on the part of Indigenous traditions, albeit one that played out in the realms of culture, society, and politics. For example, when eighteenth- and nineteenth-century Protestant missionaries in Africa and the Americas adopted Khoi-Khoi, Zulu, and Valiente terms for God in their Bible translations, they did so as agents of a diffusionist, colonial project; nevertheless, whatever the missionaries' intention, such practices *functioned* to confer recognition on those local names of God, already available in the self-understandings of Indigenous hearers, and thus valorized the Indigenous traditions themselves.[116] Sanneh generalizes this idea: "God is no further—and no closer—than the language of common discourse, which makes translation a safeguard against believers becoming strangers to God and to one another, and against reducing believers to the status only of clients; translation exists to define the ground of our adoption as God's children, a God who speaks our language and who, in forming us in the accents of birth and nurture, calls us to a united common purpose."[117] Sanneh insists elsewhere that authentic translation should be approached as an "indigenous discovery of Christianity" rather than a "Christian discovery of indigenous societies," insofar as the reception of the gospel ideally ennobles "local conceptions of religion" and facilitates a process of self-empowerment.[118] Typically, on his reading, the translation of scripture into local vernaculars by European colonialists had the ironic effect of fueling anticolonial resistance and inspiring liberation movements, particularly in the African context.[119]

Sanneh's enthusiastic view of Christian translatability is not beyond critique,[120] and there are conspicuous differences between the colonial production of a Zulu New Testament and Ādi Śaṅkarācārya's refutation of the *prasaṃkhyāna-vāda*. Nevertheless, this typology and analysis provide a useful lens to situate Advaita's distinctiveness as a missionary tradition. The inquiry in this chapter, for example, has surfaced a willingness and even enthusiasm on the part of Advaita teachers to refashion the Advaita message through various literal practices of translation, including not least Ramana's free Tamil translation of a classical Sanskrit text, the discovery and eventual English translation of a lost commentary by a revered Śaṅkarācārya of Śṛṅgeri, and the commentarial (re) translation of ancient and modern texts by Swami Chinmayananda and Swami Dayananda. More deeply, from one point of view, the Advaita tradition is *nothing except translation*—namely, the translation of experiential knowledge into various idioms of language and culture. Swami Chinmayananda, like Swami Vivekananda before him, viewed the Vedic scriptures as an indirect, mediated account of the ancient rishis' direct, experiential awareness of *ātman*,[121] and some disciples of Ramana Maharshi accord the *Upadeśa Sāram* a higher status than even the Vedas because it most faithfully encapsulates the "direct path" (*marga ārjavāt*, v. 17) that the great sage traced for them in his own experience.[122]

As noted earlier, and as we will explore further in the chapter that follows, Advaita mission movements such as the Chinmaya Mission and the Śṛṅgeri *maṭha* have sometimes described their universal significance in terms of the diffusion of a particular, Sanskrit religious culture—just as Christians, on Sanneh's reading, sometimes distorted the gospel by identifying it with Latin language or Western European religious culture. When these Advaita traditions are engaged strictly on their own terms and distinguished from other missionary traditions in the broader Hindu stream, however, their core theological claims would appear to be most consistent with a particularly radical type of "mission by translation." If Christianity is a "translated religion without a revealed language," in Sanneh's artful phrase,[123] Advaita completely elides any conceptual spaces among translation, revelation, and liberative experience in the ongoing communication and reception of its teaching.[124]

The Advaita missionary tradition purports to convince hearers of the truth of its message not by external imposition but through redirecting hearers' attention to previously unrecognized dimensions of their immanent self-awareness. The liberating reality of *ātman* is not yet truly known, but neither is it truly unknown. Commenting on *Vivekacūḍāmaṇi* 56, the Jagadguru Śri Candraśekhara Bhāratī writes: "Every person is inherently Brahman. He is free as a matter of fact. He forgets it due to overpowering *ajñāna* . . . Brahmajñāna is not *productive* of Brahmanhood, but is only *revelatory* (*abhivyañjaka*) of it . . . It is revelation of an *existent* fact, that one is and ever has been Brahman" (CBVC 58 [56]). This principle, as we have seen, generates diverse, conflicting visions of the tradition. For Candraśekhara Bhāratī, only certain persons, sharply delimited by gender, social class, and renunciant life, will ever experience this liberating recollection in its fullness. For Swami Chinmayananda and Swami Dayananda, by contrast, the fact that everyone has some experience of joy or deep sleep means that anyone can, at least potentially, hear the word of the scriptures and attain liberation. And, in a particularly dramatic instance of translatability we encountered briefly in chapter 2, disciples of Ramana Maharshi can spring up in North America, empowered by their interior experiences of liberation, with no training in the Vedas and no historical connection to the great sage or his lineage.[125] The Advaita appeal to pure experience transcends even those bounds the tradition itself might attempt to place on its translation into new contexts and new cultural idioms.

These observations, moreover, invite renewed attention to questions of translation, recollection, and religious experience in Christian theologies of mission. In building his case for Christian translatability, for example, Sanneh draws special attention to the biblical accounts of Pentecost (Acts 2:1–13) and of the Apostle Paul's preaching at the Areopagus, in Athens (Acts 17:22–1).[126] Both episodes mark key points of transition in the theological narrative of Luke-Acts, from the more particularist missionary vision of the first Jerusalem community to its universalist extension of the gospel "to the ends of the earth" (Acts 1:8).[127] Both valorize the inherent translatability of the Christian message, with reference to languages of the Mediterranean world in the case of Pentecost and Hellenistic culture in the case of the Areopagus. Both also, finally, frame the reception of the gospel as a moment of recognition or recollection on the part of its hearers. The Jews and "proselytes" (*prosēlutoi*) from every nation are amazed and puzzled that they recognize the words of the apostles, when "in our own languages we hear them speaking about God's deeds of power" (Acts 2:10–11, NRSV). And Paul invites his Athenian hearers to recollect their own religiosity, sacred fragments of their own philosophical traditions and their own deep, abiding sense of a God "who is not far from each one of us. For 'In him we live and move and have our being' " (Acts 17:27–28).[128] In both cases, some hearers are moved to accept the message and embark on a new way, while others turn away (2:37–42; 17:32–34)—possibly because these hearers do not recognize the gospel in their language, culture, and intimate experience. If there is failure here, it may be a failure of recollection, a failure to break the inexplicable, obscuring power of *ajñāna*.

But precisely what, or whom, is being recollected? Though Sanneh speaks primarily about the liberation of Indigenous cultures in the process of translation, in theological perspective the ultimate source and subject of any true liberation is God the divine self, the one in whom "we live and move and have our being." Implicit in the presence of a viable word or concept of God in a recipient culture is the active presence of God in the lived experience of those who sustain that culture and are sustained by it.[129] Thus, reflecting on the importance of religious experience in their now classic work *The Biblical Foundations of Mission*, Donald Senior and Carol Stuhlmueller write that "the ultimate justification of the decision to preach to the Gentiles is the fact that the Gentiles *respond* to the gospel. The New Testament sees this not as a lucky accident but as the manifestation of God's plan, a plan already initiated in Jesus' openness to peripheral peoples. God in his Spirit had already been at work, touching the hearts of the Gentiles and making them open to the proclamation of the gospel."[130] "This seems to imply," they conclude, "that religious experience is the great equalizer."[131] It is in moments of profound religious affect—"the prayers, hymns and poetry of Israel and the early church"—that Christians most clearly perceived the universal scope of God's saving work historically, and many contemporary Christians feel "pastoral intuitions of solidarity" with religious others at a deep, experiential level.[132]

In their discussion, Senior and Stuhlmueller are careful not to define the religious experience in question too precisely, in terms of contemplative absorption or ecstasy, for example. Any experience that acquires religious meaning, it would seem, emerges as religious experience.[133] Such modesty coheres well with the analysis conducted in this chapter. If the pure, non-dualist experience of *ātman* may be interpreted as a "great equalizer" in these Advaita traditions, it does this work asymptotically, provoking immense engagement, inspiring ever-fresh articulations in each new context, and drawing diverse disciples into its fold, while always remaining just out of view and beyond the limits of categorical inquiry. The reality of this experience is attested not directly but by the continuous emergence of new translations and the evidence of transformative recollection on the part of those who make its message their own. New hearers—and scholarly observers—remain in what Swami Chinmayananda calls a kind of liminal space, a stance of "hopeful and expectant waiting"[134] for awareness to dawn, for a word of God's deeds that rings true in one's own language and culture, for a new consciousness of a divine reality that has remained, until now, unrecognized. The labor of the missionary is no more and no less than to open these spaces of expectant waiting, and then to get out of the way.

Conclusion

In the tenth verse chapter of the *Upadeśasāhasrī*, in the course of prescribing a contemplative practice of recollection, Śaṅkara has the model disciple recite as follows: "I am always the same to [all] beings, the Lord, for I am superior to, and higher than, the perishable and imperishable. Though I have the highest *ātman* as my true nature and am non-dual, I am nevertheless covered with wrong knowledge, with ignorance" (USP 10.8). Swami Chinmayananda and Ramana Maharshi also describe the path to liberation as a process of rediscovery, recollecting a truth that has been inexplicably forgotten.[135] In this respect, all of our interpreters—ancient and modern—speak with one voice.

And for good reason. For, at stake in each of these accounts is the universality of the Advaita claim, as well as the fruitfulness and necessity of the teaching tradition. Whether one speaks in terms of a careful scriptural discernment, of the discipline of yogic Vedānta and attainment of perfect *nirvikalpa samādhi*, or of a recognition of the perduring truth behind evanescent experiences of joy or deep sleep, one engages a paradoxical tension between one's apparent, empirical condition and the revelation of one's true, liberated condition as the self of all beings, between reality as presently experienced and reality as one is coming to know it to be. The eternally liberated self of all beings is "incapable of being known by anyone," insists Ramana Maharshi, "and yet is experienced as the 'I-I' in the Heart."[136] It can never become an object of ordinary experience, and yet it promises to reshape one's experience in fundamental ways. Missionary Advaita, in one sense, emerges entirely out of this paradoxical claim, proclaiming a liberation that is already, and also not yet—in one's intellectual apprehension, in one's habitual assumptions, and in one's intimate experience of self.

5

Conquest of the Quarters?

Crossing Borders and Charting New Geographies

The shrine to Ramana Maharshi at Arunachala Ashrama, in the New York suburb of Jamaica, features an elaborate coordination of several representations of the great sage.[1] The central *mūrti*, a life-sized black stone sculpture of a young Ramana, sits on a raised platform in a lotus posture, with relaxed arms and a serene gaze. Two symbols of the formless divine have been placed in front of this image: on a lower pedestal, a bronze engraving of the intricate, mystical pattern of nine overlapping triangles called the Śrī Cakra and, at floor level, a modest Śiva *liṅgam* for ritual offerings. On the wall, directly behind Ramana's sculpted head, hangs another Śrī Cakra, this one a hand-drawn image that, according to tradition, the sage himself produced to console a devotee who had recently lost her daughter. Above this hangs a large, framed photograph of an older Ramana and, above that, a large portrait of the sacred mountain Arunachala, site of both the cave where the Maharshi sought initial refuge and the ashram that eventually developed around him.

The Ramana Mandiram or meditation hall in Nova Scotia, Canada, is quite similar, including a black stone *mūrti* of young Ramana, the Śrī Cakra, and two larger photographs, beside still another portrait of the formidable, silent Arunachala.

These various modes of presence reveal several layers of Ramana's Advaita tradition. First of all, they testify to the hybrid interpenetration of this teaching—and many forms of Advaita Vedānta—with Śaiva, Tantra, and Śrī Vidyā goddess traditions of meditation and ritual practice.[2] Second, they reflect a dialectic between a focus on Ramana Maharshi as a particular, historical individual and as the universally accessible experience of liberation to which he bore witness, symbolized by the abstract images of Śrī Cakra. Finally, both shrines suggest a complex negotiation of place. The images of Arunachala point to a sacred mountain in South India, far from these two sites in New York and Nova Scotia. At the same time, both ashrams also embody the sacred mountain Arunachala in their own particular emplacement. On one wet day in August 2017, for example, as I walked around the Canadian site with one of Ramana's prominent North American devotees, the rain and fog lifted for a moment, revealing a low, wooded ridge behind the main house. "Arunachala," whispered my guide.

A wry smile followed: "We were just lucky that there happens to be a hill behind the property."

Both the reverent pronouncement and the subsequent disclaimer revealed a profound conviction about the place of place in this Advaita mission movement. This is a random ridge behind a random homestead in the settler state of Canada. It is also Arunachala, right here, in rural Nova Scotia, on the south shore of the Bay of Fundy. As the message of Advaita spreads to new regions of the world, so does sacred Arunachala.

In this chapter, I take up questions of place, emplacement, and geographical extension in missionary Advaita. In his popular *Introduction to Hinduism*, Gavin Flood writes, "There would seem to be two forces at work within Hinduism in the modern world: on the one hand a trend toward universalization which contributes to global culture and process, yet on the other a trend towards exclusive, local or national identity formation."[3] In principle, Advaita Vedānta would seem to belong on the universalist side of this equation. We can recall, for example, Thomas Forsthoefel's account of the "perennialist" and "internalist" appeal of Ramana Maharshi's method of self-inquiry, which strips the cultural baggage and even the scriptural foundation from the Advaita teaching to render it truly universal.[4] Arguably, it is Advaita's relative freedom from any cultural or ethnic identity that renders it suitable for missionary outreach, from Swami Vivekananda's Parliament speeches to the present day.

The Ramana shrines in New York and Nova Scotia—and my guide's spontaneous pronouncement, "Arunachala"—invite a more nuanced assessment. This I attempt in the present chapter, albeit with principal reference not to Ramana Maharshi, but to Swami Chinmayananda and the Chinmaya Mission. In the first section, I establish a broad context by looking at various claims by Vedāntins to preach a religion of "no place," including the "universal religion" of Swami Vivekananda, the mechanical path of Maharishi Mahesh Yogi, and the philosophical deployment of the B-M-I chart by Swami Chinmayananda. In each case, the purported universalization of the tradition stands in some tension with their very particular cultural and geographical roots in India. The next two sections delve more deeply into the case of the Chinmaya Mission, focusing on the retelling of the *dig-vijaya* hagiographical tradition in the 1978 manifesto *Śaṅkara the Missionary*. In this work, I suggest, Advaita tradition is neither limited to its Indian geography nor divested from it. Instead, the imaginative understanding of place itself is reconfigured. The sacred "quarters" (*dik*) of the Indian subcontinent are mapped onto new geographies, both interior and exterior—thus rendering these geographies available for pilgrimage and spiritual "conquest" (*vijaya*) by the various forms of missionary Advaita.

From this analysis, following the model of the previous chapter, I attempt a comparative reconsideration of Christian mission in terms of migration and pilgrimage. The line between hegemonic conquest and authentic missionary pilgrimage is a thin one, for Christian and Advaita tradition alike. Resources for navigating this tension and engaging the Advaita theologies more critically can, I suggest, be found in theologies of missiological itineracy advanced by Gemma Tulud Cruz and David Bosch. To be missionary, on this reading, is to be on the move, both literally and spiritually, seeking not so much to conquer or encompass new geographies but simply to cross them as a continual practice of self-imposed exile and vulnerability. In this shared summons, missionary Advaita and missionary Christianity might emerge equally as both pilgrims in this present world and companions on the way.

A Religion of No Place?

In a 2002 essay, Christian missiologist M. Thomas Thangaraj considered the effect of globalization on Hinduism, both in India and in the global diaspora. Echoing the assessment of Flood and other historians of South Asia, Thangaraj identifies two typical, opposed responses to the challenges posed to Hindu tradition by the incursion of new social, political, and market forces in late modernity.[5] At one extreme stands a caste-based "bio-piety" and India-centered "geo-piety" in the rhetoric of the Vishwa Hindu Parishad and other forms of Hindu religious nationalism. The destruction of the Babari Masjid in Ayodhya by Hindutva militants in 1992 serves as a concrete example of this geo-pietistic emphasis on the sacred geography of South Asia.[6]

At another extreme lies the more expansive "Hindu universalism" of Swami Vivekananda and other modern Vedāntins, notionally free from restrictions of culture, caste, or national identity.[7] Thangaraj offers a concrete example:

> I know a swami in Atlanta who is a monk of the Ramakrishna Order. He is a white American who walks around with slacks and shirts (at times a saffron shirt). He is always quick to tell me that he is not a Hindu but a Vedantin. When I asked why he calls himself so, he told me that if he were a Hindu he would have to dress like a Hindu, go to India often, and be part of the caste system, and that he was not defined by any of those.[8]

Here the universal truth of Vedānta has been stripped not only of its association with particular institutional structures or scriptural expressions but of any intrinsic connection with its origin as a religion of South Asia. Elaine M. Fisher notes that such strategies of differentiating sectarian identities from the underlying Vedic or Hindu religious culture of South Asia have roots in the precolonial period, at least as far back as the sixteenth century CE.[9]

The actual history and lived practice of the Ramakrishna movement reveals a more complex negotiation of identity and geography. In a study of selected Western disciples, for example, Gwylim Beckerlegge notes several conflicting trends.[10] On the one hand, Swami Vivekananda would declare at the 1893 Parliament that the "universal religion" he proclaimed would "have no location in place and time," and interviews with *ācāryas* in contemporary London reveal a shared conviction that the great Advaitin "had disseminated Vedānta, and not the 'ethnic religion' of Hinduism."[11]

On the other hand, whereas some of Vivekananda's North American and British disciples retained Christian or other religious self-identifications even as they took up the study of Vedānta, others significantly "Hinduized" their participation in the tradition. The movement eventually developed "a cult centred upon Ramakrishna and the use of Hindu ritual forms and artefacts, which were not central to Vivekananda's philosophy."[12] Beckerlegge refers to the latter pattern as "imported localism."[13] In his own study of the movement in *Vedanta for the West,* Carl Jackson suggests that the Ramakrishna movement adopted a "middle way" between the cultural specificity of ISKCON, which endeavors to proselytize a distinctively Bengali form of Vaiṣṇavism and retains a very strong South Asian character in its ethics, community structures, and devotional practice, and the decontextualized universality of Transcendental Meditation, which reduced the entire teaching of Advaita to an easily transportable meditation technique.[14]

Perhaps only in TM, then, does Vedānta achieve the aspirational universality described by Thangaraj's informant and implied by Swami Vivekananda's speeches at the Parliament. But here again the picture becomes more complex on closer examination. TM scholar Cynthia Ann Humes, for example, has drawn attention to a typology developed by Jan Nattier to explain different patterns of Buddhist enculturation in the West.[15] Nattier writes: "Religions—not just Buddhism—travel in three major ways: as import, as export, and as 'baggage' . . . Religions transported according to the 'import' model are, so to speak, demand driven: the consumer (i.e., the potential convert) actively seeks out the faith. 'Export' religions are disseminated through missionary activity, while 'baggage' religions are transmitted whenever individuals or families bring their beliefs along when they move to a new place."[16] Nattier notes further differences among these groups. "Import" Buddhists, for example, tend to be cultural elites who are highly selective in their adaptation of the tradition, often focusing on meditation, whereas those who convert to one or another form of "export" Buddhism come from a wider social demographic and usually adopt a wider view of their traditions.[17]

To return to the analyses of the Ramakrishna movement by Beckerlegge and Jackson, one might argue that some Western Vedāntins have selectively taken up Advaita teaching without the

"Hindu" trappings according to an "import" pattern, others have adopted it as an "export" from India, and the movement underwent a further transformation after the 1960s when the Vedānta Societies of Europe and North America received an influx of new members from South Asia, who carried Hinduism and possibly even the distinctly Ramakrishna devotional traditions with them as "baggage."[18]

For Humes, on the other hand, Nattier's threefold typology helps to explain the cycle of rapid growth and decline in the TM movement in the last third of the twentieth century. After thirteen years of formation at the feet of "Gurudev"—Swami Brahmananda Saraswati, Śaṅkarācārya of the Jyotir *maṭha* in the foothills of the Himalayas—the young Mahesh Varma upheld a deeply traditional commitment to Advaita Vedānta and what he came to call the "Vedic Science," even as he distilled this commitment down to a simple *mantra* meditation technique and translated it into the idiom of Western science.[19] Many North American and European adherents initially took up the practice of TM through this *mantra* technique alone, as a kind of "import" religion free of the "baggage" of traditional Hinduism. Humes offers a quotation from the 1975 *TM Book*: "The TM Program is not a religion? I've heard it was just some Westernized form of Hinduism. No, no—it's absurd to assume that just because the TM technique comes from India it must be some Hindu practice . . . The TM technique is a scientific discovery which happens to come from India . . . the TM program does not involve any religious belief or practice—Hindu or otherwise."[20]

From the moment of his first successes in the United States in the 1960s, however, Mahesh—now known as Maharishi Mahesh Yogi—slowly added new layers to this simple message. These included a special devotion to Brahmananda Swaraswati for initiates, new requirements for those who advanced from basic TM to the elite TM-Sidhi technique first introduced in 1976, and, eventually, a full array of teachings, products, and practices associated with Vedic Science. Maharishi Mahesh Yogi actively promoted the ascetic life of *saṃnyāsa* for his inner circle. Over time, what had begun as a simple meditation technique emerged into "a full-fledged incarnation of a multinational Vedantic Export Religion," rooted in Indian language, culture, and ritual practice.[21] "Many of those who bought into the program as a type of Import Hinduism," Humes writes, "felt deceived when ultimately faced with Maharishi's true end: exporting not just a mantic technique, but a religion, a lifestyle, a political ideology."[22] Maharishi Mahesh Yogi reconceptualized the Advaita tradition to reach a North American audience, and one result—upon its re-emplacement as a tradition of South Asia—was tension, and even a sense of betrayal on the part of some followers.

The Chinmaya Mission would seem to be immune from this kind of negotiation and alienation insofar as Swami Chinmayananda's primary objective was always the religious renewal of the Indian nation. Nevertheless, he too sometimes presented Advaita as a religion of "no place," with only incidental connection to the land of South Asia and the religious tradition of Hinduism. On the eve of his first global tour in the mid-1960s, for example, he insisted that "I am going not as a philosopher or champion of any particular religion but as a humble disciple of Mother Shruti to advocate certain values of life as enshrined in the *Upanishads* and other ancient scriptures."[23] The teachings of Advaita may originate in the sacred texts of Hinduism, but that mere accident of birth does not make them Hindu teachings. They are, in and of themselves, universal—unrestricted by any particular geography or religion.

A good example of such a strategy of universalization can be found in the 1975 work *A Manual of Self-Unfoldment*.[24] The book's preface was penned in Cambridge, Massachusetts, in the shadow of Harvard and MIT, and Chinmayananda describes its audience as "modern university educated [and] scientific minded."[25] Perhaps unsurprisingly, given this intended audience, Chinmayananda describes the teaching of Advaita as an objective "Science of Reality," similar to the natural sciences but distinguished by its inward focus.[26] This theme runs throughout the entire *Manual*. Chinmayananda first presents a portrait of true religion as a "great science," and the ancient rishis, correspondingly, as "scientists of the spirit" and "glorious depth-psychologists."[27] He then turns, in subsequent chapters, to a systematic analysis of human experience in terms of five "sheaths" and the *vāsanās*.[28] From this foundation, he proceeds to outline preparatory ethical disciplines for cleansing the mind, practices for the conservation of energy and elimination of *vāsanās*, and, in the final chapters, detailed consideration of the threefold *sādhana* to release our mental power, including scriptural study, the disciplined repetition of mantras, and techniques for deeper meditation.[29]

Swami Chinmayananda's explicit discussion of Hindu culture and religion, though implied throughout *The Manual of Self-Unfoldment*, arises only late in the work, in chapter 10. This follows long after his initial account of human experience and identification of the "Divine-Principle" as the singular goal "advocated by all Religions,"[30] and it leads, in turn, into yet another broader, more philosophical question-and-answer about the "Composition of Man."[31] The religious culture of India is thus skillfully introduced and reinscribed into a more universal and interior understanding of religion and an easily transportable series of meditative practices. The work, appropriately, concludes with a discussion of the formation and maintenance of Chinmaya Mission study groups as yet another practice replicable anywhere in the world.[32]

In the *Manual of Self-Unfoldment*, then, Swami Chinmayananda's vision of Vedānta is deliberately and specifically abstracted from any particular physical, cultural, or religious geography. Chinmayananda wrote to a Western disciple in 1968: "In the Eternal Heart, there are no continents, there are no peoples, there is only love."[33] So also, in the *Manual*, he re-defines the place of the teaching less in terms of "continents" or "peoples" than in terms of cognitive, interior structures. This is revealed especially in his deployment of his signature B-M-I chart in this work. This distinctive visual diagram, emblematic of the Chinmaya movement, is presented twice in the *Manual*.[34] This chart offered a schematic, symbolic diagram of the teaching, visually tracing the origin of phenomenal experience—the body-mind-intellect (B-M-I) of the perceiver, with its corresponding objects, emotions, and thoughts (O-E-T)—upward to the obscuring power of *vāsanās* and, above and behind them, the divine Reality of *brahman*, sometimes symbolized by an X but more frequently by the sacred syllable *oṃ* (figure 5.1).[35] "After listening intently to Gurudev's explanation of the BMI chart," one devotee reports, "I realized that this was a uniquely simple, yet comprehensive, way to explain all that is, both Real and relative."[36] To the degree that the *Manual* locates the teaching of Vedānta in a particular geography at all, then, it is not a physical landscape but an interior geography of "all that is," schematized by abstract signifiers like B-M-I, O-E-T, X, and *oṃ*.

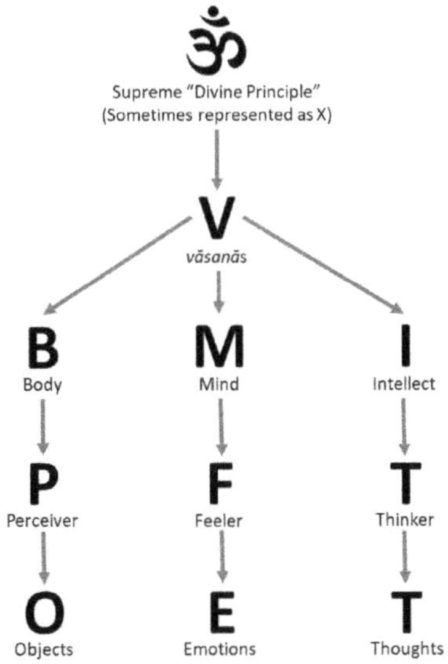

Figure 5.1. The B-M-I Chart offers a symbolic, interiorized map for the Chinmaya Mission. *Source*: Created by the author.

Swami Chinmayananda and the *Śaṅkaradigvijaya*

From one point of view, the vision of the *Manual of Self-Unfoldment* and a cognitive map like the B-M-I Chart seem ideally suited to reimagining this particular Hindu movement as a transnational, global tradition. Yet, as in the cases of the Ramakrishna Mission and Transcendental Meditation, this is not the end of the story for Swami Chinmayananda and the global Chinmaya Mission. Nor could it be, given Chinmayananda's commitment to his particular vision of cultural nationalism. It would not be sufficient to divest the teaching of Advaita of its geographical particularity. Instead, this geography itself would need to be universalized. Hence, the importance of another work, produced a few years after the *Manual*, which would provide the Mission with something like its own evangelical charter: *Śaṅkara the Missionary*.[37]

As indicated in the prefaces of both editions,[38] *Śaṅkara the Missionary* originated in 1978 as a souvenir volume to honor Swami Chinmayananda's 267th Jñāna Yagña, in the Indian city of Jamshedpur, Jharkhand. Chinmayananda ordered the souvenir to be reprinted as a full volume the same year, coinciding with the twenty-fifth anniversary of his founding of the Chinmaya Mission.[39]

With the exception of the foreword, part of the introduction, and a portion of the chapter on Śaṅkara's philosophy, very little of the work can be definitively traced to Swami Chinmayananda's own pen. He certainly gave the treatise his stamp of approval and even recommended it "to every student of *Vedānta* for a deep and sympathetic study,"[40] yet it has no place in the Mission's prescribed Scheme of Study. As an expression of Chinmayananda's teaching, then, the work possesses a distinctive role and status. One might characterize it, in both editions, as a visioning document of the Chinmaya movement. The essential features of the vision undoubtedly spring from Chinmayananda and receive his explicit commendation, but the written text is no less undoubtedly composite.

In form, *Śaṅkara the Missionary* consists of a creative representation of Śaṅkara's life as inspiration for the Chinmaya Mission and for Hindu tradition more generally. Both Chinmayananda and the publishers identify their primary source as the most influential of the Śaṅkara hagiographies: the *Śaṅkaradigvijaya* of Mādhava (ŚDV), which we have already explored in some detail in chapter 3 of this volume.[41] In its first edition, *Śaṅkara the Missionary* consisted of three major sections: (1) a synthetic narrative of the "Life" of Śaṅkara in four chapters, based substantively on the ŚDV; (2) a compilation of "Literature" attributed to the great sage, including summaries of major works and nearly one hundred pages of devotional hymns; and (3) four appendixes, including a translation of Śaṅkara's famous debate with Maṇḍana Miśra, reflections on his four primary disciples, a brief précis of his philosophy, and a list of his major compositions. In a slimmer revised edition, produced twenty years after the first edition and five years after Swami Chinmayananda's death, the work was thoroughly reorganized. All the hymns save the compact *Daśa Śloki* were removed, and the appendixes and summaries of major works were seamlessly integrated as chapters in the main narrative (see table 5.1, below). In both its versions, *Śaṅkara the Missionary* creatively deploys the legendary image of Śaṅkara and his "conquest" (*vijaya*) of South Asia, as narrated in the ŚDV, to advance Swami Chinmayananda's vision of spiritual and cultural revival.

This appropriation is neither simple nor naïve. In his introduction to the work, for example, Swami Chinmayananda credits

Table 5.1. Three Retellings of Adi Sankaracarya's Legendary Conquest

Śaṅkaradigvijaya, Mādhava-Vidyāraṇya (Skt. in Padmanaban; ET Tapasyananda) Ca. 1650–1740 CE?	*Sankara the Missionary* Central Chinmaya Mission Trust 1978	*Śaṅkara the Missionary*, revised edition Central Chinmaya Mission Trust 1998
		Foreword [Chinmayananda]
1. "Prologue" (*upoddhātaḥ*)	Foreword [Chinmayananda]	
2. "Birth of Sankara" (*ācāryajanmādikathanam*)		Preface to the Present Edition
3. "The Earthly Manifestation of Devas" (*devāvatāraḥ*)	PART I: LIFE	
4. "Boyhood Days Up to the Age of Eight" (*kaumāracaritavarṇanam*)	Introduction: Sankara, the Spiritual General [Chinmayananda]; Sankara, the Effulgent Efflorescence of India's National Genius [Ramakrishnan]	Introduction: Śaṅkara, the Spiritual General [Chinmayananda]; Śaṅkara, the Effulgent Efflorescence of India's National Genius [Ramakrishnan]
5. "Embracing Sannyasa" (*saṃnyāsagrahaṇam*)		
6. "Establishment of the Pristine Philosophy of the Self" (*ātmavidyāpratiṣṭhā*)		1. Religious Development
7. "The Meeting with Vyasa" (*vyāsadarśanādicaritavarṇanam*)	1. Religious Development in India up to the Time of Sankara	2. Early Life
8. "Controversy with Mandana" (*śrīmadācāryamaṇḍanamiśrasaṃvādaḥ*)	2. Early Life 3. Dig-vijayam	3. *Dig Vijayam*
9. "Establishing the Claim to Be the Master of All Learning" (*śrīmadācāryasarasvatīsaṃvādaḥ*)	4. The Four Mutts and the Four Disciples	4. Works of *Śaṅkara* [Chinmayananda and Others; prev. ch. 5]
10. "Acquirement of Knowledge of Sex-Love" (*rājadehapraveśādikathanam*)	PART II: LITERATURE 5. Works of Sankara [Chinmayananda and Others]	5. *Śaṅkara*'s Legacy [prev. appendix 2]
11. "Encounter with the Fierce Bhairava" (*ugrabhairavavadhaḥ*)	6. Selections from Sankara's Hymns	6. *Muṭhā-s* and Disciples [prev. ch. 4]
12. "The Coming of Some Disciples" (*hastāmalakādīnāṃ śiṣyatvena grahaṇam*)		7. Philosophy of *Śaṅkara* [prev. appendix 3]
13. "Preaching of Brahma-Vidya" (*brahmavidyāvicāra*)	APPENDIX 1. Sree Sankara's Confrontation with Mandana Misra [trans. Swami Jnanananda Bharati]	
14. "Pilgrimage of Padmapada" (*padmapādatīrthayātrāvarṇanam*)		8. *Śaṅkara* and *Maṇḍana* [trans. Swami Jñānānanda Bhāratī; prev. appendix 1]
15. "Triumphant Tour of the Land" (*ācāryakṛtadigvijayavarṇanam*)	2. Sankara's Legacy: The Four Disciples	9. *Daśa Śloki*: The Ten-Versed Hymn
16. "Accession to Saradapitha" (*śrīmadācāryāṇāṃ śāradāpīṭhavāsavarṇanam*)	3. Philosophy of Sankara 4. Compositions of Sankara [List]	10. List of Works

the great teacher with re-establishing the "true cultural basis of our nation," employing the "variety of efficient weapons in his resourceful armoury," and thereby attaining the status of a "spiritual general."[42] In this respect, he seems clearly to echo what William S. Sax has called the "*digvijaya* ideal" of unity through territorial conquest and incorporation.[43] But Chinmayananda also signals his intention to draw critically and creatively on the received portrait in the process. In the same introduction, after briefly reviewing some of the major Śaṅkara hagiographies and singling out Mādhava's ŚDV, he goes on to offer an initial application to the present moment in history:

> Today, there is throughout the country a great enthusiasm in *Śaṅkara*; the signs of revival are everywhere around us. On *Śrī Śaṅkara Jayantī* day, we find celebrations everywhere. Unfortunately, none of the thundering platforms successfully brings out the personality of this great Master from *Kālaḍy* . . . a lot is known of *Ādi Śaṅkara*, but very few know of "The *Śaṅkara*." The more we learn to adore him, not as a divine incarnation but as a sincere man inspired to serve the country and reconquer the nation from its slavery to alien ideologies, the more we shall successfully pay tribute to our own culture.[44]

The *dig-vijaya* ideal and language of conquest—or, more precisely (and ominously), re-conquest—ring out loud and clear. Yet, Chinmayananda also indicates that a new story needs to be told for contemporary persons, a shift in focus from "Ādi Śaṅkara" as an object of worship to "*The* Śaṅkara": that is, Śaṅkara the plain human person, inspired leader, and movement initiator.

The narrative unfolded in the core chapters of *Śaṅkara the Missionary* can be read as a faithful development of this vision. Its authors attempt to get behind "Ādi Śaṅkara" to arrive at "*The* Śaṅkara." This process of creative retrieval can be discerned, first and foremost, in the way the narrative of *Śaṅkara the Missionary* revises the introduction and conclusion of its primary source text. Mādhava's *Śaṅkaradigvijuyu* begins and ends not in the land of India but in a heavenly realm (see table 5.1).[45] After a literary preface (ŚDV 1.1–26), the work's prologue inaugurates Śaṅkara's life story by describing the consternation of all the celestial *devas* over the terrible degeneration of the Vedic *dharma*, which has been fragmented and poisoned through the spread of Buddhism and various Hindu *bhakti* cults. They beg the god Śiva for help, and he agrees to descend in the form of Śaṅkara to set things right (1.27–59). Similarly, at the conclusion of the work, after Śaṅkara first ascends the "throne of omniscience" as a symbol of his final victory (16.81–92), he travels to the holy site of Kedara, manifests his divine form as Śiva, and re-ascends to his divine abode, where he is greeted and celebrated by these same celestial beings (16.100–107).[46] Though there is brief mention, between these two ascensions, of Śaṅkara's continued teaching and his decision to send some of his disciples to Śṛṅgeri and "other places" to continue his work (16.93), the focus remains resolutely on the image of Śaṅkara himself as the "sacred centre" and "hub of the wheel" not only for the hagiographical narrative but also for the heavens and earth themselves.[47]

Given that the authors of *Śaṅkara the Missionary* include another important scene from Mādhava's prologue—namely, the defeat of leading Buddhists by Kumārila Bhaṭṭa (ŚDV 1.60–98)[48]—it is all the more telling that Śiva's heavenly court finds no place in its pages. Instead, the first chapter of the volume offers a brief sketch of the historical evolution of Hindu tradition, from the origins of Brahmanism in the Vedic period, through the subsequent rise of Jainism, Buddhism, and the *bhakti* traditions, to Śaṅkara's own era in the eighth century.[49] Its authors' interest in constructing a credible historical background for their narrative reappears at several points. At the end of chapter 1, for instance, *Śaṅkara the Missionary* provides a summary of evidence for and against assigning Śaṅkara's birth to the date 788 CE, and, at the end of the main narrative in chapter 3, its authors go on to list the various Śaṅkara hagiographies and even to concede their legendary character.[50] Despite an initial disclaimer that "the religious mind does not bother much for the history of religion,"[51] then, it is not the heavens but precisely this history that offers the primary interpretive context for understanding Śaṅkara's true significance.

In his foreword to *Śaṅkara the Missionary*—distinct from his introduction—Swami Chinmayananda notes that Ādi Śaṅkarācārya can and should be regarded as a divine *avatāra* beyond the reach of rational testing and inquiry. But he also suggests two alternative ways of viewing this divine figure: namely, as a "highly competent person," on the one hand, and as an "institution," on the other.[52] Both alternatives echo the brief sketch of "*The* Śaṅkara" presented by Chinmayananda in the introduction to the same treatise, and both also direct attention away from the heavens and toward the exigencies of human life and history, just as the overall narrative of *Śaṅkara the Missionary* does.

Chinmayananda's twofold perspective on Śaṅkara also, finally, leads us from the introduction of this new narrative to its conclusion. For, if the way that the authors of *Śaṅkara the Missionary* revise Mādhava's prologue emphasizes Śaṅkara's humanity and historical location, their reconfiguration of its conclusion clearly brings out the more institutional figure. It comes as no great surprise that, since Śiva does not descend from heaven at the beginning of this narrative, neither does Śaṅkara re-ascend to heaven at its end. After touring the most sacred sites of India, unifying the subcontinent through his teaching and debate, and ascending the throne of omniscience, he does indeed travel to the sacred site of Kedara, as in the *Śaṅkaradigvijaya*. In *this* narrative, however, he does so in order to organize his disciples to assume control of the four great religious centers (*maṭhas*) at Jagannātha Purī in the east, Śṛṅgeri in the south, Dvārakā in the west, and Jyotirdhāma in the north, to write a code of discipline to govern these *maṭhas*, and then to merge into "his own supreme state of perfect Bliss."[53] In the 1978 edition, moreover, this account at the end of chapter 3 is immediately followed by a fourth chapter that introduces the *maṭhas* in greater detail and tells the stories of the four great disciples, Padmapāda, Sureśvara, Hastāmalaka, and Toṭaka, surgically extracted from their integral places in Mādhava's main narrative and made to stand entirely on their own. Each disciple's story concludes, significantly, with his installment as the principal *ācārya* at one of the four *maṭhas*.[54]

It may be worth noting at this point that, in distinction from some of the other Śaṅkara hagiographies, Mādhava's *Śaṅkaradigvijaya* never explicitly mentions the four *maṭhas*. Given the work's widespread popularity and close association with the Śṛṅgeri *maṭha* in particular, its restraint on this score seems remarkable.[55] For Mādhava, the evidence suggests, the disciples are intended to be understood almost exclusively in terms of their relation to Śaṅkara as the central, divine figure of the narrative. In *Śaṅkara the Missionary*, on the other hand, these same disciples are understood primarily in terms of their role in further advancing the great teacher's mission. This role, the authors of *Śaṅkara the Missionary* carefully point out, continues unbroken into the present, through institutions such as the four *maṭhas* themselves and also, in connection with Śṛṅgeri, through the work of more modern movements such as the Ramakrishna Mission, the Divine Life Society, and the Chinmaya Mission.[56] The inclusion of such modern Vedānta organizations alongside and in close connection with a highly traditional center like Śṛṅgeri relocates these movements from the margins to the center of Brahmanical orthodoxy and, by association, the Hindu nationalist project;[57] yet, it also claims both Śaṅkara's and Śṛṅgeri's authorization for a missionary project that extends beyond the Indian subcontinent. Śaṅkara represents an absolutely crucial link in this historical chain, from the unification of India to the global spread of such movements as the Chinmaya Mission. The reader's attention is, nevertheless, turned away from his person and toward his continuing mission and historic legacy, unfolded in explicitly social and institutional terms. The vision of the hagiographies has been transposed and, thereby, subtly transformed.

A Religion of New Place

Thus far, I have confined my attention to the basic structure of *Śaṅkara the Missionary* and its creative re-presentation of "Ādi Śaṅkara" as "*The* Śaṅkara" of ordinary human history. The narrative remains resolutely focused on the land, religion, and culture of India. Yet, something *has* changed. These two alterations to the fabric of Mādhava's *Śaṅkaradigvijaya*, one at the story's beginning and the other at its end, function both to preserve the essential features of the traditional "conquest of the quarters" and to re-inscribe this same conquest within a longer arc that begins in the Vedic age, reaches a climax in the life and work of Śaṅkara, and then continues on, unabated, through the work of prominent Advaita institutions like the Śṛṅgeri *maṭha*, the Ramakrishna Mission, and the Chinmaya Mission itself.

We have already noted some of the ways that *Śaṅkara the Missionary*, though it cannot be considered a work of Swami Chinmayananda, nonetheless resonates with broad strokes of his own interpretation. Unsurprisingly, its authors' creative reorientation of the main narrative can also be seen to reflect his wider vision of spiritual renewal. Throughout many of his works, Chinmayananda accords great importance to individuals, institutions, and nations in contributing to a collective, worldwide work of spiritual progress. On the one hand, self-realized figures such as the Buddha, Vivekananda, and Śaṅkara have "alone brought into our life flashes of love and light, life and liveliness, which constitute the glory of all civilizations."[58] On the other, such extraordinary individuals do not merely exemplify universal human progress; they are also both agents and products of it. Thus, in his work *Love Divine*, Chinmayananda writes: "the collective activities, cultural contributions, personal sacrifices of all the fathers of spiritual culture, the dead ancestors, the Rishis, etc. are realized in the devotee who realizes the supreme love . . . The great one, on realizing Truth, enriches his mind with love, and becomes the very goal and culmination of a consistent and inexorable cultural march of evolution."[59] Historical figures and institutions play an important role in fostering authentic spiritual development, and this same development, though always focused on personal mental and intellectual dispositions, necessarily has social effects. Individual, societal, and universal human histories are mutually related and mutually implicating, and all are marching together, inexorably, toward their final fulfillment.

Though the authors of *Śaṅkara the Missionary* do not explicitly invoke Chinmayananda's vision of cultural and spiritual evolution in any detail, they do use their re-inscription of the *dig-vijaya* to set an interpretative trajectory that echoes its major themes. The first element of this new trajectory might simply be described as the progressive development of Hindu tradition from few to all, from a religion of the elite to a spiritual ideal for all Indians and, at least potentially, all humankind. This development is signaled at several key points in the narrative. When *Śaṅkara the Missionary* first introduces the religion of the Upaniṣads in chapter 1, it notes that "by its very nature this religion was severely individualistic; hence, it could only be the religion of the few."[60] In tracing the history from the Vedic period to Śaṅkara's own era, alongside an account of corruption, decline, and sectarian fragmentation familiar from the traditional hagiographies, these interpreters also describe the rise of Buddhism as a "second renaissance" of Hindu tradition and note that, through the emergence of Śaiva and Vaiṣṇava devotional sects, the teachings of the Upaniṣads became simplified and thereby gained wider acceptance among "the common people."[61] This is a significant alteration in the fabric of the traditional narrative. Śaṅkara's conquest, the reader is invited to infer, not only arrests the decline of *dharma* and restores the purity of the ancient tradition, as described in Mādhava's *Śaṅkaradigvijaya*, but also consolidates and further extends a progressive movement in history that includes both Buddhists and *bhaktins* in a positive way. They serve an indispensable role in facilitating the Advaita teachings' dynamic spread beyond the "few" to a wider public.

This progressive movement reaches its climax—if not its conclusion—in Śaṅkara's grand victory tour, as summarized at the beginning of chapter 3:

> The *Ācārya* conceived India as one cultural unit from the *Himālayas* to *Kanyākumārī* and from *Kāmarūpa* to *Gandhāra* (i.e., from Assam to Afghanistan). With his lofty vision of the cultural unity of *Bhārat*, and the supreme realisation of the one underlying God-principle pervading all the animate and inanimate world of beings and things, he could infuse into the people the idea of their essential oneness, in spite of the seemingly different customs, traditions and methods of worship. Thus it was truly a *dig-vijaya yātrā*, a triumphant tour and conquest, annihilating the forces of ignorance and disruption, of consolidation and establishment of the unifying forces of the universal brotherhood and mutual understanding, culminating in the goal of all pursuits, the intimate experience of the non-dual reality, no matter what paths were followed.[62]

Here, as before, the basic framework remains focused on the territorial and spiritual unity of India. But the description also hints at a more universalist vision, speaking of the one underlying reality of all "beings and things," of "universal brotherhood," and of the singular goal of all diverse spiritual pursuits. Customs, traditions, and "methods of worship" do not necessarily need to be reshaped or reformed to reconcile them with Brahmanical orthodoxy, unlike in the traditional hagiographies.[63] Śaṅkara's deeper conquest consists instead in a more radical revelation of such practices' "essential oneness," despite any appearance of diversity. To anyone familiar with Swami Chinmayananda's teachings, this language would carry a special resonance, echoing the many places where he extols the unique power of Advaita to transcend all boundaries of nation, culture, race, or religion.

In the actual text of *Śaṅkara the Missionary*, the unifying force and universal reach of Śaṅkara's vision does not translate into a literal, geographical spread conquest of the whole world. As we know from previous chapters, the Chinmaya Mission does not hesitate to describe Swami Chinmayananda's world travels as a global *dig-vijaya yātrā*,[64] and he himself not only accepted Western disciples but also explicitly identified the West as a prime candidate for cultural and spiritual transformation. Yet, nowhere does this new narrative of Śaṅkara's *vijaya* speak explicitly of extending it to include North America or Europe. Instead, as in the passage above, its authors establish a definite historical trajectory from few to all and integrate broadly universalist themes into the narrative itself. Building on the famous episode of Śaṅkara's meeting with Śiva in the form of an outcaste (*caṇḍāla*),[65] for instance, they characterize Śaṅkara as a person "whose heart throbbed with compassion and sympathy for all men and beings irrespective of whether they were rich or poor, learned or illiterate, *brāhmaṇa* or *caṇḍāla*."[66] Recounting the great teacher's composition of the *Bhaja Govindam*, they describe this hymn as "a philosophical song addressed to mankind as a whole."[67]

Finally, as we have seen earlier in this volume, the authors of *Śaṅkara the Missionary* follow the lead of another teacher, Swami Jñānānanda Bhāratī, in identifying Śaṅkara's four disciples as symbols of diverse spiritual paths to the one goal of Advaita.[68] In chapter 3, I deployed this analysis—originally an appendix in the 1978 edition—to outline four styles of Advaita mission.[69] But the authors of *Śaṅkara the Missionary* themselves read it more broadly as a validation of the principle of diversity as a spiritual ideal. "Thus," they write, "we have in these four great disciples an exemplification of the various levels and various paths, a rare phenomenon in the spiritual history of the country, nay, of the whole world."[70] We might draw a very rough analogy to the Pentecost narrative in Acts: just as the early apostles symbolized the spread of the movement to all nations by speaking many tongues in the Christian text, so too these four disciples may be read to restore unity and to symbolize the spread of Advaita to every possible kind of spiritual seeker, irrespective of geography or birth.

If the disciples of *Śaṅkara the Missionary* may be so interpreted, however, it is not because they speak the tongues of many nations. It is because they together embody different aspects of every human mind. Hence, prior to drawing correlations to the diversity of spiritual paths, the chapter on the four disciples dwells on their significance as symbols of a distinctive faculty psychology, with Padmapāda representing the "I-notion" (*ahaṃkara*), Sureśvara the discriminative intellect (*buddhi*), Hastāmalaka the passive consciousness (*citta*), and Toṭaka the "restless mind" (*manas*) pushed and pulled by worldly objects.[71] It is not merely Indians or Advaitins who possess this interior constitution—according to Swami Chinmayananda's teaching and the broader tradition, this is shared by each and every human person. Hence, the particular personalities of this Hindu narrative can be claimed to possess a universal resonance and intrinsic power of recognition well beyond their culture, circumstances, or historical era.

Such a strategy of internalization emerges even more forcefully a bit further along in the text, in the chapter entitled "the Philosophy of Śaṅkara." This chapter begins with the programmatic claim that Advaita "commands the admiration of the whole world," due in no small part to Śaṅkara's "scientific exposition of the *Upaniṣadik* philosophy."[72] After a brief précis of major Advaita teachings on the ultimate unity of self, world, and *Brahman*, the authors return to this familiar motif:

> Ours is an Age of Science, wherein we are trained to live and think with a spirit of enquiry. The modern scientists, by their wondrous discoveries in the world outside, have contributed much to usher in the Age of Enquiry. Their achievements deserve praise; but the scientists and the thinkers of the present generation have another role to

> play. They must deliver their brethren from an Age of Enquiry to an Era of Contemplation . . . Their enquiry and research have so far been in "the outer world," and now they must shift their field of enquiry from the world of the "object" to the "subject," that is, the enquirer himself. The enquiry into the "subject" cannot be done in any laboratory. Subjective enquiry should be pursued in one's own within. And, therefore, it is an enquiry with a difference: an enquiry which we choose to call "contemplation."[73]

On the one hand, this interpretation of Vedānta as a contemplative science appears only as an appendix in the original 1978 edition. On the other, by situating this in terms of a historical transition from the "Age of Enquiry" to the desired "Era of Contemplation," the authors of *Śaṅkara the Missionary* seem quite clearly to invite the reader to consider this new Era as the terminus of the historical trajectory established in the volume's main narrative. The teachings of the Upaniṣads, initially communicated only to the few in the late Vedic period, spread more widely through the rise of Buddhism and *bhakti* sectarianism and eventually, by means of Śaṅkara's eighth-century victory tour, become the spiritual and cultural basis of India. Then, through Śaṅkara's scientific systematization, this same teaching now emerges as a powerful force to set the world and science itself on a more deeply contemplative foundation. And here, for the first time in *Śaṅkara the Missionary*, the teaching is explicitly extended not merely to Hindus or Indians but to modern scientists and all who inhabit the "Age of Enquiry." From few to all, from outward inward, the great teacher's *vijaya* marches on.

The scientific reinterpretation of the *Upaniṣads*, of course, is not the work of Śaṅkara or even of his medieval hagiographers: it is the work of Swami Chinmayananda and other late modern Vedāntins. The section from which we have drawn the above quotation is titled "Self-Unfoldment," and close examination reveals that it is actually a lightly edited excerpt from Swami Chinmayananda's own *Manual of Self-Unfoldment*.[74] Even more intriguingly, the authors of *Śaṅkara the Missionary*, again following the account in the *Manual*, conclude their discussion of humankind's progressive evolution toward the Era of Contemplation with a conceptual map from and for such Contemplation: namely, the Body-Mind-Intellect (B-M-I) chart discussed above (figure 5.1).[75]

In the *Manual of Self-Unfoldment*, the presentation of the B-M-I chart leads Swami Chinmayananda into a discussion of *ātman*, the innermost self and "Divine Principle" of every living being, the realization of which carries the Advaitin disciple—and, indeed, any truly religious person—from "Manhood to Godhood." "Whether we like it or not," Chinmayananda concludes, "through a slow process of evolution, we are every hour creeping toward the goal of self-realisation."[76] Precisely as an evolutionary movement, this growth toward self-realization both fulfills the highest goals of the scientific era and purifies it of its worst materialistic excesses. "We must," Chinmayananda declares, "seek for strength within, marshal our abilities against the self-created enemies who surround us on every side."[77] Here we again encounter the language of conquest, but this time the addressee is simply humanity writ large, and the "quarters" are the self-generated ills of modern society.

Read in the light of the *Manual*, on which it partially depends, *Śaṅkara the Missionary* emerges as a work that establishes a new interpretive trajectory from the *vijaya* literature and, thereby, symbolically transforms the sacred geography of the hagiographies. Mādhava's *Śaṅkaradigvijaya*, as we have seen, begins and ends in the heavens; yet, its narrative draws together the sacred pilgrimage sites and four "quarters" of the Indian subcontinent. The new narrative offered by Chinmayananda and his collaborators, in turn, begins and reaches its climax in India; yet, its narrative strategically extends these quarters to all humankind, shifting the requisite pilgrimage and conquest inward to the mind and intellect of the inquirer. It is an intriguing coincidence that, in its 1978 edition, *Śaṅkara the Missionary*'s frontispiece displayed a map of Śaṅkara's India and its fifth-to-last page carried an image of the B-M-I chart. Taken as a whole, the work enacts a narrative shift from one map to the other, and with this shift effects a conceptual translocation of the tradition. Śaṅkara not only emerges as a missionary who re-establishes Hinduism and re-unifies India. He is also the herald of a new era of human history. Contemporary hearers of the Advaita teaching are thus encouraged to locate themselves and their spiritual home not only in a particular geography or tradition but also in a dynamic, progressive, historical movement that begins and takes shape in that geography and tradition but reaches its fullest extent only in a present and future "Era of Contemplation" for all humankind.

Reaping the Fruits:
Mission as Exterior and Interior Pilgrimage

In his elegantly titled *Place: A Short Introduction*, cultural geographer Tim Cresswell notes that our understandings of place never refer merely to physical landscapes but always include an inextricable element of human construction.[78] He writes: "The idea of being 'out-of-place' or 'in-place' is admittedly a simple one, but one that nonetheless conveys a sense of the way segments of the geographical world are meaningful and how those meanings both produce and are reproduced by people and their practices. A saying from Sri Lanka states: 'The fish don't talk about the water.' What this means is that we rarely explicitly become aware of and talk about that which we take for granted."[79] In the context of this passage, Cresswell is referring to the threats and opportunities posed by alternative sexualities. But the experience of geographical diffusion in a religious tradition is no less disruptive to settled, unnoticed grammars of place and no less fruitful for their reappropriation. Thus, a work like *Śaṅkara the Missionary* can be read as destabilizing settled, previously unnoticed understandings of Hindu tradition and the "quarters" of the hagiographies. It can also, perhaps more consistently, be read as an imaginative reassertion of this geography in and out of the already-destabilizing experience of the tradition's migration, diffusion, and universalization. Both dynamics—destabilization and reappropriation—inevitably arise and belong together, in the same moment of creative (re)interpretation.

And what might this mean for a comparative theology of mission, as attempted in this volume? At a first level of interpretation, one can search Christian tradition for comparable destabilizations and reappropriations of sacred place. In his influential 1987 work *To Take Place*, for example, Jonathan Z. Smith traces the ritual re-placement of the sacred sites of Jerusalem by their transposition into sacred moments of Christian liturgy and spiritual practice, culminating in their full interiorization by Ignatius of Loyola in his *Spiritual Exercises*.[80] A similar process of interiorization can be found in a work like Edith Stein's short reflection "On the History and Spirit of Carmel."[81]

In his study of a Cuban shrine in Miami, Thomas Tweed draws our attention to a more complex pattern of transformation, one that transcends the dualism of what he calls "*locative*" and "*supralocative*" religion.[82] Locative religion identifies the tradition with the sacred physical and cultural geography of a particular "homeland," as we see in many traditionalist Hindu formations; supralocative religion abstracts this geography so that it can be imaginatively reproduced in each and every "new land," as in the cases of Ignatius of Loyola and Edith Stein. In the "*translocative*" pattern proposed by Tweed, however, attention shifts from correspondences constructed by immigrant communities between "homeland" and "new land" to the dynamic movement back and forth that such correspondences may enable for those who participate in them.[83] The distinctive feature of a translocative religious identity, as articulated here, is the way it places "homeland" and "new land" into dynamic relation. The position of such religious persons and traditions is located not in one or another sense of place but in their continual, imaginative movement between them.

In his subsequent work *Crossing and Dwelling*, Tweed has gone on to make such metaphors of relation, position, and movement central to a general understanding of religion.[84] Like a watch or compass, he suggests, religious traditions orient their adherents in the world; yet, this very process of orientation also propels such adherents to cross geographical boundaries through pilgrimage and mission, to cross social boundaries of status, race, and gender, and, ultimately, to move across the "limits of embodied existence" and/or toward "the zenith of human flourishing," variously conceived.[85] "As spatial practices, religions are active verbs linked with unsubstantial nouns by bridging prepositions: *from*, *with*, *in*, *between*, *through*, and, most important, *across*. Religions designate where we are *from*, identify whom we are *with*, and prescribe how we move *across*."[86]

There is good reason to doubt whether Tweed's theory offers a truly comprehensive account of religion; indeed, he is refreshingly candid about the limits of this or any general theory.[87] Tweed's central metaphors of crossing, dwelling, and translocative religious identity may nevertheless help us better to assess the significance of the Chinmaya Mission's reinterpretation of the Śaṅkara hagiographical traditions, and its potential for comparative inquiry.

Chinmayananda and his disciples did not create an entirely new missionary movement, as I hope I have demonstrated in earlier chapters. What they did do was significant in its own right: they *mapped* this missionary movement in a distinctive way and, through such remapping, re-imagined the tradition in self-consciously translocative terms. In this case, the process of remapping took a different course than the oft-cited case of Pittsburgh's Śri Venkateśwara Temple, where the sacred geography and river systems of southern India are symbolically replicated in the Penn Hills.[88] Here, the new, transformed geography is more conceptual and historical than topographic or ecological. At one end of their new historical narrative stands the "homeland," the idealized religion and culture of ancient India. At the other stands the "new land," comprehending not merely new territories but the rationalized, interiorized, and "scientific" reading of Advaita that purportedly frees it to address all humankind—symbolized, above all, by the B-M-I chart. Finally, joining "homeland" to "new land," one encounters the dynamic figure of Śaṅkara and a creative retelling of his legendary *vijaya*.

Swami Chinmayananda's distinctive use of a schematic diagram like the B-M-I chart to ground one side of this dynamic relation suggests what might at first glance seem an unexpected Christian parallel: namely, the spiritual and missiological significance of labyrinths, those medieval designs that have gained new currency in the gardens and floor tiles of many Christian places of worship (see figure 5.2). As interpreted by Daniel K. Connelly, for example, the famous twelfth-century labyrinth design in the pavement of Chartres Cathedral does not offer a mythic representation of Theseus and the Minotaur or of Jesus' descent into the underworld, as other art historians have suggested. Rather, at least in its origins, it represented a specific response to a highly disruptive event in Christian history—that is, the loss of Jerusalem and the Holy Lands as a pilgrimage site in 1187.[89] Connelly writes: "Performing . . . scripted spaces of the labyrinth, enacting its turning and twisting course until finally reaching the center, encouraged participants to reflect upon their perambulations as a micro-journey to the city of Jerusalem by engaging them in well known and widely practiced mechanisms of meditational exercises. The labyrinth pavements thus provided a metaphoric access to the Holy City at a time when physical availability had been dramatically curtailed."[90] On the one hand, then, the labyrinth offered a metaphorical and contemplative map for the pilgrim who was prevented from making the journey to Jerusalem. On the other, as Connelly's belabored argument well attests, the connection between the original and the copy, between the pilgrimage route and its symbolic representation on the floor of Chartres, could become attenuated and forgotten. Eventually, the labyrinth attains a life of its own.

Figure 5.2. The floor labyrinth of Grace Cathedral, San Francisco, closely resembles that of Chartres Cathedral. *Source*: Creative Commons. David Clay Photography, CC BY-SA 4.0, https://commons.wikimedia.org/w/index.php?curid=71968496

The argument of *Śaṅkara the Missionary* can be read to address precisely this kind of concern, to ensure that the B-M-I chart remains anchored to the map of India—and the movement's global network to the sacred geography that gave it birth. It makes this sacred geography accessible even in its absence, and even in its sublation by the higher truths of the teaching. In this respect, *Śaṅkara the Missionary* exemplifies similar tensions evident in other forms of missionary Advaita, surveyed in the first part of this chapter: the diverse patterns of early Western adherents of the Ramakrishna Mission, the interplay of "import" and "export" Hinduism in the history of Transcendental Meditation, and my Nova Scotia guide's spontaneous affirmation, "Arunachala." In one of his *Eight Stanzas to Arunachala*, Ramana writes: "'Who is the seer?' When I sought within, I watched the disappearance of the seer and what survived him. No thought of 'I saw' arose; how then could the thought 'I did not see' arise? Who has the power to convey this in word when even Thou . . . couldst do so in ancient days by silence only? Only to convey by silence Thy (transcendent) state Thou standest as a hill, shining from heaven to earth."[91] Just as Swami Chinmayananda and his collaborators could draw a straight line from Śaṅkara's legendary all-India tour to the universal, transcultural reality symbolized by the B-M-I chart, so also Ramana Maharshi can evoke the universal reality of each and every conscious being by pointing to a very particular sacred, silent hill in South India.

There is, however, one quite significant difference between *Śaṅkara the Missionary* and these other Advaita negotiations of place: the explicit language of "conquest" (*vijaya*) in the Śaṅkara hagiographies and the rhetoric of the Chinmaya Mission. As William Sax and others have well documented, the *vijaya* ideal has played an important role in the articulation of nationalist, Hindu majoritarian visions of Indian identity, from Gandhi's struggles against British colonialism to the political rhetoric of the contemporary BJP.[92] Such nationalist visions are deeply threatening for many religious minorities, Dalits, *Ādivāsīs*, and other marginalized persons and communities in contemporary India.[93] The threat is real, and it offers a further, more sinister parallel to the medieval labyrinth. The fall of Jerusalem in 1187 was, after all, one moment in the history of the Crusades in Western Asia, which many interpreters—including not a few Hindu critics—view in relation to later

Christian collaboration with and legitimation of European colonial powers. One can think, for example, of the coercive theocratic regimes of the Portuguese *Padroado*, exported from the Iberian Peninsula to Goa and the Americas.[94] Contemporary missiologists have engaged in searching introspection about these histories and have striven to divest Christian mission from any intrinsic association with conquest.[95]

We may be helped here, however, by returning to the Śaṅkara hagiographies and to another closely related image of translocative religious identity brought out in both the B-M-I chart and the pavement stones of Chartres Cathedral: namely, pilgrimage. The medieval Crusades were, at least at their inception, disputes about protecting Christian pilgrimage routes rather than attempts to achieve territorial conquest,[96] and Jonathan Bader has demonstrated that the cities featured prominently in Śaṅkara's victory tour by the narratives of the ŚDV and other *vijayas* were major sites of pilgrimage in medieval India.[97] Three of the hagiographies Bader surveys in his magisterial *Conquest of the Four Quarters*, in fact, describe Śaṅkara's tour of South Asia primarily in terms of pilgrimage (*tīrtha-yātra*) rather than conquest (*vijaya-yātra*).[98]

This is also a significant theme in the teaching and lived practice of Swami Chinmayananda. Though the editors of one of the authorized histories describes Chinmayananda's first global itinerary in 1965 as a *vijaya*, he preferred to describe the same tour as a *Meru-vidhi*, an obligatory pilgrimage to the symbolic, fabled mountain Meru. He explained: "The job of the *mahatmas* (great souls) is to tour from place to place at all times. The *mahatmas* renounce all things. They give up love and hatred for worldly things in order to move about in the world from village to village, spreading the great culture, inspiring others, and themselves getting inspired. This has been the function and duty of all *mahatmas*."[99] Chinmayananda's international journeys more closely reflected this image of itinerant pilgrimage than they resembled conquest in any but the most rarefied sense.[100] Chinmayananda would typically visit a new country at the invitation of Mission members or fellow travelers already living in that region, following established patterns of migration in the South Asian diaspora. Along the way, he would give public lectures at universities, churches, and other venues, which sometimes attracted new devotees from beyond the migrant community. Where language or other barriers prevented Chinmayananda from offering direct instruction—such as, for example, in Mexico—he trusted that some organic connection would facilitate a wider, spontaneous dissemination of the Advaita message.[101]

When the *vijaya* of a work like *Śaṅkara the Missionary* is situated within the framework of pilgrimage (*tīrtha*), migration, and ascetic peregrination—as seems at least plausibly warranted by the hagiographical tradition and Chinmayananda's own missionary life practice—it assumes a less threatening visage. It also invites a reconsideration of Christian mission in terms of pilgrimage and spiritual migration.[102] The Christian scriptures frequently depict the working of God's salvation in history in terms of travel, including not only the self-consciously peripatetic ministries of figures like Paul the Apostle and Jesus himself but also the involuntary migrations of the people of Israel in the Hebrew Bible, of heroic figures like Ruth and Jonah, and of the earliest missionary apostles in Acts after the first persecution of the Jerusalem community.[103] Irish monks in the early medieval period spread the gospel by means of *peregrinatio pro Christo*, an ascetic practice of self-imposed exile from one's geographical home and from any rights or powers ordinarily conferred by social status.[104] In an extended reflection on Paul's Second Letter to the Corinthians, the influential Dutch Reformed missiologist David J. Bosch has drawn on these and other examples from Christian memory to articulate what he calls a "spirituality of the road."[105] "I believe," he writes, "that the church discovers her true nature only as she moves from one human world to another, when she crosses frontiers, whether these are geographical, cultural, ethnic, linguistic or sociological."[106] Translocative identity, on this reading, is intrinsic to the ecclesial project and, by extension, any authentically Christian theology of mission. To be a missionary church is to take on the arduous, self-emptying, and vulnerable existence of the migrant and the religious pilgrim.[107]

Few theologians, at least in the English-speaking world, have developed a vision of mission as migration at greater length or in more concrete detail than the ethicist Gemma Tulud Cruz. Whereas Bosch offers a meditative reading of the New Testament, Cruz develops her account of Christian spirituality from ethnographic encounters with those who are literally on the road: Filipina and

Indonesian domestic workers in Hong Kong, those fleeing violence in and from South Asia, and refugees from Latin America and the Caribbean in the United States and Europe.[108] Like Swami Chinmayananda and the authors of *Śaṅkara the Missionary*, Cruz engages these narratives through vital metaphors of place, evoking the language of landscape, "geographies," frontiers, boundaries, signposts, roads, and even "cartography" to describe both the concrete facts of migrant life and their liberating, feminist reinterpretation.[109] Also like Chinmayananda, Cruz situates the particular experiences of individuals and communities in a broader vision of human progress. She describes the "pilgrim church" of migrant Filipina household workers in Hong Kong as a "birthplace of a new humanity," in which deep bonds of solidarity are fostered through shared vulnerability and the interpenetration of diverse cultures.[110] Where Chinmayananda and his collaborators evoke a collective human journey toward a new "era of contemplation," Cruz speaks in the language of Christian eschatology. "To migrate," she writes, "is to wander away from home and whether we are migrants or not we are, all of us, as human beings, migrants, pilgrims or travelers on a journey to our eternal homeland, the new heaven and the new earth."[111]

This difference in idiom, between an "era of contemplation" and a "new heaven and new earth," is not trivial, and it draws our attention to distinctive elements of each missionary vision. For Chinmayananda and the Chinmaya Mission, the final end of humanity, and the ground of authentic human solidarity, is captured in the B-M-I chart, depicting an interior withdrawal and ascent from the body-mind-intellect (B-M-I) through objects-emotions-thoughts (O-E-T) to the true self, the divine *ātman*, symbolized by *oṃ*. Walking a Christian labyrinth, from the medieval period to the present day, similarly reimagines a literal or physical journey into a more rarefied, interiorized idiom of mystical ascent. Cruz, by contrast, explicitly criticizes such interpretations, in favor of a vision that figures the journey in terms of an embodied, corporeal descent into the passing, provisional, and evanescent reality of "*lo cotidiano* [daily life]."[112] The bodily death and resurrection of Jesus calls forth a revalorization of living bodies—and, in particular, the bodies of migrant women—as privileged sites of suffering and revelation.[113] In his "spirituality of the road," Bosch for his part argues that the missionary pilgrim constantly navigates a dynamic tension between what he calls a "Pilgrim's Progress Model" of otherworldly piety and a "Jonah Model" of immersion in the world.[114] For both Bosch and Cruz, the pilgrimage of mission proceeds primarily—or, at least, significantly—through an embrace of the world and the deep ambiguity of embodied experience, rather than through their contemplative sublation.

Missionary Advaita does not shrink from engaging the world. As we shall explore in the next chapter, several of the movements we have been following in this volume have mounted ambitious initiatives for charitable service and social reform, and some have even translated the teaching of Advaita into direct political action. And, on the other side of the ledger, it is important to note that Bosch and Cruz advance their argument for a more embodied and engaged spirituality of pilgrimage in critical dialogue not with an overly spiritualized Advaita but with an overly spiritualized Christianity. Both traditions are forced to navigate competing demands of this-worldly and other-worldly visions of religious pilgrimage—of the dynamic tension between "Jonah" and "Pilgrim's Progress" models, in Bosch's formulation. Nevertheless, the doctrine of the incarnation obviously takes a different view of the body and embodied existence than does the teaching tradition of Advaita Vedānta, and this in turn gives a specific, incommensurable character to the traditions' respective constructions of migration and missionary pilgrimage. Swami Chinmayananda's *Śaṅkara the Missionary* cannot be mapped directly on to Cruz's *Theology of Migration* or Bosch's *Spirituality of the Road*, even if all three engage comparable questions of place and translocative religious belonging.

Advaita and Christianity embody different, particular visions of religious life on the move, deeply embedded in different, particular places old and new, even as the question of place is continually transfigured by longer visions of human progress and transcultural ideals of human fulfilment. Both traditions must wrestle with their own ideologies of missionary conquest (*vijaya*), even as they strive to offer the more vulnerable, organic witness of the pilgrim or the migrant (*tīrthika*). Some element of contest and competition, as depicted so clearly in the *vijaya* literature and so amply revealed in the dark histories of colonial Christianity, is perhaps inevitable. But such competition can be tempered by humility, a mutual sense of self-imposed exile, and a determination to be or become good companions along the way. Missionary Christianity and missionary Advaita are perhaps most fruitfully imagined as rival pilgrims, clearly distinct one from the other yet drawn together by intersecting and interpenetrating lines of itinerant travel.[115] Both are summoned to extend their teachings not by consolidating control over new physical and conceptual geographies but by crossing them—and rediscovering themselves and their respective messages of freedom in and through their continual peregrination.

Conclusion

One of the common tropes deployed by Advaita teachers to illustrate the relationship between the ever-pure, changeless *ātman* and the phenomenal world is the magnet, which causes other objects to move in its unmoving, agentless presence.[116] Similarly, in a work like Śaṅkara's independent treatise, the *Upadeśasāhasrī*, the ideal teacher is depicted as essentially unmoving, attracting disciples to himself as they discover the futility of worldly pursuits, arrive at a self-generated desire for liberation, and seek instruction.[117]

But, of course, the Advaita tradition has moved, and continues to do so at an accelerated pace. According to the traditional hagiographies, it moved in the person of Śaṅkara as he traveled throughout the Indian subcontinent debating rivals and establishing the truth of the teaching. In late modernity, it has moved with the voluntary and involuntary migrations of South Asian devotees to new lands, in the global tours of such teachers as Swami Vivekananda, Swami Chinmayananda, and Maharishi Mahesh Yogi, and in the mystical, silent presence of Ramana Maharshi in a New York shrine and a low ridge above a modest farm in rural Nova Scotia. In a work like *Śaṅkara the Missionary*, this dynamic movement is given a distinctively Advaita theological—and missiological—rationale.

It is not quite accurate to say that the authors of *Śaṅkara the Missionary* extend Śaṅkara's *vijaya* to new lands beyond the "quarters" (*dik*) of the hagiographical tradition. These quarters are themselves made to move outward and upward, not unlike objects in the presence of a magnet, by means of a new mythic narrative and a new conceptual map of the tradition. In this transformed religious locality, North America, Europe, and indeed the whole world find their place in Śaṅkara's India, even as India rediscovers itself in a progressive, interior, and eminently transportable evolution of the mind. The result is not just a new map of reality for the Chinmaya movement but a new, dynamic understanding of Advaita as a missionary movement.

6

All Selves, and Whole Selves?

Striving for Social and Political Liberation

In 1935, the celebrated organist, historian, and missionary physician Albert Schweitzer published *Die Weltanschauung der Indischer Denker Mystik und Ethik*, later translated into English as *Indian Thought and Its Development*.[1] In this work, Schweitzer advanced the controversial claim that the religious traditions of South Asia could never, in and of themselves, motivate ethical engagement in the world. At issue was these traditions' orientation toward withdrawal from worldly matters and union with the Absolute, which distinguishes them from the more typically world- and life-affirming mystical worldviews of Western thinkers. In *Die Weltanschauung*, Schweitzer acknowledges the "naïve" dualism of much ancient and medieval Christian thought, celebrates the achievements of the *Bhagavad-Gītā* and its creative reinterpretation by such political leaders as Gandhi and Tagore, and positions his own work as an attempt to construct a new, synthetic ethic informed by both traditions.[2] Nevertheless, the Western thinkers clearly have the upper hand. "The pathway from imperfect to perfect recognised truth," Schweitzer writes, "leads through the valley of reality. European thought has already descended into this valley. Indian thought is still on the hill to this side of it."[3]

Advaita philosopher Sarvepalli Radhakrishnan, at that time Spalding Professor of Eastern Religions and Ethics at the University of Oxford, offered a strong response to Schweitzer just two years after *Die Weltanschauung*'s original German publication.[4] In his Sir George Birdwood Memorial Lecture, entitled "Mysticism and

Ethics in Hindu Thought," Radhakrishnan accuses Schweitzer of neglecting huge swaths of Christian history and even elements of Jesus' own teaching in his construction of Western thought.[5] He also indicts a certain form of this-worldly ethic as one of the culprits behind the worst excesses and brutality of late modernity.[6] Perhaps most significant, where Schweitzer perceives a logical contradiction between ethics and world-negating mysticism, Radhakrishnan proposes a fruitful dialectic. He writes: "When man [*sic*] realizes his essential unity with the whole of being, he expresses this unity in his life. Mysticism and ethics, other-worldliness and worldly work go together . . . Religion springs from the conviction that there is another world beyond the visible and the temporal with which man has dealings, and ethics require us to act in this world with the compelling vision of another."[7] Finally, although Radhakrishnan contends that any authentic religious vision can function in this way, he offers the Advaita Vedānta tradition of Ādi Śaṅkarācārya and his successors as one of the most fruitful and ethically compelling visions for the contemporary world.[8]

Various scholars have assessed the strengths and weaknesses of Schweitzer and Radhakrishnan's respective arguments.[9] What seems inarguable is that both theologians offered highly idiosyncratic readings of their respective traditions. Both no less surely embodied a profound commitment to mystical, ethical praxis in their writings and public lives, possibly because their readings were so idiosyncratic.[10] Important for my purpose in this chapter, both sides of their exchange also speak directly to questions of mission. A. L. Herman notes that one of Schweitzer's motives in presenting his critique of Indian religions was missiological—or, more precisely, counter-missiological. Writing in 1925, Schweitzer cautioned that "Several of these world religions, notably Buddhism and Hinduism, are beginning to claim to be superior to Christianity. Their representatives come to the West and are admired as the bringers of truth which Christianity (it is said) is not able to offer in the same way."[11] To respond to this challenge, according to Schweitzer, Western Christianity must discredit these new competitors, exposing their "monistic-pessimistic view of the world and life" and the weak "ethical content" of their mystical visions.[12] This is the very task Schweitzer would take up ten years later in *die Weltanschauung*. And his missionary provocation would, in turn, elicit Radhakrishnan's vigorous Advaita response.

The previous two chapters explored the claims of missionary Advaita to reach each and every human person, in the idiom of religious experience, and to encompass each and every new geography, in the idiom of pilgrimage and spiritual conquest. In this chapter, we shift our attention to yet another dimension of the tradition's universalist claim: namely, its potential to effect a change across every aspect of human life—spiritual, material, social, and political. Interpreters have sometimes identified a holistic approach to human transformation as a distinctive hallmark of Christian mission, taking the forms of missionary hospitals, schools, and programs of social change. The fourth major principle of the ecumenical proclamation "Christian Mission in a Multi-Religious World," for example, includes the affirmation that, "Acts of service, such as providing education, health care, relief services and acts of justice and advocacy are an integral part of witnessing to the gospel."[13] But the Christian impulse to bear such witness through charitable initiatives has also provoked controversy with Hindu critics, on the grounds that the promise of social improvement can become a material "enticement" to individual or group conversion.[14] The Schweitzer-Radhakrishnan debate reflects this controversy in a somewhat rarefied, academic form. At the same time, their exchange also holds out the possibility for authentic dialogue, substantive argument, and shared reflection about the social and ethical character of mission, in either or both traditions.

To extend this exchange into the present, this chapter attempts once again to follow a missiological theme across multiple layers of Advaita history, focusing in this case on Advaita visions of social transformation. In the first section, I draw out some of the ambiguities of Ādi Śaṅkarācārya's thought for constructing an activist vision of Advaita Vedānta, including some of the strategies deployed by recent interpreters to address such ambiguities and to establish his relevance to contemporary social ethics. I then jump ahead several centuries to explore the humanitarian programs of the Ramakrishna and Chinmaya Missions. A third section compares two patterns of Advaita political engagement in late twentieth- and early twenty-first-century North America: the electoral politics of the Natural Law Party, on the one hand, and the radical liberative agenda advanced by the Advaita theologian Anantanand Rambachan and the grassroots Sadhana coalition, on the other. In the chapter's final section, I draw these accounts of

Advaita social responsibility and political engagement into conversation with ongoing developments and contestations about the social mission of the Christian churches.

Ādi Śaṅkarācārya and the Social Content of Liberation

As we have seen at a number of points in prior chapters, the figure of Ādi Śaṅkarācārya looms large in the history of Advaita Vedānta. It may be fair to say he looms even larger in Christian ethical critiques of the tradition. A good example of this dynamic can be found in Albert Schweitzer's *Die Weltanschauung*, which we have touched on already. Though Schweitzer criticizes many Hindu and Buddhist traditions in this work, Śaṅkara and classical Advaita receive particularly strong censure. Schweitzer credits Śaṅkara for integrating devotional theism into his religious vision, but he also perceives in the great teacher's writings the full development—or nadir—of ancient Brahmanism and its mystical monism.[15] "There are two kinds of mysticism," he argues, "the one kind resulting from the assumption that the World-Spirit and the spirit of man [*sic*] are identical, and the other of ethical origin. The mysticism of identity, whether Indian or European, is not ethical either in origin or in nature and cannot become so."[16] Not only does the non-dualist vision of Śaṅkara compare unfavorably to a fully ethical worldview, according to Schweitzer, but it is intrinsically incompatible with such a view.

Schweitzer's harsh judgment finds some support in more recent scholarship. In his widely cited essay "The Dualism of Nondualism," for example, Lance E. Nelson observes that classical Advaita denies the intrinsic worth of the natural world, characterizes it as a source of suffering and fear, and equates liberation with the dissolution of the phenomenal world in the experience of the liberated sage. Such emphases, on Nelson's reading, discourage active engagement in the natural and social worlds, if they do not rule it out altogether.[17] Hindu theorist Rita Sherma similarly positions Śaṅkara as a striking example of a broader trend among classical traditions of South Asia to neglect "the relevance of *mokṣa* to *dharma*," setting final liberation in contrast to worldly life rather than viewing it as a resource and inspiration for the world's creative transformation.[18] Perhaps for this reason, S. L. Malhotra has noted a tendency among modern, politically engaged Advaitins to reject Śaṅkara or to reinterpret his teaching radically for the purposes of social action.[19]

One influential example of such a creative reinterpretation is that of Sarvepalli Radhakrishnan, not only in his response to Schweitzer but across many of his philosophical writings.[20] Somewhere in the background of Radhakrishnan's proposals stands the so-called "*tat-tvam-asi* ethic," first articulated explicitly by Arthur Schopenhauer (1788–1860), further developed by Schopenhauer's disciple, Orientalist Paul Deussen (1845–1919), and eventually adopted by Vivekananda and other missionary Vedāntins in the nineteenth and twentieth centuries.[21] This view contends that recognition of the same self in all beings can motivate concerned effort on behalf of others, as a parallel but stronger application of the Jewish and Christian precept to love one's neighbor as oneself. "One who has attained the insight that *Brahman* is *Atman*," writes one interpreter, "can be said to love others or to treat others with respect, justice and compassion because they are one with the self, the *Brahman-atman*."[22]

Consideration of the social content of Śaṅkara's teaching need not, however, end with the single great saying *tat-tvam-asi*. North American Advaitin Arvind Sharma, for example, has synthesized several passages from Śaṅkara's commentaries and the *dig-vijaya* literature to construct a "hermeneutic of human rights" grounded in the primordial unity of creation (*ekam eva*) and consequent value-equality of all persons (*puruṣa-mātra-sambandhi*).[23] In his 2006 study *The Immanent Divine*, John J. Thatamanil notes that many elements of Śaṅkara's teaching—including the great teacher's searing critique of egoism and distorted desire, and the value he places on virtues like compassion on the path to liberation—closely approximate features associated with ethical commitment and self-giving love.[24] Hugh Nicholson takes such arguments a step further, discerning an ontological basis for self-giving action on the part of the liberated Advaitin sage in Śaṅkara's acceptance of more general Hindu teachings on the origin of creation in the *līla* or joyous play of the Lord.[25] Firm identification of one's innermost self with *Brahman* may, on this reading, entail not merely a negation of the conventional self and empirical world but also the assumption of specific positive attributes of *Brahman* the divine self. From the assumption of such attributes will follow spontaneous positive activity in the world.

Perhaps the most thorough defense of Śaṅkara's ethical vision in the last decade can be found in Warren Lee Todd's comparative study, *The Ethics of Śaṅkara and Śāntideva*. Advaita disciples, Todd argues, "flicker" back and forth between their conventional perceptions of the world and their realization of highest truth. In the case of the seeker on the path, such "flickering cognition" is a matter of deliberate habituation, cultivated as a means to achieve liberating self-knowledge. In the case of the sage who has attained liberation while still living (*jīvan-mukti*), it follows instead from the residual effect of *prārabdha karma*, those past actions that have already begun to bear fruit in the present lifetime.[26] Either way, continuing experience of the world requires continued action in it. At the same time, knowledge of highest truth and detachment from the empirical mind, body, and personality transform the basis of such action, divesting it of egoism, self-interest, and self-regard. The result? A distinctive form of altruism. Whereas "Western altruism" presumes the reality of self and others and then "demands a temporary 'sacrifice'" of the self, the altruism of the Advaitin *jīvan-mukta* presumes the ultimate selflessness of all beings and then requires a temporary construction of other selves for the purpose of compassionate action. "This is not a simple 'other-regarding' ethics," Todd concludes: "it is an '*other-constructing*' ethics."[27]

Each of the above proposals makes a persuasive case for recognizing a coherent, intelligible, and thoroughly ethical worldview at the heart of Śaṅkara's teaching. With the possible exception of Sharma, however, none draws social or political consequences directly from the content of the teaching. Few scholars deny that Śaṅkara's views tend toward social conservatism, insofar as he upholds traditional restrictions against Vedic instruction for women or members of lower classes and reserves renunciation (*saṃnyāsa*) to Brahmin men.[28] And Todd in particular simply accepts that there is no inherent contradiction between such a conservative, dualistic view on caste and gender and the liberated self-knower's "non-duality of self-reflexive consciousness."[29] Each pertains to its own domain—respectively, conventional reality and highest truth. Todd also observes that Śaṅkara's altruism would appear to extend only to the spiritual good of others rather than to their social or material advancement.[30] If liberative self-knowledge is indeed the highest human good (*śreyas*), as Śaṅkara proclaims in his *Upadeśasāhasrī*, then it makes intuitive good sense that the most compassionate possible activity would be to make this highest good more widely known.[31]

In at least a few places, however, Śaṅkara does appear to recognize specific social consequences of the Advaita teaching in conventional reality.[32] Notably, these include his teaching on *karma-saṃnyāsa*, or formal renunciation. Śaṅkara associates the pursuit of self-knowledge with membership in an order of monasticism called *paramahaṃsa*, whose members abandon their ritual fires, break their sacrificial thread, remove their topknot, and carry either a single staff or no staff at all.[33] In some places this association is so close as, by all appearances, to restrict liberation to these persons alone.[34] Why? Intriguingly, the desirability of renunciant life for the seeker after knowledge appears to follow from Śaṅkara's conviction that this form of life, rather than others, emerges naturally or spontaneously (*artha-prāpta*) in the lives of those who have already attained self-knowledge.[35] True *saṃnyāsa* represents liberation's natural and inevitable consequence—a social expression, we might say, of the self-knower's non-dualist awareness, which no longer recognizes the structures of ordinary social life nor desires to benefit by performing worldly activity.[36]

Śaṅkara summarizes this idea in his commentary on the second chapter of the *Bhagavad-Gītā*, with reference to its description of the "person of steady wisdom" (*sthita-prajñaḥ*). "[T]he very characteristics of the perfected sage," he comments, "have been set forth as means to be cultivated [by the aspirant] . . . The blessed Lord recounted these [characteristics] that are at once the means, demanding effort, and also the marks."[37] If *saṃnyāsa* is a spontaneous, defining characteristic or mark (*lakṣana*) of the liberated sage, in other words, then it also becomes—*ipso facto*—something to be cultivated by disciples on the path. It can thus be called, analogically, a privileged means (*sādhana*) to attain that same liberated state. This is the same basic logic that Todd observes with reference to the "flickering" vision of sage and aspirant, described above: for one type of person, it follows as a consequence of liberating self-knowledge, whereas for another it functions as a means to achieve such knowledge. But the experiential phenomenon itself, and the altruistic ethic that flows from it, perdures across both states.

For Śaṅkara, this principle of marks and means would seem to apply narrowly to *saṃnyāsa*, and to those mental qualities of concentration, detachment, and equanimity closely associated with it. But there is little reason in principle why it could not be extended to include other characteristic marks of the sage's liberating self-awareness. Consider, for example, the ultimate equality of high-status Brahmins, low-status outcastes, purifying cows, and unclean dogs, as perceived by the person of steadfast wisdom in *Bhagavad-Gītā* 5.18.[38] Ethical striving against such injustices as racialized, caste, and gender inequality would seem to follow fairly naturally from the radical equality envisioned in this *Gītā* text. Such striving could be fruitfully reimagined as a social expression to the sage's liberated self-awareness, that is, as both mark and means of liberation. Core principles derived from Śaṅkara's argument for ascetic withdrawal from the world might then, ironically, provide some theological rationale for a thorough immersion in and ethical engagement of that same world. Through a creative extension of Śaṅkara's teaching, one or another form of embodied social praxis—a form of life that is arguably no less rigorous than formal renunciation in the *paramahaṃsa* monastic order—emerges as a no less privileged *sādhana* on the path of self-knowledge.

This would also, of course, exceed any interpretation offered by Śaṅkara himself. Schweitzer describes "Ethics," properly understood, as "responsibility towards all that lives—responsibility which has become so wide as to be limitless."[39] It must probably be conceded that Śaṅkara does not advocate such wide responsibility in his certainly authentic writings, and he therefore falls short of achieving "Ethics" as envisioned by Schweitzer.[40] At the same time, if we understand the great Advaita teacher in his own historical context, it may be unsurprising that he upheld conservative positions on class, caste, and gender. Such social conservatism does not distinguish him from his approximate contemporary, the Buddhist teacher Śāntideva,[41] nor from many revered bishops and theologians of Western Christianity.[42]

Of greater importance than Śaṅkara's own ethical positions, perhaps, are the materials he provides for subsequent Advaitins to deploy in their own contexts. And nowhere do we find better evidence of this than in the setting of late modernity.

"Organized Sevā" in the Ramakrishna and Chinmaya Missions

If it is difficult to identify clear themes of social engagement in Śaṅkara and classical Vedānta, it is nearly impossible to avoid them in the teaching of Swami Vivekananda, the international Ramakrishna movement, and most forms of missionary Advaita that emerged in their wake. In his 2006 study, *Swami Vivekananda's Legacy of Service*, Gwilym Beckerlegge offers a snapshot of the Ramakrishna Mission's works in India at the beginning of the twenty-first century: 176 mission centers animating fourteen hospitals, 141 "outdoor" and "mobile dispensaries," and six hundred schools and universities. Altogether, these services reach over seven million recipients each year.[43] Some scholars explain such engagement as a fairly straightforward imitation of "the spirit of the Western social order" or, more specifically, "Christian-style charity."[44] Wilhelm Halbfass writes of a creative "mediation" of Hindu tradition by Vivekananda and other late modern Vedāntins, provoked by their "encounter with the West" and motivated "by Western models and expectational horizons."[45] Sociologist Samta Pandya speaks more broadly of social service by various guru movements as a "legitimating" cultural practice, an "alternative and non-nationalistic way to 'perform' citizenship" in relation to the Indian state.[46]

From the interpretive perspective taken in this volume, there is no necessary contradiction between any Hindu tradition's adaptation of attitudes or practices from other sources—or its intelligibility in light of broader social patterns—and the tradition's historical integrity. Though Halbfass does ascribe Swami Vivekananda's renewed ethical vision to his encounter with the West, for example, he is also clear that this encounter did not determine the specific shape of the ethic he brought to expression. "In essence," Halbfass writes, "Vivekananda was not concerned with merely appending an ethical and social dimension onto Hindu thought, but rather with deriving this from the most basic principles of Hinduism itself."[47] If Advaita Vedānta can be interpreted as "essentially relational," as was suggested in conversation with the Christian theorist Kathryn Tanner in an earlier chapter, then processes of borrowing and creative reformulation should be viewed as evidence of religious vitality rather than of weakness or capitulation to a Europeanized global order.[48]

The influence of Western ethics on the Ramakrishna Mission and related organizations may, in any case, figure more prominently in the scholarly literature than it did in the actual history of the movement. One cannot, first, underestimate the precedent set by Rammohan Roy (1772–1883), Keshub Chandra Sen (1838–1884), and the Brahmo Samaj movement in forging a close connection between religious and social reform.[49] And Beckerlegge draws attention to the fact that the specific forms of philanthropy often associated with Christian traditions in colonial India were themselves a relatively recent innovation. The development of organized programs of social welfare in Christianity may thus be better interpreted as a parallel to, rather than as a cause of, the similar emphases on social welfare in the Brahmo Samaj, the Ramakrishna Mission, and other Hindu reform movements, reaching at least as far back as the eighteenth century.[50] Thus, Beckerlegge contends, the phenomenon of "organized *sevā*" and social engagement in the Ramakrishna movement is "not a simple consequence of either the relationship between Ramakrishna or Vivekananda or Vivekananda's exposure to Western Christianity."[51]

When Vivekananda and his fellow disciple Swami Akhandananda first committed the Mission to famine relief, for example, they were motivated primarily by an acute consciousness of famine itself as a new phenomenon. Looking at the evidence before them, they concluded that the late nineteenth century's "grim crescendo of death"—claiming upward of nineteen million Indian lives—was intimately related to disruptive changes of industrialism and colonial economic policy rather than mere changes in the weather. As a new problem, "modern famine" thus required new forms of religious response.[52] The relative independence of Vivekananda's thinking on service is further attested by the diverse range of Hindu sources he and Akhandananda mined to develop this new ethic, including traditional codes of gift-giving and caste duty, late medieval Vaiṣṇavism, and, of course, Advaita Vedānta.[53]

Beckerlegge further distinguishes two arguments developed by Vivekananda to motivate Advaita tradition for social engagement.[54] The first of these approaches, which Beckerlegge calls "service as worship," took shape in the period from the late 1880s through Vivekananda's first visit to the United States in 1893–1894, and focused in approximately equal parts on the economic uplift of

India and the renewal of Hindu religion. The pairing of Śaṅkara's "intellect" with the "heart" of the Vedānticized Buddha figured prominently in this development, along with a creative adaptation of Vaiṣṇava themes of loving service to commend the worship of God, *Narayana,* through care for the persons (*nara*) of the poor and weak.[55] This first argument became central to the famine relief effort, and included a sharp critique of caste discrimination and social inequity.[56] The Ramakrishna Mission in India "continues to speak of 'Nara-Narayana Seva' when referring to the feeding of those in need."[57]

Whereas the theme of "service as worship" emerged primarily from Vivekananda's experiences in India, the key tenets of what Beckerlegge views as a distinct second approach, "Practical Vedānta," were developed during his first travels in the United States and Europe in 1893–97, and they reflected a more international vision.[58] The "practicality" of this teaching refers less to its social relevance than to its simplicity and accessibility as a means of liberating self-knowledge.[59] As one component of this practical program, however, Vivekananda began to give special prominence to the *Bhagavad-Gītā* and its teaching on *karma-yoga,* the path of action, reinterpreted in terms of his earlier arguments for "service as worship." "When you are doing any work," he argues in his lectures on Karma Yoga, "do not think of anything beyond. Do it as worship, as the highest worship, and devote your whole life to it for the time being."[60] By connecting service to *karma-yoga,* Vivekananda contextualized it within a more recognizably classical Advaita frame. This led to further shifts in emphasis. In particular, Vivekananda increasingly associated worldly service with householders rather than renunciants, he softened the element of social critique, and he arguably came to view *sevā* primarily as a means of mental purification rather than as a distinct path to liberation.[61] He also, conspicuously, began to deploy the *tat-tvam-asi* ethic, discussed above, as a theoretical justification for organized *sevā* and wider social concern. Far from being the foundation of Vivekananda's ethics, this use of *tat-tvam-asi* appears to have been adopted strategically, to make the Advaita message more appealing to a Western audience.[62] The deeper roots of his social vision lay elsewhere.

Whatever its roots, Swami Vivekananda's vision of social engagement established a compelling pattern for other forms of missionary Advaita, including the social initiatives of such successor movements as the Divine Life Society and the Chinmaya Mission. As discussed in chapter 3, Swami Sivananda (1887–1963) worked for a decade as a physician prior to entering renunciant life, and the Divine Life Society was, at least in part, built around a free medical dispensary Sivananda founded in Rishikesh.[63] Eventually, this would blossom into a larger system of medical and educational institutions, including the highly successful "Yoga-Vedānta Academy."[64] Having received his initial formation in the Divine Life Society, Swami Chinmayananda was deeply influenced by the activist spirituality of his master, as well as the outreach activities and ethic of service of Swami Vivekananda and the Ramakrishna movement.

The Chinmaya Mission nevertheless adapted these earlier models in a distinctive way. Like Swami Vivekananda, Swami Chinmayananda draws on the *Bhagavad-Gītā* in constructing his ethic of *sevā*, but he does so in the context of Indian Independence and his own specific vision of cultural revival. In one 1975 commentary for youth under the title *The Art of Man-Making*, for example, he draws special attention to the work's narrative setting, in the midst of a pitched battle. "Religion," he concludes, "is never to be practised in jungles or forests alone . . . [It] must be lived at the market-place, at home, in the Parliament houses and in the polling booths."[65] He generalizes this principle to authorize a robust program of reform: "The *Bhagawad Geeta*, as a text-book of Hindu renaissance, has necessarily to carry within it the seeds of a thorough reformation, almost revolutionary in its impact. Fundamental values remaining the same, a religion that keeps pace with life has to adjust itself to accommodate current social problems and political conditions."[66] In accord with such an accommodationist ideal, the Chinmaya Mission eventually became associated with an extensive network of primary and secondary schools in India and the Caribbean, the Chinmaya Mission Hospital in Bangalore, an orphanage for young girls, and eight institutions of elder care under the auspices of the Central Chinmaya Vanaprastha Sansthan.[67]

Whereas the Ramakrishna movement's social programs were initiated directly by Swamis such as Vivekananda and Akhandananda and generally continue to operate under monastic leadership,[68] the Chinmaya Mission has more consistently emphasized lay leadership. This is particularly evident in the history of the Chinmaya Organization for Rural Development (CORD).[69] As described by its longtime director, Dr. Kshama Metre, and a senior project manager, Narender Paul, CORD owes its origins to an accident of geography. In 1977, the Chinmaya Mission founded an ashram for spiritual programs in the rural community of Sidhbari in the foothills of the Himalayas. This placed the Mission's core constituency of educated, middle-class devotees from prosperous urban centers into direct proximity with the rural poor, and this proximity fostered a desire for deeper relationship. First, perhaps with his formation with Swami Sivananda in mind, Chinmayananda invited two lay physicians from the movement to operate a free medical dispensary. Then, in 1985, through a cooperative arrangement with the Indian government and the United States Agency for International Development (USAID), the project was enlarged to provide health care throughout the Kangra Valley, becoming the Chinmaya Rural Primary Health Care and Training Centre.[70] Dr. Metre became director of the agency in 1987 and, through subsequent partnerships with the Ford Foundation and the government development agencies of Norway and Canada, expanded its focus from direct provision of health care to a more comprehensive approach to poverty reduction.[71]

With the creation of CORD in 2003, these programs were extended from Himachal Pradesh to rural communities in Odisha, Tamil Nadu, Andhra Pradesh, and Sri Lanka.[72] It maintains connections both to the wider Chinmaya movement, through its fund-raising affiliate CORD USA and a youth volunteer program, and to a range of secular partners, from state governments and other Indian NGOs to the Kelly School of Business of Indiana University.[73]

One of the distinctive aspects of CORD is its emphasis on women's empowerment. The training of community nurses was one of the pillars of the USAID program, and the organization's current work centers on the formation of "Mahila Mandals" or women's forums in every village.[74] Once established in any given community, the Mahila Mandals serve as catalysts for direct advocacy, for legal aid, for Self-Help Groups that qualify for government subsidized micro-credit, for cooperative agricultural initiatives, for youth empowerment programs, and finally, for strengthened political representation in local *Panchayat Raj* councils.[75] Metre and Paul defend CORD's focus on women in terms of its pragmatism and consonance with wider trends in international development. They write: "It is well-recognized that development will not flourish unless women are seen and heard . . . Investing in women is not just the right thing to do. It is the smart thing to do. Investing in the empowerment, dignity, and well-being of women enriches families, communities, and, ultimately, the country. CORD's Program in the villages has been based on this reality."[76] At the same time, again according to Metre and Paul, Swami Chinmayananda provided a separate motive for this focus on women, rooted in classical tradition: "The people of the Himalayas, especially women, have selflessly served the wandering *sadhus*. This will be our repaying of *ṛṣi ṛiṅ* (debt) to them. I want to serve them."[77] In the vision of CORD, best practices of international development and the legacy of the ancient *ṛṣis* seamlessly cohere.

This is not the only place where Metre and Paul highlight a point of synergy between their development work and the religious worldview of the Chinmaya Mission. First, echoing Vivekananda and the Ramakrishna movement, they speak of *sevā* as a response to the divine in each person, as well as a form of purification and preparation to receive liberating self-knowledge.[78] "Aptly," they write, "Ramana Maharishi (1879–1950) summarized the supreme goal of sevā as, 'Self-realization is the greatest service you can offer the world.' "[79] Second, they invoke the "*yajña* spirit" of self-sacrifice.[80] This is one of the significant leitmotivs of Swami Chinmayananda's *Art of Man-Making*.[81] In this commentary, *yajña* does not refer merely to ritual sacrifice or the interior practice of sacrificing selfish desire; instead, it evokes a positive, constructive "power to cooperatively work together for a desirable goal" or, more succinctly, "Hindu Socialism."[82] Acting with a "*yajña* spirit," then, is not merely acting without attachment to the results of action; it is acting with an eye to building up society and the common good. Chinmayananda cites *Gītā* 5.18—the sage's "equal vision" of Brahmin and outcaste, cow and dog, cited above in our discussion of Śaṅkara—to make this point. "Communal quarrels, party squabbles, inter-racial disturbances," as well as "caste prejudices" and "inter-religious animosities" are, according to Chinmayananda, "all due to seeing distinctions and not being able to recognize the subtle points of harmony."[83] From one point of view, then, CORD exists with the sole purpose of fostering harmonious, collective action, beginning with impoverished women, extending to whole villages, and eventually creating "ripples" in society as a whole.[84]

Finally, Metre and Paul characterize their approach to *sevā* as a collective process of individual self-unfoldment. They note, for example, that Swami Chinmayananda prescribed a Hindi translation of his *Manual of Self-Unfoldment* as the core spiritual text of their movement.[85] They detail a cumulative, shared practice of *svādhyāya* or self-study as a "spiritual thread" of all CORD's programs, beginning with *bhajan* chanting in the villages, taking a more intentional form in prescribed "center days" for spiritual discussion among workers at each site, and culminating in higher Vedāntic study for some team leaders, at their own discretion.[86] More deeply, Metre and Paul describe development work itself in terms of character development and progressive "self-unfoldment" on the part of individuals and communities.[87] This mandates an inclusive, participatory approach to the work: "To enable the poor and underprivileged to participate effectively in their own advancement and make informed decisions, their knowledge, capacities, and skills need to be built persistently, consistently, and continuously for meaningful and relevant change to occur. Such capacity-building has to be at the community's pace, with the community's insights and wisdom synergized with concurrent developmental changes, leveraging other stakeholders, including governmental organizations."[88] Elsewhere, in giving an account of the first meeting with a ground of rural women in Sri Lanka, they describe the work of CORD as having "nothing to distribute, but much to offer to help them unfold their potential."[89] The language of contemporary development theory has become inseparable from a specific vision of Advaita spiritual practice.

The Ramakrishna and Chinmaya Missions are not, of course, immune to critique and searching inquiry. In the present political moment, one of the most pressing questions may be their respective associations with the Hindu nationalist movement and militant Hindutva, whether overt or covert, intentional or circumstantial.[90] One could also seek to assess the effectiveness of their development initiatives by objective measures, or to discern their true motives. Samta Pandya, for example, cites one "senior Swami" of the Chinmaya Mission on the integration of religious teaching with *sevā*: "We make no qualms of the fact that our service has a strong and firm Hindu ideology backing it. It is actually a universal ideology—covering all facets and aspects and signifying a real way of life for adherents as well as those who benefit from our projects. Our main aim as a mission is to create a cadre of professionals who can carry the Vedanta message across—the Sankara bhasya of Advaita thought."[91] As Radhakrishnan observed in his debate with Schweitzer almost a century ago, social engagement should not be viewed as, in and of itself, an unambiguous good.[92] When a missionary tradition extends its outreach initiatives to include the full reality of human selves, it also becomes more deeply implicated in contested social and economic worlds, and becomes vulnerable to a wider cast of prospective critics. The examples of the Ramakrishna and Chinmaya Missions should not suggest that missionary Advaita operates above such concerns or exempt from such criticism. It suggests, instead, that the tradition's engagement and vulnerability to critique stem primarily from its willingness to draw new conclusions from the teaching of Advaita Vedānta rather than another source or influence.

Advaita Theologies of Perfect Government and Political Liberation

The humanitarian initiatives of the Ramakrishna and Chinmaya Missions aim, on the whole, to mitigate distress and to foster incremental change, and they focus on empowering individuals as agents of social and spiritual renewal. Swami Vivekananda sometimes spoke of a hierarchy of service, beginning with the "gift of food," followed by the "gift of learning" and eventually the "gift of knowledge" leading to spiritual liberation.[93] Though CORD sponsors legal aid clinics, and both mission movements have placed themselves in formal opposition to such injustices as gender and caste discrimination, both have also generally refrained from direct political advocacy.[94] They operate within existing structures, rather than challenging those structures. And their focus remains firmly on the needs of India and other countries of the global south, the so-called "Third World" of developing economies.

Some forms of missionary Advaita aim for deeper transformation. As discussed in chapter 2, for example, Maharishi Mahesh Yogi and the Transcendental Meditation movement have consistently affirmed the possibility and desirability of harmonizing relative reality with the Absolute.[95] Large sections of *The Science of Being and Art of Living* endeavor to demonstrate how the practice of TM can improve every aspect of life, at both personal and societal levels.[96] Early in the history of the movement, the Maharishi insisted that such social transformation would take place through the agency of ever-greater numbers of individual TM practitioners. "If this state of affairs is to be changed," he wrote in one pamphlet critical of democratic government, "individuals must change. *There is no other way.*"[97] In the early 1990s, however, he discerned that the movement should effect the necessary transformation more directly, particularly through the agency of political parties organized under the general aegis of "Natural Law"—not unlike the Christian Democratic parties of an earlier era. In the United States, the Natural Law Party experienced limited but significant success in municipal elections, in Arizona state politics, and in several third-party presidential campaigns that attracted some 2.2 million voters at their highest point, in the mid-1990s.[98]

The Maharishi lays out his political philosophy—what he calls the "Supreme Political Science"—in his 1995 book, *Maharishi's Absolute Theory of Government*.[99] Swami Chinmayananda would sometimes suggest that "If the microcosm changes, the macrocosm will also change."[100] The Maharishi closes this circle, insisting that "Microcosm *is* macrocosm."[101] Throughout the work, he deploys an array of diagrams to illustrate point-by-point correspondences between the hierarchical constitutions of the corpus of Vedic literature; the ordered cosmos; the human genetic code, brain, nerve, and circulatory systems; and any particular "national consciousness" in the form of a government bureaucracy.[102] Each of these realities can be traced immediately to its ontological substrate in the "Unmanifest Sound of self-referral consciousness" or "pure intelligence" of the universe;[103] hence, "Vedic Education"—that is, education in this "Unmanifest Sound" made manifest in the Sanskrit syllables and mantras of the Vedas—provides the key to unlocking harmony at the levels of individual, national, and global consciousness.[104] Ideally, as appeared briefly to be possible in Mozambique under the leadership of President Joaquim Alberto Chissano, the Maharishi envisions the foundation of new sovereignties on the Vedic principles of Transcendental Meditation.[105] More practically, he commends that each country constitute a "Group for Government," a designated community of "Yogic Flyers, Vedic Scientists, who have this ability to function from the self-referral level of consciousness" and thereby to foster a salutary "coherence in national consciousness."[106]

To achieve any of these objectives, at least in the context of North America, the movement would have to engage in what the Maharishi would later refer to as "damn Democracy."[107] Two works making a public case for TM's Advaita vision of political transformation were published in 1998: *A Manual for a Perfect Government*, by the Natural Law Party presidential candidate John Hagelin, and *A Reason to Vote*, by his campaign manager Robert Roth.[108] Written in the midst of his multiple campaigns for the White House, Hagelin's *Manual* advances the thesis that government functions most effectively when it empowers its subjects to become self-governing.[109] "The art of governing is . . . ," Hagelin writes, "to raise the deservability, and hence the destiny, of the people."[110] As might be expected, the primary tool for such self-improvement is the practice of TM, which works on both individual and collective levels for social transformation.[111] At the collective level, in perfect accord with the Maharishi's *Absolute Theory of Government*, both Hagelin and Roth propose the creation of "coherence-creating" groups of TM or specially skilled TM-Sidhi practitioners to influence the collective consciousness of whole cities and societies.[112]

Because they address their appeals to a wider public, however, both politicians are at some pains to show the deep affinity between these distinctive TM teachings and more widely recognized standards of authority and knowledge. For Roth, the primary reference points are drawn from the histories of the U.S. constitutional order and Greek, Roman, and eighteenth-century American traditions of natural law.[113] Hagelin, as a quantum physicist by training, is at greater pains to demonstrate the coherence of Advaita teaching with scientific accounts of the natural world.[114] On both Hagelin and Roth's readings, however, Natural Law includes common-sense understandings of what counts as "natural," alongside the higher science of TM. Roth devotes long sections of *A Reason to Vote* to arguments on behalf of alternative medicine, organic agriculture, and green energy, initiatives featured prominently in the Natural Law Party's platform.[115] Similarly, in his discussion of national defense, Hagelin begins with a sharp critique of a militarized culture, noting the threats posed by nuclear warfare, the hypocrisy of the U.S. arms trade, and even the widespread social effect of military personnel returning home with untreated PTSD.[116] His proposed solution is twofold. First, he commends a special contingent of TM-Sidhi practitioners to diffuse areas of conflict before they start—what he calls a "prevention wing of the military."[117] Second, he outlines a foreign policy that orients itself toward fostering the authentic good of rival nations, and a serious confrontation with the global arms trade.[118] Though these two strategic initiatives may seem rather different from a *vyavihārika* or conventional point of view, they are fully coherent from the perspective of the teaching. Both share a premise that the only way to achieve true "invincibility" is to remove the fundamental causes and means of military conflict.

Roth and Hagelin are citizens of the United States, and their arguments are cosmopolitan in content and style. Cynthia Ann Humes notes that a parallel electoral effort by TM's Ajeya Bharat Party in India adopted a far more nativist rhetorical posture, calling for the "Indianization of India" and a wholesale rejection of Western influence.[119] Nevertheless, at least arguably, both campaigns embodied a fundamentally similar, technocratic vision of social transformation in which an elite class of spiritual and intellectual elites bear primary responsibility for reshaping the political order according to a Vedic—and recognizably Advaitin—religious ideal. Since the empirical world is nondifferent from the Absolute and capable of harmonization with it, it makes sense to use every available tool to effect such harmonization, from education to foreign policy to organic agriculture to the continuous practice of Transcendental Meditation.

This is not the only way to imagine radical social change, of course, nor a complete account of the social implications of Advaita Vedānta. Thus, shortly after Hagelin's most successful presidential campaigns, a more grassroots, progressive account of political transformation began to be articulated by Advaitin theologian Anantanand Rambachan.[120] Rambachan is a contemporary disciple of Swami Dayananda Saraswati, with whom he studied when the latter was still associated with the Chinmaya Mission. In the contemporary academic study of Hinduism, he is perhaps most well known as one of the foremost defenders of verbal testimony (*śabda*) as a privileged means of self-knowledge and final liberation.[121] Like the Maharishi, then, Rambachan places the Vedic revelation at the center of his social and spiritual vision. But, from this positive affirmation, Rambachan has also launched a blistering assault on more experientialist constructions of Advaita, including the teachings of the Ramakrishna Mission, other Hindu reform movements of the nineteenth century, and the philosophy of Sarvepalli Radhakrishnan.[122] His book-length treatment of Vivekananda is titled *The Limits of Scripture*, and he employs the motif of "limits" in at least two ways: descriptively, as a critique of the false limits placed by some modern Vedāntins upon the Vedic scriptures; and, more prescriptively, as a call for Advaitins to reason within the strict limits these scriptures provide.

Rambachan's case against the modern liberal construction of Advaita Vedānta is complicated by his clear sympathies with many of its exponents' ambitions for social and political reform. Early in his career, he commended Swami Vivekananda for his opposition to race discrimination and his "openness to the possibilities of change and growth" in all religious traditions, including Hinduism.[123] And he has increasingly argued for an inclusive, egalitarian social ethic as the most logical correlate and consequence of the Advaita message.[124] In advancing this ethic, Rambachan does not shrink from invoking the witness of the *Upaniṣads* and other Hindu scriptures against more conservative co-religionists who might otherwise appear as allies in the defense of Vedic authority. Those censured include Vinayak Damodar Sarvarkar and the Hindu nationalist movement,[125] the leadership of the Chinmaya Mission,[126] and even Rambachan's own *parama-guru* Ādi Śaṅkarācārya.[127]

Rambachan's distinctive combination of scriptural conservatism with a progressive political agenda is on full display in his 2015 monograph, *A Hindu Theology of Liberation*.[128] This work is divided into two parts. In the first major portion, Rambachan outlines a constructive vision of Advaita, with an eye toward the various ways that it can, in principle, inform liberative social action.[129] In the second, he applies this constructive vision to issues of patriarchy, homophobia, anthropocentrism, childism, and caste oppression.[130] Throughout, Rambachan's key interpretive strategy involves a revalorization of the created world in two respects: first, as an expression of *Brahman*, the divine self, worthy of emulation and care; and, second, as an independent source of valid knowledge, informing ethical judgments and moral action.

It is on the first of these two points that we can discern the strongest parallels with the holistic vision of TM and the Natural Law Party. Just as Maharishi Mahesh Yogi argued not for retreat from relative reality but for its harmonization with the Absolute, so also Rambachan argues that creation should be regarded not as an illusion to be sublated but as the "celebrative self-expression of *Brahman*" to be valued and affirmed. The selfless, continuous act of value-conferral on the part of the divine provides a significant, character-forming "model for human action."[131] Rambachan establishes a correlation between the absolute reality of *Brahman* and the relative reality of human behavior not by appeal to quantum physics or another scientific idiom but through direct appeal to the Vedas. In his distinctive exegesis of the *Upaniṣads*, for example, Rambachan glosses the three "knots" of *avidyā*, *kāma*, and *karma* as "ignorance," "greed," and "greedful action," and the principal means for their untying as compassion, generosity, and a mindful sense of interdependence. Echoing the earlier rhetoric of Swami Chinmayananda, Rambachan terms this compassionate disposition a "*Yajña* mode of being."[132] The reciprocity and mutual relation of the higher reality of *Brahman* and the natural world does not render the latter as a field for collective influence, as in TM, but as a sphere of collective obligation.[133] The correlation here functions to shape, direct, and correct human action; it does not change the character of finite action, as such.

Rambachan's realist position on the finite character of human action resonates with the second aspect of his revalorization of the created world—that is, as a source of valid knowledge. In his insistence on the Vedas as an independent *pramāṇa* for liberative self-knowledge, Rambachan contends equally strongly for the independence of other *pramāṇas*, such as perception and inference, for knowing phenomenal reality, including "details and order of the creation of the world."[134] Thus, although Rambachan's arguments against patriarchy and caste oppression are rooted most fundamentally in the "identity of the self in all beings," regardless of gender or caste,[135] this theological conviction takes flesh in social reality through thick descriptions of empirical reality. He details the oppression of women and Dalits in history and in Hindu scriptures, and he adduces both demographic studies of literacy rates in the state of Kerala and the established fact of "everyday experience" to establish that "there is no necessary correlation between birth in a particular family and one's qualification for a particular kind of work."[136] So also, Rambachan does not shrink from historicizing common Hindu understandings of *dharma*, so as to broaden its valence to include concerns of justice and the common good.[137] By bringing historical experience and the social sciences to bear on the Vedic scriptures, Rambachan endeavors to demonstrate that ignorance and greedful injustice are not merely individual phenomena but are "embedded in the conventional structures of society" and in need of radical political transformation.[138]

Unlike Maharishi Mahesh Yogi and the TM movement, Anantanand Rambachan has not launched an electoral campaign or attempted to establish a new sovereign state on the principles of his *Hindu Theology of Liberation*.[139] This does not mean his vision is without political consequences. One example is the progressive Hindu service and advocacy organization, Sadhana. Co-founded by several New York–based activists and community organizers in 2011, Sadhana seeks "to stand up for social justice causes including environmental justice, racial and economic justice, gender equity, immigrant rights, and anti-casteism" based on its core principles of "*Ekatva*: Oneness of all," "*Ahimsa*: Nonviolence," and "*Seva*: Service."[140] Sadhana does not identify exclusively with Advaita but appeals to a wider Hindu constituency. However, Rambachan and another Advaita *ācārya*, Swami Bodhananda, have served on Sadhana's advisory board, and Rambachan's work significantly informs its vision of liberation.[141]

Among its advocacy work, the organization facilitates regular Sadhana Salons to discuss justice issues.[142] It provided support to the nation's first Hindu temple to join the Sanctuary Movement for undocumented immigrants,[143] and it partnered with the "Poor People's Campaign," originally founded by Reverend Martin Luther King Jr. in 1968, to demand "the rollback of voter suppression laws, rechanneling the defense budget into social welfare programs, recognizing Native Americans' sovereignty over their lands, a 'Medicare for all' healthcare system, and an end to mass incarceration, among many other policy planks."[144] On April 19, 2018, when Sadhana added its endorsement to a forty-day "Call to Moral Revival" launched by the Campaign, Anantanand Rambachan contributed a theological reflection, rooted in his liberative, Advaita critique of a "culture of greed."[145]

It would be fair, I think, to conclude that neither the theological vision of Anantanand Rambachan nor the political ambitions of the TM movement have had a world-changing impact. Compared with the more local, pragmatic development initiatives of the Ramakrishna and Chinmaya Missions, they are far more utopian in their visions of social transformation. But advocates of both the Natural Law Party and Advaita theologies of liberation would likely deny that the sole purpose of utopian thinking is to build actual utopias. John Hagelin and Robert Roth consistently maintained that the Natural Law Party sought as much to introduce new ideas into the public debate as to win elected office,[146] and Sadhana exists mainly as a progressive catalyst for various constituencies in and beyond the Hindu community to find common political cause.[147] In these and other ways, the teaching of Advaita Vedānta can serve a creative role in fostering social change and reshaping the political order, whether or not its vision comes definitively to shape that order. It can fulfill this role, however, only insofar as its message of freedom is understood to comprehend the full experiential reality of selfhood, from absolute to relative, from consciousness to embodiment, and from individual to community.

Reaping the Fruits: Mission as Holistic Transformation

This chapter has endeavored to trace several lines of development in missionary Advaita, with reference to questions of ethics and social engagement. Advaita Vedānta, as a missionary tradition, does not speak with one voice on these questions. At one end of a spectrum, perhaps, stands Ādi Śaṅkarācārya and a modern teacher like Ramana Maharshi, both of whom advocated withdrawal or indifference to worldly life—or, at least, a conviction that the highest good liberated self-knowers can offer to society is their living witness of detached serenity.[148] "Public speeches, outer activity, and material help," Ramana reportedly taught, "are all outweighed by the Silence of the Mahatmas. They accomplish more than others."[149] We might place TM at the other extreme of this spectrum insofar as it posits a complete transformation of cosmic, social, and political spheres. What the Maharishi calls the "Supreme Political Science" comprehends every aspect of life, and it does so in terms of the teaching of Advaita.

Though they vary in their particulars, the Ramakrishna Mission, the Chinmaya Organization for Rural Development, and the grassroots activism of Rambachan and the Sadhana coalition all differentiate clearly between liberating self-knowledge and activity in the phenomenal world, and they engage the latter more or less on its own terms. This places them somewhere in the middle of the spectrum. Tilting toward Śaṅkara, the Ramakrishna and Chinmaya social missions might be interpreted as sponsoring organized *sevā* primarily to cultivate ever-greater fitness to receive the teaching, on the part of *sevaks* and recipients alike. Thus, Swami Vivekananda would distinguish a hierarchy of service, beginning with food and culminating in religious teaching, and Metre and Paul situate the initiatives of the Chinmaya Organization for Rural Development within a cumulative, ongoing project of "self-unfoldment." Rambachan, though more traditionalist in a number of respects than Vivekananda or Chinmayananda, nevertheless privileges more radical political activism in his vision of social engagement, and he posits such activism as a direct consequence of Advaita. This puts his vision closer to that of TM.

What might these mission initiatives, in their diversity, suggest for comparative inquiry? In the course of my exposition, I have contested or at least tried to trouble one kind of comparison to Christian mission—namely, a comparison that purports to establish a genetic or historical relation of causation between the two phenomena. It can hardly be doubted that Advaita teachers have developed their programs in self-conscious awareness of comparable Christian and secular initiatives. Nevertheless, I agree with Beckerlegge and others that these developments are best approached in parallel and that, where these Advaita teachers have adopted recognizably Christian structures or rationales, such adaptation is more strategic than foundational. If one is looking to establish causes for new articulations of social mission in Christian and

Advaita traditions in the late nineteenth century and beyond, such causes are best sought in the conditions of late modernity itself, including the combined forces of colonialism, industrialism, and globalization and the creation of new forms of social inequality.

One piece of evidence that can be adduced to support this contention is the simple fact that questions of social engagement are not much more firmly settled in missionary Christianity than they are in missionary Advaita, right up to the present day. In his *Mission between the Times*, for example, Ecuadorian evangelical theologian C. René Padilla has drawn attention to perduring tensions in the interpretation of the *Lausanne Covenant*, a highly influential statement of Christian evangelical principles that emerged from the First International Congress of World Evangelism in 1974.[150] The *Covenant* consists of fifteen articles.[151] These address core principles of Trinitarian theology (nos. 1, 14), Biblical inerrancy (no. 2), and Christology (nos. 3, 15), along with practical matters of education, Indigenous leadership, inculturation, cooperation among churches, and the grim realities of opposition and persecution (nos. 7–13). Article 5 of the *Covenant* offers a strong statement on behalf of "social responsibility" as part and parcel of Christian mission. It includes the following affirmations: "Although reconciliation with other people is not reconciliation with God, nor is social action evangelism, nor is political liberation salvation, nevertheless we affirm that evangelism and socio-political involvement are both part of our Christian duty . . . The salvation we claim should be transforming us in the totality of our personal and social responsibilities. Faith without works is dead" (no. 5). This affirmation echoes, in its commitment to holistic transformation, not only the so-called Christian "social gospel" but also Advaita theologians like Swami Vivekananda and Anantanand Rambachan. Yet, on either side of this affirmation, the *Covenant* also describes evangelism in far more traditional terms as "the proclamation of the historical, biblical Christ as Saviour and Lord, with a view to persuading people to come to him personally and so be reconciled to God" (no. 4), and upholds such verbal proclamation and individual, personal conversion as "primary" in the Christian theology of mission (no. 6).

Padilla notes a profound disconnection between article 5 and other articles of the Covenant on questions of social responsibility.

He suggests that this stems in part from the fact that this article was the fruit of a relatively recent "awakening of the evangelical social conscience," which stood in contrast to those more firmly established convictions enshrined in articles 4 and 6.[152] As a prominent advocate of this reawakening, Padilla remains conscious of its fragility.[153] Thus, over a period of some four decades, he has advanced several theological arguments in support of "sociopolitical involvement" as an essential aspect of Christian mission. At the 1974 Congress, Padilla developed the theme of Christian "repentance" as "turning from sin to God not only in the individual's subjective consciousness but *in the world*," and he criticized any interpretation of Christian "otherworldliness" that positions religion as "a means of escape from present reality."[154] His argument was met with resistance from other attendees.[155]

In the years that followed, Padilla would continue to struggle against missionary strategies of "church growth" that sought to widen the reach of Christianity by preaching a gospel of individual prosperity or by deliberately leaving aside difficult questions of social equity and integration.[156] His arguments draw on scriptural accounts of the earliest Christian communities, the demands of Christian discipleship, and Paul the Apostle's vision of unity in Christ.[157] Padilla's core appeal, however, is to the eschatological preaching of Jesus and the early church, the "already-not yet" of the kingdom of God.[158] The gospel "must be proclaimed diligently," he wrote in 1984, in explicit reference to *Lausanne Covenant*'s article 6. "But the gospel is good news concerning the kingdom, and the kingdom is God's rule over the totality of life."[159] Hence, no aspect of life can be insulated from the call for radical reform.

Both C. René Padilla and the *Lausanne Covenant* come out of the evangelical movement, and thus stand at some remove from the Catholic and ecumenical Christian theologies that have served as my primary reference point in this book. They nevertheless provide a useful illustration of the tension around questions of social responsibility, as well as the key hermeneutic disagreement about whether the good news—the content of mission—does or does not embrace the "totality" of social and historical existence. The term Padilla coined to capture this sense of wholeness or totality is "integral mission," which he defines as

> a view of mission that conceives evangelization not as a means to become happy or successful according to worldly standards, but as a means to enroll people as followers of Jesus Christ engaged in God's mission to transform humankind according to God's purpose. Not as a way to impose on people a lifestyle defined in terms of microethical and religious categories, but as a way to enable people to place every dimension of life under the lordship of Jesus Christ.[160]

Though recognizably evangelical, this definition of "integral mission" resonates in broad detail with at least one major trajectory in Catholic theologies of mission. The Peruvian liberation theologian Gustavo Gutiérrez similarly describes a late twentieth-century shift from "quantitative" or "extensive" understanding of salvation toward those that identify the universal reach of the gospel in "qualitative" or "intensive" terms, giving an account of the good news that "embraces all human reality."[161] In his 1988 work *The Church We Believe In*, Francis A. Sullivan proposes the image of the church as a "sacrament of integral salvation" as a way to synthesize this theme as it emerges especially in the Magisterial teaching of popes and councils.[162] "[E]vangelization cannot but include the prophetic proclamation of a hereafter," wrote Pope Paul VI in his landmark 1971 apostolic exhortation on mission, *Evangelii Nuntiandi*. "But evangelization would not be complete if it did not take into account the unceasing interplay of the Gospel and of man's [*sic*] concrete life, both personal and social."[163]

No less than article 5 of the *Lausanne Covenant*, this Catholic commitment to an "integral" or holistic vision of mission is relatively recent, and still contested. Though Christianity like classical Hinduism has always valued charitable service and harmonious community relations, the transformations of late modernity brought about a significant shift in Catholic Social Teaching and the church's attitudes to social engagement. This shift is often traced to the 1891 encyclical *Rerum Novarum*, released by Pope Leo XIII at the very moment that Swami Vivekananda was touring India and developing his initial ideas about famine relief.[164] This development was consolidated and brought forward in the Second Vatican Council's

Pastoral Constitution on the Church in the Modern World, *Gaudium et Spes* (1965), successive meetings of the worldwide Synod of Bishops, papal encyclicals, and other Magisterial teachings, ably documented by Sullivan.

The articulation of an integral or holistic theology of Catholic mission arguably received its strongest expression—and most forceful opposition—in Latin America. In partial reaction to the rise of right-wing, authoritarian regimes throughout the region, Latin American bishops met together in Medellín, Colombia, in 1968 and articulated a broadly "liberationist" message of justice for the poor, grassroots activism, and denunciation of the globalized economic order as necessary consequences of the Christian gospel.[165] This synod provoked a conservative backlash, and struggles among liberationists, traditionalists, and centrists ensued over the scope and nature of the church's political engagement at subsequent meetings in Puebla, Mexico, in 1979, Santo Domingo, Dominican Republic, in 1992, and Aparecida, Brazil, in 2007.[166] The concluding document of Aparecida balances strong affirmation of a "preferential option for the poor" with a more traditional focus on individual holiness and lay responsibility for political and social life. With TM and the Natural Law Party in the background, it is notable that the document also adopts a focus on social and political elites that Alejandro Crosthwaite views as "very close to a managerialist solution to the problems beseeching the region."[167] Most important for our present purpose, the Aparecida document reaffirms that "the new life of Jesus Christ touches the entire human being," and the synod extends this holistic vision to include not merely human life but the whole ecological order.[168] This final extension of Christian mission has received further support from Pope Francis in his encyclical letters on ecological justice in 2015 and on social solidarity in 2020.[169]

Even from this brief exposition, it should be obvious that Christian and Advaita arguments on behalf of holistic mission are specifically different in many particulars. The doctrine of *jīvanmukti*, living liberation through firm knowledge of the eternally free and serene self of all beings, is directly contradicted by central precepts of Christian teaching, including the sanctification of history and perfection of relations in the coming reign of God. Such doctrinal differences inevitably give distinctive shape to the practice of social engagement in each tradition. Nevertheless, it is equally clear that, on the local level, many of the concrete issues of injustice addressed by both traditions and the grassroots initiatives they foster offer a wide field for collaboration. This is well demonstrated by the seamless participation of the Chinmaya Organization of Rural Development in a global culture of international development and public philanthropy that includes significant Christian partners, as well as Sadhana's promotion of a multifaith project like the Poor People's Campaign. And, at a higher level of abstraction, Advaitin and Christian interpreters adopt similar—and similarly diverse—strategies to extend their respective visions of humankind's "ultimate" soteriological end to "penultimate" realities like economic structures and political institutions, strategies that draw attention to what the Christian ethicist Miroslav Volf has called the "materiality of salvation."[170] One could easily imagine situations in which Advaitins like Kshama Metre or Anantanand Rambachan might find greater affinity with Christians like C. René Padilla or Gustavo Gutiérrez than with a range of more socially conservative critics, from either or both Advaita and Christian traditions.

More deeply, the comparison of missionary Advaita and missionary Christianity on questions of social responsibility might help steer Hindu–Christian relations beyond superficial associations of medical, educational, and developmental initiatives with material "inducement" to religious conversion.[171] Many of the Advaitins surveyed in this chapter freely admit a religious motive for their social initiatives, and they do not shrink from integrating study, meditation, and other elements of Advaita practice into their development programs. Nonetheless, the primary "conversion" for which they are striving is direct transformation of those economic, social, and political conditions that continue to hold persons in all kinds of bondage. For both those missionary Advaitins and those missionary Christians who adopt a truly holistic view, the work of social transformation possesses its own rationale and integrity. Such work may well provide various occasions for scriptural study and formation in the tradition, and it ideally functions as a living, embodied revelation of its teaching on liberation. But it is best conceived as an integral consequence of this teaching rather than as a cynical means for its further dissemination.[172]

Consistent with the fundamental teaching of Advaita, moreover, the conversion of social and political realities in light of the teaching typically takes the form of a return or rediscovery rather than new creation. People already possess the capabilities they need to build better lives, insist Metre and Paul of CORD. The work of development merely connects them to education and facilitates the emergence of Mahilal Mandals and other spaces for mutual learning, accountability, and collaboration. It thereby brings out those resources already present in the community but obscured by ignorance and discrimination. Maharishi Mahesh Yogi, the Natural Law Party, and Anantanand Rambachan each in different ways extends this insight to creation itself. "The deepest ground, in the Hindu tradition, for compassion and giving," writes Rambachan, "is the identity of self in all. These values express the deepest truth about the nature of reality."[173] Hence, it is not so much a matter of generating new understandings of equality and justice as remembering them, of owning up to those truths that humankind has inexplicably forgotten, and translating that recollection into politics, economics, and social activism.

In his encyclical letter *Laudato Si'*, Pope Francis strikes a similar chord. After analyzing the causes of the global climate crisis and developing several lines of response, he turns to a meditation on the religious significance of the Christian Eucharist. He writes:

> Grace, which tends to manifest itself tangibly, found unsurpassable expression when God himself became man [*sic*] and gave himself as food for his creatures. The Lord, in the culmination of the mystery of the Incarnation, chose to reach our intimate depths through a fragment of matter. He comes not from above, but from within, he comes that we might find him in this world of ours. In the Eucharist, fullness is already achieved; it is the living centre of the universe, the overflowing core of love and inexhaustible life.[174]

Here, Christians are called to pursue values like truth, justice, and ecological sustainability not as something imposed on the world "from above, but from within" that same world, in its full materiality. The basis of this claim stands in sharp contrast to Advaita insofar as it is profoundly Christological. It is solely in and through the Incarnation, the joining of God to material reality continually re-embodied in the Eucharistic celebration, that all material reality is infused with the life of God. Yet, the effect of the claim resonates strongly with Advaita traditions of social responsibility. Insofar as every fragment of the material world can be regarded, by grace, as nondifferent (*advaita*) from the highest good of human life, humankind is called to active care and advocacy for all of those fragments, separately and together.

Conclusion

"Any ethical theory," wrote Sarvepalli Radhakrishnan in 1937, in his response to Albert Schweitzer, "must be grounded in metaphysics, in a philosophical conception of the relation between human conduct and ultimate reality. As we think ultimate reality to be, so we behave. Vision and action go together."[175] Radhakrishnan's claim might be challenged as a fully descriptive, empirical statement about human morality and motivation. As a normative exhortation, however, it beautifully expresses a deep instinct of missionary Advaita. From Śaṅkara's teachings on renunciation and the path of knowledge in the eighth century to the public advocacy of the Ramakrishna Mission, the Chinmaya Organization for Rural Development, and the Natural Law Party well up to the present day, Advaitins have consistently judged that the metaphysical content of their teaching has ethical and social consequences. As in Christian tradition, so also in Advaita the conditions of late modernity accelerated a process of reflection and action, provoking new forms of social engagement.

At stake in these transformations, no less than in the accounts of religious experience and geographical extension detailed in previous chapters, is the universal reach of the tradition's message of liberation. On the one hand, the Advaita teaching radically relativizes all empirical reality, rendering it strictly secondary to the divine self of all beings. On the other hand, whether in the idiom of "service as worship," "social and political self-unfoldment," "harmonization of the absolute with the relative," or simply "*Ekatva*: Oneness of all," modern and contemporary Advaitins have continually discovered new applications and points of relevance in the contested, complex world of empirical existence. This is not only a matter of ethics; it is also a matter of mission, of extending the reach of the teaching to include the liberation of selves in their totality, inclusive of education and survival, politics and economics, conflict and struggle. It addresses the Advaita message not merely to all selves but also to whole selves.

7

From Lower to Higher Truth?[1]

Rethinking Conversion

In this study thus far, I have deliberately focused on the interpretive category of "mission" rather than "conversion."[2] The two concepts cannot be placed in a simple, one-to-one relationship in the case of missionary Advaita or any other tradition.[3] Nevertheless, the so-called "conversion controversy" was adduced early on as the most significant, proximate reason for initiating such an inquiry, and the question of conversion has continued to hang over intervening chapters. Why, for example, invoke Śaṅkara or the Buddha as missionary models, or why argue about pure, non-dualist experience as a cross-cultural ideal, if not to create opportunities for new disciples to hear the Advaita message and to receive the liberation it offers? How could one deploy a narrative of *vijaya* or spiritual conquest, propose a utopian ideal of perfect government, or extol the "Silence of the Mahatmas" without intending or perhaps at least anticipating some form of religious transformation?

This, then, is the focus of the present chapter: to return to the central point of controversy, to explore the dynamics of conversion in missionary Advaita. This is not, of course, a straightforward task. As we have seen on more than one occasion, advocates of the movements profiled in this volume have articulated, along with their more or less explicit missionary agendas, a no less explicit disavowal of conversion. They often insist that Advaita honors all paths equally, in a relationship of mutual harmony and ultimate transcendence.[4] But even one attentive historian of the Ramakrishna Mission detects an element of paradox, or possibly even deliberate self-deception, in such disclaimers. He writes:

"Ramakrishna swamis have answered—or perhaps managed to evade—the question [of conversion] by denying that they come as missionaries. They insist that their purpose is not to win converts to Hinduism but to preach the universal oneness of all religions. In fact, thousands of Americans have joined the Vedanta societies since 1893, in the process abandoning Christianity for a modern variety of Hinduism. Despite all protestations, the swamis appear to work as missionaries of Hinduism in the West."[5] Reinhart Hummel addresses such points of tension by differentiating conversion as a decisive break from one religious group to join another, as one witnesses in many forms of Christianity, from a more gradual transformation of religious milieu and transfer of primary loyalties, in missionary Hinduism.[6] Stephen R. Wilson has similarly proposed the language of "resocialization" to describe transformations in the tradition of Kripalu Yoga.[7] The Jesuit sociologist Rudolf C. Heredia, for his part, differentiates *ātmaparivartan*, "a metanoia, or a change of heart, within the same religious tradition" from *dharmāntar*, "a change in one's religious allegiance across such traditions," and he also highlights "conversion by gradual absorption and integration" as an alternative to "aggressive and organized proselytization."[8]

The proposals of Hummel, Wilson, and Heredia are useful insofar as they highlight the equivocal character of conversion within and across different traditions. This is also a point highlighted by Arvind Sharma in his landmark 2011 study, *Hinduism as a Missionary Religion*. In his exposition of the religious vision of Sarvepalli Radhakrishnan, for example, Sharma observes that the "missionary character" of Hinduism "tends to be obscured by the fact that its sense of mission is different from that of some other religions."[9] Central to this point of difference is the tradition's distinctive attitude toward conversion.[10] Most important, Sharma suggests, "Conversion to Hinduism does not entail the abandonment of one's previous allegiance (although it might entail a modification in the previous lifestyle)."[11]

Sharma's parenthetical comment here is important, insofar as it affirms that, even though conversion to Hinduism may not require the abandonment of prior commitments, that is not the same as saying that it does not effect—or attempt to effect—some specific form of transformation. Stated differently, the important question of interpretation may not be *whether* Hindu traditions promote or imagine a process of religious conversion, but *how* they do so, including attention to how these understandings and practices may differ specifically from those of Christianity or other traditions. The purpose of this chapter is to take up this question anew, with reference not to Hinduism in general, but only to the particular missionary traditions that we have been following throughout the present study.

Specifically, in this chapter I develop a theology of conversion that privileges the language of graduated improvement, sublation and inclusive ascent—a movement "from darkness to light," in the language of the *Bṛhadāraṇyaka Upaniṣad* or "from lower to higher truths," as suggested by Swami Vivekananda. In the first section, I offer a brief survey of several accounts of conversion as a cross-cultural category, focusing on the Christian philosophy of Bernard Lonergan and the social scientific studies of Lewis Rambo and Henri Gooren. Then, in two subsequent sections, I develop an outline of conversion in missionary Advaita, beginning with various conversion narratives and then moving to a critical retrieval of Sanskritization and non-dualist belonging as fruitful metaphors to interpret these narratives and to bring them into coherence with the explicit visions of Vivekananda, Swami Chinmayananda and other missionary Advaitins.[12] I conclude the chapter with a reconsideration of conversion in Christianity, focused on a constructive re-reading of the convert *par excellence,* Paul the Apostle.

In and out of a renewed encounter with the historical Paul, I suggest, it may become possible to reimagine Christian conversion as a vertical process of "Christification" or eschatological transformation, a process that may or may not be accompanied by a horizontal change of one's traditioned identity. Christianity and Advaita remain as religious competitors in this thought experiment, but the terrain of their competition shifts from an imagined, zero-sum scramble for new members to a broader spiritual process of mutual contestation, mutual purification and, at least potentially, mutual transformation.

What Is Conversion? Theological and Social-Scientific Perspectives

Few would dispute that the language of conversion, like that of mission, has an unmistakably Christian provenance. In most Christian worldviews, however, it carries a richer range of meanings than frequently presumed by either its most fervent advocates or its harshest critics. Frank Flinn offers a useful etymology:

> The English word "conversion" is derived from the Latin *convertere* which means "to revolve, turn around" or "head in a different direction." This basic meaning also holds for the biblical Hebrew word *shub* ("to turn, to return") and the Greek words *strepho* and *epistrepho*. Two other Greek words in the New Testament associated with the phenomenon of conversion convey overtones of repentance and regret. The first *metamelomai* ("to be anxious, regretful") describes the state of the subject undergoing a conversion experience. The second *metanoia* ("change of mind") describes the positive state or attitude of one who has undergone a conversion.[13]

It is telling that the Hebrew term that informs these Greek and Latin usages refers, first and foremost to the activity of turning back or making a return—to God, to God's covenant with Israel, to a path from which one had previously strayed. Only by extension does this come to mean something like a change in institutional affiliation. More fundamentally, it evokes communal and individual disciplines of renewal, reconciliation, and return.

One Christian theologian who has taken this clarification very much to heart is Canadian Jesuit Bernard J. F. Lonergan (1904–1984). In his 1971 *Method in Theology*, building on his earlier work in *Insight* (1957), Lonergan proposed that human living unfolds on four fundamental levels of consciousness: experiencing, understanding, judging, and deciding. Or, understood more actively, these four levels include the human imperatives to be attentive, to be intelligent, to be reasonable, and to be responsible.[14] Conversion, stated simply, consists of a radical reorientation at one or more levels of consciousness, "a transformation of the subject and his [*sic*] world."[15] Such transformation involves a change of "horizon," an opening of new possibilities of thought and action in the world.[16]

On Lonergan's reading, conversion involves the subject in a single movement of ever-greater openness, understanding and apprehension. At the same time, the intrinsic complexity of this knowing subject also implies a similarly complex process of conversion. At the level of intelligence and reason, "intellectual conversion" involves a transformation from "naïve realism"—the "myth that knowing is like looking, that objectivity is seeing what is there to be seen"—to "critical realism," which locates objectivity in the capacity of authentic knowers to make probable, verifiable judgments of fact.[17] At the level of decision, "Moral conversion changes the criterion of one's decisions and choices from satisfactions to values." At its furthest extent, such moral conversion opens into "religious conversion," variously described as "being grasped by ultimate concern," as "other-worldly falling in love," or as "total and permanent self-surrender without conditions, qualifications, reservations."[18]

Lonergan offers a distinctive perspective on religious conversion, not shared by all Catholic theologians—much less all Christians.[19] Nevertheless, Lonergan's students and interpreters have drawn creatively on this basic scheme and developed it further. Robert Doran, for example, has proposed "psychic conversion" as a further transformation at the level of experience, and Jeremy Blackwood has argued persuasively for a fifth level of consciousness, corresponding to religious conversion.[20] Walter Conn has drawn Lonergan's account into dialogue with several developmental theorists to analyze the famous conversion narratives of Thomas Merton (1915–1968) and John Henry Newman (1801–1890).[21] Preserved in each of these recensions is Lonergan's fundamental conviction that conversion, properly understood, has primarily to do with "self-appropriation" and "self-transcendence." One of the most striking elements of this vision of religious transformation is its vertical orientation. Conn notes, "In this approach, conversion is viewed from the perspective of structure rather than content, and may be understood as a *vertical* conversion: radically new questions creatively restructuring content (old or new) into a totally new horizon."[22]

In his account of intellectual, moral and religious conversion, Lonergan adopted the language of sublation, such that each level of conversion "goes beyond" the previous one, while also carrying lower levels "forward to a fuller realization within a richer context."[23] Lonergan makes clear, and subsequent interpreters have further emphasized, that this schema should be interpreted as holistic, rather than strictly linear: conversion and self-appropriation can progress from higher to lower levels of consciousness, as well as from lower to higher.[24] It seems safe, moreover, to presume that Lonergan positions baptism and Christian commitment as the ordinary telos of all religious conversion, insofar as such conversion is fully authentic.[25] Nevertheless, the emphasis of his account falls squarely on the interior transformation of the human person, rather than on any particular shift in institutional identity.

We witness a similar shift in focus in at least some social scientific studies of conversion as a cross-cultural phenomenon. In his influential 1993 work *Understanding Religious Conversion*, for example, Lewis Rambo treats conversion as "a process over time, not a single event," parsed developmentally into seven distinct stages.[26] In this schema, conversion includes not only "tradition transition" or movement between religious traditions, but also intensification or new affiliation within a home tradition, institutional movement within a broader family of traditions, and also defection or apostasy.[27] Finally, Rambo clarifies that, although conversion ordinarily moves through his proposed stages in sequence, "there is sometimes a spiraling effect—a going back and forth between stages."[28]

Building on the process-oriented contributions of Rambo and James T. Richardson,[29] Henri Gooren has advanced a similarly synthetic account of "conversion careers," comprehending "all episodes of higher or lower participation in one or more religious organizations during a person's life."[30] Rather than Rambo's scheme of seven successive stages, Gooren proposes five levels of participation in a religious tradition, including *preaffiliation* and *disaffiliation* at the lowest levels, on either end of the spectrum, and moving upward through mere institutional *affiliation* and deeper *conversion* to *confession* or "core member identity" at the highest level.[31] As a distinctive level of religious participation, conversion here refers to "a comprehensive personal change of religious worldview and identity, based on both self-report and attribution by others."[32] Such conversion can lay the ground for confession, or it can recede back to a more passive state of affiliation—and, depending upon social, individual and other factors, disaffiliation always remains an open possibility, from any other level.[33] In order to understand the complex dynamics at play in each kind of transition, Gooren argues that one must attend to the widest possible variety of "individual life histories," which he attempts with reference to a rich sample of Catholic, Pentecostal, Mormon, Muslim, and other converts and deconverts, drawn from Europe, the United States, and Latin America.[34]

Rambo and Gooren share with Lonergan and his interpreters a keen interest to distinguish conversion in its proper sense from mere affiliation with a religious tradition, whether this tradition be new to the potential convert or one in which she was raised or previously affiliated. Gooren makes this point in particularly strong terms: "researchers should be wary of simply equating recruitment with conversion. For researchers who wish to understand both the process and effects of conversion all over the world, the distinction between affiliation and conversion is critical. To a large degree, this distinction gives us greater insights into the high religious mobility of many individuals."[35] In addition to this point of commonality, all three theorists—one Christian theologian and two social scientists—construct conversion as a process that occurs over time, rather than a once-and-for-all event. For Lonergan and Gooren, moreover, albeit for strikingly different reasons, the trajectory of conversion is fundamentally vertical rather than horizontal.

Narratives of Conversion in Missionary Advaita

All three of the proposals surveyed in the previous section aspire to offer cross-cultural, explanatory theories of conversion. Nevertheless, all presume a normative Christian framework, in their own interpretive perspectives, in their data sets, or both.[36] Others have endeavored to broaden the range of the inquiry by means of historical case studies across various religious traditions, including in South Asia.[37] Rambo and Charles Farhadian's 2014 edited volume, the *Oxford Handbook of Religious Conversion*, takes this initiative a step further, with chapters on the theologies and practices of religious transformation not only in Christianity, Islam, and New Religious Movements but also diverse traditions of South and East Asia. In each case, the received, predominantly Christian understandings of conversion are reconfigured and significantly revised by their translation into a new religious framework. In their chapters on Islam, for instance, Marcia Hermansen and Karin Van Nieuwkerk both draw attention to themes of return, "reversion," or perfection of an original, innate faith,[38] and Dan Smyer Yü cites with approval Thich Nhat Hanh's vision of Buddhist liberation as a process of "spiritual homecoming" and ever-greater attainment of one's intrinsic Buddha Nature.[39] Andrea Jain describes conversion to Jainism in terms of gradual re-attunement and construction of a new religious identity that may subsume or coexist with other, prior such identities.[40] Finally, Arvind Sharma alludes briefly to the renowned Hindu scholar T. M. P. Mahadevan's vision of "*vertical* conversion . . . moving 'from the lower to the higher conception of God' and/or moving from a lower to a higher level of moral behavior" rather than from one religious tradition to another.[41]

In this essay, and elsewhere in his writings, Sharma speaks of vertical conversion as a feature of Hinduism in general.[42] Nevertheless, Mahadevan, Radhakrishnan—to whom Sharma attributes the original idea[43]—and Sharma himself are all closely associated with the study of Advaita Vedānta. The language of higher and lower conceptions of God would seem to map naturally onto Advaita constructions of lower and higher understandings of *Brahman* with (*saguṇa*) or without qualities (*nirguṇa*),[44] as well as the binary of lower, empirical experience (*vyāviharika*) and highest truth (*paramārthika*). That is, notwithstanding its resonance with other Hindu traditions, including the synthetic vision of Mohandas K. Gandhi,[45] this vertical orientation arguably corresponds most closely to a distinctively Advaita vision of final liberation.

Consider the ubiquitous mantra from *Bṛhadāraṇyaka Upaniṣad* 1.3.28, recited often during religious services in the Ramakrishna Mission:

> *asato mā sadgamaya//tamaso mā jyotirgamaya//mṛtyormā amṛtam gamaya*
>
> (Lead [us] from the unreal to the real, from darkness to light, from death to immortality.)

Striking in this mantra is the asymmetry between unreal and real, darkness and light, death, and immortality, as well as the concrete possibility of graded progress upwards from the lower to the higher categories. Such a schema is quite prominent in the teachings of Swami Vivekananda. "To the Hindu," he insisted at the 1893 World's Parliament of Religion, "man [*sic*] is not traveling from error to truth, but from truth to truth, from lower to higher truth."[46] Vivekananda did not hesitate to assign definite grades to different stages of development, with Dvaita or theist religious teachings at the lowest level on the ladder, Viśiṣṭādvaita or panentheist teachings in the middle, and Advaita as the final stage and these other teachings' perfect fulfillment.[47] But it is clear that these distinctions cut across any given historical tradition as well as between them.[48]

Often, then, Vivekananda and other missionary Advaitins speak of religious transformation in terms of graded progress and ascent. One can also find language that resonates more strongly with the Hebrew *shub*, a turning away from one way of life to embrace another. Thus, in his comment on *Vivekacūḍāmaṇi* 270, Swami Chinmayananda glosses the repeated phrase *anuvartanaṃ tyaktvā*—"having renounced one's following" of the world (*loka*), the body (*deha*) and the scriptures (*śāstra*)—as a call for radical reorientation:

> Without changing the old values of life and old ways of life, a new dimension of life and living cannot be achieved . . . stop living blindly a stamped blue-print of life, supplied by the fashions of the times or by the sensuous men who seek their fulfilment in sense-indulgences. Just living the routine life of unintelligent imitation of others in society is the surest way to a life of sensuality. For spiritual purposes, a most intelligent replanned way of life is to be followed. If you want to take up sincere sādhanā, you will have to redirect your life's flow.[49]

In the immediate context of the commentary, as well as his wider mission to "convert Hindus to Hinduism," it seems clear that Chinmayananda is referring here to what Lewis Rambo refers to as *intensification* and Heredia calls *ātmaparivartan*—that is, a transformation of religious commitment within the tradition.[50] Nevertheless, the sharp contrast between old and new ways of life, between rival paths of sensuality and spirituality, is striking, and there seems no intrinsic reason why it might not attract disciples from within and without the Hindu stream. This intuition is, in turn, confirmed by the presence of disciples from various backgrounds in Chinmaya Mission centres throughout India, Europe and the Americas.

To gain a clearer sense of the path—or paths—of conversion in missionary Advaita, it seems advisable to turn from the abstract pronouncements of a Vivekananda or Chinmayananda to narratives of actual converts, drawn from a combination of first-person and secondary accounts.[51] As Gooren notes in his *Religious Conversion and Disaffiliation*, such narratives should not be read as providing objective records of converts' actual experience. What they do reveal is, at least arguably, no less significant: such converts' "speech and reasoning" about their experiences of religious change, including their retrospective conceptualizations of these experiences as one or another form of conversion.[52]

One fruitful place to begin engaging such narratives is the spiritual journey of a figure we have encountered several times in previous chapters: the former Chinmaya Mission disciple and teacher, Swami Dayananda Saraswati (1930–2015). As recorded by one of his devotees, Dayananda's journey neither began nor ended with Chinmaya Mission; nevertheless, Chinmayananda and his Mission played a decisive role.[53] Natarajan Iyer's early life in Tamil Nadu was characterized by a paradoxical combination of two different emotions: cool dispassion in the face of his father's premature death, as well as fierce passion to defend the Hindu tradition from the attacks of teachers and schoolmates associated with the Dravidian movement.[54] Natarajan continued to fight Dravidian activists as a young journalist, first writing for the *Dhārmika Hindu* and then, after a brief stint with the Indian Air Force, seeking a more permanent position with the *Indian Express*. The decisive moment in his journey came in 1952, when, at a forty-one-day Jñāna Yajña, he encountered what he described as a "*Sannyāsī* with fire and inspiration," expounding the word of the *Muṇḍaka Upaniṣad*.

Dayananda's biographer describes the transformation that followed: "Thereafter, Natarajan's life took a totally different turn. He joined the *Veda-Paṭhasālā* to learn chanting of the *Vedaḥ*s . . . He was no longer interested in the job with the *Indian Express*. He waited only for Chinmayananda to come back."[55] He quickly moved up the ranks of the Mission, first as a typist, then as a brahmacārin and editor of the fortnightly publication *Tyagi*, and then, upon his initiation into renunciant life in 1962, as Swami

Dayananda Saraswati. Now an authorized teacher in the tradition, Dayananda continued editorial work, took up leadership at the newly established Sandeepany Sadhanalaya in Bombay and, in 1979, founded the first resident program in the United States, at Sandeepany West in Piercy, California.[56]

If the course at Piercy was the high point of Dayananda's career at the Chinmaya Mission, however, it was also the end of it: after the course, he severed his relationship with the Mission and established his own centers in Rishikesh, Coimbatore, and Saylorsburg, Pennsylvania.[57] The roots of this split can be traced to a period of intense personal conflict and doubt in the early 1960s, when Dayananda experienced what might be termed a second conversion. During this period, he called into question what he calls the "prevalent teaching" that "*Vedāntaḥ* was a theory and that we have to practise certain things to gain experience of *Ātmā*."[58] Dayananda scrambled to understand the mystic teachings of Ramana Maharshi and J. Krishnamurty, as well as William Blake, William James, and Zen Buddhism. A chance encounter with one Swami Pranavananda led him to dismiss Chinmayananda's account of *vāsanā*-destruction in favor of what he regarded as a more traditional emphasis upon the word of the *Upaniṣads*, the *śabda-pramāṇaṃ* or verbal means of liberating self-knowledge.[59] "No more is *Vedāntaḥ* a theory," Dayanananda writes. "No more a philosophy. Just as the eyes are the *Pramāṇaṃ* to see form and colour, *Vedāntaḥ* is the direct means of knowledge for me to remove my ignorance of *Ātmā* as *Brahma* . . . Afterwards, I had to go through the whole *Vedāntaḥ* again. I now had the key."[60] This he eventually did under the tutelage of another Advaitin teacher in Rishikesh, and the wisdom he acquired there led him entirely out of the Chinmaya movement.

Swami Dayananda's conversion narrative might best be characterized as a conversion not to Hinduism or even to the Chinmaya Mission but to the *Upaniṣads* and to what Dayananda came to identify as the "traditional teaching" of Advaita Vedānta. It is a fairly straightforward narrative of religious intensification. From his origins as a defender of Hinduism against Dravidian critics, Dayananda eventually became a defender of the authentic teaching of Advaita against those modernizers who were, on his reading, distorting it.[61]

At quite the other end of the spectrum, at least at first sight, lie narratives of converts who take up the study and practice of Advaita Vedānta from a more distant starting point in Christianity or another tradition, mostly though not exclusively from the West. In chapter 2, for example, we encountered Paul Brunton, Arthur Osborne, and Eckhart Tolle as Western followers of Ramana Maharshi, each of whom in his own way took the initiative to spread the message of Advaita to a wider public. Philip Goldberg, for his part, relates the story of Pravrajika Vrajaprana, who grew up "quasi-Protestant," read widely in world religions as a child, and encountered the Ramakrishna Mission teacher Swami Prabhavananda as an antiwar activist in 1967.[62] For some ten years, she remained informally associated with the Mission through the local Vedanta Society. After a near-fatal car accident, she experienced a renewed sense of commitment, joined the Sarada Convent in Southern California, and eventually took her final vows of *saṃnyāsa* in 1988. Of this transformation, Vrajaprana has written: "There was no defining moment when I became 'Hindu' . . . My own conversion was gradual enough to be nearly imperceptible. A few ideas planted by my parents were given impetus with my Vedanta Society encounter and then slowly gestated within me. Externally, I led a prosaic life—college, graduate school, career—but it was ultimately unsatisfying. The fulfillment I hoped to find in career and relationships was not the fulfillment I craved."[63] This fulfillment Vrajaprana would find only in the Ramakrishna monastic order, and she has emerged as one of the most prominent teachers of Vedānta in contemporary North America.[64]

In the first chapter of his monograph *A Vision for Hinduism*, Hindu theologian Jeffery Long offers a similar, albeit fuller account of his own journey to the Ramakrishna Mission.[65] Long self-consciously identifies as a "*religious* Hindu" who grew up "the only child of middle class, Roman Catholic parents" in small-town Missouri.[66] Like Swami Dayananda, Long lost his father at a young age, but for him this provoked a "dark night of the soul" that would unfold into his "formal affiliation to Hinduism, and eventually to the Ramakrishna tradition."[67] Having stumbled across a copy of the *Bhagavad-Gītā* at a local flea market, Long's young adulthood was marked by sustained study of Hindu texts and traditions, culminating in his decision to abandon a vocation to the Catholic priesthood and to join an informal *satsang* group.[68] His commitment was formalized through ritual purification and investiture with a sacred thread as a condition of marriage with a Hindu partner and then, still later, by taking *dikṣa* or formal initiation with a guru of the Ramakrishna Order.[69] Whereas Vrajaprana encountered Hindu tradition through the Ramakrishna Mission, Long first became Hindu and only subsequently, as a ritualized Hindu, found his way to missionary Advaita. In this sense, perhaps, his conversion account reveals some affinity with that of Swami Dayananda.

The picture, however, is still more complex. First of all, Long is explicitly and self-consciously reluctant to describe his narrative as a conversion *from* Catholicism to Hinduism. It represents, instead, an organic process of development and expansion: "As a characterization of this process, I think it would be more correct to say that my originally Catholic worldview gradually *expanded*, rather than that I *switched* worldviews at some discernible point in time. My attitude toward the Catholic Church is one of gratitude for my early spiritual formation, which ultimately prepared me for Hinduism. I am not the stereotypical, angry ex-Catholic."[70] More interestingly, despite his affiliation with the Ramakrishna Mission, Long honors the Advaita teaching of Swami Vivekananda in a paradoxical way: he contests it. Indeed, he makes the case that the tradition should reach behind Vivekananda to Vivekananda's own guru Sri Ramakrishna and highlight the more fundamental basis of the movement as an experientialist "synthesis of all previous forms of Vedānta."[71] For Long the convert and theologian, it is deeply significant that the Ramakrishna Mission is not merely an Advaita mission, but also one capable of integrating wisdom from many different sources, Hindu or otherwise. In this respect, his vision would seem to embody the disruptive, retraditionalizing missionary style of Sureśvara, as proposed in chapter 3.[72]

The stories of Pravrajika Vrajaprana and Jeffery Long represent clear instances of what Rambo calls "tradition transition"—that is, conversion to a new religious tradition, different from the tradition(s) of one's upbringing. Or, to adopt the language of Henri Gooren, both of their "conversion careers" are interpretable in terms of movement from initial periods of affiliation with the Ramakrishna Mission or Hindu tradition more broadly, through deeper experiences of conversion, to "confession" and active propagation of the teaching as renunciant nun and professional theologian, respectively. A somewhat different set of trajectories emerges in the life narratives of TM members and other Western practitioners of those "Hindu-Inspired Meditation Movements" surveyed by Lola Williamson in her *Transcendent in America*. As discussed in chapter 2, Maharishi Mahesh Yogi consistently presented Transcendental Meditation as a technique compatible with any religion. There is, at least in theory, no question of conversion to or from the Advaita tradition through this meditative practice. At the same time, we recall from that same discussion that scholars like Cynthia Ann Humes question whether the TM technique was ever really separable from Vedānta.[73] And Williamson herself, though she emphasizes the generic features of TM that unite it with other meditation movements like the Self-Realization Fellowship, argues that these movements should be regarded as religion in a robust sense, with distinctive worldviews, ethics, ritual practices, and cosmologies.[74]

With these qualifications in mind, it may come as no surprise that some disciples Williamson interviewed for her study describe their entry into TM in terms of a momentous, once-and-for-all event. As just one example, we have this account:

> When Maharishi came to the course, it was the first time I'd seen him in person. The only thing I could think when I saw him was that I knew exactly what Peter and James and John felt like when Jesus walked by them and said, "Come, follow me." There was a presence and a silence that was so loud, and I just felt that this was my path, and I knew without a doubt that I should follow him.[75]

We also recall that the first TM course, which trains new practitioners in the meditation technique and introduces them to the fundamentals, includes ritual initiation and the reception of a personal mantra. Williamson describes her own initiation experience as follows:

> After a second introductory lecture, I was asked to bring a flower and a clean white handkerchief on the day of initiation. When I entered the room where instruction was

> to occur, gifts in hand, I was greeted by a strong waft of incense. I saw an altar, draped in white, adorned with flowers and a picture of Guru Dev. I listened, standing next to my instructor, as he performed a ceremony, singing in Sanskrit, waving incense, and offering the flower and cloth I had brought, along with other items, to the picture of Guru Dev. At the end of the ceremony, I was asked to kneel in front of the altar . . . I felt as though my life had taken a sharp turnabout, and I was happy with the new direction.[76]

Though Williamson and some of her sources eventually became more critical of TM, she concedes that the majority of her subjects continue to find in these traditions "faith and the inner peace and stability needed to meet the challenges of living and dying."[77] Having entered a new religious world defined by the meditation movement, they feel no pressing need to look back.

This does not, however, exhaust the possible trajectories in and through the TM movement. Williamson observes that, while some members of these movements do leave their Christian or Jewish roots behind, others find ways to reintegrate these roots into their new worldview. One Catholic TM practitioner, for example, reports:

> I love taking communion. It's like a yajña. For years I thought communion was kind of silly. But I don't approach it from an intellectual standpoint anymore . . . I don't know how to relate all the Vedic things I've learned like Shiva and Vishnu and Brahma and the different aspects of Mother Divine and the Absolute and the supreme value of the relative. I don't know how to relate all that to the Father, Son, and Holy Ghost. But it doesn't matter. Every culture expresses divinity in a different way—whether the tree is divine, or Christ is divine, or God in the abstract is divine, or Mother Divine is divine. It's all the same. In a way, all those different forms are part of the illusion.[78]

In another, remarkable example, a TM practitioner named Donna actually converts to Catholicism, due in part to her conviction that

Catholic teachings on Mary reflect "all this Mother Divine stuff on the Hindu level."[79] In neither case, however, do these arguments for continued practice or even conversion to Catholicism strongly reflect orthodox or mainstream Christian beliefs. It seems clear that the Advaita teaching of TM—combined with generic elements of Hindu cosmology and popular psychology—has come to govern these practitioners' relation to Christianity, particularly when specifically Christian traditions are reduced to the status of mere "different forms" in the cosmic "illusion" of relative existence.[80]

So far, we have encountered narratives of conversion to missionary Advaita in its institutional forms, from both within and without the Hindu tradition, as well as some examples in which spiritual assimilation of the Advaita teaching is combined with institutional affiliation in the Christian tradition. But, as Gooren insists, the full range of conversion trajectories must also include accounts of disaffiliation.[81] Thus, for example, the prominent Anglican theologian Sarah Coakley narrates a deeply transformative encounter with TM in her mid-twenties, along with her self-conscious decision to deepen the insights she gained by turning away from TM or any form of Vedānta in favor of a renewed exploration of Christian mysticism.[82] And Robert K. C. Forman, in his autobiographical memoir *Enlightenment Ain't What It's Cracked Up to Be,* describes how the practice of TM as a young person helped him take responsibility for his life and advance in meditation until he had a profound experience of penetrating silence, at precisely 4 p.m. on January 4, 1972. This experience forced him to recharacterize the liberation he had been seeking as "the great unmingling."[83] He writes: "once I had dug myself through the 'glorious gloriousness' and 'resplendent resplendents [*sic*],' enlightenment became not some perfect life, but rather a much more specific psycho-physiological transformation . . . Enlightenment, as I was seeing it described in countless texts from every major tradition, is a *shift in the relationship between consciousness and its objects.* Enlightenment is the *unmingling of a commingled reality.*"[84] The remainder of Forman's memoir documents his varied attempts to work out the consequences of this realization in his very ordinary, empirical life as a married layperson and academic. One of these consequences would be his eventual separation from the TM movement. He continues to credit Maharishi Mahesh Yogi for showing him the way, but the very content of his experiential realization—in particular, his convictions about its universality across all spiritual traditions—ultimately made him a stranger to what he calls the "myopia" of institutional TM.[85]

Though their institutional trajectories could hardly be more different, Forman and Coakley both describe encounters with TM that propel them deeper into their own contemplative experience, beyond the explicit teachings of TM or any particular Advaita Vedānta movement. The late nineteenth century activist Margaret Noble (1867–1911), also known as Sister Nivedita, followed a similar, paradoxical path into and then out of the Ramakrishna Mission in pursuit of Indian nationalism, all the while remaining faithful, in her self-understanding, to the teaching of Swami Vivekananda.[86] In each of these three cases, the path to disaffiliation—or non-affiliation, in the case of Coakley—follows a course set by the Advaita message itself, as its full impact transcends the limits of institutional names and forms.

A still more paradoxical case of conversion to Advaita can be found in the example of the Hindu-Christian renunciant, Swami Abhishiktananda.[87] A French Benedictine, Henri Le Saux was summoned to India by his confrere Jules Monchanin in 1948 to attempt an experiment in monastic inculturation. It seems fair to venture that Le Saux took this experiment further than anyone expected. Between 1949 and 1955 he made a number of journeys to Arunachala and met Ramana Maharshi several times before the sage's death in 1950. After this, he placed himself in the care of another guru and began to have profound mystical experiences of *advaita*. In one of these, he powerfully addresses God as the abyss of the self: "There is no room in me for God and myself at once . . . There is but You in the depths of me, You in the depth of all. You who regard me, who summon me, who grant me being by calling me You, by making me your partner, other from You and yet inseparable, *akhanda, advaita* from you . . . OM! All is there. All that is, has been, will be."[88] Abhishiktananda continued to celebrate the Eucharist as a Catholic priest throughout his life, and he characterized the relationship between the historic Christ and his experience of *advaita* as a holy struggle, with no clear solution in the world of name and form.[89] Toward the end of his life, however, between 1971 and 1973, he began to articulate a newfound sense of peace in the midst of the struggle. "Here," he writes, "in solitude without and within, the solitude of the Only, in the transcendence of all uttering and all thinking, you understand *eimi*, 'I am'—the name under which Yahweh revealed himself. Then Easter becomes this awakening to nothing new, but to what is—to that reality that has neither origin nor end."[90] Easter here is figured as that dawning, experiential knowledge of God and self, deeper than Christianity, deeper than Advaita, deeper than both together. Swami Abhishiktananda remains Christian throughout his life, but his Christianity is purified and transformed by missionary Advaita.[91] He never converts to institutional Vedānta, but he is profoundly Vedānticized.

We can conclude this section by looking briefly at the 2011 spiritual memoir by Arvind Sharma, with whom we began our discussion in this section. In this work, entitled *One Religion Too Many*, Sharma describes his spiritual journey as emerging from a "Hindu phase," passing through a "comparative phase," and eventually arriving at a final, "emotive" embrace of "the world's religions in their totality as the religion of humanity."[92] Advaita features prominently in all three phases. Thus, Sharma's "Hindu" phase concludes with his first contact with the teachings of Ramana Maharshi and Swami Chinmayananda.[93] The second, "comparative" phase is punctuated by a consideration of Advaita and Zen as "systems of religious thought [that] are acutely conscious of the fact they are systems" in need of transcendence.[94] The third phase includes scholarly engagement of Advaita with the Christian philosophy of John Hick (1922–2012) and Sharma's own argument for "universalism" as a style of engagement with religious plurality that improves and ultimately transcends exclusivism, inclusivism, and pluralism.[95]

In *One Religion Too Many*, Sharma emerges as a Hindu who has arrived, through his study of Advaita and comparative religion, at a universalist perspective that declares of the religious inheritance of humankind, "all of it is ours."[96] In this sense, his journey closely mirrors that of Swami Abhishiktananda. In both cases, the fundamental trajectory of conversion is not out of their home traditions. Instead, it follows an upward, vertical transformation within these traditions, in dialogue with others. The movement is not from Christianity to Advaita, or vice versa, but more fundamentally, with an elegant simplicity, "from lower to higher truth."

Conversion as Sanskritization and Non-Dualist Belonging

The few, selected conversion narratives surveyed above do little more than scratch the surface. There is no easy way—for this interpreter, at least—to determine whether these particular, publicly available accounts are truly representative. To the degree that we may presume their normativity, however, we can risk some tentative conclusions. First, it seems evident that the narratives are, at one level, entirely recognizable. One can easily imagine converts to Christianity or other traditions who exceed the fervor or orthodoxy of those who converted them, like Swami Dayananda; who enter the tradition through an extended process of ever-greater religious intensity and fulfillment, like Pravrajika Vrajaprana; who have complex, hybrid religious identities like Swami Abhishiktananda, Arvind Sharma, and various practitioners of TM; who affiliate with the tradition only briefly, to return to their traditions of origin with a renewed appreciation, like Coakley; or who, like Long or Forman, are eventually led by their experience to challenge some core tenets of their adopted tradition.

At the same time, one also senses resistance to fixing the path in any single shape or form, both within any individual Advaita movement and between them. TM is in some ways the most restrictive, liberally exercising the institutional power of excommunication to maintain the purity of Maharishi's teaching. Yet, the vast majority of TM practitioners take only a single course and either practice entirely on their own or cycle into other movements.[97] The Chinmaya Mission and especially the Ramakrishna movement also exercise considerable flexibility in self-definition, with some individual Western *acāryas* differentiating the practice of Vedānta from the "religion" of Hinduism and, in the latter case, a high-profile attempt of some "Ramakrishnaites" to qualify as a new, minority religion in the Indian courts.[98] We can also recall that, according to Arthur Osborne, Ramana Maharshi's method of Self-inquiry is not a religion at all but a "new path" and "new hope" for all who submit to the Advaita teaching in the silence of their own hearts.[99] Such an understanding opens the door both to an Osborne, who lives out his later life at Arunachala and works assiduously in its publishing division, and to an Abhishiktananda, who visits the ashram only briefly and then sets out on his own, deeply personal journey of mystical contemplation and religious synthesis.

Scholars have used various terms and metaphors to try to render such a variety of accounts intelligible as a distinctive type or style of religious transformation. Jose Kuruvachira, whom we engaged in some detail in chapter 1, would insist on the language of conversion here, pure and simple—thereby establishing an unambiguous equivalence to conversion to Christianity or Islam.[100] Ankur Barua speaks instead of a classical Hindu strategy of "hierarchical encompassment," employed by Advaitins such as Vivekananda to position other religious traditions "as being ultimately oriented—whether or not their adherents are aware of this deep truth—to the neo-Advaitic transpersonal ultimate."[101] Rudolf Heredia adopts the formula "conversion as absorption" to describe what he regards as a distinctive form of proselytization. He writes that: "The decline of Buddhism in India is testimony to the absorptive capacity of Brahmanic Hinduism, which eventually converted and integrated Buddhism. By the ninth century AD, Buddha becomes the ninth avatar of Vishnu and the inherent contradictions between the two religious traditions are resolved by one driving out the other."[102] Whereas "hierarchical encompassment" would seem to make conversion to Advaita or any other tradition of Hinduism unnecessary and perhaps, at least in the present life, even impossible, "absorption" implies an explicit agenda of religious change—albeit one aimed at traditions as complete wholes, rather than merely at individual members of them.

Another term that might be employed to describe a distinctively Hindu and particularly Advaita understanding of conversion is also a controversial one: Sanskritization. As noted in chapter 1, the Christian theologian C. V. Mathew introduces the interrelated themes of "Sanskritization," "Aryanization," and "Brahminization" to give his account of mission and conversion in modern Hinduism interpretative heft. Drawing on the work of Sarvepalli Radhakrishnan, anthropologist M. N. Srinivas, and an anonymous 1913 article from *The Hindu Review*, Mathew suggests that "Sanskritization" involves a process of cultural transformation and, in Radhakrishnan's terms, the "gradual civilising" of lower castes, tribal communities and other cultures of South and Southeast Asia according to an ideal of perfect Brahminhood.[103] For Mathew, such a paradigm provides a broad historical background and justification for his inquiry into modern Hindu missionary movements. It can also become a basis for scathing critique, particularly on the part of Dalit theologians and theorists who advocate for de-Sanskritization and a thorough critique of caste hierarchy as a structure of oppression.[104] While accepting the legitimacy of both Mathew's analysis and especially Dalit critiques, I think Sanskritization merits closer examination, both as a social process and as a distinctive metaphor of conversion.

As a first step in this direction, we can note that modern critical theories of Sanskritization do not entirely support the simple, hierarchical image propounded by Radhakrishnan and deployed by Mathew in his description of Hindu missionary movements. When Srinivas employed the principle in his anthropological work, for example, he used it to describe not a doctrine of strict assimilation but a dynamic process by which caste groups self-consciously emulate Brahmin or other high-caste practices in order to advance their own social status, a process akin to—and sometimes in tension with—the process of Westernization under the British Raj.[105] Like Westernization, this transformation never flowed in just one direction: "Throughout Indian history Sanskritic Hinduism has absorbed local and folk elements and their presence makes easier the further absorption of similar elements. The absorption is done in such a way that there is a continuity between the folk and the theological or philosophical levels, and this makes possible both gradual transformation of the folk layer, as well as the 'vulgarization' of the theological layer."[106] Perhaps most importantly for Srinivas's analysis, Sanskritization was only rarely promoted by Brahmins, who often viewed such cultural processes as a threat to their privilege. Rather, the primary agents were those who wanted to advance their own social ambitions, and its specific shape varied enormously, depending upon local context. So great was this variety that Srinivas eventually attempted to generalize the concept and divest it of any necessary, substantive connection with Brahminism.[107] As an ideological agenda, Sanskritization implies some form of uplift within an hierarchical frame; as an actual historical process, however, it just as often functioned to disrupt such hierarchies and to establish new patterns of social relation.

Sheldon Pollock's more recent work on the emergence of a "Sanskrit Cosmopolis" in South and Southeast Asia between 300 and 1300 CE represents another insightful resource in this regard.[108] Pollock traces a process of Sanskritization in a very literal sense: namely, the expansion of Sanskrit from its earlier liturgical and scholastic domains to the realm of the public and the political, specifically in the proliferation of Sanskrit political inscriptions and the allied development of classical poetic forms (*kāvya*). Sharply critical of functionalist approaches that attempt to explain the spread of such cultural forms by appealing to their high status or their utility as tools of social legitimation—including, of course, Srinivas's own analysis—Pollock instead appeals directly to the intrinsic "textuality" of classical Sanskrit as "a language of cosmopolitan stature."[109] Certain features of this liturgical language, he claims, rendered it particularly suitable for bestowing a "permanent, indeed eternal, expression" upon the fame of political rulers: the stability of its grammar, its aesthetic qualities of metaphor and other figures of sense, its capacity "to interpret, supplement, [and] reveal reality," "to make the real somehow superreal by poetry."[110]

The cultural achievement of Sanskrit cosmopolis was, in Pollock's reading, never imposed through coercive power or any unified religious vision. It spread by means of "some far less obvious process of cultural imitation and borrowing," a process co-constitutive with the emergence of the textual form itself.[111] Contrary to the implicit and explicit claims made through the Sanskrit idiom in this period, moreover, this achievement was historically contingent from beginning to end, and it was emphatically not eternal. Thus, following its medieval heyday, Sanskrit was eventually displaced by various vernaculars.

Neither Srinivas nor Pollock is beyond reproach, and, as noted, their theories stand in mutual tension.[112] It would also be difficult if not impossible to argue that modern Advaita mission movements engage directly in one or another process of literal Sanskritization.[113] Indeed, both theorists would seem to challenge any use of this concept in terms of deliberate propagation, emphasizing as they do the relative autonomy and self-conscious patterns of imitation of those who become "Sanskritized." At the same time, I suggest it is precisely these aspects of their accounts that make the *metaphor* of Sanskritization an apt one for describing both the theological understandings and the embodied practice of conversion in these Advaita movements.

One illuminating example of Vivekananda's stance toward other religions, for example, can be found in a speech from 1900, in which he asks a question rich with missionary implications: "Is Vedanta the Future Religion?"[114] His initial response is irenic and congenial, insofar as he asserts that "with all its emphasis on impersonal principles, Vedanta is not antagonistic to anything."[115] Hence, it cannot be seen as a competitor to the other great religions of the world. At a deeper level, however, Vivekananda also questions whether Vedānta could qualify as a "future religion" on other grounds: not because of a presumed equality of religions but because Vedānta cannot really be regarded as "religion" at all.[116] It is instead the highest reality behind all individual religious claims, a saving knowledge of the way things actually are, now and eternally. In the light of this highest truth, particular positive religions can only be dismissed as mere "kindergartens of religion" at best and "foolish beliefs and superstitions" at worst.[117] "The hour comes," Vivekananda declares at the end of his address, "when great men [*sic*] shall arise and cast off these kindergartens of religion and shall make vivid and powerful the true religion, the worship of the spirit by the spirit."[118] Vedānta is not antagonistic to other religions precisely because it is the sole "true religion" to which all of them point, a reality so sublime that it transcends the category of "religion" itself.

A similar vision of religious transformation can be found in the teachings of the Chinmaya Mission. In his important work *A Manual of Self-Unfoldment*, Swami Chinmayananda offers the following account of Hinduism's diffusion throughout Asia:

> One of the particularities which deserves mention is that the Hindus never thrust their religion forcibly or by trickery on other people. Peace, love, compassion, sympathy and service were their watchwords. That point will be more significant later on when the actual details of the Hindu religion are discussed. The people of the foreign countries welcomed and hailed the superior culture of the Hindus. Thus one may say that Hinduism is the mother of civilisation in the East . . . This great

> religion of the Hindus is a Mighty force for universal good. That is why this religion has had such a glorious and brilliant record of past achievements and why the Hindus believe that their religion is destined for a greater and more glorious future.[119]

As he promises, Chinmayananda clarifies what he means by the Hindu "religion" a few pages further along in the same work: it is, of course, none other than Advaita Vedānta, the universal non-dualist teaching of the Hindu *Upaniṣads* and epics, as well as of the Christian Bible and all authentic scriptures worldwide.[120] Because of its universality, its glory and its self-evident superiority, this religion need not be "thrust" on other people by force or deceit. A contrast to colonial Christianity seems implied here even if it remains unstated.

This idea—and its implicit contrast to Christianity—emerges still more clearly later in the same volume, in a description of the small Study Groups that would become one of the signature features of the Chinmaya Mission. A question is raised: "Study Group. Is it a subtle means of conversion to the Hindu faith?" To this, the authors give the following response: "Not at all. Vedanta is not sectarian in appeal. As experienced by a number of members of study groups all over the world, this study makes one a better individual irrespective of whatever faith he or she may belong to. Vedanta does not seek converts. It is a great catalyst for a better understanding and self-integration. Its appeal is to the intellect and its application is universal. Hence is it used for self-improvement and never for conversion."[121] The language of "self-improvement," like the related idiom of "civilization," readily evokes images of Sanskritization. Just as Srinivas distinguished between Sanskritic theology or philosophy at one level and folk religion at another, so also here the teaching of Vedānta is situated at a higher level relative to participants' individual faith positions, such that it can serve as a catalyst for their intellectual understanding and ever greater personal integration.

Potential disciples in the Chinmaya Mission, according to this short exchange, need not fear that they will be asked to become Hindu. They need never be so asked because the language of the teaching is universal, interior, and intrinsically oriented to, in Pollock's terms, interpret, supplement, and reveal new dimensions of participants' lives. Participation in study groups simply "makes one a better individual." The point is not to convert; it is to become refined and reinscribed in the higher teaching of Advaita. If there is a new form of belonging associated with the Chinmaya Mission, such belonging is—like the teaching itself—in principle non-dualist. It remains unopposed to other forms of social and religious belonging precisely because it does not concede the perduring existence of such merely social or merely religious belonging beyond the lower, phenomenal reality of name and form.[122]

Though it may be in principle transcendent, the metaphor of Sanskritization still implies significant personal, intellectual, and spiritual transformation. In his short work *A Vedantin's View of Christian Concepts*, for example, Swami Dayananda—whose own story of conversion we have just witnessed—attempts to illustrate how Christians, and indeed Christianity itself, can be improved through its contact with the teaching of non-duality.[123] Dayananda, no less than Vivekananda and Chinmayananda, expresses a strong conviction that Vedānta represents a timeless truth with the power to include, to purify, and ultimately to sublate other religious claims. In practice, Dayananda also dismisses some central Christian doctrines, such as creation *ex nihilo*, as unintelligible; others, like the key narratives of salvation history, he interprets allegorically.[124] Through such exegetical strategies, he endeavors to demonstrate how such religious rivals as Christianity, though they are "not totally off the mark," must be re-imagined to prepare for the profound "shift in thinking" required by Vedānta.[125]

Like Vivekananda did before him, moreover, so also Dayananda suggests that the truth of Advaita is not new. It is already at work beyond the boundaries of India or Hinduism: "Wherever it is, if there is an equation: you are the whole, that's Vedānta, in whichever language. And it's available in whichever culture. That is Vedānta. Only thing is, we have a teaching tradition for that, to make that happen . . . And in other cultures it would remain as mysticism. They would be called mystics, if anyone made a statement like that."[126] Dayananda goes on to identify Meister Eckhart as precisely such a "mystic" who somehow "had some insight" beyond any explicit connection to Advaita teaching. To be truly enduring and effective, however, such generalized mysticism must evolve into a "teaching tradition" like that of Vedānta.[127] Total replacement is out of the question. On the contrary, any "shift of thinking" or conversion to Advaita would necessarily involve assimilating and bringing to perfection the best that Christians themselves have to offer.

Social theorists and historians would no doubt make the further observation that this eternal, universal teaching is also deeply contingent in its actual, concrete realizations in the world of name and form—very much like the Sanskrit cosmopolis, in Pollock's account of it.[128] To follow M. N. Srinivas's later analyses, the very process of Sanskritization implies a concomitant process of "vulgarization" or vernacularization, as both the "high" theological and the grassroots folk traditions are transformed by their mutual interaction.[129] And this is what we have witnessed, both in the conversion narratives of the previous section and, more broadly, in the diversification of the Advaita teaching into diverse movements like the Ramakrishna and Chinmaya Missions, Ramanasramam, Transcendental Meditation, and Dayananda's own Arsha Vidya Gurukulam. Conversion, in this sense, is not something that happens merely on the individual level, as prospective disciples drift into and out of contact with Vedānta. It is also something that manifests in and through these movements themselves, as they endeavor to transform persons and whole traditions through the liberating message of Advaita.

Reaping the Fruits: The Apostle Paul among Jews and Gentiles

In his *Religious Conversion and Disaffiliation*, Henri Gooren contends that, in order for the language of conversion "to remain a useful concept for scholars . . . it has to be carefully distinguished from its original religious—Christian—context and meanings." In particular, it has to be "thoroughly differentiated and nuanced" to free it from a deeply unhelpful "Christian idea of a unique and once-in-a-lifetime experience."[130] While it would probably go too far to declare the metaphor of Sanskritization, at least as developed in this chapter by a Catholic theologian, free from Christian baggage, it nevertheless can be read to represent a distinctively Hindu and

Advaita approach to religious transformation, and one that opens fresh interpretive space for thinking about conversion as a social phenomenon and as a theological ideal. In some distinction from commonly received Christian tropes, this vision of conversion is inclusive and integrative, ordinarily seeking not to draw its disciples out of their home traditions but to improve them within those traditions and to establish a higher, non-dualist horizon for their future knowing and living. Stated positively, in the language of Swami Dayanananda, this Advaita theology of conversion aims less for a change in institutional membership than for a more profound "shift in thinking" provoked by the liberating teaching of Vedānta.[131] This is not something that will usually happen in a single moment of transformation. It is the project of a lifetime—or even, in the teaching of most of these movements, multiple lifetimes.

It is important not to confuse the comparatively irenic character of this Advaita theology of conversion with an attitude of nondiscrimination or indifference with regard to the true nature of reality or the authentic path to liberation. To offer just one striking example from a premodern source, consider the vivid, obliquely threatening language of the *Vivekacūḍāmaṇi*: "The one who, having by some means obtained a human birth, with a male body and mastery of the Vedas to boot, is foolish enough not to exert himself for self-liberation, verily commits suicide (*ātma-han*), for he kills himself by clinging to things unreal. What greater fool is there than the one who having obtained a rare human body, and a male body too, neglects to achieve the proper end of this life."[132] In his commentary on this classic Advaita text, Swami Chinmayananda recasts it in important respects, downplaying restrictions of gender and caste and appealing to the vast expanse of evolutionary history rather than the cycle of rebirth to celebrate the unique gift of human selfhood.[133] Yet, his conclusion is similarly insistent. "[T]here can never be a greater fool," he writes, "than the one who, being blessed with a human birth and the necessary mental and intellectual capacities, does not intelligently invest them for the higher purpose of self redemption and self rediscovery."[134] Not every person will have the disposition to become a disciple of Advaita Vedānta. For those who do, however, it is a matter of some urgency.

It may be useful to linger on this point. Ankur Barua has argued persuasively that the primary difference between Christianity and non-dualist Hinduism on questions of conversion lies less with the former's arrogant assertion of its own truth than with the two traditions' different temporal frameworks. Hindus are not intrinsically more tolerant or pluralistic, on Barua's reading; they just do not confine spiritual progress to a single lifetime.[135] As we have seen repeatedly throughout this chapter and in previous chapters, most Advaitins no less than most Christians claim to announce a final truth, a truth without which no person can arrive at the fullness of liberation. Both advance programs of conversion insofar as movements in both traditions endeavor to recruit new disciples and to spread their respective messages of freedom. In this respect, Christianity and Advaita stand in a relation that Barua calls "epistemic peer conflict."[136] The critical difference, informed by both general Hindu beliefs and specifically Advaita teachings on *Brahman*, self-knowledge, and liberation, lies in these Advaitin missionaries' distinctive understandings of what constitutes authentic conversion to this final, uniquely efficacious religious path. There is no great urgency to attract converts in large numbers, presumably due to the tradition's capacious time frame,[137] and reception of the teaching ultimately sublates converts' home traditions or prior understandings rather than simply displacing them. In the words of Vivekananda, there is no question of "traveling from error to truth, but from truth to truth, from lower to higher truth."[138]

On the surface, this represents a serious point of tension between Christianity and Advaita. Most forms of Christianity do emphasize critical moments in the process of conversion, including creedal confession, baptism, and other rites of initiation. The baptismal ritual, and the Christian tradition more generally, require converts' renunciation of previous or inherited ways of life, and the biblical literature is replete with polemics against the idolatry of religious others. Yet, these typical emphases of Christianity may obscure what is actually significant depth and complexity. Christian philosopher Bernard Lonergan, as we witnessed in the first section of this chapter, is comfortable using the language of sublation to describe various levels and kinds of conversion, and the sociological accounts of Rambo and Gooren describe conversion as an extended process, with multiple stages or levels of engagement. If authentic conversion manifests as a vertical rather than horizontal movement, as Sharma, Mahadevan, and Radhakrishnan contend, one could in principle draw support for such a vision from these Christian or Christian-inflected sources, as well as from Advaita teaching.[139]

To explore this possibility further, we can turn back to the Christian scriptures, and in particular to one figure who tends to dominate Christian theologies of conversion: that is, Saul of Tarsus, also known as Paul the Apostle. It is telling, for example, that Gooren associates the momentous, "once-in-a-lifetime" interpretation of conversion—the one that he and others have attempted to correct—with the dramatic narrative of Paul on the road to Damascus, as recorded in the Book of Acts (9:1–22). Gooren writes: "The Pauline conversion experience greatly influenced both theological conversion models and psychologists of religion. Many of its principal elements—especially the bright light and the idea of surrender—still turn up in the conversion stories of believers all over the world."[140] From one point of view, then, Paul as ideal convert stands in the way of a more nuanced or capacious understanding of conversion in Christianity or any religious tradition, a difficulty made all the more problematic by the manner in which this image was reconfigured and deployed in support of colonial projects, including in British India.[141] At the very least, it seems clear that the kind of religious transformation described in Acts 9 scarcely resembles, and offers little space for dialogue with, the theologies of conversion to Advaita surveyed in this chapter.

But is this the only or primary model of conversion in the Christian scriptures, or even in the interpretation of Paul the Apostle? In her 1986 study, *From Darkness to Light*, Beverly Roberts Gaventa takes up this precise question. Gaventa proposes a rough typology of conversion in the Christian New Testament, including "alternation, pendulum-like conversion, and transformation."[142] "Pendulum-like conversion" corresponds roughly with what Gooren disparages as the "unique and once-in-a-lifetime" model, and this is indeed the type of conversion that Geventa discerns in Acts 9, in the Johannine and Petrine literature, and in much contemporary Christian, scholarly, and popular culture.[143] Elsewhere in Acts, particularly in the narratives of the Ethiopian eunuch (Acts 8) and the Roman centurion Cornelius (Acts 10), Gaventa identifies a different pattern. According to this second account, "changes . . . do not involve a rejection of the past and, indeed, actually develop out of one's past."[144] Conversion in this case represents an organic emergence from and confirmation of the values, beliefs and patterns of behaviour that have heretofore defined the convert's life. Hence, Gaventa refers to this type of conversion as "alternation." One might think here of Jeffery Long's judgment, in giving an account of his journey to the Ramakrishna Mission, that his "originally Catholic worldview gradually *expanded*, rather than that I *switched* worldviews."[145]

These are not the only two options, of course. When Gaventa turns to the certainly authentic letters of Paul the Apostle, she identifies a third pattern, with a relation to converts' past that pushes beyond the binary of continuity or rejection. She presents the following summary:

> What Paul describes in his letters is *transformation*. The revelation of Jesus as Messiah brought about in Paul a transformed understanding of God and God's actions in the world. As in the diagrams of Gestalt psychology, the "picture" Paul has of Jesus, Jesus' followers, and of Paul himself undergoes a radical change. What had once seemed unthinkable—a crucified Messiah—becomes a revelation. What once had seemed to be zealous becomes irrelevant, outdated, passé . . . In the transformation, Paul is able to see the "picture" in a new way.[146]

The analogy to Gestalt psychology is quite useful for our purposes insofar as it brings out the fundamentally cognitive, perspectival character of this type of conversion.[147] For Paul, the eschatological transformation of the cosmos in Christ is, in its most important respects, already completed. The transformation of individual believers and believing communities consists primarily in a new insight into, acceptance of and participation in this already-completed reality of grace. "The *apocalypse* of Jesus Christ," writes Gaventa, "does not require the rejection of the past, but its reinterpretation—its transformation."[148]

Gaventa's account of Paul's vision of conversion as a kind of transformative reinterpretation of the persons self-understanding and prior commitments, as distinct from dramatic "pendulum-like" change imposed on Paul's narrative by the author of Acts or the "alternation" model found elsewhere in the NT, already suggests several avenues for dialogue with the metaphor of Sanskritization. To add further depth to this exchange, however, it may be worth considering yet another, more recent and provocative account of conversion and religious belonging in the theology of the historical Paul. In a 2010 article and subsequent 2017 book, Paula Fredriksen has attempted to challenge several common tropes of Pauline scholarship.[149] In line with the so-called "New Perspective on Paul" inaugurated by E. P. Sanders,[150] Fredriksen argues for the thoroughly Jewish and thoroughly Hellenistic character of Paul's preaching, particularly with regard to the Mediterranean pagans to whom he primarily communicated his gospel. Like most people in the Hellenistic world, Fredriksen argues, Paul perceived little or no difference between religious identity and ethnic identity. "Gentile" and "Jew" are, for Paul, mutually exclusive, bounded categories, even given considerable permeability in practice and the rare conversion of pagans to Judaism. Like many apocalyptic Jews, Paul envisioned Gentiles turning to the Jewish God at the end of time, albeit as "ex-pagan pagans" or "eschatological pagans" rather than as Jews.[151] "Put differently," Fredriksen writes, "gentiles are indeed included in Israel's redemption; but they are included *as* gentiles. Put yet a third way: *inclusion is not conversion.*"[152]

So also for Paul the Apostle's communities of Gentiles baptized into the new age of Christ and awaiting its imminent fulfillment. These pagans were Judaized in some respects, receiving spiritual adoption as children of Abraham, attaining a transformed status as a "new temple" inhabited by the Spirit of God, and, importantly, giving up worship of other gods. But these Gentile believers did not become Jews, and Paul continued to insist strongly on the enduring importance of ethnic Jews, the people of Israel, and the Jerusalem Temple.[153] In a strict sense of "conversion" as a shift from one religious and ethnic identity to another, on Fredriksen's reading, Paul never converted, and neither did the Gentiles reborn in Christ—at least, not in a sense that Paul and other first-century Mediterraneans would have recognized as conversion.[154] Jews remained Jews; pagans remained pagans. Yet, both received a spirit of new life through their shared participation in the life, death, and resurrection of Christ. This first generation of Christians consisted of both Jews and pagans, distinguished by religious identity but united by what we might call their shared Christification or transformation in Christ.

Fredriksen notes that this highly fluid situation obtained only as long as members of the early Jesus movement expected an immediate, "fast approaching eschatological solution," and one cannot simply draw a straight line from this past to the present.[155] We can add to this the fact that, as Gaventa well documents, Paul's letters are not the sole source of a Christian theology of conversion. Nor do Gaventa and Fredriksen exhaust the possible reconstructions of the historical Paul.[156] Nevertheless, read together, these two scholarly accounts do provide an alternative framework for reconsidering Christian conversion, past and present. Specifically, one possible trajectory emerging from this scholarship would identify conversion not primarily with any change of religious affiliation but with a wider dynamic of Christification or eschatological transformation that comprehends such transitions without being limited to them. Following Fredriksen in particular, such an understanding of conversion as transformation might be imagined to work through, within, and beyond any explicit change in group membership. First-century Jews and pagans could, on her reading, retain the religio-ethnic identities of their birth, even as these identities themselves are radically resignified in Christ. Borrowing Gaventa's image of the Gestalt diagram, the lines and blots remain fixed on the page, but they acquire new meaning in the light of Christ and the inbreaking reign of freedom that Christ both heralds and personally embodies.

A Christian theology of conversion as Christification might thus posit an ongoing revelation of Christ throughout history, an ever-renewed invitation to individual persons and whole traditions to receive what Gaventa calls a "cognitive shift."[157] Embodying such a revelation is the special purpose of Christian mission and the Christian community. At the same time, the revelation itself can also be described as spontaneous, even agentless, insofar as it transcends the agency of limited human subjects and remains sovereignly unconstrained by the limits of human imagination. The parallels here to an Advaita theology of Sanskritization, as developed above, are reasonably self-evident and, I believe, compelling. The Christian message on this reading offers prospective disciples an interpretive key, a new perspective, with the power, in Pollock's terms, "to interpret, supplement, [and] reveal reality."[158] Or, to borrow the language of the Chinmaya Mission, the revelation of Christ can be re-membered or reconceived as a reality with a direct impact on the persons and traditions whom it encounters, an invitation to each and every hearer to become "a better individual irrespective of whatever faith he or she may belong to."[159] Inclusion in the Christian movement and institutional conversion to one or another Christian community may remain closely related, without the one invariably implying the other.

Lest this proposal about conversion in Christ appear to stand at too far a remove from contemporary Christian self-understandings, we can draw at least some support from what might seem an unlikely source: the late Pope Benedict XVI. Benedict, particularly in comparison to his successor Pope Francis, is often portrayed as a conservative thinker on questions of Christian identity and the necessity of evangelization. In his provocative 2017 essay, "Mission Impossible?," however, Emil Anton has argued that one can trace a zig-zag course of two trajectories of the emeritus pontiff's attitude toward interreligious dialogue, from the years before Cardinal Joseph Ratzinger's (1927–2022) election as Pope Benedict XVI in 2005 to his resignation from the papal office in 2012.[160] Anton identifies one of these two trajectories with the journalist John Allen's oft-cited formula, "interreligious dialogue no, intercultural dialogue yes." Anton refers to this as the "culture/values" trajectory, and he notes its basic pessimism toward the possibility of mutual learning in matters of religious truth, particularly in the dialogue between Christianity and Islam.[161] He does not, however, consider this Benedict's most enduring or mature view on the topic.[162] "A much more fitting alternative," Anton writes, "could be found in the well-known Arabic words *Allahu akbar*—God is greater," a position that requires both a categorical rejection of relativism and "an attitude of humility" that opens space for authentic, mutual learning between members of diverse religious traditions.[163]

Perhaps the strongest piece of evidence Anton adduces to support his argument is an audience Benedict hosted with Roman clergy in 2008.[164] A visiting priest from India asks the pope to clarify the relation between "qualitative" and "quantitative" understandings of the "fulness of salvation" in the Catholic Church.[165]

Benedict responds first by affirming both the vital need for interreligious collaboration and the imperative to share the gospel, out of gratitude. He then continues to make a remarkable statement, worth quoting at length:

> Exponents of non-Christian religions have said to me: the presence of Christianity is a reference point for us that helps us, even if we do not convert. Let us think of the great figure of Mahatma Gandhi: although he remained firmly bound to his own religion, the Sermon on the Mount was a fundamental reference point for him which shaped his whole life. Thus, the leaven of faith, even if it did not convert him to Christianity, entered his life. It seems to me that this leaven of Christian love which flows from the Gospel—in addition to missionary work that seeks to enlarge the spaces of faith—is a service we render to humanity.[166]

Benedict goes on, in this address, to draw an analogy to Paul the Apostle:

> Let us think of St Paul . . . Paul was moved by the Lord's word in his eschatological discourse. Before any other event, before the return of the Son of Man, the Gospel must be preached to all peoples. A condition for the world to attain perfection, for it to be open to Heaven, is that the Gospel be proclaimed to all. He devoted all his missionary zeal to ensuring that the Gospel reached everyone, possibly already in his generation, in response to the Lord's command "so that it may be announced to all the peoples." His desire was not so much to baptize all peoples as rather that the Gospel, hence, the fulfilment of history as such, be present in the world. I think that by looking at history's progress it is possible today to understand better that this presence of the Word of God, this proclamation which, like leaven, reaches everyone, is necessary in order that the world truly achieve its goal.[167]

Reading Benedict's discussion backward, as it were, one can trace an argument that closely resembles what I am proposing here under the rubric of Christification. First, the presence of the Word of God works in the world like a leaven to ensure "the fulfilment of history." "[I]n order that the world truly achieve its goal"—that is, its historical fulfillment—the gospel must be "announced to all peoples." This universal proclamation does not, at least in the vision of Paul the Apostle, require that all persons be baptized. Instead, Christians may undertake their missionary work motivated by a conviction that this "leaven of Christian love" may bear different kinds of fruit, both within and beyond formal Christian communion. The model of this latter kind of transformation—conversion without "conversion"—is the appropriation of the Sermon of the Mount by Mohandas K. Gandhi (1869–1948), on whom Benedict knowingly or unknowingly confers an aura of sainthood by the honorific "Mahatma." Had the pope included the example of Martin Luther King Jr. (1929–1968) alongside those of Gandhi and Paul, I would observe, he might have reached the further insight that Christians can both give and receive the leaven of truth in this ongoing process of historical transformation.[168]

Before concluding this exposition, we should return to Ankur Barua's notion of "epistemic peer conflict," applied here to the relation of ecumenical and Catholic Christianity with modern and contemporary missionary Advaita. It is implausible to suppose that, in his 2008 address, Emeritus Pope Benedict XVI intended to cast doubt on the truth and finality of Christ, any more than Chinmayananda, Dayananda, or the author of the *Vivekacūḍāmaṇi* offer the Advaita teaching on *Brahman* as merely one possible option in the search for freedom. These two traditions, in this respect, stand in a relation of competition and conflict, resolvable only through the actual achievement of final liberation. Until such a moment of resolution arrives, however, it matters a great deal how this competition is negotiated, both in theory and on the ground. At one level, at least in the rhetoric of a figure like Vivekananda, Advaita no less than Christianity seeks or at least anticipates the dissolution of those "kindergartens of religion" that fall short of home tradition's spiritual ideal.[169] But there is also a capaciousness in these Advaita traditions, a serene confidence that the teaching of Vedānta will inevitably improve, purify, and transform the self-understanding of all of those with ears to hear, regardless of such hearers' own identification with an Advaita lineage, with another religious movement, or with no tradition at all.

Through this brief exposition of the teaching of Paul the Apostle in the first century and Emeritus Pope Benedict XVI in the twenty-first century, I have attempted to suggest that Christians need not abandon either belief in Christ or their evangelical commitment to respond very much in kind. They too can draw on sources in Christian tradition to reconceive their missionary work with a similarly serene confidence in the transformative power of Christ and a comparably capacious understanding of cosmic history and the inbreaking reign of God. Reimagining Christianity in this way will not eliminate any sense of competition or "epistemic peer conflict" between the traditions, as we have considered here and in earlier chapters,[170] but it may nevertheless transform the tenor of the competition and open new possibilities of relationship. Christians and Advaitins may, on this reading, work assiduously to convert one another in whole or in part to the highest possible truth, and each may receive unexpected, transformative gifts of conversion, in turn. Indeed, one of these gifts may be a renewed, purified understanding of conversion itself.

Conclusion

In chapter 1 of this study, I had occasion to refer to Swami Dayananda Saraswati's 1999 open letter to Pope John Paul II, entitled "Conversion is Violence." Dayananda builds his argument in this letter on a rigid series of binaries constructed around the question of conversion. He writes:

> Among the world's religious traditions, there are those that convert and those that do not. The non-converting religious traditions, like the Hindu, Jewish and Zoroastrian, give others the freedom to practise their religion whether they agree with the others' tenets or not. They do not wish to convert. I would characterise them as non-aggressive. Religions that are committed by their theologies to convert, on the other hand, are necessarily aggressive, since conversion implies a conscious intrusion into the religious life of a person, in fact, into the religious person.[171]

Later in the letter, Dayananda insists that Hinduism, distinct from Christianity, is intrinsically non-aggressive and non-violent because it is non-converting: "We don't believe in conversion, even though certain Hindu organisations have taken back some converted people."[172]

One can approach the strong claims in Dayananda's open letter in various ways. On the one hand, one can contextualize his perspective by appealing the long history of Christian complicity in European colonialism, including such searing memories as the brutal imposition of the Inquisition in colonial Goa by Catholic authorities.[173] On the other hand, one can note the ways that Dayananda's simplistic association of Christianity and Islam with aggression and violence may in fact invite or authorize violence against them as minority traditions in India.[174] Both of these approaches are useful and persuasive, on their own terms. What I have attempted in this chapter, however, suggests a different set of questions. That is, rather than defending or critiquing Dayananda's rhetoric in this open letter, it may be possible now to test his claims about conversion empirically, with reference to the Advaita mission movements we have been following throughout this monograph.

Following this more empirical approach, it seems necessary to uncouple three descriptive binaries that Dayananda sets in close parallel, namely, "aggressive/non-aggressive," "converting/non-converting," and "violent/non-violent." The first of these binaries, I believe, holds up reasonably well. That is, it seems fair for Dayananda to characterize Christianity as very aggressive in its missionary posture, at least in comparison to missionary Advaita. Whether this follows from Advaita's intrinsic tolerance of religious diversity or from other factors, such as its powerful elitism or the wide frame provided by Hindu teachings on rebirth, is debatable. I have tried, however, to bring out one significant element of this mix: a distinctive theology of conversion that, by analogy to Sanskritization, aims for the transformation, purification, and elevation of persons and whole traditions by the teaching of Advaita Vedānta. While formal entrance into a community constructed around an Advaita lineage may be quite desirable, it is not strictly required. What is required is a thorough reshaping of prospective disciples' self-understanding in light of the teaching.

This, of course, implies a negative judgment on the second binary. It is inaccurate, in my view, to describe these Advaita mission movements as "non-converting" except in a designedly reductive sense. Sociologically, as noted by Carl Jackson at the top of this chapter, "thousands of Americans have joined the Vedanta societies since 1893, in the process abandoning Christianity for a modern variety of Hinduism."[175] Indeed, in the central section of the chapter, we surveyed the narratives of a number of such converts to the Ramakrishna Mission and other Advaita mission movements, in India, Europe, and North America. Some of these converts left their home traditions to pursue Vedānta; others returned to these home traditions, or never left. Most nevertheless revealed what Dayananda himself refers to as a fundamental "shift in thinking"[176] about the truth of self, God, and world, a shift with sufficiently profound consequences to be interpreted in terms of religious conversion.

And this, in turn, has profound consequences for assessing the third and final binary in Dayananda's analysis: "violent/non-violent." Now, it should be conceded at the outset that the association of at least some Christian missionary movements with violent means is a matter of public historical record, not to mention personal and communal repentance.[177] In that sense, missionary Christianity is, or at least has been, a perpetrator of violence. If, however, the real violence of conversion stems from its "conscious intrusion into the religious life of a person," as Dayananda suggests, then one can hardly imagine a more profound intrusion than the change of perspective demanded by Advaita Vedānta. This teaching tradition offers, and requires, a transformation of one's interior life and self-perception well beyond any mere change of religious or institutional affiliation.

Why doesn't *this* qualify as violence? It may be that, for Dayananda and other exponents of missionary Advaita, their efforts to spread the teaching of Vedānta should be considered *intrinsically* non-intrusive and, therefore, non-violent. This is not primarily because they aspire to reach only ethnic South Asians in India and the Hindu diaspora—which they do not. Nor does it follow directly from the fact that they adopt an irenic, integrative, and non-aggressive attitude toward other traditions—which they generally do. Missionary Advaitins understand their work as non-intrusive, I suggest, for a simpler reason: because they judge that Advaita alone reveals the innermost, always liberated reality of each and every conscious being. In other words, these missionary movements are inherently free from violence because the path of conversion they offer is the path that uniquely leads to highest truth.

Conclusion

The Still More Common Task

In June 1910, representatives of diverse Protestant churches and mission societies gathered for a "World Missionary Conference" in Edinburgh, Scotland. This meeting has gained legendary status as the birth of the Christian ecumenical movement, the genesis of major church unions in many parts of the world, and the reinvention of Christianity as a world tradition.[1] Though several of these claims do not survive critical scrutiny,[2] many participants in the 1910 conference undoubtedly viewed the task of global mission as a significant force for Christian unity. The American Episcopalian Silas McBee (1853–1924), for example, expressed hope that the meeting would "let the [gospel] message bear its own inherent message to the divided Churches of Christendom in the sure confidence that they would be drawn together in their witness for Christ."[3] A centenary celebration in 2010 adopted the language of a "Common Call" to characterize the message of the World Missionary Conference.[4] In his book *The Common Task,* which we encountered briefly in chapter 3, M. Thomas Thangaraj has taken this idea a step further, reimagining mission in holistic terms as a fundamental summons, shared by all persons and every religious tradition, to "responsibility," "solidarity," and "mutuality."[5]

The study I have attempted in this volume has deep affinities with Thangaraj's study, and indeed it was my reading of *The Common Task* years ago that raised the possibility of a book-length comparative theology of mission. I have, however, taken my start here not from the 1910 World Missionary Conference but from the 1893 World's Parliament of Religions and the speeches of the Hindu missionary Swami Vivekananda. I have attempted to root my account not primarily in abstract theological or philosophical principles but in the specific histories and theologies of the Ramakrishna Mission, Ramanasramam, the Chinmaya Mission, Transcendental Meditation, and the Śṛṇgeri *maṭha*. Along the way, I have also had occasion to develop themes of Christian mission that open space for relational exchange with missionary Advaita. This exchange has, in the previous chapter, culminated in an initial, tentative sketch of Christian conversion as Christification, a multilayered process that works at both individual and communal levels. Drawing on the model of Paul the Apostle, I argued in that chapter for an understanding of conversion—Christification—not primarily as a transfer of allegiance *into* one or another Christian church but as a dynamic force of transformation at work within, beyond, and across ecclesial boundaries to reshape persons and whole traditions in the image of Jesus the Christ.

The cumulative result of these reflections is not a single, comprehensive proposal in Christian missiology, such as David Bosch's unfolding of the theme of *missio Dei* in his landmark study *Transforming Mission*, Stephen Bevans's and Roger Schroeder's synthetic image of mission as "prophetic dialogue," or even Thangaraj's phenomenological account of *missio humanitatis*.[6] Nor are most of the themes developed in the second half of this study, in and of themselves, original to me or to the comparative encounter with missionary Advaita. I have drawn them from Lamin Sanneh, Gemma Cruz, René Padilla, Pope Benedict, Pope Francis, Paula Fredriksen, and others, who have in the main articulated their insights as the fruit of the historical study of Christianity, social analysis, and intra-Christian theological debate. Here, reflecting a wider tendency in contemporary comparative theology, the constructive work may consist as much or more in creative retrieval of the home tradition as in its substantive revision.[7]

Nevertheless, the themes thus retrieved are specific, distinctive in their combination and application here, and, I hope to have demonstrated, mutually coherent. Collectively, they offer a vision of Christian mission that may seem modest in some respects, such as its presumptions about the universality of God's gracious presence, as developed in chapter 4, or its self-conscious witness as pilgrim or migrant rather than world conqueror, in chapter 5. This vision may in other places seem positively chauvinistic, particularly in its insistence that every aspect of human life and all persons, regardless of religious affiliation, stand solidly within the scope of missionary striving, as developed especially in chapters 6 and 7. Christian mission, I have argued, is nothing more nor less than a human participation in the transformation of the whole creation, in and for Christ. To this ambitious vision we have added an important caveat: namely, that such Christification unfolds relationally, alongside Advaita and other mission movements, not only in our religiously pluralistic world but also in the religious experience of individuals and communities.

This vision of holistic transformation holds real promise. At the same time, it should not be regarded as unproblematic, beyond risk of distortion or potential for real harm. Thus, in the few pages that remain, I propose to dwell briefly on the deep ambivalence of Christification as a missionary ideal. To do this, I again focus on the particular, in this case yet another late modern missionary project that moved suddenly to the center of my attention, and the attention of many settler Canadians, as I was researching and writing the final chapters of this book: namely, the Indian Residential School System, operated by Catholic and Protestant churches and missionary orders from the late nineteenth century right up to the 1990s.[8]

In 1910, for example, the very same year that missionaries gathered in Edinburgh for their World Missionary Conference, the government of Canada was scrambling to respond to a series of reports about terrible health conditions among the thousands of Indigenous children removed forcibly from their families and consigned to the Residential Schools.[9] These reports were filed by Dr. Peter Bryce, chief medical officer for Indian Affairs from 1904 to 1921, and he would later publish his findings under the title *The Story of a National Crime*.[10] About a century later, as part of a legal settlement with survivors of these schools, the government of Canada struck a Truth and Reconciliation Commission to examine this national crime in all of its aspects. In its 2015 *Final Report*, the Commission documented the physical, sexual, and spiritual violence suffered by many Indigenous children in these schools, as well as the system's role as symptom, product, and privileged instrument of a wider program of "cultural genocide" with deep roots in the colonial project.[11]

Importantly for this study, the Residential School System was informed by a distinctive interpretation of Christian mission, one that aimed for nothing less than the holistic transformation of whole persons and traditions. That is, the Canadian settler state and European churches advanced a broad "civilizing mission" that seamlessly fused the proclamation of the gospel with ruthless suppression of Indigenous languages, cultures, and sacred life ways. Their aim was not merely to recruit new members but to force Indigenous peoples to conform to a very particular understanding of Christ and Christian transformation—even, we might say, to "Christify" them. The members of the Truth and Reconciliation Commission write: "Christian missionaries played a complex but central role in the European colonial project. Their presence helped justify the extension of empires, since they were visibly spreading the word of God to the heathen . . . Although missionaries often attempted to soften the impact of imperialism, they were also committed to making the greatest changes in the culture and psychology of the colonized."[12] Advaita scholar and Hindu theologian Arvind Sharma does not address the specific history of the Indian Residential School System, but he has similarly invoked the past and present imposition of European Christianity on Indigenous peoples of Turtle Island as powerful evidence against Western ideals of religious freedom.[13] And Sharma is not alone in this respect.[14]

Now, as we saw especially in chapters 3 and 5 of this study, ideals of spiritual conquest are not the exclusive preserve of Christianity, and the metaphor of Sanskritization deployed in chapter 7 to understand conversion in Advaita Vedānta carries its own obvious, grim resonance with the "civilizing mission" of the European colonial project. These Advaita theologies could and should be subjected to searching inquiry.[15] This monograph is the work of a Christian theologian, however, so it seems reasonable to linger just a bit longer on the Christian side of the ledger, to ask how a holistic vision of mission as Christification might be specified to distinguish it from the hegemonic, universalizing holism of the Indian Residential School System. Does my proposal merely re-package the old wine of imperial Christianity in a new wineskin of irenic exchange and "world religions universalism"?[16]

A partial answer to this question may be gained by recourse to a proposal advanced in the 1960s and 1970s by the prominent lay theologian and ecumenical missiologist, M. M. Thomas (1916–1996). A native of Kerala and inheritor of the ancient tradition of Thomas Christianity, in the form of the Mar Thoma Church, Thomas emerged as one of the most important public theologians of post-Independence India, serving at various points as director of the Christian Institute for the Study of Religion and Society in Bangalore, as moderator of the Central Committee of the World Council of Churches, and as governor of the northeastern Indian state of Nagaland—where he himself confronted questions of Indigeneity, mission, and settler colonialism in the Indian context.[17] Earlier in his career, however, Thomas developed a theological argument for recognizing the existence and vitality of what he called "Christ-centred secular fellowship." The outline of this proposal emerged in two books, *The Christian Response to the Asian Revolution* in 1966 and *The Acknowledged Christ of the Indian Renaissance* in 1969.[18] In *Acknowledged Christ,* written in response to the first edition of Raimond Panikkar's *Unknown Christ of Hinduism,*[19] Thomas shifted attention from the mystical Christ hidden in the classical Advaita of Ādi Śaṅkarācārya to the explicit reinterpretations of Christ by modern Hindu reformers, including Swami Vivekananda and Sarvepalli Radhakrishnan, as well as prominent Indian Christian interlocutors and supporters of the independence movement. From this creative interaction, Thomas discerns both a wider work of Christ in the Hindu community and a key insight that "[t]he Gospel of Jesus Christ is not a cult of individualistic spirituality, but is essentially a message of reconciliation of relationships, of righteousness, of right relations with God and with one another resulting in a new quality of fellowship."[20] It is this notion of new "fellowship or *koinonia*" in Christ, Thomas concludes, that represents the preeminent contribution of Christianity to Indian religion, and also to the nationalist project.[21]

This idea became a central principle of Thomas's missiology in his 1970 William Carey Lectures, published as an essay entitled "Salvation and Humanization," in a subsequent monograph of the same name and in a 1972 exchange with the legendary British missionary, theologian and Church of South India bishop Lesslie Newbigen.[22] In these works, Thomas contextualized his proposal in the new awareness among many theologians that mission includes "humanization," or the building up of human society to reflect and to anticipate the "New Humanity" offered in Christ.[23] "[S]alvation," he writes, "is the spiritual inwardness of true humanization, and . . . humanization is inherent in the message of salvation in Christ."[24] On this basis, and informed by New Testament studies of biblical *koinonia*, Thomas suggests that both "religious fellowship in the church" and "human fellowship in secular society" can and should be regarded as "created by the Gospel" and "within the reality of Christ and the history of salvation in the world."[25] The witness of Hindus who accept Christ as "decisive" for their lives without receiving baptism and fellowship in the church, moreover, implies "the building up of a Christ-centred fellowship of faith within the society, culture and religion in which they live, transforming their structures and values from within."[26] As a matter of missionary outreach, "The Church in India can extend into the religious and secular communities of India only if we are prepared to recognise partial formation of Christ-centred fellowships as valid beginnings of the form of church life itself in these communities."[27]

Compared to the themes I have discussed in previous chapters, Thomas's argument is most closely related to the ideas of integral mission discussed in chapter 6, and his writings on the topic coincided with the Catholic synodal meetings at Medillín and Puebla as well as the emergence of liberation theologies across the Americas. Nevertheless, it is possible to interpret the notion of Christification developed in the previous chapter as a generalization of Thomas's core proposal, particularly the distinction he draws between being drawn into the new humanity of Christ and explicit membership in a Christian ecclesial community. Such a generalization finds further support in Kerry San Chirico's recent study of Khrist Bhaktas, Hindu devotees of Christ, in the sacred city of Varanasi.[28] Here the religious idiom is much less occupied with secular fellowship or political "humanization," and much more firmly rooted in charismatic experience, miraculous healing, and devotional practice. Nevertheless, here too the religious leaders and bhaktas themselves are careful to distinguish between water baptism in the church and the "baptism of *viśvas*" conferred directly on Hindu devotees by the Holy Spirit.[29]

Such a distinction is also the aspect of Thomas's proposal that has provoked the most criticism. Newbigen, in his written exchange with Thomas, presses the intrinsic and necessary connection between discipleship of Christ, participation in the new humanity he presents, and the social expression of that participation in some form of explicitly Christian fellowship.[30] George R. Hunsberger identifies the relation between "conversion" and "community" as the key point of the Thomas-Newbigen debate, and he affirms the "priority" given by the latter to "the life of the community of God's people as the basis for the other aspects of its mission."[31] Sebastian Kim, in his account of the debate in *In Search of Identity*, notes Thomas's somewhat naïve assessment of secular society in post-Independence India. Kim writes that Thomas's "optimistic predictions of the disappearance of differences between religious communities, the demise of religious fanaticism, and the placing of greater value on humanization did not materialize."[32] All three, in different ways, emphasize the perduring importance of baptism and membership in the religious community as a theological imperative and sociological fact.

Retaining an emphasis on baptism and formal conversion to the church, however, need not rule out other mediations. In chapter 7, for example, we encountered Paul's vision of conversion to Christ as a holistic transformation that sublates without obliterating such ethno-religious, communitarian identities as "Jew" and "Gentile," along with Gooren's description of "conversion careers" within religious communities and Lonergan's account of intellectual, rational, moral, and religious conversion as a single, complex process that transcends the boundaries of any community, secular or religious. In his own comment on the Thomas-Newbigen debate, Alfred C. Kass observes that Roman Catholics traditionally side-stepped the strict necessity of baptism by postulating a "baptism of intention," and Karl Barth speaks of a "Spirit-baptism" that stands in a necessary but complex relation to "water-baptism."[33] Thomas responds to this reflection as follows:

> I have no doubt that baptism in the NT sense is incorporation into Christ and this congregational life. But the meaning of baptism has been distorted for long in India as a mark of transference of sociological cultural-juridical loyalties from one community to another. The real question, therefore, is how to regain the meaning of water-

> baptism. Probably it can be done by just dissociating it in time from the Spirit-baptism conceptually . . . and by considering baptism as the privilege a disciple, already in the Fellowship of the Church and participating in other privileges, including Lord's Supper, may ask for some time in the process of his [*sic*] growth in Christ.[34]

As a rite of Christian initiation and sacrament of conversion to the New Humanity of Christ, baptism is definitely included in what Thomas elsewhere refers to as the "plenitude" of the church, but he observes that such plenitude "cannot be present in the Church in all times and in all places, though it is proper to it."[35]

We will return to the question of plenitude, but it may be worth lingering first on two phrases from Thomas's response that bring us back to colonial Christianity and the Indian Residential School System. For, in his exchange with Newbingen, Thomas notes that water-baptism has become "distorted" and that "dissociating" it from "Spirit-baptism"—at least "conceptually" if not in practice—may represent a step in its own renewal.[36] Stated another way, and more forcefully, the question of ecclesial plenitude arises here from a position of weakness rather than strength, of seeking Christ's transforming grace rather than presuming to dispense it, as a pilgrim on the path of Christification rather than as its privileged or exclusive representative. This is key, for Thomas in the context of post-Independence India, for any authentic Christian response to the findings of the Truth and Reconciliation Commission of Canada, and for the missiological proposal advanced in this monograph. The contemporary Catholic Church, as one example, has proven itself quite comfortable distinguishing among diverse levels and kinds of relation to the fullness of ecclesial belonging and union with Christ, present in mystery from the foundation of the world.[37] It has even, in places, recognized the reality of God's reign at work in and through diverse religious traditions of the world.[38] But it may not yet have completely embraced the posture of weakness required to embody such teachings in its pastoral practice and self-understanding.[39]

Adopting the image of Christ as an ethical ideal or striving for authentic humanization of the social order, without baptism and incorporation into a Christian community, would certainly fall short of the plenitude of transformation in Christ. But so would mere "recruitment" into a church or "transference of sociological cultural-juridical loyalties," in the terms proposed respectively by Gooren and Thomas. Violently removing Indigenous children from their families as part of a genocidal program would seem not merely to fall short of the missionary ideal but directly to contradict it. Beyond such particular examples of partial success and catastrophic failure, however, we can also recognize that all phenomenal manifestations of Christification in this suffering world of name and form will inevitably fall short of its final plenitude. This is why Paul could refer to new Christians in the continuing present tense as those who are "being saved" (1 Cor 1:18) and medieval monastics could speak of conversion as a journey for the whole of life. The goal of Christian mission should ideally be to advance this ongoing, ever-fragile, and partial effort of Christification, inside, beyond, and across the visible boundaries of the churches, and to recognize it in humility when it presents itself in unexpected places and from sources that may stand at some distance from explicit Christian communion.

Does this work? Do such qualifications protect a holistic vision of missionary Christification from comparison or association with the similarly holistic "civilizing mission" that animated the Residential Schools? I'm not sure. Certainly, the practical consequences of such a vision would have to be worked out locally by diverse Christian communities in their own cultural and political contexts. Perhaps in some contexts, including the settler states of Canada and the United States, it may for some time entail a near-exclusive focus on penitential practices of listening and reparation.[40] But I do think it may be possible to venture a general principle or two, informed again by Arvind Sharma. At one point in his thoughtful and provocative work *Problematizing Religious Freedom*, Sharma finds himself reflecting on the resistance to proselytism in Judaism, a tradition that accepts converts but has not usually sought them out. As a kind of thought experiment, he introduces the "doctrine of double-effect . . . which distinguishes between intended and foreseen consequences."[41] If one applies this doctrine to questions of mission and conversion beyond the Jewish context, he suggests, then one "creates the possibility of religions engaging in propagating their doctrines among people beyond their ken without intending to convert them, though this action of theirs might result in a few unintended conversions. If we now combine this with the distinction between religious change being 'additive' rather than 'transplantive,' then one has a new missiology here that might take the sting out of proselytization."[42] It seems clear that Sharma intends in this passage to offer a friendly amendment to the missionary theologies of Christianity and Islam. In so doing, he also offers a creative extension of what he has called, in conversation with his former teacher Krister Stendahl, "an exemplary outpost model" of missionary outreach.[43]

In making this proposal, Sharma knowingly or unknowingly echoes other proposals from closer to the Christian mainstream, such as those of the Jesuit theologian Francis A. Sullivan. Sullivan identified the unique status of the church as a "universal sacrament of salvation" with its obligation to embody some visible sign of Christ's reconciling work in every time and place, along with its continual petition, in its Eucharistic celebrations, on behalf of all humankind.[44] Whereas a previous generation might have interpreted catholicity or universality in terms of membership numbers, geographic extent, or spiritual hegemony, here the universality of the church refers primarily to the ideal character of its public witness and the unlimited scope of its loving concern. This, it seems to me, is a useful intervention—and it resonates with key aspects of *missio Dei* theologies of mission, outlined briefly in chapter 1.[45]

In and out of the comparative study attempted in this volume, of course, we might perceive in the proposals of Thomas, Sharma, Stendahl, or Sullivan further points of resonance with Advaita texts and traditions encountered in previous chapters. Śaṅkara's vision of a compassionate teacher in his eighth-century *Upadeśasāhasrī* springs to mind, for example, along with the distinctive missionary styles of Hastāmalaka and Toṭaka, as portrayed in the *Śaṅkara-vijayas* and exemplified by Advaita teachers from the medieval period to the present day. We might be reminded of the command of Ramana Maharshi to preach in silence, or we might be inspired by the seamless integration of Advaita teaching and development theory in the formation of Mahila Mandals for women's empowerment in rural India. We could multiply such examples, while also noting counter-examples along the way. Taken together, these Advaita mission traditions testify to the profound importance of witnessing presence, along with a serene confidence that the message of liberation can and will take root in the most unlikely of places, to the extent that it is embodied in the lives of those who profess it.

At the end of the day, perhaps, this is the sole common task that truly matters, in Christianity, in Advaita, and in the ongoing process of our mutual purification.

Notes

Introduction

1. Raghvendra Rao and Rakesh Sinha, "Pushed on 'ghar wapsi,' govt calls for laws against conversion," *The Indian Express*, 12 December 2014, http://indianexpress.com / article / india / india-others / pushed-on-ghar-wapsi-govt-calls-for-laws-against-conversion. See also Gardiner Harris, "'Reconversion' of Religious Minorities Roils Indian Politics," *New York Times*, 23 December 2014. www.nytimes.com / 2014 / 12 / 24 / world / asia / india-narendra-modi-hindu-conversions-missionaries.html?_r=0

2. Press Trust of India, "Improper to ban conversion: Digvijay," *The Hindu*, 11 December 2014. www.thehindu.com / news / national / improper-to-ban-conversion-digvijay / article6682645.ece#

3. Jatin Gandhi, Varghese K. George, and Krishnadas Rajagopal, "Conversion confusion," *The Hindu*, 21 December 2014. www.thehindu.com / sunday-anchor / sunday-anchor-conversion-confusion / article10961782.ece

4. For Hindu, Christian, and secular overviews of this controversy in its several phases, see Sita Ram Goel, *History of Hindu-Christian Encounters, AD 304 to 1996* (New Delhi: Voice of India, 1996); Sebastian C. H. Kim, *In Search of Identity: Debates on Religious Conversion in India* (New Delhi: Oxford University Press, 2003); Goldie Osuri, *Religious Freedom in India: Sovereignty and (Anti) Conversion* (London & New York: Routledge, 2013); Rebecca Shah and Joel A. Carpenter, eds., *Christianity in India: Conversion, Community Development, and Religious Freedom* (Minneapolis, MN: Fortress Press, 2018); and Laura Dudley Jenkins, *Religious Freedom and Mass Conversion in India* (Philadelphia: University of Pennsylvania Press, 2019). Dudley Jenkins helpfully extends the scope of her inquiry to include conversion to Christianity, Buddhism, and Mizo Judaism.

5. See, for example, Kim, *In Search of Identity*, 139–51; Ram Swarup, *A Hindu View of Christianity and Islam* (New Delhi: Voice of India, 1992);

Ram Swarup, *Hinduism and Monotheistic Religions* (New Delhi: Voice of India, 2009); Goel, *History of Hindu-Christian Encounters*; Sita Ram Goel, *Jesus Christ: An Artifice for Aggression* (New Delhi: Voice of India, 1994); Arun Shourie, *Missionaries in India: Continuities, Changes, Dilemmas* (New Delhi: ASA, 1994); Arun Shourie, *Harvesting Our Souls: Missionaries, Their Design, Their Claims* (New Delhi: ASA, 2000).

6. See Iris Vandevelde, "Reconversion to Hinduism: A Hindu Nationalist Reaction Against Conversion to Christianity and Islam," *South Asia: Journal of South Asian Studies* 34 (2011): 31–50; Lise McKean, *Divine Enterprise: Gurus and the Hindu Nationalist Movement* (Chicago & London: University of Chicago Press, 1996), 106–8; Thomas Blom Hansen, *The Saffron Wave: Democracy and Hindu Nationalism in Modern India* (Princeton, NJ: Princeton University Press, 1999), 101–7; and the background in Kenneth W. Jones, *Arya Dharm: Hindu Consciousness in 19th-Century Punjab* (Berkeley, Los Angeles, & London: University of California Press, 1976), esp. 129–35, 202–15, and 303–12.

7. See Kim, *In Search of Identity*, 76–81; Chad M. Bauman, *Christian Identity and Dalit Religion in Hindu India, 1868–1947* (Grand Rapids, MI & Cambridge: Eerdmans, 2008), 1–5; and the comprehensive analysis by Ian Richards in "Poles Apart: The Debates on Religious Conversion in Post-Independence India," PhD dissertation, University of Toronto, 2016, as well as his shorter summary in "Anti-Conversion Laws in Post-Independence India," in *The Routledge Handbook of Hindu-Christian Relations*, ed. Chad M. Bauman and Michelle Voss Roberts (London & New York: Routledge, 2021), 155–68.

8. On Kandhmal and the broader phenomenon of violence against Christians, see especially Chad M. Bauman, "Hindu-Christian Conflict in India: Globalization, Conversion, and the Coterminal Castes and Tribes," *The Journal of Asian Studies* 72.3 (2013): 633–53; Chad M. Bauman, "Identity, Conversion, and Violence: Dalits, Adivasis, and the 2007–08 Riots in Orissa," in *Margins of Faith: Dalit and Tribal Christianity in India*, ed. Rowena Robinson and Joseph Marianus Kujur (Los Angeles: Sage, 2010), 263–90; and Chad M. Bauman, *Anti-Christian Violence in India* (Ithaca & London: Cornell University Press, 2020).

9. As just one example, see the compelling analysis in Nathaniel Roberts, *To Be Cared For: The Power of Conversion and Foreignness of Belonging in an Indian Slum* (Oakland: University of California Press, 2016).

10. See, for example, Ankur Barua, *Debating "Conversion" in Hinduism and Christianity* (London & New York: Routledge, 2015); and Arvind Sharma, *Problematizing Religious Freedom* (Dordrecht: Springer, 2011).

11. Swami Vivekananda, "The Work Before Us," *The Complete Works of Swami Vivekananda*, Mayavati Memorial Ed., vol. 3 (Calcutta: Advaita Ashrama, 1989), 277.

12. By "mainline ecumenical movement," I intend primarily the documents of, and theologians associated with, the World Council of Churches. The Catholic Church is a contributor and partner to this movement but has never become a full member of the WCC.

13. Bernard Lonergan, "First Lecture: Religious Experience," in *Third Collection: Papers*, ed. Frederick E. Crowe (New York: Paulist Press, 1985), 125.

14. See Francis X. Clooney, "Afterword," in *Comparative Theology in the Millennial Classroom: Hybrid Identity, Negotiated Boundaries*, ed. Mara Brecht and Reid B. Locklin (New York & London: Routledge, 2016), esp. 225–31.

15. Ibid., 228.

Chapter 1

1. Goldie Osuri, *Religious Freedom in India: Sovereignty and (Anti) Conversion* (London & New York: Routledge, 2013).

2. Ibid., 5.

3. Ibid., 7.

4. Chad M. Bauman, "Postcolonial Anxiety and Anti-Conversion Sentiment in the Report of the Christian Missionary Activities Inquiry Committee," *International Journal of Hindu Studies* 12.2 (2008): 181–213; J. Coleman, "Authoring (in)Authenticity, Regulating Religious Tolerance: The Implications of Anti-Conversion Legislation for Indian Secularism," *Cultural Dynamics* 20.3 (2008): 245–78; Laura Dudley Jenkins, "Legal Limits on Religious Conversion in India," *Law and Contemporary Problems* 71.2 (2008): 109–27; and Ian Douglas Richards, "Poles Apart: The Debates on Religious Conversion in Post-Independence India," PhD dissertation, University of Toronto, 2016, esp. 116–55, 280–84.

5. Osuri, *Religious Freedom in India*, 7–38; Goldie Osuri, "The Concern for Sovereignty in the Politics of Anti-Conversion," *Religion Compass* 7.9 (2013): 385–93.

6. Osuri, *Religious Freedom in India*, esp. 126–39.

7. Ankur Barua, *Debating "Conversion" in Hinduism and Christianity* (London & New York: Routledge, 2015), 36.

8. Ibid., 13–16.

9. See Ibid., 8–9, 91–94, 121–25, 144.

10. Ibid., 39.

11. See Ibid., 125–46, 201–11.

12. Sebastian C. H. Kim, *In Search of Identity: Debates on Religious Conversion in India* (New Delhi: Oxford University Press, 2003), 184–90.

13. Ibid., 179.

14. Barua, *Debating "Conversion,"* 117.

15. By highlighting this shared narrative, I am by implication conceding that conflicts between Hindus and Christians on questions of conversion are to a large extent socially constructed rather than inherent to one or both traditions. In this sense my analysis resonates with the more comprehensive theorization in Chad M. Bauman, *Anti-Christian Violence in India* (London & Ithaca: Cornell University Press, 2020), especially chapters 1 and 2.

16. Swami Dayananda Saraswati, "An Open Letter to Pope John Paul II: Conversion is Violence," *Indian Express*, 29 October 1999. https://indianexpress.com/article/news-archive/conversion-is-violence

17. Ibid.

18. See Kim, *In Search of Identity*, 155–63.

19. For further discussion, see Chad M. Bauman, "The Violence of Conversion: Proselytization and Interreligious Controversy in the Work of Swami Dayananda Saraswati," *Open Theology* 1 (2015): 175–88.

20. I have decided in this chapter to focus on the critiques of Dayananda and Goel, but they do not exhaust the full scope of critical Hindu engagements with Christian thought and practice. For wider surveys, see Richard Fox Young, "Hindu-Christian Debates in the Eighteenth and Nineteenth Centuries," in *The Routledge Handbook of Hindu-Christian Relations*, ed. Chad M. Bauman and Michelle Voss Roberts (London & New York: Routledge, 2021), 127–38; and Chad M. Bauman, "Critiques of Christianity from Savarkar to Malhotra," in ibid., 139–52.

21. Sita Ram Goel, *History of Hindu-Christian Encounters, AD 304 to 1996* (New Delhi: Voice of India, 1996), iv–v.

22. Ibid., 465–66.

23. Ibid., 10–21, 386–404; see also Sita Ram Goel, *Catholic Ashrams: Sannyasins or Swindlers?* (New Delhi: Voice of India, 1995).

24. Goel, *History of Hindu-Christian Encounters*, 446–47, 462; Sita Ram Goel, *Jesus Christ: An Artifice for Aggression* (New Delhi: Voice of India, 1994), vi, 60–66, 90.

25. Goel, *Jesus Christ*, 65.

26. Goel, *History of Hindu-Christian Encounters*, 4–6, 49–50, 88–90, 112–14, 236–38, 240–42, 252–53, 324, 367.

27. Goel, *Jesus Christ*, 68–71, 76–79.

28. C. V. Mathew, *The Saffron Mission: A Historical Analysis of Modern Hindu Missionary Ideologies and Practices* (Delhi: ISPCK, 1999); J. Kuruvachira, "Hinduism as a Missionary Religion." *Mission Today* 8 (2006): 265–84; J. Kuruvachira, "Hinduism's World Mission." *Mission Today* 9 (2007): 39–56; J. Kuruvachira, *Hindu Nationalists of Modern India: A Critical Study of the Intellectual Genealogy of Hindutva* (Jaipur: Rawat Publications, 2006); and

J. Kuruvachira, *Politicisation of Hindu Religion in Postmodern India* (Jaipur: Rawat Publications, 2008).

29. Matthew, *Saffron Mission*, esp. 6, 36–40, 121, 192–94, 196–97, 203, 284–85.

30. Kuruvachira, "Hinduism as a Missionary Religion," 266–70.

31. Kuruvachira, "Hinduism's World Mission," 39–40.

32. See especially Kuruvachira, *Hindu Nationalists*, 192–227, and Kuruvachira, *Politicisation of Hindu Religion*, 207–49.

33. Kuruvachira, *Hindu Nationalists*, 36–37, 122–23, 140, 176–77, 228–35, quotations at 36, 231.

34. Kuruvachira, "Hinduism as a Missionary Religion," 271–80, quotation at 279; Kuruvachira, *Hindu Nationalists*, 29–32; Kuruvachira, *Politicisation of Hindu Religion*, 130–77.

35. Kuruvachira, *Hindu Nationalists*, 162–63; see also ibid., 53; and Kuruvachira, *Politicisation of Hindu Religion*, 234–36.

36. Kuruvachira, "Hinduism as a Missionary Religion," 280–84; Kuruvachira, *Hindu Nationalists*, 216–17, 228–31; Kuruvachira, *Politicisation of Hindu Religion*, 209, 216–17, 230–31, 237–38; Kuruvachira, "Hinduism's World Mission," 55.

37. Kuruvachira, *Hindu Nationalists*, 36–37, 122–23, 157–59, 179; Kuruvachira, *Politicisation of Hindu Religion*, xii, 96–103.

38. See especially Kuruvachira, *Hindu Nationalists*, 222.

39. Perhaps controversially, I would contend that even the mutual accusations of Nazism have some basis in history. No one can credibly deny the roots of Hitler's anti-Semitism in earlier, Christian teachings of anti-Judaism, for example, and leading Hindu nationalists have publicly invoked fascist and Nazi ideals for emulation in India. School textbooks produced under the BJP rule in the late 1990s, for example, presented Hitler as a kind of national hero. See Martha C. Nussbaum, *The Clash Within: Democracy, Religious Violence, and India's Future* (Cambridge, MA: Belknap Press of Harvard University Press, 2007), 50–51, 160–63, 276–78.

40. Arvind Sharma, "Hinduism and Conversion," in *The Oxford Handbook of Religious Conversion*, ed. Lewis R. Rambo and Charles E. Farhadian (Oxford & New York: Oxford University Press, 2014), 429–443.

41. Ibid., 429–32. On this point, see also Arvind Sharma, *Problematizing Religious Freedom* (Dordrecht: Springer, 2011), 175–95.

42. Sharma, "Hinduism and Conversion," 437–439.

43. Robert Eric Frykenberg, *Christianity in India: From Beginnings to the Present* (Oxford & New York: Oxford University Press, 2009), 268–300.

44. Robert Eric Frykenberg, "Accounting for Fundamentalisms in South Asia: Ideologies and Institutions in Historical Perspective," in

Accounting for Fundamentalisms: The Dynamic Character of Movements, ed. Martin E. Marty and R. Scott Appleby (Chicago & London: University of Chicago Press, 1994), 600.

45. This inference is made explicit in ibid., 600–602. In *Christianity in India*, 300, Frykenberg concludes more obliquely that "the terms 'Hindu' and 'India' are linked. Not only are they twins that came into existence with the formation of the Government of India in 1773, but the systems they represent were also intermingled and overlapping from the beginning. It is hardly surprising that, in our own day, 'Hindutva' as the ideology of a political religion ferociously opposed to monotheistic traditions such as Christianity and Islam later found institutional support, especially in Maharashtra and Gujarat, as also in northern India."

46. See Sharma, *Problematizing Religious Freedom*, 217–31; Arvind Sharma, "Christian Proselytization: A Hindu Perspective," *Missiology* 33.4 (2005): 425–34, and Arvind Sharma, "Experiencing Christianity," in *One Religion Too Many: The Religiously Comparative Reflections of a Comparatively Religious Hindu* (Albany, NY: SUNY Press, 2011), 63–76.

47. Frykenberg, "Accounting for Fundamentalisms," 611.

48. Goel, *History of Hindu-Christian Encounters*, 262.

49. See Goel, *Jesus Christ*, 74–75, 90–93, quotation at 75; Goel, *History of Hindu-Christian Encounters*, 465–67.

50. Kuruvachira, "Hinduism as a Missionary Religion," 271.

51. Gauri Viswanathan, *Outside the Fold: Conversion, Modernity, and Belief* (Princeton, NJ: Princeton University Press, 1998), xi.

52. See Richard King, *Orientalism and Religion: Postcolonial Theory, India and 'The Mystic East'* (London & New York: Routledge, 1999) and Tomoko Masuzawa, *The Invention of World Religions: Or, How European Universalism Was Preserved in the Language of Pluralism* (Chicago & London: University of Chicago Press, 2005), as well as the discussion in François Böspflug, "Religions Missionaires, Religions Non-Missionaires," *Revue des sciences religieuses* 80.2 (2006): 127–54.

53. Barua, *Debating "Conversion,"* 75–79.

54. Ibid., 43–61, 66–75, 84–89, 150–71.

55. Roger P. Schoeder, *What is the Mission of the Church? A Guide for Catholics* (Maryknoll, NY: Orbis Books, 2008), 1.

56. Ibid., 2.

57. Ibid., 3.

58. The United Church of Canada, *World Mission: Report of the Commission on World Mission* (Toronto: General Council of the United Church of Canada, 1966), 128, quoted in Wilfred Cantwell Smith, "The Mission of the Church and the Future of Missions," in *The Church in the Modern World: Essays in Honour of James Sutherland Thomson*, ed. George Johnston and Wolfgang Roth (Toronto: The Ryerson Press, 1967), 165.

59. Smith, "Mission of the Church," 164–67; Schroeder, *What Is the Mission of the Church?*, 92–94; and Stephen B. Bevans and Roger P. Schroeder, *Constants in Context: A Theology of Mission for Today* (Maryknoll, NY: Orbis Books, 2004).

60. Stephen B. Bevans, "Unraveling a 'Complex Reality': Six Elements of Mission," *International Bulletin of Missionary Research* 27.2 (2003): 50.

61. Bevans and Schroeder, *Constants in Context*, 286–347; Schroeder, *What Is the Mission of the Church?*, 13–20.

62. Bevans and Schroeder, *Constants in Context*, 289–91. The International Missionary Conference merged with the World Council of Churches in 1961 to become the Commission on World Mission and Evangelism.

63. Perhaps the most significant work in this regard is David J. Bosch, *Transforming Mission: Paradigm Shifts in Theology of Mission* (Maryknoll, NY: Orbis Books, 1991). See also the discussion in Stephen B. Bevans, SVD, and Roger P. Schroeder, SVD, "Missiology after Bosch: Reverencing a Classic by Moving Beyond," *International Bulletin of Missionary Research* 29.2 (2005): 69–72, as well as the more critical, postcolonial approach to the history of missiology in Paul Kollman, "At the Origins of Mission and Missiology: A Study in the Dynamics of Religious Language," *Journal of the American Academy of Religion* 79.2 (2011): 425–58. We will return to the diversity of Christian mission paradigms in chapter 3.

64. Pontifical Council for Interreligious Dialogue, World Council of Churches, and World Evangelical Alliance, "Christian Witness in a Multi-Religious World," 28 June 2011, www.oikoumene.org/en/resources/documents/wcc-programmes/interreligious-dialogue-and-cooperation/christian-identity-in-pluralistic-societies/christian-witness-in-a-multi-religious-world. Hereafter, this document is cited by section and number in the body of the text.

65. Pope Francis, *Evangelii Gaudium* (Rome: Vatican Press, 2013). English translation available as a pdf file at http://w2.vatican.va/content/francesco/en/apost_exhortations/documents/papa-francesco_esortazione-ap_20131124_evangelii-gaudium.pdf. Hereafter cited in-text by section number. Italicized texts are in every case italicized in the original document.

66. The final phrase is a quotation from a 2007 address by Pope Benedict XVI in Aparecida, Brazil.

67. Pope Francis has since picked up the theme of pluralism in several subsequent documents, including especially his third encyclical letter, Pope Francis, *Fratelli Tutti: On Fraternity and Social Friendship*, 3 October 2020, *The Holy See*, www.vatican.va/content/francesco/en/encyclicals/documents/papa-francesco_20201003_enciclica-fratelli-tutti.html. In this connection, see also Reid B. Locklin, "Polyhedral Pluralism: Pope Francis, Deep Pluralists and the Practice of Hindu-Christian Studies," *Journal of Hindu-Christian Studies* 33 (2020): 15–26.

68. See James L. Fredericks, "The Catholic Church and the Other Religious Paths: Rejecting Nothing That Is True and Holy," *Theological Studies* 64.2 (2003): esp. 246–52.

69. Smith, "Mission of the Church," 166.

70. Ibid.

71. Masuzawa, *Invention of World Religions*, 326–27.

72. See, for example, King, *Orientalism and Religion*, esp. 35–61; Wilfred Cantwell Smith, *The Meaning and End of Religion* (Minneapolis: Fortress Press, 1991); Talal Asad, *Genealogies of Religion: Discipline and Reasons of Power in Christianity and Islam* (Baltimore: Johns Hopkins University Press, 1993); Brent Nongbri, *Before Religion: A History of a Modern Concept* (New Haven, CT: Yale University Press, 2015); and the useful survey in Daniel Dubuisson, "Exporting the Local: Recent Perspectives on 'Religion' as a Cultural Category," *Religion Compass* 1 (2007): 787–800.

73. Barua, *Debating "Conversion,"* 63–66. See also King, *Orientalism and Religion*, 96–117; Masuzawa, *Invention of World Religions*, 147–78; Brian K. Pennington, *Was Hinduism Invented? Britons, Indians, and Colonial Construction of Religion* (Oxford: Oxford University Press, 2005); and Michael J. Altman, "The Construction of Hinduism in America," *Religion Compass* 10.8 (2016): 207–16.

74. Barua, *Debating "Conversion,"* 66.

75. See ibid., 73–75, 185–91.

76. Susan Bayly, *Saints, Goddesses and Kings: Muslims and Christians in South Indian Society, 1700–1900* (Cambridge: Cambridge University Press, 1989); Selva J. Raj and Corinne M. Dempsey, eds., *Popular Christianity in India: Riting between the Lines* (Albany, NY: SUNY Press, 2002).

77. I have selected Bayly, Raj, and Dempsey as representative early figures in this scholarly movement, but the literature dedicated to the study of South Asian Christianities as distinctively South Asian has continued to grow and flourish. Important titles include Roger E. Hedlund, ed., *Christianity Is Indian: The Emergence of an Indigenous Community* (Delhi: ISPCK, 2000); Corinne G. Dempsey, *Kerala Christian Sainthood: Collisions of Culture and Worldview in South India* (Oxford & New York: Oxford University Press, 2001); Judith M. Brown and Robert Eric Frykenberg, eds., *Christians, Cultural Interactions and India's Religious Traditions* (Grand Rapids, MI: William B. Eerdmans Publishing Company; London: RoutledgeCurzon, 2002); Rowena Robinson, *Christians of India: An Anthropology of Religion* (New Delhi: Sage, 2003); Eliza F. Kent, *Converting Women: Gender and Protestant Christianity in Colonial South India* (Oxford: Oxford University Press, 2004); Paul M. Collins, *Christian Inculturation in India: Liturgy, Worship and Society* (Farnham, UK & Burlington, VT: Ashgate,

2007); Jonas Adelin Jørgensen, *Jesus Imandars and Christ Bhaktas: Two Case Studies of Interreligious Hermeneutics and Identity in Global Christianity* (Frankfurt am Main: Peter Lang, 2008); Rowena Robinson and Joseph Marianus Kujur, eds., *Margins of Faith: Dalit and Tribal Christianity in India* (New Delhi: Sage, 2010); Chad M. Bauman and Richard Fox Young, eds., *Constructing Indian Christianities: Conversion, Culture, and Caste*, ed. (London: Routledge, 2014); Timothy S. Dobe, *Hindu Christian Faqir: Modern Monks, Global Christianity, and Indian Sainthood* (Oxford & New York: Oxford University Press, 2015); Mudita Menona Sodder, RSCJ, *Reliving Christian Life in the Globalized World Today: Cultural Celebrations in Urban Churches of Mumbai* (New Delhi: Christian World Imprints, 2016): Ole Kirchheiner, *Culture and Christianity Negotiated in Hindu Society: A Case Study of a Church in Central and Western Nepal* (Oxford: Regnum, 2017); Reid B. Locklin, ed., *Vernacular Catholicism, Vernacular Saints: Selva J. Raj on 'Being Catholic the Tamil Way'* (Albany, NY: SUNY Press, 2017); Kristin C. Bloomer, *Possessed by the Virgin: Hinduism, Roman Catholicism, and Marian Possession in South India* (Oxford & New York: Oxford University Press, 2018); Clara A. B. Joseph, *Christianity in India: The Anti-Colonial Turn* (London & New York: Routledge, 2019); Kerry P. C. San Chirico, *Between Hindu and Christian: Khrist Bhaktas, Catholics, and the Negotiation of Devotion in Banaras* (New York: Oxford University Press, 2023); and Chandra Mallampalli, *South Asia's Christians: Between Hindu and Muslim* (New York: Oxford University Press, 2023).

78. Bayly, *Saints, Goddesses and Kings*, 454.

79. Selva J. Raj, "Shared Vows, Shared Space, Shared Deities: Vow Rituals among Tamil Catholics in South India," in Locklin, *Vernacular Catholicism*, 83.

80. Selva J. Raj, "The Quest for a Balanced Representation of South Asian Religions in World Religions Textbooks," *Religious Studies Review* 31 (2005): 14–16. Raj's desire eventually bore fruit in Karen Pechilis and Selva J. Raj, eds., *South Asian Religions: Tradition and Today* (London & New York: Routledge, 2013).

81. Frykenberg, *Christianity in India*, 346–50. See also Alexander Henn, *Hindu-Catholic Encounters in Goa: Religion, Colonialism, and Modernity* (Bloomington & Indianapolis: Indiana University Press, 2014), esp. 40–64.

82. David Mosse, *The Saint in the Banyan Tree: Christianity and Caste Society* (Berkeley: University of California Press, 2012), 44–53.

83. Vasudha Narayanan, "Sacred Land, Common Ground, Contested Territory: The Healing Mother of Velankanni Basilica and the Infant Jesus Shrine in Bangalore," *Journal of Hindu-Christian Studies* 17 (2004): 24–25;

Corrinne G. Dempsey, "Comparative Transgressions: Vernacular Catholicisms in Tamil Nadu and Kerala," in Locklin, *Vernacular Catholicism*, 204–6.

84. Dempsey, "Comparative Transgressions," 206.

85. See, for example, Richard Burghart, ed., *Hinduism in Great Britain: The Perpetuation of Religion in an Alien Cultural Milieu* (London & New York: Tavistock Publications, 1987); Raymond Brady Williams, *Religions of Immigrants from India and Pakistan: New Threads in the American Tapestry* (Cambridge: Cambridge University Press, 1988); Harold Coward, John R. Hinnells, and Raymond Brady Williams, *The South Asian Religious Diaspora in Britain, Canada and the United States* (Albany, NY: SUNY Press, 2000); Steven Vertovec, *The Hindu Diaspora: Comparative Patterns* (London & New York: Routledge, 2000); Diana Eck, *A New Religious America: How a "Christian Country" Has Become the World's Most Religiously Diverse Nation* (New York: HarperCollins, 2001), esp. 8–141; T. S. Rukmani, ed., *Hindu Diaspora: Global Perspectives* (Delhi: Munshiram Manoharlal, 2001); Anantanand Rambachan, "Global Hinduism: The Hindu Diaspora," in *Contemporary Hinduism: Ritual, Culture, and Practice*, ed. Robin Rinehart (Santa Barbara, CA, Denver, CO & Oxford: ABC CLIO, 2004), 381–413; Raymond Brady Williams, *Williams on South Asian Religions and Immigration: Collected Works* (Aldershot, UK: Ashgate, 2004); Michael Bergunder, ed., *Westliche Formen des Hinduismus in Deutschland* (Halle: Verlag der franckeschen Stiftungen zu Halle, 2006); John C. Hawley, *India in Africa, Africa in India: Indian Ocean Cosmopolitanisms* (Bloomington: Indiana University Press, 2008); Paul Younger, *New Homelands: Hindu Communities in Mauritius, Guyana, Trinidad, South Africa, Fiji, and East Africa* (New York & Oxford: Oxford University Press, 2010); Albert Wuaku, "Exploring the South–South Trajectory of Global Religious Flows: The Origins of Ghana's Hinduism," in *Religion on the Move! New Dynamics of Religious Expansion in a Globalizing World*, ed. Afe Adogame and Shobana Shankar (Leiden: Brill, 2013), 133–57; and the overview in Chad Bauman and Jennifer B. Saunders, "Out of India: Immigrant Hindus and South Asian Hinduism in the USA," *Religion Compass* 3.1 (2009): 116–35.

86. Vasudha Narayanan, "Extending Selva J. Raj's Scholarship to Hindu American Temples: Accommodation, Assimilation and a Dialogue of Action," in Locklin, *Vernacular Catholicism*, 234–35.

87. See ibid., 238–40; and especially Knut A. Jacobsen and Selva J. Raj, eds., *South Asian Christian Diaspora: Invisible Diaspora in Europe and North America* (Aldershot, UK: Ashgate, 2008).

88. See Vertovec, *Hindu Diaspora*, 1–2; Bauman and Saunders, "Out of India," 128–30; and Elizabeth De Michelis, *A History of Modern Yoga* (London & New York: Continuum, 2005), 9–12.

89. Maya Warrier, *Hindu Selves in a Modern World: Guru Faith in the Mata Amritanandamayi Mission* (London & New York: Routledge, 2005).

90. Srinivas Aravamudan, *Guru English: South Asian Religion in a Cosmopolitan Language* (Princeton, NJ & Oxford: Princeton University Press, 2006).

91. De Michelis, *History of Modern Yoga*; Sarah Strauss, *Positioning Yoga: Balancing Acts across Cultures* (Oxford & New York: Berg, 2005); and Andrea R. Jain, *Selling Yoga: From Counterculture to Pop Culture* (New York: Oxford University Press, 2015).

92. The study of explicitly missionary Hindu traditions has a modest scholarly literature beyond the studies of Mathew and Kuruvachira, mentioned above. See, for example, Wendell Thomas, *Hinduism Invades America* (New York: Beacon Press, 1930); P. D. Devanandan, "Hindu Missions to the West," *International Review of Mission* 48 (1959): 398–408; Reinhart Hummel, *Indische Mission und neue Frömmigkeit in Westen: Religiöse Bewegungen Indiens in westlichen Kulturen* (Stuttgart: Verlag W. Kohlhammer, 1980); and Joachim Finger, *Gurus, Ashrams und der Weste: Eine religionswissenschaftliche Untersuchung zu den Hintergründen der Internationalisierung des Hinduismus* (Frankfurt am Main: Verlag Peter Lang, 1987).

93. Karen Pechilis, ed., *The Graceful Guru: Hindu Female Gurus in India and the United States* (Oxford & New York: Oxford University Press, 2004); Thomas A. Forsthoefel and Cynthia Ann Humes, eds., *Gurus in America* (Albany, NY: SUNY Press, 2005); and Ann Gleig and Lola Williamson, ed., *Homegrown Gurus: From Hinduism in America to American Hinduism* (Albany: SUNY Press, 2013). See also Joanne Punzo Waghorne, "Global Gurus and the Third Stream of American Religiosity: Between Hindu Nationalism and Liberal Pluralism," in *Political Hinduism: The Religious Imagination in Public Spheres*, ed. Vinay Lal (New Delhi: Oxford University Press, 2009), 122–49; and Angela Rudert, "Research on Contemporary Indian Gurus: What's New about New Age Gurus?" *Religion Compass* 4.10 (2010): 629–42.

94. Sunrit Mullick, *The First Hindu Mission to America: The Pioneering Visits of Protap Chunder Mozoomdar* (New Delhi: Northern Book Centre, 2010). See also De Michelis, *History of Modern Yoga*, 51–90; Pandit Sivanath Sastri, *The Mission of the Brahmo Samaj*, 3rd ed. (Calcutta: Brahmo Mission Press, 1952); and David Kopf, *The Brahmo Samaj and the Shaping of the Modern Indian Mind* (Princeton, NJ: Princeton University Press, 1979), esp. 317–29.

95. Lola Williamson, *Transcendent in America: Hindu-Inspired Meditation Movements as New Religion* (New York & London: New York University Press, 2010).

96. E. Burke Rochford Jr., *Hare Krishna in America* (New Brunswick, NJ: Rutgers University Press, 1985); and E. Burke Rochford Jr., *Hare Krishna Transformed* (New York & London: New York University Press, 2007).

97. Harold W. French, *The Swan's Wide Waters: Ramakrishna and Western Culture* (Port Washington, NY & London: Kennikat Press, 1974); Carl S. Jackson, *Vedanta for the West: The Ramakrishna Movement in the United States* (Bloomington & Indianapolis: Indiana University Press, 1994); Gwilym Beckerlegge, *The Ramakrishna Mission: The Making of a Modern Hindu Movement* (Delhi: Oxford University Press, 2000); and Gwilym Beckerlegge, *Swami Vivekananda's Legacy of Service: A Study of the Ramakrishna Math and Mission* (New Delhi: Oxford University Press, 2006).

98. Jackson, *Vedanta for the West*, 130–37.

99. For example, he asserts that, with the advent of the Ramakrishna Mission, Hinduism has emerged from a merely "ethnic religion" to a "missionary" tradition of "world significance" (ibid., 137).

100. Peter Antes and Hans Waldenfels, SJ, "Mission in Non-Christian Religions," in *Dictionary of Mission: Theology, History, Perspectives* (Maryknoll, NY: Orbis Books, 1987), 305.

101. Böspflug, "Religions Missionaires, Religions Non-Missionaires," 152–54.

102. See, for example, ibid., 142–51; Frank Whaling, "A Comparative Religious Study of Missionary Transplantation in Buddhism, Christianity and Islam," *International Review of Mission* 70 (1981): 314–33; Max L. Stackhouse, "Missions: Missionary Activity," in *Encyclopedia of Religion*, vol. 9, ed. Lindsay Jones, revised edition (Detroit: McMillan Reference USA, 2005), 6068–76; and, with a more political and literary focus, Béatrice Bakhouche, Isabelle Fabre, and Vincente Fortier, eds., *Dynamiques de Conversion: Modèles et Résistances, Approches Inderdisciplinaires* (Turnhout, Belgium: Brepols, 2012).

103. Rambo and Farhadian, *Oxford Handbook of Religious Conversion;* Rowena Robinson and Sathianathan Clarke, eds., *Religious Conversion in India: Modes, Motivations, and Meanings* (New Delhi: Oxford University Press, 2003); Rudolf C. Heredia, *Changing Gods: Rethinking Conversion in India* (New Delhi: Penguin Books, 2007); Peter Berger and Sarbeswar Sahoo, eds., *Godroads: Modalities of Conversion in India* (Cambridge: Cambridge University Press, 2020). See also G. A. Oddie, ed., *Religion in South Asia: Religious Conversion and Revival Movements in South Asia in Medieval and Modern Times* (Columbia, MO: South Asia Books, 1977); H. Newton Malony and Samuel Southard, eds. *Handbook of Religious Conversion* (Birmingham, AL: Religious Education Press, 1992); Joseph Mathew, *Contemporary Religious Conversions* (Delhi: Authorpress, 2001); Robert Eric

Frykenberg and Alaine M. Low, eds., *Christians and Missionaries in India: Cross-Cultural Communication Since 1500, with Special Reference to Caste, Conversion, and Colonialism* (Grand Rapids, MI: W. B. Eerdmans, 2003); Antony R. H. Copley, ed., *Hinduism in Public and Private: Reform, Hindutva, Gender, and Sampraday* (New Delhi: Oxford India Paperbacks, 2009); and Shanta Premawardhana, ed., *Religious Conversion: Religion Scholars Thinking Together* (West Sussex, UK: Wiley Blackwell, 2015).

104. Klaus K. Klostermaier, "'In Every Town, Country and Village My Name Will be Sung': Hindu Missions in India and Abroad," in *Mixed Messages: Materiality, Textuality, Missions*, ed. Jamie S. Scott and Gareth Griffiths (New York: Palgrave Macmillan, 2005), 173–202.

105. Ibid., 199.

106. Aaron J. Ghiloni, ed., *World Religions and Their Missions* (New York: Peter Lang, 2015).

107. See Judith Simmer-Brown, "Christian Views: A Response," *Buddhist-Christian Studies* 17 (1997): 152–58.

108. Antes and Waldenfals, "Mission in Non-Christian Religions," 307; Böspflug, "Religions Missionaires, Religions Non-Missionaires," 131, 134–39; Stackhouse, "Missions: Missionary Activity," 6070.

109. Aaron J. Ghiloni, "Towards the Comparative Study of Mission," in Ghiloni, *World Religions and Their Missions*, 268.

110. Ghiloni, "Towards the Comparative Study," 271–89, quotation at 285.

111. Ferdinando Sardella, "Hinduism," in Ghiloni, *World Religions and Their Missions*, 161–62.

112. Arvind Sharma, *Hinduism as a Missionary Religion* (Albany, NY: SUNY Press, 2011).

113. Ibid., 129.

114. Ibid., esp. 65–83. On this point, see also Arvind Sharma, "Ancient Hinduism as a Missionary Religion," *Numen* 39 (1992): 175–92.

115. Sharma, *Hinduism as a Missionary Religion*, 134.

116. For a further discussion of Sharma's constructive Hindu missiology, see Reid B. Locklin, "A Most Uncommon Task: Arvind Sharma and the Construction of Hindu Missiology," *International Journal of Hindu Studies* 28.1 (2024), forthcoming.

117. See also Arvind Sharma, *Religious Studies and Comparative Methodology: The Case for Reciprocal Illumination* (Albany, NY: SUNY Press, 2005).

118. Ghiloni, "Towards the Comparative Study," 289–90.

119. On the problematic relationship between contemporary comparative theology and the older, Orientalist project of the same name, see

especially Hugh Nicholson, "The New Comparative Theology and the Problem of Theological Hegemonism," in *The New Comparative Theology: Interreligious Insights from the Next Generation*, ed. Francis X. Clooney (London: T&T Clark, 2010), 43–62; Hugh Nicholson, *Comparative Theology and the Problem of Religious Rivalry* (Oxford & New York: Oxford University Press, 2011); Paul Hedges, "The Old and New Comparative Theologies: Discourse on Religion, the Theology of Religions, Orientalism and the Boundaries of Traditions," *Religions* 3.4 (2012): 1120–37; Paul Hedges, "Comparative Theology: A Critical and Methodological Perspective," *Theology* 1.1 (2017): 27–58; and John J. Thatamanil, *Circling the Elephant: A Comparative Theology of Religious Diversity* (New York: Fordham University Press, 2020), 108–51.

120. Francis X. Clooney, SJ, *Comparative Theology: Deep Learning across Religious Borders* (Malden, MA: Wiley-Blackwell, 2010), 24–40. See also the discussion in Reid B. Locklin and Hugh Nicholson, "The Return of Comparative Theology," *Journal of the American Academy of Religion* 78.2 (2010): 477–514, esp. 482–89.

121. Clooney, *Comparative Theology*, 39–40.

122. In this respect, it closely resembles the "New Comparativism" advocated by William Paden and other contemporary scholars of religion in North America and Europe. See Locklin and Nicholson, "Return of Comparative Theology," 489–99.

123. Clooney, *Comparative Theology*, 16–19, 87–108.

124. See Clooney, ibid., 57–68, as well as the further conversation in Judith Gruber, "(Un)Silencing Hybridity: A Postcolonial Critique of Comparative Theology" in Mara Brecht and Reid B. Locklin, eds., *Comparative Theology in the Millennial Classroom: Hybrid Identities, Negotiated Boundaries* (New York & London: Routledge, 2016), 21–35; and Lisa Gasson-Gardner and Jason Smith, "Feeling Comparative Theology: Millennial Affect and Reparative Learning," in ibid., 113–25.

125. Francis X. Clooney, S.J., "Reading the World in Christ: From Comparison to Inclusivism," in *Christian Uniqueness Reconsidered*, ed. Gavin D'Costa (Maryknoll: Orbis Books, 1990), 70.

126. Clooney, Comparative Theology, 125–27; and Francis X. Clooney, SJ, *Beyond Compare: St. Francis de Sales and Śrī Vedānta Deśika on Loving Surrender to God* (Washington, DC: Georgetown University Press, 2008), esp. 132–41, 202–10.

127. Catherine Cornille, "The Problem of Choice in Comparative Theology," in Francis X. Clooney, SJ, and Klaus von Stosch, eds., *How to Do Comparative Theology* (New York: Fordham University Press, 2018), 19–36, with quoted passages drawn from 29–31; and the fuller enumeration of

these approaches in Catherine Cornille, *Meaning and Method in Comparative Theology* (Hoboken, NJ: Wiley Blackwell, 2020), 115–47.

128. Francis X. Clooney, SJ, *Theology after Vedānta: An Experiment in Comparative Theology* (Albany, NY: SUNY Press, 1993), 156–87.

129. Francis X. Clooney, SJ, *His Hiding Place is Darkness: A Hindu-Catholic Theopoetics of Divine Absence* (Stanford, CA: Stanford University Press, 2014).

130. Michelle Voss Roberts, *Tastes of the Divine: Hindu and Christian Theologies of Emotion* (New York: Fordham University Press, 2014), xviii–xxii.

131. See King, *Orientalism and Religion*, esp. 118–25. Of course, the choice of Catholic and ecumenical Christian theologies is no less open to critique, insofar as my choice may be read (probably accurately) to presume a theological judgment that these traditions, rather than more evangelical or conservative Protestant traditions, should be regarded as, if not the essence of Christianity, then perhaps its least inadequate expression.

132. Clooney describes the comparative theological project as a "necessarily arbitrary and intuitive practice" and commends an approach that proceeds "by intuitive leaps, according to instinct," rather than according to some grand design or theoretical agenda. See Francis X. Clooney, SJ, *The Truth, the Way, the Life: Christian Commentary on the Three Holy Mantras of the Śrīvaiṣṇava Hindus* (Leuven: Peeters, 2008), 11, 96, as well as the further discussion in Cornille, "Problem of Choice," 25–27 and Cornille, *Meaning and Method*, 118–20.

133. Sharma, *Hinduism as a Missionary Religion*, 119.

134. See Mullick, *The First Hindu Mission*, for a counternarrative.

135. Thomas A. Forsthoefel, "Weaving the Inward Thread to Awakening: The Perennial Appeal of Ramana Maharshi," in Forsthoefel and Hume, *Gurus in America*, 37.

136. Ibid., 39.

137. Leo F. Stelton, *Dictionary of Ecclesiastical Latin* (Peabody, MA: Hendrickson Publishers, 1995), 314.

138. Arvind Sharma, "Christian Proselytization," 425. See also Sharma, *Problematizing Religious Freedom*, 180–81.

139. Sharma, *Hinduism as a Missionary Religion*, 133.

140. Wesley Wildman, *Religious Philosophy as a Multidisciplinary Comparative Inquiry: Envisioning a Future for the Philosophy of Religion* (Albany, NY: SUNY Press, 2010), 126–27.

141. Ibid., 133–34, 147–52. Wildman draws these criteria from the Comparative Religious Ideas Project at Boston University, which ran between 1995 to 1999 and involved a collaborative team of ten scholars.

See Wesley Wildman, "Cross-Cultural Comparative Religious Ideas Project (CRIP)," *Wildman's Weird Wild Web*, http://people.bu.edu/wwildman/WeirdWildWeb/proj_crip.htm, as well as the three volumes produced by the project: Robert C. Neville, ed., *The Human Condition* (Albany, NY: SUNY Press, 2001); Robert C. Neville, ed., *Religious Truth* (Albany, NY: SUNY Press, 2001); and Robert C. Neville, ed., *Ultimate Realities* (Albany, NY: SUNY Press, 2001). These criteria have been developed along a different, complementary trajectory by Robert Neville himself in such works as *Defining Religion: Essays in the Philosophy of Religion* (Albany, NY: SUNY Press, 2018).

142. See Cornille, "Problem of Choice," 20–24, along with the further discussion in Cornille, *Meaning and Method*, 18–34, 186–88; and Catherine Cornille, "The Confessional Nature of Comparative Theology," *Studies in Interreligious Dialogue* 24.1 (2014): 9–17.

143. Wildman, *Religious Philosophy*, 128. The recognition of one's subject position as an interpreter also figures prominently in several recent defenses of the comparative method by anthropologists and historians of religion. See, for example, Kimberley C. Patton and Benjamin C. Ray, eds., *A Magic Still Dwells: Comparative Religion in the Postmodern Age* (Berkeley: University of California Press, 2000); Corinne G. Dempsey, *Bringing the Sacred Down to Earth: Adventures in Comparative Religion* (New York: Oxford University Press, 2012); Bruce Lincoln, *Apples and Oranges: Explorations in, on, and with Comparison* (Chicago: University of Chicago Press, 2018); and Oliver Freiberger, *Considering Comparison: A Method for Religious Studies* (New York: Oxford University Press, 2019).

144. See especially Kollman, "At the Origins," 435–45.

145. On this point, see Cornille, "Problem of Choice," 32–33 and Glenn R. Willis, "On Some Suspicions Regarding Comparative Theology," in Clooney and von Stosch, *How to Do Comparative Theology*, esp. 129–32.

146. The two parts of the book roughly correspond to what Bernard Lonergan referred to as the "mediating" and "mediated" phases of all theological inquiry, in which the interpreter first engages in the interpretation and analysis of past tradition before reformulating it constructively for the present and future. See Bernard J. F. Lonergan, *Method in Theology* (Toronto: University of Toronto Press, 1971), 133–36. Lonergan, like Wildman, envisions this as a collaborative project, beyond the capacity of any single scholar. The structure also resonates with Aaron Langenfeld's fourfold account of "elaboration," "questioning," "discourse" and "returning" phases in "The Moment of Truth: Comparative and Dogmatic Theology," in Clooney and von Stosch, *How to Do Comparative Theology*, 59–71. Though every chapter includes elements of all four phases, the

emphasis shifts steadily from elaboration in the first part to ever deeper practices of questioning and return in the chapters of the second part.

147. Cornille, *Meaning and Method*, 187.

Chapter 2

1. Swami Vivekananda, "The Work Before Us," *The Complete Works of Swami Vivekananda*, Mayavati Memorial Ed., vol. 3 (Calcutta: Advaita Ashrama, 1989), 277.

2. The main exposition of this chapter was previously published as Reid B. Locklin, "A Century of Advaita Mission: Tracing a Lineage and Opening a Conversation," *Journal of Ecumenical Studies* 52.4 (2017): 488–526. It is reused by permission of the University of Pennsylvania Press. The original article has been revised and significantly expanded for its inclusion here.

3. See, for example, Arvind Sharma, *Hinduism as a Missionary Religion* (Albany, NY: SUNY Press, 2011), 119; Ferdinando Sardella, "Hinduism," in *World Religions and Their Missions*, ed. Aaron J. Ghiloni (New York: Peter Lang, 2015), 164; and Klaus K. Klostermaier, "'In Every Town, Country and Village My Name Will be Sung': Hindu Missions in India and Abroad," in *Mixed Messages: Materiality, Textuality, Missions*, ed. Jamie S. Scott and Gareth Griffiths (New York: Palgrave Macmillan, 2005), 185.

4. Reinhart Hummel, *Indische Mission und neue Frömmigkeit in Westen: Religiöse Bewegungen Indiens in westlichen Kulturen* (Stuttgart: Verlag W. Kohlhammer, 1980), 17–19, 117–22.

5. Vivekananda, "Paper on Hinduism," in *Complete Works*, vol. 1, 13–14.

6. Vivekananda, "Is Vedanta the Future Religion?" in *Complete Works*, vol. 3, esp. 136, 140–41.

7. Corinne Dempsey offers an insightful analysis of the creative reversal of Orientalist tropes in Theosophy, Vivekananda's "Practical Vedānta," and South Asian Christianity in her *Bringing the Sacred Down to Earth: Adventures in Comparative Religion* (Oxford & New York: Oxford University Press, 2012), esp. 21–48, 109–42.

8. Philip Goldberg perceives Vivekananda's adoption of his distinctive synthesis of Advaita and Yoga, rather than the Kali devotionalism of his guru, as a deliberate, strategic choice. See his *American Veda: From Emerson and the Beatles to Yoga and Meditation—How Indian Spirituality Changed the West* (New York: Harmony Books, 2010), 80.

9. For an example of the latter approach, in addition to Hummel, see Michael J. Altman, "The Construction of Hinduism in America," *Religion Compass* 10.8 (2016): 207–16.

10. Goldberg, *American Veda*, 9–12; Elizabeth De Michelis, *A History of Modern Yoga* (London & New York: Continuum, 2005), 2–4; and Lola Williamson, *Transcendent in America: Hindu-Inspired Meditation Movements as New Religion* (New York & London: New York University Press, 2010), 3–5.

11. Hummel, *Indische Mission*, 119–21. See also Joachim Finger, *Gurus, Ashrams und der Weste: Eine religionswissenschaftliche Untersuchung zu den Hintergründen der Internationalisierung des Hinduismus* (Frankfurt am Main: Verlag Peter Lang, 1987), 19–25.

12. I will return to this point in greater detail in the next chapter.

13. Raymond Brady Williams, "Sacred Threads of Several Textures," in *A Sacred Thread: Modern Transmission of Hindu Traditions in India and Abroad*, ed. Raymond Brady Williams (Chambersburg, PA: Anima, 1992), 231–44.

14. Thomas A. Forsthoefel and Cynthia Ann Humes, eds., *Gurus in America* (Albany, NY: SUNY Press, 2005), 5.

15. Williams, "Sacred Threads," 243.

16. *Śaṅkara the Missionary*, revised edition (Mumbai: Central Chinmaya Mission Trust, 1998).

17. See William Cenkner, *A Tradition of Teachers: Śaṅkara and the Jagadgurus Today* (Delhi: Motilal Banarsidass, 1983, 1995 [reprint]); Wade H. Dazey, "Tradition and Modernization in the Organization of the Daśanāmī Saṁnyāsins," in *Monastic Life in the Christian and Hindu Traditions*, ed. Austin B. Creel and Vasudha Narayanan (Lewiston/Queenston/Lampeter: Edwin Mellen Press, 1990); Yoshitsugu Sawai, *The Faith of Ascetics and Lay Smārtas: A Study of the Śaṅkaran Tradition of Śṛṅgerī* (Vienna: Institut für Indologie der Universitat Wien, 1992); and Matthew Clark, *The Daśanāmī-Saṃnyāsīs: The Integration of Ascetic Lineages into an Order* (Leiden & Boston: Brill, 2006).

18. In this respect, all of the movements profiled here are "traditional" in their self-presentation, even if they would not all win recognition by the exponents of what Phillip Charles Lucas calls "Traditional Modern Vedanta." See his "Non-Traditional Modern Vedanta Gurus in the West and Their Traditional Modern Advaita Critics," *Novo Religio* 17.3 (2014): 6–37.

19. See Dazey, "Tradition and Modernization," 311–12; *Śaṅkara the Missionary*, 82; Cynthia Ann Humes, "Maharishi Mahesh Yogi: Beyond the TM Technique," in Forsthoefel and Humes, esp. 58–62. Though Ramana Maharshi did not receive formal renunciation, he was publicly recognized as an authentic renunciant and liberated sage by the Śaṅkarācārya of Kāñcī and other prominent Advaita personalities associated with Kāñcī, such as the renowned philosopher T. M. P, Mahadevan. See Andrew O. Fort, *Jīvanmukti in Transformation: Embodied Liberation in Advaita and Neo-Vedanta* (Albany, NY: SUNY Press, 1998), 134, 146.

20. "Places Associated with Swami Vivekananda," *Vivekananda Vedanta Society of Chicago*. http://chicagovedanta.org/vivekananda/chicago-places.html

21. De Michelis, *History of Modern Yoga*, 91.

22. Richard Hughes Seager, *The World's Parliament of Religions: The East/West Encounter, Chicago, 1893* (Bloomington & Indianapolis: Indiana University Press, 1995).

23. Ibid., 25–30.

24. Quoted in ibid., 19.

25. See the discussion in Donald H. Bishop, "Religious Confrontation, a Case Study: The 1893 Parliament of Religions," *Numen* 16 (1969): 63–76; Diana L. Eck, *Encountering God: A Spiritual Journey from Bozeman to Banares* (Boston: Beacon Press, 1993), 27–28; and Indira Choudhury-Sengupta, "Reconstructing Hinduism on a World Platform: The World's First Parliament of Religions, Chicago 1892," in *Swami Vivekananda and the Modernization of Hinduism*, ed. William Radice (Delhi: Oxford University Press, 1998), esp. 20–23.

26. Seager, *World's Parliament*, 25–30.

27. Ibid., 50.

28. Ibid., xxiii.

29. For nuanced assessments of Vivekananda's role at the Parliament, see ibid., 111–12, and Carl S. Jackson, *Vedanta for the West: The Ramakrishna Movement in the United States* (Bloomington & Indianapolis: Indiana University Press, 1994), 25–27.

30. Vivekananda, "Response to Welcome," *Complete Works*, vol. 1, 3.

31. Vivekananda, "Paper on Hinduism," *Complete Works*, vol. 1, esp. 13–14.

32. Ibid., 19.

33. Hummel, *Indische Mission*, 18–19. For overviews of previous receptions of Hinduism as a broad background for Vivekananda and the Parliament, see Jackson, *Vedanta for the West*, 6–15; and Carl T. Jackson, "Turning East: American Interest in Asian Religions since the 1890s," in *The Cyclonic Swami: Vivekananda in the West*, eds. Sukalyan Sengupta and Makarand Paranjape (New Delhi: Samvad India Foundation, 2005), 64–73.

34. Seager, *World's Parliament*, 148–53, 156–59. Vivekananda's dramatic success at the Parliament and the rapid growth of the Ramakrishna Mission have tended to obscure the work of Majumdar in particular in laying the ground through three missionary journeys in 1883, 1893, and 1900. See P. D. Devanandan, "Hindu Missions to the West," *International Review of Mission* 48 (1959): 398–408.

35. Jackson, *Vedanta for the West*, 28–30. He notes that the first Vedanta Society founded in 1894 was "so nebulous that it was entirely overlooked by early movement historians" (28).

36. Vivekananda, "Reply to the Address of Welcome at Paramakudi," *Complete Works*, vol. 3, 156.

37. For fuller histories of the movement's early development in India and the United States, see Jackson, *Vedanta in the West*; Harold W. French, *The Swan's Wide Waters: Ramakrishna and Western Culture* (Port Washington, NY & London: Kennikat Press, 1974); Cyrus R. Pangborn, "The Rāmakrishna Math and Mission: A Case Study in a Revitalization Movement," in *Hinduism: New Essays in the History of Religions* (Leiden: Brill, 1976), 98–118; George M. Williams, "The Ramakrishna Movement: A Study in Religious Change," in *Religion in Modern India*, revised edition, ed. Robert D. Baird (New Delhi: Manohar, 1989), 55–79; and the authorized account in Swami Gambhirananda, *History of Ramakrishna Math and Ramakrishna Mission* (Calcutta: Advaita Ashrama, 1983).

38. Swami Budhananda, *The Ramakrishna Movement: Its Meaning for Mankind* (Calcutta: Advaita Ashrama, 1980), 20, 34, 157.

39. Gwilym Beckerlegge has provided a helpful overview of this scholarship in *The Ramakrishna Mission: The Making of a Modern Hindu Movement* (New Delhi: Oxford University Press, 2000), esp. 27–51, and Gwilym Beckerlegge, "Swami Vivekananda (1863–1902) 150 Years on: Critical Studies of an Influential Hindu Guru," *Religion Compass* 7.10 (2013): 444–53. Working primarily from primary texts, Arpita Mitra has responded to critics and made the case for a close affinity between Vivekananda and his teacher in "Ramakrishna and Vivekananda: Two Teachings or One?" *Prabuddha Bharata* 119 (2014): 65–78, 194–203, 251–55, 259. Most difficult for the movement, perhaps, have been psychoanalytic studies of Ramakrishna's mysticism. See Sudhir Kakar, *The Analyst and the Mystic: Psychoanalytic Reflections on Religion and Mysticism* (New Delhi: Viking, 1991); Jeffrey J. Kripal, *Kālī's Child: The Mystical and the Erotic in the Life and Teachings of Ramakrishna* (Chicago & London: University of Chicago Press, 1995); and the response in Swami Tyagananda and Pravrajika Vrajaprana, *Interpreting Ramakrishna: Kālī's Child Revisited* (Delhi: Motilal Banarsidass, 2010).

40. See De Michelis, *History of Modern Yoga*, 91–126; George M. Williams, "Svami Vivekananda: Archetypal Hero or Doubting Saint?" in Baird, *Religion in Modern India*, 313–42; and Narasingha Prosad Sil, *Swami Vivekananda: A Reassessment* (Selinsgrove, PA: Susquehanna University Press, 1997).

41. See Sumitora Noma, "'The Will of the Mother,'" in *Swami Vivekananda: A Hundred Years Since Chicago*, ed. R. K. Dasgupta (Belur: Ramakrishna Math and Ramakrishna Mission, 1994), 3; Swami Cheta-

nananda, "Vivekananda: On the Way to Chicago," in ibid., 11–12; and Swami Tyagananda, "What Made Vivekananda Attend the Parliament of Religions?" in ibid., 22–23.

42. Tyagananda, "What Made Vivekananda," 22, quoting from *The Life of Swami Vivekananda by His Eastern and Western Admirers*, 3rd edition (Calcutta: Advaita Ashrama, 1970), 371.

43. Though the description of this episode comes out of the *Life of Swami Vivekananda*, 360, Vivekananda does describe his determination to persevere with the words, "I have a call from Above," in an 1893 letter from America (*Complete Works*, vol. 5, 12). In context, this remark does not seem to refer to a specific event in the past.

44. Jackson, *Vedanta in the West*, 25–26. Hummel (*Indische Mission*, 122–28) illustrates how Vivekananda's commission, which evolves during his travels in 1893–1894, is eventually retrojected back to Ramakrishna himself. See also the discussions of myth and history in Swami Tyagananda, "Rediscovering Vivekananda in the East and the West," and Makarand Paranjape, "Representing Swami Vivekananda: Some Issues and Debates," in Sengupta and Parnjape, *Cyclonic Swami*, 29–69.

45. For a fuller discussion of this concept, see Jackson, *Vedanta for the West*, esp. 68–72; and Williams, "Svami Vivekananda," 334–37.

46. Swami Vivekananda, *What Religion Is: In the Words of Vivekananda*, ed. Swami Vidyatmananda (Kolkata: Advaita Ashrama, 1972), 1.

47. As I was completing this manuscript, Swami Medhananda brought out his magisterial study, *Swami Vivekananda's Vedāntic Cosmopolitanism* (Oxford: Oxford University Press, 2022), which sets the basic teachings I cover here in a broader social and intellectual context. See also Medhananda's remarkable study of Vivekananda's teacher Ramakrishna, published before Medhananda received formal *saṃnyāsa* in the Ramakrishna Order: Ayon Maharaj, *Infinite Paths to Infinite Reality: Sri Ramakrishna and Cross-Cultural Philosophy of Religion* (Oxford: Oxford University Press, 2018).

48. See especially Vivekananda, "The Ideal of a Universal Religion," *Complete Works*, vol. 2, 384–96.

49. See, for example, Vivekananda, *Complete Works*, vol. 2, 82–83, 144–54, 252–53; Budhananda, *Ramakrishna Mission*, 42–43. For further analysis of Vivekananda's social ethic, see below, chapter 6, pp. 191–94, as well as the essays collected in Rita D. Sherma, *Swami Vivekananda: His Life, Legacy, and Liberative Ethics* (Lanham, MD: Lexington Books, 2021).

50. Vivekananda, "Practical Vedanta II," *Complete Works*, vol. 2, 325.

51. In "Maya and Freedom" (*Complete Works*, vol. 2, 123), for example, Vivekananda sets out a sharp contrast: "On the one side, therefore, is the bold assertion that this is all nonsense, that this is Maya; but along with it there is the most hopeful assertion that beyond Maya, there is a

way out. On the other hand, practical men tell us: 'Don't bother your heads about such nonsense as religion and metaphysics. Live here; this is a very bad world, indeed, but make the best of it.' Which put in plain language means, live a hypocritical, lying life, a life of continuous fraud, covering all sores in the best way you can. Go on putting patch over patch, until everything is lost and you are a mass of patchwork. This is what is called practical life. Those that are satisfied with this patchwork will never come to religion."

52. See especially Hummel, *Indische Mission*, 128–29; and Wilhelm Halbfass, *India and Europe: An Essay in Understanding* (Albany, NY: SUNY Press, 1988), 230–38.

53. Vivekananda, "The Free Soul," *Complete Works*, vol. 3, 18.

54. Vivekananda, "My Master," *Complete Works*, vol. 4, 155.

55. Richard King, *Orientalism and Religion: Postcolonial Theory, India and "The Mystic East"* (London & New York: Routledge, 1999), 93–94, 134–42; Srinivas Aravamudan, *Guru English: South Asian Religion in a Cosmopolitan Language* (Princeton, NJ & Oxford: Princeton University Press, 2006), 53–62; and Dermot Killingley, "Vivekananda's Western Message from the East," in Radice, *Swami Vivekananda and the Modernization of Hinduism*, 138–57.

56. See especially Joanne Punzo Waghorne, "Global Gurus and the Third Stream of American Religiosity: Between Hindu Nationalism and Liberal Pluralism," in *Political Hinduism: The Religious Imagination in Public Spheres*, ed. Vinay Lal (New Delhi: Oxford University Press, 2009), 125–29; and the more detailed discussions of Vivekananda's nationalism in Paul Hacker, "Swami Vivekananda's Religious Nationalism," in *Philology and Confrontation: Paul Hacker on Traditional and Modern Vedānta*, ed. Wilhelm Halbfass (Albany, NY: SUNY Press, 1995), 319–36, and Shamita Basu, *Religious Revivalism as Nationalist Discourse: Swami Vivekananda and New Hinduism in Nineteenth-Century Bengal* (New Delhi: Oxford University Press, 2002). There is some irony here insofar as both Wendall Thomas (*Hinduism Invades America* [New York: Beacon Press, 1930], 113–14) and to a lesser extent Jackson (*Vedanta for the West*, 85–87) have pointed out that the Vedanta Societies in the West are in some ways more "conservative" in their transmission of Hindu teachings than are the Ramakrishna Math and Mission in India.

57. See, for example, Pravrajika Vrajaprana, *Vedanta: A Simple Introduction* (Hollywood, CA: Vedanta Press, 1999), 82–88.

58. For explorations of some of the reasons behind the slow growth of Vedanta Societies in the West, see Jackson, *Vedanta for the West*, 108–29; Beckerlegge, *Ramakrishna Mission*, 143–79; Diana Eck, *A New Religious America: How a "Christian Country" Has Become the World's Most Religiously Diverse*

Nation (New York: HarperCollins, 2001), 101–4; and John M. Whitworth and Martin Shiels, "From Across the Black Water: Two Imported Varieties of Hinduism," in *New Religious Movements: A Perspective for Understanding Society*, ed. Eileen Barker (New York: Edwin Mellen Press, 1982), 170–71.

59. On this point, see especially Goldberg, *American Veda*, 87–108.

60. Budhananda, *Ramakrishna Mission*, 109, 133. On the broader influence of the movement, also see ibid., 100–109; and Beckerlegge, *Ramakrishna Mission*, 27–29, 109–11.

61. Paul Brunton, *A Search in Secret India* (London: Rider and Company, 1934, 1957), 10. The Ramanasramam has also published a shorter version, including only the three chapters dealing directly with Ramana Maharshi: Paul Brunton, *The Maharshi and His Message* (Tiruvannamalai, India: Sri Ramanasramam, 2009).

62. Brunton, *The Maharshi and His Message*, 10.

63. Brunton, *Search in Secret India*, 194–99.

64. Brunton, *The Maharshi and His Message*, 69–76, quotations at 76 and 72.

65. Brunton, *Search in Secret India*, 13.

66. Ramana Maharshi met with Frank H. Humphreys, a member of the British colonial government, in 1911, and Humphreys published a summary of the Maharshi's teachings in the *International Psychic Gazette* in 1913. See Arvind Sharma, *Ramana Maharshi: The Sage of Arunachala* (New Delhi: Penguin, 2006), 76–81; and the two-part account in the New York ashram's newsletter: "Whatever Became of Frank H. Humphreys?" in *The Maharshi* 27.5 (2017): 1–3 and 27.6 (2017): 1–4.

67. See Sharma, *Ramana Maharshi*, 127–28; and Fort, *Jīvanmukti in Transformation*, 137.

68. In this article, I have depended primarily on Sharma, *Ramana Maharshi*. Other accounts of Ramana's life are available in B. V. Narasimha Swami, *Self-Realisation: The Life and Teachings of Sri Ramana Maharshi* (Tiruvannamalai, India: Sri Ramanasramam, 1985 [1931]); Arthur Osborne, *Ramana Maharshi and the Path of Self-Knowledge: A Biography*, 4th edition (San Rafael, CA: Sophia Perennis, 2006); T. M. P. Mahadevan, *Ramana Maharshi: The Sage of Arunachala* (London: George Allen and Unwin, 1977); and the shorter summary in Thomas Forsthoefel, *Knowing Beyond Knowledge: Epistemologies of Religious Experience in Classical and Modern Advaita* (Aldershot, UK and Burlington, VT: Ashgate, 2002), 129–33.

69. Sharma, *Ramana Maharshi*, 10.

70. Swami, *Self-Realisation*, 20–22, quoted in Sharma, *Ramana Maharshi*, 13–14.

71. Lucy Cornelssen, *Hunting the "I"* (Tiruvannamalai, India: Sri Ramanasramam, 2009), 6–7.

72. Osborne, *Ramana Maharshi*, 35–37; and Sharma, *Ramana Maharshi*, 134–40.

73. Osborne, *Ramana Maharshi*, 40. Many of these interviews have been gathered together in Ramana Maharshi, *Talks with Sri Ramana Maharshi: Three Volumes in One*, 3rd edition (Tiruvannamalai, India: Sri Ramanasramam, 1963).

74. Ramana Maharshi, "Reality in Forty Verses," verse 30, in *The Collected Works of Sri Ramana Maharshi*, 10th edition (Tiruvannamalai, India: Sri Ramanasramam, 2009 [2007]), 119.

75. See Ramana Maharshi, *Collected Works*, 19–20, 40–41; and the discussion in Cornelsson, 28–32, 84; Fort, *Jīvanmukti in Transformation*, 141–42; and T. M. P. Mahadevan, *Ramana Maharshi and His Philosophy of Existence*, 3rd edition (Tiruvannamalai, India: Ramanasramam, 1976), 101–4.

76. Mahadevan, *Ramana Maharshi and His Philosophy*, 95.

77. Ibid., 95–96; and Sharma, *Ramana Maharshi*, 146–52. See also Ramana Maharshi, *Collected Works*, 5–7, 36–39; Brunton, *Maharshi and His Message*, 14–17, 32–34, 62; and Osborne, *Ramana Maharshi*, 117–19.

78. Ramana Maharshi, *Collected Works*, 7, 112 (v. 20), 121 (v. 40), 125 (v. 14); Mahadevan, *Ramana Maharshi and His Philosophy*, 100; and Sharma, *Ramana Maharshi*, 143.

79. Osborne, *Ramana Maharshi*, 117.

80. Sharma, *Ramana Maharshi*, 28.

81. See ibid., 107; and Cornelssen, *Hunting the "I,"* 49–50, 54.

82. Ramana Maharshi, *Collected Works*, 120 (vv. 32, 34).

83. Ibid., 208–69. Sharma (*Ramana Maharshi*, 153) notes that the expression of Ramana's teaching became more sophisticated over time, as he became more familiar with the scholastic traditions.

84. Sharma, *Ramana Maharshi*, 46–51, quotation at 48; Osborne, *Ramana Maharshi*, 109–14.

85. See the editor's gloss in Ramana Maharshi, *Collected Works*, 105–7, as well as Osborne, *Ramana Maharshi*, 60, 121–25; and Cornelssen, *Hunting the "I,"* 92–101.

86. Phillip Charles Lucas, "Neo-Advaita in America: Three Representative Teachers," in *Homegrown Gurus: From Hinduism in America to American Hinduism*, ed. Ann Gleig and Lola Williamson (Albany, NY: SUNY Press, 2013), 165–66.

87. Ibid., 166–69.

88. For a description of the structure and institutionalization of Ramanasramam, see Osborne, *Ramana Maharshi*, 93–98, 149–50; Fort, *Jīvanmukti in Transformation*, 137–38; and the list of centers and *satsang* groups at "Satsangh Centres," *Sriramanasramam*. www.sriramanamaharshi.org/centres/directory

89. See the four-part series, Dennis Hartel and Anil K. Sharma, "50th Anniversary of Arunachala Ashrama," in *The Maharshi* 26.6 (2016): 1–4; 27.1 (2017): 4–5; 27.2 (2017): 1–3; 27.3 (2017): 1–3.

90. The video is available in VHS and DVD formats, as well as on the worldwide web: John Flynn and Dennis J. Hartel, *The Sage of Arunachala: Sri Ramana Maharshi: 1879–1950* (Forest Hills, NY: Arunachala Ashrama, 1992); and "Bhagavan Sri Ramana Maharshi—The Sage of Arunachala," YouTube. www.youtube.com/watch?v=pefl9sbkKxk

91. Lucas, "Neo-Advaita in America," 171–80. See also Goldberg, *American Veda,* 256–61.

92. Ramana Maharshi, *Talks,* 243, cited in Ankur Barua, "The Silences of Ramana Maharshi: Self-Inquiry and Liberation in Sāṁkhya Yoga and Advaita Vedānta," *Religions of South Asia* 9.2 (2015): 199.

93. "Preface," in Cornelssen, *Hunting the "I,"* iii.

94. Osborne, *Ramana Maharshi,* 126, 150–51.

95. Ibid., 153.

96. Nancy Patchen, *The Journey of a Master: Swami Chinmayananda the Man, the Path, the Teaching* (Bombay: Central Chinmaya Mission Trust, 1989, 1994), 159.

97. Ibid., 159–60.

98. Ibid., 161.

99. See ibid., 163–71, quotation at 168.

100. Ibid., 94. On Chinmayananda's deliberate effort to aim the work of the Chinmaya Mission at the educated middle classes and businesspeople in India, see ibid., 91, 155–56, and Purvi Parikh, "Does Character Count: Moral Self-Fashioning in the Swadhyaya and Chinmaya Mission Movements" (PhD dissertation, University of Pennsylvania, 2014), 56. For further accounts of the *Jñāna Yajña* plan, see also Jagdhari Masih, *The Role of Swami Chinmayananda in Revitalization of Hinduism and Reinterpretation of Christianity* (Calcutta: Punthi Pustak, 2000), 86–87, and Shyamala Shiveshwarkar, "The Chinmaya Mission: Vedantic Activism," in *Dharma and Development: The Future of Survival,* ed. Makarand Paranjape (New Delhi: Samvad India Foundation, 2005), 174–76.

101. Swami Chinmayananda, *The Holy Geeta: Commentary by Swami Chinmayananda,* revised edition (Mumbai: Central Chinmaya Mission Trust, 1996, 2008). See also Margaret Dukes, David Dukes, Neena Dev, Rashmi Mehrotra, Arun Mehrrotra, and Padmashree Rao, eds., *He Did It: Swami Chinmayananda—A Legacy* (Piercy, CA: Chinmaya Mission West, 2011), xi, 3, 186–87.

102. Patchen, *Journey of a Master,* 15, 26–29, 54–58, 93–94; Shiveshwarkar, "Chinmaya Mission," 173–74; Dukes et al., 32–34, 36–53, 74–75; David M. Miller, "The Divine Life Society Movement," in Baird, *Religion*

in Modern India, esp. 92, 101; and Lise McKean, *Divine Enterprise: Gurus and the Hindu Nationalist Movement* (Chicago & London: University of Chicago Press, 1996), 177–79. Though the Divine Life Society is also rooted in Advaita Vedānta, it eventually became connected much more strongly with training teachers and disciples in yoga. See the discussion in Miller; McKean, *Divine Enterprise*, 164–84; and especially Sarah Stauss, *Positioning Yoga: Balancing Acts Across Cultures* (Oxford & New York: Berg, 2005).

103. See, for example, Swami Chinmayananda, *A Manual of Self-Unfoldment* (Mumbai: Central Chinmaya Mission Trust, 1975, 2000), 55, 150–51; and Swami Chinmayananda, *Kindle Life* (Mumbai: Central Chinmaya Mission Trust, 1990, 1996), 55–56, 73, quotation at 56.

104. Varun Khanna offers a fruitful analysis of this element of Chinmayananda's self-presentation in "Swami Chinmayananda, Hinduism and Diaspora Configurations: Identifying the Effects of a Modern Advaita-Vedāntin on the Hindu Diaspora in North America," *Nidān* 3.1 (2018): 31–49, esp. 32–36.

105. On the latter point, see especially Chinmayananda, *Manual of Self-Unfoldment*, 76–77. The analysis of the human constitution into five sheaths is taken from the *Taittirīya Upaniṣad* and recurs frequently throughout Swami Chinmayananda's writings, such as ibid., 98–106, and Chinmayananda, *Kindle Life*, 60–69.

106. See Chinmayananda, *Manual of Self-Unfoldment*, 76, 173; Patchen, *Journey of a Master*, 194; Dukes et al., *He Did It*, 101; Anita Raina Thapan, ed., *The Penguin Swami Chinmayananda Reader* (New Delhi: Penguin Books, 2004), xiii; and especially "The Genius of the Chart," in *Vedānta: Swami Chinmayananda, His Words, His Legacy*, ed. Margaret Dukes, David Dukes, Neena Dev, Rashmi Mehrotra, Arun Mehrotra, and Padmashree Rao (Piercy, CA: Chinmaya Publications, 2011), 15–21. The BMI Chart remains a defining symbol of the movement; it is rare to encounter a Chinmaya Mission teacher without one near at hand.

107. Chinmayananda, *Holy Geeta*, 2–7; Chinmayananda, *Manual of Self-Unfoldment*, 18–21, 53–56; and Chinmayananda, *Kindle Life*, 24. These two characterizations are not contradictory: since the *vāsanās* represent the basis of all thoughts, their destruction also entails the destruction of the thoughts that flow from them. What Swami Chinmayananda's teaching does reveal is a significant change in emphasis—from the immanent subjective process of self-inquiry, as promoted by Ramana Maharshi, to more objective analyses in Sanskrit and in terms set primarily by the *Upaniṣadic* scriptures.

108. See Chinmayananda, *Manual of Self-Unfoldment*, 121; Chinmayananda, *Kindle Life*, 73, 95–100; and D. J. Hoens, "The Movements of Hams Ji Mahāraj and of Chinmayānanda as Process of Change in Hin-

duism," in *Official and Popular Religion: Analysis of a Theme for Religious Studies*, ed. Pieter Hendrik Vrijhof and Jacques Waardenburg (The Hague, Paris, & New York: Mouton Publishers, 1979), 473–74. Here too, however, Chinmayananda differs from Vivekananda, insofar as, though he concedes that *bhakti* may appeal to the masses, the three *yogas* of *karma, bhakti,* and *jñāna* should be practiced simultaneously. He recognizes *haṭha yoga* as a fourth, but he consigns it to a lower level of personal development than the other three.

109. Chinmayananda, *Kindle Life*, 15 (quotation), 108; Chinmayananda, *Manual of Self-Unfoldment*, 3–5, 162–64, quotation at 162.

110. Compare, for example, the discussions in Chinmayananda, *Kindle Life*, 111–16, 212–13; and Chinmayananda, *Manual of Self-Unfoldment*, 116–18.

111. Chinmayananda, *Manual of Self-Unfoldment*, 122–57; Chinmayananda, *Kindle Life*, 55–57 (quotation at 56), 117–26 (quotation at 118); Hoens, "Movements," 474–75. For a description of the study groups and an outline of the Scheme of Study, see Chinmayananda, *Manual of Self-Unfoldment*, 180–92; and especially Anita Raina Thapan, ed., *Scripture: A Mirror—The Chinmaya Study Group* (Piercy, CA: Chinmaya Publications, 2013).

112. For an overview of Vivekananda's understanding of the Buddha and Buddhism, see Beckerlegge, *Ramakrishna Mission*, 58–60; Jeffery D. Long, "Claiming the Buddha for Hinduism: Swami Vivekananda and the Rediscovery of Buddhism in India," in Sengupta and Paranjape, *Cyclonic Swami*, 113–20, and the further discussion in the next chapter.

113. Swami Chinmayananda, "Śaṅkara—The Spiritual General," in *Śaṅkara the Missionary*, 1–3. See also Patchen, *Journey of a Master*, 173–76.

114. Chinmayananda, "Śaṅkara," 3.

115. See Patchen, *Journey of a Master*, 229–39; "Global Tours," in Dukes et al., *Vedānta*, 387–421; and Swami Chidānanda and Rukmani Ramani, eds., *Call of the Conch: The History of Chinmaya Movement* (Mumbai: Central Chinmaya Mission Trust, 2001), 69–126, and the color insert between 126 and 127 (quotation).

116. For what follows, see Masih, *Role of Swami Chinmayananda*, 87–93; Patchen, *Journey of a Master*, 203–28, 237–38; and Shiveshwarkar, "Chinmaya Mission," esp. 186–91.

117. Swami Mitrananda, Rukma Naik Sadekar, Trishna Gulrajani, and Geeta Keswani, *Youth Alone Can: Dynamic Spirituaity* (Piercy, CA: Chinmaya Mission West, 2014); Swamini Vimalananda and Vishva Sodhi, *Manifesting Divinity: Chinmaya Vision on Education* (Piercy, CA: Chinmaya Mission West, 2012); Meera Seth, *Unto Research: Chinmaya International Foundation* (Piercy, CA: Chinmaya Mission West, 2012); and *Chinmaya Vishvavidyapeeth University*, https://cvv.ac.in. For sociological studies of many

of these institutional initiatives, see Samta P. Pandya, "'Guru' Culture in South Asia: The Case of Chinmaya Mission in India," *Society and Culture in South Asia* 2.2 (2016): 204–32; Samta P. Pandya, "Promoting Spiritual Well-Being among Hindu Children in South Asian, Southeast Asian and African Countries: Bala Vihars of Chinmaya Mission," *International Journal of Children's Spirituality* 21.1 (2016): 19–37; and Samta P. Pandya, "Yoga, Emotional Awareness and Happiness in Children: A Multi-City Study of the Chinmaya Bala Vihar Programme," *Child & Youth Care Forum* 47 (2018): 897–917.

118. Shiveshwarkar, "Chinmaya Mission," 177–86; Kshama Metre and Narender Paul, *Chinmaya Sevā: CORD and Chinmaya Mission Hospital* (Piercy, CA: Chinmaya Mission West, 2014); and "CORD—Chinmaya Organisation for Rural Development," *Chinmaya Mission West*, http://chinmayamissionwest.com/cord. Though the Chinmaya Mission currently recognizes a male renunciant, Swami Swaroopananda Saraswati, at the head of its governing body, the Central Chinmaya Mission Trust (CCMT), and men still form the majority of its *ācāryas*, women are eligible to receive renunciation and serve as chief *ācārya*s of individual centers. Lay women are among the most active in the leadership of study groups, Mission center activities, the school systems, and whole enterprises, such as CORD, and Chinmayananda seems to have viewed them as in some ways more receptive to the Vedānta message and as primary agents of preserving the Hindu heritage. See, for example, Chinmayananda, *Kindle Life*, 143; Finger, *Gurus*, 197; Patchen, *Journey of a Master*, 204–5; Thapan, *Scripture*, 177–83; and Parikh, "Does Character Count," 56–57.

119. See Patchen, *Journey of a Master*, 219–20; Masih, *Role of Swami Chinmyananda*, 179–80, 186–87; Mathew, *Neo-Hinduism*, 55–57 McKean, *Divine Enterprise*, 101–2; and Peter van der Veer, *Religious Nationalism: Hindus and Muslims in India* (Berkeley, Los Angeles, & London: University of California Press, 1994), 130–37.

120. See Patchen, *Journey of a Master*, 3–12, 255; Dukes et al., *He Did It*, 23–35, 83–86, 212–25; Chinmayananda, *Manual of Self-Unfoldment*, 158–59; and Chinmayananda, *Kindle Life*, 140–42, 185–86.

121. Swami Chinmayananda, "Temple Should Be Built," *Hindu Vivek Kendra*, http://hindunet.org/hvk/articles/0801/94.html. Background on the Ayodhya conflict is available in Thomas Blom Hansen, *The Saffron Wave: Democracy and Hindu Nationalism in Modern India* (Princeton, NJ: Princeton University Press, 1999), 154–99.

122. Masih, *Role of Chinmayananda*, 275; Ramani and Chidānanda, *Call of the Conch*, 38; and Khanna, "Swami Chinamayananda," 43–45. Ramani and Chidānanda (74) note that Swami Chinmayananda was refused

permission to offer public teaching in Indonesia due to his association with the VHP.

123. Dukes et al., *He Did It*, 396–97.

124. Ibid., 215. Purvi Parikh notes that "Almost all of the informants whom I interviewed were unaware of the link between Swami Chinmayānanda and the VHP, and their reasons for engagement were not politically motivated . . ." ("Does Character Count," 31n). This has also been my experience in the movement: mention of Swami Chinmayananda's connection with the VHP usually elicits some combination of bemusement and distress.

125. Quoted in McKean, *Divine Enterprise*, 102.

126. See ibid., 106–8; Hansen, *Saffron Wave*, 101–7; and the background in Kenneth W. Jones, *Arya Dharm: Hindu Consciousness in 19th-Century Punjab* (Berkeley, Los Angeles, & London: University of California Press, 1976), 129–35, 202–15, and 303–12.

127. See "What is the Natural Law Party?" *The Natural Law Party: A Reason to Vote.* www.natural-law.org/introduction/index.html

128. "Dr. John Hagelin Launches U.S. Peace Government on July 4," *Natural Law Party News Flash*, 12 July 2003, http://natural-law.org/enews/2003_07_12.htm. See also Joseph Weber, *Transcendental Meditation in America: How a New Age Movement Remade a Small Town in Iowa* (Iowa City: University of Iowa Press, 2014), 68–69.

129. Williamson, *Transcendent in America*, esp. 80–105; Aravamudan, *Guru English*, 220–64; Goldberg, *American Veda*, 151–75; William Sims Bainbridge and Daniel H. Jackson, "The Rise and Decline of Transcendental Meditation," in *The Social Impact of New Religious Movements* (New York: Rose of Sharon Press, 1981), 135–58; Diana L. Eck, "'New Age' Hinduism in America," in *Conflicting Images: India and the United States*, ed. Sulochana Raghavan Glazer (Glenn Dale, MD: Riverdale Company, 1990), 111–42; Cynthia Ann Humes, "Maharishi Ayur-Veda™: Perfect Health™ through Enlightened Marketing in America," in *Modern and Global Ayurveda: Pluralism and Paradigms*, ed. Dagmar Wujastyk and Frederick M. Smith (Albany, NY: SUNY Press, 2008), 309–31; and Cynthia Ann Humes, "Schisms within Hindu Guru Groups: The Transcendental Meditation Movement in North America," in *Sacred Schisms: How Religions Divide*, ed. James R. Lewis and Sarah M. Lewis (Cambridge: Cambridge University Press, 2009), esp. 295–99.

130. His Holiness Maharishi Mahesh Yogi, *The Science of Being and Art of Living* (New Delhi: Allied Publishers, 1963), 4, emphasis in the original. See also Jack Forem, *Transcendental Meditation: Maharishi Mahesh Yogi and the Science of Creative Intelligence* (New York: E. P. Dutton and Co., 1973),

32–35. The language of this formulation very closely reflects some of the most important "great sayings" (*mahā-vākyas*) of Advaita, such as "I am *Brahman*" (*aham-brahma-asmi*) and "That thou art" (*tat-tvam-asi*).

131. Maharishi Mahesh Yogi, *Science of Being*, 9, 20–25, 50–52, 73–76, 106–8.

132. See ibid., 26–29, 52–56, 68–69, 136–41, 254–62; and Reinhart Hummel, "Über 40 Jahre Transzendentale Meditation," in *Westliche Formen des Hinduismus in Deutschland*, ed. Michael Bergunder (Halle: Verlag der franckeschen Stiftungen zu Halle, 2006); 111–12.

133. On this point, see especially Humes, "Maharishi Mahesh Yogi: Beyond the TM Technique," in Forsthoefel and Humes, 67; and Maharishi Mahesh Yogi, *Maharishi Mahesh Yogi on the Bhagavad-Gita: A New Translation and Commentary with Sanskrit Text, Chapters 1–6* (Middlesex, Baltimore, & Victoria: Penguin Books, 1967, 1967), 13–15.

134. Maharishi Mahesh Yogi, *Science of Being*, 202; Forem, *Transcendental Meditation*, 36.

135. Bainbridge and Jackson, "Rise and Decline," 138–41; Williamson, *Transcendent in America*, 87–91.

136. Maharishi Mahesh Yogi, *Science of Being*, 30–39; Forem, *Transcendental Meditation*, 36–42.

137. Maharishi Mahesh Yogi, *Science of Being*, 35.

138. Ibid., 40.

139. On the Self-Realization Fellowship as a broad background for TM and other meditation movements, see the discussion in Eck, *New Religious America*, 105–12; Thomas, *Hinduism Invades America*, 134–76; Williamson, *Transcendent in America*, 55–76; Hummel, "Über 40 Jahre," 119–20; Reinhart Hummel, "Reliöse Bewegungen Indiens in westlichen Kulturen," in Bergunder, *Westliche Formen*, 20–21; and Polly Trout, *Eastern Seeds, Western Soil: Three Gurus in America* (Mountain View, CA: Mayfield Publishing Company, 2001), 109–46.

140. Maharishi Mahesh Yogi, *Science of Being*, 328–31. In a significant portion of the section entitled "Art of Living," the Maharishi works systematically through the fields of health, education, crime and rehabilitation, economics, and politics (193–268) in order to demonstrate how each of them will continue to fall short of their goals until brought to completion and perfection through the practice of TM. TM has sponsored many scientific studies to substantiate these claims, but the method of these studies has been challenged by critics. See the discussion in Goldberg, *American Veda*, 163–66; Weber, *Transcendental Meditation in America*, 182–83; and Scott Lowe, "Transcendental Meditation, Vedic Science and Science," *Novo Religio* 14 (2011): 54–76.

141. Humes, "Maharishi Mahesh Yogi," 58–63. Williamson (*Transcendent in America,* 82–87) observes that the Maharishi's claims to this traditional authority were contested by Brahmananda Swaraswati's successor at Jyotir, who criticized TM strongly for indiscriminately initiating women, lower castes, and those without caste into the sacred *mantras.*

142. Bainbridge and Jackson, "Rise and Fall," 143–46; Humes, "Maharishi Mahesh Yogi," 63–68; and Humes, "Schism within Hindu Guru Groups," 287–89.

143. Williamson, *Transcendent in America,* 93–100; Bainbridge and Jackson, "Rise and Fall," 151–57; Lowe, "Transcendental Meditation," 61–64. Williamson (92–93, 103–15) also notes reports of the Maharishi's sexual impropriety and abuse of power, as well as the tendency of the TM movement to suppress any reports of scandal or negative assessments of the TM technique.

144. Humes, "Maharishi Ayur-Veda," 326. See also the further discussion in Humes, "Maharishi Mahesh Yogi," 72–75; and the similar analysis in Hummel, "Über 40 Jahre," 109–11.

145. See especially Maharishi Mahesh Yogi, *Bhagavad Gita,* 9–12, 16–17; Maharishi Mahesh Yogi, *Science of Being,* 17–18, 290–92; and Hummel, "Über 40 Jahre," 116. Lowe notes that two of the Maharishi's most explicitly religious texts from these early days were quietly suppressed by the movement in its middle period ("Transcendental Meditation," 59).

146. See especially Weber, *Transcendental Meditation in America,* 30–33, 54–57; Lowe, "Transcendental Meditation," 62–63, 74n; and "Center for Health and Wellness: Healing Traumatic Stress and Raising Performance in At-risk Populations," David Lynch Foundation. www.davidlynchfoundation.org

147. This is founded on the conviction that the entire universe is interconnected; hence, self-cultivation also represents the only sure path to work for peace in the external world. See Maharishi Mahesh Yogi, *Science of Being,* 59–64, 80–82, 191–94, 197–98, 262–68, 338–40; Forem, *Transcendental Meditation,* 227–28; Tina Posner, "Transcendental Meditation, Perfect Health, and the Millennium," in *Sickness and Sectarianism: Exploratory Studies in Medical and Religious Sectarianism,* ed. R. Kenneth Jones (Aldershot, UK: Gower, 1985), 94–112; and Reender Kranenborg, "Peace, Reconciliation and New Religious Movements," in *Religion, Conflict and Reconciliation: Multifaith Ideals and Realities,* ed. Jerald D. Gort, Henry Jansen, and Hendrik M. Vroom (Amsterdam & New York: Rodopi, 2002), esp. 357–58.

148. See Forem, *Transcendental Meditation,* 10–12; Bainbridge and Jackson, "Rise and Fall," 143; Hummel, "Über 40 Jahre," 107–8; and Posner, "Transcendental Meditation," 98–101, 105–106.

149. See Humes, "Maharishi Mahesh Yogi," 70–72; Williamson, *Transcendent in America*, 80–82; and "Global Organization," *Global Country of World Peace*, www.globalcountry.org/wp/full-width/global-administration. Cynthia Humes has traced the rise, evolution, and eventual dissolution of the Natural Law and Ajeya Bharat political organizations and the creation of the Global Country of World Peace in her chapter, "A Perfect Government." Unpublished manuscript provided by author, 28 July 2016.

150. See Scott Lowe, "The Neo-Hindu Transformation of an Iowa Town," *Novo Religio* 13 (2010): 81–91; and Joseph Weber, "Transcendental Meditation and the Remaking of an Iowa Farm Town," *Utopian Studies* 25 (2014): 341–58.

151. Forem, *Transcendental Meditation*, 8.

152. "Message from David Lynch," David Lynch Foundation. www.davidlynchfoundation.org/message.html

153. "About SVBF," Sringeri Vidya Bharati Foundation (Canada). www.svbfcanada.com/SVBF/Aboutus.html

154. See "Mahakumbhabhishekam," SVBF: Sringeri Vidya Bharati Foundation (Canada). www.svbfcanada.com/mka.html

155. "Welcome to Sringeri Vidya Bharati Foundation (Canada)," SVBF: Sringeri Vidya Bharati Foundation (Canada). http://www.svbfcanada.com

156. Williams, "Sacred Threads," 238–40.

157. "SVBF—An Introduction," YouTube. www.youtube.com/watch?v=GA9GjNaBteU&feature=youtu.be. A link is available on the SVBF webpage. www.svbfcanada.com/SVBF/Video.html

158. See "Testimonials," SVBF: Sringeri Vidya Bharati Foundation (Canada), www.svbfcanada.com/SVBF/Testimonials.html; and Gopal Krishna, "Sri Dushyanth Sridhar—Video by Gopal Krishna," YouTube, www.youtube.com/watch?v=gooS9e29OL0&feature=youtu.be. This lecture was held at SVBF, and a link is available on its webpage. www.svbfcanada.com/SVBF/Video.html.

159. See "Our Jagadgurus," SVBF: Sringeri Vidya Bharati Foundation (Canada), www.svbfcanada.com/SVBF/Jagadgurus.html; Sawai, *Faith of Ascetics*, 24–31; K. R. Venkataraman, *Samkara and His Sarada Pitha in Sringeri: A Study in Growth and Integration* (Calcutta: Kalpa Printers and Publ. Private, 1969); Sri Sarada Peetham, *The Greatness of Sringeri*, revised edition (Sringeri: Dakshinamnaya Sri Sarada Peetham, 2008), 43–121.

160. Cenkner, *Tradition of Teachers*, 114–15; Clark, *Daśanāmī-Saṃnyāsīs*, 128–38.

161. See Clark, *Daśanāmī-Saṃnyāsīs*, 183–226.

162. Venkataraman, *Samkara and His Sarada Pitha*, 32–33; Clark, 202–3; Sri Sarada Peetham, *Greatness of Sringeri*, 59–60; and Leela Prasad, *Poetics of Conduct: Oral Narrative and Moral Being in a South Indian Town*

(New York: Columbia University Press, 2007), 67–68. To the present day, the Śaṅkarācārya receives a royal coronation on his ascension to the Śrī Śāradā Pīṭhaṃ throne and holds court as a fictive emperor during the festival of *Navarātri* each fall. See Prasad, *Poetics of Conduct*, 67–70; Glenn Yocum, "The Coronation of a Guru: Charisma, Politics and Philosophy in Contemporary India," in Williams, *A Sacred Thread*, 68–91.

163. Prasad, *Poetics of Conduct*, 71–80; Venkataraman, *Samkara and His Sarada Pitha*, 33–38. The *maṭha* retained its properties until the passage of land reform legislation by the secular state of India in 1958.

164. Yocum, "Coronation of a Guru," 80.

165. Prasad, *Poetics of Conduct*, 7–8, 98–117.

166. Venkataraman, *Samkara and Sarada Peetham*, 46–47; Sri Sarada Peetham, *Greatness of Sringeri*, 76–77; and Joël André-Michel Dubois, *The Hidden Lives of Brahman: Śaṅkara's Vedānta through His Upāniṣad Commentaries, in Light of Contemporary Practice* (Albany, NY: SUNY Press, 2013), 2–8, 52–53, 170–78. Dubois underscores the specifically Advaita character of these *vidvat-sabhās*: "The Council of the Vidvats . . . showcases the most specialized of brāhmaṇa experts: paṇḍitas ("learned ones") from all parts of India, both from traditional pāṭhaśālās and secular schools, who have come to discuss advanced Saṃskṛta subjects before their peers. Many are affiliated with Śaṅkara's tradition; a few scholars of rival vedānta schools also join the discussion, but these are usually specialists in nyāya or ritual theory who therefore do not directly criticize Śaṅkara's views" (*Hidden Lives*, 170).

167. Venkataraman, *Samkara and Sarada Peetham*, 47–48; Sri Sarada Peetham, *Greatness of Sringeri*, 78–80; Sawai, *Faith of Ascetics*, 34–35.

168. See "Propagation of Sanatana Dharma," *Sri Sri Jagadguru Shankaracharya Mahasamsthanam Dakshinamnaya Sri Sharada Peetham, Sringeri.* www.sringeri.net/activities/propagation-of-sanatana-dharma

169. "History," *Sri Sri Jagadguru Shankaracharya Mahasamsthanam Dakshinamnaya Sri Sharada Peetham, Sringeri.* www.sringeri.net/history

170. See, for example, K. Suresh Kumar, *Inspiring Saint: Life and Teachings of His Holiness Jagadguru Sri Bharathi Theertha Mahaswamigal*, 2nd edition (Madras: Sri Vidyatheertha Foundation, 1998), 111–12, 117–18, 144, 152, 158–59, 178–80.

171. In an important 1989 article, Lance Nelson observed a similar pattern in the teaching of Ādi Śaṅkara, in which the great sage promoted devotional *bhakti* for most persons while restricting the actual teaching of Advaita to a small, restricted number of Brahmin renunciants. See his "Theism for the Masses, Non-Dualism for the Monastic Elite: A Fresh Look at Śaṃkara's Trans-Theistic Spirituality," in William Shea, ed., *The Struggle over the Past: Fundamentalism in the Modern World* (Lanham, MD: University Press of America, 1993), 61–77.

172. These teachings were published as a multiple series of articles in the SVBF USA newsletter, *Paramartha Tattvam*, for which their author, Dr. Yegnasubramanian, serves as editor. There is significant variation in pagination and the digital format of each work. For this reason, rather than a page number, I give a single citation for the main page of each piece and source quotations by internal section divisions. For most Sanskrit terms, I have made small modifications in transliteration.

173. S. Yegnasubramanian, "Vaidika Samskaras," Sringeri Vidya Bharati Foundation, Inc., USA, http://svbf.org/vaidika-samskaras, sections 2 and 4.

174. S. Yegnasubramanian, "Upadesa Panchakam," Sringeri Vidya Bharati Foundation, Inc., USA, http://svbf.org/newsletters/tag/upadesa-panchakam, Part I; S. Yegnasubramanian, "Tattva Bodha," Sringeri Vidya Bharati Foundation, Inc., USA, http://svbf.org/tattvabodha, section 1.1.c.2.6. "Once a person goes thru all these four stages," Yegnasubramanian writes at the end of the *Upadeśa Pañcakam*, commentary (Part III), "he attains *jīvan muktiḥ* [liberation in life] and *videha muktiḥ* [complete freedom after death]. Whether a person physically goes through stages or not, one has to mentally go through."

175. See, for example, Yegnasubramanian, "Upadesa Panchakam," Part I; "Tattva Bodha," section 1.1.

176. The sources cited from the Chinmaya Mission are the original edition of *Sankara the Missionary* (Bombay: Central Chinmaya Mission Trust, 1978) and what appears to be a 1995 reprint of Svarupa Chaitanya, *Tattva Bodha of Sankaracharya* (Bombay: Central Chinmaya Mission Trust, 1981). Yegnasubramanian also draws on several more general reference works and, in his "Vaidika Samskaras," a work published by ISKCON. But his exposition of Advaita is founded in the Chinmaya Mission and, above all, the lectures of Paramarthananda.

177. See "About Us," *Arsha Vidya Gurukulam*. www.arshavidya.org/about-us.html

178. A full video of the ceremony is available online: "Adi Shankaracharya Award Ceremony," YouTube. www.youtube.com/watch?v=warZsxYj9AM

179. I have recourse here to the translation of one Sri Prasad Krishnan, posted as "Sringeri Jagadguru on Pujya Swamiji Sri Sri Dayananda Saraswati, 24 September 2015," Shishyavrunda of Jagadguru Sri Sri Bharathithirtha Mahaswamiji—Sringeri Facebook Page, www.facebook.com/permalink.php?story_fbid=880637235319464&id=497623950287463. I have made small changes in the transliterations from the Sanskrit.

180. "Adi Shankara Vidyalaya Centre for Educational & Learning Activities," SVBF: Sringeri Vidya Bharati Foundation (Canada). www.svbfcanada.com/SVBF/freeclasses.html

181. Goldie Osuri, *Religious Freedom in India: Sovereignty and (Anti) Conversion* (London & New York: Routledge, 2013), 37.

182. Ibid.

183. Weber, *Transcendental Meditation in America*, 167–75.

184. Maharishi Mahesh Yogi, *Science of Being*, 40.

185. Vivekananda, "Practical Vedanta II," *Complete Works*, vol. 2, 325.

186. Ramana Maharshi, *Collected Works*, 119.

Chapter 3

1. This chapter was originally published as Reid B. Locklin, "Paradigms and Styles of Advaita Mission: An Experiment in Interpretation," *International Journal of Hindu Studies* 20.1 (2016): 1–49. It is reused by permission of Springer Nature and has been lightly revised for inclusion in this volume.

2. Jacqueline G. Suthren Hirst, "Images of Śaṅkara: Understanding the Other," *International Journal of Hindu Studies* 8 (2004): 157–81.

3. Ibid., 158.

4. Ibid., 173.

5. Quotation at ibid., 159.

6. See, for example, William Cenkner, *A Tradition of Teachers: Śaṅkara and the Jagadgurus Today* (Delhi: Motilal Banarsidass, 1983).

7. Suthren Hirst, "Images of Śaṅkara," 166–68.

8. See, for example, Lorilai Biernacki, "Shree Maa of Kamakkhya," in *The Graceful Guru: Hindu Female Gurus in India and the United States*, ed. Karen Pechilis (Oxford & New York: Oxford University Press, 2004), 190–91; and Elizabeth De Michelis, *A History of Modern Yoga* (London & New York: Continuum, 2005), 30–31, 83.

9. See Wendell Thomas, *Hinduism Invades America* (New York: Beacon Press, 1930); Reinhart Hummel, *Indische Mission und neue Frömmigkeit im Westen: Religiöse Bewegungen Indiens in westlichen Kulturen* (Stuttgart: Verlag W. Kohlhammer, 1980); Torkel Brekke, "The Conceptual Foundation of Missionary Hinduism," *The Journal of Religious History* 23 (1999): 203–14; J. Kuruvachira, "Hinduism as a Missionary Religion," *Mission Today* 8 (2006): 265–84; J. Kuruvachira, "Hinduism's World Mission," *Mission Today* 9 (2007): 39–56; Srinivas Aravamudan, *Guru English: South Asian Religion in a Cosmopolitan Language* (Princeton, NJ & Oxford: Princeton University Press, 2006); and Joanne Punzo Waghorne, "Global Gurus and the Third Stream of American Religiosity: Between Hindu Nationalism and Liberal Pluralism," in *Political Hinduism: The Religious Imagination in Public Spheres*, ed. Vinay Lal (New Delhi: Oxford University Press, 2009), 122–49.

10. C. V. Mathew, *The Saffron Mission: A Historical Analysis of Modern Hindu Missionary Ideologies and Practices* (Delhi: ISPCK, 1999); Arvind Sharma, "Ancient Hinduism as a Missionary Religion," *Numen* 39 (1992): 175–92; Arvind Sharma, *Hinduism as a Missionary Religion* (Albany, NY: SUNY Press, 2011).

11. Sharma, *Hinduism as a Missionary Religion*, 129.

12. Leo F. Stelton, *Dictionary of Ecclesiastical Latin* (Peabody, MA: Hendrickson Publishers, 1995), 314.

13. David J. Bosch, *Transforming Mission: Paradigm Shifts in Theology of Mission* (Maryknoll, NY: Orbis Books, 1991), 1.

14. Ibid., 226–30. Paul Kollman traces this history from the first Jesuit usage of "mission" to refer generally to all "apostolic work" to its more specialized use by colonial powers in "At the Origins of Mission and Missiology: A Study in the Dynamics of Religious Language," *Journal of the American Academy of Religion* 79.2 (2011): 425–58.

15. Bosch, *Transforming Mission*, 181–89.

16. See, for example, Alan Kreider, "Beyond Bosch: The Early Church and the Christendom Shift," *International Bulletin of Missionary Research* 29 (2005): 59–68; and Stephen B. Bevans and Roger P. Schroeder, "Missiology After Bosch: Reverencing a Classic by Moving Beyond," *International Bulletin of Missionary Research* 29 (2005): 69–70.

17. Bosch, *Transforming Mission*, 340–41. Prior to this, according to Bosch, most of the Protestant Reformers judged that "the 'Great Commission' had been fulfilled by the apostles and was no longer binding on the church" (ibid., 249, referring to the sixteenth-century Lutheran theologian Philip Nicolai). For the broader discussion, see ibid., 243–48.

18. This is the approximate distance from Serampore College, co-founded by Carey in 1800, and Belur Math, founded by Vivekananda in 1897 as the worldwide headquarters of the Ramakrishna Mission.

19. Bevans and Schroeder, "Missiology after Bosch," 69–70.

20. M. Thomas Thangaraj, *The Common Task: A Theology of Christian Mission* (Nashville, TN: Abingdon Press, 1999), 101–19.

21. Stephen B. Bevans and Roger P. Schroeder, *Constants in Context: A Theology of Mission for Today* (Maryknoll, NY: Orbis Books, 2004), 32–72.

22. Thangaraj, *The Common Task*, 47–60; Bevans and Schroeder, "Missiology after Bosch," 348–95; and Roger P. Schroeder, "Proclamation and Interreligious Dialogue as Prophetic Dialogue," *Missiology* 41 (2013): 50–61.

23. Recent studies of early modern Vedānta show promise for complicating and enriching our understanding of Advaita's historical emergence as the most influential theological tradition and purported essence of Hinduism by the colonial period. See especially Christopher Minkowski, "Advaita Vedānta in Early Modern History," *South Asian History and Culture* 2.2 (2011): 205–31; Elaine M. Fisher, *Hindu Pluralism:*

Religion and the Public Sphere in Early Modern South India (Oakland: University of California Press, 2017); and a themed issue on "New Directions in the Study of Advaita Vedānta," edited by Michael S. Allen and Anand Venkatkrishnan, *International Journal of Hindu Studies* 21.3 (2017): 271–389.

24. Bosch, *Transforming Mission*, 208–9, 236–37.

25. The idealized image of the guru, including its diversity and its centrality in South Asian religions, is the subject of Jacob Copeman and Aya Ikegame's edited collection, *The Guru in South Asia: New Interdisciplinary Perspectives* (London & New York: Routledge, 2012).

26. Francis X. Clooney, "Restoring 'Hindu Theology' as a Category in Indian Intellectual Discourse," in *The Blackwell Companion to Hinduism*, ed. Gavin Flood (Oxford & Malden, MA: Blackwell Publishing, 2003), 447–77; Jonathan Edelmann, "Hindu Theology as Churning the Latent," *Journal of the American Academy of Religion* 81 (2013): 427–66.

27. Hummel, *Indische Mission*, 119–21. See also Joachim Finger, *Gurus, Ashrams und der Weste: Eine religionswissenschaftliche Untersuchung zu den Hintergründen der Internationalisierung des Hinduismus* (Frankfurt am Main: Verlag Peter Lang, 1987), 19–25; and David Hardiman, "Assertion, Conversion, and Indian Nationalism: Govind's Movement among the Bhils," in *Religious Conversion in India: Modes, Motivations, and Meanings*, ed. Rowena Robinson and Sathianathan Clarke (New Delhi: Oxford University Press, 2003), 255–84.

28. See Srilata Raman, "Initiation and Conversion in Medieval South India: *Pañcasaṃskāra* as Historical Practice in the Śrīvaiṣṇava Post-Rāmānuja Hagiographic Literature," in *Studies in Hinduism IV: On the Mutual Influences and Relationship of Viśiṣṭādvaita Vedānta and Pañcarātra*, ed. Gerhard Oberhammer and Marion Rastelli (Wien: Verlag der Österreichischen Akademie der Wissenschaften, 2007), 263–86; and D. N. Jha, *Rethinking Hindu Identity* (London & Oakville, CT: Equinox, 2009), 27–47.

29. Andrew J. Nicholson, *Unifying Hinduism: Philosophy and Identity in Indian Intellectual History* (New York: Columbia University Press, 2010), 3–6, 166–84.

30. Ibid., 3.

31. *Śaṅkara the Missionary*, revised edition (Mumbai: Central Chinmaya Mission Trust, 1998), 45.

32. Nicholson, *Unifying Hinduism*, 5. See also Richard King, *Orientalism and Religion: Postcolonial Theory, India and "The Mystic East"* (London & New York: Routledge, 1999), 128–29.

33. See Francis X. Clooney, S.J., *Theology after Vedānta: An Experiment in Comparative Theology* (Albany, NY: SUNY Press, 1993), 102–13.

34. Hugh Nicholson, "Two Apologetic Moments in Śaṅkara's Concept of *Brahman*," *Journal of Religion* 87 (2007): 528–55; Stephen Kaplan, "Authorial Authenticity or Theological Polemics? Discerning the Implications of

Śaṅkara's Battle with the Buddhists," *International Journal of Hindu Studies* 17 (2013): 1–36; and Jacqueline G. Suthren Hirst, "Who Were the *Tārkikas*? The Place of Polemic in Śaṃkara's *Bṛhadāraṇyakopaniṣadbhāṣya*," *Journal of Hindu Studies* 4 (2011): 54–78.

35. Nicholson, *Unifying Hinduism*, 31–33; D. H. H. Ingalls, "The Study of Śaṃkarācārya," *Annals of the Bhandarkar Oriental Research Institute* 33 (1952): 8–10.

36. Suthren Hirst, "Who were the *Tārkikas*?," 68. See also Jacqueline Gaynor Suthren Hirst, "The Place of *Bhakti* in Śaṅkara's Vedānta," in *Love Divine: Studies in Bhakti and Devotional Mysticism*, ed. Karel Werner (Richmond, Surrey: Curzon Press, 1993), 26–28.

37. Sengaku Mayeda, ed. *Śaṅkara's Upadeśasāhasrī, Critically Edited with Introduction and Indices* (Tokyo: Hokuseido Press, 1973). I have followed Mayeda's English translation in *A Thousand Teachings: The Upadeśasāhasrī of Śaṅkara* (Albany, NY: SUNY Press, 1992), with small modifications. Hereafter, I cite the *Upadeśasāhasrī* directly in my exposition, in its verse portion (USP) and prose portion (USG).

38. Consistent with Śaṅkara's other works, Pūrva Mīmāṃsā represents an exception to this rule. Positions drawn from Pūrva Mīmāṃsā are given a privileged place apart from other rival traditions, as in the introductory exposition of USP 1. See also Clooney, *Theology after Vedānta*, 23–30, and Reid B. Locklin, *Liturgy of Liberation: A Christian Commentary on Shankara's Upadeśasāhasrī* (Leuven: Peeters, 2011), 47–67.

39. I have omitted the first half of verse 66 from the translation. As Mayeda notes (*A Thousand Teachings*, 159n40), the source of the stanza that Śaṅkara seems to be quoting here is obscure.

40. See also USG 1.3.

41. Tilmann Vetter argues that the differences in the descriptions of the teacher and student in USG 2 imply a different, and earlier, point of composition than USG 1. See his *Studien zur Lehre und Entwicklung Śaṅkaras* (Wien: Institut für Indologie der Universität Wien, 1979), 75–78. Even granting that the two texts may not have been written in series, I do not think that the changes in vocabulary require that they be treated as separate works.

42. Lance E. Nelson, "Living Liberation in Śaṅkara and Classical Advaita: Sharing the Holy Waiting of God," in *Living Liberation in Hindu Thought*, ed. Andrew O. Fort and Patricia Y. Mumme (Albany: SUNY Press, 1996), 24–25.

43. See also the discussion in Warren Lee Todd, *The Ethics of Śaṅkara and Śāntideva: A Selfless Response to an Illusory World* (Fornham, Surrey, & Burlington, VT: Ashgate, 2013), 163–76.

44. Ibid., 139–40.

45. Nelson, "Living Liberation," 39–44; Todd, *Ethics of Śaṅkara*, 171–72.

46. For examples, see the discussion of USG 1.25–26 in Suthren Hirst, "Who Were the *Tārkikas*?, 64–65, and of USG 2.74–79 in Kaplan, "Authorial Authenticity," 17–19.

47. See also Todd, *Ethics of Śaṅkara*, 172–76, 179–86, and Lance E. Nelson, "Theism for the Masses, Non-Dualism for the Monastic Elite: A Fresh Look at Śaṃkara's Trans-Theistic Spirituality," in *The Struggle over the Past: Fundamentalism in the Modern World*, ed. William Shea (Lanham, MD: University Press of America, 1993), 61–77. It should be noted that Śaṅkara's teaching is not univocal on this point. Though the *Upadeśasāhasrī* presumes *brāhmaṇa* renunciant males as the normal, if not exclusive, recipients of the teaching, other passages suggest wider availability of the discipline of self-knowledge by study of *smṛti* and other means. Roger Marcaurelle surveys the evidence on both sides in his *Freedom through Inner Renunciation: Śaṅkara's Philosophy in a New Light* (Albany, NY: SUNY Press, 2000), 29–40.

48. See Locklin, *Liturgy of Liberation*, 117–18.

49. Phyllis Granoff, "Holy Warriors: A Preliminary Study of Some Biographies of Saints and Kings in the Classical Indian Tradition," *Journal of Indian Philosophy* 12 (1984): 291–303; William S. Sax, "Conquering the Quarters: Religion and Politics in Hinduism," *International Journal of Hindu Studies* 4.1 (2000): 39–60.

50. Jonathan Bader, *The Conquest of the Four Quarters: Traditional Accounts of the Life of Śaṅkara* (New Delhi: Aditya Prakashan, 2000), 139.

51. It is worth noting that Sax references a Himalayan tradition that Śaṅkara "fought his Buddhist rivals 'with both *śastra* and *śāstra*,' that is, with both weapons and arguments, destroying many of them with the aid of Rājā Sudhavan's army" ("Conquering the Quarters," 47).

52. David N. Lorenzen, "The Life of Sankaracarya," in *The Biographical Process*, ed. Frank E. Reynolds and Donald Capps (Paris: Mouton & Co., 1976), 87–103; Karl H. Potter, "Śaṃkarācārya: The Myth and the Man," *Journal of the American Academy of Religion Thematic Studies* 48.3–4 (1982): 111–25; and Govind Chandra Pande, *Life and Thought of Śaṅkarācārya* (Delhi: Motilal Banarsidass, 1994).

53. See Sax, "Conquering the Quarters"; Yoshitsugu Sawai, *The Faith of Ascetics and Lay Smārtas: A Study of the Śaṅkaran Tradition of Śṛṅgerī* (Wien: Institut für Indologie der Universität Wien, 1992), 83–105; and especially Daniel Raveh, "*Śaṅkaradigvajaya*: A Narrative Interpretation of Śaṅkara's Advaita Vedānta," in *The Bloomsbury Research Handbook of Vedānta*, ed. Ayon Maharaj (London: Bloomsbury Academic, 2020), 367–90.

54. Hereafter I have cited the ŚDV in the body of my exposition. The dating of the text is by no means certain. Following the textual crit-

ical analysis of W. D. Antarkar, Bader assigns this late date due to ŚDV's apparent literary dependence upon three other hagiographies (*Conquest of the Four Quarters*, 17–70). See also Yoshitsugu Sawai, "On a Legendary Biography of Śaṅkara," *Journal of Indian and Buddhist Studies* 34.1 (1985): 454–59; and Matthew Clark, *The Daśanāmī-Saṃnyāsīs: The Integration of Ascetic Lineages into an Order* (Leiden & Boston: Brill, 2006), 149–51. Vidyasankar Sundaresan has, in turn, challenged these textual criteria in his "Conflicting Hagiographies and History: The Place of Śaṅkaravijaya Texts in Advaita Tradition," *International Journal of Hindu Studies* 4.2 (2000): 109–84. If accepted, Sundaresan's arguments could push the work's date back as far as the fourteenth century, though this still post-dates Śaṅkara by at least six centuries. Except where otherwise noted, I draw here on the free translation of the ŚDV available in Swami Tapasyananda, trans., *Sankara-Dig-Vijaya: The Traditional Life of Sri Sankaracarya, by Madhava Vidyaranya* (Madras: Sri Ramakrishna Math, 1978), in consultation with the Sanskrit Text and English translation in K. Padmanaban, trans., *Srimad Sankara Digvijayam by Vidyaranya*, 2 vols. (Madras: K. Padmanaban, 1985–1986).

55. Bader, *Conquest of the Four Quarters*, 100–104; Yoshitsugu Sawai, "The Legend of Śaṅkara's Birth," *Journal of Indian and Buddhist Studies* 36.1 (1987): 464–68.

56. Sax, "Conquering the Quarters," 51.

57. For historical context, see Hugh Nicholson, "The Shift from Agonistic to Non-Agonistic Debate in Early Nyāya," *Journal of Indian Philosophy* 38.1 (2010): 75–95.

58. Arjun Appadurai, "Kings, Sects and Temples in South India, 1350–1700 A.D." *The Indian Economic and Social History Review* 14.1 (1977): 47–73; Valerie Stoker, "Polemics and Patronage in Sixteenth-Century Vijayanagara: Vyāsatīrtha and the Dynamics of Hindu Sectarian Relations." *History of Religions* 51.2 (2011): 129–55; and Valerie Stoker, *Polemics and Patronage in the City of Victory: Vyāsatīrtha, Hindu Sectarianism, and the Sixteenth-Century Vijanagara Court* (Oakland: University of California Press, 2016).

59. Bader, *Conquest of the Four Quarters*, 183–229; Phyllis Granoff, "Scholars and Wonder-Workers: Some Remarks on the Role of the Supernatural in Philosophical Contests in Vedānta Hagiographies," *Journal of the American Oriental Society* 105.3 (1985): 459–67.

60. See Fisher, *Hindu Pluralism*, 19–27.

61. Bader, *Conquest of the Four Quarters*, 253–72, 312–13.

62. Sawai, "Legend of Śaṅkara's Birth," and Sawai, *Faith of Ascetics*, 61–82.

63. Here I am following the translation in Sawai, "Legend of Śaṅkara's Birth," 464.

64. Arvind Sharma, "Śaṅkara's Life and Works as a Source for a Hermeneutics of Human Rights," in *New Perspectives on Advaita Vedānta: Essays in Commemoration of Professor Richard De Smet, S.J.*, ed. Bradley J. Malkovsky (Leiden: Brill, 2000), 113–17.

65. The further attribution of the text to Vidyāraṇya, one of the most important *jagadgurus* or Śaṅkarācāryas of the Śṛṅgerī Maṭha in present-day Karṇataka, follows from the belief that Mādhava was Vidyāraṇya's name prior to taking *saṃnyāsa*. See Sawai 1985, "On a Legendary Biography," 457–58. Clark, *Daśanāmī Saṃnyāsīs*, 208–14, offers a persuasive critique of this attribution. For the purposes of the present chapter, it matters little whether these texts are written by the same person; together, I am suggesting, the texts reveal general patterns of late medieval and early modern Advaita tradition, regardless of their exact provenance.

66. Nicholson, *Unifying Hinduism*, 158–62, 182–83.

67. Sax, "Conquering the Quarters," 46–47; Nicholson, *Unifying Hinduism*, 190–96. See also the nuanced discussions of this thesis in Clark, *Daśanāmī Saṃnyāsīs*, esp. 236–39; Minkowski, "Advaita Vedānta," 222–23; James W. Laine, "The *Dharma* of Islam and the *Dīn* of Hinduism: Hindus and Muslims in the Age of Śivāji," *International Journal of Hindu Studies* 3.3 (1999): 299–318; and David N. Lorenzen, "Who Invented Hinduism?" in *Who Invented Hinduism? Essays on Religion in History* (New Delhi: Yoda Press, 2006), 1–36.

68. Sax, "Conquering the Quarters," 47–51.

69. Stoker, "Polemics and Patronage," esp. 132–45.

70. Daniel P. Sheridan, "The Dueling Sacred Biographies of Madhva and Śaṅkara," *Journal of Vaishnava Studies* 15.2 (2007): 123–44.

71. Torkel Brekke, *Makers of Modern Indian Religion in the Late Nineteenth Century* (Oxford: Oxford University Press, 2002): 46, quoted in Gwylim Beckerlegge "Swami Vivekananda (1863–1902) 150 Years on: Critical Studies of an Influential Hindu Guru," *Religion Compass* 7.10 (2013): 444.

72. Torkel Brekke, "The Conceptual Foundation of Missionary Hinduism," *The Journal of Religious History* 23.2 (1999): 204.

73. David Miller, "Modernity in Hindu Monasticism: Swami Vivekananda and the Ramakrishna Movement." *Journal of Asian American Studies* 34.1 (1999): 124.

74. The exposition that follows in this section draws more or less exclusively on the canonical collection of Swami Vivekananda's English works published by the Ramakrishna Mission: *The Complete Works of Swami Vivekananda*, 8 vols. (Calcutta: Advaita Ashrama, 1989); and *The Complete Works of Swami Vivekananda*, vol. 9 (Calcutta: Advaita Ashrama, 1997). Hereafter these are cited in the main prose, by volume and page

number, as CWSV. My analysis depends heavily on research completed by Ren Ito in 2009–2010, supported by the President's Research Fund of the University of St. Michael's College.

75. Andrew Nicholson also draws attention to Vivekananda's criticism of Śaṅkara in his essay, "Vivekananda's Non-Dual Ethics in the History of Vedānta," in *Swami Vivekananda: His Life, Legacy, and Liberative Ethics*, ed. Rita D. Sherma (Lanham, MD: Lexington Books, 2021), esp. 57–64.

76. Here Swami Vivekananda stands in sharp contrast to the inclusivist strategies of the doxographers. Despite their relatively irenic attitude toward rival teachings generally, for example, Mādhava and Madhusūdana Saravātī nevertheless work to suppress and marginalize rival forms of Vedānta in their doxographies. See Nicholson, *Unifying Hinduism*, 158–65.

77. King, *Orientalism and Religion*, 143–60; and Philip C. Almond, *The British Discovery of Buddhism* (Cambridge: Cambridge University Press, 1988).

78. See King, *Orientalism and Religion*, 133–35; and Paul Hacker, "Aspects of Neo-Hinduism as Contrasted with Surviving Traditional Hinduism," in *Philology and Confrontation: Paul Hacker on Traditional and Modern Vedānta*, ed. Wilhelm Halbfass (Albany: SUNY Press, 1995), 229–55.

79. Gwylim Beckerlegge, "Swami Vivekananda and the *Sangh Parivar:* Convergent or Divergent Views on Population, Religion and National Identity?" *Postcolonial Studies* 9.2 (2006): 125–26, 128.

80. In places, Vivekānanda shows a direct reliance on these earlier traditions, such as when he describes the Buddha, in an early Bengali lecture, as "the demon Gayasura" who "tried to destroy the world by showing the paths of Moksha to all" (CWSV 5:447).

81. It is worth noting that Vivekānanda may not be transposing the *vijaya* narrative from Śaṅkara to Aśoka: Aśoka well fits the model of a conquering ruler, and Buddhist hagiographies similarly present their renunciant heroes as defeating rivals in debate. See Bader, *Conquest of the Four Quarters*, 65–67.

82. Jeffery D. Long, "Claiming the Buddha for Hinduism: Swami Vivekananda and the Rediscovery of Buddhism in India," in *The Cyclonic Swami: Vivekananda in the West*, ed. Sukalyan Sengupta and Makarand Paranjape (New Delhi: Samvad India Foundation, 2005), 113–20.

83. Gwilym Beckerlegge, *The Ramakrishna Mission: The Making of a Modern Hindu Movement* (Oxford & New York: Oxford University Press, 2000), 59–60; Beckerlegge, "Swami Vivekananda and the *Sangh Parivar*," 128.

84. See Almond, *British Discovery of Buddhism*, esp. 69–77; and Tomoko Masuzawa, *The Invention of World Religions, or, How European Universalism Was Preserved in the Language of Pluralism* (Chicago: University of Chicago Press, 2005), 121–46.

85. This is not to claim that the image of the Buddha was the *sole* source of these themes. Torkel Brekke, in "Conceptual Foundation," draws attention the objectification and universalization of the concept of *dharma* by such predecessors as Baṇkim Chandra Chatterjee (1838–1894).

86. See Gwylim Beckerlegge, "The Early Spread of Vedanta Societies: An Example of 'Imported Localism,'" *Numen* 51 (2004): 296–320; Joanne Punzo Waghorne, "Global Gurus and the Third Stream of American Religiosity: Between Hindu Nationalism and Liberal Pluralism," in *Political Hinduism: The Religious Imagination in Public Spheres*, ed. Vinay Lal (New Delhi: Oxford University Press, 2009), 122–49.

87. See Hummel, *Indische Mission*, 17–18, 117–22; and Masuzawa, *Invention of World Religions*, 107–20.

88. Beckerlegge, "Early Spread of Vedanta Societies"; Carl T. Jackson, *Vedanta for the West: The Ramakrishna Movement in the United States* (Bloomington & Indianapolis: Indiana University Press, 1994).

89. On this point, see especially James Madaio, "Rethinking Neo-Vedānta: Swami Vivekananda and the Selective Historiography of Advaita Vedānta," *Religions* 8.6 (2017): 101.

90. *Śaṅkara the Missionary*, revised edition (Mumbai: Central Chinmaya Mission Trust, 1998), 80–101.

91. Ibid., 76–79.

92. Ibid., 76–77. See also ŚDV 12.87; Bader, *Conquest of the Four Quarters*, 98–99.

93. *Śaṅkara the Missionary*, 79.

94. Here I am following the theologian Kathryn Tanner, who, in her *Theories of Culture: A New Agenda for Theology* (Minneapolis: Fortress Press, 1997), defines "style" rather generally as "the specific way a practice is performed when there are other possible options" (144).

95. *Bhagavad-Gita* 4.34; *Śaṅkara the Missionary*, 77–79.

96. See ŚDV 13.70–71, 14.107–116, 166–75, as well as Karl H. Potter, *Encyclopedia of Indian Philosophies: Advaita Vedānta up to Śaṃkara and his Pupils* (Princeton, NJ: Princeton University Press, 1981), 563–64.

97. Waghorne, "Global Gurus"; Beckerlegge, "Swami Vivekananda and the *Sangh Parivar*," Paul Hacker, "Vivekananda's Religious Nationalism," in Halbfass, *Philology and Confrontation*, 319–36; Tapan Raychaudhuri, "Swami Vivekananda's Construction of Hinduism," in *Swami Vivekananda and the Modernization of Hinduism*, ed. William Radice (Delhi: Oxford University Press, 1998), 1–35; and Jyotirmaya Sharma, *A Restatement of Religion: Swami Vivekananda and the Making of Hindu Nationalism* (New Haven, CT & London: Yale University Press, 2013).

98. *Śaṅkara the Missionary*, 2.

99. Margaret Dukes, David Dukes, Neena Dev, Rashmi Mehrotra, Arun Mehrotra, and Padmashree Rao, eds., *He Did It: Swami Chinmayananda, A Legacy* (Piercy, CA: Chinmaya Publications, 2011), 84.

100. Ibid., 84–85.

101. See *Śaṅkara the Missionary*, 82, and the discussion in Mathew, *Saffron Mission*, 204–13; Peter van der Veer, *Religious Nationalism: Hindus and Muslims in India* (Berkeley, Los Angeles, & London: University of California Press, 1994), 130–37; Lise McKean, *Divine Enterprise: Gurus and the Hindu Nationalist Movement* (Chicago & London: University of Chicago Press, 1996), 101–2, 177–79; and Chetan Bhatt, *Hindu Nationalism: Origins, Ideologies and Modern Myths* (Oxford & New York: Berg, 2001), 180–83.

102. Suthren Hirst, "Images of Śaṅkara," 168–71, 173 (quotation).

103. Potter, *Encyclopedia of Indian Philosophies*, 601–2.

104. *Bhagavad-Gita* 9.34, 18.65; *Śaṅkara the Missionary*, 77.

105. Ramana Maharshi, *Talks with Sri Ramana Maharshi* (Tiruvannamalai: Sri Ramanasramam, 1994), 243, cited in Ankur Barua, "The Silences of Ramana Maharshi: Self-Enquiry and Liberation in Sāṁkhya Yoga and Advaita Vedānta," *Religions of South Asia* 9.2 (2015): 199.

106. Arvind Sharma, *Ramana Maharshi: The Sage of Arunachala* (New Delhi: Penguin, 2006), 134.

107. Andrew O. Fort, "*Jīvanmukti* and Social Service in Advaita and Neo-Vedānta," *Poznań Studies in the Philosophy of the Sciences and the Humanities* 59 (1997): 489–504.

108. See Beckerlegge, *Ramakrishna Mission*, 79–112; Gwylim Beckerlegge, "Responding to Conflict: A Test of the Limits of Neo-Vedāntic Social Activism in the Ramakrishna Math and Mission?" *International Journal of Hindu Studies* 11.1 (2006): 1–25; and Gwylim Beckerlegge, *Swami Vivekananda's Legacy of Service: A Study of the Ramakrishna Math and Mission* (New Delhi: Oxford University Press, 2007).

109. David Miller, "The Divine Life Society Movement," in *Religion in Modern India*, revised edition, ed. Robert D. Baird (New Delhi: Manohar, 1989), 83–94; Sarah Strauss, "The Master's Narrative: Swami Sivananda and the Transnational Production of Yoga," *Journal of Folklore Research* 39.2–3 (2002): 220–27.

110. Strauss, "The Master's Narrative," 226.

111. See Miller, "Divine Life Movement," 94–99; Strauss, The Master's Narrative," 233–36; and the further discussion in Sarah Strauss, *Positioning Yoga: Balancing Acts across Cultures* (Oxford & New York: Berg, 2005).

112. Swami Sivananda, *Practice of Karma Yoga*, 3rd edition (Delhi: Motilal Banarsidass, 1965), 245.

113. Ibid., 319.

114. Michael Comans, *Extracting the Essence of the Śruti: The Śrutisāra-samuddharaṇam of Toṭakācarya* (Delhi: Motilal Banarsidass, 1996).

115. *Śaṅkara the Missionary*, 77–78.

116. See especially Clooney, *Theology after Vedānta*, 14–30.

117. Locklin, *Liturgy of Liberation*, 25–27, 150–51.

118. Marcaurelle, *Freedom through Inner Renunciation*, 172–73.

119. *Śaṅkara the Missionary*, 77–78.

120. See van der Veer, *Religious Nationalism*, 137; Nancy Patchen, *The Journey of a Master: Swami Chinmayananda: The Man, the Path, the Teaching* (Bombay: Central Chinmaya Mission Trust 1989, 1994), 158–62.

121. See Swami Dayananda, *The Teaching Tradition of Advaita Vedanta* (Saylorsburg, PA: Arsha Vidya Gurukulam, 1993).

122. Anantanand Rambachan, *Accomplishing the Accomplished: The Vedas as a Source of Valid Knowledge in Śaṅkara* (Honolulu: University of Hawaii Press, 1991); Anantanand Rambachan, *The Limits of Scripture: Vivekananda's Reinterpretation of the Vedas* (Honolulu: University of Hawaii Press, 1994).

123. Anantanand Rambachan, "The Co-existence of Violence and Non-Violence in Hinduism," *The Ecumenical Review* 55.2 (2003): 115–21; Anantanand Rambachan, *The Advaita Worldview: God, World, and Humanity* (Albany, NY: SUNY Press, 2006), 2–3, 27–29; Anantanand Rambachan, "'There Are Many Branches on the Tree of Life': The Irreconcilability of Hinduism and Homophobia," in *Heterosexism in Contemporary World Religion: Problem and Prospect*, ed. Marvin M. Elison and Judith Plaskow (Cleveland: Pilgrim Press, 2007), 201–23; and the further discussion in Reid B. Locklin, "*Śabda Pramāṇa* and Prophetic Witness: Barthian and Advaitin Perspectives in Dialogue," *Journal of Religion* 94.4 (2014): 485–503.

124. Anantanand Rambachan, *A Hindu Theology of Liberation: Not-Two Is Not One* (Albany, NY: SUNY Press, 2015). We shall return to Rambachan's project in chapter 6.

125. Miller, "Divine Life Society," 106–10; Miller, "Modernity in Hindu Monasticism," 119–24.

126. Edelmann, "Hindu Theology," 442–43.

127. Ibid., 450–56.

128. Ibid., 440–42.

129. Suthren Hirst, "Images of Śaṅkara," 157–59, 174–75.

130. See Locklin, *Liturgy of Liberation*, 193–202, and especially Jacqueline Suthren Hirst, "Weaving the Strands: Cognition, Authority and Language in Śaṅkara's *Upadeśasāhasrī*," in *Paramparā: Essays in Honour of R. Balasubramanian*, ed. Srinivasa Rao and Godabarisha Mishra (New Delhi: Indian Council of Philosophical Research, 2003), 149–55.

Chapter 4

1. Thomas A. Forsthoefel, "Weaving the Inward Thread to Awakening," in *Gurus in America*, ed. Thomas A. Forsthoefel and Cynthia Ann Humes (Albany, NY: SUNY Press, 2005), 37–53. An earlier version of the essay, under the same title, was published in *Horizons* 29.2 (2002): 240–59.

2. Ibid., 38.

3. Ibid., 50–51; Thomas A. Forsthoefel, *Knowing Beyond Knowledge: Epistemologies of Religious Experience in Classical and Modern Advaita* (Hants and Burlington: Ashgate, 2002), esp. 56–71, 138–55.

4. Forsthoefel, *Knowing beyond Knowledge,* 155.

5. Forsthoefel, "Weaving the Inward Thread," 44–45.

6. Anantanand Rambachan, *The Limits of Scripture: Vivekananda's Reinterpretation of the Vedas* (Honolulu: University of Hawaii Press, 1994), 94–112; Elizabeth De Michelis, *A History of Modern Yoga: Patañjali and Western Esoterism* (London and New York: Continuum, 2005), esp. 168–80. See also the further discussion in Swami Medhananda, *Swami Vivekananda's Vedāntic Cosmopolitanism* (Oxford: Oxford University Press, 2022), 163–96.

7. Forsthoefel, "Weaving the Inward Thread," 38. For the wider context, see Steven T. Katz, "Language, Epistemology, and Mysticism," in *Mysticism and Philosophical Analysis,* ed. Steven T. Katz (New York: Oxford University Press, 1978), 22–74; Robert Forman's rebuttal in "Introduction: Mysticism, Constructivism, and Forgetting," in *Problem of Pure Consciousness: Mysticism and Philosophy,* ed. Robert K. C. Forman (Oxford: Oxford University Press, 1997), 3–49; and the further discussion in Bruce Janz, "Mysticism and Understanding: Steven Katz and His Critics," *Studies in Religion/Sciences Religieuses* 24.1 (1995): 77–94 and Philip Goldberg, *American Veda: From Emerson and the Beatles to Yoga and Meditation—How Indian Spirituality Changes the West* (New York: Harmony Books, 2010), 238–40. Though Forman broke with the TM movement early in his academic career, he attributed this to the dogmatic, close-mindedness of the Maharishi Mahesh Yogi's followers, rather than a problem with the experiential foundation of the teaching itself. See his memoir, *Enlightenment Ain't What It's Cracked Up to Be: A Journey of Discovery, Snow and Jazz in the Soul* (Winchester, UK & Washington, DC: O-Books, 2010), esp. 47–71. We will return to Forman's narrative in chapter 7.

8. His Holiness Maharishi Mahesh Yogi, *The Science of Being and Art of Living* (New Delhi: Allied Publishers, 1963), 18, 32–45.

9. Śaṅkarācārya, 1954–1989.

10. His Holiness Jagadguru Sri Abhinava Vidyatheertha Mahaswamigal, "True Advaitins and Pseudo-Advaitins are Poles Apart," in *Enlightening Expositions,* 2nd edition (Madras: Sri Vidyatheertha Foundation, 1998),

31. In *Yoga, Enlightenment and Perfection,* Abhinava Vidyātīrtha describes in some detail his step-by-step progress, as a young man, through ever more refined meditative states until he arrives at *svanubhavo' brahmānā*—glossed by his devotee R. M. Umesh as "direct realisation of Brahman." "To this day," the Jagadguru reports, "there has been no deviation from the Reality." Earlier in the narrative, moreover, Umesh describes Abhinava Vidyātīrtha's ability to convey this experience of "indescribable, non-dual bliss" directly to his disciples. See His Holiness Jagadguru Sri Abhinava Vidyatheertha Mahaswamigal, *Yoga, Enlightenment and Perfection,* ed. R. M. Umesh (Chennai: Sri Vidyatheertha Foundation, 1999), quotations at 115, 187.

11. Swami Dayananda, *The Teaching Tradition of Advaita Vedanta* (Saylorsburg, PA: Arsha Vidya Gurukulam, 1993), 9.

12. See, for example, the clarification Dayananda offers in the course of his critique of distinguishing "intellectual" from "experiential" knowledge: "The adjective 'intellectual' describing knowledge will be a necessity only when there is a nasal or dental knowledge. All forms of knowledge happen in the intellect. There is no such thing as intellectual knowledge. There can be two types of knowledge; one is direct and the other indirect. When the ātmā is invariably present, the knowledge of ātmā can only be direct" (ibid.).

13. Kathryn Tanner, "Editorial Symposium: Roman Catholic Theology of Tradition," *Horizons* 29 (2002): 309.

14. Rambachan, *The Limits of Scripture,* 113–25; Anantanand Rambachan, "Śaṅkara's Rationale for *Śruti* as the Definitive Source of *Brahmajñāna*: A Refutation of Some Contemporary Views," *Philosophy East and West* 36 (1986): 25–40; Anantanand Rambachan, *Accomplishing the Accomplished: The Vedas as a Source of Valid Knowledge in Śaṅkara* (Honolulu: University of Hawaii Press, 1991), esp. 1–14; Michael Comans, "The Question of the Importance of *Samādhi* in Modern and Classical Advaita Vedānta," *Philosophy East and West* 43 (1993): 19–38; and the further review in Alan A. Preti, "*Brahmānubhava* as *Überpramāṇa* in Advaita Vedānta: Revisiting an Old Debate," *Philosophy East and West* 64.3 (2014): esp. 720–26. It is worth noting that the leading critics of the experientialist reading of Advaita cited here, Rambachan and Comans, are both disciples of Swami Dayananda, cited at the top of the chapter as a critic of the rhetoric of self-realization.

15. Forsthoefel, *Knowing beyond Knowledge,* esp. 123–55; Arvind Sharma, *The Experiential Dimension of Advaita Vedanta* (Delhi: Motilal Banarsidass, 1993).

16. As we shall see below, Forsthoefel also notes important points of continuity between classical Vedānta, especially the teaching of the

Vivekacūḍāmaṇi, and the more thoroughly internalist orientation of Ramana Maharshi.

17. Sharma, *Experiential Dimension*, xiv.

18. Wilhelm Halbfass, "The Concept of Experience in the Encounter between India and the West," in *India and Europe: An Essay in Understanding* (Albany, NY: SUNY Press, 1981), 378–402.

19. Ibid., 395.

20. Ibid., 395–402. Halbfass is indebted to Paul Hacker for initiating this line of inquiry, although his own analysis is far more complex. For a more recent scholarly engagement on this theme, see a recent theme issue of the journal *Religions*, on "Religious Experience in the Hindu Tradition," ed. June McDaniel, www.mdpi.com/journal/religions/special_issues/hindutradition. Particularly noteworthy for their engagement of the psychology of William James and other Western theorists are Christopher K. Chapple, "Religious Experience and Yoga," *Religions* 10.4 (2019): 237, and Alfred Collins, "Religious Experience without an Experiencer: The 'Not I' in Sāṃkhya and Yoga," *Religions* 10.2 (2019): 94.

21. Ibid., 387–91.

22. *Upadesasāhasrī Padyabandha* 18. In the discussion that follows, I use the critical edition in Sengaku Mayeda, ed. *Śaṅkara's Upadeśasāhasrī, Critically Edited with Introduction and Indices* (Tokyo: Hokuseido Press, 1973) and the English translation in Sengaku Mayeda, trans., *A Thousand Teachings: The Upadeśasāhasrī of Śaṅkara* (Albany, NY: SUNY Press, 1992), with small modifications. Hereafter, I cite the *Upadeśasāhasrī* directly in my exposition, in its verse portion (USP) and prose portion (USG).

23. See Michael Comans, "Śaṅkara and the Prasaṅkhyānavāda," *Journal of Indian Philosophy* 24 (1996): 50–55; Jacqueline Suthren Hirst, "Weaving the Strands: Cognition, Authority and Language in Śaṅkara's *Upadeśasāhasrī*," in *Paramparā: Essays in Honour of R. Balasubramanian*, ed. S. Rao and G. Mishra (New Delhi: Indian Council of Philosophical Research, 2003), 143–44; and Mayeda, *A Thousand Teachings*, 196n13.

24. See Reid B. Locklin, *Liturgy of Liberation: A Christian Commentary on the Upadeśasāharī* (Leuven: Peeters, 2011), 147–52.

25. See the further discussion in Locklin, *Liturgy of Liberation*, 152–59; G. Cardona, "*Anvaya* and *Vyatireka* in Indian Grammar," *Adyar Library Bulletin* 31–32 (1967–1968), 313–52; Wilhelm Halbfass, "Human Reason and Vedic Revelation in Advaita Vedanta," in *Tradition and Reflection: Explorations in Indian Thought* (Albany: SUNY Press, 1991), 170–74; and Sengaku Mayeda, "Śaṃkara and Sureśvara: Their Exegetical Method to Interpret the Great Sentence '*Tat Tvam Asi*,'' *Adyar Library Bulletin* 44–45 (1980–1981), 147–60.

26. Comans, "Importance of *Samādhi*," 30.

27. See Swami Gambhirananda, trans., *Brahma-Sūtra-Bhāṣya of Śrī Śaṅkarācārya* (Calcutta: Advaita Ashrama, 1965, 1972), 317–19, and the discussion in Comans, "Importance of *Samādhi*," 23–24.

28. Comans, "Importance of *Samādhi*," 24–29; Jonathan Bader, *Meditation in Śaṅkara's Vedanta* (New Delhi: Aditya Prkashan, 1990), 102–5.

29. Halbfass, "Concept of Experience," 390.

30. See Karl H. Potter, "Introduction to the Philosophy of Advaita Vedānta," in *Encyclopedia of Indian Philosophies, Vol. 3: Advaita Vedānta up to Śaṅkara and His Pupils*, ed. Karl H. Potter (Princeton, NJ: Princeton University Press, 1981), 42–44.

31. Halbfass, "Concept of Experience," 393. Most scholars do not accept this work as one of Śaṅkara's certainly authentic writings, though there are exceptions to this view. Few doubt its antiquity, and it is widely accepted as an authoritative Advaita text. See the discussion in Karl H. Potter, "*Vivekacūḍāmaṇi*," in Potter, *Encyclopedia*, Vol. 3, 335; Thomas A. Forsthoefel, "Retrieving the *Vivekacūḍamaṇi*: The Poles of Religious Knowing," *Philosophy East and West* 52.3 (2002): 312–14; and John Grimes, trans., *The Vivekacūḍāmaṇi of Śaṅkarācārya Bhagavatpāda: An Introduction and Translation* (Aldershot, Hants, UK & Burlington, VT: Ashgate, 2004), 11–23.

32. In the discussion that follows, I follow the Sanskrit text and English translation in Swāmī Mādhavānanda, trans., *Vivekacūḍāmaṇi of Śaṅkaācārya* (Calcutta: Advaita Ashrama, 1995), with small modifications. Hereafter, I cite it in the main prose as VC.

33. Forsthoefel, "Retrieving the *Vivekacūḍāmaṇi*," 318–21; Francis X. Clooney, S.J., with Hugh Nicholson, "To Be Heard and Done, but Never Quite Seen: The Human Condition According to the *Vivekacūḍāmaṇi*," in *The Human Condition*, ed. Robert Cummings Neville (Albany, NY: SUNY Press, 2001), 91–93.

34. See Forsthoefel, "Retrieving the *Vivekacūḍāmaṇi*," 314–18.

35. Clooney and Nicholson, "To Be Heard," 88–90, quotation at 88.

36. Forsthoefel, "Retrieving the *Vivekacūḍāmaṇi*," 322.

37. See Eliot Deutsch, *Advaita Vedānta: A Philosophical Reconstruction* (Honolulu: University of Hawaii Press, 1969), 51–54; Karl H. Potter, *Presuppositions of India's Philosophies* (Delhi: Motilal Banarsidass, 1991), 167–82; and Pulasth Soobah Roodurmun, *Bhāmatī and Vivaraṇa schools of Advaita Vedānta: A Critical Approach* (Delhi: Motilal Banarsidass Publishers, 2002. In his *Knowledge and Liberation in Classical Indian Thought* (Basingstoke, UK & New York: Palgrave, 2001), Chakravarthi Ram-Prasad traces the distinction between these schools to different approaches to immediacy (196–209). He writes: "Where the Vivaraṇa philosophers find a foundation for their project in the relationship between text, teacher and seeker, Vācaspati [and the Bhāmatī tradition] in effect makes the teacher a mere

convenience and the text a mere vehicle. The primary commitment should be to the truth of non-duality, the primary mode of attainment should be the self-generated process of transcending dualistic consciousness" (209).

38. Andrew O. Fort, *Jīvanmukti in Transformation: Embodied Liberation in Advaita and Neo-Vedanta* (Albany, NY: SUNY Press, 1998), 84–125. See also the discussion in Ankur Barua, "Ideas of Liberation in Medieval Advaita Vedānta," *Religion Compass* 9.8 (2015): 265–68.

39. Fort, *Jīvanmukti in Transformation*, 91–95, 101–3.

40. See Locklin, *Liturgy of Liberation*, 27.

41. See Sulochana A. Nachane, *A Survey of Post-Śaṅkara Advaita Vedānta* (Delhi: Paramamitra Prakashan, 2000), 266.

42. Fort, *Jīvanmukti in Transformation*, 102–3; Swamī Vidyāraṇya, *Jīvan-Mukti-Viveka*, trans. Swamī Mokṣadānanda (Calcutta: Advaita Ashrama, 1996), 181–275.

43. Forsthoefel, "Weaving the Inward Thread," 50–51. Barua, "Ideas of Liberation," 268–69, attributes this shift, at least in part, to the increasing influence of Saṃkhya and the "substantialization" of *māyā* and *ajñāna* in late medieval Advaita.

44. Lawrence A. Babb, *Redemptive Encounters: Three Modern Styles in the Hindu Tradition* (Berkeley, Los Angeles, & London: University of California Press, 1988), 2–6.

45. Ibid., 5.

46. Ibid., 9, 206–7.

47. Ibid., 4.

48. See Kathryn Tanner, *Theories of Culture: A New Agenda for Theology*, Guides to Theological Inquiry (Minneapolis: Fortress Press, 1997), esp. 124–43, and her restatement in "Cultural Theory," in *The Oxford Handbook of Systematic Theology*, ed. John Webster, Kathryn Tanner, and Iain Torrance (Oxford & New York: Oxford University Press, 2007), esp. 529–34, 539–40. Tanner's discussion of "style" as a possible source of shared identity is somewhat more complex, but here too she ultimately decides that both the vagueness of such patterns of shared use itself and a robust Christian theology of divine sovereignty militate against presuming any "pure Christian something" that directs the process and guarantees stability in the midst of extraordinary variety (*Theories of Culture*, 144–51, quotations at 148).

49. Tanner, *Theories of Culture*, 123–24, 151–55, quotation at 154.

50. Tanner, *Theories of Culture*, 152.

51. See Babb, *Redemptive Encounters*, 9, 206–7; Tanner, *Theories of Culture*, 152, 154.

52. See especially Thomas A. Forsthoefel, "Ramaṇa Maharṣi: Mystic as Translator," *International Journal of Hindu Studies* 5.2 (2001): 109–30. For

the purposes of this exposition, I have had reference to Forsthoefel's article and the English translation of Ramana's Tamil rendition in *The Collected Works of Sri Ramana Maharshi*, 10th edition (Tiruvannamalai, India: Sri Ramanasramam, 2009 [2007]), 208–69. Hereafter, I cite this translation in my prose, by page number and, in brackets, by the corresponding verse number(s) in Swāmī Mādhavānanda's edition of the VC.

53. Śaṅkaracārya, 1912–1954.

54. Śrī Candraśekhara Bhāratī, *Vivekacūḍāmaṇi of Śrī Śaṃkara Bhagavatpāda, with an English Translation of the Commentary in Saṃskṛt by Jagadguru Śrī Candraśekhara Bhāratī Svāminaḥ*, 3rd edition, trans. S. Sankaranarayanan (Bombay: Bharatiya Vidya Bhavan, 1988), viii–x. Hereafter cited in my prose by verse number. Where the verse numbering differs from Swāmī Mādhavānanda's edition of the VC, I have included the latter in brackets.

55. See Parvathy Raman, *Words to the Wordless: The Living Legacy of Swami Chinmayananda* (Piercy, CA: Chinmaya Mission West, 2015), 56–59; and Swami Chinmayananda, *Ādi Śaṅkarācārya's Vivekacūḍāmaṇi*, revised edition (Mumbai: Chinmaya Prakashan, 2013), ii–iv. Hereafter cited in my prose by verse number. Where the verse numbering differs from Swāmī Mādhavānanda's edition of the VC, I have included the latter in brackets. This commentary has figured prominently in the Mission's signature "scheme of study" for small groups. See Swami Chinmayananda, *Manual of Self-Unfoldment* (Mumbai: Central Chinmaya Mission Trust, 1975), 192.

56. Forsthoefel, "Ramaṇa Maharṣi," 115–16, 122–23.

57. Chinmayananda, *Vivekacūḍāmaṇi*, i.

58. Forsthoefel, "Ramana Maharṣi," 118. See also the discussion in Ankur Barua, "The Silences of Ramana Maharshi: Self-Enquiry and Liberation in Sāṃkhya Yoga and Advaita Vedānta," *Religions of South Asia* 9.2 (2015): 197–99.

59. See Forsthoefel, "Ramana Maharṣi," 125–27.

60. Potter, *Presuppositions*, 36–46. I am grateful to Ankur Barua for reminding me of this account as a way to understand key disagreements in the Advaita tradition.

61. Ibid., 237–47. Potter classifies these two, along with the Buddhist Nagārjuna, as "Do-it-yourself" leap philosophers. In ibid., 247–54, he surveys a number of "Non-do-it-yourself" philosophers who attribute the sudden onset of liberation to divine grace, interestingly including Swami Vivekananda and his teacher Ramakrishna.

62. Ibid., 236.

63. See ibid., 43–44. Indeed, one could argue that all Advaita Vedāntins could be classified as leap philosophers from the perspective of highest truth, insofar as no change or development is possible in the innermost, eternally liberated self of all beings, and as progress or path

philosophers from the perspective of empirical reality, insofar as the liberating self-knowledge always arrives through some process of inquiry and practice. On this point, see especially Ankur Barua's discussion of the "paradox of practice" in "Silences of Ramana Maharshi," 187–92.

64. Barua, "Silences of Ramana Maharshi," 202.

65. Except where otherwise noted, I draw on the Sanskrit text and, with small modifications, the English translation available in *Upadesa Saram (The Essence of Spiritual Instruction), In Complete Version in Four Languages Composed by Sri Bhagavan (in Tamil, Sanskrit, Telugu and Malayalam), with Transliteration, Word-for-Word Meaning, Paraphrase and Commentary* (Tiruvannamalai: Sri Ramanasramam, 2011), 87–131. I cite the text itself in the main prose, by verse number; I cite commentary and explanatory notes from this edition in the footnotes.

66. Ibid., iv–vi.

67. Here I am following the analysis of N. A. Mohan Rao in ibid., 88–93.

68. Barua, "Silences of Ramana Maharshi," 198. On this point, see also D. M. Sastri, *Sri Maharshi's Way: A Translation and a Commentary on Upadesa Saram* (Tiruvannamalai: Sri Ramanasramam, 1989), 20: "We see here . . . a scale of excellence. Again, the Maharshi's theme is that the quieter and more internal the devotional practice, the more effective it is."

69. On this point, see especially Sastri, *Sri Maharshi's Way*, 2–3, 33, and *Upadesa Saram*, 55–56, 72.

70. See the discussion in *Upadesa Saram*, 4, 88, 135–37, 163, 215–16.

71. Ibid., vii–ix. For the purposes of the present discussion, I have confined myself to synthetic commentaries by Michael James and N. A. Mohan Rao, which take previous commentaries into account, in ibid., as well as Sastri, *Sri Maharshi's Way*.

72. Sastri, *Sri Maharshi's Way*, 24, 47.

73. *Upadesa Saram*, 77.

74. Ibid., 16, 32–33, 39–47, 240, quotation at 33.

75. Ibid., 87 (emphasis in the original).

76. Sastri, *Sri Maharshi's Way*, i. Sastri goes so far as to contend that, among the works that emerged from this experience, the *Upadeśa Sāram* should be granted the highest authority, because it is the sole text that Ramana composed in a single sitting. See ibid., 1–2.

77. *Upadesa Saram*, 87. See also ibid., iii, and Sastri, *Sri Maharshi's Way*, i–ii.

78. See Chinmayananda, *Manual*, 192. By way of contrast, although Swami Vivekananda is frequently praised and invoked as an inspiring model by teachers in the Chinmaya Mission, I know of no instances in

which his public teachings or those of his guru Sri Ramakrishna have been accorded similar, quasi-scriptural status.

79. H. H. Swami Tejomayananda, *Talks on Upadesha Sara by Bhagavan Ramana Maharshi* (Langhorne, PA: Chinmaya Publications West, 2006), DVD, 6 discs. For a further discussion and analysis of this lecture series, see Reid B. Locklin, "Performance and Engagement: Reconsidering Religious Experience in Contemporary Comparative Theology," in *The Wiley Blackwell Companion to Comparative Theology: A Festschrift in Honor of Francis X. Clooney, SJ*, ed. Axel Takacs and Joseph Kimmel (Oxford: Wiley Blackwell, 2023), 104–14).

80. For example, a series of lectures on the text by Swami Paramarthananda, apparently from 2016, are available at "Commentary on Upadesha Saram," *Hindu Online*, www.hinduonline.co/AudioLibrary/Discources/ CommentaryonUpadeshaSaramParamarthananda.html. Another recent commentary by Neema Majmudar, a disciple of Swami Dayananda who teaches in India and Europe, is available at "Upadesa Saram, Anaikatti, January 2014," YouTube. www.youtube.com/playlist?list=PLWBJlNyjM4s3MeyL92Yy7F3muMojPCOcT

81. Swami Dayananda, *Talks on Upadesa Saram (Essence of the Teaching) of Ramana Maharshi* (Rishikesh, India: Sri Gangdhareshwar Trust, 1987), 2–6, quotation at 6 (emphasis mine).

82. Ibid., 6, 1 (quotation). Also see Swami Viditatmananda's introduction in ibid., i–ii.

83. Ibid., 25, 56, 64, 70, 99–100, 139.

84. Ibid., 9, 17, 22.

85. Ibid., 58.

86. Ibid., 66.

87. Ibid., 101.

88. Ibid., 63, 77, 80–82, 86, 96–98.

89. Ibid., 79.

90. Ibid., 65.

91. Ibid., 92.

92. Ibid., 78–79, 92. Earlier, again with classical yoga in mind, Dayananda writes that meditation without scriptural teaching should not be regarded as knowledge, but "self-hypnosis" (ibid., 57).

93. Ibid., 92–93.

94. Ibid., 93.

95. Ibid., 111.

96. Ibid., 13–14, 47–48, 68.

97. Ibid., 113–14, 138.

98. Ibid., 129, 131.

99. Ibid., 138.

100. Sastri, *Sri Maharshi's Way*, 25–26.

101. Ibid., 26.

102. Forsthoefel, *Knowing beyond Knowledge*, 155.

103. On the relation between experience and universality in the Ramakrishna Mission in particular, see Jeffery D. Long, "Universalism in Hinduism," *Religion Compass* 5–6 (2011): 214–23; and Jeffery D. Long, "Religious Experience, Hindu Pluralism and Hope: *Anubhava* in the Tradition of Sri Ramakrishna," *Religions* 10.3 (2019): 210. https://doi.org/10.3390/rel10030210

104. Tanner, "Editorial Symposium," 309.

105. See Hajime Nakamura, *A History of Early Vedānta Philosophy* (Delhi: Motilal Banarsidass, 1983) and especially Richard King, *Early Advaita Vedānta and Buddhism: The Mahāyāna Context of the Gauḍapādīya-Kārikā* (Albany, NY: SUNY Press, 1995).

106. Forsthoefel, *Knowing beyond Knowledge*, 48.

107. There are of course exceptions to this rule, most significantly Ramana Maharshi himself.

108. Lamin Sanneh, *Translating the Message: The Missionary Impact on Culture*, 2nd edition (Maryknoll, NY: Orbis Books, 2009). On the comparison of Christianity and Islam, see also Lamin Sanneh, *Whose Religion Is Christianity? The Gospel beyond the West* (Grand Rapids, MI & Cambridge, UK: William B. Eerdmans, 2003), esp. 18–20, 99–100, 119–22.

109. Sanneh, *Translating the Message*, 33–34.

110. Ibid., 33.

111. Ibid., 42–43, 252–76.

112. Although her focus is different and considerably less prone to religious enthusiasm, Lydia H. Liu has similarly explored the connection between the act of translation as a historical and cultural "event" and a distinctively pluralist approach to universalism. See her "Shadows of Universalism: The Untold Story of Human Rights around 1948," *Critical Inquiry* 40 (2014): 385–417, and "The Eventfulness of Translation: Temporality, Difference, and Competing Universals," in *At Translation's Edge*, ed. Nataša Ďurovičová, Patrice Petro, and Lorena Terando (New Brunswick, NJ: Rutgers University Press, 2019), 13–30. Also useful in this respect is the development of "open-ended universalisms" in Nika Kuchuk, "Genealogies of Transnational Religion: Translation, Revelation, and Discursive Technologies in Two Female Gurus of Esoteric Vedanta" (PhD dissertation, University of Toronto, 2021), esp. 360–68, ProQuest Dissertations Publishing (28769458).

113. Sanneh, *Translating the Message*, 1; Sanneh, *Whose Religion?*, 97–98.

114. Sanneh, *Translating the Message*, 13–190; Sanneh summarizes his historical argument compactly in "Bible Translation, Culture, and Religion," in *The Wiley Blackwell Companion to World Christianity*, ed. Lamin Sanneh and Michael J. McClymond (Malden, MA: Wiley-Blackwell, 2016), 265–81.

115. Sanneh, *Whose Religion?*, 97.

116. Sanneh, *Translating the Message*, 192–99; Sanneh, "Bible Translation," 269–70; Sanneh, *Whose Religion?*, 18.

117. Sanneh, *Translating the Message*, 98.

118. Sanneh, *Whose Religion?*, 10–11, 53–57.

119. Sanneh, *Translating the Message*, 164–226; Sanneh, "Bible Translation," 274–78. The anticolonial significance of vernacular Bible translation has also been brought out by Homi K. Bhabha in "Signs Taken for Wonders: Questions of Ambivalence and Authority under a Tree Outside Delhi, May 1817," *Critical Inquiry* 12.1 (1985): 144–65.

120. See, for example, the discussion in Stanley H. Skreslet, *Comprehending Mission: The Questions, Methods, Themes, Problems, and Prospects of Missiology* (Maryknoll, NY: Orbis Books, 2012), 40–42.

121. See SCVC 7, and the discussion of Swami Vivekananda in Rambachan, *Limits of Scripture*, 41–62.

122. See, for example, Sastri, *Sri Maharshi's Way*, i.

123. Sanneh, *Whose Religion?*, 97.

124. Writing in an entirely different context, Jacques Derrida draws on Walter Benjamin to figure the process of translation as a kind of mystagogical search for "complementarity or harmony" among different tongues in his famous 1985 essay, "Des Tours de Babel," reprinted in *Acts of Religion*, ed. Gil Anidjar (New York: Routledge, 2001), 131. "And since," Derrida continues, "to complete or complement does not amount to the summation of any worldly totality, the value of harmony suits this adjustment, and what can here be called the accord of tongues. This accord lets the pure language, and the being-language of the language, resonate, announcing it rather than presenting it. As long as this accord does not take place, the pure language remains hidden, concealed (*verborgen*), immured in the nocturnal intimacy of the 'core.' Only a translation can make it emerge." If one replaces Benjamin's notion of "pure language" with liberating self-knowledge, this passage would seem to describe the Advaita missionary project astoundingly well. See also the discussion in Kuchuk, "Genealogies of Transnational Religion," 115–56.

125. See above, chapter 2, pp. 57–58, and the discussion in Phillip Charles Lucas, "Neo-Advaita in America: Three Representative Teachers," in *Homegrown Gurus: From Hinduism in America to American Hinduism*, ed. Ann Gleig and Lola Williamson (Albany: SUNY Press, 2013), 163–87.

126. See Sanneh, *Translating the Message,* 51, 53, 191–92, 262, 274–76.

127. See Donald Senior, CP and Carol Stuhlmueller, CP, *The Biblical Foundations for Mission* (Maryknoll, NY: Orbis Books, 1983), 255–79, esp. 269–70, 272; Lucien Legrand, *Unity and Plurality: Mission in the Bible,* trans. Robert R. Barr (Maryknoll, NY: Orbis Books, 1990), 74, 108–10.

128. Lucien Legrand, *The Bible on Culture* (Maryknoll, NY: Orbis Books, 2000), 159–61.

129. In his *Whose Religion?*, 82, Sanneh places the following observation on the lips of a fictive questioner: "You make a strong pitch for a personal God as the ruling power in the religions of Africa, pointing out that evidence for such a personal God exists independently of any commensurate political organization or economic system . . . You do not say this is because of special revelation à la Karl Rahner, but it fits well into that scheme." Here, Sanneh is referring to Karl Rahner's famous discussion of the notion of "anonymous Christianity." See Karl Rahner, "Christianity and the Non-Christian Religions," in *Theological Investigations, Vol. 5: Later Writings,* trans. Karl-H. Kruger (New York: Crossroad Publishing Company, 1983), 115–34; Karl Rahner, "Anonymous Christians," in *Theological Investigations, Vol. VI: Concerning Vatican Council II,* trans. Karl-H. and Boniface Kruger (New York: Crossroad Publishing Company, 1982), 390–98; and Karl Rahner, "Observations on the Problem of the 'Anonymous Christian,'" in *Theological Investigations, Vol. XIV: Ecclesiology, Questions in the Church, The Church in the World,* trans. David Bourke (New York: Seabury Press, 1976), 280–94, as well as the overview in Francis A. Sullivan, S.J., *Salvation Outside the Church? Tracing the History of the Catholic Response* (Mahwah, NY: Paulist Press, 1992), 171–81.

130. Senior and Stuhlmueller, *Biblical Foundations,* 332.

131. Ibid.

132. Ibid., 342.

133. See ibid., 329–32. Robert Cummings Neville makes this idea explicit in his *Defining Religion: Essays in Philosophy of Religion* (Albany, NY: SUNY Press, 2018), writing that "the most fundamental element for defining a class of experiences is what the experiences are about . . . Religious experiences are about something religious, which is to say, something ultimate" (87). John J. Thatamanil, a student of Neville, has helpfully refined this idea to define "the religious" in terms of "interpretative schemes" and "therapeutic regimes" in the service of one or another "comprehensive qualitative orientation." See his *Circling the Elephant: A Comparative Theology of Religious Diversity* (New York: Fordham University Press, 2020), 152–92.

134. SCVC 318.

135. See SCVC 45, 53, 292; Forsthoefel, "Ramana Maharṣi," 124–27; and the further discussion in Forsthoefel, *Knowing beyond Knowledge*, 133–38.

136. RVC, 265.

Chapter 5

1. Portions of this chapter were previously published as Reid B. Locklin and Julia Lauwers, "Rewriting the Sacred Geography of Advaita: Swami Chinmayānanda and the *Śaṅkara-dig-vijaya*," *The Journal of Hindu Studies* 2.2 (2009): 179–208; and Reid B. Locklin, "Migration and Spiritual Conquest: Emplacing Contemporary Comparative Theology in a Hindu Theology of the 'Quarters' (*dik*)," in *Strangers in this World: Multi-Religious Reflections on Immigration*, ed. Hussam S. Timani, Allen G. Jorgenson, and Alexander Y. Hwang (Minneapolis, MN: Fortress Press, 2015), 11–29. These portions are reused by permission of Oxford University Press and Fortress Press, respectively. I am particularly grateful to Julia Lauwers for her permission to re-present our co-authored work in this monograph.

2. Though I have in this volume focused on Advaita engagement and syntheses with Yoga, Vaiṣṇava, and eventually Christian interlocutors, non-dualist forms of Śaivism and Śaktism have also had a significant historical impact on the development of modern Advaita Vedānta. Significant recent work has been done on this relation in the context of early modern South India by Elaine M. Fisher and Eric Steinschneider. See Elaine Fisher, "'A Śākta in the Heart': Śrīvidyā and Advaita Vedānta in the Theology of Nīlakaṇṭha Dīkṣita," *The Journal of Hindu Studies* 8.1 (2015): 124–138; Elaine M. Fisher, "Remaking South Indian Śaivism: Greater Śaiva Advaita and the Legacy of the Śaktiviśiṣṭādvaita Vīraśaiva Tradition," *International Journal of Hindu Studies* 21.3 (2017): 319–344; Elaine M. Fisher, *Hindu Pluralism: Religion and the Public Sphere in Early Modern South India* (Oakland: University of California Press, 2017); Eric Steinschneider, "Arguing the Taste of Fresh Butter: Īcūr Caccitāṉanta Cuvāmikaḷ's Advaitic Interpretation of Tamil Śaiva Theology," *International Journal of Hindu Studies.* 21.3 (2017): 299–318; and Eric Steinschneider, "Ceṭṭiyār Vedānta: Fashioning Hindu Selves in Colonial South India," *Journal of Indian Philosophy* 48 (2020): 101–18.

3. Gavin Flood, *An Introduction to Hinduism* (Cambridge: Cambridge University Press, 1996), 273.

4. Thomas A. Forsthoefel, "Weaving the Inward Thread to Awakening," in *Gurus in America*, ed. Thomas A. Forsthoefel and Cynthia Ann Humes (Albany, NY: SUNY Press, 2005), 45–46; and Thomas A. Forst-

hoefel, *Knowing beyond Knowledge: Epistemologies of Religious Experience in Classical and Modern Advaita* (Aldershot, UK & Burlington, VT: Ashgate, 2002), 153–55.

5. M. Thomas Thangaraj, "Hinduism and Globalization: A Christian Theological Approach," in *Christ and the Dominions of Civilization*, ed. Max L. Stackhouse with Diane B. Obenchain (Harrisburg: Trinity Press International, 2002), 213–39.

6. Ibid., 218.

7. Ibid., 226–27.

8. Ibid., 229. Anecdotally, I have heard very similar expressions of one's religious identity as "Vedāntin, but not Hindu" by Anglo and Latinx devotees in the Chinmaya Mission and Arsha Vidya Gurukulam, including in at least one case a member of senior leadership.

9. Fisher, *Hindu Pluralism*, esp. 1–3, 31–56.

10. Gwilym Beckerlegge, "The Early Spread of Vedanta Societies: A Case of 'Imported Localism,'" *Numen* 51 (2004): 296–320.

11. Ibid., 301–2, 307. In one dramatic instance, related to a local dispute about governance at one of its schools, the Ramakrishna Mission sought minority religious status under the constitution of India, arguing that it was not a form of Hinduism at all. After years in the courts, however, this claim was overruled by the Supreme Court of India in 1995. For further discussion, see Peter Heehs, "Not a Question of Theology: Religions, Religious Institutions, and the Courts in India," *Comparative Legal History* 1.2 (2013): 252–55.

12. Beckerlegge, "Early Spread of Vedanta," 309–14, quotation at 314.

13. Ibid., 314.

14. Carl T. Jackson, *Vedanta for the West: The Ramakrishna Movement in the United States* (Bloomington & Indianapolis: Indiana University Press, 1994), 133–37.

15. Cynthia Ann Humes, "Maharishi Mahesh Yogi: Beyond the TM Technique," in Forsthoefel and Humes, *Gurus in America*, 56–57.

16. Jan Nattier, "Buddhism Comes to Main Street," *The Wilson Quarterly* 21.2 (1997): 74.

17. Ibid., 75–78.

18. Jackson provides an overview of the changing demographics of the movement in the United States in *Vedanta for the West*, 88–129.

19. Humes, "Maharishi Mahesh Yogi," 62–63.

20. Ibid., 66.

21. Ibid., 74. C. V. Mathew similarly differentiates between the initial self-presentation and the full vision of TM in his *The Saffron Mission: A Historical Analysis of Modern Hindu Missionary Ideologies and Practices* (Delhi: ISPCK, 1999), 250–70.

22. Humes, "Maharishi Mahesh Yogi," 74.

23. Quoted in Swami Chidananda and Rukmani Ramani, eds., *Call of the Conch: The History of the Chinmaya Movement* (Mumbai: Chinmaya Mission Trust, 2001), 70.

24. Swami Chinmayananda, *A Manual of Self-Unfoldment* (Mumbai: Central Chinmaya Mission Trust, 1975).

25. Chinmayananda, *Manual*, ii.

26. Ibid., i.

27. Ibid., 4–5.

28. Ibid., esp. 53–87.

29. For this threefold scheme, see ibid., 117–18.

30. Ibid., 75–79, 157–70.

31. Ibid., 170–79.

32. Ibid., 180–89.

33. Quoted in Margaret Dukes, David Dukes, Neena Dev, Rashmi Mehrotra, Arun Mehrrotra, and Padmashree Rao, eds., *He Did It: Swami Chinmayananda—A Legacy* (Piercy, CA: Chinmaya Mission West, 2011), 246–47.

34. Chinmayananda, *Manual*, 76, 173.

35. See Dukes et al., eds., *He Did It*, 101; and "The Genius of the Chart," in *Vedānta: Swami Chinmayananda, His Words, His Legacy*, ed. Margaret Dukes, David Dukes, Neena Dev, Rashmi Mehrotra, Arun Mehrotra, and Padmashree Rao (Piercy, CA: Chinmaya Publications, 2011), 15–21.

36. Dukes et al., eds., *Vedānta*, 19–20.

37. Except where otherwise noted, all references to this work are taken from the 1998 edition: *Śaṅkara the Missionary*, revised edition (Mumbai: Central Chinmaya Mission Trust, 1998).

38. Ibid., iii; *Sankara the Missionary* (Bombay: Central Chinmaya Mission Trust, 1978), xiii.

39. *Sankara the Missionary* (1978), iv.

40. *Śaṅkara the Missionary*, i.

41. See the discussion in *Sankara the Missionary* (1978), xiii, 6; and *Śaṅkara the Missionary*, 4.

42. *Śaṅkara the Missionary*, 2.

43. William S. Sax, "Conquering the Quarters: Religion and Politics in Hinduism," *International Journal of Hindu Studies* 4 (2000): 51.

44. *Śaṅkara the Missionary*, 4.

45. For this discussion, I have made use of two English translations of the ŚDV: Swami Tapasyananda, trans., *Sankara-Dig-Vijaya: The Traditional Life of Sri Sankaracarya, by Madhava Vidyaranya* (Madras: Sri Ramakrishna Math, 1978); and K. Padmanaban, trans., *Srimad Sankara Digvijayam by Vidyaranya*, 2 vols. (Madras: K. Padmanaban, 1985–1986), the latter of which

includes both Sanskrit text and English translation. All quotations come from Tapasyananda, though I have made small modifications. Hereafter, I cite the ŚDV directly in the text.

46. See also Jonathan Bader, *The Conquest of the Four Quarters: Traditional Accounts of the Life of Śaṅkara* (New Delhi: Aditya Prakashan, 2000), 76–77, 100–35; David N. Lorenzen, "The Life of Sankaracarya" in *The Biographical Process*, ed. Frank E. Reynolds and Donald Capps, *Religion and Reason* 11 (Paris: Mouton & Co., 1976), 87–103; and Yoshitsugu Sawai, *The Faith of Ascetics and Lay Smārtas: A Study of the Śaṅkaran Tradition of Śṛṅgerī* (Vienna: Institut für Indologie der Universität Wien, 1992), 83–116.

47. Bader, *Conquest of the Four Quarters*, 174.

48. This is recounted in *Śaṅkara the Missionary*, 33.

49. Ibid., 11–12.

50. Ibid., 18–20, 56.

51. Ibid., 11.

52. Ibid., i.

53. Ibid., 53–54. Bader and Clark discuss the ongoing dispute between the claims of the Śṛṅgerī and Kañcīpūram *maṭhas* for primacy in the Southern quarter of India in Bader, *Conquest of the Four Quarters*, 288–306; and Matthew Clark, *The Daśanāmī-Saṃnyāsīs: The Integration of Ascetic Lineages into an Order* (Leiden & Boston: Brill, 2006), 128–33. *Śaṅkara the Missionary* (83) addresses the issue by including the Kañcī *maṭha* in the list, albeit without assigning it to one of the four great disciples.

54. *Sankara the Missionary* (1978), 55–73. In the 1998 revised edition (*Śaṅkara the Missionary*, 80–101), this discussion appears in chapter 6, after the summaries of Śaṅkara's works in chapter 4 and the symbolic reflections on the four disciples in chapter 5.

55. Bader, *Conquest of the Four Quarters*, 232–44; Clark, *Daśanāmī-Saṃnyāsīs*, 150–51; Vidyasankar Sundaresan, "Conflicting Hagiographies and History: The Place of Śaṅkaravijaya Texts in Advaita Tradition," *International Journal of Hindu Studies* 4.2 (2000): 147–48.

56. *Śaṅkara the Missionary*, 82.

57. On the place of the *maṭhas* in the nationalist project, see Peter van der Veer, *Religious Nationalism: Hindus and Muslims in India* (Berkeley, Los Angeles, & London: University of California Press, 1994), 136–37.

58. Swami Chinmayananda, *Vedanta: Science of Life*, vol. 3 (Bombay: Central Chinmaya Mission Trust, 1980, 1986), 960.

59. Swami Chinmayananda, *Love Divine* (Bombay: Central Chinmaya Publications Trust, 1970, 1982), 132.

60. *Śaṅkara the Missionary*, 12.

61. Ibid., 14, 16–18.

62. Ibid., 45.

63. See Bader, *Conquest of the Four Quarters*, 253–72.

64. Chidananda and Ramani, *Call of the Conch*, 126–27 [map insert].

65. For further discussion of this episode in the context of the ŚDV, see chapter 3, p. 97.

66. *Śaṅkara the Missionary*, 30, 55–56.

67. Ibid., 49.

68. Ibid., 78–79.

69. See chapter 3, pp. 104–14.

70. *Śaṅkara the Missionary*, 79.

71. Ibid., 76–77.

72. Ibid., 102.

73. Ibid., 104–5.

74. *Śaṅkara the Missionary*, 104–6; Chinmayananda, *Manual*, 75–76.

75. Chinmayananda, *Manual*, 76; *Śaṅkara the Missionary*, 106.

76. Chinmayananda, *Manual*, 81.

77. Ibid., 115.

78. Tim Cresswell, *Place: A Short Introduction* (Malden, MA: Blackwell, 2004).

79. Ibid., 108–9.

80. Jonathan Z. Smith, *To Take Place: Toward Theory in Ritual* (Chicago: University of Chicago Press, 1987), esp. 85–95, 116–17.

81. Edith Stein, "On the History and Spirit of Carmel," in *The Hidden Life: Hagiographic Essays, Meditations, Spiritual Texts*, Collected Works of Edith Stein, Vol. 4, ed. L. Gelber and Michael Linssen, O.C.D., trans. Waltraut Stein (Washington, DC: ICS, 1992), 1–6.

82. Thomas Tweed, *Our Lady of the Exile: Diasporic Religion at a Cuban Catholic Shrine in Miami* (New York: Oxford University Press, 1997), 91–98.

83. Ibid., 94–95.

84. Thomas A. Tweed, *Crossing and Dwelling: A Theory of Religion* (Cambridge, MA: Harvard University Press, 2006).

85. Ibid., 151.

86. Ibid., 78.

87. Ibid., 13–20, 171–78.

88. See Thomas A. Tweed and Stephen Prothero, eds., *Asian Religions in America: A Documentary History* (New York & Oxford: Oxford University Press, 1999), 6; Diana L. Eck, *A New Religious America: How a "Christian Country" Has Become the World's Most Religiously Diverse Nation* (New York: HarperCollins Publishers, 2001), 123–27; and especially Vasudha Narayanan, "Creating the South Indian 'Hindu' Experience in the United States," in *A Sacred Thread: Modern Transmission of Hindu Traditions in India and Abroad*, ed. Raymond Brady Williams (New York: Columbia University Press, 1992, 1996), 147–76.

89. Daniel K. Connelly, "At the Center of the World: The Labyrinth Pavement of Chartres Cathedral," in *Art and Architecture of Late Medieval Pilgrimage in Northern Europe and the British Isles: Texts*, ed. Sarah Blick and Rita Tekippe (Leiden & Boston: Brill, 2005), 285–314. I am grateful to Forrest Clingerman for drawing my attention to this article.

90. Ibid., 309.

91. Ramana Maharshi, "Eight Stanzas to Arunachala," in *The Collected Works of Sri Ramana Maharshi*, 10th edition (Tiruvannamalai, India: Sri Ramanasramam, 2009 [2007]), 101 (v. 2).

92. See Sax, "Conquering the Quarters," esp. 39–40, 52–53; Anand Amaladass, "Conquest of the Four Quarters (*digvijaya*): The Quest for Identity," in *Crossing the Borders: Essays in Honour of Francis X. D'Sa on the Occasion of His 65th Birthday*, ed. Anand Amaladass and Rosario Rocha (Chennai: Satya Nilayam Publications, 2001), 151–67; Samta Pandya, "Charisma, Routinisation and Institution-Building: Hindu-Inspired Faith Movements in Contemporary India," *Sociological Bulletin* 62.3 (2013): 398–403; Samta P. Pandya, "Governmentality and Guru-Led Movements in India," *European Journal of Social Theory* 19.1 (2016): 86–88; Samta P. Pandya, " 'Guru' Culture in South Asia: The Case of Chinmaya Mission in India," *Society and Culture in South Asia* 2.2 (2016): 211–22; and Sathianathan Clarke, *Competing Fundamentalisms: Violent Extremism in Christianity, Islam and Christianity* (Louisville, KY: Westminster John Knox Press, 2017), esp. 95–106.

93. Among the vast number of sources that might be cited on this topic, the following works speak directly to the experiences of Dalit and *Ādivāsī* Christians and Christianity: James Massey, *Dalits in India: Religion as a Source of Bondage or Liberation with Special Reference to Christians* (New Delhi: Manohar, 1995); Sathianathan Clarke, *Dalits and Christianity: Subaltern Religion and Liberation Theology in India* (Delhi: Oxford University Press, 1998); Sathianathan Clarke and Deenabandhu Manchala, eds., *Dalit Theology in the Twenty-First Century: Discordant Voices, Discerning Pathways* (Oxford: Oxford University Press, 2010); Rowena Robinson and Josepha Marianus Kujur, eds., *Margins of Faith: Dalit and Tribal Christianity in India* (Los Angeles: Sage, 2010); Peniel Rajkumar, *Dalit Theology and Dalit Liberation* (Farnham, UK & Burlington, VT: Ashgate, 2010); and Zoe C. Sherinian, *Tamil Folk Music as Dalit Liberation Theology* (Bloomington & Indianapolis: Indiana University Press, 2014).

94. On the *Padroado* in India, see Robert Eric Frykenberg, *Christianity in India: From Beginnings to the Present* (Oxford & New York: Oxford University Press, 2008), 119–36, 344–61; Alexander Henn, *Hindu-Catholic Encounters in Goa: Religion, Colonialism and Modernity* (Bloomington: Indiana University Press, 2014), esp. 19–82; Chandra Mallampalli, *South*

Asia's Christians: Between Hindu and Muslim (New York: Oxford University Press, 2023), 62–88; and the broader, critical account in Clara A. B. Joseph, *Christianity in India: the Anti-Colonial Turn* (London & New York: Routledge, 2019).

95. See, for example, Stanley H. Skreslet, *Comprehending Mission: The Questions, Methods, Themes, Problems, and Prospects of Missiology* (Maryknoll, NY: Orbis Books, 2012), 43–68, esp. 62–63; and Marion Grau, *Rethinking Mission in the Postcolony: Salvation, Society, and Subversion* (London & New York: Continuum, 2011).

96. Keith D. Lewis, "Neither for Money nor Honor," in *The Catholic Church in History: Legend and Reality* (New York: Crossroad Publishing Company, 2006), 25–48.

97. Bader, *Conquest of the Four Quarters*, 136–82. See also Sax, "Conquering the Quarters," 51.

98. Bader, *Conquest of the Four Quarters*, 162–69, 160nn53–54.

99. Chidananda and Ramani, *Call of the Conch*, 69.

100. See ibid., 69–126, and *Chinmaya Vishwa: A Global Movement* (Mumbai: Central Chinmaya Mission Trust, 2001), esp. 1–62.

101. *Chinmaya Vishwa*, 35–39, records the story of one Luis Jauregui, a Mexican immigrant in the United States, who first encountered Swami Chinmayananda in San Francisco in 1971, began teaching Vedānta classes in the Bay area in 1973, and eventually, in 1981, received Chinmayananda's blessing to found an independent NGO, Centro Cultural y de Servicio de las América, to translate Chinmaya publications into Spanish, and to spread the teaching throughout the southwest United States, Mexico, and Latin America.

102. For an overview, see Skreslet, *Comprehending Mission*, 181–82.

103. Deidre Cornell surveys several of the major narratives in her work *Jesus Was a Migrant* (Maryknoll, NY: Orbis Books, 2014), esp. 15–28.

104. See Michael Richter, *Medieval Ireland: The Enduring Tradition*, revised edition (Dublin: Gill & Macmillan, 2005), 60–62.

105. David J. Bosch, *A Spirituality of the Road* (Scottdale, PA & Kitchener, ON: Herald Press, 1979).

106. Ibid., 58.

107. Ibid., esp. 25–39, 75–90. See also David J. Bosch, "Vulnerability of Mission," in *New Directions in Mission and Evangelization 2: Theological Foundations*, ed. James A. Scherer and Stephen B. Bevans (Maryknoll, NY: Orbis Books, 1994), 73–86; Judith Gruber, "Remembering Borders: Notes toward a Theology of Migration," in *Migration as a Sign of the Times: Towards a Theology of Migration*, ed. Judith Gruber and Sigrid Rettenbacher (Leiden: Brill, 2015), 79–106; Peter C. Phan, "Crossing the Borders: A Spirituality for Mission in Our Times," in *In Our Own Tongues: Perspectives from Asia*

on Mission and Inculturation (Maryknoll, NY: Orbis Books, 2003), 130–50; and Peter C. Phan, "*Deus Migrator*—God the Migrant: Migration of Theology and Theology of Migration," *Theological Studies* 77.4 (2016): 845–68.

108. Gemma Tulud Cruz, *An Intercultural Theology of Migration: Pilgrims in the Wilderness* (Leiden: Brill, 2010); and Gemma Tulud Cruz, *Toward a Theology of Migration: Social Justice and Religious Experience* (New York: Palgrave Macmillan, 2014).

109. These images are particularly prominent in Cruz, *Intercultural Theology*, vii–x, 8–9, 325–26.

110. Ibid., 283–84.

111. Cruz, *Toward a Theology of Migration*, 146.

112. Ibid., 144–45.

113. See especially ibid., 140–43; and Cruz, *Intercultural Theology*, 270–72.

114. Bosch, *Spirituality of the Road*, 13–16.

115. See the further development of this theme in Reid B. Locklin, *Liturgy of Liberation: A Christian Commentary on the Upadeśasāharī* (Leuven: Peeters, 2011), 215–48.

116. See, for example, *Upadeśasāhasrī Padyabandha* 17.79 [80], in Sengaku Mayeda, *A Thousand Teachings: The Upadeśasāhasrī of Śaṅkara* (Albany, NY: SUNY Press, 1992), 167.

117. See *Upadeśasāhasrī Gadyabandha* 1.1–5, 9–10; 2.45, in ibid., 211–12, 214, 234.

Chapter 6

1. Albert Schweitzer, *Indian Thought and Its Development* (London: Adam and Charles Black, 1951).

2. See ibid., 11–14, 17–18, 185–95, 225–49.

3. Ibid., 256–57.

4. This lecture became chapter 3 of S. Radhakrishnan, *Eastern Religions and Western Thought* (New York: Oxford University Press, 1959), 58–114.

5. Ibid., 68–75.

6. Ibid., 81–83, 112–14.

7. Ibid., 82.

8. Ibid., 75–76, 86–93.

9. See William F. Goodwin, "Mysticism and Ethics: An Examination of Radhakrishnan's Reply to Schweitzer's Critique of Indian Thought," *Ethics* 67.1 (1956): 25–41; Milton D. Hunnex, "Mysticism and Ethics: Radhakrishnan and Schweitzer," *Philosophy East and West* 8.3–4 (1958–1959):

121–36; A. L. Herman, "Again, Albert Schweitzer and Indian Thought," *Philosophy East and West* 12.3 (1962): 217–32; and, more obliquely, Daniel Zelinski, "From Prudence to Morality: A Case for the Morality of Some Forms of Nondualistic Mysticism," *Journal of Religious Ethics* 35.2 (2007): 291–317.

10. See Hunnex, "Mysticism and Ethics," esp. 121, 124, 127–29, 133–34.

11. Albert Schweitzer, *Christianity and the Religions of the World*, trans. Johanna Powers (New York: H. Holt and Company, 1939), 2, cited in Herman, "Again," 218.

12. Schweitzer, *Christianity*, 43–44, cited in ibid.

13. Pontifical Council for Interreligious Dialogue, World Council of Churches, and World Evangelical Alliance, "Christian Witness in a Multi-Religious World," 28 June 2011. www.oikoumene.org/en/resources/documents/wcc-programs/interreligious-dialogue-and-cooperation/christian-identity-in-pluralistic-societies/christian-witness-in-a-multi-religious-world

14. See Ankur Barua, *Debating "Conversion" in Hinduism and Christianity* (London & New York: Routledge, 2015), 90–93.

15. Schweitzer, *Indian Thought*, 164–65.

16. Ibid., 262.

17. Lance E. Nelson, "The Dualism of Nondualism: Advaita Vedānta and the Irrelevance of Nature," in *Purifying the Earthly Body of God: Religion and Ecology in Hindu India* (Albany, NY: SUNY Press, 1998), 61–88.

18. Rita Sherma, "Eros, Ethics, and Enlightenment: Toward a Reconstructive Approach to Ultimate and Penultimate Goals in Hindu Theology," *Infinity Foundation*. www.infinityfoundation.com/mandala/s_es_sherm_eros.htm

19. S. L. Malhotra, *Social and Political Orientations of Neo-Vedantism: Study of the Social Philosophy of Vivekananda, Aurobindo, Bipin Chandra Pal, Tagore, Gandhi, Vinoba, and Radhakrishnan* (New Delhi: S. Chand and Company, 1970), esp. 6, 31–33.

20. See, for example, Radhakrishnan, *Eastern Religions*, 101–102.

21. See Andrew O. Fort, "The Liberated Being and Social Service: Vivekananda, Radhakrishnan, and the Neo-Vedantic *Jīvanmukta*," in Jīvanmukti *in Transformation: Embodied Liberation in Advaita and Neo-Vedanta* (Albany, NY: SUNY Press, 1998), 172–85, as well as the further discussion in Andrew J. Nicholson, "Vivekananda's Non-Dual Ethics in the History of Vedānta," in *Swami Vivekananda: His Life, Legacy, and Liberative Ethics*, ed. Rita D. Sherma (Lanham, MD: Lexington Books, 2021), 51–71.

22. Peggy Starkey, "Agape: A Christian Criterion for Truth in the Other World Religions," *International Review of Mission* 74 (1985): 449.

This kind of argument has been roundly criticized by Paul Hacker and Karl Potter on exegetical and philosophical grounds. See Paul Hacker, "Schopenhauer and Hindu Ethics," in *Philology and Confrontation: Paul Hacker on Traditional and Modern Vedānta,* ed. Wilhelm Halbfass (Albany: SUNY Press, 1995), 273–318, and Karl H. Potter, "Introduction to the Philosophy of Advaita Vedānta," in *Encyclopedia of Indian Philosophies: Advaita Vedānta up to Śaṃkara and His Pupils* (Princeton, NJ: Princeton University Press, 1981), 36–38.

23. Arvind Sharma, "Śaṅkara's Life and Works as a Source for a Hermeneutics of Human Rights," in *New Perspectives on Advaita Vedānta: Essays in Commemoration of Professor Richard De Smet, S.J.,* ed. Bradley J. Malkovsky (Leiden: Brill, 2000), 109–21, esp. 120–21.

24. See John J. Thatamanil, *The Immanent Divine: God, Creation, and the Human Predicament* (Minneapolis, MN: Fortress Press, 2006), 121–32, 174–77.

25. Hugh Nicholson, *Comparative Theology and the Problem of Religious Rivalry* (Oxford & New York: Oxford University Press, 2011), 188–93.

26. Warren Lee Todd, *The Ethics of Śaṅkara and Śāntideva: A Selfless Response to an Illusory World* (Farnham, Surrey, & Burlington, VT: Ashgate, 2013), 24–25, 139–40, 172. In Śaṅkara's teaching, the acquisition of liberating self-knowledge immediately destroys all accumulated *karma* and prevents the liberated sage from generating any new *karma*—thus removing the possibility of rebirth. Those *karma*s that are already bearing fruit in the sage's present existence (*prārabdha karma*) continue to run their course, which is why the sage continues to live an embodied life until the point of natural death. For further discussion, see Lance E. Nelson, "Living Liberation in Śaṅkara and Classical Advaita: Sharing the Holy Waiting of God," in *Living Liberation in Hindu Thought,* ed. Andrew O. Fort and Patricia Y. Mumme (Albany, NY: SUNY Press, 1996), 31–38; A. G. Krishna Warrier, *The Concept of Mukti in Advaita Vedānta* (Madras: University of Madras, 1961), 469–528; and Yoshitsugu Sawai, "Śaṅkara's Theory of Saṃnyāsa," *Journal of Indian Philosophy* 14.4 (1986): 378–79.

27. Todd, *Ethics of Śaṅkara and Śāntideva,* 142–43.

28. See, for example, ibid., 96–108, 178–86; Patrick Olivelle, *The Āśrama System: A History and Hermeneutics of a Religious Institution* (New York & Oxford: Oxford University Press, 1993), 195–201; and especially Lance E. Nelson, "Theism for the Masses, Non-Dualism for the Monastic Elite: A Fresh Look at Śaṃkara's Trans-Theistic Spirituality," *The Struggle over the Past: Fundamentalism in the Modern World,* ed. William Shea (Lanham, MD: University Press of America, 1993), 61–77.

29. Todd, *Ethics of Śaṅkara and Śāntideva,* 186.

30. Ibid., 170–73.

31. *Upadeśasāhasrī Gadyabandha* 1.3, in Sengaku Mayeda, ed. *Śaṅkara's Upadeśasāhasrī, Critically Edited with Introduction and Indices* (Tokyo: Hokuseido Press, 1973), 191.

32. A longer version of the argument in the next two paragraphs is available in Reid B. Locklin, "Integral Samnyasa? Adi Shankaracharya and Liberation Hermeneutics," *Journal of Hindu-Christian Studies* 20 (2007): 43–51. See also Reid B. Locklin, "Ritual Renunciation and/or Ritual Innovation: Re-Describing Advaita Tradition," in *Ritual Innovation in South Asian Religions*, ed. Amy Allocco and Brian Pennington (Albany, NY: SUNY Press, 2018), 91–108.

33. Roger Marcaurelle, *Freedom through Inner Renunciation: Śaṅkara's Philosophy in a New Light* (Albany, NY: SUNY Press, 2000), 32–40, 139–42. On the *paramahaṃsa* order, see Olivelle, *Āśrama System*, 170–73, and Patrick Olivelle, *Renunciation in Hinduism: A Medieval Debate: Volume One: The Debate and the Advaita Argument* (Vienna: Institut für Indologie der Universität Wien, 1986), 33–34, 52–54.

34. See *Upadeśasāhasrī Gadyabandha* 1.2, in Mayeda, *Upadeśasāhasrī*, 191, and *Bhagavad-Gītā-Bhāṣya* 3.3, Sanskrit text and English translation in A. G. Krishna Warrier, trans., *Srīmad Bhagavad Gītā Bhāṣya of Sri Saṃkarācārya* (Madras: Sri Ramakrishna Math, 1983), 101–3.

35. See *Aitareya-Upaniṣad-Bhāṣya* introduction, Sankrit text and English translation in V. Panoli, trans., *Upanishads in Sankara's Own Words*, vol. 2, revised edition (Calicut: Mathubhumi Printing and Publishing Company, 1996), 448–49.

36. Karl H. Potter, "Śaṃkarācārya: The Myth and the Man," *Journal of the American Academy of Religion Thematic Studies* 48.3–4 (1982): 115–18. Also see Olivelle, *Āśrama System*, 224–26; and Marcaurelle, *Freedom through Inner Renunciation*, 131–47.

37. *Gītā-Bhāṣya* 2.55.0, in Warrier, *Srīmad Bhagavad Gītā Bhāṣya* 76 (modified).

38. Sanskrit text and English translation in R. C. Zaehner, trans., *The Bhagavad-Gītā* (London, Oxford, & New York: Oxford University Press, 1969), 63.

39. Schweitzer, *Indian Thought*, 262.

40. This may, of course, reveal more about Schweitzer's categories than it does about Śaṅkara's teachings. See Radhakrishnan, *Eastern Religions*, 73–75.

41. Todd, *Ethics of Śaṅkara and Śāntideva*, 187–96.

42. Consider, for example, the now classic analysis of the roles of Augustine and Aquinas in the construction of "patriarchal anthropology," in Rosemary Radford Ruether, *Sexism and God-Talk: Toward a Feminist Theology* (Boston: Beacon Press, 1983), 95–99.

43. Gwilym Beckerlegge, *Swami Vivekananda's Legacy of Service: A Study of the Ramakrishna Math and Mission* (New Delhi: Oxford University Press, 2006), 35–36. See also the further discussion in Gwilym Beckerlegge, "Vivekananda and His Organizational Legacy with Particular Reference to Seva within the Ramakrishna Math and Mission," in Sherma, *Swami Vivekananda*, 89–101.

44. Paul Hacker, "Vivekananda's Religious Nationalism," in Halbfass, *Philology and Confrontation*, 325; and Fort, "Liberated Being and Social Service," 176. See also the discussion in Beckerlegge, *Swami Vivekananda's Legacy*, 113.

45. Wilhelm Halbfass, *India and Europe: An Essay in Understanding* (Albany: SUNY Press, 1988), 239.

46. Samta P. Pandya, "'Guru' Culture in South Asia: The Case of Chinmaya Mission in India," *Society and Culture in South Asia* 2.2 (2016): 204–32, quotation at 216; and Samta Pandya, "*Seva* in Mata Amrtanandamayi Mission: Social Service as Public Face of Faith," *Implicit Religion* 19.3 (2016): 401–23, quotation at 404. See also Samta Pandya, "Charisma, Routinization, and Institution Building: Hindu-Inspired Faith Movements in Contemporary India," *Sociological Bulletin* 62.3 (2013): 389–412; Samta P. Pandya, "Governmentality and Guru-Led Movements in India: Some Arguments from the Field," *European Journal of Social Theory* 19.1 (2016): 74–93; Samta P. Pandya, "Sociality and Guru-Led Movements: Interplay of Social Issue, Action and Social Service," *Current Sociology* 64.5 (2016): 775–93; Samta P. Pandya, "Food, Faith, Social Service and Institution Building: The Annamrita Programme of the Hare Krishna Movement in India," *Religion, State and Society* 45.1 (2017): 4–22; and Maya Warrier, "The *Seva* Ethic and the Spirit of Institution Building in the Mata Amritanandamayi Mission," in *Hinduism in Public and Private: Reform, Hindutva, Gender, and Sampraday*, ed. Antony Copley (New Delhi: Oxford University Press, 2003), 254–89.

47. Halbfass, *India and Europe*, 241.

48. See chapter 4, pp. 128–29, 141–42; Kathryn Tanner, *Theories of Culture: A New Agenda for Theology*, Guides to Theological Inquiry (Minneapolis: Fortress Press, 1997), esp. 110–15; and the further development of this theme in Reid B. Locklin, *Liturgy of Liberation: A Christian Commentary on Shankara's* Upadeśasāhasrī (Leuven: Peeters, 2011), 236–48.

49. Sources that trace the organic development from the Brahmo Samaj to Swami Vivekananda and the Ramakrishna movement include Halbfass, *India and Europe*, 217–46; Otto Wolff, "Die Religiöse Aktivität Des Modernen Hinduismus," *Zeitschrift für Religions—und Geistesgeschichte* 10.4 (1958): 299–305; and Victor A. van Bijlert, *Vedāntic Hinduism in Colonial*

Bengal: Reformed Hinduism and Western Protestantism (Abingdon & New York: Routledge, 2021).

50. Beckerlegge, *Swami Vivekananda's Legacy*, 56–58, 141–50, 172–73. "[I]n discussing the development of philanthropic action during the nineteenth century, it must be recognized that social service was not simply an extension of earlier, established Christian charitable action. The Christian tradition itself had to be reread in the light of novel social circumstances" (146). See also Gwilym Beckerlegge, *The Ramakrishna Mission: The Making of a Modern Hindu Movement* (New Delhi: Oxford University Press, 2000), 103: "Vivekananda's adoption of service to humanity as an expression of spirituality did not so much follow on from established Christian practice as closely parallel the flowering of the Christian 'Social Gospel' in the last decades of the nineteenth century and the expansion of Christian missionary endeavour into a variety of forms of practical service."

51. Beckerlegge, *Swami Vivekananda's Legacy*, 258.

52. Ibid., 170–80, quotation from Ira Klein, at 170; Beckerlegge, *Ramakrishna Mission*, 79–95.

53. Beckerlegge, *Swami Vivekananda's Legacy*, 102–5, 121–26, 189–92, 201–6. Though I am following Beckerlegge closely in this discussion, the literature on Swami Vivekananda's social thought is immense. Relevant accounts of his ethics include Arun Kumar Biswas, *Swami Vivekananda and the Indian Quest for Socialism* (Calcutta: Firma KLM, 1986), 30–108; Abraham Stephen, *Social Philosophy of Vivekananda: Its Relevance to Modern India* (Delhi: ISPCK, 2005); Swami Medhananda, "From Good to God: Swami Vivekananda's Vedāntic Virtue Ethics," *International Journal of Hindu Studies* 27 (2023): 67–96; and Ankur Barua, "Living in the World by Dying to the Self: Swami Vivekananda's Modernist Reconfigurations of a Premodern Vedāntic Dialectic," *International Journal of Hindu Studies* 27 (2023): 125–148.

54. Beckerlegge, *Swami Vivekananda's Legacy*, 246–51.

55. Ibid., 164–65, 185–89, 201–6. For further discussion of the Buddha as a religious ideal in Vivekananda's teaching, see chapter 3, above, pp. 99–104.

56. Ibid., 165–69, 172–77.

57. Ibid., 202.

58. Ibid., 236–46.

59. See ibid. and the discussion in chapter 2, pp. 51–54.

60. Swami Vivekananda, "Karma Yoga," *The Complete Works of Swami Vivekananda*, Mayavati Memorial Ed., vol. 1 (Calcutta: Advaita Ashrama, 1989), 71, cited in Beckerlegge, *Swami Vivekananda's Legacy*, 231.

61. Beckerlegge, *Swami Vivekananda's Legacy*, 228–35.

62. Ibid., 218–28, 235, 249–50.

63. Otto, "Die Reliöse Activität," 312–14; David M. Miller, "The Spiritual Descent of the Divine: The Life Story of Swāmi Sivānanda," in *Hindu Spirituality: Postclassical and Modern*, ed. K. R. Sundararajan and Bithika Mukerji (New York: Crossroad Publishing Company, 1997), 351–55; David M. Miller, "The Divine Life Society Movement," in *Religion in Modern India*, revised edition, ed. Robert D. Baird (New Delhi: Manohar, 1989), 87–94.

64. See Miller, "Divine Life Society," 97–99; Sarah Strauss, *Positioning Yoga: Balancing Acts across Cultures* (Oxford & New York: Berg, 2005); and the discussion in chapter 3, pp. 109–11.

65. Swami Chinmayananda, *The Art of Man-Making: Talks on the Bhagawad Geeta* (Bombay: Central Chinmaya Mission Trust, 1978), 22.

66. Ibid., 317.

67. Samta Pandya offers an overview of these programs in "'Guru' Culture," 217–18. Fuller accounts of the educational network and elder care communities are available in Swamini Vimalananda and Vishva Sodhi, *Manifesting Divinity: Chinmaya Vision on Education* (Piercy, CA: Chinmaya Mission West, 2012); Meera Seth, *Vānaprastha: A Joyous Journey toward Liberation* (Piercy, CA: Chinmaya Mission West, 2015); and Samta P. Pandya, "Aging Spiritually: *Pitamaha Sadans* in India," *Cogent Social Science* 2 (2016): 1219212.

68. See Beckerlegge, *Swami Vivekananda's Legacy*, 37–38, 256.

69. Kshama Metre and Narender Paul, *Chinmaya Sevā: CORD and Chinmaya Mission Hospital* (Piercy, CA: Chinmaya Mission West, 2014). An alternative account of the development of CORD and other outreach initiatives of the Chinmaya Mission is available in Shymala Shiveshwarkar, "The Chinmaya Mission: Vedantic Activism," in *Dharma and Development: The Future of Survival*, ed. Makarand Paranjape (New Delhi: Samvad India Foundation, 2005), 172–92.

70. Metre and Paul, *Chinmaya Sevā*, 24–30.

71. Ibid., 31–46.

72. Ibid., 17–23. Of the 726 villages in India supported by CORD, over three-quarters are located in Himachal Pradesh, which remains the center of the organization's development efforts. The Sri Lanka program was initiated in 2005. See ibid., 207–11.

73. Ibid., 193–201, 212–17.

74. Ibid., 78–80, 103–22, 178–87.

75. Ibid., 123–69.

76. Ibid., 104–5.

77. Ibid., 27.

78. In accord with his wider interpretation of Vedānta, Swami Chinmayananda interprets the purification that arises from disinterested

service with the exhaustion of *vāsanās*. See, e.g., Chinmayananda, *Art of Man-Making*, 74–81, 85–86, and passim.

79. Metre and Paul, *Chinmaya Sevā*, xii.

80. Ibid., 55–56, 189.

81. Chinmayananda, *Art of Man-Making*, 85–89, 91–93, 154–55, and passim.

82. Ibid., 88, 91.

83. Ibid., 191.

84. Metre and Paul, *Chinmaya Sevā*, 54–56, 122.

85. Ibid., 72.

86. Ibid., 71–75, 86–87. Cf. Shiveshwarkar, "Chinmaya Mission," 183–84.

87. Metre and Paul, *Chinmaya Sevā*, 48–52, 207–8. The rhetoric of character formation and habit cultivation are strong themes in the moral teaching of the Chinmaya Mission. See Pandya, "'Guru' Culture," 222–24, and especially Purvi Parikh, "Does Character Count: Moral Self-Fashioning in the Swadhyaya and Chinmaya Mission Movements" (PhD dissertation, University of Pennsylvania, 2014).

88. Ibid., 51. On this point, Metre and Paul appear to reveal a slight tension with Chinmayananda's own social vision. While Chinmayananda does speak frequently about bringing out the hidden potential of individuals and communities, he also indulges in a more paternalistic idiom. See, for example, his discussion in *Art of Man-Making*, 101: "In short, moral beauty, cultural glory, national integrity, creative productivity, disciplined progress and such other virtues must always come from the top to the base of the social ladder. Revolution comes from the bottom to the top; evolution proceeds from the top and seeps down to the lowest level."

89. Metre and Paul, *Chinmaya Sevā*, 208.

90. Both the Ramakrishna and Chinmaya Missions have long maintained they are nonpolitical organizations. At the same time, Swami Vivekananda has been adopted as a nationalist ideal, and, as discussed in previous chapters, Swami Chinmayananda and the Chinmaya Mission have never disguised their distinctive rhetoric of cultural nationalism. See the further discussion in Pandya, "'Guru' Culture," 213–15, 220–22; Pandya, "Charisma," 399–403; Gwilym Beckerlegge, "Saffron and *Seva*: The Rashrtiya Swayamsevak Sangh's Appropriation of Swami Vivekananda," in Copley, *Hinduism in Public and Private*, 31–65; Shamita Basu, *Religious Revivalism as Nationalist Discourse: Swami Vivekananda and New Hinduism in Nineteenth-Century Bengal* (New Delhi: Oxford University Press, 2002); Jyotirmaya Sharma, *Cosmic Love and Human Apathy: Swami Vivekananda's Restatement of Religion* (Noida: HarperCollins India, 2013); and Sonia Sarkar,

"Narendra's Grab on Narendra," *The Telegraph Online*, 7 January 2018. www.telegraphindia.com/india/narendra-s-grab-on-narendra/cid/1331615

91. Pandya, "'Guru' Culture," 219.

92. Radhakrishnan, *Eastern Religions*, 112–13.

93. Beckerlegge, *Swami Vivekananda's Legacy*, 177.

94. Metre and Paul, *Chinmaya Sevā*; Beckerlegge, *Swami Vivekananda's Legacy*, 52–53.

95. See chapter 2, pp. 65–67.

96. His Holiness Maharishi Mahesh Yogi, *The Science of Being and Art of Living* (New Delhi: Allied Publishers, 1963), 193–268.

97. Emphasis in the original. This passage is quoted in Cynthia Ann Humes, "A Perfect Government," unpublished manuscript provided by author, 28 July 2016, 2.

98. See ibid., 11–13; and Joseph Weber, *Transcendental Meditation in America: How a New Age Movement Remade a Small Town in Iowa* (Iowa City: University of Iowa Press, 2014), 60–70.

99. His Holiness Maharishi Mahesh Yogi, *Maharishi's Absolute Theory of Government* (n.p., India: Maharishi Prakashan, 1995), 234.

100. Quoted in Metre and Paul, *Chinmaya Sevā*, 48.

101. Maharishi Mahesh Yogi, *Maharishi's Absolute Theory* (emphasis added).

102. Ibid., 87–97, 104–7, 122–60, 169, 241–43.

103. Ibid., 165–66, 233, 237.

104. Ibid., 230–34.

105. See ibid., 339–47, and the further discussion in Humes, "Perfect Government," 19–20.

106. Maharishi Mahesh Yogi, *Maharishi's Absolute Theory*, 50–51.

107. This is a phrase that Maharishi Mahesh Yogi used in an interview with Larry King as he was in the process of drawing down the Natural Law Party's federal campaigns. See Humes, "Perfect Government," 2–3.

108. John Hagelin, *Manual for a Perfect Government: How to Harness the Laws of Nature to Bring Maximum Success to Governmental Administration* (Fairfield, IA: Maharishi University of Management Press, 1998); Robert Roth, *A Reason to Vote: Breaking the Two-Party Stranglehold—and the Remarkable Rise of America's Fastest Growing New Political Party* (New York: St, Martin's Griffin, 1999 [1998]).

109. Hagelin, *Manual*, 11–15, 22–24, 29–30.

110. Ibid., 153.

111. Ibid., 36–39, 67–70.

112. Hagelin, *Manual*, 92–94; Roth, *A Reason to Vote*, 174–83.

113. Roth, *A Reason to Vote*, 18–59, 131–40. Humes argues for strong affinities between the Maharishi's conception of natural law and that of

Romantic philosophers, including the American transcendentalists, in "A Perfect Government," 6–8.

114. In chapter 3 of the *Manual*, for example, Hagelin offers a precis of quantum mechanics and superstring theory, arguing that the universe should be seen as a "cosmic symphony" of "vibrational states" whose sole foundation is the underlying, conceptual reality of the Quantum Field (*Manual*, 45–48). So too, drawing on cognitive science, he argues for the unity of all individual experience as a "structure of pure, self-interacting consciousness" rooted in the *chakravarti* or brain stem as the "silent witness to all mental activity" (*Manual*, 53–55). These arguments closely echo those made by the Maharishi himself, in *Maharishi's Absolute Theory*, 78–109.

115. See Roth, *A Reason to Vote*, 73–128, 253–56, 265–76; Hagelin, *Manual*, 110–19; and Humes, "A Perfect Government," 10–11.

116. Hagelin, *Manual*, 139–40.

117. Ibid., 142–45.

118. Ibid., 145–46.

119. Humes, "A Perfect Government," 13–14; and Cynthia Ann Humes, "Maharishi Mahesh Yogi: Beyond the TM Technique," in *Gurus in America*, ed. Thomas A. Forsthoefel and Cynthia Ann Humes (Albany, NY: SUNY Press, 2005), 71.

120. For a fuller account of Rambachan's ethics, on which the exposition in the next two paragraphs is based, see Reid B. Locklin, "*Śabda Pramāṇa* and Prophetic Witness: Barthian and Advaitin Perspectives in Dialogue," *Journal of Religion* 94.4 (2014): esp. 494–99.

121. See Anantanand Rambachan, *Accomplishing the Accomplished: The Vedas as a Source of Valid Knowledge in Śaṅkara* (Honolulu: University of Hawaii Press, 1991); Anantanand Rambachan, "Where Words Can Set Free: The Liberating Potency of Vedic Words in the Hermeneutics of Śaṅkara," in *Texts in Context: Traditional Hermeneutics in South Asia*, ed. Jeffrey R. Timm (Albany, NY: SUNY Press, 1992), 33–46; and Anantanand Rambachan, "*Pramāṇa*: Understanding the Authority of Scripture," in *Essays in Hindu Theology* (Minneapolis: Fortress Press, 2019), 33–45.

122. See Anantanand Rambachan, "Śaṅkara's Rationale for *Śruti* as the Definitive Source of *Brahmajñāna*: A Refutation of Some Contemporary Views," *Philosophy East and West* 36 (1986): 25–40; Anantanand Rambachan, "Is Karmayoga a Direct and Independent Means to Moksha? An Evaluation of Vivekananda's Arguments," *Religion* 15 (1985): 53–65; Anantanand Rambachan, "The Place of Reason in the Quest for *Moksha*—Problems in Vivekananda's Conceptualization of Jñānayoga," *Religious Studies* 23 (1987): 279–88; Anantanand Rambachan, "Redefining the Authority of Scripture: The Rejection of Vedic Infallibility by the Brahmo Samaj," in *Authority, Anxiety and Canon: Essays in Vedic Interpretation*, ed. Laurie L.

Patton (Albany: SUNY Press, 1995), 253–79; and Anantanand Rambachan, *The Limits of Scripture: Vivekananda's Reinterpretation of the Vedas* (Honolulu: University of Hawaii Press, 1994).

123. Anantanand Rambachan, "Interpreting Another Tradition: Vivekananda on Christ and Christianity," *Anima* 20 (1994): 128; and Anantanand Rambachan, "Swami Vivekananda: A Hindu Model for Interreligious Dialogue," in *Interreligious Dialogue: Voices from a New Frontier*, ed. M. Darrol Bryant and Frank Flinn (New York: Paragon House, 1989), 17 (quotation).

124. See Anantanand Rambachan, "Advaita Vedanta and Marcus Borg," *Hindu-Christian Studies Bulletin* 16 (2003): 35–36; Anantanand Rambachan, "The Hindu Tree on America's Sacred Ground," in *Taking Religious Pluralism Seriously: Spiritual Politics on America's Sacred Ground*, ed. Barbara A. McGraw and Jo Renee Formicola (Waco, TX: Baylor University Press, 2005), 182–85; Anantanand Rambachan, *The Advaita Worldview: God, World, and Humanity* (Albany: SUNY Press, 2006), 107–11; Anantanand Rambachan, "'There are Many Branches on the Tree of Life': The Irreconcilability of Hinduism and Homophobia," in *Heterosexism in Contemporary World Religion: Problem and Prospect*, ed. Marvin M. Elison and Judith Plaskow (Cleveland, OH: Pilgrim Press, 2007), esp. 211–14; and Anantanand Rambachan, "Are There Principles in the Hindu Tradition Consonant with Liberty, Equality and Fraternity?: *Bhagavad Gītā* 4:13 and the Caste System," in *Essays in Hindu Theology*, 147–63.

125. See Anantanand Rambachan, "Evangelization and Conversion Reconsidered in the Light of the Contemporary Controversy in India: A Hindu Assessment," *Hindu-Christian Studies Bulletin* 15 (2002): esp. 24–27; and Anantanand Rambachan, "The Co-existence of Violence and Non-violence in Hinduism," *The Ecumenical Review* 55 (2003): 115–21.

126. Rambachan, "Many Branches," 201–2.

127. See especially Rambachan, *Advaita Worldview*, 2–3.

128. Anantanand Rambachan, *A Hindu Theology of Liberation: Not-Two is Not One* (Albany, NY: SUNY Press, 2015). For a concise summary of his constructive argument, see Rambachan, "The Resources and Challenges for a Hindu Theology of Liberation," in *Essays in Hindu Theology*, 131–45.

129. Rambachan, *A Hindu Theology of Liberation*, chapters 1–4.

130. Ibid., chapters 5–9.

131. Ibid., 68–69.

132. Ibid., 76–88.

133. Ibid., 143–44.

134. Ibid., 67.

135. See especially ibid., 103–4.

136. Ibid., 105–6, 183–84 (quotation at 183).

137. Ibid., 185.

138. Ibid., 5.

139. In his introduction (ibid., 12), he writes, "Although the reader may discern the policy of implications of this discussion, this is not a work about policy. It is first and foremost a work of theology that has a twofold aim. First, to offer an interpretation of the Advaita that does not trivialize the world, but establishes its value and meaning in relation to *brahman*. Second, to retrieve from this interpretation the core guiding values that we must bring to understanding of and response to issues of contemporary concern."

140. "Mission and Vision," *Sadhana*, www.sadhana.org/mission-vision. Sailaja Krishnamurti offers a brief, appropriately critical account of Sadhana in the context of Hindu activism in North America in her essay "Race, Representation and Hindu-Christian Encounters in Contemporary North America," in *The Routledge Handbook of Hindu-Christian Relations*, ed. Chad M. Bauman and Michelle Voss Roberts (London & New York: Routledge, 2021), 190.

141. "Advisory Board," *Sadhana*, www.sadhana.org/advisory-board. Rambachan contributes frequently to Sadhana's blog, and Rambachan's works, including *A Hindu Theology of Liberation*, appear prominently in blog posts by other members, as well as in a "Sadhana Syllabus" on the organization website. See "Blog," *Sadhana*, www.sadhana.org/blog-1; and "Sadhana Syllabus," *Sadhana*, www.sadhana.org/syllabus. For a recent attempt by a young Sadhana member to develop a progressive, activist ethic from Advaita sources, see Shashank Rao, "An Asian-American Reads the Īśavāsya Upaniṣad: First Steps Toward a Hindu Diaspora Theology of Liberation," *Journal of Hindu-Christian Studies* 33 (2020): 53–62.

142. "Sadhana Salons," *Sadhana*. www.sadhana.org/salons

143. Sharon Otterman, "Hindu Temple in Queens Joins Sanctuary Movement," *New York Times*, 7 May 2017. www.nytimes.com/2017/05/07/nyregion/a-lonely-stand-hindu-temple-in-queens-joins-sanctuary-movement.html

144. Noreen Reza, "Progressive Hinduism and a New Movement against Poverty," *Kajal Magazine*, 26 June 2018. www.kajalmag.com/progressive-hinduism-and-a-new-movement-against-poverty

145. Anantanand Rambachan, "Hindus and the Poor People's Campaign: A Religious and Moral Obligation," *Sadhana*, 19 April 2018. www.sadhana.org/blog-1/2018/4/19/hindus-and-the-poor-peoples-campaign-a-religious-and-moral-obligation

146. Humes, "A Perfect Government," 11; and Roth, *A Reason to Vote*, esp. 18–21.

147. In addition to the Jewish, Christian, and other partners with whom they work on such broad initiatives as the Sanctuary Movement and the Poor People's Campaign, Sadhana's blog highlights its close con-

nections with the progressive political vision of Swami Agnivesh, former president of the Ārya Samāj; its Advisory Board includes members from ISKCON and other Hindu organizations, and it hosts its New York City events at a local Presbyterian seminary and a Unitarian congregation.

148. Andrew Fort makes the case that Ramana's views on social service and living liberation (*jīvanmukti*) cohere much more closely to classical Advaita sources than most other forms of late modern Advaita, even while he differs significantly on the question of religious experience. See Fort, "A Liberated Being Being Liberated: The Case of Ramana Maharshi," in Jīvanmukti *in Transformation,* 134–49.

149. Quoted in ibid., 143.

150. C. René Padilla, *Mission between the Times,* revised edition (Carlisle, UK: Langham Monographs, 2010, 2013).

151. *The Lausanne Covenant,* July 1974, *Lausanne Movement,* www.lausanne.org/content/covenant/lausanne-covenant#cov; hereafter cited in text, by article.

152. Padilla, *Mission between the Times,* 2–3. Padilla considered the entrenched position, rather than the newer argument on behalf of social responsibility, a postwar aberration against the wider history of the evangelical movement. "Unfortunately," he writes, "the greatest expansion of the gospel on a worldwide scale (probably the largest one in the history of the church) took place during a period marked by what David Moberg has called 'the great reversal'—the departure from social concern on the part of evangelicalism in the United States, especially during the first decades of the twentieth century—and during the decade following World War II" (3).

153. Ibid., 6–18. Padilla notes that the consultations that followed Lausanne frequently marginalized social concern and even argued that "the mission of the church can be reduced to evangelism in isolation from social responsibility" (16).

154. Ibid., 42–49, quotations at 43, 45.

155. See his response to questions and criticisms in ibid., esp. 54–66.

156. Ibid., 20–21, 158–83.

157. Ibid., 152, 156–57, 159–80.

158. Ibid., 199–211.

159. Ibid., 210.

160. Ibid., 19.

161. Gustavo Gutiérrez, *A Theology of Liberation: History, Politics, and Salvation,* revised edition (Maryknoll, NY: Orbis Books, 1988), 83–86.

162. Francis A. Sullivan, S.J., *The Church We Believe In: One, Holy, Catholic and Apostolic* (New York/Mahwah: Paulist Press, 1988), 132–51.

163. Pope Paul VI, *Evangelii Nuntiandi* nos. 28–29, 8 December 1975, *The Holy See*, https://w2.vatican.va/content/paul-vi/en/apost_exhortations/documents/hf_p-vi_exh_19751208_evangelii-nuntiandi.html. Also of central importance in this development was the teaching of the Second General Assembly of the Synod of Bishops on 30 November 1971. See Synod of Bishops, "Justice in the World," in *The Gospel of Peace and Justice: Catholic Social Teaching Since Pope John* (Maryknoll, NY: Orbis Books, 1976), 513–29.

164. Pope Leo XIII, *Rerum Novarum*, 15 May 1891, *The Holy See*. https://w2.vatican.va/content/paul-vi/en/apost_exhortations/documents/hf_p-vi_exh_19751208_evangelii-nuntiandi.html

165. See Alejandro Crosthwaite, O.P., "Aparecida: Catholicism in Latin America and the Caribbean at the Crossroads," *Journal of the Society of Christian Ethics* 28.2 (2008): 160–63.

166. Ibid., 163–67.

167. Ibid., 171.

168. See Consejol Episcopal Latinoamericano (CELAM), *Aparecido: Documento Conclusiva* nos. 366, 470–75, following the English translation. http://celam.org/aparecida/Ingles.pdf

169. Pope Francis, *Laudato Si': On Care for Our Common Home*, 24 May 2015, *The Holy See*, https://w2.vatican.va/content/francesco/en/encyclicals/documents/papa-francesco_20150524_enciclica-laudato-si.html; Pope Francis, *Fratelli Tutti: On Fraternity and Social Friendship*, 3 October 2020, *The Holy See*. www.vatican.va/content/francesco/en/encyclicals/documents/papa-francesco_20201003_enciclica-fratelli-tutti.html

170. See Sherma, "Eros, Ethics, and Enlightenment," and Miroslav Volf, "Materiality of Salvation: An Investigation of the Soteriologies of Liberation and Pentecostal Theologies," *Journal of Ecumenical Studies* 26.3 (1989): 447–67.

171. See Barua, *Debating "Conversion,"* esp. 91–94; and Sebastian C. H. Kim, *In Search of Identity: Debates on Religious Conversion in India* (New Delhi: Oxford University Press, 2003), esp. 122–26.

172. C. René Padilla summarizes the conclusions of a 1982 evangelical Consultation on the Relationship between Evangelism and Social Responsibility, as follows: "in the first place, Christian social action is a *consequence* of evangelism, since those involved in it are Christians. In fact, they must be involved because they are saved 'for good works,' and that means that social action is not only a consequence but one of the purposes of evangelism" (11). From this foundation, the document develops secondary and tertiary roles of social action as a "*bridge*" to and "*partner*" of evangelism (ibid.).

173. Rambachan, *Hindu Theology of Liberation*, 83.
174. Francis, *Laudato Si'*, no. 236.
175. Radhakrishnan, *Eastern Religions*, 80.

Chapter 7

1. Portions of this chapter were previously published as Reid B. Locklin, "Non-Dual Belonging: Conversion, Sanskritization and the Dissolution of the Multiple in Advaita Missionary Movements," *Journal of Hindu-Christian Studies* 28 (2015): 88–99; and Reid B. Locklin, "Non-Dual Conversion and Non-Dual Belonging: Trajectories of Religious Transformation in Missionary Advaita Vedānta," in *Hindu-Christian Dual Belonging*, ed. Daniel Soars and Nadya Pohran (London & New York: Routledge, 2022), 122–39. These portions are reused by permission of the *Journal of Hindu–Christian Studies* and Taylor & Francis Group, respectively.

2. See chapter 1, pp. 36–41.

3. See, for example, the discussions in Peter Antes and Hans Waldenfels, SJ, "Mission in Non-Christian Religions," in *Dictionary of Mission: Theology, History, Perspectives* (Maryknoll, NY: Orbis Books, 1987), 306–7; François Böspflug, "Religions Missionaires, Religions Non-Missionaires," *Revue des sciences religieuses* 80.2 (2006): 130–31; and Max L. Stackhouse, "Missions: Missionary Activity," in *Encyclopedia of Religion*, vol. 9, ed. Lindsay Jones, revised edition (Detroit: McMillan Reference USA, 2005), 6069–70.

4. See Arvind Sharma, *Hinduism as a Missionary Religion* (Albany, NY: SUNY Press, 2011), esp. 31–62; and Ankur Barua, *Debating "Conversion" in Hinduism and Christianity* (London & New York: Routledge, 2015), esp. 118–25.

5. Carl S. Jackson, *Vedanta for the West: The Ramakrishna Movement in the United States* (Bloomington & Indianapolis: Indiana University Press, 1994), 74. In this respect, Jackson offers a fundamentally similar judgment to that of Wendell Thomas, who differentiates between two groups of Ramakrishna adherents: a small group of Christians who enhance their Christianity through their practice of Vedanta and a second, larger group of "nominal Christians" who encounter "Hinduism as their first vital religion" and never look back. See Wendell Thomas, *Hinduism Invades America* (New York: Beacon Press, 1930), 118. "In this way," Thomas writes, "the protestation that all cults are equally true, made by Hinduism in India as a defence against the conversion of nominal Hindus to Christianity, becomes in America a subtle instrument for the conversion of nominal Christians to Hinduism, for it is precisely the Hindu method of broad generalization that entices certain doubted and creed-bound Christian

rebels into the capacious Hindu fold" (119). Both Jackson and Thomas speak more or less exclusively of Western converts to the tradition, rather than the members of the Indian diaspora, who today form the backbone of the Ramakrishna movement in the United States and Canada.

6. Reinhart Hummel, *Indische Mission und neue Frömmigkeit in Westen: Religiöse Bewegungen Indiens in westlichen Kulturen* (Stuttgart: Verlag W. Kohlhammer, 1980), 17–18. See also ibid., 239–40, and Antes and Waldenfels, "Mission in Non-Christian Religions," 307.

7. Stephen R. Wilson, "Becoming a Yogi: Resocialization and Deconditioning as Conversion Process," *Sociological Analysis* 45.4 (1984): 301–14.

8. Rudolf C. Heredia, *Changing Gods: Rethinking Conversion in India* (New Delhi: Penguin, 2007), 8, 13.

9. Sharma, *Hinduism as a Missionary Religion*, 122.

10. See especially ibid., 134–38; Arvind Sharma, "For a Sociology of India: The Place of Conversion in Hinduism," *Contributions to Indian Sociology (ns)* 11.2 (1977): 177–83; Arvind Sharma, "Ancient Hinduism as a Missionary Religion," *Numen* 39.2 (1992): 175–92; and the further discussion in Reid B. Locklin, "A Most Uncommon Task: Arvind Sharma and the Construction of Hindu Missiology," *International Journal of Hindu Studies* 28.1 (2024): forthcoming.

11. Sharma, *Hinduism as a Missionary Religion*, 137.

12. Other scholars—notably Sharma, but also Ankur Barua and C. V. Mathew—have drawn attention to similar themes, and I will continue to draw on their insights throughout the chapter. My account differs from theirs primarily in its narrow focus on the particularity of these narratives and theologies of conversion and its insistence on their distinctively Advaita character.

13. Frank K. Flinn, "Conversion: Up from Evangelicalism or the Pentecostal and Charismatic Experience," in *Religious Conversion: Contemporary Practices and Controversies*, ed. Christopher Lamb and M. Darroll Bryant (London & New York: Cassell, 1999), 51–52.

14. Bernard J. F. Lonergan, S.J., *Method in Theology*, 2nd edition (London: Darton, Longman & Todd, 1972), 6–20.

15. Ibid., 130.

16. Ibid., 237–38.

17. Ibid., 238–40.

18. Ibid., 240.

19. One of the most influential critiques, from a sympathetic interpreter, is available in George A. Lindbeck, *The Nature of Doctrine: Religion and Theology in a Postliberal Age* (London: SPCK, 1984).

20. Robert M. Doran, *Psychic Conversion and Theological Foundations: Toward a Reorientation of the Human Sciences* (Chico, CA: Scholars Press, 1981); Robert M. Doran, *Theology and the Dialectics of History* (Toronto,

Buffalo and London: University of Toronto Press, 1990), esp. 42–63; Jeremy W. Blackwood, "Sanctifying Grace, Elevation, and the Fifth Level of Consciousness," *Method: Journal of Lonergan Studies*, n.s. 2.2 (2011): 143–161; Jeremy W. Blackwood, "Eighteen Days in 1968: An Essay on the Maturation of Lonergan's Intentionality Analysis," *Method: Journal of Lonergan Studies*, n.s. 3.2 (2012): 1–26.

21. Walter Conn, *Christian Conversion: A Developmental Interpretation of Autonomy and Surrender* (New York/Mahwah: Paulist Press, 1986), esp. 159–211; Walter E. Conn, *Conscience and Conversion in Newman: A Developmental Study of Self in John Henry Newman* (Milwaukee, WI: Marquette University Press, 2010).

22. Ibid., 27.

23. Lonergan, *Method*, 241.

24. Indeed, Lonergan writes that "from a causal viewpoint, one would say that first there is God's gift of his love," and the transformation of religious conversion moves downward through the levels and elevates them by grace (*Method*, 243). See also Doran, *Theology and the Dialectics of History*, esp. 34–37, 77–82, 242–53, 548–50, and Jeremy D. Wilkins, "Grace and Growth: Aquinas, Lonergan, and the Problematic of Habitual Grace," *Theological Studies* 72.4 (2011): esp. 741–48.

25. As the Lonergan interpreter Joseph Komonchak puts the matter, "religious community sublates communities whose principle is moral responsibility, and Christian community sublates religious community." See his *Foundations in Ecclesiology* (Chestnut Hill, MA: Boston College, 1995), 44; as well as Conn, *Christian Conversion*, 212–68; Reid B. Locklin, "Toward an Interreligious Theology of Church: Revisiting Bernard Lonergan's Contribution to the 'Dialogue of Religions,'" *Journal of Ecumenical Studies* 43.3 (2008): esp. 391–96; and Donald L. Gelpi, S.J., *Charism and Sacrament: A Theology of Christian Conversion* (London: SPCK, 1976).

26. Lewis R. Rambo, *Understanding Religious Conversion* (New Haven, CT & London: Yale University Press, 1993), 5 (quotation), 16–18, 165–70. See also the further discussion of this seven-stage schema in Lewis R. Rambo, "Theories of Conversion: Understanding and Interpreting Religious Change," *Social Compass* 46.3 (1999): esp. 267 and Lewis R. Rambo and Charles E. Farhadian, "Converting: Stages of Religious Change," in Lamb and Bryant, *Religious Conversion*, 23–34.

27. Rambo, *Understanding Religious Conversion*, 12–14.

28. Ibid., 17.

29. James T. Richardson, *Conversion Careers: In and Out of the New Religions* (Beverley Hills, CA: Sage, 1978); James T. Richardson, "Conversion Careers," *Transaction: Social Science and Modern Society* 17.3 (1980): 47–50.

30. Henri Gooren, *Religious Conversion and Disaffiliation: Tracing Patterns of Change in Faith Practices* (New York: Palgrave MacMillan, 2010), 3. I am grateful to Chad Bauman for alerting me to the work of Gooren and suggesting its relevance to the present study.

31. Ibid., 48–49.

32. Ibid., 3.

33. Ibid., 49–52, 136–38.

34. Ibid., 16, 69–129.

35. Ibid., 141.

36. Lonergan writes as an explicit and self-confessed Christian philosopher and theologian, and Gooren notes that one of the weaknesses of conversion theory to date is its nearly exclusive focus on conversions to Christianity, New Religious Movements and, to a lesser extent, Islam. See ibid., 40–42, as well as Henri Gooren, "Anthropology of Religious Conversion," in *The Oxford Handbook of Religious Conversion*, ed. Lewis R. Rambo and Charles E. Farhadian (Oxford & New York: Oxford University Press, 2014), 84–116; and Reid B. Locklin, "'Rise Up and Walk': Psychology, Comparative Theology, and the *Oxford Handbook of Religious Conversion*," *Pastoral Psychology* 67.2 (2018): esp. 206–8.

37. See, for example, Heredia, *Changing Gods*; Gauri Viswanathan, *Outside the Fold: Conversion, Modernity, and Belief* (Princeton, NJ: Princeton University Press, 1998); Krickwin C. Marak and Plamthadathil S. Jacob, eds., *Conversion in a Pluralistic Context: Perspectives and Perceptions* (Pune: CMS/ISPCK, 2000); Rowena Robinson and Sathianathan Clarke, eds., *Religious Conversion in India: Modes, Motivations, and Meanings* (New Delhi: Oxford University Press, 2003); Jan N. Bremmer, Wout Jac. van Bekkum and Arie L. Molendijk, eds., *Cultures of Conversions* (Leuven: Peeters, 2006); Richard Fox Young and Jonathan A. Seitz, *Asia in the Making of Christianity: Conversion, Agency and Indigeneity, 1600s to the Present* (Leiden: Brill, 2013); Ines W. Jindra, *A New Model of Religious Conversion: Beyond Network Theory and Social Constructivism* (Leiden: Brill, 2014); and Peter Berger and Sarbeswar Sahoo, eds., *Godroads: Modalities of Conversion in India* (Cambridge, UK: Cambridge University Press, 2020). David W. Kling has recently offered a similarly comparative account of conversion by taking a diachronic approach to Christianity itself, across its full historical and geographical diversity. See his *A History of Christian Conversion* (New York: Oxford University Press, 2020) and the discussion in Ines W. Jindra, "*A History of Conversion* and Other Conversion Models: A Review Essay," *Pastoral Psychology* 70 (2021): 141–50.

38. See Marcia Hermansen, "Conversion to Islam in Theological and Historical Perspectives," in Rambo and Farhadian, *Handbook*, 633–34; and

Karin van Nieuwkwerk, "'Conversion' to Islam and the Construction of a Pious Self," in ibid., 668–69.

39. Dan Smyer Yü, "Buddhist Conversion in the Contemporary World," in ibid., 466–67.

40. Andrea R. Jain, "Conversion to Jain Identity," in ibid., 444–45.

41. Arvind Sharma, "Hinduism and Conversion," in Rambo and Farhadian, *Handbook*, 440, citing T. M. P. Mahadevan, *Outlines of Hinduism* (Bombay: Chetana, 1971), 20.

42. Other places where he takes up this theme include Sharma, *Hinduism as a Missionary Religion*, 53, and Arvind Sharma, *Problematizing Religious Freedom* (London & New York: Springer, 2011), 180.

43. Sharma, *Hinduism as a Missionary Religion*, 151n85.

44. See the critical engagement of this binary in Anantanand Rambachan, "Hierarchies in the Nature of God? Questioning the Saguna-Nirguna Distinction in Advaita Vedanta," *Hindu-Christian Studies Bulletin* 14 (2001): 13–18.

45. Sharma notes the strong resonance between Mahadevan's notion of vertical conversion and Gandhi's frequently articulated opinion that Hindu teaching seeks only that "Hindus become better Hindus, Muslims better Muslims, and Christians better Christians" through a shared commitment to nonviolence (Sharma, *Hinduism as a Missionary Religion*, 53). One might argue that Gandhi's own religious outlook, by the end of his public life, revealed strong affinities with Advaita teachings, even though he is not associated with missionary Advaita, as I have delimited the movement in this study.

46. Swami Vivekananda, "Addresses at the Parliament of Religions," in *The Complete Works of Swami Vivekananda*, vol. I (Calcutta: Advaita Ashrama: 1970), 17.

47. Swami Vivekananda, *Swami Vivekananda, What Religion Is: In the Words of Vivekananda*, ed. Swami Vidyatmananda (Kolkata: Advaita Ashrama, 1972), 105–16. See also C. V. Mathew, *The Saffron Mission: A Historical Analysis of Modern Hindu Missionary Ideologies and Practices* (Delhi: ISPCK, 1999), 124–25; Bradley J. Malkovsky, "Swami Vivekananda and Bede Griffiths on Religious Pluralism: Hindu and Christian Approaches to Truth," *Horizons* 25.2 (1998): esp. 220–27; Antonio Rigopoulos, "Tolerance in Swami Vivekānanda's Neo-Hinduism," *Philosophy and Social Criticism* 45.4 (2019): 438–60; Ankur Barua, "Vedāntic Approaches to Religious Diversity: Grounding the Many Divinities in the Unity of Brahman," in *The Bloomsbury Research Handbook of Vedānta*, ed. Ayon Maharaj (London: Bloomsbury Academic, 2020), 266–69, 272–75; and the exceptionally nuanced assessment in Jeffery D. Long, "Religions as *Yogas*: How Reflection

on Swami Vivekananda's Theology of Religions Can Clarify the Threefold Model of Exclusivism, Inclusivism, and Pluralism," *International Journal of Hindu Studies* 27 (2023): 7–32.

48. See Barua, *Debating "Conversion,"* 31, 74–75; Anantanand Rambachan, "Swami Vivekananda: A Hindu Model for Interreligious Dialogue," in *Interreligious Dialogue*, ed. M. Darrol Bryant and Frank Flinn (New York: Paragon House, 1989), 9–19; and Francis X. Clooney, "Hindu Views of Religious Others: Implications for Christian Theology," *Theological Studies* 64 (2003): 320–23.

49. Swami Chinmayananda, *Ādi Śaṅkarācārya's Vivekacūḍāmaṇi*, revised edition (Mumbai: Chinmaya Prakashan, 2013), 289–90.

50. See Rambo, *Understanding Religious Conversion*, 12–14; Heredia, *Changing Gods*, 8–10.

51. In focusing on the specifics of individual narratives, rather than statistics and demographics, I am following the model of Gooren, *Religious Conversion*, 69–129, and Heredia, *Changing Gods*, 152–224. Carl Jackson, building on Wendell Thomas, offers a more systematic survey of Western converts to Vedanta Societies in the United States and attempts to generalize some common shared features of converts, such as upper middle-class identity, Protestant background, self-identification as "spiritual seekers," female gender and often foreign birth. See Jackson, *Vedanta for the West*, 88–99; Thomas, *Hinduism Invades America*, 116–19; as well as the related discussion in Séan Carey, "Initiation into Monkhood in the Ramakrishna Mission," in *Hinduism in Great Britain: The Perpetuation of Religion in an Alien Cultural Milieu*, ed. Richard Burghart (London & New York: Tavistock Publications, 1987), 135–39.

52. Gooren, *Religious Conversion*, 16–18, 43–52, quotation at 44.

53. Padma Narasimhan, *Swami Dayananda Saraswati: Traditional Teacher of Brahma Vidyā* (Madras: TT. Maps and Publications, n.d.).

54. Ibid., 9–11.

55. Ibid., 41–42.

56. Ibid., 65–67, 89–106.

57. See especially ibid., 108.

58. Quoted in ibid., 58.

59. Though Dayananda describes this as a conflict between "traditional" and "modern" Vedānta, one can argue that it actually has its roots as far back as the difference in emphasis between Ādi Śaṅkarācārya and Maṇḍana Miśra in the eighth century. See the discussion in chapter 4, especially pp. 125–26.

60. Ibid., 61. This reassertion of scriptural testimony, and its consequences in the practice of Advaita in the centers founded by Swami

Dayananda, are developed at greater length in Neil Dalal, "Contemplative Practice and Textual Agency in Advaita Vedānta," *Method & Theory in the Study of Religion* 21 (2009): 15–27.

61. See especially his short, mildly polemical pamphlet *The Teaching Tradition of Advaita Vedanta* (Saylorsburg, PA: Arsha Vidya Gurukulam, 1993) and our discussion in chapter 4. This pamphlet is reprinted as a fitting conclusion to Dayananda's biography in Narasimhan, *Swami Dayananda Saraswati*, 213–30.

62. Philip Goldberg, *American Veda: From Emerson and the Beatles to Yoga and Meditation—How Indian Spirituality Changed the West* (New York: Harmony Books, 2010), 83–84. I have also made reference to Pravrajika Vrajaprana's own account in "The Convert—Stranger in Our Midst," in *The Stranger's Religion: Fascination and Fear*, ed. Anna Lännström (Notre Dame, IN: University of Notre Dame Press, 2004), 169–85, esp. 170–71.

63. Vrajaprana, "The Convert," 171.

64. Ibid. Vrajaprana is a frequent presence at meetings of the American Academy of Religion and the author of such works as Pravrajika Vrajaprana, *Vedanta: A Simple Introduction* (Hollywood, CA: Vedanta Press, 1999); Pravrajika Vrajaprana, *Living Wisdom: Vedanta in the West* (Hollywood, CA: Vedanta Press, 1994); and Swami Tyagananda and Pravrajika Vrajaprana, *Interpreting Ramakrishna: Kali's Child Revisited* (Delhi: Motilal Banarsidass, 2010), as well as numerous popular and academic articles.

65. Jeffery D. Long, *A Vision for Hinduism: Beyond Hindu Nationalism* (London & New York: I. B. Tauris, 2007).

66. Ibid., 5.

67. Ibid., 6.

68. Ibid., 7–8, 13.

69. Ibid., 15–16.

70. Ibid. 8.

71. Ibid., 19, as well as Jeffery D. Long, "Complementarity, not Contradiction: Swami Vivekananda's Theology of Religions," in *Swami Vivekananda: His Life, Legacy, and Liberative Ethics*, ed. Rita D. Sherma (Lanham, MD: Lexington Books, 2021), 161–73.

72. See chapter 3, pp. 111–14. Some interpreters have noted that, while the literature on conversion often focuses on the disruption to the convert's community of origin, many converts also go on to become disruptive, creative forces in the communities they join. See, for example, Vrajaprana, "The Convert," esp. 175–79; Heredia, *Changing Gods*, esp. 299–305; Timothy S. Dobe, *Hindu Christian Faqir: Modern Monks, Global Christianity, and Indian Sainthood* (Oxford & New York: Oxford University Press, 2015), and, in an entirely different context, John Connelly, *From*

Enemy to Brother: The Revolution in Catholic Teaching on the Jews, 1933–1965 (Cambridge, MA: Harvard University Press, 2012).

73. Cynthia Ann Humes, "Maharishi Mahesh Yogi: Beyond the TM Technique," in *Gurus in America*, ed. Thomas A. Forsthoefel and Cynthia Ann Humes (Albany, NY: SUNY Press, 2005), esp. 66–67.

74. Lola Williamson, *Transcendent in America: Hindu-Inspired Meditation Movements as New Religion* (New York & London: New York University Press, 2010), 12–14, 186–213, 226–28.

75. Ibid., 146.

76. Ibid., 88.

77. Ibid., 212.

78. Ibid., 192.

79. Ibid., 205.

80. See the discussion in ibid., 193, 205–6.

81. Gooren, *Religious Conversion*, 48–50, 102–10.

82. Sarah Coakley, "Prayer as Crucible: How My Mind Has Changed," *The Christian Century*, 22 March 2011, 32–40.

83. Robert K. C. Forman, *Enlightenment Ain't What It's Cracked Up to Be: A Journey of Discovery, Snow and Jazz in the Soul* (Winchester, UK & Washington, DC: O-Books, 2010), esp. 25–30, 69–75.

84. Ibid., 69.

85. Ibid., 47–55, quotation at 53. I have deliberately focused here on examples of persons who disaffiliate, but nevertheless retain a positive view of the teaching. Others, naturally, abandon the teaching and practice as a whole. See especially Joseph Weber, *Transcendental Meditation in America: How a New Age Movement Remade a Small Town in Iowa* (Iowa City: University of Iowa Press, 2014), 145–66.

86. See Heredia, *Changing Gods*, 207–22.

87. My brief exposition here follows the account and analysis in Jacques Dupuis, S.J., *Jesus Christ at the Encounter of World Religions*, trans. Robert R. Barr (Maryknoll, NY: Orbis, 1991), 67–90. The literature on Swami Abhishiktananda is quite extensive. See especially M.-M. Davy, *Henri Le Saux, Swami Abhishiktananda, le Passeur entre Deux Rives* (Paris: Editions du Cerf, 1981); Edward T. Ulrich, "Swami Abhishiktananda and Comparative Theology," *Horizons* 31.1 (2004): 40–63; Shirley Du Boulay, *The Cave of the Heart: The Life of Swami Abhishiktananda* (Maryknoll, NY: Orbis Books, 2005); Ankur Barua, "Christian Visions of Vedānta: The Spiritual Exercises of Bede Griffiths and Henri Le Saux," *Journal of Ecumenical Studies* 51.4 (2016): 524–51; and Catherine Cornille, "Abhishiktananda," in *The Routledge Handbook of Hindu-Christian Relations*, ed. Chad M. Bauman and Michelle Voss Roberts (London & New York: Routledge, 2021), 334–42.

88. Quoted in Dupuis, *Jesus Christ*, 71–72.

89. Ibid., 74–86.

90. Ibid., 86.

91. It is worth noting that this process of transformation reaches well beyond Abhishiktananda to a generation of theologians profoundly influenced by his example, notably through the public scholarship of the Jesuit theologian of religious diversity, Jacques Dupuis (1923–2004). On this influence, see the perceptive analysis in Shannon Gabrielle Wylie, "A More Inductive Method of Interreligious Theology: Joseph Ratzinger's Insights into Christian Experience in Response to Jacques Dupuis," (PhD dissertation, Toronto School of Theology, 2022), 158–68.

92. Arvind Sharma, *One Religion Too Many: The Religiously Comparative Reflections of a Comparatively Religious Hindu* (Albany, NY: SUNY Press, 2011), quotations at 1 and 3.

93. Ibid., 37–44.

94. Ibid., 97.

95. Ibid., 132.

96. Ibid., 3.

97. On the rigid insider/outsider dynamics of TM in its later developments, see Weber, *Transcendental Meditation*, 176–90; Humes, "Maharishi Mahesh Yogi," 73–74; Cynthia Ann Humes, "Schisms within Hindu Guru Groups: The Transcendental Meditation Movement in North America," in *Sacred Schisms: How Religions Divide*, ed. James R. Lewis and Sarah M. Lewis (Cambridge: Cambridge University Press, 2009), 287–305; and especially Scott Lowe, "The Neo-Hindu Transformation of an Iowa Town," *Novo Religio* 13 (2010): 81–91. Lowe estimates that, by 2007, nearly all of the TM practitioners who had moved to Fairfield "had been barred from the golden domes; only a few hundred stalwart souls were still acceptably orthodox" (88). Whitworth and Shiels noted a similar transient quality of up to a third of participants in the Ramakrishna movement in Great Britain. See John M. Whitworth and Martin Shiels, "From Across the Black Water: Two Imported Varieties of Hinduism," in *New Religious Movements: A Perspective for Understanding Society*, ed. Eileen Barker (New York: Edwin Mellen Press, 1982), 170–71.

98. On the interplay of "Hindu" and "Vedāntin" in the Ramakrishna movement, see M. Thomas Thangaraj, "Hinduism and Globalization," in *God and Globalization, Vol. 3: Christ and the Dominions of Civilization*, ed. Max L. Stackhouse with Diane B. Obenchain (Harrisburg, PA: Trinity Press International, 2002), 228–29. It has also been my experience that some Western participants in the Chinmaya Mission and Arsha Vidya Gurukulam are more comfortable self-identifying with Vedānta, or sometimes just with "the teaching," than with Hindu culture and religion. On the

court case, which stretched from 1980 to 1995, see Gwilym Beckerlegge, *The Ramakrishna Mission: The Making of a Modern Hindu Movement* (New Delhi: Oxford University Press, 2000), 61–66.

99. Arthur Osborne, *Ramana Maharshi and the Path of Self-Knowledge: A Biography*, 4th edition (San Rafael, CA: Sophia Perennis, 2006), 153.

100. See especially J. Kuruvachira, "Hinduism as a Missionary Religion," *Mission Today* 8 (2006): 271, and the discussion in chapter 1 of this volume, pp. 15–16, 18–19.

101. Barua, *Debating "Conversion,"* 121.

102. Heredia, *Changing Gods*, 35.

103. Mathew, *Saffron Mission*, 37–40. Though he does not use the idiom of Sanskritization, Arvind Sharma's account of Aryan missionary traditions in ancient India corresponds strongly to Mathew's account. See Arvind Sharma, *Hinduism as a Missionary Religion* (Albany, NY: SUNY Press, 2011), 65–83; and Arvind Sharma, "Ancient Hinduism as a Missionary Religion," *Numen* 39 (1992): 175–92.

104. See Barua, *Debating "Conversion,"* 103, and Heredia, *Changing Gods*, 27–28.

105. M. N. Srinivas, "A Note on Sanskritization and Westernization," in *Caste in Modern India and Other Essays* (Bombay: Asia Publishing House, 1962), 42–62; M. N. Srinivas, "The Cohesive Role of Sanskritization," in *The Oxford India Srinivas* (Delhi: Oxford University Press, 2009), 221–35.

106. Srinivas, "Sanskritization and Westernization," 60.

107. See Vineeta Sinha, "Problematizing Received Categories: Revisiting 'Folk Hinduism' and 'Sanskritization,'" *Current Sociology* 54 (2006): 100–3.

108. For the purposes of this chapter, I have drawn my exposition of Pollock's theory primarily from his article "The Sanskrit Cosmopolis, 300–1300: Transculturation, Vernacularization and the Question of Ideology," in *Ideology and Status of Sanskrit*, ed. Jan E. M. Houben (Leiden, New York, & Köln: E. J. Brill, 1996). The full development of this argument is available in his *The Language of the Gods in the World of Men: Sanskrit, Culture, and Power in Premodern India* (Berkeley: University of California Press, 2006).

109. Pollock, "Sanskrit Cosmopolis," 239, 243.

110. Ibid., 209–17, 238–43, quotations at 240, 212, 242.

111. Ibid., 216.

112. For criticisms of Srinivas, see Pollock, *Language of the Gods*, 513–14, and Sinha, "Problematizing Received Categories," 103–9; on Pollock, see David Shulman, "Review Essay: *The Language of the Gods in the World of Men* by Sheldon Pollock," *Journal of Asian Studies* 66 (2007): 819–73; and Rebecca Gould, "How Newness Enters the World: The Methodology of

Sheldon Pollock," *Comparative Studies of South Asia, Africa and the Middle East* 28 (2008): 533–59.

113. Though it should be noted that Swami Vivekananda and other modern Hindus did call for greater education in Sanskrit and, in some cases, Hindi as a Sanskritic language suitable for the nation of India. See Corstiaan J. G. van der Burg, "The Place of Sanskrit in Neo-Hindu Ideologies: From Religious Reform to National Awakening," in Houben, *Ideology and Status of Sanskrit*, 367–81.

114. Swami Vivekananda, "Is Vedanta the Future Religion?," in *Complete Works*, vol. 8, 122–41.

115. Ibid., 122.

116. Ibid., 122–25.

117. Ibid., 138–41.

118. Ibid., 141.

119. Swami Chinmayananda, *A Manual of Self-Unfoldment* (Mumbai: Central Chinmaya Mission Trust, 1975, 2000), 159.

120. Ibid., 159–66.

121. Ibid., 188.

122. See Locklin, "Non-Dual Belonging," 98–99.

123. Swami Dayananda Saraswati and Helmut Girndt, *A Vedantin's View of Christian Concepts: A Dialog between Swami Dayananda Saraswati and Professor Helmut Girndt* (Saylorsburg, PA: Arsha Vidya Gurukulam, 1998).

124. Ibid., 16–18, 54–60.

125. Ibid., 48–49.

126. Ibid., 62–63.

127. Ibid., 63–65.

128. See Pollock, "Sanskrit Cosmopolis," 243–47.

129. Srinivas, "Sanskritization and Westernization," 60. A highly insightful treatment of these and other Hindu movements in terms of the emergence of cosmopolitan vernaculars is available in Srinivas Aravamudan, *Guru English: South Asian Religion in a Cosmopolitan Language* (Princeton, NJ & Oxford: Princeton University Press, 2006). See also Agehananda Bharati's now classic article, "The Hindu Renaissance and its Apologetic Patterns," *Journal of Asian Studies* 29 (1969–70): 267–87 as well as Rashmi Luthra, "The Formation of Interpretive Communities in the Hindu Diaspora," in *Religion and Popular Culture: Studies on the Interaction of Worldviews*, ed. Daniel A. Stout and Judith M. Buddenbaum (Ames: Iowa State University Press, 2001).

130. Gooren, *Religious Conversion*, 10.

131. Dayananda, *Vedantin's View*, 48–49.

132. *Vivekacūḍāmaṇi* 4–5. Sanskrit text and English translation in Swāmi Mādhavānanda, trans., *Vivekacūḍāmaṇi of Śrī Śaṅkarācārya*, 2nd edition (Calcutta: Advaita Ashrama, 1995), 2–3.

133. Chinmayananda, *Ādi Śaṅkarācārya's Vivekacūḍāmaṇi*, 10–11.

134. Ibid., 12.

135. Barua, *Debating "Conversion,"* 8–9. See also Michael Stoeber, "Hindu-Christian Dialogue on the Afterlife: Swami Vivekananda, Modern Advaita Vedānta, and Roman Catholic Eschatology," *International Journal of Hindu Studies* 27 (2023): 33–65.

136. Barua, *Debating "Conversion,"* 1.

137. TM offers a bit of an exception to this general rule, due to its more aggressive recruitment agenda. Even here, however, as we noted earlier in the chapter, in practice most TM devotees have a fairly brief and oblique relation to the missionary institution, having completed only a single course.

138. Vivekananda, "Addresses at the Parliament," 17.

139. On the commonplace of multiple religious participation if not belonging, even on the part of many Christian persons and traditions, see especially the various essays in Soars and Pohran, *Hindu-Christian Belonging,* as well as the persuasive constructive argument in John J. Thatamanil, *Circling the Elephant: A Comparative Theology of Religious Diversity* (New York: Fordham University Press, 2020), 152–92.

140. Gooren, *Religious Conversion,* 11.

141. See Shinjini Das, "An Imperial Apostle? St. Paul, Protestant Conversion and South Asian Christianity," *The Historical Journal* 61.1 (2018): 103–30.

142. Beverly Roberts Gaventa, *From Darkness to Light: Aspects of Conversion in the New Testament* (Philadelphia: Fortress Press, 1986), 39.

143. Ibid, 1–8, 54–67, 130–45, 148–49.

144. Ibid., 10 (quotation), 96–129, 148.

145. Long, *Vision for Hinduism,* 8.

146. Gaventa, *Darkness to Light,* 40.

147. For a fuller discussion of perspectival transformation in Paul and the teaching of Advaita, see Reid B. Locklin, *Liturgy of Liberation: A Christian Commentary on Shankara's Upadeśasāhasrī* (Leuven: Peeters, 2011), 66–77.

148. Gaventa, *Darkness to Light,* 149.

149. Paula Fredriksen, "Judaizing the Nations: The Ritual Demands of Paul's Gospel," *New Testament Studies* 56 (2010): 232–52; Paula Fredriksen, *Paul: The Pagans' Apostle* (New Haven, CT & London: Yale University Press, 2017).

150. See E. P. Sanders, *Paul and Palestinian Judaism: A Comparison of Patterns of Religion* (Philadelphia: Fortress Press, 1977); E. P. Sanders, *Paul, the Law, and the Jewish People* (Philadelphia: Fortress Press, 1983); and E. P. Sanders, *Paul* (Oxford & New York: Oxford University Press, 1991); and the further development and clarification of these themes in

James D. G. Dunn, *The New Perspective on Paul: Collected Essays* (Tübingen: Mohr Siebeck, 2005).

151. Fredriksen, "Judaizing the Nations," 234–43, quotation at 242; Fredriksen, *Paul*, 73–77.

152. Fredriksen, *Paul*, 75 (emphasis by the author).

153. See especially Fredriksen, "Judaizing the Nations," 248–49.

154. For a general survey and a somewhat different approach to conversion in the ancient Mediterranean world, see Andrew S. Jacobs, "Interpreting Conversion in Antiquity (and Beyond)," *Religion Compass* 15.7 (2021).

155. Fredriksen, "Judaizing the Nations," 250. For an effectively argued caution against transposing categories of belonging from the first generation of Christians to the present day, see Gavin D'Costa, "Considering the Case of Catholic-Hindu Dual Belonging from a Magisterial and Dogmatic Point of View," in Soars and Pohran, *Hindu-Christian Dual Belonging*, 69–87.

156. Among the more compelling alternatives are, on the one hand, the mystical and ecstatic interpretations of Alan F. Segal, Evan Fales and Colleen Shantz, and, on the other, the reinterpretation of conversion in terms of patron-client relations of the first-century Mediterranean world. See Alan F. Segal, *Paul the Convert: The Apostolate and Apostasy of Saul the Pharisee* (New Haven, CT: Yale University Press, 1990); Zeba A. Crook, *Reconceptualising Conversion: Patronage, Loyalty, and Conversion in the Religions of the Ancient Mediterranean* (Berlin: De Gruyter, 2004); and Colleen Shantz, *Paul in Ecstasy: The Neurobiology of the Apostle's Life and Thought* (Cambridge: Cambridge University Press, 2009). I am grateful for the assistance of Lori Frias, who completed a directed research course on this topic in 2013–2014. This section is deeply informed by her work.

157. Gaventa, *Darkness to Light*, 37.

158. Pollock, "Sanskrit Cosmopolis," 212.

159. Chinmayananda, *Manual*, 188.

160. Emil Anton, "Mission Impossible? Pope Benedict XVI and Interreligious Dialogue," *Theological Studies* 78.4 (2017): 879–904.

161. Ibid., 885–889, 904 (Allen quotation).

162. Ibid., 904.

163. Ibid.

164. Ibid., 891.

165. Pope Benedict XVI, "Address of His Holiness Benedict XVI, Meeting with the Parish Priest and Clergy of the Diocese of Rome," 7 February 2008, *The Holy See*. www.vatican.va/content/benedict-xvi/en/speeches/2008/february/documents/hf_ben-xvi_spe_20080207_clergy-rome.html

166. Ibid.

167. Ibid.

168. On this point, see the beautiful discussion in Thatamanil, *Circling the Elephant*, 193–212.

169. Vivekananda, "Is Vedanta the Future Religion?," 138–41.

170. See especially the discussion in chapter 5, pp. 172–81.

171. Swami Dayananda Saraswati, "An Open Letter to Pope John Paul II: Conversion is Violence," *Indian Express*, 29 October 1999. https://indianexpress.com/article/news-archive/conversion-is-violence

172. Ibid.

173. See, for example, Anantanand Rambachan, "Evangelization and Conversion Reconsidered in the Light of the Contemporary Controversy in India: A Hindu Assessment," *Journal of Hindu-Christian Studies* 15 (2002): 20–27.

174. Chad M. Bauman, "The Violence of Conversion: Proselytization and Interreligious Controversy in the Work of Swami Dayananda Saraswati," *Open Theology* 1 (2015): 175–88.

175. Jackson, *Vedanta for the West*, 74.

176. Dayananda, *Vedantin's View*, 48–49.

177. See, for example, the discussion of Pope John Paul II's act of repentance, in the year 2000, for various sins of the church, in Francis A. Sullivan, S.J. "The Papal Apology," *America* 182.12, 8 April 2000. www.americamagazine.org/issue/288/article/papal-apology

Conclusion

1. See Peter C. Phan, "The World Missionary Conference, Edinburgh 1910: Challenges for Church and Theology in the Twenty-First Century," *International Bulletin of Missionary Research* 34.2 (2010): 105–8; and Stanley H. Skreslet, *Comprehending Mission: The Questions, Methods, Themes, Problems and Prospects of Missiology* (Maryknoll, NY: Orbis Books, 2012), 113–15.

2. Brian Stanley, "The World Missionary Conference, Edinburgh 1910: Sifting History from Myth," *Expository Times* 121.7 (2010): 325–31.

3. Cited in Stanley, "World Missionary Conference," 330.

4. Edinburgh 2010, "Common Call," *Centenary of the 1910 World Missionary Conference*. www.edinburgh2010.org/fileadmin/Edinburgh_2010_Common_Call_with_explanation.pdf

5. M. Thomas Thangaraj, *The Common Task: A Theology of Christian Mission* (Nashville, TN: Abingdon Press, 1999), esp. 12–13.

6. David J. Bosch, *Transforming Mission: Paradigm Shifts in Theology of Mission* (Maryknoll, NY: Orbis Books, 1991), 368–510, esp. 389–93; Stephen B. Bevans and Roger P. Schroeder, *Constants in Context: A Theology*

of Mission for Today (Maryknoll, NY: Orbis Books, 2004), 348–95; and Thangaraj, *The Common Task*, 47–60.

7. See Catherine Cornille, *Meaning and Method in Comparative Theology* (Hoboken, NJ: Wiley-Blackwell, 2020), esp. 124–29.

8. Truth and Reconciliation Commission of Canada, *Honouring the Truth, Reconciling for the Future: Summary of the Final Report of the Truth and Reconciliation Commission of Canada* (Toronto: Lorimer, 2015).

9. Ibid., 95–98.

10. P. H. Bryce, *The Story of a National Crime: Being an Appeal for Justice to the Indians of Canada; the Wards of the Nation, Our Allies in the Revolutionary War, Our Brothers-in-Arms in the Great War* (Ottawa: John Hope & Sons, 1922).

11. Truth and Reconciliation Commission, *Honouring the Truth*, 1.

12. Ibid., 48.

13. Arvind Sharma, *Problematizing Religious Freedom* (Dordrecht: Springer, 2011), 233–54.

14. Nicholas Shrubsole, *What Has No Place, Remains: The Challenges for Religious Freedom in Canada Today* (Toronto: University of Toronto Press, 2019).

15. As a first attempt at this kind of work, see the Advaita theologian Anantanand Rambachan's account of racialization and caste discrimination in Hindu tradition, in his "Liberation from Caste," in *A Hindu Theology of Liberation* (Albany, NY: SUNY Press, 2015), 167–85, and "Are There Principles in the Hindu Tradition Consonant with Liberty, Equality and Fraternity? *Bhagavadgītā* 4:13 and the Caste System," in *Essays in Hindu Theology* (Minneapolis: Fortress Press, 2019), 147–63. See also Akshay Gupta, "Constructing a Hindu Black Theology," *Journal of Hindu–Christian Studies* 34 (2021): 42–51.

16. See Tomoko Masuzawa, *The Invention of World Religions: Or, How European Universalism Was Preserved in the Language of Pluralism* (Chicago & London: University of Chicago Press, 2005) and Hugh Nicholson, *Comparative Theology and the Problem of Religious Rivalry* (Oxford & New York: Oxford University Press, 2011).

17. See M. M. Thomas, *Nagas Towards A.D. 2000, and Other Selected Addresses and Writings* (Madras: Centre for Research on New International Economic Order, 1992), as well as the more contemporary reflection by R. C. Jongte in his article "Rethinking the Idea of Indigeneity: An Indigenous Liberationist Response to Hindutva Cooptation and Assimilationist Agenda in Northeast India," *Journal of Hindu–Christian Studies* 35 (2022): 49–58.

18. M. M. Thomas, *The Christian Response to the Asian Revolution* (London: SCM Press, 1966); M. M. Thomas, *The Acknowledged Christ of the Indian Renaissance* (London: SCM Press, 1969).

19. Thomas, *Acknowledged Christ*, x. Panikkar's work went through several revisions, tracing the development of his creative synthesis, and it was released in its final, significantly enlarged edition in 1981. See Raimundo Panikkar, *The Unknown Christ of Hinduism: Towards an Ecumenical Christophany* (Maryknoll, NY: Orbis Books, 1981).

20. Thomas, *Acknowledged Christ*, 253.

21. Ibid.

22. M. M. Thomas, "Salvation and Humanization: A Crucial Issue in the Theology of Mission for India," *International Review of Mission* 60.237 (1971): 25–38; M. M. Thomas, *Salvation and Humanisation: Some Critical Issues of the Theology of Mission in Contemporary India* (Madras: CLS, 1971): M. M. Thomas, Lesslie Newbigen and Alfred C. Krass, "Baptism, the Church, and Koinonia," *Religion and Society* 19.1 (1972), 69–90.

23. Thomas, "Salvation and Humanization," 26–32.

24. Ibid., 31.

25. Ibid., 38.

26. M. M. Thomas, "Baptism," 72–73.

27. Ibid., 74.

28. Kerry P. C. San Chirico, *Between Hindu and Christian: Khrist Bhaktas, Catholics, and the Negotiation of Devotion* (New York: Oxford University Press, 2023). Also useful in this respect are Jonas Adelin Jørgensen, *Jesus Imandars and Christ Bhaktas: Two Case Studies of Interreligious Hermeneutics and Identity in Global Christianity* (Frankfurt am Main: Peter Lang, 2008); and Jonas Adelin Jørgensen, "'Becoming Faithful': Conversion, Syncretism, and the Interreligious Hermeneutical Strategies of the 'Faithful of Jesus' (Īsā Īmāndārs) in Today's Bangladesh," in *Asia in the Making of Christianity: Conversion, Agency and Indigeneity, 1600s to the Present*, ed. Richard Fox Young and Jonathan A. Seitz (Leiden & Boston: Brill, 2013), 269–93.

29. See San Chirico, *Between Hindu and Christian*, especially 207–8, 217–19.

30. Newbigen, "Baptism," 75–84.

31. George R. Hunsberger, "Conversion and Community: Revisiting the Lesslie Newbigin-M M Thomas Debate." *International Bulletin of Missionary Research* 22, no. 3 (July 1998), 115.

32. Sebastian C. H. Kim, *In Search of Identity: Debates on Religious Conversion in India* (New Delhi: Oxford University Press, 2003), 105.

33. Krass, "Baptism," 85.

34. Thomas, "Baptism," 89.

35. Thomas, "Baptism," 74.

36. Thomas, "Baptism," 89.

37. See, for example, the Second Vatican Council's Dogmatic Constitution on the Church, *Lumen Gentium*, esp. nos. 9–15. Latin text and

English translation available in Norman P. Tanner, S.J., ed., *Decrees of the Ecumenical Councils, Volume Two: Trent to Vatican II* (London & Washington DC: Sheed & Ward and Georgetown University Press, 1990).

38. Pontifical Council for Interreligious Dialogue, "Reflection and Orientations on Interreligious Dialogue and The Proclamation of The Gospel Of Jesus Christ," 19 May 1991, *The Holy See*, www.vatican.va/roman_curia/pontifical_councils/interelg/documents/rc_pc_interelg_doc_19051991_dialogue-and-proclamatio_en.html: "To the Church, as the sacrament in which the Kingdom of God is present 'in mystery,' are related or oriented (*ordinantur*) (cf. LG 16) the members of other religious traditions who, inasmuch as they respond to God's calling as perceived by their conscience, are saved in Jesus Christ and thus already share in some way in the reality which is signified by the Kingdom" (no. 35). Further discussion of this idea, situated in the wider context of Catholic teachings on religious diversity, can be found in Jacques Dupuis, SJ, *Toward a Christian Theology of Religious Pluralism* (Maryknoll, NY: Orbis Books, 1997), 347–57; Jacques Dupuis, SJ, *Christianity and the Religions: From Confrontation to Dialogue* (Maryknoll, NY: Orbis Books, 2001), 2016–2017; and Christiaan Jacobs-Vandegeer, "The Unity of Salvation: Divine Missions, the Church, and World Religions," *Theological Studies* 75.2 (2014): 266–69.

39. On this point, see especially Brian P. Flanagan, *Stumbling in Holiness: Sin and Sanctity in the Church* (Collegeville, MN: Liturgical Press, 2018).

40. When Pope Francis traveled to Canada in July 2022 to offer—after significant delay—the formal apology called for by the Truth and Reconciliation Commission of Canada, his week-long visit was characterized as a "penitential pilgrimage." See "Pope Francis' Penitential Pilgrimage," *Canadian Conference of Catholic Bishops*. www.cccb.ca/indigenous-peoples/pope-francis-penitential-pilgrimage

41. Arvind Sharma, *Problematizing Religious Freedom* (London & New York: Springer, 2011), 158. In this reflection, Sharma does not delve very deeply into the history of this distinctively Jewish approach to query whether it is a natural development in the tradition or an adaptation to the harsh restrictions placed on Jewish peoples in medieval Europe and, to a lesser extent, in many parts of the Muslim world.

42. Ibid.

43. Arvind Sharma, *One Religion Too Many: The Religiously Comparative Reflections of a Comparatively Religious Hindu* (Albany, NY: SUNY Press, 2011), 73. For further discussion, see Reid B. Locklin, "A Most Uncommon Task: Arvind Sharma and the Construction of Hindu Missiology," *International Journal of Hindu Studies* 28.1 (2024): forthcoming.

44. Francis A. Sullivan, SJ, *The Church We Believe In: One, Holy, Catholic and Apostolic* (New York/Mahwah, NJ: Paulist Press, 1988), 122–28.

45. See chapter 1, pp. 19–25.

Works Cited

Primary Advaita Sources

His Holiness Jagadguru Sri Abhinava Vidyatheertha Mahaswamigal. *Enlightening Expositions*, 2nd ed. Madras: Sri Vidyatheertha Foundation, 1998.

———. *Yoga, Enlightenment and Perfection*, edited by R. M. Umesh. Chennai: Sri Vidyatheertha Foundation, 1999.

"About SVBF." SVBF: Sringeri Vidya Bharati Foundation (Canada). Accessed January 29, 2018. www.svbfcanada.com/SVBF/Aboutus.html

"About Us." *Arsha Vidya Gurukulam*. Accessed February 8, 2018. www.arshavidya.org/about-us.html

"Adi Shankara Vidyalaya Centre for Educational & Learning Activities." *SVBF: Sringeri Vidya Bharati Foundation (Canada)*. Accessed February 8, 2018. www.svbfcanada.com/SVBF/freeclasses.html

"Adi Shankaracharya Award Ceremony." YouTube. Accessed February 8, 2018. www.youtube.com/watch?v=warZsxYj9AM

"Advisory Board." *Sadhana*. Accessed July 19, 2019. www.sadhana.org/advisory-board

"Bhagavan Sri Ramana Maharshi—The Sage of Arunachala." YouTube. Accessed May 27, 2016. www.youtube.com/watch?v=pefl9sbkKxk

"Blog." *Sadhana*. Accessed July 19, 2019. www.sadhana.org/blog-1

Brunton, Paul. *A Search in Secret India*. London: Rider and Company, 1934, 1957.

———. *The Maharshi and His Message*. Tiruvannamalai, India: Sri Ramanasramam, 2009.

Swami Budhananda. *The Ramakrishna Movement: Its Meaning for Mankind*. Calcutta: Advaita Ashrama, 1980.

Śrī Candraśekhara Bhāratī. *Vivekacūḍāmaṇi of Śrī Śaṃkara Bhagavatpāda, with an English Translation of the Commentary in Saṃskṛt by Jagadguru Śrī*

Candraśekhara Bhāratī Svāminaḥ. 3rd ed. Trans. S. Sankaranarayanan. Bombay: Bharatiya Vidya Bhavan, 1988.

"Center for Health and Wellness: Healing Traumatic Stress and Raising Performance in At-risk Populations." *David Lynch Foundation*. Accessed January 16, 2018. www.davidlynchfoundation.org

Chaitanya, Svarupa, trans. *Tattva Bodha of Sankaracharya*. Bombay: Central Chinmaya Mission Trust, 1981.

Swami Chidānanda and Rukmani Ramani, eds. *Call of the Conch: The History of the Chinmaya Movement*. Mumbai: Chinmaya Mission Trust, 2001.

Chinmaya Vishvavidyapeeth University. Accessed July 12, 2019. https://cvv.ac.in

Swami Chinmayananda. *Ādi Śaṅkarācārya's Vivekacūḍāmaṇi*. Revised edition. Mumbai: Chinmaya Prakashan, 2013.

———. *The Art of Man-Making: Talks on the Bhagawad Geeta*. Bombay: Central Chinmaya Mission Trust, 1978.

———. *The Holy Geeta: Commentary by Swami Chinmayananda*. Revised edition. Mumbai: Central Chinmaya Mission Trust, 1996, 2008.

———. *Kindle Life*. Mumbai: Central Chinmaya Mission Trust, 1990, 1996.

———. *Love Divine*. Bombay: Central Chinmaya Publications Trust, 1970, 1982.

———. *A Manual of Self-Unfoldment*. Mumbai: Central Chinmaya Mission Trust, 1975, 2000.

———. "Temple Should Be Built." *Hindu Vivek Kendra*. Accessed May 27, 2016. http://hindunet.org/hvk/articles/0801/94.html

———. *Vedanta: Science of Life*, vol. 3. Bombay: Central Chinmaya Mission Trust, 1980, 1986.

Chinmaya Vishwa: A Global Movement. Mumbai: Central Chinmaya Mission Trust, 2001.

Swami Chetanananda. "Vivekananda: On the Way to Chicago." In *Swami Vivekananda: A Hundred Years Since Chicago*, edited by R. K. Dasgupta, 8–19. Belur: Ramakrishna Math and Ramakrishna Mission, 1994.

Comans, Michael. *Extracting the Essence of the Śruti: The Śrutisārasamuddharaṇam of Toṭakācarya*. Delhi: Motilal Banarsidass, 1996.

"CORD—Chinmaya Organisation for Rural Development." *Chinmaya Mission West*. Accessed 15 January 2018. http://chinmayamissionwest.com/cord

Cornelssen, Lucy. *Hunting the "I."* Tiruvannamalai, India: Sri Ramanasramam, 2009.

Swami Dayananda Saraswati. "An Open Letter to Pope John Paul II: Conversion is Violence." *Indian Express*. October 29, 1999. www.indianexpress.com/Storyold/129355

———. *Talks on Upadesa Saram (Essence of the Teaching) of Ramana Maharshi*. Rishikesh, India: Sri Gangdhareshwar Trust, 1987.

———. *The Teaching Tradition of Advaita Vedanta*. Saylorsburg, PA: Arsha Vidya Gurukulam, 1993.

———, and Helmut Girndt. *A Vedantin's View of Christian Concepts: A Dialog between Swami Dayananda Saraswati and Professor Helmut Girndt*. Saylorsburg, PA: Arsha Vidya Gurukulam, 1998.

"Dr. John Hagelin Launches U.S. Peace Government on July 4." *Natural Law Party News Flash*. July 12, 2003. http://natural-law.org/enews/2003_07_12.html

Dukes, Margaret, David Dukes, Neena Dev, Rashmi Mehrotra, Arun Mehrotra, and Padmashree Rao, eds. *He Did It: Swami Chinmayananda—A Legacy*. Piercy, CA: Chinmaya Mission West, 2011.

———, eds. *Vedānta: Swami Chinmayananda, His Words, His Legacy*. Piercy, CA: Chinmaya Publications, 2011.

Flynn, John, and Dennis J. Hartel. *The Sage of Arunachala: Sri Ramana Maharshi: 1879–1950*. Forest Hills, NY: Arunachala Ashrama, 1992.

Forem, Jack. *Transcendental Meditation: Maharishi Mahesh Yogi and the Science of Creative Intelligence*. New York: E. P. Dutton and Co., 1973.

Swami Gambhirananda, trans. *Brahma-Sūtra-Bhāṣya of Śrī Śaṅkarācārya*. Calcutta: Advaita Ashrama, 1965, 1972.

———. *History of Ramakrishna Math and Ramakrishna Mission*. Calcutta: Advaita Ashrama, 1983.

"Global Organization." *Global Country of World Peace*. Accessed May 27, 2016. www.globalcountry.org/wp/full-width/global-administration

Grimes, John, trans. *The Vivekacūḍāmaṇi of Śaṅkarācārya Bhagavatpāda: An Introduction and Translation*. Aldershot, Hants, UK, & Burlington, VT: Ashgate, 2004.

Hagelin, John. *Manual for a Perfect Government: How to Harness the Laws of Nature to Bring Maximum Success to Governmental Administration*. Fairfield, IA: Maharishi University of Management Press, 1998.

Hartel, Dennis, and Anil K. Sharma. "50th Anniversary of Arunachala Ashrama." *The Maharshi* 26.6 (2016): 1–4; 27.1 (2017): 4–5; 27.2 (2017): 1–3; 27.3 (2017): 1–3.

"History." *Sri Sri Jagadguru Shankaracharya Mahasamsthanam Dakshinamnaya Sri Sharada Peetham, Sringeri*. Accessed February 7, 2018. www.sringeri.net/history

Krishna, Gopal. "Sri Dushyanth Sridhar—Video by Gopal Krishna." YouTube. Accessed Janaury 29, 2018. www.youtube.com/watch?v=gooS9e29OL0&feature=youtu.be

Krishna Warrier, A. G., trans. *Srīmad Bhagavad Gītā Bhāṣya of Sri Saṃkarācārya*. Madras: Sri Ramakrishna Math, 1983.

Krishnan, Sri Prasad. "Sringeri Jagadguru on Pujya Swamiji Sri Sri Dayananda Saraswati, 24 September 2015." *Shishyavrunda of Jagadguru Sri Sri Bharathithirtha Mahaswamiji—Sringeri Facebook Page*. Accessed

February 8, 2018. www.facebook.com/permalink.php?story_fbid=880637235319464&id=497623950287463

Kumar, K. Suresh. *Inspiring Saint: Life and Teachings of His Holiness Jagadguru Sri Bharathi Theertha Mahaswamigal*. 2nd ed. Madras: Sri Vidyatheertha Foundation, 1998.

The Life of Swami Vivekananda by His Eastern and Western Admirers. 3rd ed. Calcutta: Advaita Ashrama, 1970.

Long, Jeffery D. *A Vision for Hinduism: Beyond Hindu Nationalism*. London & New York: I. B. Tauris, 2007.

Swāmī Mādhavānanda, trans. *Vivekacūḍāmaṇi of Śaṅkaācārya*. Calcutta: Advaita Ashrama, 1995.

Mahadevan, T. M. P. *Outlines of Hinduism*. Bombay: Chetana, 1971.

———. *Ramana Maharshi and His Philosophy of Existence*. 3rd ed. Tiruvannamalai, India: Ramanasramam, 1976.

———. *Ramana Maharshi: The Sage of Arunachala*. London: George Allen and Unwin, 1977.

"Mahakumbhabhishekam." *Sringeri Vidya Bharati Foundation (Canada)*. Accessed February 7, 2018. www.svbfcanada.com/mka.html

His Holiness Maharishi Mahesh Yogi. *Maharishi's Absolute Theory of Government*. N.p., India: Maharishi Prakashan, 1995.

———. *The Science of Being and Art of Living*. New Delhi: Allied Publishers, 1963.

Majmudar, Neema. "Upadesa Saram, Anaikatti, January 2014." YouTube. Accessed June 13, 2018. www.youtube.com/playlist?list=PLWBJlNyjM4s3MeyL92Yy7F3muMojPCOcT

Mayeda, Sengaku, ed. *Śaṅkara's Upadeśasāhasrī, Critically Ed. with Introduction and Indices*. Tokyo: Hokuseido Press, 1973.

———, trans. *A Thousand Teachings: The Upadeśasāhasrī of Śaṅkara*. Albany, NY: SUNY Press, 1992.

"Message from David Lynch." *David Lynch Foundation*. Accessed January 29, 2018. www.davidlynchfoundation.org/message.html

Metre, Kshama, and Narender Paul. *Chinmaya Sevā: CORD and Chinmaya Mission Hospital*. Piercy, CA: Chinmaya Mission West, 2014.

"Mission and Vision." *Sadhana*. Accessed July 19, 2019. www.sadhana.org/mission-vision

Swami Mitrananda, Rukma Naik Sadekar, Trishna Gulrajani, and Geeta Keswani. *Youth Alone Can: Dynamic Spirituality*. Piercy, CA: Chinmaya Mission West, 2014.

Swami, B. V. Narasimha. *Self-Realisation: The Life and Teachings of Sri Ramana Maharshi*. Tiruvannamalai, India: Sri Ramanasramam, 1985 [1931].

"Our Jagadgurus." *SVBF: Sringeri Vidya Bharati Foundation (Canada)*. Accessed February 5, 2018. www.svbfcanada.com/SVBF/Jagadgurus.html

Osborne, Arthur. *Ramana Maharshi and the Path of Self-Knowledge: A Biography*. 4th ed. San Rafael, CA: Sophia Perennis, 2006.

Padmanaban, K. trans. *Srimad Sankara Digvijayam by Vidyaranya*, 2 vols. Madras: K. Padmanaban, 1985–1986.

Panoli, V., trans., *Upanishads in Sankara's Own Words*, vol. 2. Revised edition. Calicut: Mathubhumi Printing and Publishing Company, 1996.

Swami Paramarthananda. "Commentary on Upadesha Saram." *Hindu Online*. Accessed June 12, 2018. www.hinduonline.co / AudioLibrary / Discources / CommentaryonUpadeshaSaramParamarthananda.html

Patchen, Nancy. *The Journey of a Master: Swami Chinmayananda: The Man, the Path, the Teaching*. Bombay: Central Chinmaya Mission Trust 1989, 1994.

"Places Associated with Swami Vivekananda." *Vivekananda Vedanta Society of Chicago*. Accessed May 27, 2016. http://chicagovedanta.org/ vivekananda / chicago-places.html

"Propagation of Sanatana Dharma." *Sri Sri Jagadguru Shankaracharya Mahasamsthanam Dakshinamnaya Sri Sharada Peetham, Sringeri*. Accessed February 6, 2018. www.sringeri.net / activities / propagation-of-sanatana-dharma

Radhakrishnan, S. *Eastern Religions and Western Thought*. New York: Oxford University Press, 1959.

Raman, Parvathy. *Words to the Wordless: The Living Legacy of Swami Chinmayananda*. Piercy, CA: Chinmaya Mission West, 2015.

Ramana Maharshi. *The Collected Works of Sri Ramana Maharshi*. 10th ed. Tiruvannamalai, India: Sri Ramanasramam, 2009 [2007].

———. *Talks with Sri Ramana Maharshi: Three Volumes in One*. 3rd ed. Tiruvannamalai: Sri Ramanasramam, 1963.

———. *Upadesa Saram (The Essence of Spiritual Instruction), The Complete Version in Four Languages Composed by Sri Bhagavan (in Tamil, Sanskrit, Telugu and Malayalam), with Transliteration, Word-for-Word Meaning, Paraphrase and Commentary*. Tiruvannamalai: Sri Ramanasramam, 2011.

Rambachan, Anantanand. *Accomplishing the Accomplished: The Vedas as a Source of Valid Knowledge in Śaṅkara*. Honolulu: University of Hawaii Press, 1991.

———. "Advaita Vedanta and Marcus Borg." *Hindu–Christian Studies Bulletin* 16 (2003): 35–36.

———. *The Advaita Worldview: God, World, and Humanity*. Albany, NY: SUNY Press, 2006.

———. "The Co-existence of Violence and Non-violence in Hinduism," *The Ecumenical Review* 55.2 (2003): 115–21.

———. *Essays in Hindu Theology*. Minneapolis: Fortress Press, 2019.

———. "Evangelization and Conversion Reconsidered in the Light of the Contemporary Controversy in India: A Hindu Assessment." *Hindu–Christian Studies Bulletin* 15 (2002): 20–27.

———. "Hierarchies in the Nature of God? Questioning the Saguna-Nirguna Distinction in Advaita Vedanta." *Hindu–Christian Studies Bulletin* 14 (2001): 13–18.

———. *A Hindu Theology of Liberation: Not-Two Is Not One*. Albany, NY: SUNY Press, 2015.

———. "The Hindu Tree on America's Sacred Ground." In *Taking Religious Pluralism Seriously: Spiritual Politics on America's Sacred Ground*, edited by Barbara A. McGraw and Jo Renee Formicola, 182–85. Waco, TX: Baylor University Press, 2005.

———. "Hinduism, Hindutva and the Contest for the meaning of Hindu Identity: Swami Vivekananda and V. D. Savarkar." In *The Cyclonic Swami: Vivekananda in the West*, edited by Sukalyan Sengupta and Makarand Paranjape, 121–28. New Delhi: Samvad India Foundation, 2005.

———. "Hindus and the Poor People's Campaign: A Religious and Moral Obligation." *Sadhana*. April 19, 2018. Accessed July 19, 2019. www.sadhana.org/blog-1/2018/4/19/hindus-and-the-poor-peoples-campaign-a-religious-and-moral-obligation

———. "Interpreting Another Tradition: Vivekananda on Christ and Christianity." *Anima* 20 (1994): 127–33.

———. "Is Karmayoga a Direct and Independent Means to Moksha? An Evaluation of Vivekananda's Arguments." *Religion* 15 (1985): 53–65.

———. *The Limits of Scripture: Vivekananda's Reinterpretation of the Vedas*. Honolulu: University of Hawaii Press, 1994.

———. "The Place of Reason in the Quest for *Moksha*—Problems in Vivekananda's Conceptualization of Jñānayoga." *Religious Studies* 23 (1987): 279–88.

———. "Redefining the Authority of Scripture: The Rejection of Vedic Infallibility by the Brahmo Samaj." In *Authority, Anxiety and Canon: Essays in Vedic Interpretation*, edited by Laurie L. Patton, 253–79. Albany, NY: SUNY Press, 1995.

———. "Śaṅkara's Rationale for *Śruti* as the Definitive Source of *Brahmajñāna*: A Refutation of Some Contemporary Views." *Philosophy East and West* 36 (1986): 25–40.

———. "Swami Vivekananda: A Hindu Model for Interreligious Dialogue." In *Interreligious Dialogue: Voices from a New Frontier*, edited by M. Darrol Bryant and Frank Flinn, 9–19. New York: Paragon House, 1989.

———. "'There Are Many Branches on the Tree of Life': The Irreconcilability of Hinduism and Homophobia." In *Heterosexism in Contemporary*

World Religion: Problem and Prospect, edited by Marvin M. Elison and Judith Plaskow, 201–23. Cleveland, OH: Pilgrim Press, 2007.

———. "Where Words Can Set Free: The Liberating Potency of Vedic Words in the Hermeneutics of Śaṅkara." In *Texts in Context: Traditional Hermeneutics in South Asia*, edited by Jeffrey R. Timm, 33–46. Albany, NY: SUNY Press, 1992.

Roth, Robert. *A Reason to Vote: Breaking the Two-Party Stranglehold—and the Remarkable Rise of America's Fastest Growing New Political Party*. New York: St. Martin's Griffin, 1999.

"Sadhana Salons." *Sadhana*. Accessed July 19, 2019. www.sadhana.org/salons

"Sadhana Syllabus." *Sadhana*. Accessed July 19, 2019. www.sadhana.org/syllabus

Sankara the Missionary. Bombay: Central Chinmaya Mission Trust, 1978.

Śaṅkara the Missionary. Revised edition. Mumbai: Central Chinmaya Mission Trust, 1998.

Sri Sarada Peetham. *The Greatness of Sringeri*. Revised edition. Sringeri: Dakshinamnaya Sri Sarada Peetham, 2008.

Sastri, D. M. *Sri Maharshi's Way: A Translation and a Commentary on Upadesa Saram*. Tiruvannamalai: Sri Ramanasramam, 1989.

"Satsangh Centres." *Sriramanasramam*. Accessed 27 May 2016. www.sri-ramanamaharshi.org/centres/directory

Seth, Meera. *Unto Research: Chinmaya International Foundation*. Piercy, CA: Chinmaya Mission West, 2012.

———. *Vānaprastha: A Joyous Journey Toward Liberation*. Piercy, CA: Chinmaya Mission West, 2015.

Swami Sivananda. *Practice of Karma Yoga*. 3rd ed. Delhi: Motilal Banarsidass, 1965.

"SVBF—An Introduction." YouTube. Accessed January 29, 2018. www.youtube.com/watch?v=GA9GjNaBteU&feature=youtu.be

Swami Tapasyananda, trans. *Sankara-Dig-Vijaya: The Traditional Life of Sri Sankaracarya, by Madhava Vidyaranya*. Madras: Sri Ramakrishna Math, 1978.

H. H. Swami Tejomayananda. *Talks on Upadesha Sara by Bhagavan Ramana Maharshi*. Langhorne, PA: Chinmaya Publications West, 2006. DVD, 6 discs.

"Testimonials." *SVBF: Sringeri Vidya Bharati Foundation (Canada)*. Accessed January 29, 2018. www.svbfcanada.com/SVBF/Testimonials.html

Thapan, Anita Raina, ed. *The Penguin Swami Chinmayananda Reader*. New Delhi: Penguin Books, 2004.

———, ed. *Scripture: A Mirror—The Chinmaya Study Group*. Piercy, CA: Chinmaya Publications, 2013.

Venkataraman, K. R. *Samkara and His Sarada Pitha in Sringeri: A Study in Growth and Integration*. Calcutta: Kalpa Printers and Publishers Private, 1969.

Swamī Vidyāraṇya, *Jīvan-Mukti-Viveka*. trans. by Swamī Mokṣadānanda. Calcutta: Advaita Ashrama, 1996.

Swami Vidyatmananda, ed. *What Religion Is: In the Words of Vivekananda*. Kolkata: Advaita Ashrama, 1972.

Swamini Vimalananda, and Vishva Sodhi. *Manifesting Divinity: Chinmaya Vision on Education*. Piercy, CA: Chinmaya Mission West, 2012.

Swami Vivekananda. *Complete Works of Swami Vivekananda: Vols. 1–9*. Calcutta: Advaita Ashrama, 1989–1997.

———. *Swami Vivekananda, What Religion Is: In the Words of Vivekananda*, edited by Swami Vidyatmananda. Kolkata: Advaita Ashrama, 1972.

Vrajaprana, Pravrajika. "The Convert—Stranger in Our Midst." In *The Stranger's Religion: Fascination and Fear*, edited by Anna Lännström, 169–85. Notre Dame, IN: University of Notre Dame Press, 2004.

———. *Living Wisdom: Vedanta in the West*. Hollywood, CA: Vedanta Press, 1994.

———. *Vedanta: A Simple Introduction*. Hollywood, CA: Vedanta Press, 1999.

"Welcome to Sringeri Vidya Bharati Foundation (Canada)." *SVBF: Sringeri Vidya Bharati Foundation (Canada)*. Accessed March 15, 2018. www.svbfcanada.com

"What Is the Natural Law Party?" *The Natural Law Party: A Reason to Vote*. Accessed May 27, 2016. www.natural-law.org/introduction/index.html

"Whatever Became of Frank H. Humphreys?" *The Maharshi* 27.5 (2017): 1–3; 27.6 (2017): 1–4.

Yegnasubramanian, S. "Tattva Bodha." Sringeri Vidya Bharati Foundation, Inc., USA. Accessed February 8, 2018. http://svbf.org/tattvabodha

———. "Upadesa Panchakam." Sringeri Vidya Bharati Foundation, Inc., USA. Accessed February 8, 2018. http://svbf.org/newsletters/tag/upadesa-panchakam

———. "Vaidika Samskaras." Sringeri Vidya Bharati Foundation, Inc., USA. Accessed February 7, 2018. http://svbf.org/vaidika-samskaras

Zaehner, R. C., trans. *The Bhagavad-Gītā*. London, Oxford, & New York: Oxford University Press, 1969.

Other Sources

Allen, Michael S. and Venkatkrishnan, Anand, eds. "New Directions in the Study of Advaita Vedānta." *International Journal of Hindu Studies* 21.3 (2017): 271–389.

Almond, Philip C. *The British Discovery of Buddhism*. Cambridge: Cambridge University Press, 1988.

Altman, Michael J. "The Construction of Hinduism in America." *Religion Compass* 10.8 (2016): 207–16.

Amaladass, Anand. "Conquest of the Four Quarters (*digvijaya*): the Quest for Identity." In *Crossing the Borders: Essays in Honour of Francis X. D'Sa on the Occasion of His 65th Birthday*, edited by Anand Amaladass and Rosario Rocha, 151–167. Chennai: Satya Nilayam Publications, 2001.

Antes, Peter, and Hans Waldenfels, SJ. "Mission in Non-Christian Religions." In *Dictionary of Mission: Theology, History, Perspectives*. Maryknoll, NY: Orbis Books, 1987.

Anton, Emil. "Mission Impossible? Pope Benedict XVI and Interreligious Dialogue." *Theological Studies* 78.4 (2017): 879–904.

Appadurai, Arjun. "Kings, Sects and Temples in South India, 1350–1700 A.D." *The Indian Economic and Social History Review* 14.1 (1977): 47–73.

Aravamudan, Srinivas. *Guru English: South Asian Religion in a Cosmopolitan Language*. Princeton, NJ & Oxford: Princeton University Press, 2006.

Asad, Talal. *Genealogies of Religion: Discipline and Reasons of Power in Christianity and Islam*. Baltimore: Johns Hopkins University Press, 1993.

Babb, Lawrence A. *Redemptive Encounters: Three Modern Styles in the Hindu Tradition*. Berkeley, Los Angeles, & London: University of California Press, 1988.

Bader, Jonathan. *The Conquest of the Four Quarters: Traditional Accounts of the Life of Śaṅkara*. New Delhi: Aditya Prakashan, 2000.

———. *Meditation in Śaṅkara's Vedanta*. New Delhi: Aditya Prakashan, 1990.

Bainbridge, William Sims, and Daniel H. Jackson. "The Rise and Decline of Transcendental Meditation." In *The Social Impact of New Religious Movements*, edited by Bryan Wilson. 135–58. New York: Rose of Sharon Press, 1981.

Bakhouche, Béatrice, Isabelle Fabre, and Vincente Fortier, eds. *Dynamiques de Conversion: Modèles et Résistances, Approches Inderdisciplinaires*. Turnhout, Belgium: Brepols, 2012.

Barua, Ankur. "Christian Visions of Vedānta: The Spiritual Exercises of Bede Griffiths and Henri Le Saux." *Journal of Ecumenical Studies* 51.4 (2016): 524–51.

———. *Debating "Conversion" in Hinduism and Christianity*. London & New York: Routledge, 2015.

———. "Ideas of Liberation in Medieval Advaita Vedānta." *Religion Compass* 9.8 (2015): 262–71.

———. "Living in the World by Dying to the Self: Swami Vivekananda's Modernist Reconfigurations of a Premodern Vedāntic Dialectic." *International Journal of Hindu Studies* 27 (2023): 125–148.

———. "The Silences of Ramana Maharshi: Self-Enquiry and Liberation in Sāṁkhya Yoga and Advaita Vedānta." *Religions of South Asia* 9.2 (2015): 186–207.

———. "Vedāntic Approaches to Religious Diversity: Grounding the Many Divinities in the Unity of Brahman." In *The Bloomsbury Research Handbook of Vedānta*, edited by Ayon Maharaj, 255–80. London: Bloomsbury Academic, 2020.

Basu, Shamita. *Religious Revivalism as Nationalist Discourse: Swami Vivekananda and New Hinduism in Nineteenth-Century Bengal*. New Delhi: Oxford University Press, 2002.

Bauman, Chad M. *Anti-Christian Violence in India*. Ithaca & London: Cornell University Press, 2020.

———. *Christian Identity and Dalit Religion in Hindu India, 1868–1947*. Grand Rapids, MI, & Cambridge: Eerdmans, 2008.

———. "Critiques of Christianity from Savarkar to Malhotra." In *The Routledge Handbook of Hindu–Christian Relations*, edited by Chad M. Bauman and Michelle Voss Roberts. London & New York: Routledge, 2022, 139–52.

———. "Hindu–Christian Conflict in India: Globalization, Conversion, and the Coterminal Castes and Tribes." *The Journal of Asian Studies* 72.3 (2013): 633–53.

———. "Identity, Conversion, and Violence: Dalits, Adivasis, and the 2007–08 Riots in Orissa." In *Margins of Faith: Dalit and Tribal Christianity in India*, edited by Rowena Robinson and Joseph Marianus Kujur, 263–90. Los Angeles: Sage, 2010.

———. "Postcolonial Anxiety and Anti-Conversion Sentiment in the Report of the Christian Missionary Activities Inquiry Committee." *International Journal of Hindu Studies* 12.2 (2008): 181–213.

———. "The Violence of Conversion: Proselytization and Interreligious Controversy in the Work of Swami Dayananda Saraswati." *Open Theology* 1 (2015): 175–88.

Bauman, Chad M., and Jennifer B. Saunders. "Out of India: Immigrant Hindus and South Asian Hinduism in the USA," *Religion Compass* 3.1 (2009): 116–35.

Bauman, Chad M., and Richard Fox Young, eds. *Constructing Indian Christianities: Conversion, Culture, and Caste*. London: Routledge, 2014.

Bayly, Susan. *Saints, Goddesses and Kings: Muslims and Christians in South Indian Society, 1700–1900*. Cambridge: Cambridge University Press, 1989.

Beckerlegge, Gwilym. "The Early Spread of Vedanta Societies: A Case of 'Imported Localism.'" *Numen* 51 (2004): 296–320.

———. *The Ramakrishna Mission: The Making of a Modern Hindu Movement*. Delhi: Oxford University Press, 2000.

———. "Responding to Conflict: A Test of the Limits of Neo-Vedāntic Social Activism in the Ramakrishna Math and Mission?" *International Journal of Hindu Studies* 11.1 (2006): 1–25.

———. "Saffron and *Seva*: The Rashrtiya Swayamsevak Sangh's Appropriation of Swami Vivekananda." In *Hinduism in Public and Private: Reform, Hindutva, Gender, and Sampraday*, edited by Antony R. H. Copley. New Delhi: Oxford India Paperbacks, 2009.

———. "Swami Vivekananda (1863–1902) 150 Years on: Critical Studies of an Influential Hindu Guru." *Religion Compass* 7.10 (2013): 244–53.

———. "Swami Vivekananda and the *Sangh Parivar:* Convergent or Divergent Views on Population, Religion and National Identity?" *Postcolonial Studies* 9.2 (2006): 121–35.

———. *Swami Vivekananda's Legacy of Service: A Study of the Ramakrishna Math and Mission*. New Delhi: Oxford University Press, 2006.

———. "Vivekananda and His Organizational Legacy with Particular Reference to Seva within the Ramakrishna Math and Mission." In *Swami Vivekananda: His Life, Legacy, and Liberative Ethics*, edited by Rita D. Sherma, 89–101. Lanham, MD: Lexington Books, 2021.

Pope Benedict XVI. "Address of His Holiness Benedict XVI, Meeting with the Parish Priest and Clergy of the Diocese of Rome." February 7, 2008. *The Holy See*. Accessed August 22, 2020. www.vatican.va/content/benedict-xvi/en/speeches/2008/february/documents/hf_ben-xvi_spe_20080207_clergy-rome.html

Berger, Peter, and Sarbeswar Sahoo, eds. *Godroads: Modalities of Conversion in India*. Cambridge, UK: Cambridge University Press, 2020.

Bergunder, Michael, ed. *Westliche Formen des Hinduismus in Deutschland*. Halle: Verlag der franckeschen Stiftungen zu Halle, 2006.

Bevans, Stephen B. "Unraveling a 'Complex Reality': Six Elements of Mission." *International Bulletin of Missionary Research* 27.2 (2003): 50–53.

Bevans, Stephen B., and Roger P. Schroeder. *Constants in Context: A Theology of Mission for Today*. Maryknoll, NY: Orbis Books, 2004.

———. "Missiology After Bosch: Reverencing a Classic by Moving Beyond." *International Bulletin of Missionary Research* 29 (2005): 69–70.

Bhabha, Homi K. "Signs Taken for Wonders: Questions of Ambivalence and Authority under a Tree Outside Delhi, May 1817." *Critical Inquiry* 12.1 (1985): 144–65.

Bharati, Agehananda. "The Hindu Renaissance and its Apologetic Patterns." *Journal of Asian Studies* 29 (1969–70): 267–87.

Bhatt, Chetan. *Hindu Nationalism: Origins, Ideologies and Modern Myths*. Oxford & New York: Berg, 2001.

Biernacki, Lorilai. "Shree Maa of Kamakkhya." In *The Graceful Guru: Hindu Female Gurus in India and the United States*, edited by Karen Pechilis, 180–202. Oxford & New York: Oxford University Press, 2004.

van Bijlert, Victor A. *Vedāntic Hinduism in Colonial Bengal: Reformed Hinduism and Western Protestantism*. Abingdon & New York: Routledge, 2021.

Bishop, Donald H. "Religious Confrontation, a Case Study: The 1893 Parliament of Religions." *Numen* 16 (1969): 63–76.

Biswas, Arun Kumar. *Swami Vivekananda and the Indian Quest for Socialism*. Calcutta: Firma KLM, 1986.

Blackwood, Jeremy W. "Eighteen Days in 1968: An Essay on the Maturation of Lonergan's Intentionality Analysis." *Method: Journal of Lonergan Studies*, n.s. 3.2 (2012): 1–26.

———. "Sanctifying Grace, Elevation, and the Fifth Level of Consciousness." *Method: Journal of Lonergan Studies*, n.s. 2.2 (2011): 143–161.

Bloomer, Kristin C. *Possessed by the Virgin: Hinduism, Roman Catholicism, and Marian Possession in South India*. Oxford & New York: Oxford University Press, 2018.

Bosch, David J. *A Spirituality of the Road*. Scottdale, PA & Kitchener, ON: Herald Press, 1979.

———. *Transforming Mission: Paradigm Shifts in Theology of Mission*. Maryknoll, NY: Orbis Books, 1991.

———. "Vulnerability of Mission." In *New Directions in Mission and Evangelization 2: Theological Foundations*, 73–86, edited by James A. Scherer and Stephen B. Bevans. Maryknoll, NY: Orbis Books, 1994.

Böspflug, François. "Religions Missionaires, Religions Non-Missionaires," *Revue des sciences religieuses* 80.2 (2006): 127–154.

Brekke, Torkel. "The Conceptual Foundation of Missionary Hinduism." *The Journal of Religious History* 23.2 (1999): 203–14.

———. *Makers of Modern Indian Religion in the Late Nineteenth Century*. Oxford: Oxford University Press, 2002.

Bremmer, Jan N., Wout Jac. van Bekkum, and Arie L. Molendijk, eds. *Cultures of Conversions*. Leuven: Peeters, 2006.

Brown, Judith M., and Robert Eric Frykenberg, eds. *Christians, Cultural Interactions and India's Religious Traditions*. Grand Rapids, MI: William B. Eerdmans Publishing Company; London: RoutledgeCurzon, 2002.

Bryce, P. H. *The Story of a National Crime: Being an Appeal for Justice to the Indians of Canada; the Wards of the Nation, Our Allies in the Revolutionary War, Our Brothers-in-Arms in the Great War*. Ottawa: John Hope & Sons, 1922.

van der Burg, Corstiaan J. G. "The Place of Sanskrit in Neo-Hindu Ideologies: From Religious Reform to National Awakening." In *Ideology and Status of Sanskrit*, edited by Jan E. M. Houben, 367–81. Leiden, New York, & Köln: E. J. Brill, 1996.

Burghart, Richard, ed. *Hinduism in Great Britain: The Perpetuation of Religion in an Alien Cultural Milieu*. London & New York: Tavistock Publications, 1987.

Cardona, G. "*Anvaya* and *Vyatireka* in Indian Grammar," *Adyar Library Bulletin* 31–32 (1967–1968): 313–52.

Carey, Séan. "Initiation into Monkhood in the Ramakrishna Mission." In *Hinduism in Great Britain: The Perpetuation of Religion in an Alien Cultural Milieu,* edited by Richard Burghart, 134–56. London & New York: Tavistock Publications, 1987.

Cenkner, William. *A Tradition of Teachers: Śaṅkara and the Jagadgurus Today.* Delhi: Motilal Banarsidass, 1983, 1995 [reprint].

Chapple, Christopher K. "Religious Experience and Yoga." *Religions* 10.4 (2019): 237.

Choudhury-Sengupta, Indira. "Reconstructing Hinduism on a World Platform: The World's First Parliament of Religions, Chicago 1892." In *Swami Vivekananda and the Modernization of Hinduism.* SOAS Studies on South Asia, edited by William Radice, 17–35. Delhi: Oxford University Press, 1998.

Clark, Matthew. *The Daśanāmī-Saṃnyāsīs: The Integration of Ascetic Lineages into an Order.* Leiden & Boston: Brill, 2006.

Clarke, Sathianathan. *Competing Fundamentalisms: Violent Extremism in Christianity, Islam and Christianity.* Louisville, KY: Westminster John Knox Press, 2017.

———. *Dalits and Christianity: Subaltern Religion and Liberation Theology in India.* Delhi: Oxford University Press, 1998.

Clarke, Sathianathan, and Deenabandhu Manchala, eds. *Dalit Theology in the Twenty-First Century: Discordant Voices, Discerning Pathways.* Oxford: Oxford University Press, 2010.

Clooney, Francis X. "Afterword." In *Comparative Theology in the Millennial Classroom,* edited by Mara Brecht and Reid B. Locklin, 219–33. New York & London: Routledge, 2016.

———. *Beyond Compare: St. Francis de Sales and Śrī Vedānta Deśika on Loving Surrender to God.* Washington, DC: Georgetown University Press, 2008.

———. *Comparative Theology: Deep Learning across Religious Borders.* Malden, MA: Wiley-Blackwell, 2010.

———. "Hindu Views of Religious Others: Implications for Christian Theology." *Theological Studies* 64 (2003): 306–33.

———. *His Hiding Place is Darkness: A Hindu–Catholic Theopoetics of Divine Absence.* Stanford, CA: Stanford University Press, 2014.

———. "Reading the World in Christ: From Comparison to Inclusivism." In *Christian Uniqueness Reconsidered,* edited by Gavin D'Costa, 63–80. Maryknoll: Orbis Books, 1990.

———. "Restoring 'Hindu Theology' as a Category in Indian Intellectual Discourse." In *The Blackwell Companion to Hinduism,* edited by Gavin Flood, 447–77. Oxford & Malden, MA: Blackwell Publishing, 2003.

———. *Theology after Vedānta: An Experiment in Comparative Theology*. Albany, NY: SUNY Press, 1993.

———. *The Truth, the Way, the Life: Christian Commentary on the Three Holy Mantras of the Śrīvaiṣṇava Hindus*. Leuven: Peeters, 2008.

Clooney, Francis X., with Hugh Nicholson. "To Be Heard and Done, But Never Quite Seen: The Human Condition According to the *Vivekacūḍāmaṇi*." In *The Human Condition*, edited by Robert Cummings Neville, 73–99. Albany, NY: SUNY Press, 2001.

Coakley, Sarah. "Prayer as Crucible: How My Mind Has Changed." *The Christian Century*, 22 March 2011, 32–40.

Coleman, J. "Authoring (in)Authenticity, Regulating Religious Tolerance: The Implications of Anti-Conversion Legislation for Indian Secularism." *Cultural Dynamics* 20.3 (2008): 245–277.

Collins, Alfred. "Religious Experience without an Experiencer: The 'Not I' in Sāṃkhya and Yoga." *Religions* 10.2 (2019): 94.

Collins, Paul M. *Christian Inculturation in India: Liturgy, Worship and Society*. Farnham, UK & Burlington, VT: Ashgate, 2007.

Comans, Michael. "Śaṅkara and the Prasaṅkhyānavāda." *Journal of Indian Philosophy* 24 (1996): 49–71.

———. "The Question of the Importance of *Samādhi* in Modern and Classical Advaita Vedānta." *Philosophy East and West* 43 (1993): 19–38.

Conn, Walter. *Christian Conversion: A Developmental Interpretation of Autonomy and Surrender*. New York/Mahwah: Paulist Press, 1986.

———. *Conscience and Conversion in Newman: A Developmental Study of Self in John Henry Newman*. Milwaukee, WI: Marquette University Press, 2010.

Connelly, Daniel K. "At the Center of the World: The Labyrinth Pavement of Chartres Cathedral." In *Art and Architecture of Late Medieval Pilgrimage in Northern Europe and the British Isles: Texts*, edited by Sarah Blick and Rita Tekippe, 285–314. Leiden & Boston: Brill, 2005.

Connelly, John. *From Enemy to Brother: The Revolution in Catholic Teaching on the Jews, 1933–1965*. Cambridge, MA: Harvard University Press, 2012.

Consejol Episcopal Latinoamericano (CELAM). *Aparecido: Documento Conclusiva*. Accessed September 13, 2019. http://celam.org/aparecida/Ingles.pdf

Copeman, Jacob, and Ikegame, Aya, eds. *The Guru in South Asia: New Interdisciplinary Perspectives*. London & New York: Routledge, 2012.

Copley, Antony R.H, ed. *Hinduism in Public and Private: Reform, Hindutva, Gender, and Sampraday*. New Delhi: Oxford India Paperbacks, 2009.

Cornell, Deidre. *Jesus was a Migrant*. Maryknoll, NY: Orbis Books, 2014.

Cornille, Catherine. "Abhishiktananda." In *The Routledge Handbook of Hindu–Christian Relations*, edited by Chad M. Bauman and Michelle Voss Roberts, 334–42. London & New York: Routledge, 2021.

———. *Meaning and Method in Comparative Theology*. Hoboken, NJ: Wiley Blackwell, 2020.

———. "The Confessional Nature of Comparative Theology," *Studies in Interreligious Dialogue* 24.1 (2014): 9–17.

———. "The Problem of Choice in Comparative Theology." In *How to Do Comparative Theology*, edited by Francis X. Clooney and Klaus von Stosch, 19–36. New York: Fordham University Press, 2018.

Coward, Harold, John R. Hinnells, and Raymond Brady Williams. *The South Asian Religious Diaspora in Britain, Canada and the United States*. Albany, NY: SUNY Press, 2000.

Cresswell, Tim. *Place: A Short Introduction*. Malden, MA: Blackwell, 2004.

Crook, Zeba A. *Reconceptualising Conversion: Patronage, Loyalty, and Conversion in the Religions of the Ancient Mediterranean*. Berlin: De Gruyter, 2004.

Crosthwaite, Alejandro, O.P. "Aparecida: Catholicism in Latin America and the Caribbean at the Crossroads." *Journal of the Society of Christian Ethics* 28.2 (2008): 159–80.

Cruz, Gemma Tulud. *An Intercultural Theology of Migration: Pilgrims in the Wilderness*. Leiden: Brill, 2010.

———. *Toward a Theology of Migration: Social Justice and Religious Experience*. New York: Palgrave Macmillan, 2014.

Dalal, Neil. "Contemplative Practice and Textual Agency in Advaita Vedānta." *Method & Theory in the Study of Religion* 21 (2009): 15–27.

Das, Shinjini. "An Imperial Apostle? St. Paul, Protestant Conversion and South Asian Christianity." *The Historical Journal* 61.1 (2018): 103–30.

Davy, M.-M. *Henri Le Saux, Swami Abhishiktananda, le Passeur entre Deux Rives*. Paris: Editions du Cerf, 1981.

Dazey, Wade H. "Tradition and Modernization in the Organization of the Daśanāmī Saṁnyāsins." In *Monastic Life in the Christian and Hindu Traditions*, edited by Austin B. Creel and Vasudha Narayanan, 281–321. Lewiston/Queenston/Lampeter: Edwin Mellen Press, 1990.

D'Costa, Gavin. "Considering the Case of Catholic–Hindu Dual Belonging from a Magisterial and Dogmatic Point of View." In *Hindu–Christian Dual Belonging*, edited by Daniel Soars and Nadya Pohran, 69–87. London & New York: Routledge, 2022.

De Michelis, Elizabeth. *A History of Modern Yoga: Patañjali and Western Esoterism*. London & New York: Continuum, 2005.

Dempsey, Corinne G. *Bringing the Sacred Down to Earth: Adventures in Comparative Religion*. New York: Oxford University Press, 2012.

———. "Comparative Transgressions: Vernacular Catholicisms in Tamil Nadu and Kerala." In *Vernacular Catholicism, Vernacular Saints: Selva J. Raj on "Being Catholic the Tamil Way,"* edited by Reid B. Locklin, 195–208. Albany, NY: SUNY Press, 2017.

———. *Kerala Christian Sainthood: Collisions of Culture and Worldview in South India*. Oxford & New York: Oxford University Press, 2001.

Derrida, Jacques. "Des Tours de Babel." In *Acts of Religion*, edited by Gil Anidjar, 104–34. New York: Routledge, 2001.

Deutsch, Eliot. *Advaita Vedānta: A Philosophical Reconstruction*. Honolulu: University of Hawaii Press, 1969.

Devanandan, P. D. "Hindu Missions to the West." *International Review of Mission* 48 (1959): 398–408.

Dobe, Timothy S. *Hindu Christian Faqir: Modern Monks, Global Christianity, and Indian Sainthood*. Oxford & New York: Oxford University Press, 2015.

Doran, Robert M. *Psychic Conversion and Theological Foundations: Toward a Reorientation of the Human Sciences*. Chico, CA: Scholars Press, 1981.

———. *Theology and the Dialectics of History*. Toronto, Buffalo, & London: University of Toronto Press, 1990.

Du Boulay, Shirley. *The Cave of the Heart: The Life of Swami Abhishiktananda*. Maryknoll, NY: Orbis Books, 2005.

Dubois, Joël André-Michel. *The Hidden Lives of Brahman: Śaṅkara's Vedānta through His Upāniṣad Commentaries, in Light of Contemporary Practice*. Albany, NY: SUNY Press, 2013.

Dubuisson, Daniel. "Exporting the Local: Recent Perspectives on 'Religion' as a Cultural Category." *Religion Compass* 1 (2007): 787–800.

Dunn, James D. G. *The New Perspective on Paul: Collected Essays*. Tübingen: Mohr Siebeck, 2005.

Dupuis, Jacques, S.J. *Christianity and the Religions: From Confrontation to Dialogue*. Maryknoll, NY: Orbis Books, 2001.

———. *Jesus Christ at the Encounter of World Religions*, translated by Robert R. Barr. Maryknoll, NY: Orbis, 1991.

———. *Toward a Christian Theology of Religious Pluralism*. Maryknoll, NY: Orbis Books, 1997.

Eck, Diana L. *Encountering God: A Spiritual Journey from Bozeman to Banares*. Boston: Beacon Press, 1993.

———. "'New Age' Hinduism in America." In *Conflicting Images: India and the United States*, edited by Sulochana Raghavan Glazer, 111–142. Glenn Dale, MD: Riverdale Company, 1990.

———. *A New Religious America: How a 'Christian Country' Has Become the World's Most Religiously Diverse Nation*. New York: HarperCollins Publishers, 2001.

Edelmann, Jonathan. "Hindu Theology as Churning the Latent." *Journal of the American Academy of Religion* 81.1 (2013): 427–66.

Edinburgh 2010. "Common Call." *Centenary of the 1910 World Missionary Conference*. Accessed June 26, 2020. www.edinburgh2010.org/file admin/Edinburgh_2010_Common_Call_with_explanation.pdf

Finger, Joachim. *Gurus, Ashrams und der Weste: Eine religionswissenschaftliche Untersuchung zu den Hintergründen der Internationalisierung des Hinduismus*. Frankfurt am Main: Verlag Peter Lang, 1987.

Fisher, Elaine M. *Hindu Pluralism: Religion and the Public Sphere in Early Modern South India*. Oakland: University of California Press, 2017.

———. "Remaking South Indian Śaivism: Greater Śaiva Advaita and the Legacy of the Śaktiviśiṣṭādvaita Vīraśaiva Tradition." *International Journal of Hindu Studies* 21.3 (2017): 319–44.

———. "'A Śākta in the Heart': Śrīvidyā and Advaita Vedānta in the Theology of Nīlakaṇṭha Dīkṣita." *The Journal of Hindu Studies* 8.1 (2015): 124–38.

Flanagan, Brian P. *Stumbling in Holiness: Sin and Sanctity in the Church*. Collegeville: Liturgical Press, 2018.

Flinn, Frank K. "Conversion: Up from Evangelicalism or the Pentecostal and Charismatic Experience." In *Religious Conversion: Contemporary Practices and Controversies*, edited by Christopher Lamb and M. Darroll Bryant, 51–72. London & New York: Cassell, 1999.

Flood, Gavin. *An Introduction to Hinduism*. Cambridge: Cambridge University Press, 1996.

Forman, Robert K. C. *Enlightenment Ain't What It's Cracked Up to Be: A Journey of Discovery, Snow and Jazz in the Soul*. Winchester, UK and Washington, DC: O-Books, 2010.

———. "Introduction: Mysticism, Constructivism, and Forgetting." In *Problem of Pure Consciousness: Mysticism and Philosophy*, edited by Robert K. C. Forman, 3–49. Oxford: Oxford University Press, 1997.

Forsthoefel, Thomas A. *Knowing beyond Knowledge: Epistemologies of Religious Experience in Classical and Modern Advaita*. Aldershot, UK & Burlington, VT: Ashgate, 2002.

———. "Ramaṇa Maharṣi: Mystic as Translator." *International Journal of Hindu Studies* 5.2 (2001): 109–30.

———. "Retrieving the *Vivekacūḍamaṇi*: The Poles of Religious Knowing," *Philosophy East and West* 52.3 (2002): 311–25.

———. "Weaving the Inward Thread to Awakening." In *Gurus in America*, edited by Thomas A. Forsthoefel and Cynthia Ann Humes, 37–53. Albany, NY: SUNY Press, 2005.

———. "Weaving the Inward Thread to Awakening." *Horizons* 29.2 (2002): 240–59.

Forsthoefel, Thomas A., and Cynthia Ann Humes, eds. *Gurus in America*. Albany, NY: SUNY Press, 2005.

Fort, Andrew O. "*Jīvanmukti* and Social Service in Advaita and Neo-Vedānta." *Poznań Studies in the Philosophy of the Sciences and the Humanities* 59 (1997): 489–504.

———. *Jīvanmukti in Transformation: Embodied Liberation in Advaita and Neo-Vedanta*. Albany, NY: SUNY Press, 1998.

Pope Francis. *Evangelii Gaudium*. Rome: Vatican Press, 2013.

———. *Fratelli Tutti: On Fraternity and Social Friendship*. October 3, 2020. *The Holy See*. Accessed July 20, 2021. www.vatican.va/content/francesco/en/encyclicals/documents/papa-francesco_20201003_enciclica-fratelli-tutti.html

———. *Laudato Si': On Care for Our Common Home*. May 24, 2015. *The Holy See*. Accessed September 13, 2019. https://w2.vatican.va/content/francesco/en/encyclicals/documents/papa-francesco_20150524_enciclica-laudato-si.html

Fredericks, James L. "The Catholic Church and the Other Religious Paths: Rejecting Nothing That Is True and Holy." *Theological Studies* 64.2 (2003): 225–54.

Fredriksen, Paula. "Judaizing the Nations: The Ritual Demands of Paul's Gospel." *New Testament Studies* 56 (2010): 232–52.

———. *Paul: The Pagans' Apostle*. New Haven, CT & London: Yale University Press, 2017.

Freiberger, Oliver. *Considering Comparison: A Method for Religious Studies*. New York: Oxford University Press, 2019.

French, Harold W. *The Swan's Wide Waters: Ramakrishna and Western Culture*. Port Washington, NY & London: Kennikat Press, 1974.

Frykenberg, Robert Eric. "Accounting for Fundamentalisms in South Asia: Ideologies and Institutions in Historical Perspective." In *Accounting for Fundamentalisms: The Dynamic Character of Movements*, edited by Martin E. Marty and R. Scott Appleby, 591–616. Chicago & London: University of Chicago Press, 1994.

———. *Christianity in India: From Beginnings to the Present*. Oxford & New York: Oxford University Press, 2008.

Frykenberg, Robert Eric, and Alaine M. Low, eds. *Christians and Missionaries in India: Cross-Cultural Communication Since 1500, with Special Reference to Caste, Conversion, and Colonialism*. Grand Rapids, MI: W. B. Eerdmans, 2003.

Gandhi, Jatin, Varghese K. George, and Krishnadas Rajagopal. "Conversion Confusion." *The Hindu*. 21 December 2014. Accessed September 18, 2021. www.thehindu.com/sunday-anchor/sunday-anchor-conversion-confusion/article10961782.ece

Gasson-Gardner, Lisa, and Jason Smith, "Feeling Comparative Theology: Millennial Affect and Reparative Learning." In *Comparative Theology in the Millennial Classroom*, eds. Mara Brecht and Reid B. Locklin. New York & London: Routledge, 2016.

Gaventa, Beverly Roberts. *From Darkness to Light: Aspects of Conversion in the New Testament*. Philadelphia: Fortress Press, 1986.

Gelpi, Donald L. S.J. *Charism and Sacrament: A Theology of Christian Conversion*. London: SPCK, 1976.

Ghiloni, Aaron J, ed. *World Religions and Their Missions*. New York: Peter Lang, 2015.

Gleig, Ann, and Lola Williamson, eds. *Homegrown Gurus: From Hinduism in America to American Hinduism*. Albany, NY: SUNY Press, 2013.

Goel, Sita Ram. *Catholic Ashrams: Sannyasins or Swindlers?* New Delhi: Voice of India, 1995.

———. *History of Hindu–Christian Encounters, AD 304 to 1996*. New Delhi: Voice of India, 1996.

———. *Jesus Christ: An Artifice for Aggression*. New Delhi: Voice of India, 1994.

Goldberg, Philip. *American Veda: From Emerson and the Beatles to Yoga and Meditation—How Indian Spirituality Changed the West*. New York: Harmony Books, 2010.

Goodwin, William F. "Mysticism and Ethics: An Examination of Radhakrishnan's Reply to Schweitzer's Critique of Indian Thought." *Ethics* 67.1 (1956): 25–41.

Gooren, Henri. "Anthropology of Religious Conversion." In *The Oxford Handbook of Religious Conversion*, edited by Lewis R. Rambo and Charles E. Farhadian, 84–116. Oxford & New York: Oxford University Press, 2014.

———. *Religious Conversion and Disaffiliation: Tracing Patterns of Change in Faith Practices*. New York: Palgrave MacMillan, 2010.

Gould, Rebecca. "How Newness Enters the World: The Methodology of Sheldon Pollock." *Comparative Studies of South Asia, Africa and the Middle East* 28 (2008): 533–59.

Granoff, Phyllis. "Holy Warriors: A Preliminary Study of Some Biographies of Saints and Kings in the Classical Indian Tradition." *Journal of Indian Philosophy* 12 (1984): 291–303.

———. "Scholars and Wonder-Workers: Some Remarks on the Role of the Supernatural in Philosophical Contests in Vedānta Hagiographies." *Journal of the American Oriental Society* 105.3 (1985): 459–67.

Grau, Marion. *Rethinking Mission in the Postcolony: Salvation, Society, and Subversion*. London & New York: Continuum, 2011.

Gruber, Judith. "Remembering Borders: Notes toward a Theology of Migration." In *Migration as a Sign of the Times: Towards a Theology of Migration*, edited by Judith Gruber and Sigrid Rettenbacher, 79–106. Leiden: Brill, 2015.

———. "(Un)Silencing Hybridity: A Postcolonial Critique of Comparative Theology." In *Comparative Theology in the Millennial Classroom*, edited by Mara Brecht and Reid B. Locklin, 21–35. New York & London: Routledge, 2016.

Gupta, Akshay. "Constructing a Hindu Black Theology." *Journal of Hindu–Christian Studies* 34 (2021): 42–51.

Gutiérrez, Gustavo. *A Theology of Liberation: History, Politics, and Salvation*. Revised edition. Maryknoll, NY: Orbis Books, 1988.

Hacker, Paul. "Aspects of Neo-Hinduism as Contrasted with Surviving Traditional Hinduism." In *Philology and Confrontation: Paul Hacker on Traditional and Modern Vedānta*, edited by Wilhelm Halbfass, 229–55. Albany, NY: SUNY Press, 1995.

———. "Schopenhauer and Hindu Ethics." In *Philology and Confrontation: Paul Hacker on Traditional and Modern Vedānta*, 273–318. Edited by Wilhelm Halbfass. Albany, NY: SUNY Press, 1995.

———. "Swami Vivekananda's Religious Nationalism." In *Philology and Confrontation: Paul Hacker on Traditional and Modern Vedānta*, edited by Wilhelm Halbfass, 319–36. Albany, NY: SUNY Press, 1995.

Halbfass, Wilhelm. *India and Europe: An Essay in Understanding*. Albany, NY: SUNY Press, 1988.

———. *Tradition and Reflection: Explorations in Indian Thought*. Albany, NY: SUNY Press, 1991.

Hansen, Thomas Blom. *The Saffron Wave: Democracy and Hindu Nationalism in Modern India*. Princeton, NJ: Princeton University Press, 1999.

Hardiman, David. "Assertion, Conversion, and Indian Nationalism: Govind's Movement among the Bhils." In *Religious Conversion in India: Modes, Motivations, and Meanings*, edited by Rowena Robinson and Sathianathan Clarke, 255–84. New Delhi: Oxford University Press, 2003.

Harris, Gardiner. "'Reconversion' of Religious Minorities Roils Indian Politics." *New York Times*. December 23, 2014. Accessed September 7, 2017. www.nytimes.com/2014/12/24/world/asia/india-narendra-modi-hindu-conversions-missionaries.html? r=0

Hawley, John C. *India in Africa, Africa in India: Indian Ocean Cosmopolitanisms*. Bloomington: Indiana University Press, 2008.

Hedges, Paul. "Comparative Theology: A Critical and Methodological Perspective." *Theology* 1.1 (2017): 27–58.

———. "The Old and New Comparative Theologies: Discourse on Religion, the Theology of Religions, Orientalism and the Boundaries of Traditions." *Religions* 3.4 (2012): 1120–37.

Hedlund, Roger E. Hedlund, ed. *Christianity is Indian: The Emergence of an Indigenous Community*. Delhi: ISPCK, 2000.

Heehs, Peter. "Not a Question of Theology: Religions, Religious Institutions, and the Courts in India." *Comparative Legal History* 1.2 (2013): 243–61.

Henn, Alexander. *Hindu–Catholic Encounters in Goa: Religion, Colonialism, and Modernity*. Bloomington & Indianapolis: Indiana University Press, 2014.

Heredia, Rudolf C. *Changing Gods: Rethinking Conversion in India*. New Delhi: Penguin Books, 2007.

Herman, A. L. "Again, Albert Schweitzer and Indian Thought." *Philosophy East and West* 12.3 (1962): 217–32.

Hermansen, Marcia. "Conversion to Islam in Theological and Historical Perspectives." In *The Oxford Handbook of Religious Conversion*, edited by Lewis R. Rambo and Charles E. Farhadian, 632–66. Oxford & New York: Oxford University Press, 2014.

Hoens, D. J. "The Movements of Hams Ji Mahāraj and of Chinmayānanda as Process of Change in Hinduism." In *Official and Popular Religion: Analysis of a Theme for Religious Studies*, edited by Pieter Hendrik Vrijhof and Jacques Waardenburg, 462–86. The Hague, Paris & New York: Mouton Publishers, 1979.

Houben, Jan E. M. *Ideology and Status of Sanskrit*. Leiden, New York & Köln: E. J. Brill, 1996.

Humes, Cynthia Ann. "Maharishi Ayur-Veda™: Perfect Health™ through Enlightened Marketing in America." In *Modern and Global Ayurveda: Pluralism and Paradigms*, edited by Dagmar Wujastyk and Frederick M. Smith, 309–31. Albany, NY: SUNY Press, 2008.

———. "Maharishi Mahesh Yogi: Beyond the TM Technique." In *Gurus in America*. Eds Thomas A. Forsthoefel and Cynthia Ann Humes, 79–137. Albany, NY: SUNY Press, 2005.

———. "A Perfect Government." Unpublished manuscript, July 28, 2016.

———. "Schisms within Hindu Guru Groups: The Transcendental Meditation Movement in North America." In *Sacred Schisms: How Religions Divide*, edited by James R. Lewis and Sarah M. Lewis, 287–305. Cambridge: Cambridge University Press, 2009.

Hummel, Reinhart. *Indische Mission und neue Frömmigkeit im Westen: Religiöse Bewegungen Indiens in westlichen Kulturen*. Stuttgart: Verlag W. Kohlhammer, 1980.

———. "Reliöse Bewegungen Indiens in westlichen Kulturen." In *Westliche Formen des Hinduismus in Deutschland*, edited by Michael Bergunder, 10–30. Halle: Verlag der franckeschen Stiftungen zu Halle, 2006.

———. "Über 40 Jahre Transzendentale Meditation." In *Westliche Formen des Hinduismus in Deutschland*, edited by Michael Bergunder, 107–20. Halle: Verlag der franckeschen Stiftungen zu Halle, 2006.

Hunnex, Milton D. "Mysticism and Ethics: Radhakrishnan and Schweitzer." *Philosophy East and West* 8.3–4 (1958–59): 121–36.

Hunsberger, George R. "Conversion and Community: Revisiting the Lesslie Newbigin-M M Thomas Debate." *International Bulletin of Missionary Research* 22.3 (July 1998): 112–17.

Ingalls, D. H. H. "The Study of Śaṃkarācārya." *Annals of the Bhandarkar Oriental Research Institute* 33 (1952): 8–10.

Jackson, Carl T. "Turning East: American Interest in Asian Religions since the 1890s." In *The Cyclonic Swami: Vivekananda in the West*, edited by Sukalyan Sengupta and Makarand Paranjape, 64–73. New Delhi: Samvad India Foundation, 2005.

———. *Vedanta for the West: The Ramakrishna Movement in the United States*. Bloomington & Indianapolis: Indiana University Press, 1994.

Jacobs, Andrew S. "Interpreting Conversion in Antiquity (and Beyond)." *Religion Compass* 15.7 (2021).

Jacobsen, Knut A., and Selva J. Raj, eds., *South Asian Christian Diaspora: Invisible Diaspora in Europe and North America*. Aldershot, UK: Ashgate, 2008.

Jacobs-Vandegeer, Christiaan. "The Unity of Salvation: Divine Missions, the Church, and World Religions." *Theological Studies* 75.2 (2014): 260–83.

Jain, Andrea R. "Conversion to Jain Identity." In *The Oxford Handbook of Religious Conversion*, edited by Lewis R. Rambo and Charles E. Farhadian, 444–58. Oxford & New York: Oxford University Press, 2014.

———. *Selling Yoga: From Counterculture to Pop Culture*. New York: Oxford University Press, 2015.

Janz, Bruce. "Mysticism and Understanding: Steven Katz and His Critics." *Studies in Religion/Sciences Religieuses* 24.1 (1995): 77–94.

Jenkins, Laura Dudley. "Legal Limits on Religious Conversion in India." *Law and Contemporary Problems* 71.2 (2008): 109–127.

———. *Religious Freedom and Mass Conversion in India*. Philadelphia: University of Pennsylvania Press, 2019.

Jha, D. N. *Rethinking Hindu Identity*. London & Oakville, CT: Equinox, 2009.

Jindra, Ines W. "*A History of Conversion* and Other Conversion Models: A Review Essay." *Pastoral Psychology* 70 (2021): 141–50.

———. *A New Model of Religious Conversion: Beyond Network Theory and Social Constructivism*. Leiden: Brill, 2014.

Jones, Kenneth W. *Arya Dharm: Hindu Consciousness in 19th-Century Punjab*. Berkeley, Los Angeles & London: University of California Press, 1976.

Jongte, R. C. "Rethinking the Idea of Indigeneity: An Indigenous Liberationist Response to Hindutva Cooptation and Assimilationist Agenda in Northeast India." *Journal of Hindu–Christian Studies* 35 (2022): 49–58.

Jørgensen, Jonas Adelin. *Jesus Imandars and Christ Bhaktas: Two Case Studies of Interreligious Hermeneutics and Identity in Global Christianity.* Frankfurt am Main: Peter Lang, 2008.

———. "'Becoming Faithful': Conversion, Syncretism, and the Interreligious Hermeneutical Strategies of the 'Faithful of Jesus' (Īsā Īmāndārs) in Today's Bangladesh." In *Asia in the Making of Christianity: Conversion, Agency and Indigeneity, 1600s to the Present,* edited by Richard Fox Young and Jonathan A. Seitz, 269–93. Leiden & Boston: Brill, 2013.

Joseph, Clara A. B. *Christianity in India: The Anti-Colonial Turn.* London & New York: Routledge, 2019.

Kakar, Sudhir. *The Analyst and the Mystic: Psychoanalytic Reflections on Religion and Mysticism.* New Delhi: Viking, 1991.

Kaplan, Stephen. "Authorial Authenticity or Theological Polemics? Discerning the Implications of Śaṅkara's Battle with the Buddhist." *International Journal of Hindu Studies* 17 (2013): 1–36.

Katz, Steven T. "Language, Epistemology, and Mysticism." In *Mysticism and Philosophical Analysis,* edited by Steven T. Katz, 22–74. New York: Oxford University Press, 1978.

Kent, Eliza F. *Converting Women: Gender and Protestant Christianity in Colonial South India.* Oxford: Oxford University Press, 2004.

Khanna, Varun. "Swami Chinmayananda, Hinduism and Diaspora Configurations: Identifying the Effects of a Modern Advaita-Vedāntin on the Hindu Diaspora in North America." *Nidān* 3.1 (2018): 31–49.

Killingley, Dermot. "Vivekananda's Western Message from the East." In *Swami Vivekananda and the Modernization of Hinduism,* SOAS Studies on South Asia, edited by William Radice, 138–57. Delhi: Oxford University Press, 1998.

Kim, Sebastian C. H. *In Search of Identity: Debates on Religious Conversion in India.* New Delhi: Oxford University Press, 2003.

King, Richard. *Early Advaita Vedānta and Buddhism: The Mahāyāna Context of the Gauḍapādīya-Kārikā.* Albany, NY: SUNY Press, 1995.

———. *Orientalism and Religion: Postcolonial Theory, India and "The Mystic East."* London & New York: Routledge, 1999.

Kirchheiner, Ole. *Culture and Christianity Negotiated in Hindu Society: A Case Study of a Church in Central and Western Nepal.* Oxford: Regnum, 2017.

Kling, David W. *A History of Christian Conversion.* New York: Oxford University Press, 2020.

Klostermaier, Klaus K. "'In Every Town, Country and Village My Name Will be Sung': Hindu Missions in India and Abroad." In *Mixed Messages: Materiality, Textuality, Missions,* edited by Jamie S. Scott and Gareth Griffiths, 173–202. New York: Palgrave Macmillan, 2005.

Kollman, Paul. "At the Origins of Mission and Missiology: A Study in the Dynamics of Religious Language." *Journal of the American Academy of Religion* 79.2 (2011): 425–58.

Komonchak, Joseph. *Foundations in Ecclesiology*. Chestnut Hill, MA: Boston College, 1995.

Kopf, David. *The Brahmo Samaj and the Shaping of the Modern Indian Mind*. Princeton, NJ: Princeton University Press, 1979.

Kranenborg, Reender. "Peace, Reconciliation and New Religious Movements." In *Religion, Conflict and Reconciliation: Multifaith Ideals and Realities*, edited by Jerald D. Gort, Henry Jansen and Hendrik M. Vroom, 356–64. Amsterdam & New York: Rodopi, 2002.

Kreider, Alan. "Beyond Bosch: The Early Church and the Christendom Shift." *International Bulletin of Missionary Research* 29 (2005): 59–68.

Kripal, Jeffrey J. *Kālī's Child: The Mystical and the Erotic in the Life and Teachings of Ramakrishna*. Chicago & London: University of Chicago Press, 1995.

Krishna Warrier, A. G. *The Concept of Mukti in Advaita Vedānta*. Madras: University of Madras, 1961.

Krishnamurti, Sailaja. "Race, Representation and Hindu–Christian Encounters in Contemporary North America." In *The Routledge Handbook of Hindu–Christian Relations*, edited by Chad M. Bauman and Michelle Voss Roberts, 180–92. London & New York: Routledge, 2021.

Kuchuk, Nika. "Genealogies of Transnational Religion: Translation, Revelation, and Discursive Technologies in Two Female Gurus of Esoteric Vedanta." PhD dissertation, University of Toronto, 2021. ProQuest Dissertations Publishing (28769458).

Kuruvachira, J. "Hinduism as a Missionary Religion." *Mission Today* 8 (2006): 265–84.

———. *Hindu Nationalists of Modern India: A Critical Study of the Intellectual Genealogy of Hindutva*. Jaipur: Rawat Publications, 2006.

———. "Hinduism's World Mission." *Mission Today* 9 (2007): 39–56.

———. *Politicisation of Hindu Religion in Postmodern India*. Jaipur: Rawat Publications, 2008.

Laine, James W. "The *Dharma* of Islam and the *Dīn* of Hinduism: Hindus and Muslims in the Age of Śivāji." *International Journal of Hindu Studies* 3.3 (1999): 299–318.

Lamb, Christopher, and M. Darrol Bryant. *Religious Conversion: Contemporary Practices and Controversies*. London: Cassell, 1999.

Langenfeld, Aaron. "The Moment of Truth: Comparative and Dogmatic Theology." In *How to Do Comparative Theology*, edited by Francis X. Clooney and Klaus von Stosch, 59–71. New York: Fordham University Press, 2018.

The Lausanne Covenant. July 1974. *Lausanne Movement*. Accessed August 29, 2019. www.lausanne.org/content/covenant/lausanne-covenant #cov

Legrand, Lucien. *The Bible on Culture*. Maryknoll, NY: Orbis Books, 2000.

———. *Unity and Plurality: Mission in the Bible*. Trans. By Robert R. Barr. Maryknoll, NY: Orbis Books, 1990.

Pope Leo XIII. *Rerum Novarum*. May 15, 1891. *The Holy See*. Accessed September 13, 2019. https://w2.vatican.va/content/paul-vi/en/apost_exhortations/documents/hf_p-vi_exh_19751208_evangelii-nuntiandi.html

Lewis, Keith D. "Neither for Money Nor Honor." In *The Catholic Church in History: Legend and Reality*, 25–48. New York: Crossroad Publishing Company, 2006.

Lincoln, Bruce. *Apples and Oranges: Explorations in, on, and with Comparison*. Chicago: University of Chicago Press, 2018.

Lindbeck, George A. *The Nature of Doctrine: Religion and Theology in a Postliberal Age*. London: SPCK, 1984.

Liu, Lydia H. "Shadows of Universalism: The Untold Story of Human Rights around 1948." *Critical Inquiry* 40 (2014): 385–417.

———. "The Eventfulness of Translation: Temporality, Difference, and Competing Universals." In *At Translation's Edge*, edited by Nataša Ďurovičová, Patrice Petro, and Lorena Terando, 13–30. New Brunswick, NJ: Rutgers University Press, 2019.

Locklin, Reid B. "A Century of Advaita Mission: Tracing a Lineage and Opening a Conversation." *Journal of Ecumenical Studies* 52.4 (2017): 488–526.

———. "Integral Samnyasa? Adi Shankaracharya and Liberation Hermeneutics." *Journal of Hindu–Christian Studies* 20 (2007): 43–51.

———. *Liturgy of Liberation: A Christian Commentary on Shankara's Upadeśasāhasrī*. Leuven: Peeters, 2011.

———. "Migration and Spiritual Conquest: Emplacing Contemporary Comparative Theology in a Hindu Theology of the 'Quarters' (*dik*)." In *Strangers in this World: Multi-Religious Reflections on Immigration*, edited by Hussam S. Timani, Allen G. Jorgenson, and Alexander Y. Hwang, 11–29. Minneapolis, MN: Fortress Press, 2015.

———. "A Most Uncommon Task: Arvind Sharma and the Construction of Hindu Missiology." *International Journal of Hindu Studies* 28.1 (2024): forthcoming.

———. "Non-Dual Conversion and Non-Dual Belonging: Trajectories of Religious Transformation in Missionary Advaita Vedānta." In *Hindu–Christian Dual Belonging*, edited by Daniel Soars and Nadya Pohran, 122–39. London & New York: Routledge, 2022.

———. "Non-Dual Belonging: Conversion, Sanskritization and the Dissolution of the Multiple in Advaita Missionary Movements." *Journal of Hindu–Christian Studies* 28 (2015): 88–99.

———. "Paradigms and Styles of Advaita Mission: An Experiment in Interpretation." *International Journal of Hindu Studies* 20.1 (2016): 1–49.

———. "Performance and Engagement: Reconsidering Religious Experience in Contemporary Comparative Theology." In *The Wiley Blackwell Companion to Comparative Theology: A Festschrift in Honor of Francis X. Clooney, SJ,* edited by Axel Takács and Joseph Kimmel, 104–14. Oxford: Wiley Blackwell, 2023.

———. "Polyhedral Pluralism: Pope Francis, Deep Pluralists and the Practice of Hindu–Christian Studies." *Journal of Hindu–Christian Studies* 33 (2020): 15–26.

———. " 'Rise Up and Walk': Psychology, Comparative Theology, and the *Oxford Handbook of Religious Conversion." Pastoral Psychology* 67.2 (2018): 205–13.

———. "Ritual Renunciation and/or Ritual Innovation: Re-Describing Advaita Tradition." In *Ritual Innovation in South Asian Religions,* edited by Amy Allocco and Brian Pennington, 91–108. Albany, NY: SUNY Press, 2018.

———. "*Śabda Pramāṇa* and Prophetic Witness: Barthian and Advaitin Perspectives in Dialogue." *Journal of Religion* 94.4 (2014): 485–503.

———. "Toward an Interreligious Theology of Church: Revisiting Bernard Lonergan's Contribution to the 'Dialogue of Religions.' " *Journal of Ecumenical Studies* 43.3 (2008), 383–410.

———, ed. *Vernacular Catholicism, Vernacular Saints: Selva J. Raj on "Being Catholic the Tamil Way."* Albany, NY: SUNY Press, 2017.

Locklin, Reid B., and Julia Lauwers. "Rewriting the Sacred Geography of Advaita: Swami Chinmayānanda and the *Śaṅkara-dig-vijaya." The Journal of Hindu Studies* 2.2 (2009): 179–208.

Locklin, Reid B., and Hugh Nicholson, "The Return of Comparative Theology." *Journal of the American Academy of Religion* 78.2 (2010): 477–514.

Lonergan, Bernard J. F. *Method in Theology.* 2nd ed. London: Darton, Longman & Todd, 1972.

———. "First Lecture: Religious Experience." In *Third Collection: Papers,* edited by Frederick E. Crowe, 113–28. New York: Paulist Press, 1985.

Long, Jeffery D. "Claiming the Buddha for Hinduism: Swami Vivekananda and the Rediscovery of Buddhism in India." In *The Cyclonic Swami: Vivekananda in the West,* edited by Sukalyan Sengupta and Makarand Paranjape, 113–120. New Delhi: Samvad India Foundation, 2005.

———. "Complementarity, not Contradiction: Swami Vivekananda's Theology of Religions." In *Swami Vivekananda: His Life, Legacy, and*

Liberative Ethics, edited by Rita D. Sherma, 161–73. Lanham, MD: Lexington Books, 2021.

———. "Religions as *Yogas*: How Reflection on Swami Vivekananda's Theology of Religions Can Clarify the Threefold Model of Exclusivism, Inclusivism, and Pluralism." *International Journal of Hindu Studies* 27 (2023): 7–32.

———. "Religious Experience, Hindu Pluralism and Hope: *Anubhava* in the Tradition of Sri Ramakrishna." *Religions* 10.3 (2019): 210.

———. "Universalism in Hinduism." *Religion Compass* 5/6 (2011): 214–23.

Lorenzen, David N. "The Life of Sankaracarya." In *The Biographical Process*, edited by Frank E. Reynolds and Donald Capps, 87–103. Religion and Reason 11. Paris: Mouton & Co., 1976.

———. *Who Invented Hinduism? Essays on Religion in History*. New Delhi: Yoda Press, 2006.

Lowe, Scott. "The Neo-Hindu Transformation of an Iowa Town," *Novo Religio* 13 (2010): 81–91.

———. "Transcendental Meditation, Vedic Science and Science." *Novo Religio* 14 (2011): 54–76.

Lucas, Phillip Charles. "Neo-Advaita in America: Three Representative Teachers." In *Homegrown Gurus: From Hinduism in America to American Hinduism*, edited by Ann Gleig and Lola Williamson, 163–87. Albany, NY: SUNY Press, 2013.

———. "Non-Traditional Modern Vedanta Gurus in the West and Their Traditional Modern Advaita Critics." *Novo Religio* 17.3 (2014): 6–37.

Luthra, Rashmi. "The Formation of Interpretive Communities in the Hindu Diaspora." In *Religion and Popular Culture: Studies on the Interaction of Worldviews*, edited by Daniel A. Stout and Judith M. Buddenbaum. Ames: Iowa State University Press, 2001.

Madaio, James. "Rethinking Neo-Vedānta: Swami Vivekananda and the Selective Historiography of Advaita Vedānta." *Religions* 8.6 (2017): 101–113.

Maharaj, Ayon. *Infinite Paths to Infinite Reality: Sri Ramakrishna and Cross-Cultural Philosophy of Religion*. Oxford: Oxford University Press, 2018.

Malony, H. Newton, and Samuel Southard, eds. *Handbook of Religious Conversion*. Birmingham, AL: Religious Education Press, 1992.

Malhotra, S. L. *Social and Political Orientations of Neo-Vedantism: Study of the Social Philosophy of Vivekananda, Aurobindo, Bipin Chandra Pal, Tagore, Gandhi, Vinoba, and Radhakrishnan*. New Delhi: S. Chand and Company, 1970.

Malkovsky, Bradley J. "Swami Vivekananda and Bede Griffiths on Religious Pluralism: Hindu and Christian Approaches to Truth." *Horizons* 25.2 (1998): 217–37.

Mallampalli, Chandra. *South Asia's Christians: Between Hindu and Muslim.* New York: Oxford University Press, 2023.

Marak, Krickwin C., and Plamthadathil S. Jacob, eds. *Conversion in a Pluralistic Context: Perspectives and Perceptions.* Pune: CMS/ISPCK, 2000.

Marcaurelle, Roger. *Freedom Through Inner Renunciation: Śaṅkara's Philosophy in a New Light.* Albany, NY: SUNY Press, 2000.

Masih, Jagdhari. *The Role of Swami Chinmayananda in Revitalization of Hinduism and Reinterpretation of Christianity.* Calcutta: Punthi Pustak, 2000.

Massey, James. *Dalits in India: Religion as a Source of Bondage or Liberation with Special Reference to Christians.* New Delhi: Manohar, 1995.

Masuzawa, Tomoko. *The Invention of World Religions: Or, How European Universalism was Preserved in the Language of Pluralism.* Chicago & London: University of Chicago Press, 2005.

Mathew, C. V. *Neo-Hinduism, a missionary religion.* Madras: Church Growth Resource Centre, 1987.

———. *The Saffron Mission: A Historical Analysis of Modern Hindu Missionary Ideologies and Practices.* Delhi: ISPCK, 1999.

Matthew, Joseph. *Contemporary Religious Conversions.* Delhi: Authorpress, 2001.

Mayeda, Sengaku. "Śaṃkara and Sureśvara: Their Exegetical Method to Interpret the Great Sentence '*Tat Tvam Asi*.'" *Adyar Library Bulletin* 44–45 (1980–81): 147–60.

Swami Medhananda. "From Good to God: Swami Vivekananda's Vedāntic Virtue Ethics." *International Journal of Hindu Studies* 27 (2023): 67–96.

———. *Swami Vivekananda's Vedāntic Cosmopolitanism.* Oxford: Oxford University Press, 2022.

McDaniel, June. "Religious Experience in the Hindu Tradition." *Religions* 10.5 (2019): 329.

McKean, Lise. *Divine Enterprise: Gurus and the Hindu Nationalist Movement.* Chicago & London: University of Chicago Press, 1996.

Miller, David M. "The Divine Life Society Movement." In *Religion in Modern India*, edited by Robert D. Baird, 86–117. Revised edition. New Delhi: Manohar, 1989.

———. "Modernity in Hindu Monasticism: Swami Vivekananda and the Ramakrishna Movement." *Journal of Asian American Studies* 34.1 (1999): 111–126.

———. "The Spiritual Descent of the Divine: The Life Story of Swāmi Sivānanda." In *Hindu Spirituality: Postclassical and Modern*, edited by K. R. Sundararajan and Bithika Mukerji, 351–55. New York: Crossroad Publishing Company, 1997.

Minkowski, Christopher. "Advaita Vedānta in Early Modern History." *South Asian History and Culture* 2.2 (2011): 205–31.

Mitra, Arpita. "Ramakrishna and Vivekananda: Two Teachings or One?" *Prabuddha Bharata* 119 (2014): 65–78, 194–203, 251–55, 259.

Mosse, David. *The Saint in the Banyan Tree: Christianity and Caste Society*. Berkeley: University of California Press, 2012.

Mullick, Sunrit. *The First Hindu Mission to America: The Pioneering Visits of Protap Chunder Mozoomdar*. New Delhi: Northern Book Centre, 2010.

Nachane, Sulochana A. *A Survey of Post-Śaṅkara Advaita Vedānta*. Delhi: Paramamitra Prakashan, 2000.

Nakamura, Hajime. *A History of Early Vedānta Philosophy*. Delhi: Motilal Banarsidass, 1983.

Narasimhan, Padma. *Swami Dayananda Saraswati: Traditional Teacher of Brahma Vidyā*. Madras: TT. Maps and Publications, n.d.

Narasimha, Swami B. V. *Self-Realisation: The Life and Teachings of Sri Ramana Maharshi*. Tiruvannamalai, India: Sri Ramanasramam, 1985 [1931].

Narayanan, Vasudha. "Creating the South Indian 'Hindu' Experience in the United States." In *A Sacred Thread: Modern Transmission of Hindu Traditions in India and Abroad*, edited by Raymond Brady Williams, 147–76. New York: Columbia University Press, 1992, 1996.

———. "Extending Selva J. Raj's Scholarship to Hindu American Temples: Accommodation, Assimilation and a Dialogue of Action." In *Vernacular Catholicism, Vernacular Saints: Selva J. Raj on "Being Catholic the Tamil Way,"* edited by Reid B. Locklin, 225–42. Albany, NY: SUNY Press, 2017.

———. "Sacred Land, Common Ground, Contested Territory: The Healing Mother of Velankanni Basilica and the Infant Jesus Shrine in Bangalore." *Journal of Hindu–Christian Studies* 17.1 (2004): 20–32.

Nattier, Jan. "Buddhism Comes to Main Street." *The Wilson Quarterly* 21.2 (1997): 72–80.

Nelson, Lance E. "The Dualism of Nondualism: Advaita Vedānta and the Irrelevance of Nature." In *Purifying the Earthly Body of God: Religion and Ecology in Hindu India*, 61–88. Albany, NY: SUNY Press, 1998.

———. "Living Liberation in Śaṅkara and Classical Advaita: Sharing the Holy Waiting of God." In *Living Liberation in Hindu Thought*, edited by Andrew O. Fort and Patricia Y. Mumme. Albany, NY: SUNY Press, 1996.

———. "Theism for the Masses, Non-Dualism for the Monastic Elite: A Fresh Look at Śaṃkara's Trans-Theistic Spirituality." In *The Struggle over the Past: Fundamentalism in the Modern World*, edited by William Shea, 61–77. Lanham, MD: University Press of America, 1993.

Neville, Robert C. *Defining Religion: Essays in the Philosophy of Religion*. Albany, NY: SUNY Press, 2018.

———, ed. *The Human Condition*. Albany, NY: SUNY Press, 2001.

———, ed. *Religious Truth*. Albany, NY: SUNY Press, 2001.

———, ed. *Ultimate Realities*. Albany, NY: SUNY Press, 2001.

Nicholson, Andrew J. *Unifying Hinduism: Philosophy and Identity in Indian Intellectual History*. New York: Columbia University Press, 2010.

———. "Vivekananda's Non-Dual Ethics in the History of Vedanta." In *Swami Vivekananda: His Life, Legacy, and Liberative Ethics*, edited by Rita D. Sherma, 51–71. Lanham, MD: Lexington Books, 2021.

Nicholson, Hugh. *Comparative Theology and the Problem of Religious Rivalry*. Oxford & New York: Oxford University Press, 2011.

———. "The New Comparative Theology and the Problem of Theological Hegemonism." In *The New Comparative Theology: Interreligious Insights from the Next Generation*, edited by Francis X. Clooney, 43–62. London: T&T Clark, 2010.

———. "The Shift from Agonistic to Non-Agonistic Debate in Early Nyāya." *Journal of Indian Philosophy* 38.1 (2010): 75–95.

———. "Two Apologetic Moments in Śaṅkara's Concept of *Brahman*." *Journal of Religion* 87 (2007): 528–555.

van Nieuwkwerk, Karin. "'Conversion' to Islam and the Construction of a Pious Self." In *The Oxford Handbook of Religious Conversion*, edited by Lewis R. Rambo and Charles E. Farhadian, 668–86. Oxford & New York: Oxford University Press, 2014.

Noma, Sumitora. "'The Will of the Mother.'" In *Swami Vivekananda: A Hundred Years Since Chicago*, edited by R. K. Dasgupta, 3–7. Belur: Ramakrishna Math and Ramakrishna Mission, 1994.

Nongbri, Brent. *Before Religion: A History of a Modern Concept*. New Haven, CT: Yale University Press, 2015.

Nussbaum, Martha C. *The Clash Within: Democracy, Religious Violence, and India's Future*. Cambridge, MA: Belknap Press of Harvard University, 2007.

Oddie, G. A., ed. *Religion in South Asia: Religious Conversion and Revival Movements in South Asia in Medieval and Modern Times*. Columbia, MO: South Asia Books, 1977.

Olivelle, Patrick. *Renunciation in Hinduism: A Medieval Debate: Volume One: The Debate and the Advaita Argument*. Vienna: Institut für Indologie der Universität Wien, 1986.

———. *The Āśrama System: The History and Hermeneutics of a Religious Institution*. New York: Oxford University Press, 1993.

Osuri, Goldie. "The Concern for Sovereignty in the Politics of Anti-Conversion." *Religion Compass* 7.9 (2013): 385–393.

———. *Religious Freedom in India: Sovereignty and (Anti)Conversion*. London & New York: Routledge, 2013.

Otterman, Sharon. "Hindu Temple in Queens Joins Sanctuary Movement." *New York Times*, May 7, 2017. Accessed July 19, 2019. www.nytimes.com/2017/05/07/nyregion/a-lonely-stand-hindu-temple-in-queens-joins-sanctuary-movement.html

Padilla, C. René. *Mission between the Times*. Revised edition. Carlisle, UK: Langham Monographs, 2010, 2013.

Pande, Govind Chandra. *Life and Thought of Śaṅkarācārya*. Delhi: Motilal Banarsidass, 1994.

Pandya, Samta P. "Aging Spiritually: *Pitamaha Sadans* in India." *Cogent Social Science* 2 (2016): 1219212.

———. "Charisma, Routinization, and Institution Building: Hindu-Inspired Faith Movements in Contemporary India." *Sociological Bulletin* 62.3 (2013): 389–412.

———. "Food, Faith, Social Service and Institution Building: The Annamrita Programme of the Hare Krishna Movement in India." *Religion, State and Society* 45.1 (2017): 4–22.

———. "Governmentality and Guru-Led Movements in India." *European Journal of Social Theory* 19.1 (2016): 74–93.

———. "'Guru' Culture in South Asia: The Case of Chinmaya Mission in India." *Society and Culture in South Asia* 2.2 (2016): 204–32.

———. "Promoting Spiritual Well-Being among Hindu Children in South Asian, Southeast Asian and African Countries: Bala Vihars of Chinmaya Mission." *International Journal of Children's Spirituality* 21.1 (2016): 19–37.

———. "*Seva* in Mata Amrtanandamayi Mission: Social Service as Public Face of Faith." *Implicit Religion* 19.3 (2016): 401–23.

———. "Sociality and Guru-Led Movements: Interplay of Social Issue, Action and Social Service." *Current Sociology* 64.5 (2016): 775–93.

———. "Yoga, Emotional Awareness and Happiness in Children: A Multi-City Study of the Chinmaya Bala Vihar Programme." *Child & Youth Care Forum* 47 (2018): 897–917.

Pangborn, Cyrus R. "The Rāmakrishna Math and Mission: A Case Study in a Revitalization Movement." In *Hinduism: New Essays in the History of Religions*, 98–119. Leiden: Brill, 1976.

Panikkar, Raimundo. *The Unknown Christ of Hinduism: Towards an Ecumenical Christophany*. Maryknoll, NY: Orbis Books, 1981.

Paranjape, Makarand. "Representing Swami Vivekananda: Some Issues and Debates." In *Cyclonic Swami: Vivekananda in the West*, eds. Sukalyan Sengupta and Makarand Parnjape, 39–63. New Delhi: Samvad India Foundation, 2005.

Parikh, Purvi. "Does Character Count: Moral Self-Fashioning in the Swadhyaya and Chinmaya Mission Movements." PhD dissertation, University of Pennsylvania, 2014.

Patton, Kimberley C., and Benjamin C. Ray, eds. *A Magic Still Dwells: Comparative Religion in the Postmodern Age*. Berkeley: University of California Press, 2000.

Pope Paul VI. *Evangelii Nuntiandi*. December 8, 1975. *The Holy See*. Accessed September 13, 2019. https://w2.vatican.va/content/paul-vi/en/apost_exhortations/documents/hf_p-vi_exh_19751208_evangelii-nuntiandi.html

Pechilis, Karen, and Selva J. Raj, eds. *South Asian Religions: Tradition and Today*. London & New York: Routledge, 2013.

———, ed. *The Graceful Guru: Hindu Female Gurus in India and the United States*. Oxford & New York: Oxford University Press, 2004.

Pennington, Brian K. *Was Hinduism Invented? Britons, Indians, and Colonial Construction of Religion*. Oxford: Oxford University Press, 2005.

Phan, Peter C. "Crossing the Borders: A Spirituality for Mission in Our Times." In *In Our Own Tongues: Perspectives from Asia on Mission and Inculturation*, 130–50. Maryknoll, NY: Orbis Books, 2003.

———. "*Deus Migrator*—God the Migrant: Migration of Theology and Theology of Migration." *Theological Studies* 77.4 (2016): 845–68.

———. "The World Missionary Conference, Edinburgh 1910: Challenges for Church and Theology in the Twenty-First Century." *International Bulletin of Missionary Research* 34.2 (2010): 105–8.

Pollock, Sheldon. *The Language of the Gods in the World of Men: Sanskrit, Culture, and Power in Premodern India*. Berkeley: University of California Press, 2006.

———. "The Sanskrit Cosmopolis, 300–1300: Transculturation, Vernacularization and the Question of Ideology." In *Ideology and Status of Sanskrit*, edited by Jan E. M. Houben. Leiden, New York, & Köln: E. J. Brill, 1996.

Pontifical Council for Interreligious Dialogue, World Council of Churches, and World Evangelical Alliance. "Christian Witness in a Multi-Religious World." June 28 2011. www.oikoumene.org/en/resources/documents/wcc-programmes/interreligious-dialogue-and-cooperation/christian-identity-in-pluralistic-societies/christian-witness-in-a-multi-religious-world

Pontifical Council for Interreligious Dialogue. "Reflection and Orientations on Interreligious Dialogue and The Proclamation of The Gospel Of Jesus Christ." May 19, 1991. *The Holy See*. Accessed 21 August 2020. www.vatican.va/roman_curia/pontifical_councils/

interelg/documents/rc_pc_interelg_doc_19051991_dialogue-and-proclamatio_en.html

Posner, Tina. "Transcendental Meditation, Perfect Health, and the Millennium." In *Sickness and Sectarianism: Exploratory Studies in Medical and Religious Sectarianism*, edited by R. Kenneth Jones, 94–112. Aldershot, UK: Gower, 1985.

Potter, Karl H. "Śaṃkarācārya: The Myth and the Man." *Journal of the American Academy of Religion Thematic Studies* 48.3–4 (1982): 111–25.

Potter, Karl H. *Encyclopedia of Indian Philosophies, Vol. 3: Advaita Vedānta up to Śaṅkara and His Pupils*. Princeton, NJ: Princeton University Press, 1981.

———. *Presuppositions of India's Philosophies*. Delhi: Motilal Banarsidass, 1991.

———. "Śaṃkarācārya: The Myth and the Man." *Journal of the American Academy of Religion Thematic Studies* 48.3–4 (1982): 111–25.

Prasad, Leela. *Poetics of Conduct: Oral Narrative and Moral Being in a South Indian Town*. New York: Columbia University Press, 2007.

Premawardhana, Shanta, ed. *Religious Conversion: Religion Scholars Thinking Together*. West Sussex, UK: Wiley Blackwell, 2015.

Press Trust of India. "Improper to ban conversion: Digvijay." *The Hindu*. December 11, 2014. Accessed September 7, 2017. www.thehindu.com/news/national/improper-to-ban-conversion-digvijay/article6682645.ece#

Preti, Alan A. "*Brahmānubhava* as *Überpramāṇa* in Advaita Vedānta: Revisiting an Old Debate." *Philosophy East and West* 64.3 (2014): 718–39.

Rahner, Karl. "Anonymous Christians." In *Theological Investigations, Vol. VI: Concerning Vatican Council II*. Trans. by Karl-H. and Boniface Kruger, 390–98. New York: Crossroad Publishing Company, 1982.

———. "Christianity and the Non-Christian Religions." In *Theological Investigations, Vol. V: Later Writings*. Trans. by Karl-H. Kruger, 115–34. New York: Crossroad Publishing Company, 1983.

———. "Observations on the Problem of the 'Anonymous Christian,'" in *Theological Investigations, Vol. XIV: Ecclesiology, Questions in the Church, The Church in the World*, Trans. by David Bourke, 280–94. New York: Seabury Press, 1976.

Raj, Selva J. "Shared Vows, Shared Space, Shared Deities: Vow Rituals among Tamil Catholics in South India." In *Vernacular Catholicism, Vernacular Saints: Selva J. Raj on "Being Catholic the Tamil Way,"* edited by Reid B. Locklin, 69–91. Albany, NY: SUNY Press, 2017.

———. "The Quest for a Balanced Representation of South Asian Religions in World Religions Textbooks," *Religious Studies Review* 31 (2005): 233–46.

Raj, Selva J., and Corinne M. Dempsey, eds. *Popular Christianity in India: Riting Between the Lines*. Albany, NY: SUNY Press, 2002.

Rajkumar, Peniel. *Dalit Theology and Dalit Liberation*. Farnham, UK & Burlington, VT: Ashgate, 2010.

Raman, Srilata. "Initiation and Conversion in Medieval South India: *Pañcasaṃskāra* as Historical Practice in the Śrīvaiṣṇava Post-Rāmānuja Hagiographic Literature." In *Studies in Hinduism IV: On the Mutual Influences and Relationship of Viśiṣṭādvaita Vedānta and Pañcarātra*, eds. Gerhard Oberhammer and Marion Rastelli, 263–86. Wien: Verlag der Österreichischen Akademie der Wissenschaften, 2007.

Rambachan, Anantanand. "Global Hinduism: The Hindu Diaspora." In *Contemporary Hinduism: Ritual, Culture, and Practice*, edited by Robin Rinehart. Santa Barbara, CA, Denver, CO, and Oxford: ABC CLIO, 2004.

Rambo, Lewis R. "Theories of Conversion: Understanding and Interpreting Religious Change." *Social Compass* 46.3 (1999): 269–71.

———. *Understanding Religious Conversion*. New Haven, CT & London: Yale University Press, 1993.

Rambo, Lewis R., and Charles E. Farhadian. "Converting: Stages of Religious Change." In *Religious Conversion: Contemporary Practices and Controversies*, edited by Christopher Lamb and M. Darrol Bryant, 23–34. London: Cassell, 1999.

———, eds. *The Oxford Handbook of Religious Conversion*. New York: Oxford University Press, 2014.

Ram-Prasad, Chakravarthi. *Knowledge and Liberation in Classical Indian Thought*. Basingstoke, UK, & New York: Palgrave, 2001.

Rao, Shashank. "An Asian-American Reads the Īśavāsya Upaniṣad: First Steps Toward a Hindu Diaspora Theology of Liberation." *Journal of Hindu–Christian Studies* 33 (2020): 53–62.

Rao, Raghvendra, and Rakesh Sinha. "Pushed on 'ghar wapsi,' govt calls for laws against conversion." *The Indian Express*. December 12, 2014. Accessed September 7, 2017. http://indianexpress.com/article/india/india-others/pushed-on-ghar-wapsi-govt-calls-for-laws-against-conversion

Raveh, Daniel. "*Śaṅkaradigvajaya*: A Narrative Interpretation of Śaṅkara's Advaita Vedānta." In *The Bloomsbury Research Handbook of Vedānta*, edited by Ayon Maharaj, 367–90. London: Bloomsbury Academic, 2020.

Raychaudhuri, Tapan. "Swami Vivekananda's Construction of Hinduism." In *Swami Vivekananda and the Modernization of Hinduism*, edited by William Radice, 1–35. Delhi: Oxford University Press, 1998.

Reza, Noreen. "Progressive Hinduism and a New Movement against Poverty." *Kajal Magazine*. June 26, 2018. Accessed July 19, 2019. www.kajalmag.com/progressive-hinduism-and-a-new-movement-against-poverty

Richards, Ian. "Anti-Conversion Laws in Post-Independence India." In *The Routledge Handbook of Hindu–Christian Relations*, edited by Chad M. Bauman and Michelle Voss Roberts, 155–68. London & New York: Routledge, 2021.

———. "Poles Apart: The Debates on Religious Conversion in Post-Independence India." PhD dissertation, University of Toronto, 2016.

Richardson, James T. "Conversion Careers." *Transaction: Social Science and Modern Society* 17.3 (1980): 47–50.

———. *Conversion Careers: In and Out of the New Religions*. Beverley Hills, CA: Sage, 1978.

Richter, Michael. *Medieval Ireland: The Enduring Tradition*. Revised edition. Dublin: Gill & Macmillan, 2005.

Rigopoulos, Antonio. "Tolerance in Swami Vivekānanda's Neo-Hinduism." *Philosophy and Social Criticism* 45.4 (2019): 438–60.

Roberts, Nathaniel. *To Be Cared For: The Power of Conversion and Foreignness of Belonging in an Indian Slum*. Oakland: University of California Press, 2016.

Robinson, Rowena. *Christians of India: An Anthropology of Religion*. New Delhi: Sage, 2003.

Robinson, Rowena, and Joseph Marianus Kujur, eds. *Margins of Faith: Dalit and Tribal Christianity in India*. New Delhi: Sage, 2010.

Robinson, Rowena, and Sathianathan Clarke, eds. *Religious Conversion in India: Modes, Motivations, and Meanings*. New Delhi: Oxford University Press, 2003.

Rochford, E. Burke, Jr. *Hare Krishna in America*. New Brunswick, NJ: Rutgers University Press, 1985.

———. *Hare Krishna Transformed*. New York & London: New York University Press, 2007.

Roodurmun, Pulasth Soobah. *Bhāmatī and Vivaraṇa Schools of Advaita Vedānta: A Critical Approach*. Delhi: Motilal Banarsidass Publishers, 2002.

Rudert, Angela. "Research on Contemporary Indian Gurus: What's New about New Age Gurus?" *Religion Compass* 4.10 (2010): 629–42.

Ruether, Rosemary Radford. *Sexism and God-Talk: Toward a Feminist Theology*. Boston: Beacon Press, 1983.

Rukmani, T. S., ed. *Hindu Diaspora: Global Perspectives*. Delhi: Munshiram Manoharlal, 2001.

San Chirico, Kerry P. C. *Between Hindu and Christian: Khrist Bhaktas, Catholics, and the Negotiation of Devotion*. New York: Oxford University Press, 2023.

Sanders, E. P. *Paul*. Oxford & New York: Oxford University Press, 1991.
———. *Paul, the Law, and the Jewish People*. Philadelphia: Fortress Press, 1983.
———. *Paul and Palestinian Judaism: A Comparison of Patterns of Religion*. Philadelphia: Fortress Press, 1977.
Sanneh, Lamin. "Bible Translation, Culture, and Religion." In *The Wiley Blackwell Companion to World Christianity*, edited by Lamin Sanneh and Michael J. McClymond. Malden, MA: Wiley-Blackwell, 2016.
———. *Translating the Message: The Missionary Impact on Culture*. 2nd ed. Maryknoll, NY: Orbis Books, 2009.
———. *Whose Religion is Christianity? The Gospel beyond the West*. Grand Rapids, MI and Cambridge, UK: William B. Eerdmans, 2003.
Sardella, Ferdinando. "Hinduism." In *World Religions and Their Missions*, edited by Aaron J. Ghiloni, 153–81. New York: Peter Lang, 2015.
Sarkar, Sonia. "Narendra's Grab on Narendra." *The Telegraph Online*, 7 January 2018. Accessed 8 June 2023. www.telegraphindia.com/india/narendra-s-grab-on-narendra/cid/1331615
Sastri, Pandit Sivanath. *The Mission of the Brahmo Samaj*. 3rd ed. Calcutta: Brahmo Mission Press, 1952.
Sawai, Yoshitsugu. *The Faith of Ascetics and Lay Smārtas: A Study of the Śaṅkaran Tradition of Śṛṅgerī*. Wien and Vienna: Institut für Indologie der Universität Wien, 1992.
———. "The Legend of Śaṅkara's Birth." *Journal of Indian and Buddhist Studies* 36.1 (1987): 464–68.
———. "On a Legendary Biography of Śaṅkara," *Journal of Indian and Buddhist Studies* 34.1 (1985): 454–59.
———. "Śaṅkara's Theory of Saṃnyāsa." *Journal of Indian Philosophy* 14.4 (1986): 371–87.
Sax, William S. "Conquering the Quarters: Religion and Politics in Hinduism." *International Journal of Hindu Studies* 4.1 (2000): 39–60.
Schroeder, Roger P. "Proclamation and Interreligious Dialogue as Prophetic Dialogue." *Missiology* 41 (2013): 50–61.
———. *What is the Mission of the Church? A Guide for Catholics*. Maryknoll, NY: Orbis Books, 2008.
Schweitzer, Albert. *Christianity and the Religions of the World*. Translated by Johanna Powers. New York: Henry Holt, 1939.
———. *Indian Thought and Its Development*. London: Adam and Charles Black, 1951.
Seager, Richard Hughes. *The World's Parliament of Religions: The East/West Encounter, Chicago, 1893*. Bloomington & Indianapolis: Indiana University Press, 1995.
Segal, Alan F. *Paul the Convert: The Apostolate and Apostasy of Saul the Pharisee*. New Haven, CT: Yale University Press, 1990.

Senior, Donald, CP and Carol Stuhlmueller, CP. *The Biblical Foundations for Mission*. Maryknoll, NY: Orbis Books, 1983.

Shah, Rebecca and Joel A. Carpenter, eds. *Christianity in India: Conversion, Community Development, and Religious Freedom*. Minneapolis, MN: Fortress Press, 2018.

Shantz, Colleen. *Paul in Ecstasy: The Neurobiology of the Apostle's Life and Thought*. Cambridge: Cambridge University Press, 2009.

Sharma, Arvind. "Ancient Hinduism as a Missionary Religion." *Numen* 39 (1992): 175–92.

———. "Christian Proselytization: A Hindu Perspective," *Missiology* 33.4 (2005): 425–34.

———. *The Experiential Dimension of Advaita Vedanta*. Delhi: Motilal Banarsidass, 1993.

———. "For a Sociology of India: The Place of Conversion in Hinduism." *Contributions to Indian Sociology (ns)* 11.2 (1977): 177–83.

———. "Hinduism and Conversion." In *The Oxford Handbook of Religious Conversion*, edited by Lewis R. Rambo and Charles E. Farhadian, 430–43. Oxford & New York: Oxford University Press, 2014.

———. *Hinduism as a Missionary Religion*. Albany, NY: SUNY Press, 2011.

———. *One Religion Too Many: The Religiously Comparative Reflections of a Comparatively Religious Hindu*. Albany, NY: SUNY Press, 2011.

———. *Problematizing Religious Freedom*. Dordrecht: Springer, 2011.

———. *Ramana Maharshi: The Sage of Arunachala*. New Delhi: Penguin, 2006.

———. *Religious Studies and Comparative Methodology: The Case for Reciprocal Illumination*. Albany, NY: SUNY Press, 2005.

———. "Śaṅkara's Life and Works as a Source for a Hermeneutics of Human Rights." In *New Perspectives on Advaita Vedānta: Essays in Commemoration of Professor Richard De Smet, S.J*, edited by Bradley J. Malkovsky, 109–21. Leiden: Brill, 2000.

Sharma, Jyotirmaya. *Cosmic Love and Human Apathy: Swami Vivekananda's Restatement of Religion*. Noida: HarperCollins India, 2013.

———. *A Restatement of Religion: Swami Vivekananda and the Making of Hindu Nationalism*. New Haven, CT & London: Yale University Press, 2013.

Sheridan, Daniel P. "The Dueling Sacred Biographies of Madhva and Śaṅkara." *Journal of Vaishnava Studies* 15.2 (2007): 123–44.

Sherinian, Zoe C. *Tamil Folk Music as Dalit Liberation Theology*. Bloomington & Indianapolis: Indiana University Press, 2014.

Sherma, Rita. "Eros, Ethics, and Enlightenment: Toward a Reconstructive Approach to Ultimate and Penultimate Goals in Hindu Theology." *Infinity Foundation*. Accessed 17 February 2006. www.infinityfoundation.com/mandala/s_es_sherm_eros.htm

———, ed. *Swami Vivekananda: His Life, Legacy, and Liberative Ethics*. Lanham, MD: Lexington Books, 2021.

Shiveshwarkar, Shyamala. "The Chinmaya Mission: Vedantic Activism." In *Dharma and Development: The Future of Survival*, edited by Makarand Paranjape, 145–171. New Delhi: Samvad India Foundation, 2005.

Shourie, Arun. *Harvesting Our Souls: Missionaries, Their Design, Their Claims*. New Delhi: ASA, 2000.

———. *Missionaries in India: Continuities, Changes, Dilemmas*. New Delhi: ASA, 1994.

Shulman, David. "Review Essay: *The Language of the Gods in the World of Men* by Sheldon Pollock." *Journal of Asian Studies* 66 (2007): 819–73.

Shrubsole, Nicholas. *What Has No Place, Remains: The Challenges for Religious Freedom in Canada Today*. Toronto: University of Toronto Press, 2019.

Sil, Narasingha Prosad. *Swami Vivekananda: A Reassessment*. Selinsgrove, PA: Susquehanna University Press, 1997.

Simmer-Brown, Judith. "Christian Views: A Response," *Buddhist–Christian Studies* 17 (1997): 152–158.

Sinha, Vineeta. "Problematizing Received Categories: Revisiting 'Folk Hinduism' and 'Sanskritization.'" *Current Sociology* 54.1 (2006): 98–111.

Skreslet, Stanley H. *Comprehending Mission: The Questions, Methods, Themes, Problems, and Prospects of Missiology*. Maryknoll, NY: Orbis Books, 2012.

Smith, Jonathan Z. *To Take Place: Toward Theory in Ritual*. Chicago: University of Chicago Press, 1987.

Smith, Wilfred Cantwell. *The Meaning and End of Religion*. Minneapolis: Fortress Press, 1991.

———. "The Mission of the Church and the Future of Missions." In *The Church in the Modern World: Essays in Honour of James Sutherland Thomson*, edited by George Johnston and Wolfgang Roth, 154–70. Toronto: The Ryerson Press, 1967.

Soars, Daniel, and Nadya Pohran, eds. *Hindu–Christian Dual Belonging*. London & New York: Routledge, 2022.

Sodder, Mudita Menona. RSCJ, *Reliving Christian Life in the Globalized World Today: Cultural Celebrations in Urban Churches of Mumbai*. New Delhi: Christian World Imprints, 2016.

Srinivas, M. N. "The Cohesive Role of Sanskritization." In *The Oxford India Srinivas*, 221–35. Delhi: Oxford University Press, 2009.

———. "A Note on Sanskritization and Westernization." In *Caste in Modern India and Other Essays*, 42–62. Bombay: Asia Publishing House, 1962.

Stackhouse, Max L. "Missions: Missionary Activity." In *Encyclopedia of Religion*, vol. 9, edited by Lindsay Jones, 6068–76. Revised edition. Detroit: McMillan Reference USA, 2005.

Stanley, Brian. "The World Missionary Conference, Edinburgh 1910: Sifting History from Myth." *Expository Times* 121.7 (2010): 325–31.

Starkey, Peggy. "Agape: A Christian Criterion for Truth in the Other World Religions." *International Review of Mission* 74 (1985): 425–63.

Stein, Edith. *The Hidden Life: Hagiographic Essays, Meditations, Spiritual Texts*, Collected Works of Edith Stein 4. Edited by L. Gelber and Michael Linssen, O.C.D. Translated by Waltraut Stein. Washington, DC: ICS, 1992.

Steinschneider, Eric. "Arguing the Taste of Fresh Butter: Īcūr Caccitāṉanta Cuvāmikaḷ's Advaitic Interpretation of Tamil Śaiva Theology." *International Journal of Hindu Studies* 21.3 (2017): 299–318.

———. "Ceṭṭiyār Vedānta: Fashioning Hindu Selves in Colonial South India." *Journal of Indian Philosophy* 48 (2020): 101–18.

Stelton, Leo F. *Dictionary of Ecclesiastical Latin*. Peabody, MA: Hendrickson Publishers, 1995.

Stephen, Abraham. *Social Philosophy of Vivekananda: Its Relevance to Modern India*. Delhi: ISPCK, 2005.

Stoeber, Michael. "Hindu–Christian Dialogue on the Afterlife: Swami Vivekananda, Modern Advaita Vedānta, and Roman Catholic Eschatology." *International Journal of Hindu Studies* 27 (2023): 33–65.

Stoker, Valerie. *Polemics and Patronage in the City of Victory: Vyāsatīrtha, Hindu Sectarianism, and the Sixteenth-Century Vijanagara Court*. Oakland: University of California Press, 2016.

———. "Polemics and Patronage in Sixteenth-Century Vijayanagara: Vyāsatīrtha and the Dynamics of Hindu Sectarian Relations." *History of Religions* 51.2 (2011): 129–55.

Strauss, Sarah. "The Master's Narrative: Swami Sivananda and the Transnational Production of Yoga." *Journal of Folklore Research* 39.2–3 (2002): 217–42.

———. *Positioning Yoga: Balancing Acts Across Cultures*. Oxford & New York: Berg, 2005.

Sullivan, Francis A., S.J. *The Church We Believe In: One, Holy, Catholic and Apostolic*. New York/Mahwah: Paulist Press, 1988.

———. "The Papal Apology." *America* 182.12. April 8 2000. Accessed 27 September 2021. www.americamagazine.org/issue/288/article/papal-apology

———. *Salvation Outside the Church? Tracing the History of the Catholic Response*. Mahwah, NY: Paulist Press, 1992.

Sundaresan, Vidyasankar. "Conflicting Hagiographies and History: The Place of Śaṅkaravijaya Texts in Advaita Tradition." In*ternational Journal of Hindu Studies* 4.2 (2000): 109–84.

Suthren Hirst, Jacqueline G. "Images of Śaṅkara: Understanding the Other." *International Journal of Hindu Studies* 8 (2004): 157–81.

———. "The Place of *Bhakti* in Śaṅkara's Vedānta." In *Love Divine: Studies in Bhakti and Devotional Mysticism*, edited by Karel Werner, 117–45. Richmond, Surrey: Curzon Press, 1993.

———. "Weaving the Strands: Cognition, Authority and Language in Śaṅkara's *Upadeśasāhasrī*." In *Paramparā: Essays in Honour of R. Balasubramanian*, edited by S. Rao and G. Mishra, 141–66. New Delhi: Indian Council of Philosophical Research, 2003.

———. "Who Were the *Tārkikas*? The Place of Polemic in Śaṃkara's *Bṛhadāraṇyakopaniṣadbhāṣya*." *Journal of Hindu Studies* 4 (2011): 54–78.

Swarup, Ram. *A Hindu View of Christianity and Islam*. New Delhi: Voice of India, 1992.

———. *Hinduism and Monotheistic Religions*. New Delhi: Voice of India, 2009.

Synod of Bishops. "Justice in the World." In *The Gospel of Peace and Justice: Catholic Social Teaching Since Pope John*, 513–29. Maryknoll, NY: Orbis Books, 1976.

Tanner, Kathryn. "Cultural Theory." In *The Oxford Handbook of Systematic Theology*, edited by John Webster, Kathryn Tanner, and Iain Torrance, 527–42. Oxford & New York: Oxford University Press, 2007.

———. "Editorial Symposium: Roman Catholic Theology of Tradition," *Horizons* 29 (2002): 303–11.

———. *Theories of Culture: A New Agenda for Theology*. Minneapolis: Fortress Press, 1997.

Tanner, Norman P., S.J., ed. *Decrees of the Ecumenical Councils, Volume Two: Trent to Vatican II*. London & Washington DC: Sheed & Ward and Georgetown University Press, 1990.

Thangaraj, M. Thomas. *The Common Task: A Theology of Christian Mission*. Nashville, TN: Abingdon Press, 1999.

———. "Hinduism and Globalization: A Christian Theological Approach." In *God and Globalization, Vol. 3: Christ and the Dominions of Civilization*, eds. Max L. Stackhouse with Diane B. Obenchain, 213–39. Harrisburg: Trinity Press International, 2002.

Thatamanil, John J. *Circling the Elephant: A Comparative Theology of Religious Diversity*. New York: Fordham University Press, 2020.

———. *The Immanent Divine: God, Creation, and the Human Predicament*. Minneapolis, MN: Fortress Press, 2006.

Thomas, M. M. *The Acknowledged Christ of the Indian Renaissance*. London: SCM Press, 1969.

———, Lesslie Newbigen and Alfred C. Krass. "Baptism, the Church, and Koinonia." *Religion and Society* 19.1 (1972), 69–90.

———. *The Christian Response to the Asian Revolution*. London: SCM Press, 1966.

———. *Nagas Towards A.D. 2000, and Other Selected Addresses and Writings*. Madras: Centre for Research on New International Economic Order, 1992.

———. "Salvation and Humanization: A Crucial Issue in the Theology of Mission for India." *International Review of Mission* 60.237 (1971): 25–38.

———. *Salvation and Humanisation: Some Critical Issues of the Theology of Mission in Contemporary India*. Madras: CLS, 1971.

Thomas, Wendell. *Hinduism Invades America*. New York: Beacon Press, 1930.

Todd, Warren Lee. *The Ethics of Śaṅkara and Śāntideva: A Selfless Response to an Illusory World*. Farnham, Surrey, & Burlington, VT: Ashgate, 2013.

Trout, Polly. *Eastern Seeds, Western Soil: Three Gurus in America*. Mountain View, CA: Mayfield Publishing Company, 2001.

Truth and Reconciliation Commission of Canada. *Honouring the Truth, Reconciling for the Future: Summary of the Final Report of the Truth and Reconciliation Commission of Canada*. Toronto: Lorimer, 2015.

Tweed, Thomas A., and Stephen Prothero, eds. *Asian Religions in America: A Documentary History*. New York & Oxford: Oxford University Press, 1999.

Tweed, Thomas A. *Crossing and Dwelling: A Theory of Religion*. Cambridge, MA: Harvard University Press, 2006.

———. *Our Lady of the Exile: Diasporic Religion at a Cuban Catholic Shrine in Miami*. New York: Oxford University Press, 1997.

Swami Tyagananda. "Rediscovering Vivekananda in the East and the West." In *Cyclonic Swami: Vivekananda in the West*, edited by Sukalyan Sengupta and Makarand Parnjape, 29–38. New Delhi: Samvad India Foundation, 2005.

———, and Pravrajika Vrajaprana. *Interpreting Ramakrishna: Kālī's Child Revisited*. Delhi: Motilal Banarsidass, 2010.

———. "What Made Vivekananda Attend the Parliament of Religions?" in *Swami Vivekananda: A Hundred Years Since Chicago*, edited by R. K. Dasgupta, 20–34. Belur: Ramakrishna Math and Ramakrishna Mission, 1994.

Ulrich, Edward T. "Swami Abhishiktananda and Comparative Theology." *Horizons* 31.1 (2004): 40–63.

United Church of Canada. *World Mission: Report of the Commission on World Mission*. Toronto: General Council of the United Church of Canada, 1966.

Vandevelde, Iris. "Reconversion to Hinduism: A Hindu Nationalist Reaction Against Conversion to Christianity and Islam." *South Asia: Journal of South Asian Studies* 34.1 (2011): 31–50.

van der Veer, Peter. *Religious Nationalism: Hindus and Muslims in India*. Berkeley, Los Angeles, & London: University of California Press, 1994.

Vertovec, Steven. *The Hindu Diaspora: Comparative Patterns*. London & New York: Routledge, 2000.
Vetter, Tilman. *Studien zur Lehre und Entwicklung Śaṅkaras*. Wien: Institut für Indologie der Universität Wien, 1979.
Viswanathan, Gauri. *Outside the Fold: Conversion, Modernity, and Belief*. Princeton, NJ: Princeton University Press, 1998.
Volf, Miroslav. "Materiality of Salvation: An Investigation of the Soteriologies of Liberation and Pentecostal Theologies." *Journal of Ecumenical Studies* 26.3 (1989): 447–67.
Voss Roberts, Michelle. *Tastes of the Divine: Hindu and Christian Theologies of Emotion*. New York: Fordham University Press, 2014.
Waghorne, Joanne Punzo. "Global Gurus and the Third Stream of American Religiosity: Between Hindu Nationalism and Liberal Pluralism." In *Political Hinduism: The Religious Imagination in Public Spheres*, edited by Vinay Lal, 122–149. New Delhi: Oxford University Press, 2009.
Warrier, Maya. *Hindu Selves in a Modern World: Guru Faith in the Mata Amritanandamayi Mission*. London & New York: Routledge, 2005.
———. "The *Seva* Ethic and the Spirit of Institution Building in the Mata Amritanandamayi Mission." In *Hinduism in Public and Private: Reform, Hindutva, Gender, and Sampraday*, edited by Antony Copley, 254–89. New Delhi: Oxford University Press, 2003.
Weber, Joseph. *Transcendental Meditation in America: How a New Age Movement Remade a Small Town in Iowa*. Iowa City: University of Iowa Press, 2014.
———. "Transcendental Meditation and the Remaking of an Iowa Farm Town," *Utopian Studies* 25 (2014): 341–58.
Whaling, Frank. "A Comparative Religious Study of Missionary Transplantation in Buddhism, Christianity and Islam." *International Review of Mission* 70 (1981): 314–333.
Whitworth, John M., and Martin Shiels. "From Across the Black Water: Two Imported Varieties of Hinduism." In *New Religious Movements: A Perspective for Understanding Society*, edited by Eileen Barker, 155–172. New York: Edwin Mellen Press, 1982.
Wildman, Wesley. "Cross-Cultural Comparative Religious Ideas Project (CRIP)." *Wildman's Weird Wild Web*. Accessed March 1, 2018. http://people.bu.edu/wwildman/WeirdWildWeb/proj_crip.htm
———. *Religious Philosophy as a Multidisciplinary Comparative Inquiry: Envisioning a Future for the Philosophy of Religion*. Albany, NY: SUNY Press, 2010.
Wilkins, Jeremy D. "Grace and Growth: Aquinas, Lonergan, and the Problematic of Habitual Grace." *Theological Studies* 72.4 (2011): 723–49.

Williams, George M. "The Ramakrishna Movement: A Study in Religious Change." In *Religion in Modern India,* edited by Robert D. Baird, 55–79. Revised edition. New Delhi: Manohar, 1989.

———. "Svami Vivekananda: Archetypal Hero or Doubting Saint?" In *Religion in Modern India,* edited by Robert D. Baird, 313–42. Revised edition. New Delhi: Manohar, 1989.

Williams, Raymond Brady. *Religions of Immigrants from India and Pakistan: New Threads in the American Tapestry.* Cambridge: Cambridge University Press, 1988.

———. "Sacred Threads of Several Textures." In *A Sacred Thread: Modern Transmission of Hindu Traditions in India and Abroad,* edited by Raymond Brady Williams, 231–44. Chambersburg, PA: Anima, 1992.

———. *Williams on South Asian Religions and Immigration: Collected Works.* Aldershot, UK: Ashgate, 2004.

Williamson, Lola. *Transcendent in America: Hindu-Inspired Meditation Movements as New Religion.* New York & London: New York University Press, 2010.

Willis, Glenn R. "On Some Suspicions Regarding Comparative Theology." In *How to Do Comparative Theology,* edited by Francis X. Clooney and Klaus von Stosch, 122–33. New York: Fordham University Press, 2018.

Wilson, Stephen R. "Becoming a Yogi: Resocialization and Deconditioning as Conversion Process." *Sociological Analysis* 45.4 (1984): 301–14.

Wolff, Otto. "Die Religiöse Aktivität Des Modernen Hinduismus." *Zeitschrift für Religions- und Geistesgeschichte* 10.4 (1958): 299–305.

Wuaku, Albert. "Exploring the South–South Trajectory of Global Religious Flows: The Origins of Ghana's Hinduism." In *Religion on the Move! New Dynamics of Religious Expansion in a Globalizing World,* edited by Afe Adogame and Shobana Shankar, 133–57. Leiden: Brill, 2013.

Wylie, Shannon Gabrielle. "A More Inductive Method of Interreligious Theology: Joseph Ratzinger's Insights into Christian Experience in Response to Jacques Dupuis." PhD dissertation, Toronto School of Theology, 2022.

Yocum, Glenn. "The Coronation of a Guru: Charisma, Politics and Philosophy in Contemporary India." In *A Sacred Thread: Modern Transmission of Hindu Traditions in India and Abroad,* edited by Raymond Brady Williams, 68–91. Chambersburg, PA: Anima, 1992.

Young, Richard Fox, and Jonathan A. Seitz, eds. *Asia in the Making of Christianity: Conversion, Agency, and Indigeneity, 1600s to the Present.* Leiden: Brill, 2013.

Young, Richard Fox. "Hindu–Christian Debates in the Eighteenth and Nineteenth Centuries." In *The Routledge Handbook of Hindu–Christian*

Relations, edited by Chad M. Bauman and Michelle Voss Roberts, 127–38. London & New York: Routledge, 2021.

Younger, Paul. *New Homelands: Hindu Communities in Mauritius, Guyana, Trinidad, South Africa, Fiji, and East Africa*. New York & Oxford: Oxford University Press, 2010.

Yü, Dan Smyer. "Buddhist Conversion in the Contemporary World." In *The Oxford Handbook of Religious Conversion*, edited by Lewis R. Rambo and Charles E. Farhadian, 465–87. Oxford & New York: Oxford University Press, 2014.

Zelinski, Daniel. "From Prudence to Morality: A Case for the Morality of Some Forms of Nondualistic Mysticism." *Journal of Religious Ethics* 35.2 (2007): 291–317.

Index

Abhishiktananda, Swami, 351n87; conversion of, 231; religious experience of, 231–32; *See also* Arunachala
Ācārya: as mission paradigm, 88–94
Ādivāsī (Tribal), 2, 9, 16, 176, 298. *See also* Caste
Advaita, *see* Vedānta
Ajeya Bharat Party, 70, 201, 298n149
Arunachala: Abhishiktananda visit to, 231, 233–34; Brunton, Paul visit to, 54–55; New York ashram, 58, 151; Osborne, Arthur at, 233; Ramana Maharshi and, 56, 176, 231; sacred geography of, 152, 176
Ārya Samāj, 2, 64, 341n147
Ātman: Dayananda on, 139, 225, 313n12; liberation and, 57, 78, 122, 132; non-dualist awareness of, 141–42, 147; recollection of, 134, 144, 148; Śaṅkara on, 91, 97, 125, 148, 181; translation of, 142; universal presence of, 97. See also *Brahman*; Chinmayananda, Swami; Experience, Religious
Babb, Lawrence A., 128–29
Barua, Ankur: on the "Conversion Controversy," 10–12, 19, 241–42; on "epistemic peer conflict," 242, 249; on "hierarchical encompassment," 234, 241–42; on the ideological construction of Hinduism, 27; on Ramana Maharshi, 134, 317n58, 318n63; on Vivekananda, 335n53, 348n47, 349n48
Bayly, Susan, 27–28
Beckerlegge, Gwilym, 100–101, 154–56, 191–93, 206, 286n39, 335n50, 335n53
Belonging, Non-dualist: Advaita Vedānta and, 3, 11, 44, 117; Chinmayananda and, 132, 135, 238–39; as conversion, 233–42; Dayananda and, 138, 140 239; Missionary Advaita and, 44, 83, 135, 141–42, 147, 215, 217; Ramana Maharshi and, 121–22, 124; in Śaṅkara, 89, 126, 140, 186, 188–89; Schweitzer, Albert on 183, 186; Transcendental Meditation and, 66, 141
Belonging, Religious: in Christianity, 262, 356n155;

Belonging, Religious *(continued)* interreligious, 355n139; Paul the Apostle and, 245; translocative, 180; in the teaching of Śaṅkara, 89
Benedict XVI, Pope, 247–50
Bevans, Steven B., 21, 86–87, 88, 115, 256
Bharatiya Janata Party (BJP), 1, 2, 176, 271
Bhagavad-Gītā: Chinmayananda and, 61, 129, 194; Jñānānanda Bhāratī, Swami and, 105; Ramana Maharishi and, 69; Śaṅkara's commentary on, 189–90; *Sankara the Missionary* and, 111–12; Schweitzer, Albert on, 183; Vivekananda on, 193
Bhakti, 292n108; Hinduism and, 46; Śaṅkara and, 299n171; in *Sankara the Missionary*, 163, 167, 170; Vaiṣṇavism and, 98. *See also* Chinmayananda, Swami
Body-Mind-Intellect (B-M-I) Chart, 61, 132, 153, 158, 171, 174, 176, 177, 179, 292n106. *See also* Chinmayananda, Swami
Bosch, David, 4, 84–88, 95–96, 104, 115, 153, 178–80, 256, 273n63
Brahman: Abhinava Vidyātīrtha on, 122, 313n31; Advaita Vedānta and, 52, 117, 142, 222, 242, 249, 295n130; *Ātman* and, 91, 142, 187–88, 225; in the B-M-I Chart, 158; in Chinmaya Mission, 46–47, 169; Candraśekhara Bhāratī on, 130, 133, 145–46; Chinmayananda on, 158, 249; conversion and, 242; Dayananda on, 249; Ramana Maharshi on, 131; Rambachan, Anantanand on, 203, 341n139; Śaṅkara on, 81, 91–94, 108; social restrictions and, 133; Vivekananda on, 44; *Vivekacūḍāmaṇi* on, 130–31 *See also* Liberation, Social; Liberation, Spiritual
Brahmanism: Advaita Vedānta and, 47; Buddhism and, 234; Brahminization and, 122; and mission, 15, 17; and nationalism, 165; Śaṅkara and, 91–94, 186; Sanskritization and, 235; Schweitzer, Albert on, 186; in Vedic period, 163. *See also* Caste
Brahmo Samāj, 30, 44, 50, 192, 334n49
Brunton, Paul, 54–56, 226, 289n61
Buddha: as avatar of Vishnu, 234; Chinmayananda on, 166; liberation and, 222; as mission paradigm, 83, 99–104, 215; Vivekananda and, 44, 83, 99–104, 109, 111, 115, 193, 293n112, 308n80, 309n85
Buddhism: absorption into Hinduism, 234; caste system and, 103; Chinmaya Mission and, 167; conversion and, 222; Dayananda and, 225; inculturation in the West, 155; missionary aspects of, 25, 31–32, 62; Orientalist depictions of, 100, 104, 111; Ramakrishna Mission and, 103; in *Sankara the Missionary*, 163, 167, 170; Śaṅkara's relation to, 89–90, 92–93, 95, 163; Schweitzer, Albert and, 184; Vivekananda's attitude toward, 99–104, 293n112; at World's Parliament of Religions, 49. *See also* Liberation, Spiritual

Candraśekhara Bhāratī: on liberation, 123, 134; on religious

experience, 130, 132–35, 142; on social status, 146; *Vivekacūḍāmaṇi* commentary, 129–30, 132–33, 141, 145
Caste: Chinmaya Mission and, 196, 198, 241; *dharma* fulfillment and, 74; Hinduism and, 33, 60, 64, 74; and indigenization, 19; and liberation, 188; Radhakrishnan on, 234; Rambachan, Anantanand on, 113, 202–204, 358n15; in re-conversion practices, 64; Śaṅkara on, 93–94, 97, 168, 188, 190; Sanskritization and, 2, 234–35; Transcendental Meditation and, 297; Vivekananada and, 103, 154, 192–93. *See also* Brahmanism; Liberation, Social
Catholicism: baptism in, 261; conversion in, 21, 88; Hinduism and, 28, 37, 231–32, 227, 229–31, 249; inculturation of, 21, 28; interreligious dialogue in, 262, 360n38; liberation theology in, 209–10, 260; Long, Jeffery on, 226–27, 244; service, role in, 209; as theological lens for this book, 281n131; Transcendental Meditation and, 229–30. *See also* Missiology, Christian; Christianity; Colonialism; Francis, Pope; John Paul II, Pope; Leo XIII, Pope; Paul VI, Pope; Second Vatican Council
Chinmaya Mission, 59–65; Advaita Vedānta and, 46, 60, 233, 352n98; *Brahman* and, 169; Buddhism and, 168; character formation in, 337n87; study groups of, 238–39, 293n111, 284n118, 317n55; Christianity and, 247; conversion and, 237–39; Daśanāmī Order and, 47, 71; Dayananda, relationship with, 75, 113, 138, 225; lay leadership in, 194–95; nationalism and, 197–98, 337n90; Ramana Maharshi and, 58, 159; *Sankara the Missionary*, 105–106, 153, 159–74, 176, 178–82; social service and, 185, 191–98; relation to Śṛṅgeri *maṭh*, 47, 75–76, 105 145, 165; role of women in, 294; resignification of place by, 5, 153, 157–58, 165, 168, 173, 176; Transcendental Meditation and, 159; Vivekananda and, 99, 318n78; Vishva Hindu Parishad (VHP) and, 63–64. *See also* Chinmayananda, Swami
Chinmaya Organisation for Rural Development (CORD), 195–97; creation of, 195, 336n69; interreligious cooperation and, 211; liberation and, 198, 206; Mahila Mandals, 195–96, 212, 264; role of women in, 63, 195–97, 294n118
Chinmayananda, Swami: Advaita Vedānta and, 62, 153, 157–60, 166–68, 170, 237–38, 292n107, 336n78; *Art of Man-Making*, 194, 196, 337n88; on *Ātman*, 132, 141–42, 145, 171, 179; on *Bhakti*, 292n108; conversion and, 223; Dayananda and 138, 140, 146; Divine Life Society and, 194; Jñāna Yajña ideal of, 59–65; as founder of the Vishva Hindu Parishad (VHP), 63–64, 294n122, 295n124; *Manual of Self-Unfoldment*, 157–59, 170–71, 197, 237–38, 292n105; mission of, 59–60, 62–65, 84, 107–109, 148, 157, 174, 177–81, 291n100;

Chinmayananda, Swami (*continued*)
and "Mother Śruti," 60–62, 157; nationalism of, 63–64, 77, 113, 157, 159, 165, 194; as pilgrim, 177; Ramana Maharshi and, 58; Śaṅkara and, 62–63, 89, 107–108, 159–65; Sharma, Arvind and, 232; Sivananda and, 195; social service and, 194, 196, 336n78; Transcendental Meditation and, 66, 68, 199; universal vision of, 146, 153, 157–59, 166–71, 179, 196, 241; *Vivekacūḍāmaṇi*, commentary on, 129–37, 141, 145, 223–24, 241; Vivekananda and, 60–62, 99, 292n108. *See also* Body-Mind-Intellect (B-M-I) Chart; Chinmaya Mission
Christianity: conversion and, 10, 13, 19–22, 24, 217, 347n36; discipleship in, 128–29; Ecumenical, 281n 131; Evangelical, 5, 17, 207–209, 281n131; indigeneity and, 27–29, 36, 274n77; as ideological construct, 27; as identity category, 128, 220, 247, 316n48; social service, role in, 206–13, 335n50; translation in, 143–44; Vivekananda's characterization of, 44, 49. *See also* Catholicism; Colonialism; Missiology, Christian
Christian Ashram Movement, 14
"Christian Witness in a Multi-Religious World," 22, 24, 25.
Christification, *see* Conversion
Clooney, Francis X., 6, 34–35, 39, 82, 88, 126–27, 281n132
Coakley, Sarah, 230
Colonialism: "Conversion Controversy" and, 1–2, 9, 17; missiology, influence on, 39, 85–86, 115, 143–44, 176–77, 180, 238, 243, 251; religious experience and, 124–25, 133; translation and, 144, 321n119, 321n124; and "world religion" category, 26
Colonialism, Settler: in the Indian Residential School System, 257, 262–63; in South Asian context, 259. *See also* Truth and Reconciliation Commission
Conquest: Chinmayananda on, 63, 171, 176–77; "Conversion Controversy" and, 11–18, 36; in the Crusades, 176–77; nationalism and, 77, 107; missiology and, 153, 171, 176–77, 180; in relation to pilgrimage, 153; in Śaṅkara hagiographies, 77, 93–99, 160–62, 165, 167–68, 176; in speeches of Vivekananda, 15, 43, 99, 101–102, 107
Conversion: as absorption, 234; in antiquity, 356n154, 356n156; baptism and, 20, 220, 249, 260–62; Benedict XVI's account of, 247; as Christification, 217, 246, 249, 256–58, 260, 262–63; as cross-cultural category, 217, 220; definitions of, 11, 18, 77, 216–21, 225, 227, 240, 243–44; de-nationalism and, 28; disaffiliation, 231, 351n85; ethnic identity and, 245–46; intrareligious 89, 220, 223; as liberation, 211, 215; material enticements for, 185, 211; as

reconversion, 2, 15, 16, 18, 77; in Śaṅkara, 95–96; Sanskritization and, 237, 240; as transformation, 232, 243, 249, 251–52, 256, 352n91; as violence, 12–18, 250, 252; vertical movement of, 222, 232, 242. *See also* Missiology, Comparative; Missiology, Christian; Missiology, Hindu
Conversion Controversy, 1, 6, 28, 35–36; anti-conversion legislation, 1–3, 9, 268n7, 269n4; as impetus for this book, 1–3, 215; missiology and, 35, 39; "Nazism" accusations, 14, 16, 271n39; scholarly accounts of, 9–12
Cruz, Gemma Tulud, 153, 178–80

Dalit, 9, 16, 28, 176, 204, 235. *See also* Caste
Daśanāmī Order, 47, 71, 97, 105, 107
David Lynch Foundation, 69–70
Dayananda Saraswati, Swami: Advaita Vedānta, and, 225, 239–40, 349n59, 349n60; Chinmaya Mission and, 75, 113, 138, 224–25; "conversion controversy" and, 12–16, 36, 241, 252; as convert, 224–27, 233, 239; critique of religious experience, 122, 135, 138–42, 313n12; liberation and, 138–41; open letter to John Paul II, 12–13, 250–52; Rambachan, Anantanand and, 201–202, 313n14; *Upadesa Sāram*, commentary on, 138–41, 145; yoga and, 319n92
Dempsey, Corinne, 27–28, 283n7
De Nobili, Roberto, 14, 34
Divine Life Society, 109–11; as Advaita mission movement, 47, 58, 165, 291n102; Ramakrishna Mission and, 113; Ramana Maharshi and, 61; social service in, 110, 194

Edelmann, Jonathan, 88, 144
Enlightenment. *See* Belonging, Non-Dualist; Liberation, Spiritual; Ultimate Reality.
Experience, Religious: *Ātman* and, 122–23, 125, 134, 142, 145, 147; Chinmayananda on, 61–62, 129–40, 145–46; in classical Advaita Vedānta, 122–41; colonialism and, 124–25; definitions of, 147–48, 322n133, as "gospel," 141–42; Katz-Forman debate, 122; mysticism as, 186, 239, 183–84, 186; Ramana Maharshi on, 4, 121–22, 124, 129–40; self-realization and 57, 67, 122, 137; in Transcendental Meditation, 65–67, 122; renunciation and, 189; mission and, 128–29, 134, 141–42, 148–49; Candraśekhara Bhāratī on, 130, 132–35. *See also* Belonging, Non-Dualist; Liberation, Spiritual
Evangelization: Francis on, 23–24; as "integral mission," 208–209; Paul VI on, 21. *See also* "Christian Witness in a Multi-Religious World"; Conversion; Mission; Missiology, Christian

Forman, Robert K. C., 122, 230–31, 233
Forsthoefel, Thomas A., 37, 46, 121–22, 124, 126–28, 141, 152

Francis, Pope: Benedict XVI and, 247; *Evangelii Gaudium*, 22–25, 31, 39 273n65; *Laudato Si'*, 210, 212; *Fratelli Tutti*, 210, 273n67; Penitential Pilgrimage to Canada of, 360n40
Fredriksen, Paula, 245–46, 256
Frykenberg, Robert Eric, 17, 28, 272n45

Gaventa, Beverly Roberts, 243–46
Gandhi, Mohandas K., 2, 176, 183, 222, 248–49, 348n45
Ghiloni, Aaron J., 32, 33, 37, 38
Goel, Sita Ram, 2, 12, 14 15–18, 27, 36
Gooren, Henri, 217, 220–21, 224, 230, 240, 242–43, 263
Gospel: of Advaita Vedānta, 47, 50; of inner experience, 141–42, 147; as fellowship, 260; as *kerygma*, 22–24, 38, 84, 86; liberation, social and, 208–10
Gutiérrez, Gustavo, 209, 211. *See also* Catholicism; Liberation Theology

Hagelin, John, 65, 69–70, 200–201, 205, 339n114. *See also* Natural Law Party; Transcendental Meditation
Hastāmalaka, 111, 164, 169, 264; as a missionary style, 108–109, 115–16
Heredia, Rudolf C., 32, 216, 223, 234
Hindu-Inspired Meditation Movements, 30, 45, 228; Self-Realization Fellowship, 30, 67, 228, 296n139; *See also* Transcendental Meditation; Williamson, Lola
Hinduism: Buddhism and, 32, 234; conversion in, 89, 215–17, 226, 237–38; ethnic identity and, 152, 154, 173; ideological construction of, 26–27; rites of reconversion in, 64, 77; sectarianism in, 89; as transnational, 29–30, 43; universalism of, 33, 37, 152, 172–73; Vedic, 33, 68–69, 73, 163, 188, 199, 202, 229. *See also* Missiology, Hindu; Śaṅkara; Vedānta, Advaita; World Religion(s)
Humes, Cyntha Ann, 46, 68, 155–57, 201, 228, 298n149
Hummel, Reinhart, 43, 44, 50, 88, 216

International Society of Krishna Consciousness (ISKCON), 16, 30, 37, 155, 341n147
Islam, 98; Christianity and, 247; conversion in, 143, 221–22, 347n36

Jackson, Carl T., 30, 155, 252, 288n56, 344n5
John Paul II, Pope: act of repentance by, 357n177; Dayananda's open letter to, 12–13, 250; *Ecclesia in Asia*, 13; *Redemptoris Missio*, 21, 23

Karma: theory of, 10, 66, 92, 188, 332n26; *karma-yoga*, 52, 67, 110, 130, 193, 292n108
Kim, Sebastian, 12, 261
Klostermeier, Klaus K., 32–33, 37
Kuruvachira, Jose, 15–16, 18, 234

Leo XIII, Pope, 209

Liberation, Social: Advaita theologies of, 198–204; altruism and, 188–90; *Brahman* and, 203; ethics and, 185–90; as holistic transformation, 185, 205–13; Ramabachan, Anantanand on, 201–203; renunciation and, 189–90; as social service, 185, 191–98, 213; *tat-tvam-asi* ethic, 125, 187, 193

Liberation, Spiritual: in Advaita Vedānta, 78, 186, 242, 265; *Ātman* and, 132, 139; in Buddhism, 222; Candraśekhara Bhāratī on 123, 34; *Brahman* and, 46–47, 52, 131, 142, 145–46, 187–88, 222; in Christianity, 242; Chinmayananda on, 61, 129–34, 148; as conversion, 241–42; Dayananda on, 138–41; "Direct Path" of, 134–41; Ramana Maharshi on, 130–37, 148, 151; Śaṅkara on, 82, 123–27, 133–34, 141, 148–49, 186–90, 332n26; self-knowledge and, 225; as "thought-extinction," 61, 126, 136, 139–40; as translation, 141–48; Vivekananda on, 129–34, 317n61; yoga and, 127. *See also* Experience, Religious; Ultimate Reality

Lonergan, Bernard, 3, 217–20, 221, 242, 261, 282n146, 346n25, 347n36

Long, Jeffery, 226–27, 233, 244

Mahā Bodhi Society, 50

Maharishi Mahesh Yogi: *Absolute Theory of Government*, 200; and celebrities, 65–66; classical Advaita Vedānta and, 65–69, 157; Ramana Maharshi and, 58; Rambachan, Anantanand and, 201, 203–204; political activity of, 69–70, 199–200, 206, 338n107; scandals, 297n143; *Science of Being and Art of Living*, 199, 296n140; travels of, 181; *Vivekacūḍāmaṇi* and 129–33, 141; *Upadeśa Sāram* and, 135–41, 145; Vivekananda and, 58. *See also* Transcendental Meditation

Majumdar, Protap Chandra, 30, 50, 285n34

Maṭha: Daśanāmī Order, 47; Śaṅkara and, 63, 105, 164–65; Śṛṅgeri *Maṭh*, 71–76, 98, 127, 133, 145, 164–65; nationalism and, 326n57

Mathew, C. V., 14–15, 83, 234–35

Mission: definitions of, 95, 115; migration and, 178–79; as pilgrimage, 153, 171, 172–81; as holistic transformation, 205–13; religious experience and, 128–29, 134, 141–42, 148–49; as translation, 123, 141–48, 320n112. *See also* Missiology, Comparative; Missiology, Christian; Missiology, Hindu

Missiology, Comparative, 19, 25, 31, 35–41, 115–16, 143, 172–73, 179–81, 206, 255–56, 270n15. *See also* Conversion

Missiology, Christian: Catholic, 20–24, 31, 38, 40; "Christian Witness in a Multi-Religious World," 22, 24, 25, 39, 185; as "civilizing mission", 258, 263; Colonialism and, 85–86; conversion and, 19–25, 84–86, 185, 207; definitions of, 84–87; Goel's account of 14, 18; "Great Commission" and,

Missiology, Christian *(continued)* 86, 302n17; as humanization, 259–61, 262; Islam and, 143; *Lausanne Covenant*, 207–209, 342n153; *missio Dei*, 20–23, 256, 274; paradigms and models of, 84–87; Pentecoast and, 169; translation and, 143–44, 146–47. *See also* Conversion
Missiology, Hindu: conversion and, 33, 64–65, 89, 95–96; discipleship in, 128–29; distinctive qualities of, 30, 78, 104–14, 122–27; imperialism and, 17; paradigms of, 87–104; as problematic, 38–39; in Śaṅkara, 90–94; Sharma, Arvind on, 33, 38, 82–83, 360n43; styles of, 104–14; as transhistorical, 33; Vivekananda on, 99–104

Nationalism: Christianity and, 259; "Conversion Controversy" and, 1–2, 9, 15–16; 27, 53, 154, 176, 272n45; of Chinmayanada, 63–64, 77, 107, 113, 159; cultural, 62–65, 159; Missionary Advaita and, 63–64, 77, 165, 176, 197, 231; Rambachan, Anantanand and 202; Vivekananda and, 53, 107, 337n90. *See also* Bharatiya Janata Party (BJP); Vishva Hindu Parishad (VHP)
Natural Law Party, 65, 69–70, 199–201, 203, 205, 210, 212, 213, 298n149
New Age, 66, 70
Noble, Margaret, 231

Orientalism, 18–19, 26, 29, 32, 34, 37, 283n7; Buddhism and, 100, 104; comparative theology and, 279n211; and the "mystic east," 44, 53, 54
Osuri, Goldie, 9–10, 77

Padilla, C. René, 207–209, 211, 256, 342n152, 343n172
Padmapāda, 105–106, 164, 169; as a missionary style, 106–108, 115–16
Panikkar, Raimond, 259, 359n19
Parāvartan (Rite of Conversion), 2, 77
Paul the Apostle, 85, 143, 146, 178, 208, 217, 246, 256, 263, 355n147; Benedict XVI's reflections on, 248–50; conversion experience of, 243–44
Paul VI, Pope, 21, 64, 209
Proselytization: in Advaita Vedānta, 95, 101; definition of, 38; *Evangelii Gaudium*'s critique of, 24; and Judaism, 263–64. *See also* Conversion; Mission

Radhakrishnan, Sarvepalli: Christ, interpretation of, 259; conversion and, 216, 222, 242 Schweitzer, Albert, debate with, 183–85, 198, 213; *tat-tvam-asi* ethic, 187
Rambachan, Anantanand, 201–205; and Chinmayananda, 203; ecology and, 212; *A Hindu Theology of Liberation*, 202, 341n139; Maharishi Mahesh Yogi and, 201, 203–204; on political transformation, 201–205, 339n120; and Sadhana, 204, 341n141; Transcendental Meditation and, 201, 203–204, 206; on Vivekananda and the Ramakrishna Mission, 202, 206

Ramana Maharshi, 54–59; and Abishiktananda, 231; and Brunton, Paul, 54; conversion experience of, 55–56; Dayananda on, 138–41; *Eight Stanzas to Arunachala*, 176; and the Hastāmalaka style of mission, 109; on liberation, 130–37, 148, 152; mission of, 58–59; "Ramana effect," 58; *Reality in Forty Verses*, 56–57; in relation to classical Advaita Vedānta, 57, 124, 151–52, 290n83, 313n16, 342n148; and religious experience, 121–22, 124, 129, 130–37, 140; as renunciant, 284n19; self-inquiry, method of, 56–57, 233; Sharma, Arvind on, 55, 232; as teacher, 138–40; *Vivekacūḍāmaṇi* translation, 129–33, 141, 145; universalism of, 121, 141; *Upadeśa Sāram*, 135–41, 318n76. *See also* Silence
Ramanasramam, 47, 56, 58, 136–37, 290n88. *See also* Ramana Maharshi
Raj, Selva J., 27–28, 275n80
Ramakrishna, Sri, 51
Ramakrishna Math, *see* Ramakrishna Mission
Ramakrishna Mission, 47–54, 113, 352n97; Advaita Vedānta and 155, 156, 176, 202, 324n11, 352n98; Buddhism and, 103; Christians in, 344n5; as "ecumenical," 46; ethnic identity and, 104, 154, 278n99; conversion and, 215–16, 222, 226–27, 231, 244, 252; ISKCON and, 155; mission, theology of 54, 109, 278n13; nationalism and, 77, 97–98, 231, 337n90; Ramakrishna Order, 154, 226–27; Sanskritization and, 15, 83; self-definition, 233; Sringeri Vidya Bharati Foundation (SVBF) and, 76; social service in, 53, 109, 185, 191–94, 196, 198; Vedanta Societies, 216, 226, 252, 288n56, 58, 349n51. *See also* Vivekananda, Swami
Rambo, Lewis R., 220–21, 223, 227, 242
Rashtriya Swayamsevak Sangh (RSS), 1, 15, 17, 64
Religion, Theory of: 'import/export/'baggage' categorization, 155–56, locative, supralocative, and translocative religion, 173–74, 178, 180. *See also* Theology, Comparative.

Sadhana (social justice organization), 204–205, 206, 211, 341n140–41, 341n147
Śaivism, 167, Advaita Vedānta and, 44, 89, 323n2
Saṃpradāya, 30, 45, 71, 89
Śaṅkara: Chinmayananda and 62–63, 77, 89, 99, 124; conquest and, 77, 83, 94–99, 100, 160–62, 165, 167–68, 176; Dayananda and, 113, 141; disciples of, 105–15; doxographers and, 100, 308n76; "externalist" teaching of, 121, 124, 128; hagiographies of, 94–99, 115, 173, 177, 181, 305n55; as mission paradigm, 3–4, 87–99, 215; Pūrva Mīmāṃsā and, 97, 304n38; Rambachan, Anantanand on 113; Ramana Maharshi and, 57, 124; on renunciation, 213; "The Śaṅkara," 47, 162, 164–65; in the

Śaṅkara *(continued)*
Śaṅkaradigvijaya (SDV), 84, 88, 94–99, 106–12, 127, 159–67, 171, 177, 307n65; social ethics of, 185, 187–89, 191; social restrictions of, 188–89, 305n47; Suthern Hirst's account of, 81–82, 89–90, 116; as teacher, 90–94, 162, 181, 264; *Upadeśasāhasrī*, 83, 90–98, 99–100, 103, 106, 181, 189, 305n47; victory tour (*vijaya*) of, 73, 167–68, 177, 181; *Vivekacūḍāmaṇi* and, 126, 315n31. *See also* Conquest; Liberation, Spiritual; *Sankara the Missionary*
Sangh Parivar (Hindu nationalist movement), 2, 15
Sanneh, Lamin, 143–47
Sanskritization: Chinmaya Mission and, 238–39; conversion as, 234–40, 246; Mathew, C. V. on, 15, 83, 234–35, 353n103; as metaphor, 236–37, 239–40, 245, 251, 258; Pollack, Sheldon on, 236, 240, 247; politics and, 2, 78, 236; Radhakrishnan, Sarvepalli on 235; Sharma, Arvind, on 83, 353n103; Srinivas, M. N. on, 234–236, 238, 240
Schroeder, Roger P., 19–21, 86–88, 115–16, 256
Schweitzer, Albert, 183–87; Radhakrishnan, debate with, 183–85, 187, 198, 213; on Śaṅkara, 186, 190, 333n40
Second Vatican Council, 21, 54; *Ad Gentes*, 21–22; *Gaudium et Spes*, 209–10
Self-Realization Fellowship, *see* Hindu-Inspired Meditation Movements
Service: in Advaita Vedānta, 52–53, 102, 104; in "Christian Witness in a Multi-Religious World," 22, 185; Toṭaka and, 109–11, 116; as "Organized Sevā," 191–98; hierarchy of, 198, 206; as worship, 213. *See also* Liberation, Social
Sharma, Arvind 33, 38, 55, 83, 87, 124, 187, 216, 222, 242, 232, 258, 263–64, 345n12
Silence: Hastāmalaka and, 108–109, 111; liberation, means of 108–109, 178, 215, 230; preaching in, 56, 58, 108–109, 264; Ramana Maharshi and, 56–59, 68 176, 206, 228, 233, 264; "Silence of the Mahatmas," 206, 215
Smith, Wilfred Cantwell, 25, 31
Society of Jesus, 14, 28, 34, 85, 302n14; Ignatius of Loyola, 172–73; Francis Xavier, 14, 34
Sringeri Vidya Bharati Foundation (SVBF), 47, 70–71, 73–75; nationalism and, 77
Sivananda, Swami, 109–11, 113, 194, 195
Śuddhi (Rite of Conversion), 2, 15, 64, 77
Sureśvara, 72, 105, 164, 227; as a missionary style, 111–16
Suthren Hirst, Jacqueline, 81–83, 88, 89, 108, 116–17

Tanner, Kathryn, 123, 128–29, 141, 191, 309n94, 316n48
Thangaraj, M. Thomas, 5, 86–87, 115, 153–55, 255–56
Theology, Comparative: Clooney, Francis X. on, 33–36, 281n131; as "confessional," 39–40;

Comparative Religious Ideas Project, 281n141; fruitful tension in, 116–17; heuristic patterns of, 35; as retrieval, 256. *See also* Missiology, Comparative.
Thomas, M. M., 259–63
Toṭaka, 164, 264; as missionary style, 105, 109–11, 115–16
Transcendental Meditation, 65–70; Advaita Vedānta and 46, 65–70, 77, 199, 201, 228–29; Chinmaya Mission and, 205; Christianity and, 210, 229–30; Converts, experiences of, 228–31; excommunication in, 233, 352n97; Forman, Robert K. C. and, 122, 230–31, 312n7; Global Country of World Peace of, 70, 76; initiation rituals in, 228–29; political engagements by, 199–202; Ramakrishna Mission and, 205; Vedic elements of, 68, 156, 199–201; "Yogic flying" in, 68–69, 200. *See also* Maharishi Mahesh Yogi; Natural Law Party
Transcendentalism, American, 43, 338n113
Truth and Reconciliation Commission of Canada, 257–58, 262, 360n40
Tweed, Thomas, 173–74

Ultimate Reality, 122, 213. *See also* Belonging, Non-Dualist; *Brahman*; Liberation, Spiritual
United Church of Canada: *World Mission Report*, 20, 22

Vaiṣṇavism: *avatāra* in, 101; *bhakti* traditions of, 98; Clooney, Francis X. on 35; in the ISKCON movement, 155; missionary elements of, 32, 37, 89, 95, 111; as Śaṅkara's rivals, 90, 92; Vivekananda and, 101, 111, 155, 192–93
Vedānta, Advaita: Buddhism and, 62, 100–102, 167, 234; Christianity and, 180, 242; cross-cultural appeal of, 4, 37, 76–77, 140, 178, 180; conversion in, 215–16, 221–32, 240, 258; definition of, 44–47; as "essence" of Hinduism, 37, 49, 302; missiology of, 11, 46, 51, 77–78, 82–83, 145; missionary paradigms of, 87–104; missionary styles of, 104–17; nationalism and, 77–78, 107; as Neo-Vedānta, 3, 105, 124, 284n3; the place of place in, 151–53, 155, 157, 165–72, 176, 180–82; relational character of, 191; religious experience in, 122–41, 149; role of authorized teachers in, 88–114, 148; social engagement in, 109–11, 185–86, 192, 206; and translation, 144–48; and Yoga, 45, 52, 61, 110, 125, 127, 139, 141; universality of, 104, 114, 148, 152, 154, 168. *See also* Hinduism; Śaṅkara
Vedanta Society, *see* Ramakrishna Mission
Vijayanagara Empire, 72, 97–98
Violence: Advaita Vedānta and, 253; of Christianity and Islam, 251; conversion as, 12–18, 250, 252–53; in Kandhmal, 2, 17, 268n8; mission and, 143, 252; Residential School System, 257; in *Sankara the Missionary*, 106

Vishva Hindu Parishad (VHP), 2, 15, 63, 107, 154, 294n122, 295n124
Vivekananda, Swami, 48–54; Advaita Vedānta and, 44–48, 193; Buddhism and, 99–104, 308n80, 308n81; Christianity and, 104, 259; on conversion, 3, 15, 217, 222, 234, 242; Dayananda and, 113; as Hindu missionary, 27, 37, 43, 51, 86, 99–104; "practical Vedānta" of, 51–54, 283n7, 287n51; Ramakrishna and, 227; Ramana Maharshi and, 55–58, 181; Śaṅkara and, 99, 104, 124; social service and, 191–94, 334n50, 53; spiritual experience in, 122; Transcendental Meditation and, 66; universal religion of, 153–55, 283n8; on Yoga, 45, 57, 283n8; "The Work Before Us," 43, 102; at the World's Parliament of Religions, 43–44, 47–51, 54, 102, 152, 154, 223, 256, 285n25, 285n29, 285n33, 285n34. *See also* Ramakrishna Mission
Vivekacūḍāmaṇi, 126–27, 128, 241; Candraśekhara Bhāratī on, 129–30, 132–33, 134, 141, 145; Chinmayananda on 129–37, 141, 223; Ramana Maharshi on, 57, 129–33, 141, 313n16; social restrictions in, 130–31
Vrajaprana, Pravrajika, 226–27, 233, 350n62

Wildman, Wesley, 38–39, 281–82n141
Williamson, Lola, 30, 228–29
World Council of Churches: "Christian Witness in a Multi-Religious World," 22; Commission on World Mission and Evangelization, 21; ecumenism and, 269n12; Thomas, M. M. and, 259
World Evangelical Alliance, 22
World Missionary Conference, 21, 255, 257, 273n62
World Religion(s): Buddhism as, 19; Christianity as, 19, 48, 255; and colonialism, 26–31; Hinduism as, 43–44 Orientalist roots of term, 19; Advaita Vedānta as, 104, universalism and, 258
World's Parliament of Religions, 30, 43–44, 47–51, 54, 102–107, 152–55, 223, 256. *See also* Vivekananda, Swami

Xavier, Francis, *see* Society of Jesus

Milton Keynes UK
Ingram Content Group UK Ltd.
UKHW042145131124
451149UK00002B/345

9 781438 497419